WAR ON WASTE

WAR ON WASTE

President's Private Sector Survey on Cost Control

MACMILLAN PUBLISHING COMPANY

New York

Macmillan Publishing Company
866 Third Avenue, New York, N.Y. 10022

ISBN 0-02-074660-1

10 9 8 7 6 5 4 3 2 1

Printed in the United States of America

January 12, 1984

The Honorable Ronald Reagan
President of the United States
The White House
Washington, D.C.

Dear Mr. President,

Following your directive to identify and suggest remedies for waste and abuse in the Federal Government, the President's Private Sector Survey (PPSS) offers recommendations which would save:

• $424 billion in three years, rising to

• $1.9 trillion *per year* by the year 2000.

These proposals would transform the Federal debt situation as follows:

	Federal Debt ($ trillions)		Annual Interest on Federal Debt ($ billions)	
	Without PPSS	With PPSS	Without PPSS	With PPSS
1990	$ 3.2	$2.0	$ 252.3	$89.2
1995	6.2	2.2	540.9	62.3
2000	13.0	2.5	1,520.7	75.1

You asked the American people to help you get the Government "off their backs." If the American people realized how rapidly Federal Government spending is likely to grow under existing legislated programs, I am convinced they would compel their elected representatives to "get the Government off their backs." In our survey to search out ways to cut costs in the Government, great emphasis was placed on the spending outlook, which is as follows:

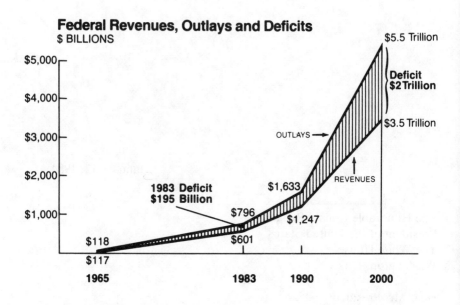

Federal Revenues, Outlays and Deficits
$ BILLIONS

If fundamental changes are not made in Federal spending, as compared with the fiscal 1983 deficit of $195 billion, a deficit of over ten times that amount, $2 trillion, is projected for the year 2000, only 17 years from now. In that year, the Federal debt would be $13.0 trillion ($160,000 per current taxpayer) and the interest alone on the debt would be $1.5 trillion per year ($18,500 per year per current taxpayer).

Mr. President, these projections are the result of a joint effort between PPSS and a leading U.S. economic forecasting firm. They are the result of very careful study and drove us to seek out every possible savings opportunity, "like tireless bloodhounds," as you requested.

In the course of the search by our 36 Task Forces, chaired by 161 top executives from around the country and staffed by over 2,000 volunteers that they provided, we came up with 2,478 separate, distinct, and specific recommendations which are the basis for the carefully projected savings. For practical purposes, these savings, if fully implemented, could virtually eliminate the reported deficit by the 1990's versus an alternative deficit of $10.2 trillion in the decade of the 1990's if no action is taken.

Equally important, the 2,478 cost-cutting, revenue-enhancing recommendations we have made can be achieved without raising taxes, without weakening America's needed defense build-up, and without in any way harming necessary social welfare programs.

Because we are starting from a deficit of $195 billion, every dollar we can stop spending is a dollar that the Government does not have to borrow. With future Government borrowing costs at 11 percent (versus 10.75 percent now and 14.5 percent when you took office) and inflation taken at 6 percent per year over the longer run, these savings compound quickly.

Applying these interest and inflation rates, the result is that a dollar saved today accumulates to $32 over 12 years and $71 over 17 years. Thus, any potential saving made, as compared to not making the saving, translates into a difference in cumulative spending of 32 times that amount through 1995 and 71 times that amount through the end of the century.

Therefore, $100 billion in reduced Government spending in year one equates cumulatively to $7.1 trillion in the year 2000. And since borrowings are decreased by this amount, so will the national debt decrease.

This is, of course, a horrendous prospect. If the American people understood the gravity of the outlook, they would not, I believe, support representatives who might let it happen.

Mr. President, you have been so correct in resisting attempts to balance the budget by increasing taxes. The tax load on the average American family is already at counterproductive levels with the underground economy having now grown to an estimated $500 billion per year, costing about $100 billion in lost Federal tax revenues per year.

The size of the underground economy is understandable when one considers that median family income taxes have increased from $9 in 1948 to $2,218 in 1983, or by 246 times. This is runaway taxation at its worst.

Importantly, any meaningful increases in taxes from personal income would have to come from lower and middle income families, as 90 percent of all personal taxable income is generated below the taxable income level of $35,000.

Further, there isn't much more that can be extracted from high income brackets. If the Government took 100 percent of all taxable income beyond the $75,000 tax bracket not already taxed, it would get only $17 billion, and this confiscation, which would destroy productive enterprise, would only be sufficient to run the Government for seven days.

Resistance to additional income taxes would be even more widespread if people were aware that:

- One-third of all their taxes is consumed by waste and inefficiency in the Federal Government as we identified in our survey.

- Another one-third of all their taxes escapes collection from others as the underground economy blossoms in direct proportion to tax increases and places even more pressure on law abiding taxpayers, promoting still more underground economy—a vicious cycle that must be broken.

- With two-thirds of everyone's personal income taxes wasted or not collected, 100 percent of what is collected is absorbed solely by interest on the Federal debt and by Federal Government contributions to transfer payments. In other words, all individual income tax revenues are gone before one nickel is spent on the services which taxpayers expect from their Government.

Our survey studied the small as well as the major items of cost savings, items of broad national impact as well as those of a more localized nature. I believe you will be interested in a few random examples of what we found:

- In the Northwest, the Federal Power Marketing Administration is selling subsidized power at one-third of market rates. If the Federal power were priced at market, there would be a three-year increase in revenues of $4.5 billion, which equates to the three-year personal income taxes of 676,000 median income American families who are thus subsidizing a discrete group in one part of the country.

- The Civil Service and Military Retirement Systems provide to participants three times and six times the benefits, respectively, of the best private sector plans. The Government's civilian and military employees retire at an earlier age, typically age 55 and 40, respectively, versus 63 to 64 in the private sector, with substantially more liberal benefit formulas than their private sector counterparts. In addition, the pensions of Federal retirees are fully indexed for inflation—a rarity in the private sector. Modifying major Federal pensions to provide benefits comparable to those of the best private sector plans, slightly better in the case of military pensions, would result in three-year savings of $60.9 billion, equivalent to the three-year income taxes of 9.2 million median income families.

- A relatively small item in the overall, but representative of many, is the prohibition of competitive bidding on the movement of military personnel household goods to and from Alaska and Hawaii, despite a DOD test showing that competitive bidding would reduce costs by as much as 26 percent. Elimination of this provision would save $69.5 million in three years, equivalent to the three-year income taxes of 10,400 median income families.

- We found Congressional interference to be a major problem. For example, because Congress obstructs the closing of bases that the military wants to close, the three-year waste is $367 million. In total, PPSS recommends three-year savings of $3.1 billion by closing excess military bases, equivalent to the three-year income taxes of 466,000 median income families.

Mr. President, these are just a few of the absurd situations that we found throughout the Government that add up to billions of dollars per year and where the opportunities for savings are clearly available.

Some of the recommendations made by PPSS have been made before. Others are entirely new. Regardless of their origins, the focus must now be on implementation. The current economic trends are simply too serious to delay action any longer.

PPSS has submitted 36 major Task Force reports and 11 studies on special subjects such as subsidies and retirement. In total, these reports substantiate three-year ongoing savings of $424.4 billion, plus cash accelerations of $66 billion. These are all analyzed and supported in great detail. Capsuled in terms of the functional problems to which they relate, the savings are as follows:

PPSS Savings Recommendations

	$ Billions	% of Total
Program Waste	$160.9	37.9%
System Failures	151.3	35.7
Personnel		
Mismanagement	90.9	21.4
Structural Deficiencies	12.7	3.0
Other Opportunities	8.6	2.0
Total	$424.4	100.0%

These data confirm our findings that system failures and personnel mismanagement together comprise well over one-half, 57.1 percent, of the total savings possibilities. They are at the foundation of inefficiencies in the Federal Government. Program waste, which accounts for 37.9 percent of the savings recommendations, would also be substantially eliminated if proper systems and personnel management were in place.

The above underscores one of our most important recommendations, which is the establishment of an Office of Federal Management in the Executive Office of the President. This Federal Government top management office would include OMB, GSA and OPM and have Government-wide responsibility for establishing, modernizing, and monitoring management systems.

If it is set up and staffed properly, it could go a long way to avoid in the future the thousands of deficiencies and examples of waste that we have identified. We would not feel our task complete if we just identified past deficiencies without recommendations for a management and organizational structure that would be best suited for preventing the errors of the past.

Additionally, the establishment of this new office would be beneficial in the implementation process of the PPSS recommendations.

In this regard, we believe that your Cabinet Council on Management and Administration, working in concert with the Office of Cabinet Affairs, is uniquely suited to lead a Government-wide effort to restore sound principles of management and efficiency to the Federal Government. While the Cabinet Council already has taken a leadership role in this regard, we urge you to call upon it to make implementation of the PPSS recommendations Government-wide its highest priority.

Mr. President, it was a great honor to have been asked by you to engage in this effort to identify ways to eliminate inefficiency, waste and abuse in the Federal Government. The project was structured and staffed to effect enduring improvement so that our children and grandchildren would not inherit a situation that would be devastating to them and to the values of our economic and social system. It was in this vein that we were able to enlist the 161 top executives from private business and other organizations to chair and to staff our 36 Task Forces at a cost to the private sector of over $75 million and at no cost to the Government.

All the participants join with me in thanking you for the opportunity to be of service and in looking forward to whatever additional help we may be able to provide to assure that the greatest practical results are obtained from the work of this Commission.

Respectfully,

J. Peter Grace
Chairman

Contents

VOLUME I

I

PREFACE

MOST REPORTS of Presidential Commissions begin with lengthy introductions detailing the origins, premises, and methodologies of their studies before focusing on the results of the study. We are omitting such matters because we do not want to risk losing even one reader who might be turned away by having to wade through such preliminary material.

Those of us who worked on PPSS took seriously the President's call for a thoroughgoing survey of the Federal Government's operations to identify opportunities for cost savings and improved management efficiencies. We welcomed the chance to bring to bear on the Executive Branch of Government our experience and expertise acquired in managing private sector business enterprises. There were 161 of us who came from top corporate, academic, and labor positions all across America, and we were assisted by more than 2,000 capable volunteers from virtually every segment of the private sector. The time, money, and materials needed for us to conduct this survey, estimated at more than $75 million, were provided at no cost to the Federal Government. It was funded and staffed entirely by the private sector.

Our work has resulted in 2,478 recommendations designed to bring about cost savings of $424.4 billion over three years, cash accelerations of $66 billion over a similar period, and overall managerial improvements. The ultimate impact of what we have proposed will depend on whether the American taxpayer can be persuaded that the problems are real and serious, the need for action pressing, the possibilities for reform promising, and the time for action at hand. If successful, then those same citizens can be depended upon to let their elected representatives and appointed officials know that "business as usual" in the Federal Government can no longer be tolerated, and that rapid and extensive reforms must be instituted.

In hopes of stimulating just such a broadly based consensus for change, we turn at once to the substance of our findings and recommendations.

II

THE URGENT NEED FOR CHANGE

THIS CHAPTER (1) summarizes the economic impact of implementing PPSS's recommendations, particularly the results of a Data Resources, Inc.(DRI)/PPSS cooperative project to forecast the course of Federal expenditures, revenues, and deficits to the year 2000; (2) highlights the cost savings and revenue enhancement opportunities PPSS has developed; and (3) details the adverse effect that certain kinds of Congressional involvement have on cost savings initiatives similar to those reported here.

It is abundantly clear to anyone who reads through the 47 PPSS reports and this Report to the President that the Federal Government is suffering from a critical case of inefficient and ineffective management, evidenced particularly by the hemorrhaging of billions of tax dollars and mounting deficits. For decades the Federal Government has not managed its programs with the same eye to innovation, productivity, and economy that is dictated by private sector P&L statements and balance sheets.

It is with private sector management tenets in mind that the PPSS findings have been developed. PPSS reports contain 2,478 specific recommendations, covering 784 issues, whose implementation could result in net savings of $424.4 billion over three years and prevent the accumulation of *$10.5 trillion* of additional deficits over the 17 years to year 2000.

None of the PPSS recommendations endanger the substance or legislated intent of Federal programs, although few programs and major functions would remain unaffected in their implementation methodologies. The overwhelming majority of the actions involve reductions in outlays made possible by improved management practices, more efficient methods of operation, and better direction of spending on program targets.

The cooperative DRI/PPSS project was undertaken to translate into dollars a view of the future if current trends in Federal revenues and outlays continue—and to portray, as well, what the alternative would be if PPSS recommendations were implemented.

Simply stated, the DRI analysis revealed that the economic problems the Nation now faces will be completely out of control over the next two decades if we go about business as usual. These projections show *annual* Federal deficits approaching a staggering *$2 trillion* by the end of the century—in only 17 years.

The upside of this special DRI analysis is that, if PPSS recommendations are adopted in full, the fiscal crisis can be overcome, with the resulting benefits of favorable non-inflationary growth. Instead of reaching new highs, budget deficits would soon begin to decline and become manageable (in the $26 billion to $62 billion range) during 1990–2000. This would also depend, of course, on maintaining a cost conscious and fiscally responsible attitude throughout the Government, so that other economic hemorrhages do not develop while we are staunching the flow from those that afflict us now.

In this regard, this section includes a discussion of the current involvement of the Congress in the day-to-day management of the Federal Government—and of the adverse impact this has on the cost of Government. Without disputing the constitutional right of the Congress to become engaged in dealing with the smallest of operational matters, it needs to be recognized that this often entails massive dollar costs in unnecessary spending and lost savings opportunities. Every billion dollars of such activity wastes (squanders) the Federal income taxes of 450,857 median income families.

The American taxpayers will continue to have to shoulder the burden of the deficient management of the Federal Government until the Congress and the Executive Branch begin to work together more effectively to achieve the common purpose of bringing the cost of Government under control.

A. The Economic Impact of PPSS

The need for a major undertaking to reduce government spending is widely perceived as witnessed by the public's present concern that budget deficits are out of control and are expected to run at about $200 billion a year indefinitely. In fact, an analysis undertaken by the respected economic consulting firm Data Resources, Inc. (DRI) in collaboration with PPSS shows that the problem in both the short and long run will considerably worsen.

The following table, derived from the DRI study, indicates that current government policies will lead to deficits approaching $2 trillion by the end of the century with spending at between 34% and 35% of GNP.

The projected deficit of $2.0 trillion in 2000 equates to 35.5% of projected Federal spending (24.6% now) and 12.2% of projected GNP (6.1% now), and up from 2.3% in 1980.

Summary of Federal Finances,
1962–2000: Status Quo of Current Policies
($ Billions)

	(1)	(2)	(3)	(4)	(5)	(6)	(7)
			Outlays			Deficit	
						As a % of	
Fiscal Year	Money GNP	Revenues	Amount	% of GNP	Amount	Outlays	GNP
(1) 1962	$ 548.2	$ 99.7	$ 106.8	19.5%	$ (7.1)	(6.6)%	(1.3)%
(2) 1980	2,575.8	517.1	576.7	22.4	(59.6)	(10.3)	(2.3)
(3) 1983	3,229.5	600.6	795.9	24.6	(195.4)	(24.6)	(6.1)
(4) 1985	3,852.5	754.8	939.9	24.4	(185.1)	(19.7)	(4.8)
(5) 1990	6,110.5	1,246.5	1,633.3	26.7	(386.7)	(23.7)	(6.3)
(6) 1995	9,946.9	2,089.2	2,864.6	28.8	(775.4)	(27.1)	(7.8)
(7) 2000	16,066.1	3,567.3	5,533.3	34.4	(1,966.0)	(35.5)	(12.2)
Avg. Ann. % Inc./(Dec.)							
(8) 1962–1983	8.8%	8.9%	10.0%	0.2%pt	17.1%	0.9%pt	0.2%pt
(9) 1980–1983	7.8	5.1	11.3	0.7	48.6	4.8	1.3
(10) 1983–2000	9.9	11.0	12.1	0.6	14.5	0.6	0.4

Note: Totals and percentages in this and subsequent tables in this section have been calculated using unrounded numbers.

The all-time record levels projected for the period through 2000 will slow economic growth, reallocate funds away from investment, and feed inflation. And that is only part of the story, as shown in the following:

The "True" Federal Deficit,
1976–2000
($ Billions)

		(1)	(2)	(3)	(4)	(5)
			Unfunded Past Service Liabilities		Memo: Civil Service	
				Annual Charge to Amortize	and Military Retire-	The
	Fiscal Year	Reported Deficit	Amount	Over 40 Years	ment Outlays	"True" Deficit
(1)	1976	$ (66.4)	$ 1,010.5	$ (67.2)	$ 15.6	$ (133.6)
(2)	1980	(59.0)	2,205.5	(146.6)	26.6	(205.6)
(3)	1983	(195.4)	2,880.6	(186.1)	36.9	(381.5)
(4)	1984	(197.2)	3,051.3	(202.8)	39.2	(400.0)
(5)	1985	(185.1)	3,502.9	(232.8)	42.2	(417.9)
(6)	1990	(386.7)	6,984.5	(464.2)	95.1	(850.9)
(7)	1995	(775.4)	13,926.6	(925.6)	131.3	(1,701.0)
(8)	2000	(1,966.0)	27,768.7	(1,845.5)	229.4	(3,811.5)

The annual charges required to amortize the unfunded liabilities of Social Security and Government pension plans shown in column 3 are rarely, if ever, mentioned in the media. In 1983, these charges amounted to $186.1 billion (up by $118.9 billion from $67.2 billion in 1976), which, when added to the regular deficit of $195.4 billion, produced a "true" deficit of $381.5 billion. By 2000, this "true" deficit is projected to reach $3.8 trillion—almost twice the regular deficit—making it imperative for the PPSS recommendations on personnel and retirement systems to be acted on.

These annual charges represent what the government should—but does not—set aside each year in order to liquidate or amortize existing (for prior years' service) Social Security and pension liabilities over 40 years. Until 1976, the government itself did not even know the true magnitude of these future liabilities, which had been completely ignored— yet another example of the "information gap" encountered throughout PPSS.

The DRI study indicates that a major turnaround in this outlook can be achieved by the implementation of the PPSS recommendations. Apart from the total three-year saving of $424 billion projected by PPSS through implementing its recommendations, the PPSS recommendations are of such scope that savings will tend to expand throughout the projection period, and have significant impacts throughout the economy. Highlights of the DRI study include:

• If PPSS recommendations are implemented, $424 billion in cost savings can be achieved in the first three years after implementation commences. These savings will increase through the year 2000 when they will have reached over $1.9 trillion a year and will have accumulated to $10.5 trillion in the 17-year period (excluding the unfunded past service pension and Social Security liability).

• In the "PPSS Case," by 2000, the deficit will have been reduced to essentially zero versus nearly $2 trillion if the "Status Quo" is maintained.

• Implementation of PPSS recommendations will result in the following projected benefits by 2000:

—31% decline in real Federal spending
—5% higher revenues in real dollars
—36% higher rate of real economic growth
—14% lower inflation rate
—23%–37% lower interest rates
—64% higher rate of growth of industrial production
—60% faster rate of growth of real business fixed investment
—38% more housing starts
—2% larger civilian labor force and 2 million more people employed.

These highlights are discussed in the remainder of this section.

The following table, based on the DRI analysis, compares Federal finances projected on a current policies basis to the end of the century—the Status Quo Case—with the PPSS Savings Case in which the only changes from the Status Quo Case are the implementation of the PPSS recommendations.

As shown, the net effect of the PPSS recommendations would be to save the Federal government $1.9 trillion per year by 2000 (col. 3, line 15) and $10.5 trillion cumulatively over the period. Initial savings would, of course, be more modest. Outlays in the PPSS Savings Case are lower than those in the Status Quo Case by $46 billion in 1985 (line 7)—while recommendations are still being implemented. The savings then increase to $433 billion in 1990, $994 billion in 1995, and $2.4 trillion in 2000. These outlay reductions are partially offset by lower revenue projections to arrive at the net savings figure—i.e., the reduction in the deficit.

Accumulating these savings over the projection period (lines 16–21) tells a very compelling story indeed. Implementing the PPSS recommendations will save U.S. taxpayers:

• A total of over $10.5 trillion—or about $130,000 per taxpayer—over the 1984–2000 period.

• Over $619 billion—or about $7,700 per taxpayer—per year.

The total savings of $10.5 trillion are the net of outlays being reduced by $13.8 trillion, or 33.3%, and revenues being reduced by $(3.3) trillion, or about (10.9)%. On an annual basis, the $810.9 billion per year average

Summary of Federal Finances, 1983–2000:
Status Quo of Current Policies vs. PPSS Savings
($ Billions)

		(1)	(2)	(3)	(4)
				PPSS Fav./(Unfav.) to Status Quo	
	Fiscal Year	Status Quo of Current Policies	PPSS Savings	Amount	%
	Revenues				
(1)	1983A	$ 600.6	$ 600.6	—	—
(2)	1985	754.8	758.5	$ 3.6	0.5%
(3)	1990	1,246.5	1,173.2	(73.4)	(5.9)
(4)	1995	2,089.2	1,807.8	(281.4)	(13.5)
(5)	2000	3,567.3	3,052.7	(514.6)	(14.4)
	Outlays				
(6)	1983A	$ 795.9	$ 795.9	—	—
(7)	1985	939.9	894.2	$ 45.7	4.9%
(8)	1990	1,633.3	1,199.8	433.5	26.5
(9)	1995	2,864.6	1,870.3	994.3	34.7
(10)	2000	5,533.3	3,089.9	2,443.4	44.2
	Deficit				
(11)	1983A	$ (195.4)	$ (195.4)	—	—
(12)	1985	(185.1)	(135.7)	$ 49.3	26.7%
(13)	1990	(386.7)	(26.6)	360.1	93.1
(14)	1995	(775.4)	(62.6)	712.8	91.9
(15)	2000	(1,966.0)	(37.1)	1,928.8	98.1
	17 Years, 1984–2000				
	Cumulative				
(16)	Revenues	$29,731.5	$26,479.1	$(3,252.4)	(10.9)%
(17)	Outlays	41,370.5	27,585.9	13,784.6	33.3
(18)	Deficit	(11,639.0)	(1,106.9)	10,532.2	90.5
	Average Per Year				
(19)	Revenues	$ 1,748.9	$ 1,557.6	$ (191.3)	(10.9)%
(20)	Outlays	2,433.6	1,622.7	810.9	33.3
(21)	Deficit	(684.6)	(65.1)	619.5	90.5

> 17 year deficit—$(11.64) trillion ex PPSS and $(1.1) trillion with PPSS—saving $10.5 trillion or $620 billion per year for 17 years

saving in outlays is $15 billion more than total U.S. outlays of $795.9 billion in 1983 (col. 1, line 6), while the $619.5 billion average annual reduction in the deficit is $18.9 billion more than total 1983 revenues of $600.6 billion (col.1, line 1).

The seeming paradox of lower revenues resulting from the PPSS recommendations—which include revenue enhancements—can be explained by two factors: the loss of stimulus resulting from lower government spending, at least in the early years of the projections, and the lower rate of inflation brought about by the savings in the PPSS Case —5.9% per year, 1983–2000, vs. 7.2% in the Status Quo Case. It should be noted that a lower inflation rate reduces Federal revenues, even though personal income taxes are indexed, because of its impact on corporate profits and taxes and on ad valorem excise taxes and duties. The following shows the same data in constant 1983 dollars.

Summary of Federal Finances, 1983–2000:
Status Quo of Current Policies vs. PPSS Savings
(Constant 1983 $ Billions)

	Fiscal Year	(1) Status Quo of Current Policies	(2) PPSS Savings	(3) PPSS Fav./(Unfav.) to Status Quo Amount	(4) %
	Revenues				
(1)	1983A	$ 600.6	$ 600.6	—	—
(2)	1985	692.1	696.1	$ 4.0	0.6%
(3)	1990	854.7	850.8	(3.9)	(0.5)
(4)	1995	966.9	971.2	4.3	0.4
(5)	2000	1,098.2	1,154.3	56.0	5.1
	Outlays				
(6)	1983A	$ 795.9	$ 795.9	—	—
(7)	1985	861.8	820.7	$ 41.1	4.8%
(8)	1990	1,119.8	870.1	249.7	22.3
(9)	1995	1,325.8	1,004.8	321.0	24.2
(10)	2000	1,703.5	1,168.3	535.2	31.4
	Deficit				
(11)	1983A	$ (195.4)	$ (195.4)	—	—
(12)	1985	(169.7)	(124.6)	$ 45.1	26.6%
(13)	1990	(265.1)	(19.3)	245.8	92.7
(14)	1995	(358.9)	(33.6)	325.3	90.6
(15)	2000	(605.2)	(14.0)	591.2	97.7

In real terms, the recommendations do result in higher revenues— with the PPSS Case yielding $56 billion (constant 1983 dollars) more than the Status Quo Case in 2000 as a result of the stronger economy brought on by the savings. The $4.0 billion improvement in 1985 over the Status Quo reflects the phased-in impact of cash accelerations. The lower revenues in the early 1990's result from the loss of fiscal stimulus provided by government spending at a time when the long-term benefits of investment, employment, etc., from such lower spending are not yet fully felt.

Thus, the PPSS recommendations, if adopted in full, can effectively overcome the prospective budget crisis. As shown in the following table which gives DRI's estimates of future budgets, the deficits, instead of rising to new highs, begin to decline as a result of the PPSS recommendations—to $136 billion by 1985 and to $37 billion by 2000.

Summary of Federal Finances, 1962–2000: PPSS Savings
($ Billions)

	(1)	(2)	(3)	(4)	(5)	(6)	(7)
			Outlays			Deficit	
						As a % of	
Fiscal Year	Money GNP	Revenues	Amount	% of GNP	Amount	Outlays	GNP
(1) 1962	$ 548.2	$ 99.7	$ 106.8	19.5%	$ (7.1)	(6.6)%	(1.3)%
(2) 1980	2,575.8	517.1	576.7	22.4	(59.6)	(10.3)	(2.3)
(3) 1983	3,229.5	600.6	795.9	24.6	(195.4)	(24.6)	(6.1)
(4) 1985	3,793.3	758.5	894.2	23.6	(135.7)	(15.2)	(3.6)
(5) 1990	5,694.7	1,173.2	1,199.8	21.1	(26.6)	(2.2)	(0.5)
(6) 1995	8,671.4	1,807.8	1,870.3	21.6	(62.6)	(3.3)	(0.7)
(7) 2000	13,541.1	3,052.7	3,089.9	22.8	(37.1)	(1.2)	(0.3)
Avg. Ann. % Inc./(Dec.)							
(8) 1962–1983	8.8%	8.9%	10.0%	0.2%pt	17.1%	0.9%pt	0.2%pt
(9) 1980–1983	7.8	5.1	11.3	0.7	48.6	4.8	1.3
(10) 1983–2000	8.8	10.0	8.3	(0.1)	(9.3)	(1.4)	(0.3)

As shown, the budget deficit drops to 3.6% of GNP by 1985 and to a virtual balance by 1990 and subsequent years. At the same time, Federal expenditures ease to a range of 21%–23% of GNP in the period 1990–2000, a level well below the range of 27%–34% projected for the 1990–2000 decade in the Status Quo Case, as shown in the following which compares the above data on Federal finances with comparable data from the Status Quo Case:

Comparison of Federal Finances, 1983 and 2000:
Status Quo of Current Policies vs. PPSS Savings
($ Billions)

		(1)	(2)	(3)	(4)	(5)
				2000		
					PPSS Fav./(Unfav.) To Status Quo	
			Status Quo	PPSS Savings		
		1983			Amount	%
(1)	Revenues	$ 600.6	$ 3,567.3	$3,052.7	$ (514.6)	(14.4)%
	Outlays					
(2)	Amount	$ 795.9	$ 5,533.3	$3,089.9	$2,443.4	44.2%
(3)	% of GNP	24.6%	34.4%	22.8%	11.6%pts.	33.7
	Deficit					
(4)	Amount	$(195.4)	$(1,966.0)	$(37.1)	$1,928.8	98.1%
(5)	% of Outlays	(24.6)%	(35.5)%	(1.2)%	34.3%pts.	96.6
(6)	% of GNP	(6.1)	(12.2)	(0.3)	12.0	97.8

As shown, in 2000 outlays in the PPSS Savings Case are $2.4 trillion, or 44.2%, favorable to the Status Quo. Expressed as a percentage of GNP, the improvement is 11.6% points, or 33.7%. The comparison between the deficits in the two cases is even more striking—virtually 100%. As a percent of total outlays, the deficit in 2000 is projected at 1.2% in the PPSS Case—34.3% points, or 96.6%, favorable to the Status Quo. As a percent of GNP, the deficit in 2000 is only 0.3% in the PPSS Case, a 97.8% improvement from the 12.2% under the Status Quo.

The salutary economic effects of the Federal spending cuts on the U.S. economy as projected by the DRI model are summarized in the table on the following pages.

As shown, *real GNP* in the PPSS Savings Case gets off to a relatively slow start compared to the Status Quo Case—growing at 3.8% per annum, 1983–1985, compared to 4.6% for the Status Quo Case—as a result of the reduction in the stimulus provided by government spending. Thereafter, however, longer run elements begin to fall into place—e.g., lower interest rates, which stimulate investment, and a greater share of resources devoted to growth of the private sector. Growth under the PPSS Savings assumptions accelerates and runs 0.5% point higher than

Comparison of Key Economic Variables,
Status Quo and PPSS Savings Cases

		(1)	(2)	(3)	(4)
		Status Quo of Current Policies	PPSS Savings	PPSS Fav./(Unfav.) to Status Quo	
				Amount	%

		Average Annual % Increase/(Decrease)			
	Money GNP				
(1)	1983–1985	9.2%	8.4%	(0.8)% pts.	(8.7)%
(2)	1985–1990	9.7	8.5	(1.2)	(12.4)
(3)	1990–1995	10.2	8.8	(1.4)	(13.7)
(4)	1995–2000	10.1	9.3	(0.8)	(7.9)
(5)	1983–2000	9.9	8.8	(1.1)	(11.1)
	Real GNP				
(6)	1983–1985	4.6%	3.8%	(0.8)% pts.	(17.4)%
(7)	1985–1990	3.5	3.5	—	—
(8)	1990–1995	1.9	2.4	0.5	26.3
(9)	1995–2000	1.4	1.9	0.5	35.7
(10)	1983–2000	2.5	2.7	0.2	8.0
	Inflation				
(11)	1983–1985	4.4%	4.4%	—	—
(12)	1985–1990	6.0	4.8	1.2% pts.	20.0%
(13)	1990–1995	8.2	6.2	2.0	24.4
(14)	1995–2000	8.5	7.3	1.2	14.1
(15)	1983–2000	7.2	5.9	1.3	18.1

	High-Grade Corporate Bond Rate	Average for Period			
(16)	1984–1985	11.68%	11.19%	0.49% pts.	4.2%
(17)	1986–1990	11.88	9.95	1.93	16.2
(18)	1991–1995	12.38	10.05	2.33	18.8
(19)	1996–2000	14.75	11.33	3.42	23.2
(20)	1984–2000	12.85	10.53	2.32	18.1

	3-Month T-Bill Rate	Average for Period			
(21)	1984–1985	9.37%	8.09%	1.28% pts.	13.7%
(22)	1986–1990	10.21	6.22	3.99	39.1
(23)	1991–1995	10.77	6.78	3.99	37.1
(24)	1996–2000	14.32	8.99	5.33	37.2
(25)	1984–2000	11.48	7.42	4.07	35.4

	Unemployment Rate				
(26)	1984–1985	8.30%	8.65%	(0.35)% pts.	(4.2)%
(27)	1986–1990	6.46	7.40	(0.94)	(14.6)
(28)	1991–1995	5.82	6.68	(0.86)	(14.8)
(29)	1996–2000	6.50	7.10	(0.60)	(9.2)
(30)	1984–2000	6.50	7.25	(0.75)	(11.5)

Comparison of Key Economic Variables,
Status Quo and PPSS Savings Cases *(continued)*

		(1)	(2)	(3)	(4)
		Status Quo of Current Policies	PPSS Savings	PPSS Fav./(Unfav.) to Status Quo	
				Amount	%
	Industrial Production	Average Annual % Inc./(Dec.)			
(31)	1983–1985	7.8%	6.4%	(1.4)% pts.	(18.0)%
(32)	1985–1990	4.8	4.9	0.1	2.1
(33)	1990–1995	2.2	2.9	0.7	31.8
(34)	1995–2000	1.4	2.3	0.9	64.3
(35)	1983–2000	3.4	3.7	0.3	8.8
	Real Business Fixed Investment				
(36)	1983–1985	5.3%	4.9%	(0.4)% pts.	(7.6)%
(37)	1985–1990	2.9	5.1	2.2	75.9
(38)	1990–1995	1.8	3.1	1.3	72.2
(39)	1995–2000	1.5	2.4	0.9	60.0
(40)	1983–2000	2.4	3.7	1.3	54.2
	Housing Starts	Average for Period (000 Units)			
(41)	1984–1985	1,704	1,728	24	1.4%
(42)	1986–1990	1,587	1,690	103	6.5
(43)	1991–1995	1,357	1,606	249	18.4
(44)	1996–2000	1,101	1,521	420	38.2
(45)	1984–2000	1,390	1,620	230	16.6

the Status Quo Case during the 1990's—a gain of 26.3% over the Status Quo for 1990–1995, and 35.7% for 1995–2000.

Although *inflation* tends to accelerate under both cases, the large deficits in the Status Quo Case lead to a rate of inflation of 8.6% in 1995 and averaging 8.5% per year, 1995–2000. By comparison, inflation in the PPSS Savings Case rises to 7.3%, 1995–2000—1.2% points, or 14.1%, less than the Status Quo. For the period 1983–2000 as a whole, the PPSS Savings Case at 5.9% a year is 1.3% points, or 18.1%, below the 7.2% inflation rate projected by DRI for the Status Quo Case.

Despite the greater growth of real GNP in the PPSS Savings Case, the more favorable—i.e., lower—rate of inflation which accompanies it results in slower growth of money, or nominal, GNP than under the Status Quo. Over the 1984–2000 projection period, nominal GNP rises an average of 8.8% per year in the PPSS Savings Case compared to 9.9% per year in the Status Quo Case.

As would be expected, with lower inflation, *interest rates* in the PPSS Case are lower as well. The rate for high grade corporates is projected to drop from an 11.19% average, 1984–1985, to 9.95% in 1986–1990 before inflation pushes it back to 11.33% in 1996–2000. The rate on T-Bills is more reactive, dropping from 8.09% in 1984–1985 to 6.22% in 1986–1990, and then rising to 8.99% for 1996–2000. By comparison, in the Status Quo Case, yields increase steadily to average 14.75% on corporates, and 14.32% on T-bills during 1996–2000. *Real rates*—i.e., interest rates after adjusting for inflation—are also lower in the PPSS Case.

Real interest rates on both short and long-term debt are projected to be in an uptrend under the Status Quo, rising to over 8% by 2000, as the continually growing deficits and rekindling of inflation lead to expectations of even higher rates of inflation. In contrast, in the PPSS Savings Case, the real rate on high grade corporates remains in a fairly narrow range, with no discernable trend until the late 1990's when it rises to 5.24% in 2000. For the entire 1984-2000 period, the real rate in the PPSS Case averages 4.68%, 143 basis points, or 23.4%, lower than the Status Quo. Similarly, in the PPSS Case, the average real yield on T-Bills over the 1984–2000 period is 1.54% in the PPSS Savings Case, 301 basis points, or 66.2%, favorable to the Status Quo.

The lower real interest rates resulting from the PPSS recommendations lead to more rapid growth of both *industrial production* and *real business fixed investment* than occurs given the Status Quo of Current Policies. As shown in the Comparison of Key Economic Variables table, industrial production, mirroring real GNP, grows more slowly at first in the PPSS Case, although growth of 6.4% per year, 1983–1985, is still healthy. By the late 1990's, however, when the economy stalls under the Status Quo, industrial production growth in the PPSS Case is 2.1% per year—0.7% point, or 50% higher. Over the entire 1983–2000 period, industrial production in the PPSS Case grows at 3.7% per year, 0.3% point, or 8.8%, faster than under the Status Quo.

The pickup in industrial production has a multiplier effect on real business fixed investment. From 1983 to 1985, fixed investment grows 4.9% per year, (0.4)% point slower than under the Status Quo. This accelerates to 5.1% per year, 1985–1990, 1.76 times the Status Quo rate. During the 1990–1995 period, investment growth slows to 3.1% per year, but this is still 1.3% points, or 72.2%, faster than under the Status Quo.

Housing starts also benefit from the lower interest rates and are consistently higher if the PPSS recommendations are implemented. The difference is slight at first—just 24,000 starts per year—or 1.4%—during 1984–1985. By 1996–2000, however, there are an average 420,000 more starts per year—38.2% higher—in the PPSS Savings Case than under the Status Quo, and the average improvement of 230,000 starts per year translates into 3.9 million more houses over the entire 1984–2000 period in the PPSS Case than under the Status Quo.

Unlike the other key economic variables, the *unemployment rate* is higher as a result of the recommendations than it would have been under the Status Quo. This is true for all periods shown, with unemployment averaging 7.2%, 1984–2000, in the PPSS Savings Case—0.7% point, or 11.5%, higher than under the Status Quo. However, this higher unemployment rate does not reflect fewer people working, but rather more people in the labor force.

As a result of the more rapidly growing real GNP and business fixed investment that follow from the PPSS recommendations, by 2000, 2.2 million jobs are created that would not have been under the Status Quo. Also, as a result of the improved economy, 2.7 million more people are induced to join the labor force than would have been under the Status Quo. The unfavorable variance in the unemployment rate resulting from the PPSS recommendations reflects the difference between these numbers, and should be considered in the context of 2.2 million additional people at work.

In net, as analyzed by DRI in a Federal budget model specifically designed for this analysis and by use of its large econometric model of the U.S. economy, the PPSS savings have a broadly positive effect on the growth and development of the U.S. economy. Apart from reducing the deficit to near balance, it results in greater overall economic growth, lower inflation, lower interest rates, increased housing, and greater investment in the economy over the period to the end of this century than would result from sticking with the trend of current policies. Further details on the methodology and data used in the analysis are contained in Volume II.

B. Highlights of Cost Saving and Revenue Enhancement Opportunities

The 47 PPSS reports contain 2,478 specific recommendations on 784 different issues. Their implementation could result in net savings and revenue enhancements of $424.4 billion over three years, after eliminating about $120.6 billion in savings and revenue overlap.

The opportunities for realizing these savings pervade the entire structure of the Federal Government. They involve better management through introduction of proven business techniques. They include provision of more timely data focused for use in decision making. They concern every major management function, especially human resources, fiscal affairs, procurement, facilities, and organization management. Nearly three-quarters (72.5 percent) of the projected savings require Congressional action if they are to be realized. Another 19.6 percent can be acted on by individual departments and agencies, while 7.9 percent require Presidential action.

Virtually every department and agency in the Federal Government is involved in some way, especially when considering such cross-cutting functional areas as personnel management, automated data processing, and financial management. The projected savings are big where expenditures are big, and thus they are concentrated in such departments as

Defense and Health and Human Services, and in Government-wide functions involving personnel, procurement, and financial management.

There are some striking "big ticket" items included in the total. One such item deals with the need for improved management of subsidized programs. Currently, some 79 percent of all the taxes collected, including personal and corporate, are used by Government contributions to transfer payments ($408 billion in FY 1983) and pay interest on the Federal debt ($88.9 billion in net interest in FY 1983). That leaves only 21 percent of taxes collected available to run the Government, and some $60 billion of that goes for the administrative costs of delivering these subsidized programs. PPSS estimates that three-year savings of $59 billion could be achieved in the area of means-tested subsidy programs alone.

In addition to the projected savings and revenue enhancements, PPSS has projected ·cash acceleration opportunities totalling some $66 billion over three years. These have to do with situations in which monies due the Government can be collected more expeditiously, thereby reducing the requirement for Government borrowings. Consequent savings in interest costs have been tallied with overall projected savings and revenue enhancements.

In the chapters that follow, there will be discussions of duplicated and unduplicated savings and revenues. Duplicated savings refers to the aggregation of gross cost saving and revenue enhancement opportunities identified by the 47 individual reports. Since some of the Task Forces looked at cross-cutting issues that involve more than one Governmental department or agency, they have, in some cases, identified savings that were also claimed by the agency-focused Task Forces. This overlap has been netted out in this Report to arrive at unduplicated savings totals.

Table II-1 identifies total cost saving and revenue enhancement opportunities over three years of $545.0 billion (duplicated) for each of the 47 reports released by PPSS. Table II-2 shows a breakdown of the $120.6 billion in overlapping savings, by major functional area, contained within the gross amount of $545.0 billion. The difference between the

TABLE II-1
PPSS Reports
Savings and Revenue Enhancement Opportunities
Three Year Totals (Duplicated)
($ Millions)

Reports	(1) Savings	(2) Revenue	(3) Total
1. Program Subsidies	$ 58,900.0	$ 0.0	$ 58,900.0
2. Federal Retirement Programs	58,100.0	0.0	58,100.0
3. Defense—OSD	44,508.4	248.2	44,756.6
4. Personnel Management	39,270.1	0.0	39,270.1
5. Federal Health Care Costs	28,900.00	0.0	28,900.0
6. Privatization	11,190.9	17,226.2	28,417.1

TABLE II-1
PPSS Reports
Savings and Revenue Enhancement Opportunities
Three Year Totals (Duplicated)
($ Millions) *(continued)*

	(1)	(2)	(3)
Reports	Savings	Revenue	Total
7. Air Force	27,603.7	0.0	27,603.7
8. Financial Asset Management	13,776.7	9,726.2	23,502.9
9. Procurement	20,271.0	0.0	20,271.0
10. Automated Data Processing/OA	19,062.6	0.0	19,062.6
11. Beyond PPSS	10,773.2	5,174.0	15,947.2
12. Army	13,400.3	0.0	13,400.3
13. Health & Human Svcs./HCFA/PHS	12,676.5	662.0	13,338.5
14. Agriculture	12,237.3	606.3	12,843.6
15. Research & Development	12,089.8	0.0	12,089.8
16. Federal Hospital Management	9,191.4	2,721.1	11,912.5
17. Wage Setting Laws	11,650.0	0.0	11,650.0
18. Treasury	2,366.8	9,139.5	11,506.3
19. User Charges	0.0	10,210.9	10,210.9
20. Banking	1,616.6	7,782.0	9,398.6
21. Health & Human Svcs./SSA	8,407.0	980.0	9,387.0
22. Congressional Encroachment	7,755.3	1,070.0	8,825.3
23. Navy	7,185.0	0.0	7,185.0
24. Low Income Standards	5,887.3	0.0	5,887.3
25. Federal Construction	5,446.0	0.0	5,446.0
26. Transportation	2,712.5	1,705.3	4,417.8
27. Energy	2,789.6	1,290.9	4,080.5
28. Labor	3,718.2	0.0	3,718.2
29. Business	2,366.6	929.0	3,295.6
30. Veterans Administration	2,120.0	953.3	3,073.3
31. Education	2,827.8	0.0	2,827.8
32. Housing & Urban Development	2,460.3	357.5	2,817.8
33. Real Property	2,361.9	0.0	2,361.9
34. EPA/SBA/FEMA	1,660.3	199.3	1,859.6
35. Travel & Transportation Mgmt.	1,850.0	0.0	1,850.0
36. Publ's, Printing & Audio Visual	1,463.0	264.8	1,727.8
37. Interior	271.2	1,022.1	1,293.3
38. Justice	183.2	666.9	850.1
39. State/U.S. Information Agency	382.8	360.0	742.8
40. Commerce	258.8	471.0	729.8
41. Land & Facilities Management	200.7	426.2	626.9
42. Health & Human Services/Other	601.7	0.0	601.7
43. Federal Feeding	259.6	38.8	298.4
44. Information Gap	0.0	0.0	0.0
45. Federal Financial Management	0.0	0.0	0.0
46. Federal Management Systems	0.0	0.0	0.0
47. Anomalies	0.0	0.0	0.0
TOTALS: Duplicated	$470,754.1	$74,231.5	$544,985.6
LESS: Duplicated Amounts	(112,786.1)	(7,848.2)	(120,634.3)
TOTALS: Unduplicated	$357,968.0	$66,383.3	$424,351.3

TABLE II-2
PPSS Reports
Duplicated Savings and Revenue Enhancement Opportunities
Three Year Totals by Function
($ Millions)

	(1)	(2)	(3)
Functional Areas Affected	*Savings*	*Revenue*	*Total*
1. Federal Retirement Programs	$ 37,322.2	$ 0.0	$ 37,322.2
2. Weapons Systems Acquisition	14,351.6	0.0	14,351.6
3. Medicare/Medicaid	8,940.0	0.0	8,940.0
4. OMB Circular A-76	8,807.7	0.0	8,807.7
5. Automated Data Processing/OA	7,964.0	0.0	7,964.0
6. Power Marketing Administration	785.3	5,833.8	6,619.1
7. Federal Subsidies	6,392.5	0.0	6,392.5
8. Inventory Management—Military	6,033.0	0.0	6,033.0
9. Commissary Operations	3,481.7	0.0	3,481.7
10. Davis-Bacon Act	3,330.5	0.0	3,330.5
11. Service Contract Act	2,383.0	0.0	2,383.0
12. Research and Development	2,286.6	0.0	2,286.6
13. Weapons Systems Cost Estimating	1,883.0	0.0	1,883.0
14. Coast Guard Services—User Fees	1,259.4	418.2	1,677.6
15. Walsh-Healey Act	1,671.5	0.0	1,671.5
16. Veterans Admin. Hospitals	1,436.5	0.0	1,436.5
17. Military Base Support	918.0	0.0	918.0
18. Military Health Care	744.7	0.0	744.7
19. Spare Parts Break-out	689.4	0.0	689.4
20. Tax Exempt Bonds	0.0	662.0	662.0
21. Cash Management	492.2	0.0	492.2
22. Unnecessary Military Bases	337.0	30.0	367.0
23. Cargo Preference Act	357.5	0.0	357.5
24. Foreign Military Sales	0.0	248.2	248.2
25. Recreation Fees	0.0	226.9	226.9
26. Debt Collection Management	180.0	19.3	199.3
27. FCC User Charges	0.0	132.4	132.4
28. Freight Transportation Audit	130.2	0.0	130.2
29. Public Rangelands/Grazing Fees	0.0	125.4	125.4
30. Direct Lending Phaseout—SBA/FMHA	100.0	0.0	100.0
31. Government Printing Offices	99.3	0.0	99.3
32. Vehicle Fleet Management	86.5	0.0	86.5
33. Small Business Act Sec. 8(a)	76.8	0.0	76.8
34. Military Moves to Alaska & Hawaii	69.5	0.0	69.5
35. Military Reserves Dual Pay	66.2	0.0	66.2
36. Firewood Fees	0.0	63.6	63.6
37. Government Employee Travel	51.5	0.0	51.5
38. Annual Loan Guaranty Fee	0.0	42.7	42.7
39. Direct Loan Application Fees	0.0	23.2	23.2
40. Soil Survey Fees	0.0	22.5	22.5
41. Consumables Management—Military	20.0	0.0	20.0
42. Purchase of Foreign Currency	17.1	0.0	17.1
43. Max. Loan Guaranty Rate—SBA/FMHA	11.2	0.0	11.2
44. Military Accrued Leave Pay	6.3	0.0	6.3
45. Certified Lenders' Program	4.2	0.0	4.2
TOTALS	$112,786.1	$7,848.2	$120,634.3

gross reported three-year savings/revenue opportunities of $545.0 billion and the overlap of $120.6 billion is the net (unduplicated) three-year savings and revenue opportunities reported by PPSS of $424.4 billion.

The overriding theme of the recommendations in these Task Force reports is that the Federal Government has significant deficiencies from managerial and operating perspectives, resulting in hundreds of billions of dollars of needless expenditures that taxpayers have to bear each year. The reports make clear that these deficiencies are not the result of a lack of competence or enthusiasm on the part of Federal employees. Rather, responsibility rests squarely on the Executive Branch and the Congress, which in the final analysis are the joint architects of the Federal Government's management systems, policies, and practices.

It is, admittedly, a staggering task to manage an organization whose size dwarfs even the largest private sector corporations. Still, the Federal Government is also an organization with human and financial resources of gigantic dimensions, and it would appear that one Administration after another has simply not been as effective as it should have been in productively employing those resources. The thousands of PPSS recommendations attest to the work that can be done—and needs to be done right now—to bring the management of the Federal Government under control.

At the same time, it is important to recognize that inefficient management practices and procedures in the Federal Government are not always the result of shortcomings in the Executive Branch. Indeed, Congressional involvement in day-to-day management decisions has frequently delayed or prevented achievement of efficiencies proposed by program managers, thus costing the taxpayers billions of dollars in unnecessary expense. Congress may have every constitutional right to involve itself in the details of routine Government operations; PPSS certainly has no competence or desire to argue such constitutional issues. It is critical for the Congress to realize, however, that exercising this right can prove costly, counterproductive, and ultimately disabling to Executive Branch managers—who are trying to employ as they see best the personnel and other resources allocated to them to accomplish their missions.

Why does Congressional micro-management occur? Primarily, of course, it is because the American political system places members of the Congress in the very difficult position of balancing the local concerns of their constituents with the overall needs of the entire Nation—interests that are not always congruent. It is hardly surprising that in such an environment Senators and Congressmen generally make every effort to keep Federal funds, Federal offices, and military bases firmly ensconced in their particular states and districts, even if shifting them elsewhere (or cutting them out of the budget entirely) would make better sense from a managerial, and a national, perspective.

Because of the complex interactions in our checks and balances system, it is not always easy to identify which branch of Government has been responsible for individual shortfalls in Federal operations. Nor is it particularly fruitful to try to make such distinctions. However, it is a relatively straightforward matter to determine which branch has the authority to implement the PPSS recommendations designed to remedy these shortfalls. Congress has primary authority to take action that could realize 72.5 percent of the PPSS savings, the President has authority over 7.9 percent, and agencies/departments (over which the President obviously exerts considerable influence) have over 19.6 percent. Their willingness to exercise that authority, and to work together in doing so, will determine how quickly the potential savings will begin having an impact on Federal deficits.

Ultimately, of course, it is the American voter who will decide whether we continue along the same overcommitted path we have been on for the past two decades—and thereby court fiscal disaster—or make the significant changes required to put our fiscal house in order. Some, but by no means all, of those changes are imbedded in the 2,478 recommendations put forward by PPSS which have the potential to save taxpayers $424.4 billion over three years. The extent to which the public impresses on both the Executive Branch and the Congress the importance of implementing these recommendations will perhaps give some indication of how committed we are to practicing as a Nation the same prudence we seek to bring to the management of our businesses and our individual financial affairs. Our survival as a free and prosperous Nation depends upon it.

Before turning to the detailed descriptions of the PPSS findings, conclusions, and recommendations, it is perhaps useful to give some "reality" to the PPSS savings figures because it is difficult for any of us to understand exactly what it means to have $10 million, much less $1 billion or more. One way of getting a handle on these vast sums is to consider that instances of unnecessary expenditures identified by PPSS mean that the equivalent of the following tax revenues are being wasted:

- $10 million   = Federal income taxes paid in 1983 by about 4,509 median income families

- $100 million = Federal income and Social Security taxes paid in 1983 by 26,089 median income families

- $500 million = enough to reduce Federal income taxes by 31.3% for each of the lowest 23.5 million returns in 1981

- $1 billion   = total Federal income taxes paid in 1981 by residents in either Alaska, Maine, or Rhode Island; and more than paid by residents in any of 7 other states

- $20 billion   = total Federal income taxes paid in 1981 by individuals in all eight Rocky Mountain states plus Washington state—a total of 5.4 million tax returns

- $50 billion = total Federal income taxes paid in 1981 by all taxpayers earning under $20,000

- $100 billion = almost all the Federal income taxes paid in 1981 by individuals residing in states west of the Mississippi

INDEX

III

WHAT WE FOUND AND WHY

THIS CHAPTER includes savings and revenue enhancement opportunities which could result in three year savings of $424 billion, equivalent to the three year tax liability of 63.8 million median income families.

PPSS, in collaboration with Data Resources, Inc. (DRI), the largest economic forecasting firm in the United States, projected the outlook for Federal finances, assuming a continuation of present policies through the 17 years ending in the year 2000. Details on this projection may be found in Section VII, Volume II, "Long-Term Economic Impact of PPSS Savings." The net of the forecast is as follows:

Federal Deficit,
Debt and Interest, 1980–2000
(\$ Billions)

	Year	(1) Deficit	(2) Debt	(3) Interest on Debt
(1)	1980	\$ (59.6)	\$ 914.3	\$ 52.5
(2)	1983	(195.4)	1,381.9	87.8
(3)	1985	(185.1)	1,764.1	120.9
(4)	1990	(386.7)	3,211.0	252.3
(5)	1995	(775.4)	6,156.7	540.9
(6)	2000	(1,966.0)	13,020.9	1,520.7
(7)	2000 as a Multiple of 1980	33.0X	14.2X	29.0X

Present policies are driving the deficit from $59.6 billion in 1980 to 33 times that level, or to almost $2 trillion in the year 2000. This escalation of the deficit would bring the Public Debt to an incredible $13.0 trillion in

2000, about four times our entire 1983 GNP. The interest burden alone would be over $1.5 trillion in the year 2000.

With that background, it was the judgment of PPSS that the United States, as we enter the mid-1980's, is in a new ballgame—one where many of the old rules no longer apply and where many of the "sacred cows" will have to be sacrificed. It is the PPSS view that, if the taxpaying public were to realize how serious the condition of Federal Government finances is, they would demand drastic action from their elected representatives. American taxpayers, however, are not aware of the crisis proportions of the impending deficits and, therefore, have never seriously questioned the need for and effectiveness of the myriad programs for which hard-earned tax dollars are expended.

For example, it is certain that the average American family, paying income taxes of $2,218/year, would not tolerate retirement benefits to Government employees which are from 3 to 6 times what is offered in the best private sector plans and which provide lifetime benefits of up to $1.5 million to Government annuitants.

The all important point in the entire PPSS effort is the context in which its recommendations are considered. If the situation is not very crucial, why touch, for example, Federal pensions? On the other hand, if the taxpayers see a financial debacle, everything will be looked at and, if unfairness exists—injustice that hurts the average taxpaying American family—it will be redressed.

Further, the taxes of all families would have to be increased by 38% to offset the average annual Federal deficits of the years 1980–1983. With the DRI forecast of a deficit approaching $2 trillion in the year 2000, personal income taxes would have to be increased by 122% to balance the budget in that year.

Clearly, it is inconceivable that American taxpayers would permit themselves to be subjected to near confiscatory tax rates. That is why PPSS has felt that there should be no holds barred—no "sacred cows" —with reference to what it should study or what it should recommend.

Indeed, it is hoped and expected that the American taxpayer will address this issue in correspondence with his or her legislative representative and that the latter will carefully consider all of the PPSS recommendations within the context of the realities of the next 17 years.

In addressing Government operations, major focus has been on restoring financial stability, and not on whether the identified opportunity is old or new, controversial or acceptable. PPSS believes that opportunities viewed as controversial and unacceptable in the past can give rise to public debate which will result in:

• Better ideas, which can stimulate

• New approaches, and provide

• Answers to long-standing problems, while gaining

• Acceptance of needed corrective measures.

Efficiency and effectiveness have long been recognized as the essence of any well managed operation. PPSS recommendations are designed to increase efficiency with improved effectiveness while continuing to be fully responsive to the needs of the Nation. Specifically, the PPSS opportunities stress the need for cost savings, particularly in this period of heightened concern about Federal deficits. This focus on efficiency however, is coupled with the recognition that promoting greater competence and incentives in Government, i.e., improving effectiveness, is as important as holding the line on expenditures. The opportunities in this chapter are grouped under the major management headings of structure, systems, programs, and people for ease of implementation and follow-up control.

To implement PPSS recommendations and to achieve resulting savings will require a continuing, organized, and systematic process. Since money, manpower, and time are always limited, priorities must be established and adhered to. The work of individuals and organizations assigned responsibility for implementing PPSS recommendations will require coordination, communication, and control and will be dependent on:

• The concurrence of Administrative and Congressional leaders; and

• The cooperation and hard work of Government employees at all levels.

The opportunities described in the following pages are the most pressing, telling stories across Government. They require immediate attention. Many are dependent on institutional changes to bring about long-term improvement. If the problems identified are left uncorrected, they can only deteriorate and result in "opportunities lost," leading to the loss of national vitality and the erosion of freedoms.

They are the savings and revenue opportunities that can:

a) reduce Federal Debt in the year 2000, just 17 years from now, from an estimated $13 trillion to $2.5 trillion, a reduction of $10.5 trillion.

b) reduce the annual interest expense in 2000 from $1.5 trillion to $75 billion.

c) reduce the Federal Deficit in 2000 from $2.0 trillion to $37 billion.

d) reduce the percent increase in Federal income taxes necessary to balance the budget from 122% to 2%.

III. A.   The Federal Structure: Why It Produces Inefficiency and Waste and What Must Be Done

PPSS in analyzing Federal Government operations and seeking and identifying opportunities to cut costs, concluded that a major obstacle to improving the efficiency and effectiveness of the Government is the Federal structure itself. PPSS identified the need for a mechanism at the top level of the Government to provide much greater emphasis on management improvement. Accordingly, PPSS recommended the establishment of an Office of Federal Management (OFM) in the Executive Office of the President, responsible for policies and programs throughout the Government to improve financial management information systems, to coordinate reporting policies and procedures, to assure effective management of human resources and for planning and budgeting.

In FY 1983, the Government spent $19.8 billion in the specific areas covered by PPSS recommendations, with spending estimated to increase to $96.6 billion by the year 2000 if present policies are continued. Implementing PPSS recommendations would reduce spending to $56.9 billion in 2000, a saving of $39.7 billion or 41.1%.

No single department or agency is responsible for overall Executive Branch administrative direction and policy setting. Responsibilities for property, financial management, human resources, and ADP management are distributed among many agencies. This condition results from a long history of uncoordinated and often conflicting legislation and administrative actions. Major structural defects include:

• Lack of centralized financial and administrative management;

• Lack of government-wide management information; and

• Lack of continuity in key management positions.

There is no centralized management for financial and accounting functions. The Federal Government accounts for more than one-quarter of all economic activity in the United States. No agency, however, is clearly responsible, for example, for developing and coordinating financial management policies. As a result, the Government has experienced significant difficulties in establishing procedures for effective cash management, debt and receivables collection, inventory management, and financial reporting.

The lack of government-wide management information inhibits the ability of central agencies to improve administrative functions. Without key indicators of performance, agencies tend to "control" operations by standardizing procedures and promulgating regulations. Problems are obscured because the information that would identify them is not available.

Tenure in key management positions is short, resulting in a lack of continuity in management. The average tenure for political appointees in agencies and departments is 18 months. In the General Services Administration, for example, there have been 9 administrators, 10 deputy administrators, and 14 commissioners for procurement activities in the past ten years.

Improving the management of administrative activities should be based on (a) centralized responsibility for policy development and direction in the areas of financial management, and budgeting and planning; (b) effective management information systems; and (c) the appointment of senior officials with extensive managerial experience for long-term service.

Q. What conclusions were reached and what recommendations did PPSS propose to overcome these problems?

A. PPSS concluded that resolution requires establishment of an *Office of Federal Management* with responsibilities and authorities that would enable it to introduce management changes throughout the Government.

Q. What are some specific examples of recommendations PPSS made regarding the structure of the Federal Government?

A. Examples of cost savings that could be achieved through modification of the structure include the following:

• The Department of Agriculture has three agencies that perform duplicative research analysis. Consolidation of the Economic Research Service, the Foreign Agricultural Service, and the World Agricultural Outlook Board into a single entity and elimination of the overlap in functions could save $22 million over three years.

• Three agencies of the Department of Agriculture—the Soil Conservation Service, the Agriculture Stabilization and Conservation Service, and the Farmers Home Administration—often have separate offices in the same counties. Consolidation could save $194 million over three years.

• The structure of an organization is, of course, frequently determined by the nature of the services it is charged to deliver. Thus, changes of mission can result in scaled back requirements for services and facilities, permitting structural changes that can produce economies. For example, administration of the Railroad Retirement Board's (RRB) field offices can be transferred to the Social Security Administration; the RRB would then no longer require a separate field service and could consolidate other functions, resulting in savings over three years of $26 million.

• Reorganization of the structure of the Federal Home Loan Bank Board, reducing the number of district banks in the system, would increase efficiency and effectiveness and produce savings of $20 million over three years.

• Air passengers and cargo entering the United States are inspected at their ports of entry by as many as six Federal agencies. Consolidation of port-of-entry inspection services would eliminate duplications in overhead, improve coordination of functions, and produce economies of scale for savings of $48 million over three years. Improved service to travelers could also eliminate delays that have been estimated to cost more than $80 million.

- Consolidating Department of Transportation (DOT) regions from ten to six and reducing related staffs would produce savings of $45 million in three years without reduction in effectiveness.

- Even more significant savings could be achieved in DOT through consolidation of certain Federal Aviation Administration activities, reducing the number of regions from nine to seven and the number of air traffic control centers from 22 to 15 with total three year savings of $445 million.

- Closing or restructuring the operation of low-volume air traffic control towers, to include defederalization of certain low and moderate activity facilities, would save the FAA an additional $151 million over three years. Similarly, consolidation of Flight Service Stations, closing approximately 100 in the process, would save FAA another $40 million over three years.

Q. Are these savings likely to be achieved, since they require Congressional action?

A. The GAO, Congress' own investigative agency, has issued numerous reports urging Congress to streamline the structure of agencies. Two examples were an April 1979 study suggesting that the Agriculture Department consolidate many of its field offices, and an October 1978 study suggesting that the Customs Service reduce the number of regional offices. Congress has not acted on GAO recommendations for structural reorganization.

GAO has documented that in some cases the opposition to structural reform comes from Government employees directly affected by reorganization. Employees encouraged Congressional intervention using such tactics as: emphasizing human and financial losses when an office within their district is closed or consolidated; applying pressure through protest marches, letters and telephone calls; using alliances between Congressional staff and agency personnel; and enlisting support and influence of former employees of affected agencies.

Q. What conclusions and recommendations did PPSS draw from analysis of Federal regulatory processes?

A. Certain regulatory procedures and processes could be made more effective, for example:

- Mitigation policies are intended to avoid or reduce environmental damage. Costs of mitigation can be a substantial addition to Federal construction expenditures. Although some mitigation is desirable, excesses occur due to overlapping and duplicative regulations and jurisdictional authorities. PPSS recommended that these practices and policies be reviewed to eliminate unnecessary mitigation and establish a systematic and consistent enforcement policy. Savings over three years are estimated at $993 million.

• Construction costs and time delays can be reduced by integrating National Environmental Policy Act (NEPA) reviews with other special purpose environment review requirements. These special reviews sometimes duplicate the NEPA reviews. By integrating the special purpose environmental reviews into the NEPA process, PPSS estimates savings of $339 million over three years.

Q. What recommendations did PPSS make in streamlining the structure of the Department of Defense?

A. Opportunities for cost savings through structural reform of defense activities include:

• The Department of Defense (DOD) distribution system includes 30 wholesale depots with a total attainable storage capacity of 665 million cubic feet, of which only 499 million cubic feet is occupied, for a 68% utilization rate. While some allowance must be made for necessary surge capacity to accommodate changes in demand, significant opportunities for depot consolidation exist. Upgrading the reporting system so that the department has accurate data on warehouse capacity and utilization, and consolidation as recommended, would produce savings of $116 million over three years.

• The Department of Defense operates 29 depot-level maintenance facilities, where heavy maintenance on a variety of systems is performed. The work requires extensive investment in fixed facilities, specialized tools, and complex test equipment. In FY 1983, expenditures for the maintenance performed at such facilities amounted to $12.4 billion. Yet, despite an apparent consensus in DOD that consolidation of depot maintenance facilities offers cost savings opportunities, progress in implementing such changes in the management and delivery of heavy maintenance services has been unsuccessful because of the reluctance of individual Services to give up control. The savings which could be achieved through elimination of redundant management and systems overhead, greater professionalism in the management of industrial activities, and better utilization through elimination of excess capacity amount to $589 million over three years.

• The DOD maintains some 5,600 separate installations and properties worldwide. While the department's military and civilian employee population has decreased from roughly five million people to about three million since 1968, significant base realignments and closures have virtually ceased since the mid-1970s.

Q. Don't base realignments and closures require Congressional action?

A. Every state and almost 60% of all Congressional districts contain, or are adjacent to, military bases or other installations. The payrolls and procurement from these bases provide extensive benefits to the communities.

Few would argue that all of DOD's 5,600 installations and properties worldwide are necessary, efficient or economical. In fact, some proportion of these facilities and the estimated $20 billion a year spent to operate them could be better utilized elsewhere.

Congress has restricted DOD's control of facilities by imposing restrictions which, per DOD, make it "virtually impossible to close any military installation in the country."

The CBO has issued studies and reports suggesting Congress pursue base realignments and closings. The GAO has made similar suggestions. Congress, however, has not acted.

PPSS recommended establishment of a Presidentially appointed bipartisan commission to study the opportunities for base realignments and closures, and estimated that $2.732 billion could be saved in this area over three years by effective action without weakening our defense capabilities.

Q. How will the proposed Office of Federal Management compare with the present management structure, and what will be its new responsibilities?

A. On the following pages are shown the current functional organization of the Office of Management and Budget and the PPSS-recommended functional organization of an Office of Federal Management, along with a discussion of its responsibilities.

Problems of organization and process now hamper effective Government within the Executive Branch because responsibilities for developing and implementing administrative policies are not clearly assigned. Duplications, conflicts and blurred lines of authority are common. For example, the Office of Management and Budget (OMB) and the General Services Administration (GSA) have procurement policy responsibilities. OMB, GSA and the Department of Commerce have government-wide policy-making responsibility for automated data processing.

Just as there is confusion and overlap in terms of assigned responsibility for management policy development in some areas, there is an absence of direction and coordination in other key areas for which no entity has responsibility. No agency is clearly responsible, for example, for developing and coordinating financial management policies. As a re-

EXECUTIVE OFFICE OF THE PRESIDENT

- White House Office
- Office of Policy Development
- Office of Administration
- Council on Environmental Quality
- Regulatory Information Service
- Council of Economic Advisors
- National Security Council
- Office of the U.S. Trade Representative
- Office of Science and Technology Policy

OFFICE OF MANAGEMENT AND BUDGET

OTHER
- Legislative Review/Reference
- Public Affairs
- Other

FEDERAL PROCUREMENT POLICY
- Procurement

MANAGEMENT
- PCIE
- Intergovernmental Affairs
- Coordination of Selected Financial Functions
- Other Management Improvements

MANAGEMENT REFORM TASK FORCE
- Reform 88

INFORMATION AND REGULATORY AFFAIRS
- Regulatory Review
- Implementation of Paperwork Reduction Act

BUDGET
- Budget Preparation and Analysis
- Other Budget Responsibilities

Cabinet Level Departments

Department of Agriculture
Department of Commerce
Department of Defense
Department of Education
Department of Energy
Department of Health and Human Services

Department of Housing and Urban Development
Department of the Interior
Department of Justice
Department of Labor
Department of State
Department of Transportation
Department of the Treasury

Independent Establishments, Corporations, Boards and Commissions

Civil Aeronautics Board
Environmental Protection Agency
Federal Emergency Management Agency
General Services Administration (GSA)
Office of Personnel Management (OPM)
Etc.

Office of Federal Management
Recommended Functional Organization

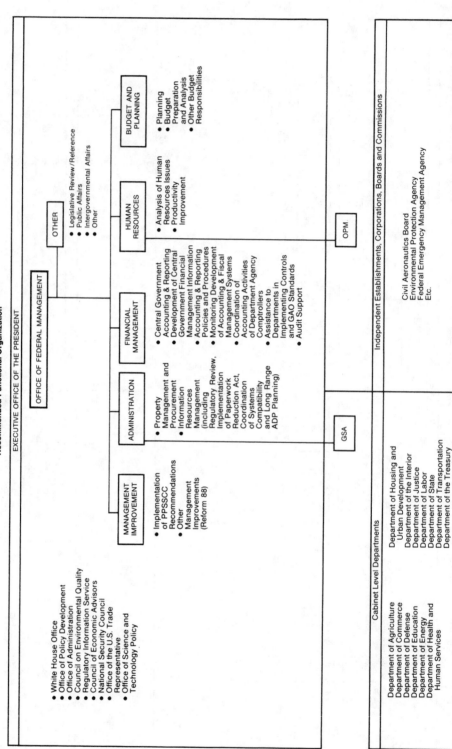

EXECUTIVE OFFICE OF THE PRESIDENT

- White House Office
- Office of Policy Development
- Office of Administration
- Council on Environmental Quality
- Regulatory Information Service
- Council of Economic Advisors
- National Security Council
- Office of the U.S. Trade Representative
- Office of Science and Technology Policy

OFFICE OF FEDERAL MANAGEMENT

OTHER
- Legislative Review/Reference
- Public Affairs
- Intergovernmental Affairs
- Other

MANAGEMENT IMPROVEMENT
- Implementation of PPSSCC Recommendations
- Other Management Improvements (Reform 88)

ADMINISTRATION
- Property Management and Procurement
- Information Resources Management (including Regulatory Review, Implementation of Paperwork Reduction Act, Coordination of Systems Compatibility and Long Range ADP Planning)

FINANCIAL MANAGEMENT
- Central Government Accounting & Reporting
- Development of Central Government Financial Management Information
- Accounting & Reporting Policies and Procedures
- Monitoring Development of Accounting & Fiscal Management Systems
- Coordination of Accounting Activities of Department Agency Comptrollers
- Assistance to Departments in Implementing Controls and GAO Standards
- Audit Support

HUMAN RESOURCES
- Analysis of Human Resources Issues
- Productivity Improvement

BUDGET AND PLANNING
- Planning
- Budget Preparation and Analysis
- Other Budget Responsibilities

GSA

OPM

Cabinet Level Departments

Department of Agriculture
Department of Commerce
Department of Defense
Department of Education
Department of Energy
Department of Health and Human Services

Department of Housing and Urban Development
Department of the Interior
Department of Justice
Department of Labor
Department of State
Department of Transportation
Department of the Treasury

Independent Establishments, Corporations, Boards and Commissions

Civil Aeronautics Board
Environmental Protection Agency
Federal Emergency Management Agency
Etc.

— 32 —

sult the Government has experienced significant difficulties in establishing procedures for effective cash management, debt and receivables collection, inventory and other asset management, and financial reporting to senior officials.

The overall management function delegated to OMB was originally intended to provide the needed direction and coordination of Executive Branch management activities. PPSS findings indicated, however, that this objective has not been achieved. OMB continues to be preoccupied with the annual budgetary process, which claims most of its resources and drives most other activities. When such opportunities are systematically addressed, the results can be dramatic. Specifically, PPSS has identified a total of $68.940 billion in cash acceleration opportunities over a three-year period, largely accounting for a projected interest saving of some $23.662 billion over the same period.

The PPSS recommendations, centering on creation of an Office of Federal Management, are based on a business-like approach that will create an organization capable of effectively directing and coordinating Executive Branch management activities.

The proposed Office of Federal Management would be responsible for policy development and direction in the areas of financial management, budgeting and planning, human resources, administration (including information resources management, procurement and property management), and management improvement. It would consolidate the current fragmented and overlapping management responsibilities into an organizational structure with clearly assigned lines of authority and specific responsibilities.

OFM would include the budget functions of OMB and serve as the President's management staff for effecting major improvements in processes and systems, communications and information flow. It would establish a unit responsible for systematically identifying and implementing management improvements on an ongoing basis, an essential function for sustaining such improvement and ensuring timely implementation of PPSS recommendations.

GSA and the Office of Personnel Management (OPM) would report directly to OFM for policy direction in carrying out their primary roles of developing and implementing procedures and regulations in their respective areas. Such a reporting relationship is based on the general private sector model that employs a corporate staff to ensure a coordinated administrative structure. This includes having the GSA and OPM transferring to departments and agencies responsibility for all operating functions (such as maintenance of office buildings) that are cost justified.

Currently no central Government organization is responsible for directing and coordinating the Federal Government's accounting and financial reporting activities. This missing link in financial management has been the cause of inadequate agency and government-wide financial accounting and reporting. It has permitted inconsistent application of accounting procedures among agencies and resulted in the inability to extract from systems reliable and useful financial data. Thus, the financial management function of OFM would include the accounting and reporting activities of the Department of the Treasury, OMB, and GSA (for government-wide property reporting).

As matters now stand, in virtually all administrative areas—payroll, personnel, accounting, and asset management, to name a few—departments and agencies have developed independent information systems and related procedures, taking little advantage of the experience or work done by other elements. These methods of development and operation have proven to be inefficient, often counterproductive, and very costly.

In addition to the cost involved, there is frequently no commonality or compatibility of data across departments and agencies, leaving those at senior levels of Government with no practical means of obtaining summarized management and financial information. As a result, it has been exceedingly difficult to extract from existing systems timely financial and management data concerning such matters as collection of amounts due the Government, location and utilization of real and personal property, inventories of supplies and materiel, and even the data processing systems currently in use.

To deal with these problems, OFM would be charged to develop common government-wide ADP software systems and related procedures for use in such administrative areas as payroll, accounts receivable, retirement and pensions, general accounting and accounts payable, and fixed asset accounting. Since there are currently more than 300 payroll systems in use in the Federal Government, PPSS recommended that implementation of a common payroll system receive the highest priority. Benefits of OFM activity in this area would include reduced cost of developmental and duplicative activities by Federal departments and agencies and the advantage of having government-wide information with which to manage more effectively.

Effective planning and management of resources are virtually impossible because of the current one year budget requirement; this annual budgeting and appropriations process focuses concern on only the subsequent fiscal year. As a further consequence, the management of Government assets, in such activities as capital planning and cash management, receives little attention, contributing to problems such as deterioration of facilities and loss of funds through inadequate cash management.

OFM would deal with these problems by issuing mission objectives to departments and agencies, outlining the specific objectives of the Administration in relevant program and administrative areas. Action plans for accomplishing assigned objectives would then be prepared by agencies and monitoring of performance would be integrated with OFM's ongoing budget and management activities. As a means of addressing the many opportunities for improving the effectiveness of the audit function, the OFM would establish an audit support activity to coordinate allocation of audit resources across the Government, develop performance standards and audit programs and guidelines, and provide technical assistance in such audit specialty areas as ADP auditing and statistical sampling.

Other related PPSS recommendations include OFM's institution of a Federal planning and budgeting process for capital expenditures and strengthening the budget process to improve its utility for government-wide management, which would include revising appropriation classifications to better match management needs and integrating the financial management and budget processes. The cumulative effect of the recommendations would be to make possible more rigorous and systematic evaluations of Federal programs to provide results-oriented data for more effective program management.

PPSS also concluded that the current annual budget process hinders agency managers' ability to conduct comprehensive planning and analysis of programs beyond the current fiscal year. PPSS therefore has recommended further study of the feasibility of adopting a biennial budget process so as to provide more consideration of long-term management needs.

Because of the rapid turnover of key executives, a condition endemic to the political process, Government functions lack continuity of management. Key appointed officials change every 18 to 24 months. It is not possible to implement and sustain meaningful management improvement in an environment characterized by persistent changes in management. Private sector profit incentives for superior management performance are not present in Government service, nor has the Government developed its own motivational approaches such as widespread senior level recognition for successful accomplishment of goals and objectives.

To assist in overcoming this built-in disadvantage, PPSS recommended that key OFM officials be appointed on a long-term basis and that they have demonstrated strong management capabilities. PPSS recommended a new "contractual" approach for second-tier OFM officials in the fields of financial management, human resources, administration, budget and planning, and management improvement that would provide the security and tenure necessary to carry out long-term improvements. OFM should also have a role in assisting departments and agencies in selection of key administrative officials, such as assistant secretaries for management, comptrollers, and the like, based on their technical and managerial qualifications to work toward a more cohesive and integrated management team across Government.

In what may be one of the most basic deficiencies of the current structure and the manner in which it permits the Executive Branch to function, PPSS found that communication of Administration and agency objectives, plans and accomplishments is lacking within the Executive Branch. Career professionals and employees are not provided with suitable insights into what their agencies plan to accomplish and, as a result, valuable human resources are wasted on misdirected efforts. Thus, it is recommended that OFM direct a systematic communications program that will ensure positive and direct communication from senior Executive Office and agency officials to Government employees, including the possible use of survey and feedback systems to increase upward communication, and an expanded orientation program for appointed officials to assist them in becoming more effective in their new roles more quickly and easily.

It is apparent that current Federal management activities have evolved over many years with little recognition of the need to provide central guidance and direction to achieve a well-coordinated overall process.

Serious structural and procedural problems in Executive Branch management processes, organization, information flow, budgeting, planning and evaluation procedures, continuity of management, and communication practices are documented in the body of the report. What is needed to deal with them effectively is an entity with a clear-cut charter and the continuity of personnel and direction to carry it out.

Several of the recommendations contained in this section can be implemented under authority vested in the Executive Branch. Others, however, will require Congressional approval. To expedite the implementation process and to avoid unnecessary delays, PPSS urges that as many recommendations as possible be implemented by the Executive Branch and *only* those recommendations requiring Congressional approval undergo this more complex and time-consuming process.

> The three-year total of all the recommendations in this section, after elimination of duplication and overlap among issues, is $12.644 billion—equal to the three-year taxes of 1.9 million median income families.

III. B.   The Federal Systems Maze:
How to Chart a Path

Although there are differences in operating styles and requirements between the public and private sectors of our economy, it is imperative that a business-like approach be taken in the management of the Executive Branch. PPSS conducted its study and developed its recommendations on the principle that private sector approaches can help improve managing the Government's business.

The absence of the right information, at the right time, in the right amounts, to make the right decision, renders the Government incapable of effectively assessing its strengths and weaknesses and achieving any reasonable degree of managerial efficiency. Key information concerning budget, programmatic, managerial, administrative, and financial operations is frequently lacking or, when available, is outdated, incomplete, or inaccurate.

In brief, PPSS identified the following weaknesses inherent in the current management process:

Organization and process—within the Executive Branch, responsibilities for developing and implementing administrative policies are not clearly assigned. Duplications, conflicts, and blurred lines of authority among the various units within the Executive Branch abound. For example, both the Office of Management and Budget (OMB) and the General Services Administration (GSA) have procurement policy responsibilities; OMB, GSA, and the Department of Commerce have government-wide automated data processing (ADP) policymaking responsibilities; and GSA shares real property disposition policymaking with the Property Review Board.

Significantly, there is also an absence of direction and coordination in key areas. For example, no agency is clearly responsible for developing and coordinating financial management policies. The result is that the Government has experienced significant difficulties in establishing procedures for effective cash management, debt and receivables collection, inventory and other asset management, and financial reporting to senior officials.

Management information systems—in virtually all administrative areas—payroll, personnel, accounting, and asset management, for example—departments and agencies have developed independent information systems and related procedures, taking little advantage of the experience or work of other departments and agencies. Joint agency operation of systems or the use of private service bureaus to process transactions are rarely considered. Current methods of development and operations are inefficient, often counterproductive, and very costly.

In addition to the cost involved, there is frequently no commonality or compatibility of data across departments and agencies, leaving the senior levels of Government without a practical means of collecting summarized management information.

Budgeting, planning, and evaluation—planning for future years is largely ignored at both the agency and central Government levels. Identifying, communicating, and monitoring the accomplishments of major Administration objectives is often ineffective.

Evaluation of program results and collection of program data for planning and management purposes are also not carried out in a rigorous and systematic manner. Reliable information is not available to enable the Administration to choose among alternative program options.

The budget is not fully used as a "management" tool by OMB or the departments and agencies. Accounting for actual expenditures is usually a separate process from budget preparation and analysis, and budget appropriation classifications are not related to the needs and practices of agency management. Differing from the private sector, the Government stresses budget preparation, while putting less emphasis on budget execution and control.

Reliance on Federal systems and employees to perform functions which could be performed more efficiently and at less cost by the private sector. Government must perform many activities which only a Government can perform. And PPSS has made numerous recommendations for the more efficient operation of those activities within Government. But, if a Government activity can be performed by the private sector, there is no surer way of ensuring that economies will be realized than by turning to the private sector.

Turning to the private sector whenever practical would result in cutting back the size of Government. The use of private contractors to perform commercial activities could, PPSS estimates, reduce the Federal work force, excluding Postal employees, by more than one-fifth. Added to that, if Government were to discontinue or transfer those services which the private sector is already providing or could provide, another major segment of the Federal work force would be eliminated. Perhaps more properly stated, part of the Federal work force would be transferred to private employment.

The size and complexity of Government is staggering, and many aspects are beyond the capabilities of truly effective management, given the inherent constraints of our form of Government—including national priorities, fiscal limitations, Congressional involvement, and legislative restrictions. Reducing the size of Government would be a major step in promoting a more efficient and more responsive Government. This is what reliance upon the private sector can offer.

Aggressively applying the key elements of the business-like approach recommended by PPSS will:

- create an organization and process capable of effectively directing and coordinating Executive Branch management activities;

- foster the development of management information systems which can provide reliable, timely, and compatible information to senior Government managers;

- redirect and expand the budgeting, planning, and evaluation process;

- overcome the weaknesses inherent in current systems resulting from a lack of management continuity;

- develop mechanisms for effective communication of policies and objectives between the Executive Office of the President and executive departments and agencies;

- turn around the trend of increasing the size of Government and implement the policy of reliance upon the private sector.

The Information Gap

A major deficiency of Federal Government management is the lack of information within agencies and across the Government that is essential for planning and control purposes. The GAO has repeatedly cited inadequate planning, budgeting and financial controls and insufficient user involvement as a fundamental problem.

PPSS recommended that the Government's current information management procedures be restructured and that a four-part approach to closing the information gap be implemented. The centerpiece of this is an Information Management Office in the proposed Office of Federal Management and information coordinators in major departments and agencies. Steps needed to close the information gap include assessing the information needs of each department and agency; establishing uniform reporting standards to ensure data accuracy, timeliness, and completeness; upgrading the computer systems used to analyze the data; and effective use of the collected information.

PPSS reviewed issues developed by its Task Forces and noted that cost savings and revenue enhancements of $78.6 billion are possible by correcting some of the Government's information gap problems. Since these problems are pervasive, cost reductions from implementing PPSS recommendations in specific agencies are discussed elsewhere throughout this report; no additional savings are claimed.

As noted at the outset of this report, the purpose of PPSS was to search out waste and inefficiency in the Executive Branch of the Government and to recommend ways in which modern business practices could be put to work to make Government more efficient and effective.

It became immediately apparent that the information essential to this purpose was often not available or was out of date, incomplete, or inaccurate.

Enormous quantities of numbers and other data are generated by the Government, but little of it has been processed and organized for management purposes. For example, within the Air Force Logistics Command, one system generates 500,000 pounds of paper each month, or six million pounds per year, but PPSS found these data of limited value and recommended savings in this one instance of $581 million over three years.

The lack of information, the "information gap," in the Federal Government is widespread. There are two basic aspects to the problem. The first is a major leadership void in the overall management of information. There is no focal point to provide the direction, coordination, and standardization needed to operate effective information systems in the individual agencies. Further, and of a potentially critical nature, there is no central authority integrating individual information systems into a coherent, management information system necessary to support decisionmaking in the Executive Office of the President (EOP).

Coupled with the leadership void are four barriers which inhibit the development and flow of information:

• failure to define the information needed to manage the Government;

- incomplete, inconsistent, and inaccurate data;

- inadequate computer based systems; and

- failure to properly analyze or utilize the available data.

The information gap in the Federal Government is so serious that nobody knows, for example:

- what cash balances are, where they are located, and what total Federal funds have been committed to individual states or localities;

- where real and personal property is located and what it is being used for; and

- how much money is owed to the Government by any one individual or corporation and how long it has been outstanding (in fact, definitions of common lending terms such as deliquencies and defaults vary from agency to agency, thus precluding meaningful government-wide analysis).

The list could go on and on.

Information gaps of this magnitude are not tolerated in the private sector; any company which did not solve the problem quickly would be out of business in short order. Yet, these gaps persist and grow in the Federal Government.

The cost to the Government of these information gaps can only be approximated. PPSS estimated three-year savings opportunities and revenue enhancements of *$78.598 billion by correcting some of these problems*. More importantly, however, the gaps inhibit effective management, fundamental to combatting waste and inefficiency.

PPSS has recommended restructuring the leadership of information management by:

- creating a Presidential Task Force which would be responsible for setting the goals and commitments of the Executive Branch to overcome information deficiencies;

- designating an information coordinator in major departments and agencies to facilitate data collection, information processing, and report dissemination; and

- establishing an Information Management Office in the proposed Office of Federal Management to implement the goals and commitments established by the Presidential Task Force and the Executive Office of the President (EOP).

To proceed with the recommended restructuring, each department and agency needs to assess its information requirements. The private sector has recognized that often a limited amount of carefully selected information can serve to manage essential functions. PPSS found many instances where individual managers in the Government had not recognized this concept and had not identified their most critical information requirements. The situation within agencies ranges from too much to insufficient data. Accounts receivable managers, for example, do not have information on the age of delinquencies to effectively take action on the $37.8 billion of overdue accounts as of 1982. In HUD, PPSS found that some managers are not even aware of the information needed for informed decisions.

The data necessary to generate information needs to be collected. Standards for relevant, complete, timely, accurate, and consistent data are, in many cases, non-existent. The Department of Justice, for example, does not routinely gather basic information on the number, type, and status of cases and investigations in the divisions and offices of U.S. Attorneys. As a result, it is virtually impossible to balance the work load among individual U.S. Attorneys. The Department of Education does not have accurate and timely data to ensure the integrity of its educational grant programs, which dispense $14.5 billion annually. And, in the Small Business Administration, officers receive information on loans over 30 days past due five to six weeks after the delinquency is noted.

Current information systems in the Federal Government are generally based on computer designs of the 1950's and early 1960's. PPSS emphasized the need to apply today's technology as essential to overcoming information gaps. A deterrent in this regard is the extreme time lag in acquiring the latest technology due to Congressional obstacles, as noted further on.

The potential for profitable use of available data has been realized to a limited degree only. For example, in the area of identifying and eliminating fraud and abuse in Federal assistance programs, matching computer files (to identify the numerous instances of overpayments under multiple programs) can be very effective but, with the exception of the Office of the Inspector General at the Department of Health and Human Services, very little has been done in this regard.

Q. In what critical areas is the information system most deficient?

A. The Government lacks essential data in the following major areas:

   • financial and accounting transactions and records;

   • organization and industrial relations;

   • support services; and

   • general administration.

Q. What examples of information gap problems did PPSS note in these areas?

A. There were over 125 specific examples that PPSS noted; the following illustrate a few of the problems found:

   1. Financial and Accounting Transactions and Records

• The Department of Justice (DOJ) has insufficient information to effectively carry out its mission of collecting the Federal Government's defaulted accounts receivable. At the end of 1982, DOJ was responsible for over $1 billion in receivables. Approximately 99% of that amount originated in other agencies. DOJ collection efforts are hindered by a lack of uniformity in the data supplied by originating agencies, accounting terms used, and definitions of "overdue" accounts. Three-year savings/revenue enhancements of $631 million are possible by adopting a uniform reporting system.

• In the Department of Defense (DOD), information for managing $40 billion of spare parts, medical and operating supplies is frequently inaccurate or not available on time. This results in excessive and obsolete inventories and the inefficient movement of supplies. For example, the Air Force has estimated that, with improved inventory management, it could field an additional 40– 60 aircraft at all times. Improving inventory management in DOD could save $6.074 billion over three years.

• The Social Security Administration (SSA) collects income data on potential beneficiaries. Poor internal controls have resulted in an SSA suspense file (income items which cannot be posted to specific accounts) of about 138 million items valued at $89 billion. Paying benefits correctly is contingent on the ability to record earnings correctly. PPSS recommended redesigning the computer systems used to collect and process income data.

• The Air Force Logistics Command (AFLC) uses 104 archaic and costly computer systems that do not provide up-to-date, accurate information to manage a $24.5 billion inventory. Further, AFLC has not taken action to correct these deficiencies. PPSS recommended that efforts to eliminate obsolete hardware and software be instituted immediately, resulting in three-year savings of $581 million.

2. Organization and Industrial Relations

• Federal agencies recognize only a part of their true personnel costs. For example, in FY 1981, agencies were charged with benefit costs equal to 27.8% of gross payroll while total payments from all Government sources, on a comparable basis, were equal to 65.3%. Understated personnel costs, resulting from failure to allocate costs on a realistic basis, can result in: grossly inaccurate budgets, misdirection of management attention, failure to understand the reasons for increasing costs and to recognize potentials for cost savings, and improper cost comparisons to the private sector.

The current systems for allocating and funding total personnel costs of the civilian work force often result in improper assignment of costs to individual programs and functions and, thus, in waste and misdirection of effort.

3. Support Services

• The Pension Benefit Guaranty Corporation (PBGC) is unable to publish verifiable financial statements. In particular, there is a lack of control over accounting for investments, and the pension payment and verification process. PBGC has attempted—with limited success—to apply the kinds of controls used in the private sector. By using private industry services, PBGC can increase its efficiency and save $132 million over three years.

4. General Administration

• With regard to the $4.6 billion spent by Executive agencies on freight transportation, poor management information systems prevent consolidation of government-wide shipping data, hampering the negotiation of freight discounts. Improving data collection systems and their use can result in three-year savings of $530 million. An automated system needs to be developed to provide adequate transportation data to traffic managers throughout Government so that an estimated 3% savings on all transportation costs, and a 2%–5% savings on large volume, large dollar shipments, can be achieved.

Q. What other savings are possible from improvements in the Government's management information systems?

A. Substantial savings are possible in specific programs as noted by the following examples:

• Little historical data is collected by the National Flood Insurance Program (NFIP) to establish a sound basis for anticipating future needs. Without adequate information, NFIP cannot ensure the accomplishment of its objectives. PPSS estimates that three-year savings of $662 million can be achieved by increasing premium rates, raising deductibles, and putting the program on a sound actuarial basis, reducing subsidized rates.

• The VA's budgeting system does not have the information necessary to project future hospital work loads. PPSS recommended that the patient treatment file be expanded and used as a basis for budgeting. In addition, reducing the time patients spend in VA hospitals by approximately one-third (so that average hospital stays are comparable to those in the private sector) and reducing the number of beds available can result in three-year savings of $4.888 billion.

- The Federal Government does not know the total amount that is being spent on training costs due to information gaps in this area. PPSS estimated savings of $66 million over three years if information is developed and used to eliminate duplicate training programs.

Q. Why is so much "knowledge" missing from the Government's information systems?

A. There are many problems with the current information systems. For example:

- An excessive amount of data is produced by some departments and agencies. Much of it is of little value or use to Government decision makers. This proliferation of data tends to impede rather than facilitate the management information process.

For example, for each of the past 17 years, GSA has converted paper and computer tapes detailing the properties owned and leased by Federal agencies into a series of annual reports. The annual report is a 2,000- to 3,000-page document that cannot be used by Federal decision makers because the data about any one property are not integrated.

- Important external information is not monitored; for example, environmental trends and conditions which can affect Federal Government programs. As a result, decisions are made concerning the direction of program activities and the use of resources which are less than effective.

For example, appraisals of technological developments are not properly coordinated with the Department of Defense weapons acquisition process. Decisions about the technologies to be employed in weapons systems are made based on incomplete information.

- Government efforts are often aimed at getting the job done without due concern for efficiency. Considerable time and effort are committed to deciding what is to be done, but all too often a comprehensive post audit is not conducted and no follow-up action is taken. In the private sector, post audit follow-up is considered a critical element in assessing the success or failure of a project and in achieving greater future efficiencies.

For example, of the 28,000 pension checks distributed monthly by the Pension Benefit Guaranty Corporation, only 18,000 are verified as correct. No one knows whether the other 10,000 are accurate.

- Federal department and agency managers do not analyze daily operations on an ongoing basis. This practice inhibits informed decision-making because essential information (such as employee or program performance data, inventory levels, and cash balances) is unavailable.

The Department of Interior's cash management system often takes more than two weeks to collect, record, and deposit payments. Comparable private sector processing is typically accomplished in one or two days. As a result of the time lag (a period during which the cash position is unknown), the Treasury does not have use of the funds and must borrow to fulfill short-term cash needs, incurring interest expenses.

Q. Doesn't the Government have sufficient computers to solve these types of problems?

A. Yes, if you look only at the numbers of computers. It is estimated that there are more than 17,000 computers in the Government. But part of the problem is that they are too old to do the job that needs to be done. The Government's computers are, on average, approximately 6.7 years old. In the private sector, the average age is approximately 3–3.5 years.

In addition to the age problem, the fact that the systems are incompatible—that is, data can't be readily exchanged between them—results in many inefficiencies. For example, because computer systems are not integrated the Government cannot verify the income levels of recipients in needs based programs. As a result, there were overpayments estimated at $4.1 billion in just five programs during 1982.

Q. Are there instances where state-of-the-art computers exist and there are still problems?

A. Yes. The Urban Mass Transportation Administration (UMTA) had FY 1982 obligations of $3.4 billion and, by the end of that year, controlled $25 billion in active, ongoing grants. UMTA spent $10 million on a computer to keep track of these grants. Nevertheless:

• UMTA has been unable to close its books since 1979.

• There have been no account reconciliations since 1977.

• There are no accounts payable or accounts receivable subsidiary records, meaning there is no central ledger detailing who owes what to whom.

• When PPSS asked UMTA to provide financial data for 1972–1982, they did it manually and could only provide records for 1980–1982.

• The computer is unable to display funds carried over from previous years. It cannot immediately update balances.

Q. PPSS noted that one problem area was the lack of consistent definitions from program to program and agency to agency. How can definitional inconsistencies obstruct communication and cause an information gap?

A. One example of this is the variety of meanings both within and across agencies applied to terms used in Federal loan and insurance programs such as "guarantee," "insurance," "delinquency," "default," "forbearance," "subsidy," and "contingent liability."

Inconsistencies in terminology and definitions limit the ability of the Executive Branch and Congress to meaningfully interpret information on program operations. For example, with regard to the definition of "default," if a particular loan is in "default," that could mean several things. Under the Maritime Administration's Federal Ship Financing Program, it would mean the loan has been in default for 30 days and extensive remedial efforts are probably underway. If the loan was guaranteed under the Veterans Administration (VA) program for housing loans, the default has just become reportable since the VA definition of reportable default is a loan on which three monthly payments have been missed. The definition of default under the Guaranteed Student Loan Program (GSLP) even goes so far as to require that the Commissioner of Education make some judgement as to whether "a borrower no longer intends to honor his obligation to repay."

This inconsistent treatment of "default," and the unique data and information which result therefrom, precludes government-wide analyses.

Q. With all of the data available to the Government, why can't it do a better job of management?

A. "Data" and "information" are not synonymous and, while the Government may have an abundance of data, it suffers a dearth of information. PPSS found that much of the Government's data are useless for management purposes because they are inadequate, inaccurate, and untimely. For example:

• Savings of $6.074 billion are possible in DOD if accurate and current management information were available to improve inventory planning. One segment of the DOD inventory system generates the previously described six million pounds of computer output annually—much data, not much information.

• The Department of Justice could save taxpayers $50 million and accelerate cash collections by $244 million if it had information on total assets seized as a result of FBI, IRS, and other agency investigations.

• The Veterans Administration pays $15 billion per year to six million claimants. Yet, it has no information to measure the accuracy of these payments even though it knows the error rate exceeds $500 million per year.

Q. Does Congress itself contribute to the "information gap"?

A. It does. While there is no question that Congress is entitled to information from agencies on Federal programs so as to properly discharge its constitutional responsibilities, many of the reports Congress requires of the Executive Branch are ill-timed, excessively costly to produce, no longer relevant, and often not even read or used by their intended audience.

The Executive Branch has attempted to reduce the paperwork burden on the American public, but Congress has made no similar attempt to limit the paperwork burden imposed on the Executive Branch. Almost every piece of legislation carries with it new requirements for Federal managers to report to Congress on the status of a program, a research project, or some other Executive Branch activity. This is in addition to the program and budgetary information that each agency must compile and present to Congress. On top of this are requests for "ad hoc" reports from Committee or Subcommittee Chairmen seeking information on Executive Branch programs and plans.

Q. What's the extent of these Congressional reporting requirements?

A. In the U.S. Department of Agriculture (USDA), for example, reporting requirements jumped 68% from 1980 to 1983. In one USDA area it was estimated that it required some 80,982 hours of work to prepare 58 reports, for an average 1,396 hours per report, or the equivalent of nearly 35 employees working a full year on nothing but those reports.

PPSS determined that there are an estimated 30 reports that duplicate or overlap, cost too much for what they produce, and are of low value in terms of useful information. The cost to develop and produce these reports totals over $35 million, with over 200,000 staff hours devoted to preparation.

Q. This discussion has shown that the information gap is pervasive throughout the Government. Will PPSS solutions bridge the information gap once and for all?

A. The Federal information gap is a dynamic problem that will continue. PPSS has identified many information gaps. There are many more. When one gap is bridged, another will appear. The recommended solution recognizes this problem. By creating a structure for information management and by identifying and emphasizing the processes needed to solve today's problem, tomorrow's problems can be managed and, perhaps, even avoided.

Too often in the past, the Government has focused its attention on a very specific problem rather than its cause which may lead to the same problem in other areas of the Government. This narrow focus can result in overlooking major issues. For example, both the Executive and Legislative Branches have directed their attention toward controlling the acquisition and cost of computers. This is important, but the benefit side of the cost/benefit relation has too often been neglected.

For example, a *Washington Post* article dated November 30, 1983, reported that the Internal Revenue Service estimated a 1981 annual "tax gap" of $81.5 billion. How much of this revenue loss could have been collected through more effective use of computer systems? While the answer cannot be quantified, modern computer systems can substantially reduce lost revenue by expanded use of sampling techniques and by increased matching of actual and reported earnings. The correct focus should be on the additional revenues that can be collected (an annual "tax gap" of $81.5 billion) rather than on the cost of the computers.

The technological revolution of the last 30 years has made a vast amount of new information available to managers. New technologies have radically altered the amount, type, and speed at which information is available. Many corporations are investing considerable time and energy to accumulate better information and improve decision-making. Based on its review, PPSS concluded that the Federal Government does not manage its information well and that managing it better could save at least $78.6 billion over three years.

Financial Management

Federal financial management procedures have little in common with accepted private sector accounting principles. Budgeting; accounting; and cash, loan, and debt management; as well as auditing functions are conducted in the Federal Government largely independent of one another. As a result, the interrelationships between responsibilities for programs and action authorities are unclear and this is an invitation to inefficiencies, abuse, and fraud.

To correct these deficiencies, PPSS has recommended that the proposed Office of Federal Management take responsibility for formulating and coordinating financial management policies and practices throughout the Federal Government.

In FY 1983, the Government spent $120.8 billion in the specific areas covered by PPSS recommendations, with spending estimated to increase to $1.833 trillion by the year 2000 if present policies are continued. Implementing PPSS recommendations would reduce spending to $376.2 billion in 2000, a saving of $1.456 trillion, or 79.5%.

The Federal Government is involved in financial transactions amounting to *$6.8 billion each working day*. This is $34.0 billion per week, $146.2 billion per month, and over $1.7 trillion per year. The monthly figure is 32 times total Federal expenditures when FDR became President in 1933. Despite the enormous sums and number of transactions involved, the Federal Government is years behind the private sector in developing modern budgeting, accounting, and management information systems.

Within the Executive Branch of the Government, no single department or agency is responsible for overall financial administrative direction and policy. Financial management responsibilities are primarily shared in the Executive Branch by the Office of Management and Budget (OMB), the Department of the Treasury, and the General Services Administration (GSA); and in the Legislative Branch by the General Accounting Office (GAO).

Individual agency and department accounting systems have led to the use of diverse methods and standards, making government-wide oversight, comparisons, and evaluations extremely difficult, if not impossible.

Also, the functional independence of agencies and departments results in very little mutual sharing of pertinent financial data.

The diversity of approaches and the lack of centralized controls in Federal loan programs has fostered management practices which lead to oversights, procedural mistakes, abuses, and, in the worst cases, the opportunity for fraud.

Under the PPSS proposal, a Financial Management Office would be set up within the Office of Federal Management (OFM), the proposed new management arm of the President. OFM would be responsible for policy development and government-wide direction in the areas of budgeting and planning, human resources, administration (including approval of management information systems), financial management, and management evaluation and incentives. The current Office of Management and Budget would serve as the core of OFM, performing the budget functions. The Office of Personnel Management (OPM) and the GSA would be part of OFM and would continue to direct efforts in the areas of human resources and administration.

Within this context, the responsibilities of a newly created Financial Management Department would be similar to those of a private sector corporate headquarters financial staff: directing and coordinating the Federal Government's overall accounting and financial reporting policy and activities, and developing a systematic program to identify and implement government-wide financial management improvements on an ongoing basis.

If PPSS recommendations are implemented, the following benefits, which are discussed in detail in the body of this section, would result:

• Improved coordination of practices and systems across departments and agencies;

- Greater compliance with GAO accounting standards by departments and agencies;
- Clarification of reporting responsibilities;
- Improved quality of information available to the central agencies— i.e., the General Services Administration, the Office of Personnel Management, and the Office of Management and Budget;
- Improved overall quality of financial management and reporting in Government and, thus, increased accuracy, reliability, and timeliness of financial data.

PPSS conclusions and recommendations in the area of Government financial operations are based on identifying the structural, procedural, and control problems in budgeting, accounting, cash management, loan and debt management, and auditing procedures. These areas are discussed individually below.

BUDGETING

The annual Federal budget is a political document, issued primarily as a statement of spending priorities, but of limited usefulness as a vehicle for planning, control, or evaluation. Further, the budget has a short-term orientation and is primarily concerned with current expected spending levels. Conversely, private sector budgeting is directed toward the measurement of results versus plan within the context of achieving long-term objectives. Important aspects of long-term planning in the private sector include: communication of primary objectives from top management to other levels of management; identification of alternative means of accomplishing objectives; formulation of detailed plans to implement the best alternatives; and the monitoring of progress toward achieving these objectives.

Problems which have been identified many times in the Government budget process include the following:

- Difficulties encountered by senior officials in attempting to continously monitor progress toward accomplishment of major Administration goals;
- Emphasis on a one-year budget process without an accompanying effective multiyear analysis of programs and resource levels by the various agencies and the Executive Office of the President (EOP); and
- Difficulties in communicating and implementing changes in policies and practices by new administrations.

Q. How can the current budget process be made more effective?

A. The budget is not fully used as a management tool by OMB or the departments and agencies. Accounting for actual expenditures is largely separate from budget preparation and analysis. Differing from the private sector, the Government stresses budget preparation, while putting minimal emphasis on budget execution and control.

Q. How would adopting private sector budget practices help the Government?

A. Implementing an Executive Branch planning system similar to those existing in the private sector would increase the Administration's ability to accomplish its major objectives and more effectively allocate its overall resources.

An Executive Branch planning system would assist agencies and the proposed OFM in ensuring that long-term issues are considered, major Administration initiatives are highlighted, resources are allocated properly, and progress toward accomplishing Presidential goals are assessed. In net, plans would:

• Communicate objectives, strategies, and detailed instructions to Federal managers; and

• Measure progress toward achieving objectives—an integral part of keeping management aware of linkages between long-term goals and current budgets.

Q. Were most of the identified budgeting problems the result of short-term planning?

A. Most, but not all. For example, in the Agriculture Department, the Commodity Credit Corporation's (CCC) accounting procedures allow other agencies to underreport their spending significantly. Among the ways the CCC provides price support to producers of agricultural goods is the purchase and storage of agricultural commodities. Some commodities purchased by CCC are then donated to other agencies. Such donations in FY 1983 are estimated at $728 million. However, there is an increasing tendency by recipient agencies to use these donations to supplement programs which are limited by budgeting constraints and pressures to reduce Government costs. If the Administration is reducing appropriations to a program, it is because other programs have higher priority, and circumventing these priorities by accounting manipulations destroys managerial control and is counterproductive.

Q. What recommendations does PPSS propose?

A. PPSS recommended that recipient agencies pay for CCC commodities with appropriated funds. This would result in greater control since agencies would more carefully assess their requirements if funding of commodity purchases were brought within the budget process. PPSS estimates savings would be $1.205 billion over three years. That's enough to purchase 931 million pounds of ground beef, or 27.1 pounds for every person below the poverty level.

Q. Is it common for agencies to mask their spending?

A. It's not clear that common is the right word, but it does happen. In the Environmental Protection Agency (EPA) much budgeting time is spent on processing change notifications, which are defined as minor balancing adjustments from one spending classification to another. These change notifications reduce the visibility of budget overruns that should receive management attention. PPSS recommended that change notifications be eliminated to simplify budgeting procedures and to allow problem areas to be identified. Staff savings alone would be $600,000 over three years.

Q. What problems exist in the Federal capital budgeting process?

A. PPSS noted three major problems with the Federal capital budgeting process:

1. Capital investments are understated since capital outlays are net of related receipts. This is a major departure from sound accounting principles.

2. Federal capital investment outlays, as reported, are not complete since they do not include a number of off-budget agencies such as the U.S. Postal Service.

3. Definitions of capital assets differ, resulting in data that are not comparable among the more than 60 departments and agencies of the Federal Government.

Q. What do you mean when you say capital outlays are net of related receipts?

A. For example, if the Government builds a dam with power generating facilities, *projected* revenues from selling the power are subtracted from the estimated cost of the plant to determine the total capital investment. This policy substantially understates actual capital requirements. Again, a major departure from sound accounting principles.

Also, excluding off-budget agencies from the budget process results in an understatement of both capital and operating costs. Off-budget agencies are those which are Federally owned and controlled but their spending has been removed from the budget process for various reasons by acts of Congress. As a result, their outlays are not included in reported budget totals or deficits. For a fuller discussion of off-budget agencies and their outlays see the section of this report on "Will the Real Budget Please Stand Up."

Off-budget *outlays*, which have the same impact on Government finances as the on-budget deficit, have been as high as $21 billion and would have increased the reported on-budget deficits by as much as 45% over the 1978-1983 period. Excluding off-budget items in reporting the deficit is contrary to generally accepted accounting principles and distorts the Government's true financial condition.

Q. Why does it matter if the Government doesn't report its capital spending in the same way as a private sector company?

A. It's more than just a matter of accountability, although that is important in its own right. Accurate capital budgeting is needed for effective analysis of alternatives and reporting of public expenditures. The failure to implement comprehensive capital planning at the Federal level has contributed to the deterioration of the Nation's physical infrastructure, e.g., roads, bridges, dams, and public buildings. As a result, governments at the Federal, state, and local levels face unplanned capital expenditures of as much as *$3 trillion* in this decade alone, if the current level of service and safety is to be maintained.

Q. How can this situation be kept from getting worse?

A. What is needed is a standardized, Government-wide capital budgeting process. In addition, PPSS recommended that a comprehensive capital analysis be included in the annual budget. This analysis should include an estimate of aggregate capital investments, sources of funding, and public works investment priorities. Departments and agencies should use a standard format in their capital investment analyses. Individual capital expenditures—including those administered by state and local governments through Federal grant programs—should be shown separately for each department and agency in the President's budget.

ACCOUNTING

Accounting systems in both public and private sector organizations consist of two parts: (1) the formal set of accounts, supporting records, documents, and reports; and (2) the related procedures and standards used to ensure both consistency of recordkeeping and also adherence to the accounting profession's generally accepted practices. An adequate accounting system should meet the following basic objectives:

• *Comparability*—Transactions must be accounted for in a consistent fashion across all units of an entity. Similarities and differences appearing in financial statements need to reflect basic conditions and not merely differences in the accounting treatment of transactions.

• *Timeliness*—Information must be available when decisions need to be made.

• *Completeness*—Accounting information should fully disclose an entity's activities in a manner that facilitates understanding and avoids misleading implications.

• *Verifiability*—Substantially the same results should be reached by different accountants working independently and observing the same principles of measurement.

To meet the above goals in the Federal Government, the General Accounting Office (GAO) prescribes the principles and standards for accounting systems. However, GAO has no authority to force departments and agencies into compliance. Reflecting this lack of authority, 123 accounting systems—37.0% of all systems subject to GAO approval—have not been approved. As a result, many departments and agencies in the Government do not have accounting systems that are on a par with accepted business standards and practices. Without appropriate systems, Federal department and agency accounting systems are frequently incapable of producing the timely, accurate, and complete financial reports required to properly manage assets, control funds, and evaluate performance versus goals.

As a first step toward upgrading Federal accounting systems, a central controllership function, similar to that in the private sector, needs to be established in the proposed new Office of Federal Management to follow through on GAO guidelines for Executive Branch departments and agencies. This position should develop comprehensive accounting policy, financial reporting, and internal control standards to serve as guidelines for greater integration and coordination of Federal accounting systems. As an additional measure, legislation should be introduced mandating that departments and agencies comply with GAO's accounting systems approval process within a specified period of time.

Q. Is it that important for departments and agencies to meet GAO accounting standards?

A. GAO has shown that departments and agencies which devote the time, effort, and resources to designing and implementing approved accounting systems have fewer difficulties and are able to carry out their financial management functions more efficiently. A very important area on which GAO focuses during its approval process is an accounting system's internal controls. While an approved accounting system cannot by itself ensure that there will be no fraud or abuse, these problems are much less likely to occur when a system has tight internal controls and adequate audit trails.

Q. In what ways do inefficient payroll systems contribute to higher costs?

A. In some Government agencies, antiquated and time-consuming punchcard systems are still in use. Further, the abundance of incompatible systems means that any change to payroll reporting requirements necessitates that many systems be adjusted instead of just a few. As a result of inefficient payroll systems, the cost to the Army to process each payroll check is $4.20. The same expense for the

Interior Department's Bureau of Reclamation is $3.75. In the private sector, the costs to process payroll checks generally range from 75¢ to $2.00 per check—about one half of the Federal cost. In addition, with so many accounting and payroll systems each time there is a change in requirements, each system has to be modified individually, which is a serious waste of staff time.

Q. How much would implementation of payroll systems, based on standardized software and procedures, save the Government?

A. Implementation of a common payroll system would require an investment in the first three years, but it would achieve significant savings by the time the system was installed government-wide. Specifically, the acquisition of a common payroll system would cost $3.3 million in the first year, $3.6 million in the second, and $4.1 million in the third. However, by year thirteen (after full implementation), the Government would have achieved a cumulative net savings of $735 million with a decrease of approximately 2,000 staff-years of payroll clerical effort.

Q. How would the PPSS recommendation to establish a central controllership function help in this area?

A. Under the leadership of the proposed Office of Federal Management, the Executive Branch should develop a centralized program to replace agency-unique systems with compatible systems.

Payroll should be designated the first common system primarily because payroll systems are generally similar across departments and agencies, and requirements for payroll systems tend to change frequently. Thus, changes in the future would not have to be made to each system individually. Following payroll, other high-priority common systems are accounts receivable, retirement/pension, accrual accounting, accounts payable, fixed asset systems, and budgeting.

Q. Are accounting and payroll systems within agencies compatible?

A. Not often. The situation is worse in agencies like the Department of Energy (DOE), which was created in 1977 from parts of several other agencies. As a result of inadequate coordination, DOE financial offices don't close their monthly books on the same day, and payrolls are processed independently at eight locations.

If standard accounting and payroll systems were developed so that all data could be consolidated, DOE accounting and payroll staffing alone could be reduced by approximately 80 people, with savings amounting to $12 million over three years.

Q. Are there any other examples of agency problems with accounting systems?

A. Yes. Because of poor information systems, Small Business Administration loan officers often don't know that a loan payment is 30 days overdue until five or six weeks after the fact. Similarly, the Commerce Department's Economic Development Agency cannot track either the number or the amount of loans that have been granted extensions on repayment.

Q. Are there also problems with the follow-up process in accounting systems?

A. Yes. Most management attention is focused on the programming and budgeting process with insufficient attention paid to actual expenditures. In addition, there is a failure to charge the cost of all resources to the units which consume those resources, thus creating a lack of incentives for efficient resource management.

Q. Why isn't something done to correct this?

A. Something was done. Congress passed a law, P.L. 84-863, requiring that accounting be shifted from an obligations basis to an accrual accounting basis. What this means is that currently when a consumable good is purchased its cost is recorded at that time—e.g., when the Air Force buys jet fuel, it is recorded as an expense even though it might sit in a storage depot for a year. With accrual accounting an expense is only recorded when resources (material, labor, etc.) are consumed. With accrual accounting the actual consumers of material are more readily identifiable and chargeable, and as a result are more likely to exercise managerial control. In review of the Air Force's operations, PPSS found that the use of an obligation accounting system rather than an accrual accounting system also results in:

• Inefficient use of personnel, who are considered "free" by operating units because the units are not charged for their use.

• A year-end rush to obligate all budgeted funds, which can result in very inefficient spending.

PPSS recommended that the law requiring the use of accrual accounting be actively enforced, which it currently is not. In addition, a system should be developed to report the total operating expenses of each organizational unit, including all personnel-associated costs —e.g., pension costs—to ensure more prudent use of resources. In the Air Force alone, savings are estimated at $1.159 billion over three years.

CASH MANAGEMENT

The last consolidated financial statement of the U.S. Government showed that its cash balance was $54 billion on December 31, 1980. Unfortunately, the Government cannot determine on a current basis what its cash balance is at any point in time. Each year the Government spends or collects *$1.7 trillion*—almost $971 million every working hour, $16.2 million every minute. With this magnitude of cash flow, the manner in which the Government handles its transactions can have a major financial effect on taxpayers. Three working days of movement is $20 billion, and the interest on this is over $2 billion per year—equal to the annual income taxes of 917,431 median income families.

Q. What improvements could the Federal Government make in order to manage its cash flow more effectively?

A. The underlying principles in managing cash positions are straightforward, and not very different conceptually for individuals or for private sector companies than they should be for the Federal Government:

- Do not pay bills until they are due unless early payment is sufficiently beneficial to cause one to do so.

- At all times, deposit checks that you receive from others immediately.

- Keep as little money as possible in bank accounts that do not earn interest and as much money as possible in interest-bearing instruments.

Q. What are some examples of how these principles could be applied?

A. Currently, the Treasury Department's Bureau of Government Financial Operations pays bills and issues checks on a first-in, first-out basis regardless of when the money is due. If bills were paid and checks issued only when they were due, the Treasury could save $1.309 billion over three years.

In addition, many states withdraw funds made available by the Federal Government before the money is needed for specified purposes. If Congress would allow the Treasury to charge interest and penalties when funds are withdrawn prematurely, $1.103 billion could be earned over three years.

The Federal Government could even save money when it pays its current and former employees by using direct deposit and electronic funds transfer. The Government makes approximately 580 million salary and benefit payments per year. This is 48.3 million payments a month. Using direct deposit/electronic funds transfer to allow the funds to remain on deposit longer would save the Government $635 million over three years.

Q. Is there any room for improvement in the way the Government collects money?

A. Yes. For example, the Treasury Financial Communications System (TFCS) is a telecommunications network that allows the Government to access the nationwide banking system instantaneously, thus accelerating its cash receipts. Currently, this system is mainly used when transactions exceed $50,000 and as a result the system is operating at only 10% of its capacity. If the TFCS were commonly used for transactions as small as $10,000, an additional $40 billion would be deposited more quickly in Government interest-bearing accounts.

Q. How long does it currently take to deposit receipts?

A. The most widely used alternative is direct mail which averages from two to four days. With an additional three days required for the check to clear, the total time in which the money is not earning the Government interest is six days.

Q. What is the cost of this six-day lag from receipt to deposit?

A. Speeding up the collection of $40 billion by just six days would earn the Government $221 million more in interest over three years. These collections do not include the collection of estimated taxes that certain individuals—mainly the self-employed—have to pay each quarter totalling over $14 billion. If these payments were made using an electronic Federal Tax Deposit System, interest gained would equal $156 million over three years on accelerated receipts of $470 million.

Q. Where else can electronic funds transfer (EFT) systems be used to accelerate receipts?

A. Applying EFT to excise taxes paid by the alcohol and tobacco industries as well as eliminating the current payment deferral period of about one month would accelerate receipts by $911 million over three years with corresponding interest earnings of $294 million.

Applying electronic funds transfer to customs duties and eliminating the current ten day grace period would earn $114 million in interest over three years by accelerating payments of $344 million.

Most banks in the private sector use automatic account withdrawal systems where feasible for installment payments. If the Government used such a system, the amount of delinquent debt owed the Government would decrease by approximately 10%, because it would keep the Government more in touch with its loan portfolio, i.e., a computer won't forget that someone owes it money. If automatic account withdrawal were used in conjunction with EFT, the Government would accelerate its receipts by $4.072 billion over three years and would earn interest of $821 million over the same period.

The combined effect of using advanced electronic cash collection practices, which are common in the banking industry—and keep in mind the Government is by far the nation's biggest lender—would be to accelerate cash flow by $6.464 billion and increase interest earnings by $1.581 billion over three years. The interest earnings alone would pay the average salaries of 86,486 elementary school teachers in 1982.

Q. Why hasn't the Government done this on its own?

A. There isn't any incentive, i.e., profit motive, in the Government. PPSS recommended that the Office of Federal Management—proposed by PPSS—establish cash management goals for each department and agency. To provide incentive, performance in this area should be used as a bonus criterion.

Q. Are there other examples where Government collections could be accelerated?

A. Yes. Prompt collection and deposit of Federal receipts, when electronic funds transfer is not practical, can alternatively be accomplished by use of a lockbox. A lockbox, widely used in the private sector, is a Postal Service rental box to which mail is delivered. Its principal purpose is to collect payments faster, generally 2.5 to 4 days faster.

Q. How much would lockbox systems save the Government?

A. If results from a test program conducted by the Customs Bureau are extrapolated government-wide, receipts would be accelerated by $4.900 billion on which interest earnings would be $1.622 billion over three years.

Another area for improvement is the way in which the Government collects Social Security withholdings (FICA) taxes. Private companies with monthly FICA liabilities greater than $3,000 must make payments within three banking days after the end of the month. States, on the other hand, are allowed up to 30 days after the end of the month to make their payments to the Federal Government—i.e., ten times as much time as private companies are allowed.

Q. How much does it cost the Government for states to have that extra time?

A. PPSS estimates that the Government's cash flow would be accelerated by $1.250 billion and interest earnings would be increased by $414 million over three years. That's enough money to cover the clothing and other personal care costs for 313,829 lower income four-person families.

Q. The Internal Revenue Service (IRS) is responsible for most of the Government's collections. Is it handling tax receipts efficiently?

A. No. IRS procedures could be changed to reduce the amount of time between the receipt of a remittance and its deposit into an interest-bearing account. Currently, the IRS processes remittances automatically, checks for errors, corrects any errors manually, then deposits the money. The IRS system for processing checks is considered state-of-the-art, but waiting for any errors to be corrected manually defeats the purpose of using high-technology computers for processing. PPSS recommended that entries be verified after the checks are deposited. This would speed deposits by an average $661 million while increasing interest earnings by $219 million over three years.

Another recommendation made by PPSS is that during the Internal Revenue Service's non-peak months, it share its advanced check processing capacity with other agencies that have substantial check processing requirements such as the Farmers Home Administration and the Small Business Administration.

Q. How effective is the IRS at collecting taxes owed to the Government?

A. Taxes receivable, which have grown from $8 billion at the end of 1977 to $28.5 billion in 1982, are in addition to the growing "tax gap," which is money lost to the Government through taxpayer non-compliance—estimated at $81.5 billion in 1981. In addition, the accounts receivable balance of $28.5 billion excludes the interest penalty for delinquent taxes, estimated to be at least $2 billion. In total, revenues that should be collected by the IRS, but are not, are about $112 billion—almost 20% of all Government revenues collected in FY 1983.

During FY 1977 through FY 1982, the number of tax filings increased from 88 million to 103 million, an increase of 17.0%, while IRS examination staff increased by only 1.9%. Largely as a result of the rapid increase in workload, the percentage of returns examined fell from 2.44% in FY 1977 to 1.67% in FY 1983. During the same 1977–1982 period, IRS accounts receivable increased by 180% but the number of revenue officers responsible for collecting these funds owed the Government decreased by 15%. As a result, total uncollected tax revenues have increased to $112 billion, as mentioned previously.

Q. Why doesn't the Government hire more people to increase collections?

A. The Government has made provision to increase the Collection Division by 4,000 staff years during FY 1982–1984, in addition to an 882 staff year increase in the Examination Division. However, PPSS found that these increases were inadequate considering the growing amount of tax dollars that remain to be collected. In addition, PPSS notes that IRS has no consistent system-wide method to determine the optimum level of personnel to maximize its revenue collections. There are problems in the methods used to determine personnel levels in various IRS programs. For example, measurement of yields and costs for individual programs are generally inconsistent, and some programs use average revenue and cost data which may not be a realistic approximation of what additional costs and benefits are.

Q. What does PPSS recommend?

A. PPSS recommended that within twelve months a computer model be designed to determine comprehensive IRS staffing needs. This model should take into consideration the importance of the interaction of the various IRS programs—i.e., it would recognize that a change in one program will affect potential benefits and costs of other programs. It must also base its conclusions on incremental, or additional, costs and benefit data to show what the impact of each additional employee hired will be.

Q. Until that is accomplished, what interim measures can be taken?

A. Until that model is completed, PPSS recommended that clerical support for IRS Revenue Officers, responsible for collecting delinquent taxes, be increased to offset some of their increased workload. In addition, payroll deductions or automatic bank transfers should be used in installment agreements.

Also, the $81.5 billion in taxes lost through non-compliance—e.g., underreporting of income—merits immediate attention. Until the proposed computer model is operational, IRS should plan to add 2,500 employees to its Examination Division staff each year for three years. At least $17 million should be reallocated to the document matching program which has proven to be the most effective method of identifying taxpayers who underreport their income.

Over three years, collections would increase by $5.732 billion, or 22% of the *total* taxable income of the lowest 25% of taxpayers.

Q. What are some specific cases where other agencies don't manage their cash and assets efficiently?

A. A good example is in the Justice Department which, as a result of its crime-fighting activities, seized $317 million in cash and physical assets such as cars and planes in FY 1982. Cash seizures represented about 25% or $79 million of that amount. Currently, seized cash is not placed in interest-bearing accounts and, because of slow processing, other non-cash assets depreciate in value as much as 65% before they are sold off.

Q. Would it be legal for the Government to deposit cash seized in criminal investigations?

A. Not only legal, but efficient. Over three years, seized cash could earn $50 million while the decision as to its eventual disposition is made.

Other specific examples where PPSS found that agency cash management could be improved include the following:

- In a review of only nine Transportation Department grant recipients, it was determined that $473 million was paid to contractors by grantees an average of 13 days earlier than necessary, resulting in added interest costs to the Government of $3 million. If procedures were enforced requiring that all bills be paid by grantees only when due, and if excess cash were aggressively collected from grantees, the Transportation Department could save $144 million over three years.

- In the Education Department, there is a lack of timely account balance information. If payments were made only when specifically authorized, $62 million in interest could be earned over three years.

- In the Interior Department, the use of electronic funds transfer to collect bid deposits on Federal offshore minerals leases and other fiscal improvements could earn $23 million over three years.

- In the Agriculture Department, requiring a deposit for timber sales could earn $460 million over three years. In addition, prioritizing Farmers Home Administration cash collections on the basis of dollar amounts and allowing decentralized deposit of collections could earn $57 million over the same period.

- In the State Department, if foreign currency requirements were provided for before they were actually needed, $17 million in exchange losses could be avoided over three years. When the tide turns against the U.S. dollar, the Government should delay purchasing foreign currencies.

LOAN AND DEBT MANAGEMENT

Total credit outstanding under Federal lending programs has increased rapidly over the past decade and in 1984 is expected to be about *$1 trillion*, as shown in the following table.

The rapid growth in the Government's lending programs has enabled it to maintain its place as, far and away, the nation's largest lender. At the end of FY 1981, the Federal Government had loans and loan guarantees outstanding of $676.3 billion—$51.8 billion, or 8.3%, greater than the $624.5 billion of *combined* loan portfolios of the nation's 50 largest commercial banks.

Loans Outstanding Under
Federal Lending Programs
($ Billions)

		(1)	(2)	(3)
				1984B as Multiple of 1974
		1974	*1984B*	
(1)	Direct Loans	$ 61.5	$210.9	3.4X
(2)	Government-Sponsored Loans	71.0	337.3	4.8
(3)	Guaranteed Loans	153.2	435.8	2.8
(4)	Total	$285.7	$984.0	3.4X

There are three ways in which the Federal Government extends credit:

- Direct Lending—the Government supplies funds to the private sector and assumes full responsibility for loan administration.

- Guaranteed Lending—the Government guarantees some specified portion—usually 75% to 90%—of loans made by private sector lenders and assumes very little responsibility for loan administration unless a loan goes into default.

- Government-Sponsored Lending—Government-sponsored enterprises are privately owned financial institutions originally founded by the Government to provide credit to specific segments of the economy—primarily agriculture, housing and education. They are subject to Federal supervision and they consult with the Treasury Department when they issue debt securities to raise funds. While the Government has no responsibility for administering loans made by these enterprises, their lending tends to distort credit markets in favor of their targeted groups to the detriment of other sectors of the economy, such as industry.

The following compares 1974 and 1982 Federal gross new lending:

Federal Lending FY 1982 vs. FY 1974

		(1)	(2)	(3)
		Gross New Loans		
		1974	*1982*	*1982 as a*
		($ Billions)		*Multiple of 1974*
(1)	Direct Loans	$15.8	$ 28.6	1.8X
(2)	Guaranteed Loans	26.0	85.8	3.3
(3)	Government-Sponsored Enterprise Loans	38.4	133.2	3.5
(6)	Total New Loans	$80.2	$247.6	3.1X

Total Federal lending in 1982 was more than three times the amount lent in 1974, with guaranteed and Government-sponsored lending accounting for most of the growth. Lending by Government-sponsored enterprises in FY 1982 was 4.7 times the level of direct lending. To place in perspective the Government's lending activities, the following shows the growth in net Federal credit—i.e., gross loans minus loan repayments—in comparison to the total funds advanced in U.S. credit markets:

Federal Share of Credit Advanced

		(1) 1974	(2) 1982	(3) 1983E
		($ Billions)		
(1)	Net Federal Lending*	$ 25.5	$ 87.6	$130.9
(2)	All Other Net Lending	202.2	400.9	420.1
(3)	Total Net Credit Advanced in U.S. Credit Market	$227.7	$488.5	$551.0
(4)	Net Federal Lending as a % of Total Net Credit Advanced	11.2%	17.9%	23.8%

* Includes direct loans, guaranteed loans, and loans of Government-sponsored enterprises.

The Federal share of credit advanced in U.S. markets has risen steadily to an estimated 23.8% in 1983. This growth in targeted Federal lending has corresponded to a steady decline of the U.S. industrial base in comparison to our major trading partners such as Japan.

Among the major recommendations made by PPSS to improve the management of Federal loan programs are to:

• Substitute guaranteed for direct lending wherever possible to avoid tying up Federal funds. The maximum amount of the Federally-guaranteed portion should also be set at 75% of the loan amount—down from 90% in many cases currently.

• Include guaranteed loans and Government-sponsored loans as Federal commitments since it is Government policies that reallocate credit toward Federally- selected users at more favorable terms than are otherwise available. This would also give these lending programs more exposure to Congressional review, which should act to check their rapid growth.

These recommendations should also act to reduce Federal costs of administering loan programs as well as to reduce the exposure to default, which in some programs runs as high as 40%—e.g., the Farmers Home Administration farm loan programs. For a more complete discussion of Federal lending programs see the section on Government Lending Programs.

Federal audit operations reviewed by PPSS fall into three categories:

1. Internal reviews of Government operations—e.g., PPSS reviewed Inspector General (IG) auditing procedures. IGs are internal department and agency audit and investigative staffs.

2. Government audits in the normal course of doing business—e.g., PPSS reviewed freight bill auditing, the Federal procedure for reviewing charges to the Government by private sector freight companies.

3. Government audits of private sector or state and local operations that are Federally funded—e.g., PPSS reviewed the Aid to Families with Dependent Children program. These audits are meant to ensure compliance with Federal regulations.

A centralized administrative function is necessary to monitor and assess the performance and the allocation of resources among the various IGs; to achieve consistency in planning, procedures, and reporting; and to promote the most effective use of audit and investigative techniques.

Freight bill audits need to be performed before payment instead of afterwards and computer assistance is necessary to reduce the backlog which may be as long as 15 months.

Improvements need to be made in Government auditing of non-Federal operations—e.g., duplication in bank examining activities can be avoided saving $24 million over three years and limiting state Aid to Families with Dependent Children (AFDC) errors to 3% of payments could save $241 million over three years.

Q. How does the Inspector General (IG) function operate within Federal departments and agencies?

A. The Inspector General Act of 1978 established an Office of Inspector General in 12 departments and agencies. Since then, IGs have been established in seven additional agencies. The 19 IGs operate with a total staff of approximately 7,400 auditors and investigators and a total budget of about $400 million annually. While no precise division of the amounts between audit and investigative activities is readily available, approximately 70% of these resources appear to be applied to the audit function and the remainder to investigative activities.

Under their current organization structure, the IGs report to a sufficiently high level of management to achieve and maintain an appropriate level of auditor and investigator independence and at the same time serve the needs of senior management in an effective manner.

Q. What improvements in IG operations are necessary?

A. With regard to the audit system, PPSS recommendations are to:

- Establish an office responsible for coordinating the activities of IGs, providing technical assistance to them, as needed, and assuring that IG personnel and budget resources are adequate;

- Develop more joint training, technology development, and exchange programs to improve the effectiveness of IG functions and to encourage innovative approaches; develop a formal mechanism for exchanging the best IG management ideas with the sub-Cabinet level agencies not having statutory IG offices;

- Maintain a central reference file of IG reports and findings for the use of all IGs; and

- Include IGs in the legislative development process so that new legislation contains appropriate audit and cost-monitoring provisions.

Q. In what specific areas is there room for improved IG auditing reviews?

A. IG audit staffs should increase their level of attention to internal control evaluation and coordinate such efforts with independent control evaluation performed by management. This will also require upgrading personnel capabilities in this area.

Regarding improvements within the audit functions of specific agencies, it is recommended that the Department of Defense (DOD) establish a Procurement Audit Service (PAS) which will be solely responsible for performing internal reviews of DOD procurement practices. The PAS should report to the DOD Inspector General (IG). Existing DOD audit agencies would concentrate on non-procurement matters. The Defense Contract Audit Agency (DCAA)—which is an external audit function—should remain in the DOD Comptroller's organization and not be assigned to the IG. The proposed PAS should review the quality, accuracy, and scope of DCAA activities in the course of its normal internal audit reviews. Savings over three years are expected to be $1.655 billion based on a projected 0.5% productivity improvement through improved audit and reviews.

Q. Is the IG audit function cost effective?

A. Yes. In the Department of Energy (DOE), for example, internal reviews indicate that hundreds more auditors are required for full coverage, but the budget provided for a 20% reduction in outlays. Measured savings from fiscal 1982 audit recommendations amounted to $23 million in cost avoidance and recoveries—a return of more than $6.50 for each $1.00 spent. PPSS recommended hiring additional entry level staff (of the current staff of 88 professionals, 64 are partner or manager equivalent level). At the indicated cost recovery rate, adding 190 additional auditors could net DOE $73 million in savings over three years.

Q. How can freight auditing procedures be improved?

A. Since 1975, the General Services Administration (GSA) has been responsible for post-payment rate audits of freight bills, and also for recovering freight rate overcharges. A rate audit is an analysis that determines whether the charge reflects the correct application of often highly complex tariffs, tenders, contract rates, routing, etc. Claims for overcharges must be made within three years after payment. Overcharges are common in both the Government and the private sector.

However, the private sector identifies and recovers rate overcharges averaging 1.75% of total freight billings, while the Federal Government identifies overcharges averaging only 0.37%; its recovery rate is 87% of the overcharges identified, or 0.32% of billings, i.e., one-fifth the private sector recovery rate.

The Government's recovery rate is one-fifth that of the private sector for several reasons: its use of postpayment audits probably encourages overcharges or carelessness in billing, whereas a prepayment audit discourages billing errors that could serve to delay payment; the Government doesn't have available computer-assisted auditing techniques and relies on manual comparisons; and the volume of bills results in as much as a 15-month backlog of work which, together with the 7-month delay in the bills being sent to GSA, means that bills may not be audited until 22 months after payment has been made, making any recovery attempts more difficult.

Q. What improvements does PPSS propose?

A. PPSS recommended using private sector auditing capacity to reduce the current audit backlog, bringing audits to a current basis. PPSS also recommended a study to assess benefits from improved in-house efficiency through automation versus continuing with a private sector contractor on a long-term basis. In addition, postpayment legislative audit requirements should be repealed. Savings are estimated at $165 million over three years.

Q. How can the auditing function save money in the Aid to Families with Dependent Children (AFDC) Program?

A. In FY 1981, 3.8 million families received benefits totalling $12.7 billion under the AFDC program, with the Federal portion accounting for approximately $6.8 billion, or 53.5%. In addition, the Federal Government reimburses states for 50% of any administrative costs of the AFDC program—resulting in an approximate $800 million subsidy in FY 1981. SSA's Office of Assessment is responsible for quality and control of state payment accuracy. The Tax Equity and Fiscal Responsibility Act (TEFRA) contains a provision that states should reduce their payment error rate to 3% by September 30, 1983, or face fiscal sanctions. However, in the past HHS administrators have been reluctant to impose similar sanctions.

Since the states have wide discretion over AFDC benefit levels and eligibility standards and are responsible for its proper administration, the Federal Government should not be financially liable for state payment errors. HHS should impose fiscal sanctions for payment errors in excess of 3% as mandated by TEFRA.

Also, HHS should withhold an estimated amount from states based upon projected payments and error rates. Total savings are estimated at $241 million over three years.

This "gift" to the states represents all the Federal income taxes over 3 years of 36,219 American median income families of four but the "givers" are never consulted.

Q. How extensive is the bank examination process in the Federal Government?

A. Five Federal agencies regulate 36,000 financial institutions. Thus, the examination process involves at least 36,000 examinations conducted by a combined force of over 6,000.

Regulatory bank examinations carried on by the Federal Reserve Board, the Office of the Controller of the Currency, and the Federal Deposit Insurance Corporation are costly. The Federal Reserve Board examinations cost $22,000 per bank on average; the Office of the Controller of the Currency spends an average $18,000. Not only are these examinations expensive, they are also duplicative.

Q. How can these costs be reduced?

A. PPSS recommended consolidating these agencies' bank examinations to avoid duplication. This would save $24 million over three years.

In addition, examination expenditures can be reduced by 10% over three years by: requiring certified public audits and accrual accounting for all banks and S&Ls and also for credit unions with assets over $2 million; requiring audit engagement letters to identify specific requirements of the audit process and list specific tests that ensure compliance with Federal regulations and statutes; increasing use of state examinations; improving computerized monitoring; and using common training courses among all regulatory agencies.

PPSS recommendations are aimed at centralizing and coordinating the current auditing efforts. With total budget outlays of approximately

$800 billion in 1983, it is imperative that Federal auditing functions, personnel, and procedures be improved.

In addition to the specific topics included in the preceding discussion on Federal Government financial management, PPSS addressed thirty-two additional issues which can be categorized as follows:

- Budgeting improvements—In addition to those discussed previously, PPSS found several other examples where improved budgeting techniques could result in savings of $12.237 billion over three years.

- Cash management—PPSS found many cases where prudent handling of liquid assets could yield cumulative interest savings of $2.872 billion over three years.

- Tax status—PPSS reviewed several entities which currently enjoy tax exempt status, such as credit unions and the Farm Credit System, and found this benefit to be unwarranted, giving these entities an unfair advantage over other credit institutions. Removing their tax exempt status would generate $1.163 billion in additional revenue over three years.

- Accounting methods—Improved accounting techniques could save $944 million over three years in the Treasury Department and the Energy Department.

- Audit activities—Improved audit measurement and standard reporting in the Medicare program and elsewhere could save $514 million over three years.

> The three-year total of all the recommendations in this section, after elimination of duplication and overlap among issues, is $30.037 billion—equal to the three-year taxes of 4.5 million median income families.

Will the Real Budget Please Stand Up

> Budgeted Federal expenditures significantly understate the true level of Federal activity by excluding or only partially including major spending commitments. The Government's practice of netting or "offsetting" outlays by amounts collected for loan repayments, property sales, etc. distorts true spending levels. Similarly, the off-budget Federal Financing Bank conceals spending by on-budget agencies by providing a "back door" to the U.S. Treasury. Guaranteed loans and Government sponsored enterprises receive favorable treatment in credit markets as implicit Government obligations. However, neither guaranteed lending nor the lending activities of Government sponsored enterprises are adequately disclosed and controlled.

Fully reflecting these items as part of a more encompassing view of Federal spending results in commitments for FY 1984 of $1.8 trillion —more than double the budgeted outlays of $848 billion. There are no quantifiable savings from changing Federal accounting procedures to reflect all Federal commitments. What would change, however, is the level of scrutiny given to budgeted programs which would ensure that financial resources are allocated according to national priorities.

Within the Federal Government, formation and review of the budget is the single most important process by which continuing operations, program priorities, and policy changes are examined by the President, the Congress, and the public. The budget should provide a framework for allocating funds among various Government programs, thereby balancing the country's needs and goals against the estimated availability of funds from taxes and other sources, such as the incurring of new Federal debt. In addition, the budget system should provide useful information to department/agency managers who are responsible for efficient program implementation. Moreover, it should present fairly to the general public the complete story concerning estimated Government spending and the use of tax dollars.

For the Federal budget to serve adequately as a review of program priorities and as a method of controlling and accounting to the public for all Government activity, the design of the budget has to be comprehensive. The basic concept followed by PPSS is that if a spending activity is carried out directly or indirectly by the Federal Government, it belongs in the budget.

From this perspective, the budget as currently presented neither reflects all Federal expenditures nor accurately shows spending by function since:

1. For certain kinds of Federal business-type activities (such as making loans, renting facilities, and selling hydroelectric power), the Government does not separate in its budget presentation the revenues generated from the costs incurred. Instead, it calls the revenues or loan repayments "offsetting collections," and it "nets" them against its expenditures or loan disbursements. In this way, one never sees or can examine or weigh the full expenditure picture.

2. Many Federal activities are omitted entirely from the official budget. Some, like the Postal Service, are considered "off-budget" entities. Others, such as the Federal National Mortgage Association, are credit institutions called "Government-sponsored enterprises"; they are the vehicles for carrying out Federal programs in fields such as housing, agriculture and education.

3. The Government does not differentiate between lending and spending. Off-budget Federal entities, new guaranteed loans, Government sponsored enterprises, and a large portion of total budget outlays are associated with lending activities. Offsetting collections are primarily repayments of loans which are redistributed as additional new loans. These amounts are used for the acquisition of assets which would offset losses in the event of default. In the private sector, direct loans are carried on the balance sheet as assets; guaranteed loans and loans by Government sponsored enterprises would be contingent liabilities. The Government, however, does not have a balance sheet, and direct lending activities, on- and off- budget, are considered expenses. Guaranteed lending and the lending activities of Government sponsored enterprises are inadequately controlled, in large part, due to deficient Federal budgetary and accounting procedures.

The Federal budget for FY 1984 estimates that outlays (or "net" expenditures) will be $848.5 billion. However, when the items discussed above are taken into account—and a timing adjustment is made to reflect when spending commitments are authorized rather than when bills are actually paid—the true size of the Federal Government's commitments for FY 1984 more than doubles to $1.8 trillion. The Government has no accounting measure similar to "commitments" which, as used here, include gross outlays of all on- and off-budget Federal entities, guaranteed lending under Federal auspices, and the Government's liabilities under pension and other programs (private sector companies are required by law to record the amount necessary to fund future pension liabilities as expenses). The effect of individual items is shown in the table on the following page.

As the table shows, budgeted outlays account for only 46.8% of total Federal commitments of $1.812 trillion, leaving $963.5 billion with little visibility and limited control by Congress or the Executive Branch. To create a budget which fully reflects the level of Federal spending and commitments, PPSS recommended the following:

1. Discontinue the practice of "offsetting" outlays by related collections, i.e., report gross rather than net spending.

2. Include off-budget Federal entities in all future budgets.

3. Include guaranteed loans and Government-sponsored enterprises as budget commitments.

4. Include the full cost of funding Federal retirement and disability plan liabilities in all future budgets.

Whether the Government borrows money directly or causes money to be borrowed for a preferential purpose, such as student loans, is not material. It is all money being spent *because* of Government and

U.S. Government Commitments, FY 1984
($ Billions)

		(1) *Amount*	(2) *% of Total Adjusted Gov't Budget*
(1)	Total budget outlays (official budget)	$ 848.5	46.8%
(2)	Offsetting collections which are netted against outlays in the official budget	330.5	18.2
(3)	Timing adjustment between authorizations and spending	42.4	2.3
(4)	Off-budget Federal entities not included in outlays	68.4	3.8
(5)	New guaranteed loans outside the official budget—money the Government causes to be spent	126.0	7.0
(6)	Government-sponsored enterprises outside the budget—money the Government causes to be spent	193.4	10.7
(7)	Amortization of unfunded pension liabilities neither accrued nor established in reserves	202.8	11.2
(8)	Total commitments—representing money the Government spends, money the Government causes to be spent, and accrued expenses	$1,812.0	100.0%

has the same impact on credit markets as Government borrowing to finance its on-budget deficit. Current budgetary treatment disguises the extent of Federal participation in U.S. credit markets.

The first three items above are discussed in detail in the following pages. The fourth item, including the unfunded pension liability in budget data, is discussed in the section entitled "Retirement Systems."

Q. PPSS recommended that all spending activities be included in the Federal budget, creating a unified budget. No doubt this is good practice if only for truth in spending. But how will unifying the budget reduce spending?

A. The primary benefit of having a so-called "unified" budget—including all Federal taxes and spending—is that it helps ensure Federal expenditures truly reflect priorities and that there is a means to assess and control the overall level of Government spending. Programs that are omitted from the budget are inevitably less scrutinized, even though they receive Federal funds and/or rely on Federal credit as much as on-budget programs. As a result, spending in these areas is not as responsive to Federal policies and priorities.

Offsetting collections are the funds the Federal Government receives from the public as a result of transactions that are of a business nature, such as the sale of Government property and products, loan repayments, rents, and royalties for the use of Federal land. Excluding these receipts in FY 1984, Government expenditures would be $330.5 billion higher than currently reported. This represents an increase of 39% on reported Government expenditures.

For budget purposes, the Federal Government treats these payments differently than the funds it raises from the public through taxes. The latter are called "governmental receipts," and they constitute the revenue side of the official Government budget (Receipts − Outlays = Deficit). By contrast, offsetting collections are not shown in the budget as revenues. Rather, they are "netted" against the collecting department's expenditures.

The "netting" of offsetting collections against reported expenditures occurs in agencies and functions throughout the Federal Government. To show the impact of this approach, here's how the Government went from total spending (i.e., total obligations) to net spending (i.e., outlays) in 1982 at the Export-Import Bank:

Export-Import Bank
Obligations to Outlays—1982
($ Millions)

		Fiscal 1982
(1)	Total Obligations (Total Spending)	$5,054
(2)	Less Offsetting Collections	(3,108)
(3)	Net Obligations (Net Spending)	$1,946
(4)	Timing Adjustments	(773)
(5)	Outlays (Official Budget)	$1,173

As shown, offsetting collections reduce expenditures for the Export-Import Bank by $3.1 billion. Stated another way, after accounting for timing adjustments, outlays represented only 23% of what the Export-Import Bank actually spent in 1982.

Q.　PPSS recommended that offsetting collections be included in both the revenue and outlay totals in the budget. While this will present a clearer picture of program/agency spending, there do not seem to be any tangible benefits. How will this save the Government money?

A.　There are no quantified savings from changing the accounting treatment of collections. Treating collections as revenues rather than as offsets to expenditures would have no impact on the budget deficit, since the effect would be to increase both reported budget revenues and reported budget expenditures by the same amount. What would change are both the level of scrutiny given to programs that are large in "gross" terms but small on a "net" basis, and the perception of how Government allocates its funds.

Changing the accounting treatment to show budget expenditures before offsetting collections would also facilitate the spotting of real trends in expenditures, not affected year-to-year by movements in collections.

Q. Why is looking at "gross" rather than "net" program expenditures helpful?

A. Netting not only presents an incomplete picture, but leads to a misjudgment of the economic impact and risks related to individual activities. The PPSS recommendation applies the same approach as in the private sector where evaluations of companies take into consideration the components that lead to the bottom line.

OFF-BUDGET FEDERAL ENTITIES

Off-budget Federal entities are Federally owned and controlled, but their transactions are excluded from the Federal budget by law. Therefore, their spending and subsequent deficits are not reflected in either budget expenditures or the budget deficit regardless of their current or long-range impacts. In addition, appropriation requests for their programs are not included in the budget and their expenditures are not subject to the targets set by the Congressional budget resolutions. However, if these entities operate at a deficit, their shortfall is covered by the U.S. Treasury (through the Federal Financing Bank), which borrows the money from the public—thus increasing the national debt. In short, having these entities off-budget misleads the public as to the true magnitude of the Federal Government's spending as well as permitting these entities to escape the normal scrutiny and control of Congress.

Until 1971, the Federal Government used the unified budget concept as the foundation for its budgetary analysis and presentation. The first departure from the unified budget concept occurred in August 1971, when the Export-Import Bank was excluded by statute from the budget. Further departures followed in the next few years as the Postal Service Fund, the Rural Telephone Bank, and the Rural Electrification and Telephone Revolving Funds were removed from the budget. Furthermore, from their inception, the Federal Financing Bank (FFB), the U.S. Railway Association, the Pension Benefit Guaranty Corporation, and the Synthetic Fuels Corporation, were established as off-budget Federal entities. In FY 1984, off-budget Federal entities account for $68.4 billion in additional expenditures.

Following are the off-budget Federal entities and increases in their obligations from 1974 to 1982.

Gross Obligations of Off-Budget Federal Entities
($ Millions)

		(1) 1974	(2) *Ranked* 1982	(3) As a % of Total in 1982	(4) 1982 as Multiple of 1974
(1)	Federal Financing Bank	$ 603	$44,843	61.1%	74.4X
(2)	Postal Service Fund	11,610	23,152	31.6	2.0
(3)	Strategic Petroleum Reserve Account	—	3,677	5.0	ND
(4)	Rural Electrification and Telephone Revolving Fund	758	1,321	1.8	1.7
(5)	Rural Telephone Bank	164	248	0.3	1.5
(6)	Board of Governors of Federal Reserve System	44	60	0.1	1.4
(7)	U.S. Railway Association	—	28	—	ND
(8)	Synthetic Fuels Corporation	—	12	—	ND
(9)	Total	$13,179	$73,341	100.0%	5.6X

Source: Appendix to the Budget of the U.S. Government, FYs 1976 and 1984.

As shown, the FFB and the Postal Service Fund accounted for approximately 93% of the $73.3 billion in off-budget obligations during 1982. Of particular concern is the growth in the FFB's activities from $603 million in 1974 to $44.8 billion in 1982—obligations increased 74.4 times in eight years in just this one off-budget agency.

The FFB began operations as an off-budget entity in 1974. At that time, as many as 18 agencies or programs were offering debt securities to the public independently of each other and independently of the Treasury. The FFB was established to centralize and reduce the cost of agency borrowing and to coordinate such borrowing within Federal economic and fiscal policies. All borrowing would be directly by the Treasury, and the money would then be channeled to the individual agencies through FFB.

In practice, the FFB serves as an intermediary (middleman) for the financing of loans issued, sold or guaranteed by on-budget Federal agencies.

The FFB generally operates in two ways:

(1.) It purchases loans which have been made by Federal agencies; this converts what would have been on-budget loans by Federal agencies into off-budget FFB loans; and

(2.) It makes direct loans to institutions, but only when these loans have been guaranteed by a Federal agency. This converts what would otherwise be on-budget guaranteed loans into off-budget direct loans.

FFB operations of these kinds involved obligations of $44.8 billion in FY 1982, none of which was included in the Federal Government's budgeted outlay figure for the year.

In essence, the FFB arranges financing for Federal agencies through the "back door" to the U.S. Treasury. The effect of the off-budget Federal entities, particularly the FFB, is to give the appearance that money is not being spent when in fact it is, and to reduce the size of the deficit by transferring on-budget spending to off-budget entities.

Q. Has the FFB accomplished its original goal of consolidating all Federal borrowing?

A. The FFB has fulfilled its intended function of marketing Federal loans more effectively by consolidating into one agency the various financing operations of other Federal agencies. However, its off-budget status has made it more difficult for the Government to control credit activities under Federal direction.

Q. Why is it more difficult to control credit with the FFB off-budget than it would be on-budget?

A. Congress originally made the FFB off-budget under the premise that no other Federal agency's budget would be increased as a result. The FFB was only intended to be a financial clearinghouse. In reality, however, the FFB has made it possible for agencies to make more loans and still stay within budget ceilings. They do this by selling their loans to the FFB. An example of a Federal agency that has accelerated its lending activity is the Farmers Home Administration (FmHA). In 1974, the FmHA had $3.2 billion in direct loans outstanding and had guaranteed another $9.8 billion in loans held by others—for a total of $13.0 billion. By the end of 1982, it had only $1.4 billion in direct loans on its books, but it had guaranteed $53.7 billion in FFB loans—for a total of $55.1 billion. The FmHA was thus able to more than quadruple its loans and guarantees outstanding without showing any increase in net outlays for new loans over the 1974–1982 period.

Q. What is the impact of FFB lending activities on Federal borrowing?

A. Although the FFB's loans are not included in the Federal budget totals, and thus are not part of the official deficit, they do increase the amount of money being borrowed by the Government—since all the FFB funds come from the Treasury.

In turn, this increased borrowing by the Government creates a situation in which private sector borrowers are subject to being "crowded out" or have to pay higher interest rates. This is shown in the following:

Federal Borrowing Monopolizing Savings
($ Billions)

	FYs	(1) Direct Federal Borrowing	(2) Federally Guaranteed Borrowing	(3) Total	(4) Net Total Savings	(5) Total Federal Borrowings As % Net Total Savings
		Federal Borrowing				
(1)	1974	$ 18	$ 21	$ 39	$100	39.0%
(2)	1977	77	27	104	173	60.1
(3)	1980	81	56	137	167	82.0
(4)	1981	90	46	136	203	67.0
(5)	1982	143	66	209	212	98.6
(6)	1983E First Half Oct.'82-Mar.'83 Annualized	205	109	314	226	138.9
(7)	1983E First Half As Multiple of 1974	11.4X	5.2X	8.1X	2.3X	3.6X

Result is historically high real interest rate—prime rate of 7.0% after adjusting for inflation

Since 1974, Federal borrowing has grown faster than the pool of savings available to finance the borrowing. Federal borrowing as a percent of net total savings increased from 39% in 1974 to 98.6% in 1982, and is estimated to be 138.9% in 1983—which leaves nothing for private sector borrowers.

NEW GUARANTEED LOANS AND GOVERNMENT-SPONSORED ENTERPRISES

The size of the Federal Government and its influence on the U.S. economy extend beyond the on- and off-budget obligations discussed above. They include guarantees of private sector loans and lending by Government-sponsored enterprises, both of which contribute to Federal involvement in credit markets. A guarantee of a loan occurs when a Government agency makes a pledge that commits the Federal Government to repay a private lender in the event that a particular borrower defaults. Since no Federal expenditures are involved unless a default occurs, the guarantee commitments themselves are not included in budget outlays nor in future contingencies. By contrast, direct Federal loans are considered as outlays in the year they are made. Most of the guaranteed loan activity occurs in the areas of housing, education, energy, and income security (for example, subsidized low-rent housing).

Government-sponsored enterprises are privately owned financial institutions which were originally founded and funded by the Government to provide credit to selected segments of the economy—primarily agriculture, housing and education. They are subject to Federal supervision and they consult with the Treasury Department when they issue debt securities to raise funds. These enterprises include the Student Loan Marketing Association (SLMA), the Federal National Mortgage Association (FNMA), the Farm Credit Administration and the Federal Home Loan Bank System (FHLBS). Activities are primarily funded through the issuance of debt securities, which are not guaranteed by the U.S. Government, although they are referred to as "agency loans." The Government has given these loans special characteristics which differentiate them in the credit market. Certain tax exemptions exist, and the financial instruments may be used as investments by Federally-regulated institutions. These advantages allow the enterprises to borrow at rates only slightly higher than those available to the Treasury and, of course, at considerably lower interest rates than would otherwise be possible.

The following table shows the total credit extended through Federal or Federally-sponsored programs in 1982, including direct loans, guaranteed loans, and loans made by Government-sponsored enterprises:

Federal Lending FYs 1974 and 1982
($ Billions)

		(1)	(2)	(3)	(4)	(5)	(6)
		New Loans		Repayments		Net Loans	
		1974	1982	1974	1982	1974	1982
	Direct Loans						
(1)	On-Budget Agencies	$14.8	$ 13.8	$(11.5)	$ (4.7)	$ 3.3	$ 9.1
(2)	Off-Budget Agencies	1.0	14.8	(0.2)	(0.5)	0.8	14.3
(3)	Subtotal	$15.8	$ 28.6	$(11.7)	$ (5.2)	$ 4.1	$23.4
(4)	Guaranteed Loans	26.0	85.8	(15.7)	(64.9)	10.3	20.9
(5)	Loans by Government Sponsored Enterprises	38.4	133.2	(27.3)	(89.9)	11.1	43.3
(6)	Total Lending under Federal Auspices	$80.2	$247.6	$(54.7)	$(160.0)	$25.5	$87.6

Of the $247.6 billion in new loans made in 1982 only $13.8 billion (5.6%) were carried by on-budget agencies. Moreover, because the on-budget loan expenditures were offset by loan repayments, only the $9.1 billion "net loans" figure was part of the official budget outlays.

Budgeted loan expenditures in FY 1982 of $9.1 billion greatly distort the true amount of Federal lending. In addition, current budgetary treatment of Federal lending activities, and consequent borrowing to finance these actions, disguises the extent of Federal participation in U.S. credit markets.

PPSS recommended that Government-sponsored enterprises and all new guaranteed loan activities be fully disclosed in the Federal budget. The obligations of these entities already exist, but they are not acknowledged as Federal commitments. It should be noted that PPSS is not recommending greater Federal participation in the operation of these Federally-sponsored enterprises. We are not questioning their management philosophy, nor are we suggesting increased Federal oversight. Rather, our comments and recommendations focus on the impact that the financial transactions of these agencies have on U.S. credit markets and the accounting treatment of these transactions in the Federal budget. Federally guaranteed loans and Government-sponsored enterprise activities receive a favorable rate in U.S. credit markets—substantially better than others could receive. Reflecting these activities in the budget would provide a truer representation of the financial obligations of the Federal Government.

Q. You mentioned that Federal borrowing creates a crowding-out effect in the U.S. credit market. How does this occur?

A. Total Federal participation in the country's capital markets has two major components: funds it directly borrows to cover on-budget and off-budget activities; and funds borrowed by Government-sponsored enterprises and others to cover their lending activities. When the Government's on-budget outlays are greater than its revenues—as they have been in every year but one over the past two decades—it has to borrow money to make up the difference. This borrowing is handled by the Treasury, which issues securities that are purchased by individuals, by pension funds, and by other investors who want to put their money in a safe investment. In addition, private institutions whose loans carry Federal guarantees and Government-sponsored enterprises also borrow funds from investors.

However, individuals and institutions only have so much money (i.e., their savings) to invest. If the Government and associated entities are getting a large share of those funds to cover their programs, there is less to go around for others at affordable interest rates. This is what is called "crowding out." It means, for example, that corporations and small businesses that need to borrow money to replace worn-out equipment, to make technological improvements, or to expand their operations—all things that increase employment and productivity and make the economy stronger—may have difficulty obtaining all the money they need at an interest rate that is reasonable. Alternatively, interest rates may wind up increasing in order to entice people to save more money rather than spend it, thus increasing the pool of funds available to meet everyone else's borrowing needs. Smaller companies and less financially secure corporations may not be in a position to borrow at these higher interest rates. Once again, therefore, they are "priced out." Moreover, because overall interest rates have increased to help generate the funds required by all those who want to borrow, everyone winds up paying higher interest rates than they would otherwise—and that includes individuals who are obtaining car loans, home mortgages, and credit lines on their credit cards.

Q. How serious is the problem of crowding-out? Is Federal participation in credit markets increasing?

A. The extent of crowding-out caused by Government direct lending and guarantees has been increasing over the past decade. The following shows the amount of net new credit advanced in the U.S. credit market in 1974 and 1982, and the proportion which has been lent under Federal auspices.

		(1)	(2)	(3)
($ Billions)		1974	1982	1983E
(1)	Net Federal Loans (a)	$ 25.5	$ 87.6	$130.9
(2)	All Other Net Lending	202.2	400.9	420.1
(3)	Total Net Credit Advanced in U.S. Credit Market	$227.7	$488.5	$551.0
(4)	Federal Net Lending as a % of Total Net Credit Advanced	11.2%	17.9%	23.8%

(a) Includes on- and off-budget loans, guaranteed loans, and loans of Government-sponsored enterprises.

The proportion of loans related to Federal Government activities grew from 11.2% in 1974 to 17.9% in 1982, and in the FY just ended, the participation is estimated to have increased by 5.9% points more, to 23.8%. The key consideration in evaluating the Government's role in preempting almost one-fourth of net new lending—as opposed to this credit being allocated by free market forces—is how well the Government chooses the programs and individuals/institutions that receive credit. This is why it is critical that, at a minimum, all Government credit activities be formally and stringently reviewed, which can only be accomplished if all credit activities are included in the budget.

In summary, the Federal budget does not accurately reflect the financial condition of the Government. Offsetting collections are used to distort true spending levels; off-budget entities such as the FFB conceal spending by on-budget agencies; and guaranteed loans and Government-sponsored enterprises receive favorable treatment in credit markets as implied obligations of the U.S. Government, but are not acknowledged as such.

As shown here, the official budget understates Federal commitments by more than half—*$848 billion* per the FY 1984 budget vs *$1.8 trillion* actual commitments.

PPSS found Federal automated data processing activities to be disorganized and inefficient, falling far short of the potential for productivity improvements and consequent savings that exist in state of the art computer systems. More than half of all Federal ADP systems are obsolete, with an average age about twice that in the private sector. Further, ADP systems are not acquired with coordinated planning and the Government's computer systems are, therefore, generally incompatible. In addition, the Government's ADP performance has been impaired by the inability to attract and retain qualified personnel. PPSS recommendations center on the establishment of a Federal Information Resources Manager who would direct a coordinated government-wide effort to upgrade and replace existing systems and, along with the Office of Personnel Management and the General Services Administration, develop incentives to recruit and retain qualified ADP personnel.

In FY 1983, the Government spent $53.6 billion in the specific areas covered by PPSS recommendations, with spending estimated to increase to $266.3 billion by the year 2000 if present policies are continued. Implementing PPSS recommendations would reduce spending to $192.9 billion in 2000, a saving of $73.4 billion, or 27.6%.

The Federal Government is by far the world's largest user of computer and automated office equipment. PPSS identified over 17,000 computers in the Government and a workforce of more than 250,000 people who operate them—a workforce exceeding the entire population of St. Petersburg, Florida. Operating costs of government-wide automated data processing (ADP), including teleprocessing and office automation (OA), are at least $12 billion annually. ADP improvements, however, could potentially result in savings far in excess of the related expenditures. PPSS identified $29.5 billion in three-year ADP related savings before adjusting for duplication that could be achieved by improved utilization of ADP systems. PPSS found that, in general, the Government's ADP efforts were handicapped by:

- Obsolete equipment—over 50% of Federal ADP hardware is obsolete.
- Incompatible systems—the majority of Federal ADP systems are incapable of interfacing or communicating with other systems government-wide.
- High turnover of qualified ADP personnel.

As a result, Federal ADP systems are generally unresponsive to user needs and inhibit attempts to improve the level of operating efficiency.

Attainment of the goal of increased efficiency in the Federal Government is highly dependent on substantial new investment in computer-driven management systems. The Federal Government is falling far short of realizing the full productivity and cost savings potential of ADP/OA, despite the ready availability and proven value of feasible, installable, state of the art computer systems.

PPSS concluded that a flexible, well-coordinated, and integrated government-wide ADP/OA strategy linked to department and agency goals could play a major role in increasing productivity and reducing the costs of Government. However, a void currently exists in the central direction of Federal ADP activities and PPSS, therefore, recommended:

- The position of Federal Information Resource Manager (FIRM) should be established as a first step in changing the Federal ADP environment. FIRM should be a facilitator, expeditor, coordinator, and leader in the development of both short- and long-term government-wide plans for information technology. FIRM should have the authority to expedite funding for cost-effective systems and should also be able to deny funding for agency systems which are not compatible or cost justified. This position should not add another layer to the ADP bureaucracy but rather it should act to cut vertically through the bureaucracy to allow improvements in ADP systems to be achieved expeditiously.

- The Office of Personnel Management and the General Services Administration should seek ways to speed up the hiring cycle for ADP personnel. In addition, to retain qualified personnel, the use of bonuses for rewarding good performance should be increased.

The discussion that follows indicates how these improvements can affect specific departments and agencies.

Q. Does the Government spend too much on computers?

A. Generally, PPSS found that Federal ADP problems cannot be simply categorized as a matter of spending too much, but rather spending in a manner that is not achieving the productivity increases which are typical of private sector experience. Federal spending on computer activities of over $12 billion annually represents a huge expenditure in absolute terms, yet relatively it represents only 1.4% of total 1984B Federal spending of $848 billion. Effective use of even this $12 billion could save the Government many more billions of dollars by increasing productivity and by providing the means for better managing its finances. In the case of computers, it doesn't pay to be penny wise when potential results prove that you are being very pound foolish.

Q. How can you tell that the Government's spending on ADP is inefficient?

A. There are many indicators. For example, the average age of the Government's computer equipment—or hardware—is 6.7 years, which is roughly twice the average age of equipment in the private sector. The capability of a new, state of the art computer could be many times greater than that of one that's 6.7 years old. The relatively advanced age of Federal ADP equipment highlights the Government's propensity to buy rather than lease its systems. In view of rapidly changing technology, leasing is common practice in the private sector.

In addition, some of the Government's computers are so old that their manufacturers no longer service them; the Government thus is forced to keep on its staff employees specially trained to maintain these obsolete computers.

Q. It was mentioned previously that many Government ADP systems are incompatible. Why does the Government buy incompatible computers?

A. Mainly because there is a lack of coordinated planning at both the agency level and government-wide. As a result, when new computers are purchased, their compatibility with existing computers is seldom considered. As an example of the consequences of poor planning at the agency level, the regional Office of Health and Human Services in New York alone uses ten different brands of incompatible equipment.

During the 1960's, the Federal Government was considered a leader in the efficient application of computer technology. Congress virtually assured an end to the Government's leadership position by passing the Brooks Act in 1966, which was intended to control the acquisition of computers. In practice, however, the Act merely slowed the acquisition process to an average of two and a half to four years—by which time the computer, which may have been state of the art in the acquisition planning stage, is well on its way to obsolescence. This Act is an excellent illustration of what PPSS does not want to happen as a result of its recommendations—another layer of bureaucracy. Central direction by FIRM should not imply central control of ADP purchases.

At the same time, PPSS recommended that the Office of Management and Budget undertake a thorough review of the Brooks Act to determine which of its provisions are appropriate to ensure efficient ADP procurement, and which merely act to delay unnecessarily the procurement process.

Q. How, specifically, do ADP improvements save money?

A. In four major ways:

- By providing managers with the timely and accurate information necessary to make informed decisions.

- By increasing the productivity of workers, i.e., the amount of work each worker is able to accomplish in a given period of time.

- By providing a means of improving performance in such mechanical tasks as checking errors on tax returns and eliminating duplicate payments to Social Security recipients.

- By providing access to outside information which enables managers to orient themselves in evaluating how well they have performed in relation to other managers.

The Social Security Administration's (SSA) automated data processing operation is a good example of a system that is grossly inadequate to meet user needs. For example, consider the following data for 1982:

Social Security Administration

		(1) Average Monthly Workload	(2) Available Capacity	(3) Workload As Multiple of Capacity
(1)	Hours of Processing Required	4,500	2,000	2.3X
(2)	Daily Teleprocessing Transactions	700,000	410,000	1.7

SSA processing requirements, which are greater than the total claims operations of the six largest insurance companies, were 2.3 times as great as its available capacity in 1982. In an effort to meet its user needs, SSA is undertaking a $479 million five-year effort to modernize its system. SSA's modernization plan will make significant and necessary improvements in SSA's operations only if it continues to receive management attention and uninterrupted financial support. PPSS concluded, however, that it is unlikely the plan can be implemented in the expected time-frame.

The Defense Department's inventory management is another good example of significant savings which could be realized through ADP improvements. Inadequacies in computer support result in larger than necessary inventories, while improved systems would reduce inventory levels and the associated holding costs. In addition, a more efficient inventory information system could increase weapons availability by 5% to 15%. Thus the Defense Department could, for example, field an additional 40 to 50 aircraft at all times.

Q. How much would a better system save?

A. PPSS estimated a state of the art inventory system could allow purchases of inventory in monthly lot sizes, thereby reducing the total amount of inventory that would have to be maintained. Three-year savings of $6.074 billion include a one-time reduction in inventory size as well as ongoing efficiencies, and are net of $1.4 billion in implementation costs.

Another ADP-related problem in the Defense Department was found in the Navy, where the implementation cycle for ADP projects is so long that the potential for timely cost savings is eliminated and most systems are virtually obsolete by the time they are brought on line. This is illustrated by consideration of some of the major ADP projects on which the Navy is now working:

• The Naval Aviation Logistics Command Management Information System (NALCOMIS) project. Begun in 1970, it is scheduled for completion in 1990.

• The Shipboard Non-Tactical ADP Support Systems project. Begun in the early 1970's, it is targeted for completion in 1988.

• The Integrated Disbursing and Accounting Financial Management System project. Begun in 1976, it is targeted for completion in 1988.

With some projects taking as long as 20 years to be fully operational, the Navy does not appear to be acquiring ADP resources in an expeditious and cost-effective manner.

In the private sector, when a company makes an investment in ADP, it typically recovers its investment in cost savings within three years. Now, if the Navy takes ten years to complete a project, it does not start realizing the full savings potential of that project for at least ten years, and that's not efficient. PPSS found that the Navy could shorten considerably the total time necessary to have a new ADP system in operation by:

• Consolidating the current acquisition review process.

• Acquiring general purpose computers instead of specially designed computers.

• Anticipating certain ADP needs before they are specifically identified based on experience and general planning factors.

By more expeditiously and effectively acquiring ADP resources, savings from ADP investments could be realized sooner. The Navy could save an average of about $500 million per year over a ten-year period, or about $1.5 billion over three years.

Q. What about the Army's computers?

A. The Army by itself is one of the world's largest users of general purpose computers, spending $2–$3 billion on ADP related activities annually at 900 computer installations. In addition, the Army operates 700 different software (the actual computer program) systems for personnel management. Despite its spending on ADP, over 50% of the Army's computer hardware is of 1975 vintage or earlier. As a result, there is still widespread use of inefficient and costly punch-card entry systems.

Q. Why are such systems costly to the Army?

A. As an example, the cost to the Army of issuing one payroll check is $4.20, about four times the cost of issuing a payroll check in the private sector. It therefore costs the Army $40 million extra per year just to process its payroll checks.

PPSS also found that the ineffective application of the Army's ADP resources is worsened by the lack of career potential for ADP personnel in the Army.

Q. How can the Army adjust to make better use of its ADP resources?

A. First, PPSS recommended that a major command be established to maximize ADP productivity potential throughout the Army. To highlight the importance of ADP, it should be accorded specific and formal budget recognition. With these changes, ADP strategy should be developed Army-wide.

Secondly, the Army Chief of Staff should upgrade the current limited potential for an ADP career in the Army. This would encourage qualified ADP personnel to stay in the Army rather than leave for higher paying jobs in the private sector.

Over three years, our recommendations will save the Army $828 million, which would be enough money to buy 339 new M-1 tanks, 26% of the number of M-1 tanks currently in service.

Q. Retaining qualified ADP personnel is a serious concern in the private sector. What experience has the Government had in this regard?

A. PPSS found that there is a chronic shortage of qualified, experienced data processing personnel throughout the Federal Government. The two major reasons for this shortage are noncompetitive Federal salaries for ADP personnel and the deteriorating work environment—i.e., ADP personnel prefer to work with state of the art equipment so their skills will not become obsolete. An additional factor contributing to the Government's poor success in attracting qualified ADP professionals is the cumbersome job classification process, which sometimes results in prospective candidates taking other jobs before Government employment can be finalized. To illustrate the seriousness of the problem, a recent recruiting effort by the Social Security

Administration to fill 600 ADP positions resulted in only a handful of applicants.

To improve the Government's ability to attract or retain ADP personnel, the Office of Personnel Management and the General Services Administration should modify the job classification system to allow more timely hiring and maximize the use of cash incentives to retain qualified personnel. Other PPSS recommendations discussed in this section would act to improve the work environment for ADP personnel by modernizing equipment, thereby eliminating the disincentives resulting from the likely erosion of skills associated with work on antiquated equipment.

Q. What ADP areas did PPSS analyze outside of the Defense Department?

A. PPSS reviewed activities in major departments and agencies throughout Government. For example, efforts to dismantle the Education Department included a hiring freeze which resulted in an exodus of qualified ADP personnel. In addition, the organizational structure which came about when the Department was formed in 1980 resulted in there being several ADP staffs with unclear divisions of responsibility. Further, obsolete equipment continues to be used. Needless to say, the Education Department is not getting its money's worth for its ADP spending of $60–70 million per year.

PPSS recommended that responsibility for ADP functions be assigned to a separate staff unit reporting directly to the Under Secretary. The new ADP staff unit should be responsible for upgrading the current ADP system to one appropriate to the Department's needs. Closer attention should also be paid to ADP work that is contracted out to see that technical, cost, and schedule performance is as agreed.

Q. How much would these actions save the Education Department?

A. In the Education Department alone, with total ADP spending representing less than 1% of total Federal ADP spending, savings would be $19 million over three years, which is enough to pay the average salaries of 342 elementary school teachers for three years.

Q. Aren't there cases where the level of ADP spending in an agency is too high?

A. Yes. A good example of that is in the Census Bureau of the Commerce Department, where PPSS found that a major system acquisition which is currently in progress is too large in scope and includes unnecessary costs. A more appropriate acquisition strategy would save $15 million over three years.

Q. How else can better information save the Government money?

A. Another good example is in the Department of Housing and Urban Development (HUD). HUD is a financial organization which currently has no consolidated financial control. Reflecting this lack of control, accounting systems within HUD are primarily updated manually, even though the $2.4 billion investment fund portfolio of the Federal Housing Authority (FHA) places it among the top five funds in the private sector. HUD has been attempting to design the hardware and software for an improved accounting system since 1970 without success. The deficient accounting system is costing HUD approximately $173 million per year.

In addition, more funds are wasted because HUD has no effective automated system to verify the eligibility of program beneficiaries. One study found that 12% to 17% of tenants applying for HUD funds are not eligible and file false information to obtain benefits.

Improving the capabilities of HUD's automated information systems, as well as other management improvements, would save HUD $185 million over three years and would result in a $351 million increase in revenues over the same period, for a total favorable three-year impact of $536 million on HUD's budget.

Q. How can ADP improvements help increase productivity?

A. The Customs Bureau in the Treasury Department handled 4.6 million shipments of merchandise into the United States in 1981. This was up 84% from 2.5 million shipments in 1969, while staff levels have remained fairly constant. Since staff is not increasing, each worker is expected to do almost twice as much. PPSS recommended rapid implementation of systems currently being tested that reduce paperwork and allow for selective examination of international shipments so that time is not wasted examining domestic shipments. Savings are estimated at $84 million over three years.

Q. Are there any other general problems with Federal management of its ADP resources?

A. Yes. One other problem was identified by several Task Forces—the sharing of computer resources among and within agencies is generally inadequate. With over 17,000 computers currently being used by the Government, it is clear that some are being used at more efficient rates than others. Sharing computer resources means that an agency which has too much work for its own computer to handle could share the computer of another agency that is underutilizing its computer resources. This would save money by allowing the first agency to meet its demand for more computer resources without having to expand its current system or buy a new system.

Q. Any specific examples to illustrate the potential for cost reduction through the sharing of computer resources?

A. The Department of Transportation (DOT) is a highly decentralized organization with nine separate administrations. Several small administrations—e.g., the National Highway Traffic Safety Administration and the Maritime Administration—do not have adequate personnel resources to procure ADP equipment cost effectively. As a result, ADP quality and compatibility within DOT is inconsistent and uncontrolled. If the ADP functions of DOT's administration were consolidated as PPSS recommended, savings of $46 million over three years would result. This would allow DOT's ADP equipment to be procured more cost effectively and would increase the sharing of resources within DOT, reducing the use of costly commercial services.

Further, if ADP resource sharing were increased at the Department of Energy (DOE) facilities, savings of $38 million could be achieved over three years.

Q. Do all ADP savings fall into the categories of resource sharing and productivity improvements?

A. Most, but not all. Federally-funded highway construction projects must meet certain noise level requirements and this is accomplished by constructing noise barriers at a current cost of about $565,000 per mile (in 1980 dollars). PPSS found that by using computer analyses, the cost of meeting noise level limits could be significantly reduced, with three-year savings estimated at $703 million. That's enough to build 100 miles of new interstate highways in rural areas.

PPSS recommended another unique application of ADP resources in the U.S. Postal Service. Computer studies should be made on the optimum methods of moving mail, i.e., surface versus air transportation. Based on experience with similar studies in the private sector, net savings are conservatively estimated at $179 million over three years.

As noted above, the savings potential is tremendous and wide-ranging.

Q. How does office automation differ from automated data processing?

A. The basic difference is that office automation focuses on the activities of people in the office—white collar, clerical, and professional workers. Over 50% of the workforce is now employed in offices and about 80% of them handle information. Office automation results in improvements in obtaining, analyzing, storing, retrieving, and communicating information. Specifically, these improvements reflect better information handling by making maximum use of conferencing, activity management, personnel processing, and information retrieval.

— 89 —

Until very recently, managers and other professionals, despite their mounting information needs, have had to rely on the same resources —pen, paper, typewriter, telephone, mail—as those of previous generations. Rapidly advancing information technology is likely to yield enhanced productivity.

Q. What are some examples?

A. Here are some ways PPSS found that office automation could aid the professional employee:

Report preparation. In the conventional method of report preparation, an author uses different types of personnel (typist, graphics developer, clerical staff) and does a substantial amount of coordination of these personnel. With a reasonably sophisticated professional work station, all of these steps can be performed by the author unassisted, with cost savings in both professional and clerical time.

Internal mail. Transmission of memoranda typically requires typing, proofing, and distribution and involves a total elapsed time of two to five business days from drafting to receipt. Communications sent by an electronic mail network can be received in an hour following drafting.

Information storage and retrieval. Automated storage of information allows rapid retrieval, access by any authorized individual from any location, immediate availability of critical data, compact storage of voluminous information, minimum reformatting of data for different users, and minimum handling of documents.

Personal computer functions. Automated office systems may make available personal computer functions such as an electronic spreadsheet for budgeting and financial tracking, list keepers (e.g., for distribution of information), an appointment calendar, etc.

The above would save time for both the professional and clerical employee.

Q. How much could this save the Government?

A. If office automation were effectively implemented throughout the Government, PPSS estimated savings at $6.537 billion over the first three years.

Other areas not specifically developed in the preceding discussion but where PPSS identified significant ADP related savings opportunities include:

• Replacement of obsolete hardware—three year savings estimated at $4.612 billion.

• Implementation of hardware systems where none exist currently— three year savings estimated at $3.249 billion.

- Implementation of income verification systems—three year savings $3.249 billion. Improved ADP capabilities are key to more effective management of subsidy programs. For more on this topic see the Subsidized Programs section of this report.

- Improved management of ADP resources—three year savings estimated at $413 million.

- Implementation of office automation where none exists currently— three year savings estimated at $46 million.

The speed and accuracy with which the Federal Government processes information are measures of its efficiency, whether it is collecting taxes, registering pesticides, or issuing Social Security checks. The loss of the Government's previous position of leadership in managing state of the art ADP/OA is a source of serious concern.

While establishment of a Federal Information Resource Manager would be a significant step toward resolving many of the problems discussed in the preceding pages, it will take a firm commitment from the White House and all department and agency heads to ensure that modern systems are implemented in a timely and cost- effective manner.

> The three-year total of all the recommendations in this section, after elimination of duplication and overlap among issues, is $22.633 billion—equal to the three-year taxes of 3.4 million median income families.

The Impact of Not Buying Prudently

> The Federal Government purchased $159 billion in goods and services in FY 1982. More than 130,000 Federal employees were involved in these purchases which were governed by millions of individual contracts.
>
> Despite the massive scale of Government procurement, PPSS found that purchases were neither efficiently nor cost-effectively handled because of excessive and inconsistent regulations; limited and often inaccurate information; decentralized, uncoordinated, and poorly-planned acquisitions; and disincentives to good management.
>
> PPSS recommendations would centralize and coordinate policy and oversight responsibilities, increase competition for Federal contracts, and improve contractor efficiency while eliminating managerial disincentives.
>
> In FY 1983, the Government spent $56.3 billion in the specific areas covered by PPSS recommendations, with spending estimated to increase to $406.4 billion by the year 2000 if present policies are continued. Implementing PPSS recommendations would reduce spending to $247.6 billion in 2000, a saving of $158.8 billion or 39.1%.

In 1982, the Federal Government wrote 18.9 million procurement contracts totaling more than $159 billion which accounted for 22% of total Federal spending. Total 1982 procurement was up by 18.2% from the $134.5 billion spent in 1981. In addition, Government agencies held more than $88 billion worth of inventories stored in hundreds of locations.

Compared with the private sector, the Government spends more on procurement than the total sales of the big three auto makers—General Motors, Ford, and Chrysler—and the two largest chemical companies—Dupont and Dow—combined.

The process by which these purchases are made is extremely complex, both because of the wide variety of goods and services obtained and because of the statutory and regulatory environment in which the more than 130,000 Federal procurement personnel operate. There are more than 80,000 pages of instructions governing Federal procurement, with more than 20,000 new or revised pages produced each year.

The potential for waste, fraud, and abuse in current Federal procurement systems can be seen in the results of a November 1983 Senate Committee on Governmental Affairs investigation. The committee noted that a contract for spare parts for the F-16 fighter aircraft had been cancelled because of excessive costs. The contractor, which only channeled the sale of spare parts through its offices, increased subcontractor prices by 70.8% to 84.6%, as shown below:

		(1)	(2)	(3)
		Per Item Cost		
	Spare Part	Subcontractor Price to Contractor	Contractor Price to Air Force	Percent Markup
(1)	Antenna Hexagon Wrench	$5,205	$ 9,609	84.6%
(2)	Antenna Clamp Alignment Tool	5,618	10,137	80.4
(3)	Antenna Pulley Puller Tool	6,005	10,630	77.0
(4)	Antenna Puller Height Gauge	6,972	11,911	70.8

In reference to the above, the November 20 *New York Times* quoted a Pentagon official as follows:

> The horrible truth, however, is that everything is priced about the same way. The rip-off of taxpayers on the big items—weapons, engines, aircraft—is as bad as on spares.

> Everyone in the system responds in a totally rational fashion to the incentives in the system . . . the military procurement system has inverted punishments and rewards.

The result is inefficiency and waste. As the article noted:

> . . . five experienced Defense Department auditors expressed the belief that it would be possible to save as much as half of the $84.4 billion set aside in the next Defense budget for procurement, plus more money on other parts of the total $247 billion military spending bill.

PPSS recommendations for the procurement process are directed at reducing costs, overlap, and duplication, as well as correcting poorly managed systems and procedures.

The largest single procurement activity in the Federal Government ($60 billion annually) is the acquisition of major weapons systems (e.g., planes, tanks, submarines, and missiles). Weapons needs are generally determined by each military service, which is responsible for design, contractor selection, research, and full-scale development and production. In limited cases of common need, joint systems are developed, such as the Sidewinder missile used by the Army, Air Force, and Navy. It is not uncommon for a weapons system to take 10 to 20 years to develop.

The remainder of DOD's procurement activities relate to non-weapon items and services. The FY 1983 DOD budget request for these goods and services exceeded $95 billion.

As of September 1981, DOD reported a total inventory value of $88 billion. This included $47 billion in items associated with weapons systems and fuel. The remaining $41 billion consisted of repairables and other consumables (consumables are all items except explosive ordnance, major end-use equipment, and repairable equipment).

Civilian agency procurement ($34 billion) is conducted by many agencies, including, centrally, the General Services Administration (GSA), and the Departments of Energy, Transportation, and Agriculture, the Veterans Administration, the Tennessee Valley Authority, and the National Aeronautics and Space Administration.

GSA influences all civilian procurement through its policy-making authority in two basic ways: by establishing regulations for procurement practices and by mandating when GSA is the required source of supply for procurement needs.

GSA provides supplies to non-defense agencies as well as to DOD, with the latter accounting for more than 70% of GSA business. GSA currently has an average of about $250 million in inventory in its warehouses.

In order to provide procurement policy coordination and improved buying efficiency in both military and civilian agencies, Congress created the Office of Federal Procurement Policy (OFPP) in 1974. OFPP was created in response to a perceived lack of leadership in procurement policy and the corresponding fragmentation in procurement practices across departments and agencies. The goal of a strong OFPP presiding over a working, uniform Government procurement system has not, however, been realized.

Management of Executive Branch procurement is shared by many agencies.

- The Office of Federal Procurement Policy (OFPP) in OMB provides overall guidance and direction in government-wide procurement.

- The General Services Administration (GSA) establishes government-wide policies for civilian agencies and administers Federal Procurement Regulations and Federal Property Management Regulations. GSA also provides centralized buying and distribution functions for common-use items, including items for DOD.

- The Department of Defense (with NASA and the Coast Guard) administers the Defense Acquisition Regulations which govern defense purchases.

Limited government-wide information is available to support effective overall management of procurement. GAO noted in a recent study that "better reporting is essential to controlling cost growth . . . and that accurate information on the status of major acquisitions would provide a first step for measuring progress and early identification of real and potential problems." GAO also found that:

- The cost of 376 projects reviewed increased 140.0%, from $226.8 billion to $544.4 billion, or by $317.6 billion, over the agencies' initial budget justifications;

- The cost of 465 additional projects reviewed increased 78.7%, from $327.2 billion to $584.7 billion, or by $257.5 billion, over the initial agency budget estimates adjusted for changes in scope; and

- Over 130 of the 170 projects reviewed for schedule data exceeded their completion dates by more than six months.

In another study, the GAO found that the Defense Department and the Armed Services can "improve their processes for determining requirements for supplies and spare parts . . . [because] oftentimes, computed requirements were not based on accurate data. As a result, the requirements were overstated and understated by millions of dollars."

Even when data are collected, they may not provide good information. PPSS found that GSA collects information on the timeliness of its procurement operations (e.g., fill-rates, work-in-process, back orders), rather than information on the efficiency of operations (e.g., discounts negotiated in the current year versus the prior year).

Procurement regulations are excessive and, in some cases, inconsistent. A survey of nineteen agencies conducted by OFPP in 1978 and 1979 found 485 offices which regularly issued procurement regulations, as well as 877 different sets of procurement regulations (including directives, bulletins, instructions, and similar documents).

Also, during legislative hearings on procurement and the creation of

OFPP, evidence was cited that 110 different provisions exist in the Government on the use of experts and consultants, and 80 separate provisions exist on access to records.

The Commission on Government Procurement noted 30 discrepancies between the two major Government procurement statutes: the Armed Services Procurement Act (ASPA) and the Federal Property and Administrative Services Act (FPASA).

The preceding procurement patterns have produced duplicated efforts, inconsistent and excessive regulations, limited control, and excessive costs.

Q. PPSS recommendations regarding procurement appear to concentrate mainly on Defense spending. Is PPSS proposing cuts in the Defense budget?

A. PPSS has not recommended cuts in defense systems, nor has it taken any stand on policy. PPSS recommended ways to manage procurement in DOD and all other Government agencies with increased efficiency and reduced costs.

Major weapons systems represent the largest single procurement activity in the Federal Government (13 million of the Federal Government's 18.9 million contracts in 1982). The 1983 DOD budget projected over $60 billion in outlays on major weapons systems procurement, equivalent to about 8% of the total Federal budget and over one-fourth of the total DOD budget. Thus, DOD is a major consideration whenever the Federal procurement process is studied.

OVERALL PROCUREMENT ISSUES—STRENGTHENING
AND CENTRALIZING THE PROCUREMENT PROCESS

Insufficient action has been taken to integrate OFPP into the existing budget and program review processes of the Office of Management and Budget (OMB). PPSS recommended that this be done in order to strengthen OFPP's policy role. When OFPP was established, it was intended to have regulatory authority in the area of procurement. As it has evolved, however, OFPP has established little authority to implement changes in the procurement process.

In 1982, OFPP submitted a proposal for a Uniform Federal Procurement System (UFPS) designed to unify Government procurement policies, streamline the process, introduce greater competition, improve professionalism, and clarify responsibility and accountability in the procurement management structure. PPSS supports the proposed UFPS, with the additional improvement of multiyear procurement (purchasing goods or services over a period of years under a single contract).

PPSS also concluded that the acquisition and distribution responsibilities of the General Services Administration (GSA) for civilian agencies should be enhanced by enforcing the policy that civilian agencies use GSA facilities, where and when feasible. The policy-making role of GSA in this area should be shifted to OFPP so that GSA can concentrate on providing efficient and effective support to other Government agencies.

PPSS also found that the vast volume buying power of the Federal Government is not being adequately used to obtain the lowest possible prices. By negotiating volume purchases, the Government should be able to centrally purchase a wide variety of goods and services at bulk discount rates.

Non-weapons procurement for DOD is generally centralized in the Defense Logistics Agency (DLA), with the individual services responsible for procurement of weapons systems. Civilian agency procurement, however, is conducted by many agencies. Even within agencies, procurement may be decentralized. For example, in the Department of Agriculture, all items except for ADP equipment are procured on an individual basis by over 4,000 Agriculture offices throughout the country.

Q. What is the volume of common use, or general purpose, items purchased centrally through GSA?

A. In FY 1981, total Government procurement was $134.5 billion, of which $14.9 billion, or 11.1%, were common use items. Of this $14.9 billion, only $5.2 billion, or 34.9%, was procured centrally through GSA. PPSS estimated that the Government could save $242 million annually upon full implementation by increasing the number of civilian agency common use items purchased centrally through GSA.

Q. Since there are so many diverse agencies in the Federal Government, how can one organization know what to buy for so many different kinds of users?

A. One of the main reasons large organizations centralize purchasing operations is to gain economies from volume purchases. Increasing centralization, however, often leads to a decline in the quality of service and distribution. The trade-off between economy and service quality, therefore, is normally limited to an organization's common use items. These items include such things as office supplies, certain ADP equipment, automobiles, and other items in common use in most organizations.

PPSS recommended that GSA identify items which could be more efficiently and economically purchased through a centralized procurement process. PPSS estimated that an increase in centralized purchasing of common use items could save civilian agencies $312 million over three years.

Q. A central coordinating point regarding Federal purchases is required because of the need for the Government to purchase goods and services in a more economical and cost-effective manner and to present uniform rules, regulations, and practices to the private sector. How does the proposed Uniform Federal Procurement System (UFPS) address these issues?

A. In February 1982, OFPP submitted to Congress the Reagan Administration's proposal for procurement reform—incorporated in the UFPS. Its four major goals are:

- streamlining and simplifying the procurement process through a single set of Federal Acquisition Regulations and increased use of simplified bid specifications,

- emphasizing new concepts of competition based on total program costs,

- establishing new standards of professionalism in the procurement work force through career management and development programs, and

- creating in each agency an executive position responsible for procurement activities.

Achieving these goals requires:

- a management structure with clear lines of authority and accountability, a simplified procurement process, a professional workforce, and performance standards and feedback mechanisms;

- OFPP responsibility to put the new procurement system into operation;

- legislation to bring Federal procurement practices into line with modern methods and requirements, ensuring that current policies are formalized and followed; and

- OFPP policy authority over all agency procurement, authority to rescind agency regulations that do not conform to policy, and leadership responsibility to develop simplified government-wide regulations.

Q. How does PPSS propose to enhance the role of OFPP through the Uniform Federal Procurement System (UFPS)?

A. PPSS proposed the following:

- Continue efforts for substantial reforms of the Federal procurement process through UFPS, with the addition that specific multiyear contracting authority be granted to civilian agencies (the military is already granted authority to enter into multiyear contracts).

- Integrate OFPP fully into the budget process of the Office of Management and Budget (OMB)—i.e., incorporate OFPP and procurement reform objectives into the annual OMB budget and program review process.

In 1981, Deputy Secretary of Defense Frank C. Carlucci identified 32 actions for improving the acquisition process in the Department of Defense. This Acquisition Improvement Program (AIP), also known as the Carlucci Initiatives, focused on procedures and controls over program planning, and the inflexibility and inefficiency of the weapons procurement process. Taking into account the numerous studies of the acquisition process in recent years, the AIP was intended to emphasize solutions rather than just study problems.

PPSS recommended accelerating implementation of the most promising areas of the Carlucci Initiatives. These improvements include actions to increase use of multiyear contracting and to expand the concept to other areas, such as automated data processing, photocopying, and building services. Expanded use of multiyear contracting could save $3.415 billion over three years throughout the Government, of which $2.958 billion, or 86.6%, would occur in DOD. Moreover, program prioritization, i.e., establishing spending priorities for defense programs based on defense requirements, would result in a more efficient weapons procurement process in DOD.

PPSS further noted that $3.442 billion could be saved just in the Air Force and Navy by dual sourcing (introducing competition into the acquisition of major weapons systems by maintaining at least two competitive sources during the production life of a weapons system).

Q. The AIP was initiated over two years ago. Why is a mid-term reappraisal required? Have the services not complied with the program?

A. PPSS found that there are too many AIP initiatives to be effectively managed and implemented within a short time. The major initiatives could be more effectively implemented by focusing management attention on those that offer the greatest reward.

PPSS considered the following issues most promising, encompassing nearly half the initiatives contained in the AIP:

• multiyear contracting;

• improvements in cost estimating (risk management, inflation, probable costs);

• improvements in contracting (competition, source selection, contract type);

• program management; and

• program stability and priorities in meeting Defense needs.

One of the major provisions of the Acquisition Improvement Program is the increased use of *multiyear contracting (MYC)* in place of the more common Federal Government practice of writing procurement contracts on a year-to-year basis. MYC increases stability in the procurement process, which affords contractors opportunities for long-range planning. This results in a number of major benefits to the purchaser, including lower procurement costs due to economies of scale. MYC also encourages contractors to make productivity enhancing investments, increases competition for the initial contract award, and reduces the administrative burden to the contractor and the purchaser. PPSS found, however, that current use of MYC is very limited and that only a few major weapons systems—the primary opportunity area for MYC cost savings—have been approved for MYC by Congress. In addition, the Defense Department is currently restricted from entering into MYCs for "commercial items."

PPSS recommended expanded use of multiyear contracting in all Federal agencies, not only in DOD. In the area of weapons procurement, PPSS noted 31 programs which met the criteria for MYC. Potential savings in procuring these systems of $1.6 billion annually are possible upon full implementation of MYC. In addition to weapons systems, PPSS found opportunities for MYC in both defense and civilian agencies in areas such as ADP equipment and photocopying leases, and building maintenance services. Over three years, increased use of MYC could save $2.958 billion in weapons system procurement and $457 million in the procurement of non-weapons items in DOD and civilian agencies.

Q. Is multiyear contracting a new concept for the Federal Government?

A. Not at all. The Government has studied and used the concept for a number of years. PPSS found, however, that legislation governing MYC is not uniform across all Federal agencies. In the Defense Department, for example, a multiyear contract, by regulation, can extend from two to five years. In general, civilian agencies cannot obligate the Government to spend money beyond the current year. Therefore, unless specifically authorized by law, civilian agencies cannot enter into multiyear contracts.

Q. If multiyear procurement has been around for a number of years and the savings are so dramatic, particularly in weapons systems acquisition, why hasn't there been more use of the process?

A. In procuring weapons systems, there are several impediments to the use of MYC.

Up-front funding for purchases of components and materials is required. Procurement of more than one year's needs must be budgeted in the current year. Thus, there is a feeling that funds used in the current year remove funds from other programs.

The services are reluctant to identify programs for MYC because of the dynamic nature of technology. MYC, therefore, may restrict future DOD and Congressional flexibility if priorities change since funds will have been committed to specific programs.

None of these problems is insurmountable if adjustments are made to current budget and procurement procedures. Not all programs are candidates for MYC. Specific criteria for selecting MYC candidates should be established (e.g., mature, stable weapons programs using well-developed technologies), and there should be strict adherence to these criteria. Borderline candidates should not receive MYC status due to cancellation possibilities which result in additional costs, unfavorable publicity, Congressional loss of confidence, and resultant increased hesitancy on the part of DOD to employ MYC in the future.

Another way to improve the acquisition of weapons systems recommended by the Acquisition Improvement Program is *prioritizing weapons systems* while they are still in the development stage. Prioritizing programs ranks them according to need, taking into account cost/benefit relations.

Establishing priorities and determining financial affordability of proposed new systems early in the budgetary cycle is critical to achieving program stability and avoiding cost overruns. Before a new weapons system is approved, DOD should consider the impact of adding that system to systems currently being acquired or in production in view of the limited funds available for all weapons systems.

This "weeding-out" process with weapons systems is currently almost nonexistent. PPSS found that, once underway, programs develop constituencies made up of contractors and Congressmen in addition to the services. These combined forces make it virtually impossible to cancel a program. The easier and more costly decision to "stretch out" a program is often made rather than the more politically painful decision to eliminate it. Program "stretch out" occurs when a weapons system is purchased over a greater number of years than originally planned, or when fewer items are purchased under the contract—i.e., buying 50 tanks rather than the 100 originally contracted for.

PPSS did not quantify savings directly identified with program prioritization, but did recommend that DOD develop a Stable Programs List identifying and setting priorities for major weapon systems programs, and bringing more discipline and analysis into the decision-making process.

DOD policy does not require that a major system be demonstrated to be affordable through the full-scale development and production phases in order to obtain approval as a new start. It need only be shown to be affordable through the early development phases.

Early development phases have the lowest financial requirements and are easily funded. Therefore, far more programs are started each year than can be carried through the full-scale development and production phases. Because it is almost impossible to terminate these programs after they are started, too many programs end up competing for limited production funding. This, in turn, leads to inefficient production quantities, program stretch outs, and cost overruns. As a result, the systems may become obsolete and units may be built in insufficient numbers to meet mission requirements.

As of June 30, 1982, there were 39 programs approved for full-scale development with projected total acquisition costs of $450 billion. OMB has indicated that the total projected cost of *all* programs is approximately 230% of the funds that are likely to be available. PPSS proposed that DOD limit such overprogramming to 140% as of the time of the new start decision, with progressively lower percentages for later decision points. A reduction from the current average overprogramming of 230% to a level of 140% would result in a 40% reduction in Research, Testing, and Development expenditures, a three-year savings of $1.523 billion.

Q. What specific changes did PPSS recommend?

A. PPSS made the following specific recommendations:

- Require the Office of the Secretary of Defense (OSD) and the services to develop a Stable Programs List, a DOD-wide ranking for high and low priority programs. Programs at the top of the list could be candidates for multiyear contracting while marginal programs could be deleted.

- Clearly identify changes in current programs required to fund new program starts. Greater control over new programs in their early years is necessary before resources become committed. Also, the number of new programs or starts should be restricted.

- Update the budget whenever program costs deviate materially from forecast. At that time, programs that require modification should be identified, and additional funding sources required to meet initial objectives should be developed.

PPSS found three primary areas of *weapons systems program management* where considerable savings could be realized from improved management methods and procedures. These included improved weapons systems planning, improved contracting procedures, and improved cost estimating and scheduling.

In the area of systems planning, PPSS recommended that OSD and the services emphasize timely development of comprehensive Program Management Plans (PMPs) and Acquisition Plans (APs) at the program level. These improvements include expanding the scope of these plans and maintaining them as working documents, using the plans as the basis for cost and schedule estimates, and delegating authority to contract and manage programs on a decentralized basis. Based on these recommendations, PPSS estimated savings of $2.940 billion over three years.

In contracting for weapons systems, PPSS found insufficient emphasis on the potential total cost of major weapons programs. As a result of these findings, PPSS recommended that OSD streamline the source selection process, making it more efficient and effective by selecting contractors based on the lowest total cost. Potential cost savings of $980 million over three years were identified by PPSS from these recommendations.

In the area of cost estimating and scheduling, PPSS recommended that DOD institute more discipline over cost estimates and schedule development to produce accurate cost forecasts, and improve "early warning" indicators of cost overruns and scheduling problems. PPSS also recommended that DOD consider sharing cost overruns with contractors to encourage more realistic program estimates. PPSS estimated that savings of $2.940 billion could be realized over a three-year period.

Q. What's wrong with the current controls (Program Management Plans [PMP] and Acquisition Plans [AP]) in DOD weapons procurement?

A. PMPs are not fully effective as management tools; they are not always completely developed and sometimes do not exist at all. They frequently are not updated for changing program circumstances and often fall into disuse.

The roles, responsibilities, and authorities of the various individuals and organizations involved in the acquisition process are not always well-defined in the PMP, or followed in practice.

The scope of the PMP is somewhat limited. It often does not cover the program's total life cycle. Program risks, i.e., those associated with the production and deployment phases are infrequently and inadequately addressed, while technical risks during the research and development phase, when considered, tend to be narrowly focused.

Program management and acquisition strategies are often developed at high levels, i.e., "top-down" planning rather than planning at the program level. As a consequence, the PMP and AP do not always consider the complete range of options available. Instead, they tend simply to record decisions which have been made.

PMPs could be improved if they were updated frequently, contained more specifically defined roles for individuals and organizations, and covered the program's total life cycle. These improvements would allow DOD to delegate authority to contract and manage programs to line management personnel.

PPSS estimated that these recommendations could save $1.5 billion annually, or approximately 2%–3% of annual spending for major weapons systems, upon full implementation.

Q. What specific problem areas were noted regarding contracting for weapons systems acquisition?

A. Some of the problems PPSS noted were:

- Insufficient consideration given to the contractor's past performance on other weapons programs when awarding contracts.

- Bidders discouraged or prevented from offering alternative proposals which might yield cost, schedule, or technical advantages.

- A source selection process that takes too long, involves too many review and approval steps, and requires too many people.

- Subcontractors "buying-in" (i.e., submitting deliberately low bids to obtain initial contracts) with the hope of recouping losses and making a profit on subsequent contracts.

- Depending on the prime contractor to do a good job in subcontracting and doing little to appraise or upgrade the performance of the prime contractor in its subcontracting activities.

PPSS recommended that DOD select contractors based on the lowest total cost and strengthen efforts to monitor and upgrade the prime contractor's subcontracting activities.

Annual savings are estimated at $500 million upon full implementation based on a 1% reduction in annual spending for weapons systems.

Q. The lack of effective management over contractor bids and operations contributes to problems in controlling weapons systems costs. However, why does this prevent the Government from producing realistic estimates of costs?

A. As the budgetary process is structured, there are pressures or incentives for producing low estimates: early estimates are based largely on input from technologists so there is a tendency to see only the merits of new technology and overlook implementation difficulties; program managers are judged in part by how well they convince their superiors that funding should be provided for their programs; and the services can get more programs started for a given funding level if estimates are on the optimistic side.

Based on a review of three major weapons systems, the following indices of company estimates, bids, and final costs were noted:

	System	(1) Company Estimate	(2) Bid	(3) Final Cost	(4) Final Cost as Multiple of Bid
(1)	A	1.0	0.75	2.2	2.9X
(2)	B	1.0	0.43	4.0	9.3
(3)	C	1.0	0.45	2.0	4.4

Taking into account underbidding, company estimates of final costs are still not accurate indicators of how much weapons systems will cost.

Q. What are some of the reasons that major weapon systems prices go so far over the initial estimates?

A. The escalating costs of these programs result from "program turbulence," which includes poor initial cost estimates, stretched and delayed production schedules, engineering changes, quantity changes, and poor contractor performance. As noted before, in some cases, contractors "underbid" to get a foot in the door. Work then proceeds on the program, and original estimates are doubled and tripled. At that point, it is too late to stop the process. PPSS found that final costs have been as much as 400% greater than initial bids.

Q. How much does program turbulence contribute to increased weapon systems costs?

A. PPSS reviewed 25 major weapons programs and found that their total costs, including inflation, were up 223% from the original estimate of $105 billion to a current estimate of $339 billion. The table below shows how these cost increases arose:

Weapons Systems Cost Increases

		(1)	(2)
		($ Billions)	*Percent of Revised Estimate*
(1)	Development Estimate	$104.8	30.9%
(2)	Inflation	42.3	12.5
(3)	Program Changes	129.4	38.1
(4)	Other Changes	62.7	18.5
(5)	Subtotal	$234.4	69.1%
(6)	Revised Estimate	$339.2	100.0%

$129.4 billion of the $234.4 billion increase in costs, or 55.2%, was due to program changes. These increases could be significantly reduced through better program management in all phases of the development and production of these weapons systems.

Q. What needs to be done to improve cost estimates?

A. Consolidate all resources within each of the services which are devoted to reviewing and checking program estimates into one unit. This would ensure that the resources of the services are concentrated on preparing estimates and would define a single point of responsibility for the quality of estimates.

Consolidate the scheduling functions with the estimating functions, recognizing the strong link between costs and scheduling.

Employ risk analysis techniques to cover potential risks during all phases of the program from research and development through production and deployment. Use this approach to produce "most likely" estimates. Use the Program Management Plan (PMP) to mitigate or eliminate the adverse effects of the risks that are identified.

Savings of $1.5 billion annually upon full implementation reflect a 2%–3% reduction in annual spending on weapons systems.

Q. Why is dual sourcing such an important issue in weapons acquisition?

A. A former Deputy Assistant Secretary of Defense for Acquisition summarized the current situation regarding dual sourcing as follows:

> Perhaps the single most important difference between defense business and civilian business stems from the all-too-frequent absence of alternatives in the military procurement process.
>
> This does not mean more of the sort of "onetime" competition presently used. It means dual sourcing throughout the program.
>
> In defense, there customarily is a fierce rivalry during the initial competition for an award of a research and development contract. After this initial competition—frequently awarded based on a firm's "buy-in"—the winner becomes the sole developer and producer for the military system over the next 20 years. Thus, a program—such as a missile system—may once have had an initial competition, but after the first step there is no alternative source for this much-needed piece of equipment. Therefore, the sole-source producer increases the price; the Government has little choice but to attempt to "negotiate" and basically to accept the cost increases.

In addition to reducing costs, dual sourcing enhances the industrial base by providing additional contractors and subcontractors to meet Defense requirements (e.g., during surges and mobilizations). It can also eliminate delays caused when an increase in the number of units needed exceeds the production capacity of a single source. Moreover, dual sourcing can provide contractors with added incentive to resolve program problems. These additional advantages can sometimes be adequate justification for using two production sources even in the absence of cost savings.

Q. Why isn't dual sourcing used more frequently in acquiring weapons systems?

A. PPSS found that only a small percentage of weapons systems are purchased through dual sourcing, resulting in lost savings opportunities. There were three primary obstacles to using dual sourcing. These are an attitude that dual sourcing is still an exception to, rather than a normal competitive business practice; that near-term, or "up-front," costs associated with qualifying a second source can be significant, especially in the production phase; and that dual sourcing can be a very complex and time-consuming process.

PPSS found potential savings in the use of dual sourcing in the types of programs where they have been successful in the past, such as procuring missiles, electronics, and munitions. Were the dual sourcing concept expanded more fully in these areas and, to a lesser degree, into areas such as aircraft procurement, PPSS estimated that $3.442 billion could be saved over three years in the Air Force and Navy alone.

IMPROVED INVENTORY MANAGEMENT

PPSS reviewed the ordering, controlling, and stockpiling of the approximate $41 billion of supplies, parts, and components known as consumables and repairables which the Federal Government currently has on hand, most of which is in DOD.

PPSS recommended DOD compliance with the Economic Order Quantity (EOQ) system, a method to reduce inventory carrying costs by determining the optimum quantities to be purchased and the frequency of purchases. PPSS also recommended modernizing computer systems which support inventory management, and adopting private sector inventory-taking techniques. The overall objective of these recommendations was to reduce the amount and the cost of holding the inventory while maintaining adequate supplies on hand.

Implementing these recommendations could result in an estimated onetime reduction in inventory of about $4.5 billion with a resulting $1.333 billion reduction in the carrying cost of the remaining inventory over three years.

Q. What is an economic order quantity system (EOQ) and how does it reduce costs?

A. An EOQ system is used to determine how often and how much to buy of each item. If purchasing and inventory carrying costs are correctly calculated and future demand is accurately projected, the EOQ system will result in an average inventory that minimizes purchasing costs and the costs of holding inventory in stock. It is, therefore, critical to inventory management to assess and update these costs.

Q. Why are inventory levels far higher than the EOQ system would direct?

A. PPSS found the following shortcomings in inventory management:

The EOQ system is commonly overridden by inventory managers, increasing quantities ordered and decreasing the frequency of ordering. Inventory managers override the EOQ system to reduce work loads.

Purchasing and inventory carrying costs are not assessed and adjusted regularly.

Inventory managers are evaluated according to their fill rates (percent of required inventory on hand). A high stock level factor leads to a high fill rate. Thus, there is no incentive to maintain inventories at an economical level.

Q. What solutions did PPSS propose?

A. To correct the problem in the Department of Defense, PPSS recommended that DOD require strict compliance with the EOQ system and eliminate variation in each Service with respect to forecasting demand and using EOQ. An audit program should be initiated to ensure compliance.

Further, PPSS recommended that DOD:

• establish guidelines for the services to regularly assess and adjust purchasing and inventory carrying costs.

• expedite the modernization of computer facilities to provide accurate inventory estimates and to improve the accuracy of demand forecasts.

• determine what inventory is required for readiness purposes and encode all items with a relative essentiality factor.

• include in its criteria for rating inventory managers demand forecast accuracy and stock usage as well as fill rates.

Q. One of the keys to controlling inventory levels is having accurate and timely information. Why is there insufficient data concerning DOD inventories?

A. The ADP facilities supporting inventory control in the Defense Department are well below the quality used in private industry. Inventory management decisions are less than optimal because the data are not timely and have high error rates. Current ADP facilities are outdated and the pace of modernizing them is inadequate. Modernization plans are less than ideal because it takes too long to buy the equipment (by which time it may be obsolete) and because of overly complex systems requirements.

PPSS recommended the following:

• Use commercial ADP services and equipment where feasible and concentrate on pilot programs that can be implemented in a short period of time.

• Emphasize existing or planned systems in DOD to avoid extended development time.

Q. How do current inventory-taking procedures in DOD differ from standard private sector practices?

A. The practice of taking "wall-to-wall" inventories, common in the private sector, is not used in DOD. This method inventories the entire facility at one time, requiring a shutdown of normal activities for a brief period and strict cutoffs on the movement of material and documentation. Not taking "wall-to-wall" inventories results in inaccurate inventory counts, unidentified obsolete inventory, and misstated records which require adjustment. In 1981, differences between DOD accounting records and inventory counts exceeded $2 billion, 4% of average inventory held.

Q. What solutions did PPSS propose?

A. DOD should initiate a program of "wall-to-wall" inventory taking on a periodic basis. PPSS believes that taking "wall-to-wall" inventories is feasible and cost effective. Since this represents a great change, however, a pilot program to establish its feasibility is needed.

Q. Is it true that inventory reductions are sometimes impossible because of special interest considerations?

A. Special interests are certainly a factor affecting good inventory management. For example, legislation introduced in both the House and Senate would hamstring GSA's and the President's ability to administer the metals stockpile by forcing GSA to purchase copper from domestic producers for the National Defense Stockpile. Legislation pending in the Senate directs GSA to acquire $85 million of domestic copper within one year while the House version specifies $300 million in purchases.

GSA opposes these bills because they blatantly violate provisions of the Stock Piling Act which stipulate that the stockpile cannot be used to subsidize specific industries—i.e., the purpose of the pending legislation—and because they are wasteful of defense funds.

INCREASING EFFICIENCY OF
GOVERNMENT PROCUREMENT AND CONTRACTING

Savings could be realized by improving the policies and procedures for determining whether certain commercial activities should be carried out by the Government or private enterprise, as provided for in Office of Management and Budget Circular A-76. For a detailed discussion of this area see "Optimizing the Use of the Private Sector," discussed elsewhere in this report.

PPSS also recommended consolidating DOD contract administration activities within a single organization (reducing staff) and modernizing

Automated Data Processing (ADP) systems (improving the contract administration process, providing current and uniform data about contractor activities). Three-year savings are projected at $185 million.

Q. What benefits would result from consolidating DOD contract administration activities?

A. Consolidating contract activities within one organization would reduce headquarters personnel, facilitate better allocation of personnel, and enhance flexibility to respond to changing needs. Consolidation would also increase consistency in executing DOD policies.

Also, substantial benefits are available through greater automation of the contract administration process. The productivity of contract administration personnel would be improved if they had access via terminals to accurate, up-to-date contract data on a current basis. Greater automation of contract administration activities would reduce reconciliation efforts at various buying locations, and provide more timely and accurate data pertaining to contract status and contractor performance.

PPSS recommended consolidating all DOD contract administration activities in a single organization and making terminals available to contract administrators, providing them with accurate, up-to-date contract data.

SPARE PARTS AND COMMON PARTS AND STANDARDS

The services purchase over $13 billion a year in spare parts for weapons systems and other equipment. PPSS found, however, that the Air Force, the biggest buyer of spare parts ($4.8 billion in 1982), purchases less than 25% of replenishment spare parts through the use of spare parts "breakout" (purchasing parts directly from their manufacturer or from a competitor of the weapon system's contractor). PPSS estimated that savings of $689 million can be realized over three years in the Air Force alone through spare parts breakout.

In addition, PPSS noted that procurement officials are not sufficiently selective in citing military specifications (MILSPECS) requirements in contracts. MILSPECS are developed for a wide range of items being procured, including various parts, components, and material. MILSPECS define the technical characteristics required in the production of such items. Generally, it is more costly to produce an item to a MILSPEC than to a normal commercial standard.

Also, use of standard, off-the-shelf component equipment, subsystems, and field operational support systems can reduce weapons system development lead time, permitting earlier deployment of more sustainable weapons systems, and lower acquisition and life-cycle costs.

Requiring the use of common parts in weapons systems and tailoring MILSPECS for specific systems could save $7.330 billion over three years.

Q. Why don't the services insist on competitive contracts for spare parts if they can buy them so much cheaper that way?

A. One of the major problems is the legal aspect of patents, data, and copyrights. The patents and proprietary data of the contractor, developed as a result of its research and development (R&D), is the property of the contractor, even though the R&D is done at Government expense. PPSS recommended that DOD establish a formal process to obtain engineering and technical data when weapons systems are acquired. A change in the Defense Acquisition Regulations is required to gain access to this data and reduce the excessive amounts often spent for spare parts.

Q. What examples of excessive spare parts costs did PPSS note?

A. A few examples present the scope of the problem. The Pentagon has been buying screws for $91 which can be purchased for 3¢, breather caps for compressors for $100 each which can be purchased for 25¢, and silicon electric cells at $114 each when they can be purchased for 9 1/2¢. The Navy's Training Equipment Center, Orlando, Florida, has paid $511 for lamps which cost 60¢. A supplier in Mississippi bought a gravity timer from the sole manufacturer for $11 and sold it to the Navy for $256, a tidy 2,227% markup.

Q. What is meant by "common parts"? What is the potential for savings in this area?

A. The term "common parts" has a broad meaning. It includes commercially available aircraft purchased for training purposes as well as commercially distributed machine screws.

Different weapons systems frequently include elements and parts (e.g., computers, radars, tracking devices), which serve the same purpose, but are specially developed and produced for each system. The objective in this area is for the services to use, wherever possible, elements from one weapons systems that can be modified for a particular use in other weapons systems at minimum cost.

Q. PPSS concluded that DOD has not adequately addressed the lack of common parts in weapons systems and the excessive use of military specification requirements (rather than normal commercial standards) in contracts. Aren't MILSPECS necessary to ensure quality standards in weapons systems?

A. The problem has been that if a military specification exists, it will be cited as a requirement in any contract, even though the particular item procured does not need to meet all such specifications. Procurement officials are not sufficiently selective in choosing only the particular military specifications that are truly needed in relation to the item being procured.

A landmark military-civilian study (1974-1976 Shea Task Force) concluded that the high cost of complying with MILSPECS results from a failure to use specifications in a reasonable and selective way, rather than from a fundamental problem with the specifications.

To improve the situation, PPSS recommended the following:

• DOD should carry out military hardware design standardization studies and initiate joint-service development of military hardware and software.

• DOD should consider only MILSPECS related to the item being procured. All other MILSPECS for material, parts, and components included in the end item should be simply reference documents, and not mandatory, unless individually justified and separately listed in the purchase contract. This is the reverse of present procedure which considers all MILSPECS to be contractual requirements unless formal exception is taken.

• DOD should authorize the use of financial incentives to encourage contractors to challenge unimportant or irrelevant "standard" data requirements.

In addition to the issues and agencies discussed above, PPSS reviewed other aspects of the Federal procurement process. These areas can be broadly categorized as Organizational Controls, Competition, Excessive Regulations and Specifications, and Miscellaneous Procurement Activities.

PPSS recommendations regarding organizational controls included revising the management structure for controlling procurement activities (e.g., in the Army and Department of Labor), establishing career paths for procurement personnel, and involving business and financial experts in decisions regarding production of weapons systems. PPSS also recommended increasing the number of DOD consumable items purchased by the Defense Logistics Agency since it is more efficient at procurement than the services. Implementing PPSS recommendations would save $1.955 billion over three years in this area.

Competition can be increased by requiring adherence to regulations on competitive bidding, motivating contractors to invest in more productive plants and equipment, establishing a data base on contractor performance to avoid repeat business with unsatisfactory vendors, and comparing price quotes from vendors for civilian common use items before awarding contracts. Savings of $1.885 billion over three years can be achieved by implementing PPSS recommendations.

Eliminating unnecessary specifications in civilian procurement and unnecessary contract provisions in buying petroleum products for DOD ($12.6 billion in 1981), and raising the threshold for complying with regulations covering socio-economic programs (designed to aid American workers and small and minority-owned businesses) to $25,000, could save $1.499 billion over three years.

Also, improving controls over Air Force procurement of consulting services, coal procurement practices in the Tennessee Valley Authority, and Navy training programs regarding weapons systems could save $270 million over three years.

The three-year total of all the recommendations in this section, after elimination of duplication and overlap among issues, is $34.528 billion—equal to the three-year taxes of 5.2 million median income families.

Managing the Government's Facilities

The Federal Government owns about one-third of all the land in the United States, leases 83 million square feet of office space, controls 318,000 cars and trucks, and stores the equivalent of 111 billion letters. Despite the magnitude of the Government's real and personal property holdings, PPSS found little attention being directed at developing and applying managerial techniques to ensure efficient and effective usage. Recommendations were made accordingly.

In FY 1983, the Government spent $4.7 billion in the specific areas covered by PPSS recommendations, with spending estimated to increase to $19.8 billion by the year 2000 if present policies are continued. Implementing PPSS recommendations would reduce spending to $4.0 billion in 2000, a saving of $15.8 billion, or 79.8%.

REAL PROPERTY

At the end of FY 1980, the Federal Government owned real property and structures valued at $104 billion, including 744 million acres of land valued at $10 billion, $42 billion in buildings, and $52 billion in structures (such as dams and power plants). This $104 billion appraisal is conservative since it includes Federal lands valued at an average of about $13 an acre, and the replacement value or market value of the land, buildings and structures would be substantially greater.

As a basic concern to PPSS, there is no central office within the Government specifically designated to manage real property holdings. This lack of centralized direction is exacerbated by inadequate information systems, a lack of government-wide, comprehensive planning, and a failure to establish clearly defined objectives.

For perspective, the following are indicative of the scope of the Government's property management activities and of areas for potential savings:

• During FY 1983, the General Services Administration (GSA) expects to incur approximately $300 million in utility and fuel costs ($225 million in direct costs, the balance attributable to GSA's "tenant" agencies). The Department of Defense (DOD) spends $2.5 billion annually on utilities—over $285,000 an hour, 365 days a year.

DOD has installed approximately 150 Energy Management Control Systems (EMCS)—electronic data processing systems providing automated energy management capability for a building or complex of buildings. PPSS found that a three-year net savings in energy costs of $385 million could be realized if GSA were to install and DOD were to expand its use of EMCS and employ other commercially available energy management techniques.

• As of September 30, 1982, GSA was leasing 83 million square feet of office space, housing about 400,000 Federal employees. GSA's leasing authority for FY 1983 was $770 million which is expected to increase to more than $1 billion in FY 1985.

GSA's cumbersome system of leasing, which includes detailed specifications of cleaning requirements, leasehold improvements, etc., results in rental rates as much as $7 per square foot higher than prevailing market rates. GSA has established a goal of completing lease negotiations in 283 days versus an average of 180 days in the private sector. PPSS estimated that reducing inefficiencies by more closely following private sector practices could result in three year savings of $144 million.

The table on the following page compares the General Services Administration's property management function with that of a private sector company.

Compared to a large life insurance company with comparable assets and facilities, GSA's Public Buildings Service spends 6 times as much for relatively incomplete, inaccurate, and outdated information; has 17 times the number of administrative and professional personnel; and has a total management cost that is 14 times greater.

In order to correct the basic problem in the Government's approach to real property management, four elements need to be considered:

• goals of the management effort;

• planning (both for procedures and communication of decisions and data);

• roles and responsibilities of various segments of the Federal Government (inside and outside GSA) in the execution of all activities related to real property management; and

Real Property Management Comparison

	GSA—Public Buildings Service	Property management division of a large life insurance firm
Assets:	$9 billion	$8 billion
Number of facilities:	8,600	10,000
Objective:	Provide space for Federal employees and operations	Obtain and manage property in such a way that it is financially self-sustaining and produces long-term gain
Management:	Decentralized, lacks effective information flow	Centralized, uses few people to make and implement decisions
Planning:	Projects numbers, principally for budget estimation	Forecasts positions of maximum gain; seeks ideas to improve efficiency
Data:	Incomplete, inaccurate, slow	Accurate, fast response, continual updating
Computerized information system:	$6 million annual equipment lease; hardware & software developed as needed	$1 million for commercially available hardware & software packages directed toward "landlord" management
Management personnel:	500 Central Administration 4500 professionals in leasing, construction and contracting—5000 in total	100 Central Administration 200 contracted professionals in leasing, construction and contracting—300 in total
Average cost/ employee:	$25,000	$30,000
Total management cost:	$125 million	$9 million

- measurement of performance, as compared with the stated goals and the management plan.

Within this framework, PPSS recommended that the Government:

- Establish in writing a clear, concise goal for Federal real property management. This would serve as a guide to planning and execution. At present, from a management standpoint, no one knows clearly and completely what is to be achieved, how it is to be achieved, who is responsible, or the amount of time that should be allowed to complete each part of a job.

- Correct and update the real property data base within 18 months.

- Select and obtain the most appropriate computer software and hardware for handling real property data. PPSS found that the Federal

Government (GSA in particular) is years behind the private sector in the use of computerized information systems. Standard packages for property management are available for much less than the $6 million current cost of GSA's outdated systems.

- Order an in-depth internal study of duplication within GSA, culminating in a report to the Office of Management and Budget (OMB) within one year. This would identify inefficiencies and overlap and provide the detail necessary to formulate a plan to streamline operations.

- Eliminate the unnecessary duplication between GSA and tenant agencies in facility management functions. The present situation of ''mini-GSAs'' forming in tenant agencies is wasteful.

The comparison between GSA and the private sector insurance company discussed previously, and the additional cost incurred by the agencies in managing property, led PPSS to conclude that by implementing the above recommendations, savings of $62 million dollars over a three-year period can be achieved—an amount sufficient to lease approximately 2 million square feet of office space for three years.

Q. Does the Federal Government know how much real property it owns?

A. The Federal Government maintains no overall inventory of its capital assets and their current condition. GSA maintains an inventory of public buildings and their associated assets, but it is not used as part of government-wide planning. Other agencies maintain inventories of various components of total capital assets. The Department of Transportation (DOT), for example, prepares an inventory and assessment of the condition of highways. However, no complete aggregate data on Federal capital investments are available.

Q. What is the Government's goal in the management of its real property holdings?

A. There is no clearly defined goal for Federal real property management and PPSS, therefore, suggested the following:

Manage real property and related interests in a manner consistent with valid user needs—charging ''tenants'' the equivalent of fair-market rates for commercial space and maintenance, but minimizing the total expense to the Federal establishment over the long term.

Q. In one of the recommendations regarding computer software and hardware, PPSS suggested obtaining the ''most appropriate system.'' What exactly does that mean?

A. Standardized hardware and software packages are commercially available which are superior and less costly than GSA's outdated property management system.

Q. PPSS recommended that the tenant agencies' duplication of GSA management functions be eliminated. How can that be accomplished?

A. The Office of Management and Budget should examine the existing duplication of property management functions between GSA and all Federal tenant agencies, with a goal of eliminating all overlapping staff. The only assignments that should be left in agencies are those essential to providing management services unique to a particular agency's needs.

PERSONAL PROPERTY

PPSS also reviewed the Government's management of personal property, defined as any property other than real property owned or leased by the Federal Government. In this area, fleet vehicle management is of particular importance.

The Federal Government has the world's largest fleet of motor vehicles. The Federal fleet, primarily automobiles and light trucks, includes over 318,000 vehicles. The General Services Administration (GSA) controls 90,000 of these vehicles. The other 228,000 vehicles are divided into more than 100 motor pools. The Department of Defense (DOD) motor fleet is the largest, with 137,000 vehicles. (While the U.S. Postal Service has an additional fleet of 118,000 vehicles, PPSS excluded it from this study because of the quasi-independent status of USPS and because of the specialized nature of its vehicles.) Average utilization of Federal vehicles is 9,000 miles per year, 64% less than the 25,000 miles per year that private rental firms consider to be effective utilization. In FY 1981, $731 million was spent on motor vehicles management—excluding rental costs and reimbursement costs for private vehicle use.

There is inadequate cooperation and coordination among the fleet managers, resulting in inefficient, duplicative and costly vehicle operations. Further, there is a serious lack of data with which to perform meaningful cost comparisons among agencies or with private fleets. As a result, no answer is currently available to the fundamental question—should the Federal Government maintain a vehicle fleet?

If the Government continues to maintain a fleet, PPSS recommended correction of three basic problems:

- There is no centralized, government-wide, motor fleet management, or management information system.

- GSA is not notified of any agency's vehicle requirements until after appropriations are approved. This limits the opportunity for standardization and negotiation of acquisitions based on volume purchases.

- GSA and DOD sell vehicles in lots on an "as is/where is" basis. Resale prices normally don't exceed wholesale prices because of the poor condition of the vehicles. Only GSA-owned vehicles are reconditioned prior to sale. Private sector experience indicates that there is a $2.00 increase in value for every $1.00 spent on reconditioning.

To correct these problems, PPSS recommended that:

- The Federal fleet be immediately reduced by 100,000 vehicles, or by 31.4%, to increase average utilization to levels more in line with the private sector. GSA and DOD should increase vehicle resale revenues by implementing a reconditioning program for all decommissioned vehicles prior to sale.

- The Office of Management and Budget analyze existing reports and data within one year and propose improvements in accounting and management standards. These standards should be implemented for the entire Federal fleet under existing Executive Branch authority.

- A government-wide fleet management information system be established to address the fundamental question of the extent to which the Federal Government should be in the business of owning and operating a motor vehicle fleet.

- GSA maximize volume purchasing leverage by utilizing a competitive, once-a-year, fixed price/indefinite quantity contract for each FY's planned quantity of new vehicles.

Q. Should fleet management be centralized?

A. The case for centralization cannot be evaluated without comparison to alternative structures, and such comparisons are not possible without adequate data for analysis. That is why the PPSS recommendations stress data collection so heavily.

Q. Do the benefits of a reconditioning program for all decommissioned vehicles justify the costs?

A. The amount of reconditioning needed obviously varies depending upon the use and wear on each particular vehicle. As stated previously, a $2 increase in value can be expected for each $1 spent on reconditioning. Since the Federal fleet is older and more worn than many private sector fleets, the actual reconditioning cost per vehicle would be higher than private sector experience, although the 2 to 1 ratio could still be expected to apply. The actual increase in revenue will vary according to the size and type of each vehicle and will depend upon how well a particular vehicle has been maintained during Government use.

Implementation of these recommendations could save taxpayers a total of $1.536 billion over a three-year period.

PPSS reviewed "Property Associated Functions," which includes space and records management.

Utilization of space within the Federal Government represents both a problem and an opportunity. The Federal Government owns 2.6 billion square feet of office space or about four times the office space in the nation's ten largest cities. A reduction of only one square foot of office space per Federal employee would save taxpayers $11 million annually. The GSA goal is to attain a 20% reduction in office space utilization to 135 square feet per employee.

PPSS also found that records storage represents a serious problem in the Federal Government. At the end of FY 1981, Federal records occupied over 37 million cubic feet of space—roughly equal to 193 football fields of records stacked 10 feet high. With one cubic foot of storage holding approximately 3,000 pieces of letter-sized paper, the Government is storing the equivalent of 111 billion letters.

Q. What must be done to achieve the targeted 20% reduction in office space utilization?

A. PPSS made five recommendations to help achieve GSA's space utilization goal and thereby reduce costs:

• Remove the ceilings on Standard Local User Charges (SLUC), i.e., the "rent" paid by agencies in GSA-managed buildings. Termination of legislation setting a ceiling on SLUC should be sought because the present ceiling reduces the incentive for tenant agencies to use space more efficiently.

• Prepare formal plans for GSA space surveys. These surveys should cover every Federal agency and every region in the United States.

• Establish space utilization goals independently and realistically for each agency and executive department.

• Include space utilization objectives, reporting, and review as part of the budgeting process.

• Streamline the current prospectus requirement to allow GSA to take advantage of favorable leasing conditions when they arise.

Q. Where are Federal records stored now?

A. National Archives and Record Service operates 14 records centers throughout the country where low-cost storage and reference service for inactive records is provided, and where records no longer required for administrative or historical purposes are destroyed in accordance with approved schedules. About 2.3 million cubic feet, or nearly 16%, of the records stored in records centers have no disposition schedule. PPSS recommended that a disposition schedule be established for all records.

PPSS also reviewed Federal activities related to the disposal of surplus real property. The General Services Administration holdings of excess property on June 30, 1982 totaled $903 million in value on a cost basis.

Q. The General Services Administration is ostensibly responsible for excess property identified by civilian agencies. How does the disposal of excess property work?

A. Periodically, all executive departments and agencies survey their real property holdings to identify surplus property. Other agencies are consulted to determine whether property, identified as surplus by one agency, can fill the "space" requirements of another agency. If not, it is classified as surplus and offered first to local and state governments and then to the public.

   PPSS recommended two general actions for improving the sales and the returns on this property:

   1. Extend credit assistance to buyers in order to accelerate sales and maximize the sales price.

   2. Permit a portion of the sales proceeds to flow back to the selling agency to motivate decisive action.

   Providing incentives to the agencies and facilitating credit arrangements for prospective purchasers would permit realistic sales goals to be met.

Q. How is excess property disposed of now?

A. Surplus property has traditionally been disposed of (1) by transferring the property at a discount from fair market price to other Federal agencies; (2) by no-cost conveyance of the property to state and local governments; and (3) by negotiated and competitive sales to the public.

   By law, each Federal agency is required to report excess real property under its control to the General Services Administration. In February 1982, Executive Order #12348 was issued initiating a new program under the Property Review Board (PRB) which eliminated discounted transfers within the Federal Government, required state and local Government to pay 100% of fair market value, and accelerated the disposition of surplus properties.

   By establishing incentives for agencies to identify surplus property, more property will be made available for sale. The availability of financing should result in additional and more rapid sales (i.e., some surplus Government property could not be sold without financing) and, thus, reduce the Government's cost of maintaining property. Additional sales over a three year period would increase revenues by $231 million. The cash generated would reduce the Government's borrowing requirements with a resulting three-year interest savings of $49 million. In addition, the Government's cost of maintaining property would be reduced by $15 million over three years.

Q. Do any of the 744 million acres of Federally-owned land qualify as surplus? Wouldn't sale of some of this land represent a substantial source of income?

A. Yes, it does, but the sale of Federal land must be a carefully conducted process. PPSS concentrated on the Interior Department, which administers approximately 520 million acres, or about 70% of all Federal land. Based on evaluations of past Federal reviews of these land holdings, PPSS estimated that 11.5 million acres, or about 2.2% of all land under Interior Department control, could be classified as surplus. Of this amount, a rough estimate suggests one-third, or 3.8 million acres—0.5% of all Federal land—is likely to be marketable in the near term.

Q. Wouldn't such a massive land sale be costly to administer?

A. PPSS realized a land sale of this magnitude would impose significant administrative costs on the Department of Interior. Based on the experience of the General Services Administration and the U.S. Postal Service in selling surplus property, it is estimated Interior will incur an increase in administrative costs equal to 10% of the selling price of the land. Some marketing costs will also be necessary. PPSS estimated the net income resulting from the land sale at $900 million over three years ($1.028 billion gross receipts less $128 million in increased costs).

Q. What recommendations were made in the area of strategic stockpiles such as the Strategic Petroleum Reserve (SPR) and stockpiles of other raw materials such as silver?

A. After review of the SPR, PPSS determined that the Congressionally-mandated fill rate of 300,000 barrels per day exceeded current permanent storage capacity and would require costly temporary storage to be used. In addition, the relaxed state of the world oil market is expected to continue for some time, mitigating the need for an accelerated stockpiling program. Petroleum stored in the SPR as of September 30, 1983 totalled 360 million barrels, enough to replace average U.S. oil imports from Arab OPEC countries during the first eight months of 1983 for over two years. PPSS recommended a lower fill rate which would not exceed existing permanent storage capacity, as well as other management improvements, which could save $1.281 billion over three years.

PPSS also found the strategic silver stockpile to be in excess of requirements. Sale of surplus silver would generate $1.040 billion.

Other recommendations in this area include:

- Management improvements at Tennessee Valley Authority facilities.

- Better management of property acquired at foreclosure sales by the Department of Housing and Urban Development and the Veterans Administration.

Potential savings identified in these areas total $470 million over three years.

The three-year total of all the recommendations in this section, after elimination of duplication and overlap among issues, is $6.048 billion—equal to the three-year taxes of 908,927 median income families.

The Cost of Not Watching the Store

PPSS concluded that support operations in the Federal Government (housekeeping, travel, freight, mailing, printing, etc.) do not receive adequate attention, resulting in excessive costs and low productivity. These items, while relatively insignificant within the context of total Government spending, nevertheless amount to tens of billions of dollars annually and could be reduced significantly through implementing private sector procedures and controls to increase productivity, streamline operations, and develop the necessary information to determine how much is being spent, for what, and by whom.

In FY 1983, the Government spent $14.4 billion in specific areas covered by PPSS recommendations, with spending estimated to increase to $77.5 billion by the year 2000 if present policies are continued. Implementing PPSS recommendations would reduce spending to $56.4 billion in 2000, a saving of $21.1 billion or 27.2%.

Studies of the organization and management of the Federal Government focus mainly on such highly visible functions as defense, welfare programs, and agriculture subsidies, that account for the bulk of expenditures and have demonstrable impact on the lives of individuals, the economy, and the social structure. These, in turn, command the attention of the media, the Congress, the business community, and citizen groups.

Much less attention is given to the essential underlying infrastructure of Government which provides housekeeping and logistical support to facilitate the operations of Government. These include mailing and shipping, printing and publishing, travel arrangements, handling correspondence, collecting trash, and a thousand other strictly support activities which cannot otherwise be categorized.

As proprietors of small businesses know, these activities are a vital part of financial viability, requiring close management attention on a continuing basis. In very large, diversified organizations, however, there is a tendency to slight these matters, to delegate them to the lowest level of attention or, worse, to largely disregard them on the erroneous assumption that they do not have an attractive cost/benefit ratio. Whatever that ratio may be elsewhere, the sheer size of the Federal Government escalates the cost of inattentiveness in many of these areas to great financial significance.

A major reason for lack of attention to housekeeping in the Federal Government is the absence of incentive. The simple fact is that the Federal Government does not adequately reward those who are "minding the store." Honors, rewards, pay increases, and promotions are passed out to those involved with policy and mission-oriented functions. Not even the oversight agencies such as the Office of Management and Budget (OMB) and the General Accounting Office (GAO) find the time or resources to examine such routine housekeeping and logistical matters sufficiently.

Should anyone care if they are left unattended? How many shipping overcharges or underutilized printing plants does it take to add up to something significant in an organization which spends more than $850 billion annually?

Most of the activities of Government under discussion here are so far beneath the concerns of senior management that they do not know how much money is spent on them, where it is spent, or who to contact in the various agencies to find out. If one wanted to know how much the Federal Government spends annually on garbage collection or postage, there is no central source for that information, no central data-collection point, and no list of the agencies or officials to contact on the subject. In general, they are neither budgeted nor controlled by the Government's financial management and accounting systems.

There are, however, some functions in this general category about which enough is known to permit their use as illustrations of the results of this failure of management and what could be done to remedy some of the problems, such as:

• The Government spent $3.5 billion on housekeeping and general maintenance in FY 1983. PPSS concluded that attainable increased worker productivity and better supervision and scheduling could cut these costs by $1.125 billion over three years.

• Official travel, civilian and military, cost taxpayers $4.8 billion in FY 1982. PPSS concluded that reducing the number of "no shows" on prepaid flights, increasing the use of overseas contract rates by non-defense agencies, and centralizing the travel function to take advantage of bulk discounts could save $984 million over three years. Improved expense accounting and reimbursement procedures could save an additional $171 million over three years.

• Shipping and freight costs of the Federal Government were $4.6 billion in FY 1982. The PPSS conclusion: automating and consolidating the freight management system could save $530 million over three years. Additional savings of $165 million could result from adopting audit procedures more in line with private sector practices.

• The direct cost of Government mailings was $900 million in FY 1982, and indirect costs (envelopes, processing, etc.) amounted to another $900 million. PPSS concluded that consolidating mailing lists, better mail management, and accountability could reduce costs by $645 million over three years.

• Printing and publishing cost $760 million in FY 1982. Eliminating unnecessary and obsolete plants, consolidating facilities, and increasing contracting out could save $159 million over three years. Improved publications management could save an additional $331 million over three years.

• It costs nearly $50 million annually to print new and destroy old Food Stamp coupons. PPSS estimates savings of $30 million over three years from increasing denominations on individual coupons and increasing the value of coupon books.

In these six examples, PPSS estimates that there is potential to save $4.140 billion over three years.

HOUSEKEEPING

Housekeeping encompasses many small, relatively unglamorous activities such as cleaning and repair services, painting, emptying waste-baskets, dusting, vacuuming—things which are usually taken for granted. Most of the $3.5 billion in FY 1983 was spent by the Department of Defense and the General Services Administration, with about $1.4 billion (41%) contracted out to the private sector.

The General Services Administration (GSA) is charged with providing, among other things, most of the workspace for Federal departments and agencies. GSA controls nearly one-quarter of a billion square feet, or 5,739 acres, of building space, either through Government ownership or by lease. Its property portfolio is valued at approximately $8 billion. GSA's payments for utilities and fuel during FY 1983 were estimated at about $224 million, and its outlay for custodial services was expected to exceed $190 million. Its annual bill for property maintenance runs about $100 million.

Property related expenditures by the Department of Defense (DOD) make those of GSA appear modest. DOD spends $2.5 billion annually on utilities—nearly $5,000 a minute. Real property maintenance costs DOD nearly $3.2 billion a year, and yearly custodial costs are about $1.5 billion.

Q. PPSS has cited the lower productivity of Federal versus private sector maintenance workers as a prime factor contributing to the $1.7 billion annual custodial costs. How were productivity levels determined?

A. PPSS compared worker productivity in Government to that in the private sector. General maintenance services are primarily performed by the GSA in all civilian and some defense facilities, including the Pentagon. GSA cleans the buildings, pays the utility bills, and generally runs the "house."

Productivity percentages gauge the level of productive activity observed through statistical work-sampling. It is the ratio of people observed working to the total number under survey, with the sampling being done with sufficient frequency and over an adequate length of time to offer high confidence in its accuracy. No observations are recorded during periods contractually provided for rest breaks, clean-up time, etc. A 100% productivity rating should never be expected in maintenance activities because of unavoidable delays involved in waiting for materials, equipment, and job assignments, as well as other inherent problems. However, anything less than 50% falls in the "low" range by private sector standards.

Q. Are Government workers less productive than their private sector counterparts?

A. Outside consultants and internal observers generally agree that government-wide productivity in carrying out in-house maintenance averages between 40% and 45% of potential. The private sector industry average is about 62%, or about one-half again higher. This is for a variety of reasons. A worker might be ready and willing to get the job done, but because the supervisor didn't schedule effectively, that worker is standing around waiting for equipment—a vacuum cleaner, a paint brush—which has to come from a different department. This is not a question of capability or of diligence on the part of individual Government workers. PPSS believes that the main reasons for low productivity lie in such areas as planning, estimating and scheduling techniques, as well as in training Government maintenance managers to understand the principles of productivity and in providing incentives for better performance. The potential payoff from improved productivity is great.

Q. Does this mean that better supervisory personnel are the answer?

A. Only in part. What is really needed is a reorientation on the part of supervisors and managers toward administration. The key requirement across the Government is "incentive." There is very little incentive for supervisors to improve their scheduling/administrative abilities, because promotions customarily come from being good mechanics rather than good administrators—i.e., the managers are too busy doing the job to supervise it, and the result is that it doesn't get done in the most productive way.

Q. What does PPSS recommend to improve the productivity of maintenance personnel?

A. To begin with, a government-wide program should be instituted. Each agency should have a person or unit responsible for planning, monitoring, and evaluating maintenance operations. For too long, these functions have been removed from the individual agencies and handled at GSA. Performance goals should be established; planning and scheduling skills upgraded. The Government should also draw on expertise from the private sector. There is no good reason Government productivity in the maintenance area should lag behind the private sector by 20%, or that the private sector should be 46% more productive.

Q. Assuming Federal worker productivity increases to the private sector average of 62%, how much could be saved on annual custodial costs?

A. Maintenance costs for real property in the Federal Government were about $3.5 billion in FY 1983. Of this total, 41% ($1.4 billion) was contracted out. About 50% of the remainder ($1.05 billion) represents in-house labor, whose productivity could be improved. PPSS made a basic assumption that productivity could increase from the present Federal Government average of about 42% to the private sector average of about 62%. This would reduce in-house labor costs to $711 million, for a saving of approximately $340 million annually, and $1.125 billion over three years.

TRAVEL

In FY 1982, the Federal Government spent $4.8 billion on employee travel, including $1.3 billion for air travel. About 45% of the Federal travel dollar is spent on transportation, about 39% on subsistence, and the remainder on taxis, limos, phone calls, tolls, and miscellaneous. Government travelers take more than 15 million trips each year and utilize trip cash advances of more than $288 million, about half of which are outstanding over 90 days.

About three-quarters of Federal travel expenditures—$3.4 billion in 1982—are incurred by the defense agencies, but all agencies incur some travel expense. The table on the next page shows the breakdown.

Defense travel includes troop movements and relocations, which occur on a regular basis. Relocations, R&R, and emergency leaves can sometimes involve moving families around the world. On international flights, the Department of Defense uses commercial carriers when pos-

**Travel and Transportation
of Persons**
($ Millions)

	Agency/Department	(1) 1982E	(2) % of Total
(1)	Defense—Military & Civilian	$3,449	71.5%
(2)	Transportation	171	3.5
(3)	Agriculture	154	3.2
(4)	Treasury	136	2.8
(5)	Veterans Administration	117	2.4
(6)	Justice	106	2.2
(7)	Health & Human Services	104	2.2
(8)	Interior	103	2.1
(9)	Other Independent Agencies	97	2.0
(10)	State	73	1.5
(11)	Subtotal	$4,510	93.5%
(12)	All Other	316	6.5
(13)	Total	$4,826	100.0%

sible, and to save money, the Military Airlift Command (MAC) will buy a block of seats as much as a year in advance to obtain the best rate. Problems arise when all of the seats purchased are not used.

Most unused seats result because of "no shows"—the seats are booked, but then the traveler doesn't show up and doesn't cancel. The seat has already been paid for, so Defense absorbs the cost of an empty seat. In the private sector, the "no show" rate on commercial airlines runs about 2% to 6%, which means that 94% to 98% of all reservations made are used. "No shows" are a fairly insignificant number. Seat utilization on MAC flights averages about 88%—12% of seats go empty because of "no shows." This is 3 times the private sector "no show" rate.

Q. What did PPSS recommend to reduce the "no show" rate?

A. Reservations for MAC flights are made through transport officers at various defense installations. Because these installations do not have to pay for "no show" flights, the practices of double booking and not cancelling flights continue. PPSS recommended that, when a booked seat goes empty because of a "no show," the installation originating the reservation be charged a penalty for the seat. The charge should be sufficient to provide incentive for travel officers to reduce booking errors and for agencies to encourage passengers to meet travel commitments. The flights are paid for whether used or not. PPSS estimates that the utilization rate could increase to 94% if more care were exercised by travel officers at installations. That 6% increase in utilization translates into a $50 million cost reduction over three years.

Q. If the flights are paid for anyway, how are there any savings?

A. "No shows" are often double-booked reservations or simply missed flights. The traveler is still traveling. Because there are limited seats available, those unable to travel on the MAC bookings have to resort to regular commercial flights—which can cost more. The savings result because additional commercial flight seats would not be necessary.

Additional three-year savings of $20 million could be achieved if low-cost overseas rates provided through the Military Airlift Command (MAC) operation were made available to personnel of other Federal agencies. MAC round-trip costs are about one-third the unrestricted coach fare on international flights.

Travel procurement in the Federal Government is very decentralized, and not all travel divisions are aware of the most recent rates or special fares. While certain general guidelines have been established pertaining to Government travel, they often deal with limitations and restrictions and have little bearing upon the efficient and economical procurement of travel services. Each agency administers its own travel budget and procures its own travel and related services. Since 1955, as a result of a ruling by the Comptroller General, Government agencies have been prohibited from using private sector travel agent services and have thus been deprived of this source of professional assistance.

Even if special fares were always used, which would certainly be a step in the right direction, a customer as large as the Federal Government should be able to negotiate additional discounts. Travel procurement, especially after airline deregulation, is highly complex and constantly changing; it demands full-time professional attention in order to ensure the purchase of the most efficient travel services at the lowest cost. In recent years, the Federal Government has instituted certain studies and pilot programs, but thus far they fall short of achieving comprehensive managerial control over the Federal travel function. As deregulation proceeds, the opportunities for significant cost savings and management improvements in the procurement of Federal travel services continue to increase. The Government should be provided with the structure and tools to take maximum advantage of these opportunities.

Q. What did PPSS recommend be done to reduce Government travel costs?

A. PPSS recommended that the travel functions for all agencies be centralized—creating a central travel bureau that can negotiate for volume discounts in hotel/motel chains, car rental companies, and transport lines.

The Federal Government requires professional, centralized in-house travel service capability. Since the Federal Government's annual expenditure for travel ($4.8 billion, $1.3 billion for air travel alone) is far larger than that of the largest private sector organizations, it is in a better position to profit from maintaining a professional, in-house travel procurement capability equipped with automated data processing necessary for current information retrieval and transfer. With limited exceptions, the Government generally pays for travel on the basis of publicly available rates, and not necessarily the lowest of those. This professional capability will permit the Government to search out the best current travel value. In addition, the Government's travel volume gives it the leverage to negotiate the lowest available prices if such information is centrally gathered, organized, and applied in global contract negotiations.

The Government should prepare to take advantage of the removal of regulatory restrictions which have in the past hampered its freedom to structure an efficient travel procurement program. Deregulation should benefit the Government as well as the private sector. The 1955 Comptroller General's ruling against use of commercial travel agents has been waived for test purposes, and such waiver should be expanded and extended. The CAB prohibition against negotiation of discounts in lieu of agent commissions on air fares will become history on December 31, 1984.

It is estimated that the establishment of central travel centers and centralized negotiation of rates could achieve three-year savings of $984 million.

Virtually every Federal agency engages in significant travel, and each handles its travel administration, cash advances, expense accounting, and reimbursement in its own way. While certain Federal travel rules have general application (mostly of a limiting nature, e.g., classes of travel, per diem allowances, etc.) and while some oversight responsibility rests with the Office of Management and Budget (OMB), the General Services Administration (GSA), and the General Accounting Office (GAO), travel administration resides at the agency level and usually receives too little management attention.

The Federal Government's travel expense accounting and reimbursement process is inefficient and wasteful for several reasons:

- Decentralized, non-integrated expense accounting systems do not hold individuals or agencies sufficiently accountable for Government advances and expenditures, and do not offer sufficient incentives for timely clearance of expense accounts.

- Excessive administrative effort is expended on reconciling expense reports, partly because of inadequate reporting and accounting systems.

- Excessive time elapses in clearing travel accounts.

- Government lacks centralized control and an audit of agency travel practices.

Although there are several efforts underway to improve travel procurement, accounting, and reimbursement systems, these efforts do not adequately address the problem of a lack of timely accountability by employees and agencies for monies advanced and travel tickets purchased, nor the lack of incentives for timely reporting and clearing of travel expenditures. There is excessive use of cash advances which remain outstanding too long—in FY 1982, the Government issued $288 million in cash advances, about half of which remained outstanding over 90 days—and substantial advances in the form of airline and rail tickets which are exchanged or unused without timely application for refund.

Q. What did PPSS recommend to improve government-wide travel accounting and reimbursement procedures?

A. PPSS recommended that the Government establish an integrated expense reporting system which will ensure prompt and inclusive accounting for all expenses properly attributable to Government travelers, including clearance of cash advances and accounting for unused or exchanged tickets.

Efforts currently underway to streamline the expense reimbursement process through consolidation of forms and simplification of procedures must also address the fundamental problem of insufficient accountability of the individual traveler.

Unnecessarily large and longstanding cash travel advances are partially caused by excessive delays in processing travel accounts and partially by lack of a system requiring prompt, complete, and frequent accounting by the traveler.

The Federal Government should emulate the private sector in establishing more efficient expense accounting and reimbursement policies. One private sector device that could improve public sector efficiency is greater use of Government-sponsored charge cards with direct employee billing for use by frequent travelers.

Travel reimbursement policies such as the use of flat rate, locality-based per diem subsistence allowances in lieu of accounting for actual expenses would speed up the accounting and reimbursement process. The introduction of agency-sponsored personal charge cards issued to qualified Government travelers would reduce the need for cash advances and provide an additional incentive to the traveler to process ticket refunds and clear expense accounts expeditiously.

Simplified voucher and reimbursement systems, improved accounting procedures, and reduced turnaround time for travel expense accounts could save $171 million over three years.

Shipping is a big expense in Government—$4.6 billion in 1982. The Federal Government is one of the largest movers of freight in the world. The Defense Department accounts for about 78%, or $3.6 billion, of all freight costs. GSA is responsible for the remaining 22% ($1 billion).

Traffic management in the Federal Government includes the rating and routing of more than six million shipments annually, and current procedures are neither uniform government-wide nor sufficiently automated to take advantage of volume discounts or lower rates. Furthermore, there is inadequate data gathering, lack of cooperation between DOD and GSA, and insufficient coordination to negotiate special rates based on overall volume.

The Federal Government has not taken sufficient advantage of the tremendous leverage which the huge size of its freight volumes ($4.6 billion) give it in order to achieve economies in the movement of cargo and the negotiation of favorable freight transportation rates. The deregulated rail and motor carrier environment, for example, now offers wider competitive choices and greater cost saving opportunities than ever before. However, deregulation is accompanied by increasing complexity in the proliferation of carriers, transportation rates, tenders and routes, and greater differences in the quality of service. Until recently, most of the Government's traffic management has been handled manually. However, the proliferation of rates and services has made automation a virtual necessity for cost-effective operation. Automation is now widely utilized in the private sector and is under development at the Department of Defense (DOD), which accounts for 80% of Government cargo.

Q. How would automating information of Federal freight shipments reduce costs?

A. Centralized automated information capability would not only enable the selection of optimum routing from the millions of routes and rates and the thousands of tenders, but would also permit consolidation of simultaneous shipments from various agencies and the negotiation of rates based on government-wide volume, and provide the data necessary for efficient audits of freight bills. An automated system will also enable all Government shippers to know the newest, most competitive rates offered by various carriers.

Q. Will automating the shipping function put Federal practices on a basis similar to those in the private sector?

A. Partly, but more is needed. Private sector firms utilize combined automated tariff libraries and rating and routing systems for selecting the most appropriate carriers, minimizing charges, and maximizing service. In addition, a private sector firm will audit carrier charges before paying for services. That is a sound business practice, but the Government is legislatively mandated not to perform audits before paying its bills. PPSS recommendations urging a reversal of this practice are set forth in the section on "Managing Its Systems—Federal Financial Management."

On the basis of results achieved in the private sector, estimated three year net savings of $530 million can be achieved through implementation of an automated, centralized freight management system. Industry experts generally agree that net savings in excess of 3% of total payments for all Government transportation could be achieved through automation of the monitoring and control of traffic practices government-wide. In addition, identifying the lowest tendered or negotiated rates and the best routes could achieve 2% to 5% savings on large volume, large dollar shipments.

MAILINGS

Federal Government direct postal charges were estimated at $900 million in 1982 and are expected to top $1 billion in 1983, although the extent of actual postage and mail-related expenditures is not known. That is the cost of actual mailing—equivalent to stamps or messenger services. The indirect costs—envelopes, processing, etc.—ran another $900 million in 1982. In an election year, they are even higher.

Most Federal agencies do not buy stamps or use postage meters. Their postage costs are determined by a periodic survey of mail volume. Each agency is charged an annual fee for its mailings. Strict systems for maintaining Federal postal accountability do not exist, and there is no concentrated effort to improve postal management. The U.S. Postal Service has been experimenting with postage meters and stamps at some Government locations, and some Federal agencies have instituted their own postal management programs, but much more can be done to reduce unnecessary costs in this area.

Q. What are the problems with controlling mailing costs? Why doesn't the Government know how much this function costs?

A. There are several reasons. Poor mail management starts at the lowest levels and spreads upward. Many agencies follow uneconomical mail practices—they use first class or priority mail services when second or third class would suffice. For example, GSA found that the Census Bureau was sending copies of surveys and publications by first-class mail, when third class was sufficient, resulting in extra costs of $400,000 per year.

In addition, the responsibility for mail management is not clearly defined in many agencies, procedures are not widely disseminated, and personnel are often unaware of procedures for economical mailings.

— 131 —

The best way to reduce the costs of Government mailings is to make divisions accountable for their postage costs, which are not currently included in program budgets. Government managers do not have the accounting records necessary to control and reduce postal costs. Making personnel more aware of postage costs can be accomplished in several ways:

- The Office of Management and Budget (OMB) should direct all agencies to evaluate mail practices and eliminate those that result in excessive costs.

- An official should be designated in each agency with primary responsibility for postage/mail management.

- GSA should work with the Postal Service to improve measurement of agency postal costs and provide technical assistance for improving mail management.

Better management and awareness of the cost of mail services could result in substantial savings.

A GSA study identified possible savings of 10% annually. PPSS reduced that estimate to exclude Congressional mailings—only the Executive Branch was reviewed—and came up with three year savings of $550 million. Consolidating and updating mailing lists could result in additional savings.

The Government distributes hundreds of millions of free publications annually to recipients on thousands of mailing lists. The free mailing program wastes millions of dollars every year because erroneous or outdated mailing lists cause costly production, mailing, handling, and distribution of unwanted or unnecessary copies.

A successful program to correct the mailing lists of the Human Development Services (HDS) Division of the Department of Health and Human Services (HHS) saved a projected $1.2 million per year in printing and mailing costs. In spite of the potential savings, other HHS divisions (with free mailing programs 16 times the size of HDS) have not followed the HDS example to bring their own mailing lists up to date. As a result, HHS alone may be wasting over $19 million per year on unnecessary mailings. Consolidating and updating the Government's mailing lists could save $96 million over three years.

Q. Everyone at some point ends up getting two copies of a mail order catalog or some kind of junk mail. How can reducing duplicate mailings save so much money?

A. Savings are large in an absolute sense because the Government is large. For example, in HDS 128 separate mailing lists with over 90,000 names were reduced to a single list of 29,000 names—one third the size. In another instance, PPSS found that 29 copies of the same publication were regularly mailed to a single addressee.

Q. What did PPSS recommend to improve mailing list management throughout Government?

A. First, OMB should issue a directive requiring mailing list consolidation. In addition, the HDS software package should be publicized and personnel trained in its use. A special job classification for publications distribution management should be set up so that all lists are compatible and can be consolidated and checked without major production. Remember, one division of one agency had 128 separate lists; multiplied across all divisions and all agencies the problem reaches immense proportions.

PRINTING/PUBLISHING

The Government publishes and prints books, pamphlets, and other reports on a myriad of topics ranging from housing and health to finance and education. In FY 1982, the Documents Sales Service of the Government Printing Office (GPO) distributed 17 million copies of free Government publications. It also mailed over 25 million publications for Executive Branch agencies. Through GSA's Consumer Information Center in Pueblo, Colorado, just under 14 million copies of free and paid consumer publications were distributed. Executive Branch agencies distribute unknown millions of copies of their own publications. There are also various forms with large distributions, such as the annual Income Tax forms. As another example, the Government spends $50 million annually to print food stamp coupons. The Government can save money on all these publications, printed forms, and coupons.

Q. Wouldn't savings on food stamps more likely come from better program management and stricter eligibility rules? How much can you save on the printing of the coupons?

A. Because of changes in food stamp issuance patterns since 1975, changes in the stamp denominations should be made. The highest denomination now is $10, and books total $65. However, the average recipient now receives $102 in monthly food stamps. Changing denominations to, say, $20 and issuing books of $100, reduces printing costs. PPSS estimates savings of $30 million over three years— enough to feed 7,463 families of four for a year. Food stamps are just one area of Government printing; there is much more to be saved in the printing of Government reports at the GPO and at Executive Branch print shops.

Q. Does the Government publish its own reports?

A. A large number of Government reports are published and printed through the GPO. Actually, GPO does not have figures on the number of reports, only the number of titles produced. GPO's sales inventory contains some 16,000 titles of Government publications. Not all of these are published on site at the GPO. GPO contracts out to the private sector about 71% of its total printing and binding work. The remaining work is done at the GPO and Executive Branch printing plants.

Q. How many printing plants does the Government operate?

A. In addition to the main GPO plant located in Washington, D.C., and six regional GPO printing plants located across the country, the Government operates 235 Executive Branch agency in-house printing plants. There are 37 in Washington, D.C. and 20 in suburban Maryland and Virginia, giving the Washington, D.C. metropolitan area the largest concentration of printing plants in the U.S.

Q. How much does Executive Branch printing cost?

A. Total Executive Branch printing costs were $760.4 million in FY 1981, divided among agency printing plants, the GPO, and contracting out to the private sector. Agency printing plants produced 11.5 billion production units (one sided, 8 1/2" x 11" sheets of paper) at a total cost of $191 million. 80% of GPO's work in 1981 was performed for Executive agencies, valued at $554 million. GPO contracted out the bulk of its Executive agency work to the private sector. The agency print shops contracted out an additional $15.4 million.

Q. Could this printing be done more efficiently and at less expense?

A. Yes. Plant eliminations and consolidations, increased contracting out to the private sector, and operation of a central printing plant could save $159 million over three years. Most of PPSS's recommendations reiterate earlier suggestions by GAO and other agencies— these potential solutions to the problems and the cost saving measures have been recognized by Government for the last ten years, without any action being taken.

Q. What is the bottleneck?

A. The GPO and Executive Branch printing plants fall under the administration and regulation of Congress—the Joint Committee on Printing (JCP). Agencies have no control over the cost of printing at the GPO, and they are mandated by law to send their work to the GPO, unless it can be printed in-house (with size and volume restrictions) or they can contract it out themselves (if the job is less than $500 in value). Agencies further have minimal control over the operations of their own in-house plants because so many decisions, concerning such matters as machinery, etc., require JCP approval.

Q. Why does Congress have jurisdiction over GPO?

A. Legislative Branch policy and regulatory control over all Government printing has a long and unique history. Prior to the administration of Abraham Lincoln, printing was virtually the only way to preserve and disseminate information. The Government's printing needs then originated almost wholly in the Legislative Branch.

Q. Who did the printing before GPO?

A. Printing was contracted out to private printers, but it became costly and rampant with graft and corruption. GPO was a good idea when it was established in 1860, and it was appropriate for Congress to oversee its operation—more than 90% of GPO's work that year was for Congress, and in its first full year of operation, the Government's printing bill was cut in half.

Q. What has changed?

A. The Federal Government, 123 years later, is still attempting to function under an industrial manufacturing system designed to meet the printing needs of Congress, and driven by a labor-intensive, in-house production capacity. Today, the Executive Branch, not Congress, has the greatest printing need—more than 90% of Federal printing originates in the Executive Branch. In addition, printing today is an increasingly high technology industry, but GPO remains a ponderous, labor-intensive organization that has not adapted to the demands of changing technology.

Q. How has technology changed?

A. "Printing" is no longer the only way of producing and preserving information. Where words and symbols on paper are required, computerized electronic and photographic production has now replaced the old methods. Advances such as laser printing, satellite transmission, and others still in the laboratory stage will further drastically revolutionize information technology.

Q. What did PPSS suggest to keep Government from falling farther behind the new technology?

A. Several things. First, obsolete and underutilized plants should be closed or consolidated. OMB should seek to work with the JCP to identify such plants and request that JCP collect information on each plant so as to effectively monitor resource utilization and plan accordingly. New audit procedures are necessary to make oversight functions more systematic. Equipment should be upgraded, since most GPO printing machinery is outdated. Nearly 40% of the equipment is rated "fair," "poor," or "unserviceable" by the agencies. This inefficient equipment also contributes to high costs for in-house printing because of downtimes to repair slower, less efficient machinery. In addition, the Government should contract out to the private sector all unrestricted printing needs.

Q. Does contracting out to private companies save money?

A. Yes. GPO sends out 71% of its work to private contractors. According to GPO records, commercial bid prices have been consistently lower than GPO in-house costs of production: GPO prices have been, on average, 31% higher than the highest bid price, and 70% higher than the lowest bid price. GAO determined that 23% of the work that remained in-house at the *agency* print shops could have been contracted out—and at 32% less cost. Said differently, it cost 47% more to retain these jobs in-house.

Q. You stated earlier that PPSS recommendations restate earlier GAO recommendations. Why is PPSS duplicating GAO's work?

A. GAO has made valid, cost-effective suggestions, some as far back as 1974, but the agencies and the JCP have not acted on these suggestions. PPSS is supporting GAO's findings and has estimated the savings which would result from implementation—$159 million over three years.

Another area of the publishing/printing function reviewed by PPSS is publications management. This activity includes the decision to publish, planning, design, audience targeting, writing, editing, procurement of printing and binding, promotion, and marketing. Executive Branch publishing costs have declined by $30 million between 1979 and 1982, from $1.372 billion to $1.342 billion, primarily as a result of pressure from OMB to reduce costs. However, OMB's cost reduction directives have not been fully implemented and did not cover all types of publications. Publications management remains decentralized within the agencies. This decentralization results in a lack of information regarding the inventory of Government publications and the lack of a standardized accounting system for total publishing costs.

Q. What did PPSS recommend to make publications management more effective?

A. Government agencies should adopt an organizational structure which includes unified responsibilities for publishing functions, and coordination between publication and administrative managers. OMB should strengthen agencies' guidelines regarding types of publications appropriate for agency publication programs. These standards should help to prevent agencies from unnecessary, inappropriate, or wasteful publishing. OMB, in collaboration with GAO, should develop model accounting procedures to track and report now-hidden publishing costs, such as personnel, postage, and overhead.

Savings from instituting more effective publications management are estimated to be $331 million over three years.

In addition to issues already discussed in this section, PPSS has reviewed numerous other support operations of the Federal Government. Recommendations include:

- Improve management and accounting procedures for purchase and use of audiovisual, telecommunications, and copying and duplicating equipment.

- Standardize Federal operations relating to security and vehicle fleet operation.

- Reduce warehousing and storage costs for commodities, records and files, and idled DOD industrial plant equipment.

- Reduce ocean freight differential payments on commodity shipments; expedite Federal Maritime Commission review of ocean carrier rates; facilitate procurement of inland container transport and reduce container detention charges; expand contracted-out transport of military personnel household goods to include shipments to Alaska and Hawaii.

- Consolidate DOD freight traffic management and base support operations such as fire protection, housing management, accounting, and security across service lines.

- Improve management and accountability for DOD aviation maintenance/readiness; and institute standardized, periodic reports on aviation and combat vehicle maintenance costs, personnel, and scheduling.

- Reduce costs of printing and engraving currency by adopting a common Federal Reserve seal on all bills, and using offset rather than intaglio printing on backs of $1 bills. Contract-out coinage strip manufacturing and eliminate the uneconomical strip production unit at the Philadelphia Mint.

- Improvements in planning; centralized organizational structures for marketing, procurement, and transportation; and accelerated automation of mail processing and delivery systems could produce savings and increased revenues for the U.S. Postal Service of $2.401 billion over three years. While not directly affecting Federal expenditures, implementation of PPSS recommendations could improve Postal Service efficiency and keep the costs of mailing from increasing.

The three-year total of all the recommendations in this section, after elimination of duplication and overlap among issues, is $10.105 billion—equal to the three-year taxes of 1.5 million median income families.

Opportunities for Increasing Revenues

User charges are the fees collected from recipients of Government goods and services which are not shared by the general public. A high level of uncertainty exists in the Executive Branch about what charges can be collected for Government products and services because of court decisions and unclear administrative policy. Practices in the Federal Government do not provide sufficient information and accountability for efficient and effective management of user charges and, as a result, the Federal Government frequently fails to recover full costs. PPSS believes user charge programs are similar to commercial businesses and should be conducted in a business-like manner. To accomplish this, PPSS recommended that a centralized service and product planning function be established to continually bring to management's attention opportunities for initiating or revising charges.

In FY 1983, the Government spent $9.8 billion in the specific areas covered by PPSS recommendations, with spending estimated to increase to $43.5 billion by the year 2000 if present policies are continued. Implementing PPSS recommendations would reduce spending to $24.6 billion in 2000, a saving of $18.9 billion or 43.4%.

The Federal Government provides a variety of services and products to the public which are of a commercial nature. PPSS identified more than 1,500 commercial activities performed by the Government, including the printing and sale of publications, maintenance of camping and recreational facilities, and the provision of survey, inspection and appraisal services.

The sale of these products and services generated approximately $40 billion for the Government in 1981. The pricing, i.e., "user charge," of these products and services, however, frequently does not recover the Government's costs.

Because of court decisions and unclear administrative policy, there is great uncertainty and confusion in the Executive Branch about what amounts can and should be collected for Government products and services. This is despite authorizing statutes, an implementing OMB circular, and more than $40 billion collected annually.

Section 483a of Title 31 of the U.S. Code (Independent Offices Appropriation Act of 1952) provides the statutory authorization for user charges. Agency heads can establish, by regulation, fees for services or products provided to the public, "taking into consideration" direct and indirect costs to the Government, value to the recipient, public policy or interest served, and other factors. However, since 1974, the Supreme Court and several lower courts have heard cases and rendered decisions which, in the process of defining the scope of "fees," have provided differing methodologies for determining the amounts and the beneficiaries.

The responsibility for user charge policy and implementation at the central Government level rests with OMB. There is one OMB official whose duties include monitoring user charge activities in the Federal Government. Merely compiling the collected statistics on user charges takes all of the time available. Implementing and monitoring policy directives is left to budget examiners and otherwise fragmented within OMB.

In attempting to recover the cost of providing services, PPSS found that agencies inconsistently apply general pricing principles established by OMB. For example, both the National Aeronautics and Space Administration (NASA) and the Department of Defense (DOD) maintain wind tunnels for research and development by the Government and the private sector. NASA charges $2,000 per hour for the use of its wind tunnels, whereas DOD charges $6,000 per hour. NASA has taken the position that certain indirect costs should not be included in their charges, whereas DOD includes them. The obvious result of this inconsistency is that private sector industries, as well as Government agencies, including DOD, overuse the NASA facilities. The NASA interpretation of Government policy results in loss of revenue to the Federal Government. The DOD interpretation is in line with the pricing principles used by the private sector to the extent that full cost recovery is sought. As another example, the Interstate and Defense Highway System recovers, through a schedule of excise taxes, the full cost of the Interstate Highway System. By comparison, the excise tax scheduled for the inland waterways and the airport and airways systems recovers only about 5% and 85% of the cost of those systems, respectively.

The user charge system is complicated and leads to misunderstandings. More than half of the program managers interviewed by PPSS were critical of the existing system. The primary objection is the perception that the accounting systems are unable to meet the day-to-day needs of program management. These shortcomings include the inability to give credit or recognition for the collection of the receipts, lack of clarity as to appropriate accounting methods, difficulty in determining the amount of funds available for program operation, difficulty in determining accountability for program performance, and inability to allocate between user charge, business-type activities and general public purpose programs.

PPSS's analyses confirmed the findings of a number of previous studies conducted by the General Accounting Office (GAO) and the Congressional Budget Office (CBO) that user charge policies and procedures are inconsistently applied in Executive Branch programs. As discussed earlier, Supreme Court decisions, which provide differing methodologies and factors for determining amounts of fees and beneficiaries, have created confusion and misunderstanding about user charge authority. But even in those situations where there should be no question as to the application of guidelines and principles, systems employed do not provide adequate program guidance. PPSS found that management information systems, accounting systems, program evaluation, and accountability are generally ineffective and, in some cases, confusing.

It should be remembered that user charges, whether sufficient or insufficient, are paid by a discrete section of the population. For a broad range of Government-provided commercial services, there is no justification for the population as a whole—and for taxpayers as a group—to subsidize a small section of clearly identifiable beneficiaries.

User charge programs are similar to commercial businesses and should be conducted in a "business-like" manner. To meet this objective, PPSS recommended that:

- A centralized service and product planning function similar to that found in the business community be established in the departments and agencies and in the Office of Management and Budget. This function would:

  —continually bring to management's attention opportunities for establishing or revising charges for services and products;
  —maintain sufficient information and accountability for the production of those products and services to recommend regular price adjustments as needed;
  —monitor comparable business activities, making recommendations for program incentives and improvements; and
  —provide incentives to those with decision-making power to conduct the Government's commercial activities in a business-like manner.

- The pricing of Government products and services incorporates the standard economic principles used to develop market clearing prices for goods whenever possible. Market prices should generally be set for the sale or rental of Government products and property, *with a goal of full cost recovery.*

- Deposit of receipts into revolving fund accounts to:

  —provide more visibility to the transaction by relating expenses to revenues;
  —provide incentives to program managers by recognizing accomplishments and/or evaluating management results; and
  —assure users that funds will be available to maintain or enhance the product or level of service.

- Employment in user charge programs should not be subject to the general personnel freezes and ceilings used as budget controls provided these positions are, at a minimum, self-sustaining.

- The statute authorizing the collection of user charges should be amended to overcome the difficulties in determining amounts of user charges and identifying beneficiaries. The amendments should clarify the scope of the issue of user charges and minimize the inconsistencies in application.

The opportunities identified by PPSS for increased user charge revenue generation can be accomplished through clarification and restatement of user charge policies and procedures, improved management and accountability, and Congressional action to remove existing prohibitions or to grant expanded authority to implement fees.

PPSS identified potential user charge increases which would generate revenues of $20.721 billion over three years before consolidation of overlapping and duplicate recommendations. These revenue increases come primarily from increases in existing fees, as well as the identification of existing programs for which new fees should be charged. Major categories for revenue increases include sales of products and services, transportation, special services, recreation, regulation and licensing, and inspection and grading.

The *sales* activities of the Federal Government provide the potential for additional revenues of more than $5 billion over three years through more appropriate pricing of products. In one area alone, electricity sales, revenues could increase by $4.543 billion over three years if Power Marketing Administration prices were brought more in line with private sector utility rates.

Q. What are Power Marketing Administrations?

A. Power Marketing Administrations (PMAs) are five divisions in the Department of Energy (DOE) that administer Federal power generating facilities and sell "surplus" power. The PMAs sell between 6% and 8% of all the electricity generated in the United States, making DOE the largest single seller of electricity in the Nation. Most of the power sold is hydroelectric. Rates are supposed to cover operation and maintenance costs, interest, and capital expenses (construction). Those served by PMAs are receiving a Government benefit because the ratemaking process includes an improper allocation of capital costs.

Q. How much are PMA customers paying for their power?

A. User rates charged by PMAs are about one-third the national wholesale rate charged by non-Federal utilities (1¢/kwh vs. 3.3¢/kwh national average).

Q. Didn't PPSS recommend elsewhere that the Power Marketing Administrations be sold, i.e., privatized?

A. Yes. But that is likely to involve a long process. In the interim, rates should be brought more in line with those charged by the private sector.

Q. Why has the improper allocation of capital costs at PMAs continued? Is there resistance in Government to fairly allocating capital costs?

A. Congress has effectively blocked any action on, or even discussion of, rate changes. A bill was passed in 1982 prohibiting the use of any funds for the purpose of conducting "any studies relating to or leading to the possibility of changing from the currently required 'at cost' to a 'market rate' method for the pricing of hydroelectric power" by the PMAs.

The possibility of even broaching the subject had been choked off, as PPSS discovered during the summer of 1983. OMB officials stated that they could not discuss PMA rate-setting since to do so would constitute a specifically prohibited expenditure of Federal funds in the form of the salaries earned during the discussion.

Q. Has PPSS recommended higher prices for all Government products?

A. The greatest problem with Government sales of products and natural resources has been the difficulty of establishing prices. From appraisal of timber to selling maps, from firewood to soil survey reports, existing prices are too low or fees are non-existent. Activities are also inconsistent in the application of established policies and principles.

Q. What are the problems in pricing Government products and services?

A. Two major problems were identified, one of which centers on insufficient management accountability and control. Most agencies which provide products and services do not have the systems which are needed to account for and allocate true costs. Without this basic information, it is impossible to establish proper prices.

A second reason is that Congressional controls often prohibit fees or, in the case of grazing fees and power, establish formulas for setting prices that don't include all of the cost components.

Q. What examples of inconsistent pricing policy did PPSS note?

A. Prices for grazing on Federal lands are established under the same system for the Departments of Agriculture and Interior, but for military and Indian controlled lands the prices are set independently.

As another example, publications are distributed free by one agency while a fee is collected by another, and in some instances this occurs for the same publication.

Q. What other sales programs have potential for higher revenue?

A. There are 82 separate budget accounts containing receipts from the sale of Government products. PPSS has reviewed several of these in depth and has also identified two additional candidates for new fees. In four specific areas—grazing fees, firewood, soil surveys, and foreign military sales—there is potential to increase Federal revenues by $547 million over three years.

Grazing fees for the Agriculture and Interior Departments are currently tied to a formula set by Congress. Revising current policies to increase grazing fees would raise revenues by $125 million over three years.

Initiating fees for firewood collected on Government lands and charging a nominal fee for soil surveys could increase revenues an additional $91 million over three years.

Charging foreign customers additional amounts to cover administrative costs of the services provided by the Defense agencies would save $331 million over three years.

In dollar terms, the *transportation user charge* programs of the Federal Government are some of the largest. The Highway Trust Fund amounted to $8 billion in FY 1983 and is expected to grow to $12 billion in FY 1984. It accounts for more than 40% of the total budget of the Department of Transportation. The potential user charges for inland waterways and ports and channels exceed $1 billion annually.

The Army Corps of Engineers (COE) and the Tennessee Valley Authority construct and maintain locks, dams, and channels that facilitate commercial traffic on U.S. inland waterway systems. The COE is responsible for most of the Government activity in this program. The FY 1981 budget obligations for construction, operation, and maintenance were approximately $850 million. User charges recovered only about $24 million, or less than 3% of the total 1981 obligations.

By comparison, the Federal Highway Program has been funded over the past 24 years through a system of user fees based primarily on a fuel tax. Until recently, the collected user fees provided for 100% of the program costs. In 1981, however, this dropped to 82%. Legislation approving an increase in the tax was passed at the end of 1982, bringing the user fee back to the 100% level.

As demonstrated by these two examples, inconsistent application of user charge policy by the Federal Government results in user fees funding 100% of the Highway Land Transportation System, for example, but only

3% of the Waterway Transportation System, requiring the U.S. taxpayer to pay 97% of the costs.

PPSS recommended that user charges on inland waterways be increased over a five-year period to obtain 100% cost recovery of operations, maintenance, and construction. Revenue increases are estimated to be $601 million over three years after full implementation.

In addition, PPSS recommended that user fees be collected for maintenance, operation, and construction of deep draft harbors and channels (deep draft harbors and channels are defined by the COE as those having a depth in excess of 14 feet).

Deep draft harbors and channels of the United States serve a major role in domestic and foreign commerce. As calculated in 1981 and reported by the Senate Environment and Public Works Committee, over 1.8 billion tons of merchandise moved through these harbors and channels.

No user fees are currently levied for the operation and maintenance work on deep draft harbors and channels performed by the Corps of Engineers. In addition, construction of deep draft harbors is usually financed by the Federal Government for local port authorities over 50 years at 3% annual interest.

PPSS recommended that user fees be initiated on deep draft harbors and channels to recover 100% of the cost of operations and maintenance. In addition, the Federal Government should end its role in financing harbor construction, especially large projects such as giant coal harbors. If the Government does continue financing construction projects, the interest on the loans should be at the market rate. Implementing PPSS recommendations could increase Federal revenues by $747 million over three years.

Q. PPSS stated that the Army Corps of Engineers (COE) is responsible for the operation and maintenance of the U.S. waterways. How did this become their responsibility?

A. For over 150 years, COE has been responsible for many of our Nation's water projects, including navigation, harbor erosion, and Federal flood control. These tasks fell upon COE because at the time it was the only group of organized engineers in the country.

The responsibilities of COE are usually divided between construction and operations and maintenance of inland waterways and deep harbors and channels.

Q. How much is spent annually on the operation, maintenance, and construction of the U.S. waterways?

A. A total of almost $1.2 billion is spent annually on the inland waterways and deep draft harbors and channels. Based on historical data from the COE, about $500 million a year will be spent on construction ($120 million) and operation and maintenance ($380 million) of deep draft harbors and channels. An additional $670 million is spent on construction ($400 million) and operation and maintenance ($270 million) of the inland waterway system.

Implementing PPSS recommendations would enable the Federal Government to recover 100% of these costs.

PPSS has also identified 108 Special Services provided by the Government to specific beneficiaries. Time and manpower constraints limited the PPSS review to three such services. Increasing user charges for these services could raise an additional $1.0 billion over three years. The three areas identified are:

User fees for Coast Guard services;
Charges for Freedom of Information requests; and
Fees for customs inspections of international aircraft entering the U.S.

Q. What services does the Coast Guard perform that are user-specific? Is PPSS suggesting that beneficiaries pay for search and rescue operations?

A. PPSS recommended that beneficiaries pay for operations associated with non-life-threatening incidents, such as supplying gas or towing. It is recommended that user charges be collected for other Coast Guard activities, including short-range navigation aids, domestic ice breaking, recreational boating safety, and bridge administration. These programs benefit a specific, readily identifiable segment of the public.

Q. How much additional revenue could be generated by instituting user charges for these Coast Guard services?

A. PPSS estimates increased revenues of $418 million over three years.

Q. PPSS estimates increased revenues of $232 million over three years from charging a fee for Freedom of Information Act requests. Isn't there already a charge for this service?

A. The Freedom of Information Act (FOIA) allows the public to request information from the Government. If the request is considered in the general public interest, no charge is made. In other cases, a charge is made to cover the search time, and the costs of copying the document. However, the charges do not cover the costs of reviewing the document to remove material which is proprietary or classified, as well as information protected by the Privacy Act.

The practice of requesting information under FOIA has become part of regular market research. Industry is taking advantage of Government resources to obtain information that is of economic benefit to them.

In fact, since passage of the Act, some companies have specialized in filing FOIA requests for others. These companies provide their services primarily to business and industrial clients at fees that are frequently three to four times the charges of the Government agencies.

Q. What services does the Customs Service provide which should be funded from user charges?

A. Customs is engaged in a number of special activities and services that provide benefits to identifiable users. The services include entry of vessels, clearance of vessels, issuing permits to foreign vessels to proceed from district to district, receiving a manifest of foreign vessels on arrival from another district, and granting a permit to unload.

A good portion of the services are being reimbursed through existing user fees, but some are in need of upward adjustment. For example, in the case of entry and clearance of general aviation aircraft, the existing fee is established by Congress at a maximum of $25, and that can be charged only after normal working hours. Based upon Customs calculations as to the amount of time spent in processing aircraft and passengers in FY 1981, $3.15 million is obligated for this activity. Under the existing fee system, $376,945 was collected in FY 1981, only 12% of the cost of this special service.

In other cases, Customs is not charging a fee for its services, so that the implementation of new charges would result in 100% cost reimbursement plus the additional cost of collecting the fee.

Q. How much additional revenue would be collected from increasing charges for Customs Services?

A. Over three years, additional revenue generated from PPSS recommendations would be $364 million.

Recreational activities provided by the Government include facilities for camping, swimming, and skiing; picnic areas; wilderness areas; trails; ramps for river and lake access; and special attractions such as visitor centers and exhibits.

Seven Federal land-management agencies provide recreational activities:

1. Bureau of Land Management

2. Bureau of Reclamation

3. Fish and Wildlife Service

4. National Park Service

5. Army Corps of Engineers

6. Forest Service

7. Tennessee Valley Authority

The National Park Service and the Forest Service provide recreational activities as part of their missions, while the other five agencies primarily perform services which result in recreational activities as a by-product.

PPSS's recommendations centered on increasing fees for all Federal recreational facilities and channeling these revenues back to the operation and maintenance of these facilities.

Q. How much could Federal revenues increase through higher charges for recreational facilities?

A. PPSS estimates a three-year revenue increase of $528 million. Before these revenues can be realized, however, better accounting procedures and program management are necessary.

Q. Why are accounting and management improvements needed before revenues can increase?

A. The mixed resources and functions of the seven agencies with recreation facilities result in difficulties in administering recreational programs. Program managers have to exercise judgment in allocating costs between those that benefit the public at large and those that benefit specific groups. To make these decisions, good management information systems are critical.

Q. What information systems did PPSS recommend?

A. The seven agencies involved should institute precise accounting for all costs attributable to recreation facilities, including the capital cost of equipment, improvements, personnel costs, operation, and maintenance. A single product or service planner should be responsible for overseeing the Federal recreation fee program, and steps should be taken to establish a "single passport" concept, allowing the purchaser entrance into all Federal recreation areas.

Q. Will consolidating control of recreational facilities and better accounting bring about a system where recreational fees collected would cover the costs of operating all Federal parks and wilderness areas?

A. No. The collection of user fees of all kinds represents only a small portion of total funding for recreation programs. That's because there is a substantial public benefit derived from maintaining our national forest and wilderness areas for present and future generations which cannot be assessed to specific users.

In addition to sales, transportation, special services, and recreation activities, two other activities, inspection and grading, and regulation and licensing, offer potential revenue increases of $246 million over three years.

Q. Aren't inspection and grading activities performed for the public good? How can a user charge be attached to such services?

A. The Government conducts many inspection and grading activities across a wide spectrum of products. Many, such as meat inspections, are mandatory and benefit the general public. Others, however, are voluntary (for example, meat grading and grain inspection) and are performed by the Government at the request of the user. This distinction between voluntary and mandatory activities should determine whether a user fee should apply. PPSS has identified voluntary inspection programs where user fees should be updated or instituted; three examples follow:

- Update the fee schedule of the Agricultural Marketing Service to include fees for cotton grading and licensing and for cotton and tobacco newsletters and other activities (revenue increase of $29 million over three years).

- Increase Federal grain inspection service fees to recover 100% of costs (revenue increase of $6 million over three years).

- Update the HUD fee schedule for manufactured (Mobile) home inspections to recover the full cost of inspection and administrative costs, and allocate funds collected to offset administrative costs and enforcement of the Manufactured Housing Program (revenues are estimated to increase by $1 million over three years).

In addition to instituting user charges for inspections and gradings, there are instances where inspections could be done without direct Federal involvement, such as inspection of dairy plants.

Q. Aren't there Federal requirements for dairy inspections?

A. Dairy inspections are now made by the USDA, the FDA, and state agencies. By relying on state inspections, performed under cooperative inspection agreements utilizing Federal standards, the entire cost would be borne by the states, and the state inspectors could monitor all requirements, Federal and state. Transferring this function to the states could save $5 million in Federal funds over three years.

Q. What are the potential revenue increases from increasing user fees for Federal regulatory and licensing activities?

A. PPSS has found two programs where regulatory and licensing fees could be increased to generate additional revenue of $209 million over three years. First, PPSS recommended that the Federal Communications Commission (FCC) institute application fees and user charges for licensing and regulating activities in interstate and foreign communications. Second, the Federal Energy Regulatory Commission (FERC) should increase user fees to recover the costs of regulatory services.

PPSS has developed many other recommendations to allocate the costs of services to specific beneficiaries in areas as wide ranging as increasing the costs of Federal publications, including maps and charts, and increasing concessioner franchise fees in the National Parks, increasing loan origination fees on Federally guaranteed loans and on GNMA mortgages, and increasing fees at the Metropolitan Washington Airports. Additional Government products and services which benefit a readily identifiable group and which should be funded through user charges include the following:

- Initiate user fees for issuance of SBA-guaranteed debentures of the Small Business Investment Companies and on Federal Home Loan Bank borrowings which, as a result of their agency status, can be issued at reduced rates, and initiate transaction fees to cover the operating costs of the Commodity Futures Trading Commission;

- Eliminate credit to timber purchasers for funds spent on Forest Service road construction; use National Service Life Insurance and Veterans Special Life Insurance fees to pay for the administrative costs of these self-supporting programs, costs which are currently paid from Federal revenues; and

- Institute user fees for safety assessments and R&D services performed for railroads; recover the costs of regulatory services provided by the Federal Energy Regulatory Commission to identifiable users; and increase user fees for services provided by the Agricultural Cooperative Service.

> The three-year total of all the recommendations in this section, after elimination of duplication and overlap among issues, is $10.867 billion—equal to the three-year taxes of 1.6 million median income families.

Optimizing the Use of the Private Sector

> Government manages best those things that are closest to its traditional functions of providing for the general welfare and security. There are numerous functions and services currently performed by the Federal Government which could more efficiently and cost-effectively be performed outside. However, Congressionally imposed limitations on transferring functions to the private sector, opposition from Federal employees, and a lack of centralized, systematic, and continuous concern have resulted in a continuing expansion of the Government's commercial activities. PPSS concluded that privatization and contracting out provide significant savings opportunities, and recommends the establishment of a central Executive Branch authority to identify and facilitate work toward their realization.

> In FY 1983, the Government spent $38.9 billion in the specific areas covered by PPSS recommendations, with spending estimated to increase to $209.8 billion by the year 2000 if present policies are continued. Implementing PPSS recommendations would reduce spending to $145 billion in 2000, a saving of $64.8 billion, or 30.9%.

Privatization involves the transfer of an activity, or part of an activity, currently performed by the Federal Government to a private entity. Privatization increases efficiency by targeting Government resources to those activities best performed by Government while turning over to the private sector those activities that can be more efficiently performed outside of Government.

In some cases, the Government has become involved in businesses or initiated services because there were no alternative private sector sources available. However, as these services become established, and as alternative sources for providing these services develop, privately or at the local Government level, Federal resources are no longer necessary.

With a FY 1983 operating budget of approximately $850 billion, the Federal Government is the largest conglomerate in the world. It is the largest power producer; insurer, lender, and borrower; hospital system operator; landowner and tenant; holder of grazing land and timberland; owner of grain; and warehouse operator, shipowner, and truck fleet operator.

Many of the services provided by the Federal Government could be provided more effectively and at less cost by the private sector. The Government, by directly producing services which could be produced in the private sector, creates a separate, uncompetitive market with no pressure to control costs.

Q. Doesn't the Government provide many services, such as electric power, at less cost than private industry, and why shouldn't it continue to do so?

A. The low cost of such Federally financed and operated facilities is a fallacy. As an example, the Bonneville Power Administration, which provides "low cost" power in the Washington/Oregon/Idaho area, generated cash deficits of between $500 million and $1 billion in each of the last five years. A primary reason for this shortfall is that the rate making process does not fully reflect the costs of producing and transmitting electricity, including the amortization of the capital investment. Customers are being provided with power at about one-third the cost charged by private power companies, but that is because taxpayers across the country are subsidizing electric customers.

Another example is Veterans Administration (VA) medical care. When the VA is unable to provide nursing home beds to veterans, it frequently uses private sector nursing homes. In FY 1981, the average cost for patient care in private nursing homes used by VA was $45 per day. The cost incurred within VA's own facilities for similar care was $109 per day, or 2.4 times as much.

PPSS recommended that an Office of Federal Management (OFM) be established, with primary responsibility for identifying opportunities for privatization across Government. Within the structure of the OFM, there should be processes for:

- pursuing existing opportunities for privatization and identifying additional Government-produced products or services which can be privatized;

- ensuring that agencies and those engaged in the legislative process routinely consider privatization as an option; and

- soliciting private sector proposals for privatizing Government functions. Procedures should provide for soliciting, accepting, evaluating, and monitoring such private sector proposals.

Fundamental to the process, privatization should be established as an option when program objectives are debated, molded, and implemented. In addition to working to move programs from the Government to the private sector, the process should also work at the national policy level to ensure that the privatization option is considered early in a program's life cycle.

Q.   Why are Federal costs for similar services so much higher?

A.   One of the primary reasons is that there are no incentives to operate efficiently because Federal services have the ultimate safety net— they cannot fail financially. PPSS has found three conditions which tend to promote operational inefficiency: (a) inefficient management tends to be rewarded with higher appropriations and more staff; (b) Government businesses are insulated from competitive pressures and thus need not address fundamental changes; and (c) powerful constituencies exist within and outside the Government that can and do effectively lobby to prevent change while taxpayers, all 90 million of them, remain moot. For example:

- Budget allocations are made to individual VA hospitals on the basis of the number of patient-days each hospital records during the year. This creates an incentive to increase admissions and delay discharge until there is another patient to fill the vacated bed. Any hospital that fails to meet its target patient-day workload loses a portion of its budget appropriations—a reverse incentive, the burden of which must be borne by the taxpayer.

- Once the Government decided to provide the military with the benefit of less expensive food, it chose to implement this service by establishing a complete retail grocery system. This duplication of private sector services is inefficient because there are no driving forces of marketplace competition. The Government, by directly producing the commissary service, creates a separate, uncompetitive market with no pressure to control costs.

Q. How did military commissaries come about?

A. Military commissaries were established to serve soldiers in frontier posts situated miles from the nearest city. The program has evolved so far beyond its original intent that today there are 238 commissaries in the continental U.S. alone—including six in such "outposts" as Washington, D.C.; five in San Francisco; four in San Diego; four in Norfolk, Virginia, and five in San Antonio—costing taxpayers $758 million for FY 1983 in appropriated funds, inventory carrying charges, sales and excise taxes foregone, and miscellaneous other costs.

Q. How much could be saved by terminating commissary operations?

A. Closing commissaries in the continental U.S. could save $973 million over three years. A preferable alternative to closure, however, would be to privatize the commissaries—i.e., rent out the space on military bases to private firms. This would offer opportunities for rental income, tax revenues, while eliminating subsidies. It would also get the Department of Defense (DOD) and the armed services personnel out of the grocery business. And the revenue potential is great—$2.447 billion in cost reductions and revenue enhancements over three years.

Q. The rationale for the privatization of the commissary system is straightforward. Why hasn't something been done previously to get the Government "out of the grocery business"?

A. The commissary system continues and, in fact, grows because vested interests voice their opposition to privatization while the vast majority of taxpayers, who are subsidizing the commissary system, remain silent.

For example, when PPSS recommended the elimination of taxpayer subsidies to commissaries, the following appeared in the August 15, 1983, issue of *Exchange and Commissary News*:

> It's time for this market to wake up and stop waiting for the House Armed Service Committee to constantly stop everything negative from becoming law. Our associations and key industry leaders must anticipate rather than react to head off moves to contract out or close the commissaries.

One strategy to maintain the status quo is the expansion of the number of potential beneficiaries of the commissary system. The more beneficiaries, the more pressure and votes that can be brought to bear to resist change.

Following the announcement of PPSS findings, three pieces of legislation were introduced, the effect of which would be to expand the number of users of the commissaries:

1. On June 13, 1983, an amendment was introduced to allow the use of commissary stores by all those persons who have left the military, are entitled to retired pay, but have not yet reached retirement age.

2. On July 13, a proposal to open commissaries to "former spouses" of military personnel was introduced.

3. The FY 1984 Defense Department Appropriations bill establishes a test program for the use of commissary stores by military reservists. This program, if fully implemented, could bring *950,000 new patrons* to the commissary system.

The military services build new commissaries from sales proceeds without having to seek construction money from Congress. No oversight has been exercised by Congress to prevent the emergence of new commissaries in metropolitan areas or the duplication of services. In the San Antonio (Texas) metropolitan area, for instance, where five commissaries can be found, two are on Lackland and Kelly Air Force Bases, which literally border one another.

Once new commissaries are constructed, the House Armed Services Committee has routinely raised commissary appropriations to provide these new stores with employees and inventories. The result has been to make commissary expansion self-perpetuating. With at least another 25 new commissary construction or renovation projects already under way, long-term and even higher levels of taxpayer support appear likely in the absence of corrective action.

Finally, the centralized review process which PPSS has recommended should identify programs that, due to costs or project magnitude, had to be initiated in the public sector, but which could now be shifted to the private sector. An example is the Space Shuttle program, the magnitude, cost, and risk of which made private sector development impractical. Now that the spacecraft is operating, an option to begin the privatization of the program through private sector funding and technology transfer could prove reasonable and cost-efficient for the Government.

PPSS identified sizable savings from privatization, including:

• greater private sector participation in the NASA Space Shuttle program, with an estimated $1.523 billion in Federal funds replaced by private sector resources over three years.

• less Government involvement in processing and disseminating LANDSAT satellite data. Selling the unprocessed data, which is commercially used to create maps and charts, to private firms for processing and distribution could save operating costs and increase revenues by $47 million and $450 million, respectively, over three years.

- reduced funding of market development organizations. Phasing out Government funding for groups such as the U.S. Wheat Association, where the membership is large enough to support the organization without Federal subsidy, can save $37 million over three years.

- closure or privatization of all military commissaries in the United States. Revenue potential from renting out commissary space on military bases could be as much as $2.447 billion over three years.

- sale of the Metropolitan Washington Airports (MWA) to a local airport authority. MWA is currently owned, operated, and regulated by the Federal Aviation Administration (FAA) and the Department of Transportation (DOT). This puts the Government in the role of supplier and regulator of services at MWA, which inhibits long-range planning and financing of improvements. Combined revenues and savings to the Federal Government from this sale could be $455 million over three years.

Savings and revenue enhancements from privatizing only the five above-mentioned areas are estimated to be $4.959 billion over three years.

Q. Did PPSS recommend that the Space Shuttle Program be privatized?

A. PPSS recommended that private industry be allowed to participate through financial investment in NASA's National Space Transportation System (NSTS), which operates the shuttles, so that commercial applications can be developed.

The space industry represents the world's next major advanced technological business frontier and an important economic base for the United States and other developed countries. Currently, the United States is a leader in the space industry market. An important support service needed for the development of the space industry is space transportation. The U.S. Space Shuttle system, in particular, is essential to the development of future commercial space activities. For example, the shuttle would be instrumental in the construction of permanent orbiting space stations as well as facilities for manufacturing and solar energy generation.

A commercial world market for space-related industries already exists. Three major market segments are the satellite industry, space launching services, and Materials Processing in Space (MPS). The satellite business industry is represented mainly by communication satellites that are used for such functions as data transmission. Expendable Launch Vehicles (ELVs) are the major space launch hardware used, as they have been operational longer than the Space Shuttle system. ELV space launching services are dependent primarily on an increased need for communication satellite launches, while the shuttle would also benefit significantly from increased space science research and space applications such as MPS. The most recent space application technology, MPS represents manufacturing in the near-zero gravity environment of space that may produce new alloys and unusually pure crystals, drugs, and lenses. It is expected that when it is proven to be viable commercially, MPS will become a major space industry requiring the construction of orbiting manufacturing facilities.

Q. Would it distort NASA's mission in the areas of research and national security to have private interests involved in the program?

A. No, it would enhance NASA's ability to concentrate on its mission. Private sector involvement would mean private sector funding, technological expertise, and management input, freeing NASA for more research and development activity and allowing Federal funds to be reallocated to other developmental space projects.

Q. Involving the private sector in the Space Shuttle program appears to be a very novel idea; is there a precedent for such involvement?

A. Federal research and development funds have traditionally been used to create new technologies that have been transferred to the private sector for commercial application. For example, aviation is a recent Government-developed transportation technology that was turned over to the private sector. Weather and remote sensing satellites could be the next space technology to be privatized. The National Space Transportation System is a Government-developed transportation and space technology system that can begin to be transferred to the private sector. This transfer would be in support of U.S. policy to encourage domestic commercial exploitation of space capabilities, technology, and systems for national economic benefit.

In the past 25 years, the United States has maintained a virtual monopoly on space launch services. Recently, however, Europe and Japan have developed space launch activities to the point of challenging the U.S. in the Expendable Launch Vehicle field. Cooperative Government/industry arrangements that include major incentives are the primary reason for the growth of these foreign programs.

Commercial European space launch activities are conducted by Arianespace, a private firm created and subsidized by the European Space Agency, NASA's equivalent. Arianespace does not require customers for its Ariane ELV launches to pay until revenue is generated from the launched satellite's operations. Currently, Arianespace's attractive financing terms have led American firms such as Western Union and GTE to sign contracts for Ariane ELV launches.

Q. How much could be saved if the Space Shuttle program were funded by private rather than public sources?

A. There are currently two space shuttles in operation, and two additional shuttles are scheduled for construction. PPSS recommendations and savings estimates are based on the construction/operation of a fifth shuttle and all shuttles built after it. Each shuttle costs approximately $2.3 billion. By funding a fifth shuttle from private sector sources, the Government could acquire increased space transportation capacity without additional cost. PPSS estimates that $1.5 billion of Federal funds could be replaced by private sector investment over three years.

Q. PPSS also mentioned that weather and remote sensing satellites could be privatized. Is this another PPSS recommendation?

A. Privatizing weather and land sensing satellites has been recommended by many sources, including the General Accounting Office, the National Oceanic and Atmospheric Administration of the Department of Commerce, and PPSS. PPSS recommendations relate primarily to privatizing the land sensing satellite program (LANDSAT).

Q. What is the purpose of the LANDSAT program?

A. The raw data collected from the LANDSAT satellite is used to create maps and charts used in agricultural forecasting, mineral and petroleum exploration, and water and land use planning.

Q. Did PPSS recommend that the satellites be sold to private interests?

A. No. PPSS recommended eliminating Government involvement in any phase of satellite land remote sensing beyond the collection and storage of raw, unprocessed data. Specifically, the Government should no longer be involved in converting raw data into computer tapes or other usable forms. PPSS recommended that the Government sell the rights to process, price, and commercially sell this raw data to the private sector.

Q. How much money could this proposal save the Federal Government?

A. As noted above, the Government will save the operating costs of processing and distributing the LANDSAT data—about $47 million over three years. In addition, the Government can collect royalties from the sale of this data. PPSS estimates that Federal revenues could increase by $450 million over three years by transferring this function to the private sector.

Q. Are there other Federal programs that could be transferred to the private sector?

A. There are many programs in areas that include agricultural marketing and research, National Laboratories, and environmental research and development that can and should be transferred to the private sector.

Q. Could you elaborate?

A. As one example, the Foreign Agricultural Service Cooperator Funding Program funds market development organizations such as the U.S. Wheat Association and the American Soybean Institute to help develop and expand foreign markets for U.S. agricultural products. In 1982, 52 special-interest groups received funding of $24 million through this program. Contributions from the Federal Government were at one time valid as "seed" money to establish such market organizations, but as these organizations grew in usefulness and membership, funding should have been provided by the members, not the Government.

Q. How much could be saved if the funding for these organizations stopped?

A. We recommend that funding be completely phased out over four years, for savings of $37 million over the first three years and an additional $24 million in the fourth year. This is just one example of savings from privatizing Federal activities; there are many more.

Q. What are some of the other areas where privatization should be considered?

A. Other prime candidates for privatization are the National Oceanic and Atmospheric Administration's (NOAA) weather radio station and the research activities of both the National Bureau of Standards (NBS) and the Federal Trade Commission (FTC).

NOAA weather radio duplicates similar data disseminated by regular radio and TV coverage and extensive Coast Guard and Navy transmissions. By discontinuing the NOAA Weather Program, the Government could save $11 million over three years in transmitter costs, wire service costs, and contracts for radio taping.

The National Bureau of Standards (NBS) and the Federal Trade Commission (FTC) both perform research activities extraneous to their missions and which duplicate research being performed in the private sector. In addition to developing measurement standards and standard reference materials, the NBS has evolved into a multipurpose research laboratory which addresses technological problems in areas such as chemical engineering, fire research, building technology, and analytical chemistry. The FTC conducts independent analyses of issues concerning the performance of the economy. The research does not contribute to the primary mission of the agencies and in many instances duplicates efforts of the private sector. Limiting the amount of extraneous research could reduce Federal expenditures by $50 million over three years—that's equivalent to the taxes paid on 18,776 average tax returns in 1980.

The preceding is just a sampling of programs that could be privatized. Fourteen PPSS task forces have identified areas where privatization should be considered, with potential savings of $11.2 billion over three years. These PPSS recommendations include:

- Phase out Veterans Administration construction and management of hospitals. Hospitals should be constructed by private companies and then leased back to VA. VA should then contract with private sector firms for management of these hospitals. In addition, VA should utilize private sector nursing homes rather than construct additional capacity ($1.436 billion three-year savings);

- Reduce the Federal vehicle fleet, provide private sector management, and increase the use of privately owned and leased vehicles where cost effective ($1.460 billion three-year savings);

- Privatize the National Fertilizer Development Center and eliminate Federal funding ($84 million three-year savings); and

- Declare a moratorium on new DOD construction of family housing in the U.S. and suspend housing acquisitions. Rely on Variable Housing Allowances to enable service families to rent suitable housing in adjacent civilian communities ($209 million three-year savings).

The areas for potential privatization cut across all agencies and functions. As discussed earlier, as a service becomes established, or as a private sector alternative becomes available, Federal resources should be shifted away from these areas. Alternatively, Government services can be performed by the private sector while control remains with the Government through the process of contracting out.

Q. Several of PPSS's recommendations involve "contracting out." What specifically is involved?

A. One of the ways the Government can procure goods and services is by contracting with private sector companies to provide them. The Office of Management and Budget (OMB) is responsible for establishing, monitoring, and revising policies, regulations, and procedures for Federal procurement. OMB Circular A-76 defines the policies and procedures to be followed in determining whether a specific commercial activity should be carried out by the Government or contracted out to the private sector. A-76 pertains to commercial and industrial activities currently performed by Government employees, such as food service, maintenance, security, fire fighting, laundry and dry cleaning, etc. It does not apply to major systems acquisitions or inherently governmental functions such as agency administration and management or national defense.

From its inception in 1955, the policy of transferring the Government's commercial activities to the private sector has been poorly implemented. The GAO found in 1978 and again in 1981 that compliance had been "inconsistent and relatively ineffective," with little progress between those years. The Director of OMB noted in 1981 that billions of dollars were being spent annually to perform thousands of activities which the private sector could perform at a cost saving to the Government.

There are an estimated 11,000 commercial activities now being performed in the Government at a cost of about $20 billion a year. Currently, of the 1.9 million Federal employees in the U.S., excluding Postal employees, more than one in every four is engaged in a commercial activity. In 1983, OMB estimated that adhering to the policies set forth in Circular A-76 could save $5 billion annually five years after implementation.

PPSS recommended the following actions to carry out these policies and to realize the savings they offer:

- The Administration should seek to have Congress enact as law the Government's long-standing policy of relying upon the private sector for commercial services.

- The Administration should seek legislation eliminating the various restrictions Congress has imposed on the Executive Branch's ability to carry out that policy.

- OMB should amend Circular A-76, revoking the 1979 stipulation that requires at least a 10% cost savings versus the cost of in-house operations before transferring an activity to the private sector.

- OMB and Executive Branch Agencies should ensure that work performance statements and invitations to bid are not biased against contracting out, and that cost comparisons are fairly and accurately conducted. As part of this process, OMB should promulgate new and accurate Federal personnel costs, especially with respect to retirement, for use in A-76 comparisons.

- Strong leadership, beginning with the President and extending through OMB to agency heads and officials, should be exerted to enforce the policy and implement the directives.

Each of these areas is discussed in further detail below.

While the Department of Defense (DOD) has led other agencies in implementing the A-76 program, it has been subject to Congressional restrictions and requirements not imposed on civilian agencies. Civilian agencies need no cost studies to contract out when the annual operating costs are under $100,000, while DOD has no cost study threshold. Congress requires that DOD report activities that are scheduled for contracting out and provide details of cost study results after completion. In addition, DOD is required to present annual reports to Congress on its contracting-out efforts.

The DOD A-76 program suffered a setback when Congress passed a moratorium on A-76 reviews for FY 1978. In 1982, Congress passed a DOD restriction forbidding the use of appropriated funds in connection with any new A-76 study between October 1, 1982, and March 31, 1983. DOD was also forbidden to enter into any new contract for the performance of fire fighting or security guard functions on any military bases or facilities during FY 1982. Beginning with FY 1984, DOD is under a two year moratorium for contracting out fire fighting and security services.

Regarding civilian agencies, Congress prevented the General Services Administration (GSA) from contracting for guards, custodians, elevator operators and messengers during FY 1983, and Congress permanently barred the Veterans Administration from contracting for patient care.

Q.   How has Congress been able to obstruct the Government's goal of relying on the private sector for goods and services?

A.   Part of the problem lies in the fact that Congress has never legislated a national policy supporting reliance on the private sector. The absence of a legislated policy has enabled members of Congress to add riders containing piecemeal legislative restrictions onto appropriation bills.

Q.   Did PPSS note examples where contracting out to the private sector had resulted in cost savings?

A.   Yes. Since 1960, the Air Training Command (ATC) has contracted with a predecessor corporation of Northrop Worldwide Aircraft Services, Inc., to provide base support functions for Vance Air Force Base at Enid, Oklahoma. Performance standards in the contract specified what Northrop must accomplish, but not how to do it. The contract has been periodically renewed. The current contract with Northrop, at a fixed cost of $28.8 million annually, covers most of the base support services required at Vance.

A primary responsibility of Northrop is to perform maintenance on the T-38 and T-37 training aircraft on the base. But also included in the single, umbrella-type contract are such base support functions as civil engineering, recreation services, food services, publications, fire protection, transportation, and housing.

ATC has concluded that the Northrop umbrella contract for base support services saves over $8 million annually (or about 22%) from the costs of performing the same services using Federal employees. Northrop is able to perform the functions more efficiently and at less cost due to lower manpower requirements, flexible personnel procedures and policies, and a more stable trained work force.

Q. How do services supplied under Northrop compare to those at other military bases which do not rely on the private sector?

A. Northrop performs maintenance on T-38 and T-37 training aircraft using only 60% and 73%, respectively, of the manpower used by the Air Training Command (ATC) system-wide on those planes. Similarly, Northrop performs the supply function at Vance using only half the number of personnel utilized at a comparable ATC airbase where Federal employees perform this function.

Using fewer employees, Northrop performs the maintenance and the supply functions better or more quickly than ATC performs these functions system-wide on the same aircraft. For example, Northrop has only 18.8% of the T-38's and 14.3% of the T-37's sidelined for maintenance, compared to 21.5% and 15.4%, respectively, for ATC system-wide. Similarly, Northrop has only 12.7% of the T-38's and 4.6% of the T-37's not fully mission capable compared to 16.0% and 7.5%, respectively, for ATC system-wide.

Despite such successful contracting out experience, there has been little movement in the Government in this area. Aircraft maintenance, for example, is still being performed in-house at most other airbases, at much higher costs and not as well.

Since Circular A-76 was initially issued in 1966, agencies have been required to identify all commercial positions within their agencies as the first step in applying A-76 procedures. A commercial activity is defined as an activity which provides a product or service which could be obtained from a private sector source.

Currently, the Government has identified 203,000 commercial positions. Of that number, 160,000 are in DOD and the remaining 43,000 in civilian agencies.

Q. Have agencies listed all their commercial positions?

A. No. PPSS concurred in OMB's estimate that there are about 500,000 commercial positions in Government (2.5 times the number of employees currently identified) performing services which could be obtained from the private sector. Agencies have yet to identify about 300,000 of those positions.

Q. Why have agencies not identified all their commercial positions, as directed?

A. Many Federal managers are opposed to contracting out. Some managers of affected activities are concerned with loss of their job security or possible demotion. Others anticipate opposition from members of Congress or employee unions, and the effect that might have on their own positions or responsibilities.

Apart from the general resistance to contracting out, the biggest obstacle is the extensive management review that is required. Currently, it takes 9-12 months, on average, to complete an A-76 study. A-76 studies are also costly. The Norfolk Navy Yard spent $588,000 during FY 1982, and Fort Polk, Louisiana, expects to spend $2 million over the next two years on A-76 studies.

Since there are limitations on the number of qualified personnel to conduct such reviews, on the funds available, and on the time available for managers to take from their program responsibilities to spend on reviews, it is understandable that the A-76 cost comparisons now required are avoided where possible by Federal managers and even agency heads.

Q. Since A-76 studies are so expensive, can't they be eliminated where cost savings are obvious?

A. They can be, but they aren't. For example, the General Services Administration (GSA) requested a waiver from OMB on cost studies of its in-house custodial activities because extensive experience with contractors pointed to assured savings by converting to contract. The waiver was withheld because of anticipated Congressional and Civil Service opposition. As a result, GSA estimated it will spend $1 million on in-house custodial A-76 reviews.

Q. Don't agencies exercise control over A-76 policy implementation?

A. Agencies have not exercised sufficient guidance or control to implement A-76 policy. This is demonstrated by the inconsistencies within agencies. At the Department of Energy (DOE) facilities at Oak Ridge, the guard services are contracted, whereas the DOE Albuquerque facility considers guard services to be "inherently governmental" and not subject to contract. Conversely, Albuquerque contracts for airport services, whereas the Bonneville Power Administration considers such services to be "inherently governmental."

Q. What did PPSS recommend to obtain a complete identification of all commercial positions?

A. Strong leadership is the key. Agency heads must ensure that all commercial positions within agencies are identified. There must be clear guidance as to the type of agency activities which are considered commercial, and proper application of A-76 exceptions and exclusions. Agency officials can expedite the process by identifying the activities which can be procured in ordinary business channels or which have already been successfully contracted, and then impose on managers the burden of demonstrating that contracting out their particular responsibility is not a feasible or viable possibility.

Also, OMB must exercise stronger central oversight and direction to see that agencies are complying with Circular A-76 directives to identify commercial positions.

After identifying the commercial positions within the agency, the next step is for agencies to conduct cost comparisons to determine whether it is more economical to contract out such functions or to perform them in-house.

The 1979 amendments to Circular A-76 introduced a new basis for the comparisons. Contractor bids were no longer to be compared to established in-house costs but to *theoretical* costs of the most efficient in-house operations.

Further, before any in-house activity could be converted, the contract costs had to be at least 10% below those of the theoretically most efficient in-house operation.

Q. Have agencies performed cost comparisons as directed by Circular A-76?

A. Agencies have been slow to conduct these cost comparisons. Since FY 1979, DOD has performed about 1,300 cost comparisons, involving about 25,000 positions, and contracted for roughly half that number. Based on DOD's current listing of 160,000 commercial positions, the Department has completed cost comparisons involving only 15% of such positions. Based on a more realistic estimate of 400,000 DOD commercial positions, cost comparisons have been performed on only 6% of such positions.

The record of civilian agencies' conducting cost comparisons is even worse. Accurate data on the total number of A-76 studies performed by civilian agencies are not available. OMB has a possibly incomplete record of about 100 cost comparison studies performed by all civilian agencies since FY 1979. Civilian agencies, as a group, have lagged far behind DOD in making A-76 cost comparisons.

Q. Has requiring cost saving comparisons to the theoretically most efficient in-house operations resulted in savings to the Government?

A. No. To develop what would be the theoretically most efficient in-house operation requires an extensive management review. A lengthy OMB Handbook prescribes detailed instructions for completing such studies. Currently, the total elapsed time to complete an A-76 study normally runs from 9 to 12 months.

How efficient or inefficient an in-house operation is does not matter in the current A-76 process. Moreover, Federal managers are not reprimanded if the A-76 process uncovers and documents inefficiencies, regardless of how long the manager has tolerated such waste.

As a result, until the studies are completed, this type of theoretical comparison reduces the stimulus and motivation for Federal managers to make their operations more efficient. If contractor bids were compared against the established costs of Federal operations as they exist, then Federal managers would have an incentive to improve their operations in order to meet the competitive threat from the private sector. That is the competitive stimulus private corporations and managers face every day.

Q.   What percent of activities are contracted out following A-76 cost comparisons at the present time?

A.   Within DOD, that percentage has dropped in recent years from about 65% in FY 1981 to about 50% in FY 1982, and to 41.5% in FY 1983. The 41.5% of the activities contracted for in FY 1983 accounted for 58% of the positions involved, indicating that contracting out was more successful as the size of the operation increased.

Q.   Have A-76 comparisons resulted in reduced in-house costs even where activities were not contracted to the private sector?

A.   Yes. If the activity remains in-house after the cost comparison study, substantial cost savings may result from the streamlining or "management review" process (especially within DOD). Where such management reviews are obligatory, there is evidence of savings. During the period 1979-1981, DOD streamlined activities which remained in-house after A-76 analyses at a savings of $14 million. Among civilian agencies, by contrast, data on streamlining savings are scarce due to the infrequency of A-76 studies for FY 1979-1981 and the inconsistent application of management reviews. Under the present circular, streamlining is encouraged but not required for civilian agencies.

Q.   What did PPSS conclude about the 1979 change which rules out contracting unless contract costs are at least 10% below in-house costs?

A.   This new requirement contradicts the announced policy of A-76 to rely on the private sector to supply commercial services and to keep Government out of business. The 10% cost differential requirement is incompatible with announced policy goals.

Even before this 10% differential is imposed, there are other major add-ons to the contract bid for comparison purposes. First, Federal contract administration costs are added, which range from 2% to 9%. Next, a *minimum* 2% is added to cover costs of severance, retraining, or relocating Federal employees who would be affected by contracting out. Such adjustments are logical for developing accurate costs of contracting for A-76 comparison purposes. But it makes no sense to impose an additional 10% penalty differential for contractors to overcome if the Government really means to rely on them for commercial services.

Q. Did PPSS uncover evidence of other impediments in the A-76 process against contracting?

A. Yes. Federal personnel costs—specifically the element of retirement costs—have been understated to reduce in-house costs. OMB prescribes in Circular A-76 the retirement benefit factor, stated as a percentage of gross salary, which agencies are required to use for A-76 cost comparisons.

The retirement benefit factor, as originally established for government-wide use in March 1966, was 7%. In March 1979, it was increased to 20.4%, the current factor. The original 7% figure was simply the charge levied against agency budgets and, as was known, did not represent the full costs to the Government of retirement benefits (see the "Retirement" section of this report).

For 1979, the Civil Service Commission (CSC), predecessor of the Office of Personnel Management (OPM), determined that the retirement factor should be 55%. OMB dismissed that and ordered CSC to submit another figure. CSC came up with a new figure of 34%. That too OMB rejected. OMB then promulgated the 20.4% factor without reference to any published cost data.

By way of comparison, OPM, as part of its annual financial report to Congress, calculated the Government contribution for Federal retirement in 1982 as 33.2%, and the long-term Government cost for Civil Service retirement as 29%. Despite being discredited, the 1979 figure of 20.4% still remains in effect for A-76 cost comparisons.

Q. What savings are possible if PPSS recommendations are implemented?

A. Based upon phased implementation, PPSS projects first year savings of $1.15 billion and cumulative first three year savings of $7.39 billion. When fully implemented (after four years), savings will exceed $5 billion annually, as shown below:

**Government Savings
from Contracting Out**
(\$ Billions)

	Year	(1) Annual	(2) Cumulative
(1)	1	$1.15	$ 1.15
(2)	2	2.42	3.57
(3)	3	3.82	7.39
(4)	4	5.36	12.75

Without the changes in Circular A-76 recommended by PPSS, savings only in the millions—not billions—are likely. With the recommended changes, savings of $5 billion annually become possible, after full implementation.

A four-year implementation period would require making A-76 determinations covering an average of 125,000 positions in each of those years, or more than 10 times the number now contemplated for completion during that period. PPSS estimated that about 80% of the positions analyzed will be eliminated. This will mean 100,000 Federal employee positions will be eliminated each year, or a total over the four years of about one-fifth of the Federal civilian work force, excluding the Postal Service.

In summary, A-76 cost comparison studies, and the contracting out that should result, have not been fully implemented by Federal agencies because of:

- Agency perceptions that A-76 is not a serious policy due to inconsistent support from successive Presidential administrations and opposition within Congress.

- Resistance from managers and staff conducting cost studies who perceive a loss of job security or possible demotion if their operation is contracted out.

- Complex, time consuming, cumbersome, costly, and inaccurate procedures for A-76 cost comparison studies.

- Concern over Congressional opposition leading to OMB delays and a concomitant reduction in savings.

For 28 years, there has been no real movement towards implementing A-76 policies. As a result, over that period the number of commercial activities performed by the Government has greatly expanded. PPSS recommended changes will provide large cost savings, but it must be recognized that they will significantly reduce the size of the Federal work force and that opposition from Congress and Federal employees will occur. If the long-standing, long-stalled policy of reliance upon the private sector is to be fully implemented, the President will have to direct the way.

The preceding pages discussed some of the major areas where privatization and contracting out present viable options for services currently performed by the Government. Additional areas where services could be transferred from Government to the private sector include:

- Increased application of A-76 by defense agencies, the Coast Guard, and the General Services Administration.

- Reduced Federal housing and hospital construction. Greater reliance on the private housing market to meet the needs of military personnel, and contracting out for additional hospital bed capacity required by the Veterans Administration.

- Discontinuation of the agency status of both the Federal National Mortgage Association and the Farm Credit System.

- Transference of the freight forwarding activities of the USDA to the private sector.

> The three-year total of all the recommendations in this section, after elimination of duplication and overlap among issues, is $37.078 billion—equal to the three-year taxes of 5.6 million median income families.

III. C. Selected Federal Programs: How to Make Them Deliver While Reducing the Cost to Taxpayers

The efficiency or inefficiency with which Government conducts its business is most clearly evident in individual programs.

Repeatedly it is brought to the attention of the general public that subsidy programs have error rates far in excess of what might reasonably be expected. It has been estimated that ten cents of every dollar in the Food Stamp program is wasted. The Farmers Home Administration has a delinquency rate on its loans 10 times greater than private lenders— and 70% of the FmHA borrowers and two-thirds of its programs are for non-farm purposes. Wage laws, enacted by the Federal Government to ensure that workers under Federal contracts are adequately compensated, result in wages that are significantly higher than those prevailing in the local market—$11.650 billion higher over three years. Federal insurance programs offer coverage totalling *$2.1 trillion*, yet premiums on these programs do not reflect the relative risks of those insured, and reserves are insufficient to cover potential claims. Federal research and development efforts, costing over $44 billion in 1983, are uncoordinated and are often initiated at the lower levels of department and agency management. As a result, programs are started without adequate consideration of national goals and priorities and are often duplicative of research efforts being conducted elsewhere in the Federal maze. All are indicative of Government deficiencies in the design, execution and management of Federal programs.

PPSS recommendations in these areas are intended to focus Federal management policy not on the gross amount of benefits these programs provide to selected recipients, but rather on the net benefit provided to those truly in need above the financial cost to the general taxpayer.

In lending programs this would involve greater attention to loan repayment than the current emphasis on loan origination. In subsidy programs this would involve greater accounting for total benefits received through various programs.

For research and development it would involve the formulation of strategy to achieve coherent national goals and the integration of department and agency research efforts into this strategy. For insurance programs it would involve realistic assessment of risks, and insurance premiums fully reflecting those risks.

Full acceptance of this philosophy would result in legislative initiatives to repeal the three major wage laws, the Davis-Bacon Act, the Walsh-Healey Act and the Service Contract Act, since these laws provide few real benefits to the public at an unconscionable cost to the taxpayer.

Subsidized Programs

In 1982, the Federal Government spent $124 billion to reduce poverty. The reduction in poverty as a result of this expenditure was $37 billion—about 30% of the amount expended. PPSS noted that benefits appear to be misdirected and are not being received by intended recipients. Adequate information does not exist to fully assess subsidy programs. PPSS recommended that the Federal Government centralize the administration of these programs and develop an accounting system which will provide information on all the benefits distributed to each recipient. A statement of both cash and non-cash benefits, similar to a W-2 form, should be prepared for all recipients and provide the basis for managing subsidy programs.

In addition, PPSS has made specific recommendations to (a) improve administration of Social Security; (b) reduce overlapping and duplicative Food Stamp benefits; and (c) control long-term Federal health care costs through system reform.

In FY 1983, the Government spent $222.3 billion in the specific areas covered by PPSS recommendations, with spending estimated to increase to $1,355.4 billion by the year 2000 if present policies are continued. Implementing PPSS recommendations would reduce spending to $1,099.5 billion in 2000, a saving of $255.9 billion or 18.9%.

OVERVIEW

A useful way of viewing Federal expenditures is to distinguish between outlays that are clearly made for the traditional functions of Government (such as those for national defense, interest on the public debt, and such general Government functions as the administration of justice, legislative and executive activities, and fiscal management), and those non-traditional outlays which are targeted to specific classes of individuals, businesses, or institutions. The following chart shows the growth in traditional and non-traditional outlays over the 1962-1982 period. The figures are in constant 1982 dollars in order to identify the "real" growth, rather than the growth associated with inflation.

Traditional vs. Non-Traditional Outlays
(millions of constant 1982 dollars)

		(1)	(2)	(3)
			Outlays	
		Targeted (Non-Traditional)	Non-Targeted (Traditional)	Total
(1)	1962	$147,471	$164,975	$312,446
(2)	1972	289,193	192,559	481,752
(3)	1977	407,385	186,844	594,229
(4)	1982	461,801	266,574	728,375
	Avg. Ann. % Increase			
(5)	1962–1982	5.9%	2.4%	4.3%
(6)	1962–1972	7.0	1.6	4.4
(7)	1972–1982	4.8	3.3	4.2
		As a % of Total Outlays		
(8)	1962	47.2%	52.8%	100.0%
(9)	1972	60.0	40.0	100.0
(10)	1977	68.6	31.4	100.0
(11)	1982	63.4	36.6	100.0

As shown, targeted or non-traditional outlays grew at an average annual rate of 5.9% over the 1962-1982 period, or 2.5 times as fast as the 2.4% growth rate for traditional expenditures. As a result, targeted outlays went from 47.2% of all outlays in 1962 to 63.4% in 1982. The fastest growth rate in targeted outlays was in the decade from 1962-1972 (7.0% per year versus 4.8% in the next decade). However, in terms of dollars, the constant dollar increase was actually greater in the decade 1972-1982 at $173 billion versus $142 billion in the decade 1962-1972.

The table on the following page shows how these non-traditional targeted outlays were distributed on a functional basis.

As shown in the chart, five functional areas continue to absorb about 83%-88% of targeted outlays. By far the largest category is Income Security, which increased from 46.7% of total targeted outlays in 1962 to 57.0% in 1982. Over the same period Veterans benefits declined from 11.2% to 5.2%. The biggest functional change was in Health, which increased from $3 billion or 2.4% of targeted outlays in 1962 (when it did not rank in the top five) to $74 billion or 16.0% by 1982 (when it ranked

Non-Traditional Targeted Outlays
Top Five Functions in 1962, 1972 & 1982
(millions of constant 1982 dollars)

		(1)	(2)
			% of Targeted
		Amount	Outlays
	1962		
(1)	Income Security	$ 68,918	46.7%
(2)	Veterans Benefits	16,454	11.2
(3)	International Affairs	16,384	11.1
(4)	Transportation	12,508	8.5
(5)	Agriculture	10,393	7.0
(6)	Subtotal	124,657	84.5
(7)	All Other	22,814	15.5
(8)	Total	$147,471	100.0%
	1972		
(9)	Income Security	$141,589	49.0%
(10)	Health	33,680	11.7
(11)	Education, Training	26,145	9.0
(12)	Veterans Benefits	22,409	7.7
(13)	Transportation	17,517	6.1
(14)	Subtotal	241,340	83.5
(15)	All Other	47,853	16.5
(16)	Total	$289,193	100.0%
	1982		
(17)	Income Security	$263,281	57.0%
(18)	Health	74,017	16.0
(19)	Education, Training	26,300	5.7
(20)	Veterans Benefits	23,955	5.2
(21)	Transportation	20,560	4.5
(22)	Subtotal	408,113	88.4
(23)	All Other	53,688	11.6
(24)	Total	$461,801	100.0%

second). Of note, Income Security and Health outlays represented only 4.5% of GNP in 1962 versus 11.0% in 1982.

All these breakdowns do not, however, reflect the value of the subsidies which are inherent in most of these targeted outlays. In certain cases, the subsidies comprise all of the payments—as in means-tested programs geared primarily to the poor or near-poor, and in crop support payments to farmers. In other cases, such as Social Security and Medicare, the benefits in part reflect the return of money that beneficiaries and their employers put into funds, but primarily reflect non-contributory outlays.

In still other cases, the payments reflect either mainly the return of contributed funds (such as with unemployment insurance) or form part of total compensation, such as the benefits paid to retired military and civilian employees.

As noted previously, 63.4% of 1982 total Federal Government outlays represented funds targeted primarily to eradicate poverty, provide retirement benefits to the elderly, and assist farmers and selected other businesses and individuals through direct aid, credit, preferential tax treatment, or some combination of the three.

Q. Given that the Federal Government is spending such a large proportion of its outlays for these social purposes, why is it that the poverty rate, for example, has been increasing?

A. The Federal Government first began measuring poverty in the early 1960's, when the U.S. was considered a relatively affluent society. Yet, an estimated 22% of the population in 1959—39.5 million Americans—were deemed poor. During the next 14 years, the combination of Great Society programs and sustained economic growth (per capita real GNP increased by an average of 2.7% per year over the entire period) resulted in the poverty rate falling to a low of 11.1% in 1973. During the balance of the 1970's, the poverty rate remained in the 11%-12.5% range, and then gradually increased during the recessions that followed to reach 15% in 1982. The obvious question is why the poverty rate is still this high in spite of transfer payments having quintupled in real dollars over the 1959-1982 period and means-tested programs specifically geared to the poor having increased more than six-fold.

Part of the answer is statistical: poverty is defined by and limited to cash income—earnings, social security, retirement benefits, and cash assistance to the poor. However, a large percentage of all transfer payments and the majority of means-tested programs are now in non-cash forms, including in-kind medical benefits, housing assistance, food stamps, and school lunches. The table on the following page, based on OMB statistics, shows the rise in non-cash transfer payments in constant 1982 dollars, in total and for the major means-tested programs.

As shown in the chart, in real terms, i.e., excluding inflation, non-cash payments increased 82.2 times overall and 43.4 times for major means-tested programs. By 1983, non-cash transfers accounted for 29.5% of all transfer payments and 71.6% of benefits under major means-tested programs.

However, the non-cash items are not included in the poverty statistics by the Bureau of the Census, which determines how poverty will be measured. *OMB estimates that adding the cash value of these non-cash benefits to other sources of income would have*

	(billions of constant 1982 $)	(1)	(2)	(3)	(4)
		All Transfer Payments			Memo: Non-Cash as a % of Total
		Cash	Non-Cash	Total	
(1)	1959	$ 71.9	$ 1.3	$ 73.2	1.8%
(2)	1966	106.2	6.8	113.0	6.0
(3)	1973	180.8	50.0	230.8	21.7
(4)	1983	255.4	106.9	362.3	29.5
(5)	1983 as a multiple of 1959	3.6X	82.2X	4.9X	N.A.
		Major Means-Tested Programs (a)			
(6)	1959	$ 11.3	$ 1.3	$ 12.6	10.3%
(7)	1966	13.4	6.8	20.2	33.7
(8)	1973	23.0	29.3	52.3	56.0
(9)	1983	22.4	56.4	78.8	71.6
(10)	1983 as a multiple of 1959	2.0X	43.4X	6.3X	N.A.

(a) Major means-tested cash includes Aid to Families With Dependent Children and Supplemental Security Income, while non-cash includes Medicaid, Food Stamps, Child Nutrition, and Housing Assistance.

caused the reported poverty rate in 1982 to drop from 15.0% to 9.6%. It should also be noted that the household surveys that the Census Bureau conducts every year to measure the poverty level are based on voluntary responses by those surveyed. OMB's comparisons between survey responses and program data indicate that there is significant underreporting of benefits—at rates of about 19% of all benefits and 33% for means-tested benefits—which could result in $62 billion in total benefits and $24 billion in means-tested benefits not being reported. That's enough to make a significant dent in the poverty rate.

The issues addressed by PPSS are how well program objectives are being met and what operational improvements can be instituted to increase the effectiveness and efficiency of the programs.

Q. What conclusions did PPSS draw from its analyses?

A. A central conclusion is that, despite the magnitude of the dollars expended in these targeted areas, adequate information does not exist to determine the degree to which the intended recipients of these subsidy programs are receiving sufficient benefits or, conversely, the degree to which benefits are being bestowed upon undeserving recipients to the detriment of all taxpayers. Indeed, there is no way to identify all the subsidies a particular person receives. Major public policy decisions regarding the poor are therefore made on the basis of sample data obtained through annual census surveys —which show significant underreporting of both income and benefits. Moreover, there are numerous programs which aren't even included in these reports. The census surveys cover only the major means-tested programs (such as Food Stamps and Medicaid) and exclude over 60 other programs, with over $40 billion in expenditures, that have income eligibility tests.

The situation is similar in farm and other business credit programs and subsidies, where no records are kept regarding all the benefits received from the variety of programs of which businesses or individuals can take advantage. For example, most agency accounting systems are unable to determine the total amount owed government-wide by a debtor when the debtor has many loans or other amounts due. There is limited ability to share credit information on Government debtors among Federal agencies, among various programs within an agency, or with the private sector. Consequently, when a loan application is being reviewed for credit worthiness, agencies cannot determine if the applicant has other outstanding Government credit, is current in his repayments, or is delinquent or in default on other Government credit. Further examples of how inadequate information contributes to mismanagement of Federal programs can be found in the "Information Gap" section of this report.

In addition to major gaps in bottom-up information gathering, there are also major shortfalls in subsidy management. The sheer number of programs, the decentralization of responsibilities, the lack of coordination among administrative and legislative functions, and the complex, inconsistent, and sometimes conflicting program eligibility criteria all contribute to a lack of control. The administrative management of programs for the poor, for example, is based on different pieces of legislation passed over the last 30 years. In fact, many Federal agencies are unable to determine total administrative costs associated with providing these subsidies. In contrast, few private sector companies would operate without knowing their total overhead costs of providing a product. The fact that the whole effort could be better managed and administrative costs reduced by combining certain programs never seems to be considered as a serious option, even though it could improve the targeting effectiveness and result in greater success in meeting overall goals.

PPSS was able to aggregate sufficient data to conclude that this lack of control has resulted in significant mistargeting of benefits, as exemplified by the following:

• Despite expenditures of $123.9 billion in 1982 on means-tested programs for the poor, such as Aid to Families with Dependent Children (AFDC), Food Stamps, and Medicaid, the poverty gap was reduced by only $37.4 billion—from $50.1 billion before means-tested transfer payments to $12.7 billion after all these transfer payments had been made. In theory, the $123.9 billion should have not only brought all households out of poverty, but should have been sufficient to bring all households to 125% of the poverty level with $47.5 billion left over for other purposes such as reducing the Federal deficit. This failure to target effectively is also reflected in an OMB analysis which showed that 42.4% of those receiving benefits from major means-tested programs in 1981 actually had total incomes (including cash benefits such as AFDC and in-kind benefits such as Food Stamps and Medicaid) in excess of 150% of the poverty line.

• Despite massive unfunded liabilities and the prospect of confiscatory payroll taxes on future workers, $76.1 billion in social insurance payments were made to elderly persons who were above the poverty line—above and beyond what these retirees and their employers contributed to these programs plus all accumulated interest. Indeed, 75% of social insurance payments (primarily Social Security) are in excess of what these retirees and their employers paid in, including interest, and thus constitute a major Federal subsidy.

• There appears to be no ongoing data gathering effort on the total benefits received by each family or corporate farmer from the many forms of farm subsidy. It has been estimated that as much as 50% of the Farmers Home Administration loan portfolio could be replaced by private sector lenders.

• Another area of subsidy examined was the adequacy of user charges for Federal goods and services. Due in part to unclear administrative policies and insufficient data regarding the full costs incurred by the Government to provide goods and services, the users of Government goods and services often pay only a small fraction of the Government's full cost, with taxpayers not benefitting from these services having to absorb the majority of the expense.

Problems will not be solved by minor changes in, or fine-tuning of, subsidy programs. Controlling the growth of these programs will require an analysis of the entire field of subsidy programs. However, as noted previously, timely, complete, and accurate information does not even exist to determine the degree to which these subsidies are reaching those truly in need or, conversely, providing benefits to those who are not in need, to the detriment of all taxpayers.

Q.   What recommendations did PPSS make based on these conclusions?

A.   For the purpose of improving targeting and administration of means-tested programs, PPSS recommended (1) the increased use of computer matching of information between programs to verify income of program recipients and (2) consolidating Federal administrative funding and requirements for the Aid to Families with Dependent Children (AFDC), Medicaid, and Food Stamp Programs. PPSS believed these concepts can be expanded further in the area of targeted outlays and recommended that a form, similar to a W-2 form issued to wage-earners, be issued by each Federal department or agency providing a subsidy to a specific beneficiary, with a copy going to the IRS. All Federal payments shown on this form would be added to the beneficiary's earnings to arrive at total income.

Additionally, the concept of consolidating benefit programs should be pursued, particularly in areas such as feeding and housing, where many uncoordinated programs are attempting to serve the same objective. This could substantially reduce administrative costs and improve targeting of benefits.

PPSS also recommended that Federal agency accounting systems be improved in order to provide accurate data on total administrative cost for subsidy programs. Additionally, poverty statistics should be redefined to include in-kind Federal transfer payments such as Food Stamps and Medicaid.

Q. What savings will be achieved as a result of these recommendations?

A. PPSS identified savings of $58.9 billion over three years which could be achieved through improved targeting of means-tested benefits.

As noted earlier, $123.9 billion in means-tested program money has not been able to close a $50.1 billion poverty gap. In theory, the $123.9 billion should have been sufficient not only to bring all households out of the poverty level but also to have brought these and all other households up to 125% of the poverty level (at an additional cost of about $26.3 billion)—and still have $47.5 billion left over for other purposes such as reducing the Federal deficit. Since about 75% of means-tested benefits represents Federal funds and about 25% state/local money, the Federal share of the $47.5 billion left over amounts to $35.6 billion. Even if savings are half these amounts, the Federal Government could reduce costs by $17.8 billion in year 1, $19.6 billion in year 2, and $21.5 billion in year 3 (assuming 10% inflation)—or by $58.9 billion over three years while doing a better job of targeting funds to the truly poor and near-poor.

Major subsidized programs are discussed below.

SOCIAL SECURITY

The public perception is that Social Security is self supporting, with payments to beneficiaries met through payments to trust funds set up specifically to meet the financial obligations of Social Security programs.

This is no longer true. The following compares payments to Old Age and Survivors Insurance (OASI) and Disability Insurance (DI) beneficiaries with payments made into the trust funds:

Social Security
($ Billions)

	Fiscal Year	(1) Trust Fund Receipts	(2) Program Payments	(3) Social Security Surplus/(Deficit) Amount	(4) Social Security Surplus/(Deficit) %
(1)	1958	$ 8.0	$ 8.2	$ (0.2)	(2.4)%
(2)	1970	33.5	29.7	3.8	12.8
(3)	1975	62.5	63.6	(1.1)	(1.7)
(4)	1978	85.4	92.2	(6.8)	(7.4)
(5)	1979	98.0	102.6	(4.6)	(4.5)
(6)	1980	113.2	117.1	(3.9)	(3.3)
(7)	1981	130.2	138.0	(7.8)	(5.7)
(8)	1982	143.5	154.1	(10.6)	(6.9)
(9)	1983E	147.8	168.3	(20.5)	(12.2)
	1983E As A Multiple of:				
(10)	1958	18.5X	20.5X	102.5X	5.1X
(11)	1970	4.4	5.7	ND	ND

Social Security has experienced growing deficits, despite continuously increasing revenues, i.e., revenues in 1983E are up 4.4 times from 1970 but payments are up by 5.7 times. However, these deficits represent only that portion of Social Security benefits subsidized directly by the Federal Government. All current contributors to Social Security are, in effect, subsidizing all current recipients since the benefits paid out are far in excess of the amounts (employee and employer contributions and accumulated earnings on those contributions) paid in. For example, Social Security beneficiaries who retired in 1981 receive more than 75% of their benefits in the form of a subsidy, as shown in the following table:

**Social Security As
A Subsidy Program**
(Constant 1981 dollars)

	Annual Income	(1) Lifetime Social Security Payments(a)	(2) Lifetime Social Security Benefits	(3) Payments As a % of Benefits	(4) Percent of Social Security Benefits Subsidized	(5) Ratio of Benefits To Payments
(1)	$10,000	$27,842	$144,735	19.2%	80.8%	5.2X
(2)	20,000	48,960	217,630	22.5	77.5	4.4
(3)	50,000	55,248	235,581	23.5	76.5	4.3

(a) Paid by the employee and employer and including the value of interest over the period.

To avoid distortions resulting from inflation—a dollar contributed in 1937 at the outset of the Social Security program was worth 571% more than the dollar paid out in 1981—all amounts are in constant 1981 dollars. Said differently, the 1981 dollar was worth 17.5¢ in 1937. As brought out in the preceding, even a beneficiary who made the 1981 dollar equivalent of $50,000 every year of his or her working life and paid the maximum Social Security tax each year receives 76.5% of his/her benefits in the form of a subsidy. In other words, the beneficiary receives benefits 4.3 times the combined value of employee/employer contributions plus interest on these contributions. In FY 1983E, 76%, or $127.9 billion, of total Social Security payments of $168.3 billion represented subsidies to the recipients.

Moreover, this subsidy does not necessarily go to those in need. The following illustrates the impact of total Federal social insurance expenditures—including Medicare and Railroad Retirement—on the "poverty gap" of elderly Americans. The poverty gap is the amount by which the incomes of elderly Americans are below the Government's official poverty level. In 1982, the elderly poor had incomes $44.1 billion below the poverty level, as summarized below:

Distribution of
Social Insurance
Benefits to the Elderly
($ Billions)

(1)	Poverty Gap of Elderly Poor Before Social Insurance (a)	$ 44.1
(2)	Poverty Gap of Elderly Poor After Social Insurance (a)	3.0
(3)	Net Impact on Elderly Poor	$ 41.1
(4)	Total Social Insurance Payments to Elderly	160.2
(5)	Payments to Elderly Not Affecting Elderly Poor	$119.1
(6)	Memo: Percent of Payments to Elderly Not Affecting Poor	74.3%

(a) The cumulative amount by which the incomes of the elderly are below the poverty level, i.e., not the average but the total amount by which individual incomes are below the poverty level.

The two previous tables show that approximately three-quarters of all social insurance payments to the elderly—mainly Social Security—are made to those above the poverty level. Since over three-quarters of all Social Security payments represent a subsidy, the three-quarters of Social Security payments in excess of contributions can be viewed as subsidies to elderly Americans above the poverty level.

PPSS recommendations are aimed at improving the efficiency of Social Security Administration (SSA) programs. Legitimate payments, as required by current law, will not be reduced as a result of our recommendations, which include the following:

• Reduce erroneous payments, which totalled approximately $14.6 billion over the FY 1980 to FY 1982 period.

- Close field offices which are no longer cost-effective.

- Restructure the disability appeals process.

- Simplify and condense the 25,000-page Program Operations Manual System.

Erroneous payments, even when ultimately identified and eventually repaid, are still costly. For example, assuming a 10% interest rate, the $14.6 billion estimated overpayments between 1980 and 1982 cost the Government $1.46 billion in interest.

Q. How did PPSS propose that this situation be corrected?

A. SSA already has the power to sharply reduce erroneous payments. To determine the amount for which a beneficiary is eligible, an Annual Earnings Test, showing the applicant's alternative sources of income, must be submitted. In general, overpayments do not result from inaccurate reporting of income, but because some beneficiaries fail to report income at all.

PPSS recommended two actions:

- SSA should computerize data on all Old Age and Survivors Insurance (OASI) beneficiaries aged 62 to 69, as well as on all Disability Insurance (DI) recipients, to monitor current earnings. This would allow more timely identification of overpayment to OASI beneficiaries and would also bring to light any Disability Insurance recipients who are working and are therefore, by definition, not eligible for DI payments.

- SSA should require prospective income estimates from beneficiaries so that benefits could be adjusted in a timely manner, thus reducing overpayments. To encourage accurate income estimating, SSA should exercise its current authority to charge interest on overpayments.

Q. How much would that save?

A. SSA could reduce costs by $2.977 billion and increase revenues by another $980 million over three years, a combined total of $3.957 billion—if PPSS recommendations were adopted.

In addition to the OASI and DI trust funds, SSA also administers Aid to Families with Dependent Children (AFDC) and Supplemental Security Income (SSI). The AFDC program is administered by the states, but the Federal Government, through SSA, pays for at least 50% of all costs of benefits plus administration. The average cost of administering the AFDC program at the state level varies from a low of $20 to a high of $126 per average monthly case load—a variance of 530%, i.e., the high is 6.3 times the low. The quality of administration also varies among states, with the Federal share of incorrect AFDC payments estimated at $370 million in

FY 1983. By law, the Federal Government is allowed to impose fiscal sanctions on states that have excessive payment error rates. However, under the current system, 1.5 to 2 years go by before the Federal Government collects this penalty, with resulting interest costs to the taxpayer.

In the Supplemental Security Income Program (SSI), the Federal Government gives states the option of either administering supplementary state contributions or having the Federal Government disburse the funds for them. SSI provides benefits to the aged, blind, and disabled. Twenty-seven states, including the District of Columbia, have elected to have the Federal Government administer these additional benefits. The Federal Government pays the states for erroneous payments made from these funds. However, the cost of calculating the Federal fiscal liability (FFL), i.e., the amount of erroneous payment made by the Federal Government or the cost of sampling payments for errors, is inordinately high relative to the total amount of state contributions. For example, in two of the 17 states where FFL determinations are calculated for SSI, Iowa and Delaware, sampling costs are 10% of total state SSI payments.

Q. What did PPSS recommend to correct these situations?

A. Where the Federal Government is obligated by law to pay 50% of all administrative and benefit costs, the SSA should more aggressively collect penalties from states and eliminate the current 1.5 to 2 year delay. In the SSI program, where the Federal Government administers the states' supplementary contribution, PPSS felt Federal fiscal liability for erroneous payment was unwarranted. If all PPSS recommendations are implemented, $147 million could be saved over three years.

In SSA's current field office system, there are 4,852 offices, 70% of which are contact stations manned by a staff of three to six employees who are expected to be well versed in all SSA programs. However, as the number and complexity of SSA administered programs has grown, this has become less and less possible. Moreover, PPSS found that the personal contacts made at these stations could be handled just as easily over the phone.

Q. How did PPSS recommend the situation be changed?

A. PPSS determined that 4,352, or 90%, of SSA field offices and contact stations could be consolidated into larger district offices, which would reduce personnel and overhead costs by $287 million over three years, or an amount equivalent to the Social Security taxes paid by 177,709 median income families in 1983.

Q. Why hasn't consolidation been effected in the past?

A. PPSS found that many SSA managers have submitted consolidation plans which have been rejected due to political considerations. Closing 4,352 offices in congressional districts across the Nation has political ramifications which tend to overwhelm the financial benefits no matter how obvious they may be.

While the PPSS review concentrated on major areas of potential savings, smaller, more specific possibilities in the Social Security Administration were also examined. For example, PPSS found that SSA's Program Operations System includes a 25,000 page manual that is maintained by approximately 45,000 recipients—SSA supervisors, claims analysts, etc. It is intended to cover all contingencies related to the processing of an SSA claim. To put the amount of paper involved in perspective, if all 45,000 recipients of this manual stacked their copies atop one another, the pile would be 34 miles high. There are 12,000 pages of revisions to this manual each year, which means 12,000 pages for each of 45,000 manuals, or 540 million pages per year that need to be replaced. (On average, each employee has to insert new pages at a rate of 60 pages per day.) Largely as a result of this manual, SSA printing and reproduction costs have increased at a rate of 12.5% per year in the decade from 1972 to 1982 to $21 million.

Q. How can this situation be corrected?

A. It was readily apparent to PPSS that all 45,000 recipients of this manual do not need the level of detail provided. PPSS recommended that a less detailed version of this manual of about 1,000 pages be distributed to most employees to handle day-to-day problems, while an unabridged version be distributed to about 2,000 supervisory employees.

PPSS estimated savings of $83 million over three years.

The current disability claims system needs improvement. A person denied a disability claim may appeal that decision 3 times within SSA, and another 3 times in the U.S. court system. The first two reviews within SSA are considered as if no previous decisions had been made.

Because cases are considered at each level independently and because inconsistent standards are applied at different levels of review, the reversal rate on decisions is high. At the second level of review, the Administrative Law Judge (ALJ) level, 60% of decisions are reversed. Claimants will naturally appeal adverse decisions if they have better than a 6 in 10 chance of obtaining a more favorable decision at progressively higher levels of review.

As a result of the high Administrative Law Judge reversal rate, the backlog of cases at this level has grown from 90,000 cases at the end of 1976 to 150,000 cases by 1982—an increase of 67%—and costs at this level of review alone have increased from $76 million in 1975 to an estimated $229 million in 1983.

Q. What is the explanation for the backlog and resulting cost increases?

A. This problem is largely the result of three factors:

(1) Inconsistencies in standards and criteria applied by the different review levels.

(2) Treatment of each review as a new case.

(3) Inability to make final decisions quickly.

Q. What did PPSS recommend to alleviate this problem?

A. The following summarizes PPSS recommendations:

(1) A uniform set of substantive laws, regulations, and rules should cover all levels of appeal.

(2) Appeals should not be handled as if no previous decision had been made. If a decision is reversed, each fact used in the determination at the initial level should be accepted or reversed.

(3) Administrative Law Judges should be able to issue quick summary affirmations of previous decisions. In addition, there should be no oral argument or testimony on disability claims.

(4) Finally, PPSS recommended that there be only one level of appeal within SSA, compared to three levels currently.

PPSS estimates such action would save $3.647 billion over three years.

FOOD STAMPS

The Food Stamp Program began in 1961 as a pilot project to provide supplemental nutritional assistance to families below the poverty line. In 1962, $14 million was spent on the program. In 1982, 20 years later, outlays exceeded $11 billion, summarized as follows:

Food Stamp Program

| | | (1) | (2) Number of | (3) |
	Fiscal Year	Outlays ($ millions)	Recipients (000)	Outlays per Recipient
(1)	1962	$ 14.0	143	$ 98
(2)	1982	11,014.1	21,717	507
(3)	Average Annual Percent Increase	39.6%	28.6%	8.6%
(4)	1982 as a Multiple of 1962	786.7X	151.9X	5.2X

During FY 1982, the program cost approximately $11.0 billion and paid benefits to almost 22 million people—about 10% of the total population. The rate of growth in outlays averaged 40% compounded annually, 1962-1982. Enrollment has grown 29% per year and average outlays per recipient increased from $98 in 1962 to $507 in 1982, approximately 5 times higher. After adjusting for grocery price inflation, average outlays per recipient were 1.7 times higher in 1982 than in 1962.

The Food Stamp Program is extremely large as measured in almost any context. For example, the Food and Nutrition Service (FNS), which administers the Food Stamp Program and other related nutrition programs, spent $15.2 billion in 1982, or 42% of the $36.2 billion total expenditures of the U.S. Department of Agriculture (USDA). FNS spending was almost twice as large as the sales of all McDonald's fast food stores throughout the world. The money spent on FNS programs is as large as the sales of Safeway Stores, the largest retail food chain in the United States.

FNS spending is expected to increase to $17.4 billion in 1983. If FNS were a country, and its expenditures were equivalent to GNP, the FNS would have approximately the 44th largest GNP in the world.

In reviewing the Food Stamp Program and other nutrition programs, PPSS concentrated on two major, interrelated problems:

1) Formulas for nutritional assistance to individuals and families are structured in such a way as to result in overlapping and duplicative benefits.

2) The Food Stamp Program has an excessively high error rate—10%, or about twice as high as Medicaid—attributable to an elaborate and complicated system for determining eligibility and distributing benefits.

PPSS recommended that changes be made in the Food Stamp Program to eliminate overlapping benefits provided by various Federal nutrition programs, and that unnecessary administrative expenses be reduced or eliminated. PPSS believes these objectives can be accomplished without adverse effect on the truly needy.

PPSS focused on the following procedural and administrative aspects of the Food Stamp program:

• updating the base for computing Food Stamp benefits;

• eliminating overlapping benefits from various nutrition programs;

• utilizing alternative Food Stamp distribution systems; and

• correcting administrative shortcomings of the program.

The Food and Nutrition Service (FNS) provides Food Stamp benefits through allotments or payments to qualified recipients. These payments are based on the FNS Thrifty Food Plan (TFP). The Thrifty Food Plan is a profile which determines the Food Stamp allotments necessary to meet a typical or average family's nutritional requirements. Currently, the base is a family of four consisting of a man and a woman (both 20-54 years old), one child 6-8 years old, and another 9-11 years old. The individual allotments for these four persons are added together, and this average family's food allotment is used to determine benefits. Benefits for smaller and larger households are calculated from this base, and are adjusted for differing family sizes by using economies of scale adjustment factors computed by FNS. Basically, these adjustment factors recognize that smaller households require more dollars per individual than larger households.

Q. What problems were identified by PPSS in the procedure for determining Food Stamp benefits?

A. Since the TFP base "family" was established in 1971, the average Food Stamp household has changed from the so-called "family of four" to only 2.6 persons. The system based on the outdated family of four should be redesigned to account for this demographic change.

PPSS recommended calculating a new weighted-average benefit *per person* by using the individual allotments and frequency distribution, i.e., participation by age/sex grouping tabulated by FNS and then multiplying it by four to create a weighted-average *family of four* that will serve as the new TFP base.

The TFP base allotment for a family of four, which consists of a man and a woman both 20-54 years old, a child 9-11 years old and a child 6-8 years old, total $253/month. PPSS proposed computing an individual allotment based on a weighted-average recipient profile. This average would be $237/month for a family of four.

This is a simple method and realistically reflects the individual characteristics of beneficiaries. Depending on family size, monthly benefits would be reduced by $4 to $28. Savings of $3.439 billion would accrue over a three-year period if this change were adopted.

Q. What else did PPSS recommend to reform benefit formulas?

A. PPSS also recommended changing the Thrifty Food Plan economies of scale adjustment factors. FNS applies those factors to the allotment of the base family of four to adjust for differing family sizes. The economies of scale factors in the TFP assume that large households have lower food costs per person than smaller households. Studies indicate this may be the result of food substitution as well as economies, and may also reflect the fact that smaller households simply consume larger quantities of food per person. PPSS recommended that adjustment factors be based on how people should, rather than how they do, spend their Food Stamp money.

Using results of a study on differences in purchasing power by family size, large households would gain $12 to $31 per month, but the more numerous small households would lose $7 to $8. Savings are expected to be $835 million over three years.

It is possible to meet the income eligibility requirements for the Food Stamp Progam and yet still have too much income to qualify for any Food Stamp benefits. However, minimum monthly Food Stamp benefits of $10 are provided to one- and two-member households even if their benefits calculate to zero. The minimum benefit was intended to increase the Food Stamp participation rates of the elderly, but it has not been successful. One- and two-person households that meet eligibility qualifications will receive $10 in Food Stamps even if their benefits calculate to zero. Currently, 240,000 households whose calculated benefit is zero are receiving the $10 minimum. An additional 195,000 one- and two-person households whose benefits should be between $1 and $9 receive the $10 minimum. PPSS recommended eliminating the $10 monthly minimum, for savings of *$138 million* over three years.

Q. Why hasn't the minimum benefit been successful in increasing the participation rate of the elderly?

A. Approximately 50% of the elderly who qualify for Food Stamps do not participate in the program, due to reluctance to undertake what is perceived to be the complex qualifying procedures. The elderly also frequently cite embarrassment and moral opposition as reasons for avoiding the program. Payment of minimum benefits does nothing to overcome these reasons for failure to participate.

Only 35% (1,466,000) of all one- and two-person households in the Food Stamp Program contain elderly persons. The remaining 65% (2,758,000) do not contain elderly individuals, but, if qualified, would be entitled to receive the $10 minimum benefit.

PPSS also recommended changes to eliminate the payment of overlapping benefits under the Food Stamp program and other nutrition programs offered by the USDA. The following table shows the expenditures of FNS by program:

FNS Outlays by Program—FY 1982

		(1) Amount ($ millions)	(2) As a % Of Total
(1)	Food Stamp Program	$11,014	72.5%
(2)	Child Nutrition Programs	3,020	19.9
(3)	Special Supplemental Food Programs (WIC)	930	6.1
(4)	Food Donations Program	121	0.8
(5)	Food Program Administration(a)	88	0.6
(6)	Special Milk Program	23	0.1
(7)	Total FNS Outlays	$15,196	100.0%

(a) Overall administrative expenses of the Food and Nutrition Service; the Federal portion of state administrative expenses are included in the totals for each program.

In addition to $11.0 billion spent on Food Stamps, spending on Child Nutrition Programs totalled $3.0 billion, or 20% of total FNS spending of $15.2 billion in 1982. Expenditures for Child Nutrition Programs include School Lunch, School Breakfast, Special Meal Assistance, Child Care Feeding, Summer Feeding, and other nutritional assistance and administrative expenses.

Special Supplemental Food Programs (WIC) outlays in 1982 were $930 million, or 6.1% of total FNS spending. These programs provide benefits to pregnant and breastfeeding women, infants, and children (WIC) who are at nutritional risk and have inadequate incomes.

PPSS examined child nutrition programs and recommended eliminating the overlapping benefits paid under various FNS programs.

Q. What specifically did PPSS recommend?

A. PPSS recommended elimination of the overlapping benefits provided by the School Lunch and Food Stamp Programs. Currently, Food Stamp laws do not take into account other Food and Nutrition Service programs, such as school lunches, when determining the Food Stamp benefit. In computing Food Stamp benefits, practically every other type of benefit provided by the Federal Government (e.g., Aid for Families with Dependent Children and Social Security) is included as income. Overlap of approximately $1.7 billion in benefits exists for children covered by school lunch and Food Stamp Programs. PPSS recommended including school lunch benefits as income when determining Food Stamp eligibility and benefits. This results in a Food Stamp benefit reduction of $7 per month per child, although each child would continue receiving $25 worth of food through the school lunch program. Savings of $1.724 billion are expected over three years.

In addition, PPSS recommended inclusion of other child nutrition benefits as income in calculating Food Stamp entitlements. As previously stated, current laws mandate that other child nutrition benefits, such as School Breakfast, Child Care Food, and the Summer Food Service Program, not be taken into account when determining Food Stamp eligibility. However, 69% of households in which children receive school breakfasts also receive school lunches and Food Stamps. PPSS recommended adding other FNS benefits as income when determining Food Stamp benefits, specifically, School Breakfast, Child Care Feeding, and Summer Feeding. Food Stamp benefits would be reduced by 30% of the value of child nutrition programs. Savings of $536 million are expected over three years.

Q. Why is PPSS advocating benefit cuts?

A. PPSS does not advocate cutting benefits to the truly needy. PPSS does, however, urge strong action to reduce the amount of benefits paid to those who do not require subsidies for their nutritional well being.

— 185 —

Of the total of 6,769,000 households receiving Food Stamps in 1980, 34.5% had incomes above the poverty line.

It should be noted that Food Stamps are only one element of means-tested benefits and, more specifically, of the non-cash or in-kind benefits available, e.g., housing assistance, Medicaid, etc.

Only 21.2% of Food Stamp households received Food Stamps alone, i.e., no other form of non-cash assistance. The majority of Food Stamp households—78.8%, or 5,337,000 in 1980—received additional forms of non-cash assistance. Further, of the 6,769,000 households receiving Food Stamps in 1980, 4,208,000 households, or 62.2%, also received public assistance in cash in the form of Supplemental Security Income (SSI), Aid to Families with Dependent Children (AFDC), or other cash assistance.

The Food Stamp Program has suffered from widespread and highly publicized abuse. Federal estimates of erroneous payments are about 10% of total program costs. This high error rate is primarily attributable to the complex benefit formula, administrative difficulties due to complicated eligibility requirements, and an inadequate delivery system for distributing benefits.

FNS prints and distributes food coupons to the states and monitors participation in the program by retail food outlets and other eligible establishments. Although funding and eligibility requirements come from the Federal Government, the program is administered at the state and local levels. In general, Federal and state Governments share expenses equally for administering the program. Exceptions to this 50-50 match include higher Federal payments (75%) for establishing automated systems and fraud-control activities.

By providing benefits in the form of food coupons to ensure that recipients purchase food, an elaborate system has been developed. These distribution systems include ATP (Authorization to Participate) cards, direct mail, direct pick-up, and on-line computer authorization. The potential for theft and fraud is greater in ATP and direct mail distribution systems than with the use of checks because coupons provide a less effective paper trail.

The following shows the proportion of benefits delivered by each method:

Distribution of Food Stamps

		% of Total Benefits
(1)	An authorization to receive Stamps is delivered by mail (ATP)	59%
(2)	Stamps are delivered by mail	26
(3)	Direct pick-up and other distribution of Stamps	15
(4)	Total	100%

In the ATP (Authorization to Participate) method participants receive a card (ATP) through the mail which entitles them to Food Stamps. The card can be redeemed at an eligible distribution center such as a bank or the local project office for Food Stamp coupons.

According to the FNS, 9.75% of the dollar value of Food Stamp benefits are erroneous payments. This breaks down as follows:

(1)	Certification of ineligible recipients	4.61%
(2)	Overissuance of benefits to eligible recipients	5.14
(3)	Total error rate	9.75%

Based on FY 1981 Food Stamp expenditures of $10.7 billion excluding administrative costs, errors resulted in estimated losses of over $1 billion.

Error rates in the Food Stamp Program of 9.75% are high in comparison to other programs such as Medicaid and AFDC (Aid to Families with Dependent Children):

		(1)	(2)
			Food Stamps as a Multiple of
		Error Rate	Other Programs
(1)	Food Stamps	9.8%	1.0X
(2)	AFDC	7.3	1.3
(3)	Medicaid	4.1	2.4

The high level of erroneous payments in the Food Stamp Program results, in part, from the complex eligibility requirements. Equally important, however, is the fact that states do not suffer financial losses from these overpayment errors, since funding comes from the Federal Government. Because states share 50% of the administrative expense, any efforts to improve eligibility certification, and thus reduce errors, may result in higher state expenditures. There is very little incentive for states to reduce these errors because of the potentially higher administrative costs that may be incurred.

Q. How can $1 billion in Food Stamps, or 10% of the total, be erroneously paid?

A. Most errors result from poor state and local administration. New York City, for example, issued 27,000 replacement ATP cards in a single month without checking or verifying that the original cards were not in use.

Q. How do some people qualify when they shouldn't?

A. Some recipients understate their income and overstate family size to increase their allotment of stamps. Cheats have also concocted phony names, worn disguises, invented entire families, and collected benefits for years from more than one welfare office, county or state. For example, between April and September 1981, a Minneapolis man was on the Food Stamp rolls of 13 counties in Iowa, Minnesota, North and South Dakota, and Wisconsin.

Much of this fraud goes undetected because most welfare offices lack facilities to verify claims.

Q. What's being done to mitigate abuses of the Food Stamp Program?

A. In 1980, Congress enacted 14 anti-fraud provisions. However, it took the FNS nearly two years to implement all the anti-fraud measures.

Specifically, where computers were used to match lists of Food Stamp recipients with tax and unemployment rolls, more fraud indictments and convictions were obtained. As a result of computer matching, 83 convictions were made in Memphis. In Los Angeles, over 1,600 cases of potential fraud are identified every month by computer matching. According to a regional inspector of the USDA:

> The court system can't accommodate the hundreds of cases we have under review. But indictment puts cheats on notice that we are serious about going after fraud.

In certain areas, recipients must present I.D.'s with photographs in order to receive Food Stamps.

Also, all states are required to check information from tax or unemployment offices against Food Stamp rolls. States must also require that Food Stamp households report monthly on changes in family size and income.

In addition, experiments are now under way to use a magnetically encoded photo I.D. card that can be checked through a central computer to make sure that the holder receives the proper Food Stamp allotment.

Q. There are a number of alternatives to distributing Food Stamps that have been suggested. What did PPSS recommend?

A. PPSS recommended that pilot projects aimed at developing alternatives to Food Stamps as a means of providing nutritional assistance be continued on an accelerated basis. Some of these projects include the cash-out approach (direct payment of cash instead of coupons), electronic benefit transfers, and block grant programs. Although savings have not been quantified, the successful development of a better distribution system would reduce improper benefit (i.e., fraud, abuse, and errors) and reduce administrative costs.

In the area of administration, PPSS recommended the establishment of a Combined Welfare Administration (CWA) which would reduce costs by providing an umbrella agency to distribute benefits and administer programs such as AFDC, Medicaid, and Food Stamps.

The average monthly cost per case by program varies widely by state. For example, from state to state the average monthly cost per case ranges from a low of $9 to a high of $94 in the Food Stamp program. This compares to $20-$126 in the AFDC program and $18-$91 in the Medicaid program. Combining welfare programs under a single agency would reduce administrative costs.

In addition, using computer models would enhance the ability of state and local officials to verify recipient-supplied information. This would reduce the costs associated with increased participation in other programs. Computer models would greatly facilitate the use of a central data bank so states could obtain information on a particular applicant at one point. This would be accomplished by permitting disclosure of wage data maintained by Social Security and the IRS. Use of Social Security numbers and copies of income tax returns should be a condition of eligibility for these programs. The use of standardized data would ensure that income verification procedures are consistent throughout all localities and that information is used efficiently. Results from pilot projects that utilize computer matching yield benefit/cost ratios as high as 20:1.

As discussed above in the Overview, PPSS recommended consolidating benefit programs and integrating reporting systems so that total benefits provided to subsidy recipients can be determined.

To summarize, current Food Stamp benefits are subject to waste, fraud, and abuse; overlap other nutrition programs; and are difficult to administer. Revising the benefit formula, eliminating overlapping benefits, and reducing erroneous payments will not only save money but also help redirect aid to those who still suffer nutritionally.

HEALTH CARE

Total U.S. health care expenditures have grown 8 times from $41.7 billion in 1965 to $322.4 billion in 1982, or by 12.8% per year—an increase of $280.7 billion, or $16.5 billion per year. This growth rate in total health care expenditures was about 40% faster than the overall economic growth rate of 9.2% in total GNP. Consequently, health care costs have absorbed a larger and larger portion of total GNP, increasing from 4.4% in 1950 to 6.0% in 1965 and 10.5% in 1982.

Based on population trends and expected advances in technology, it seems likely that total U.S. health care expenditures will continue to grow considerably faster than the total economy. Based on present Government financing arrangements, this would, in effect, tie Government health care expenditures to a dynamic growth industry, since the Federal, state, and local Governments pay for a substantial share of total health care costs. In 1982, Federal Government spending financed 28.9% of total U.S. health care costs, and state and local Governments another 13.5%.

Thus, tax levy funds financed 42.4% of the country's total $322.4 billion health care bill, or $136.7 billion.

Tying Government expenditures to the dynamic health care sector has, of course, led to a rapid increase in Federal expenditures. From a base of $5.5 billion in 1965, Federal expenditures on health care increased to $93.1 billion by 1982, up 16.9 times, or by 18.1% per year. These increased Federal expenditures played a crucial role in extending medical insurance coverage to population groups needing improved health care—particularly the poor through Medicaid and elderly and disabled people through Medicare—and in promoting scientific research which has contributed to advances in medical technology.

However, over the long term, it would not seem to be desirable to continue to tie together Federal spending and health care expenditures under the present reimbursement financing arrangements. The current system raises several key long-term issues:

- What can be done to address the fiscal problems caused by rapid growth in health care spending?

- How can Federal budget problems be addressed without destroying the fundamental social, economic, and technological advances which underlie growth in health care expenditures?

Potential savings of $28.9 billion are the estimated results of proposed long-term changes in Federal health care financing and reimbursement systems.

The key factors underlying these expected savings are changes in Federal programs intended to create effective competitive markets for the delivery of health care by:

- Increasing the latitude of *consumer choice* in making decisions on the scope of health insurance coverage and treatment plans.

- Creating profit/(loss) incentives for providers to undertake the *competitive bidding risks* involved in making financial commitments to deliver health care to the beneficiaries of Federal programs.

Q. PPSS proposed long-term reforms in Federal health care financing systems which target savings of $28.9 billion over three years. What are the major changes proposed versus current Federal spending practices?

A. PPSS recommended that Federal spending on all health care programs be controlled by a ''prospective'' budgeting system based on the following key elements:

- Total Federal spending on all health care programs combined should be limited to yearly spending increases which do not exceed the overall growth rate in the total U.S. economy.

- Within this budget constraint, the available Federal dollars would be allocated to each Federal program based on the number of persons served by Medicare and Medicaid in each region. Per capita spending rates may differ among programs.

- Federal funds made available for each program would be used to finance the medical care needs of the populations served by means which promote competitive bidding and the development of effective markets for health care. A primary means for doing this would be the use of prepaid health plans, such as Health Maintenance Organizations (HMOs) and vouchers, which provide for the total health care needs of their participants.

Total health care expenditures, as noted, have risen from $41.7 billion in 1965 to $322.4 billion in 1982, an increase of 12.8% per year. Meanwhile, Federal spending on health care has grown from $5.5 billion in 1965 to $93.1 billion in 1982, up 18.1% per year; up from 13.2% of total national health care expenditures in 1965 to 28.9% in 1982.

Q. What has accounted for the increased expenditures on health care on both the national and Federal levels?

A. Increased expenditures on health care have resulted from many factors, e.g., general inflation, health care price inflation in excess of general inflation, population growth, increased usage of health care services per person, rapidly changing medical technology, and the intensity of medical services provided.

Q. Why hasn't there been more consumer resistance to rapidly escalating health care costs?

A. Most consumers have been insulated from much of the rising cost of health care through third party insurance coverage. Private and Government insurance reimbursement, e.g., Medicare and Medicaid, pay for 88% of total hospital care and 63% of doctors' services and about 70% of all medical care. Most reimbursement rates are essentially based on costs, another inflationary factor. In addition, doctors, hospitals, and other providers get paid usually on a fee-for-service basis, i.e., for each treatment. Thus, costs are on a piecework basis, and encourage delivery of more services, for which consumers are usually covered.

Q. What does the word "prospective" mean as applied to health care reimbursement and/or budgeting?

A. Prospective means setting the reimbursement rate and/or the total amount to be spent at the beginning of a period. Thus, prospective means setting the financial limits *before* the expenditure takes place.

This approach can be used as a powerful restraint on health care costs, as compared with the present practice of basing reimbursement rates and total spending on costs. In other words, a prospective system of budgeting would do away with inflationary, open-ended spending resulting from the reimbursement of costs.

Q. Isn't this same objective met by the expanded use of Diagnosis Related Groups (DRGs)?

A. New regulations were recently passed which required the Secretary of Health and Human Services (HHS) to establish prices for inpatient hospital stays of Medicare patients. Prices are set for 470 Diagnosis Related Groups (DRGs). Each hospital stay will be classified into one of these 470 DRGs, based on the principal diagnosis or illness treated during a given episode. Thus, for Medicare, the Secretary will be setting the price paid to the hospital for every type of illness, in every part of the U.S. Similar approaches are being considered for setting other types of third-party hospital and doctor fees.

PPSS has endorsed the prospective rate system being implemented for Medicare and recommended that it be extended to other forms of hospital care and doctors' fees. PPSS continues to support these initiatives as a short-term response to what is perceived to be a financial budget crisis. However, in the longer term, the key effort will need to be directed at correcting the underlying causes of medical care inflation and, with it, the replacement of cost-based, fixed-rate pricing.

While DRGs are a step in the right direction, they are still a cost-based reimbursement system. In order to more effectively restrain health care costs, control will have to be placed on per capita usage and wider and intensive use of medical technology. As documented and noted further on, most of the increase in health care expenditures in excess of inflation has resulted from increased volume and technological complexity of medical services rendered, not health care prices rising at rates faster than inflation. During the period 1960-1982, health care expenditures rose from $26.9 billion to $322.4 billion, an increase of $295.5 billion. While general inflation accounted for 46.6% of the increase, health care increases in excess of general inflation accounted for only 9.2%. Increased usage and technology accounted for 44.2%.

Q. Why aren't DRGs the long-term solution to rising health care costs?

A. Hospitals will be forced to "unbundle" all or most of the multiple diagnoses now treated during single hospital admissions. This will increase costs, decrease efficiency, and may lead to unnecessary multiple admissions. Also, even where a single illness is the cause of an admission, the elderly and poor may experience the adverse

— 192 —

effects of the financial pressures on hospitals to reduce lengths-of-stay under the DRG system.

Q. Why won't price constraints be enough to control costs?

A. Because about 70% to 80% of the increase in health care costs over the period from the mid-1960's to 1982, in excess of the general inflation rate, was due to increased usage in real terms and new technology, not price inflation. This is summarized in the following table:

		(1)	(2)	(3)
			Health Care Expenditure Increases in Excess of General Inflation	
	Portion of Total Cost Increase Due To:	1960–1982 Increase	1965–1982 Increase	1975–1982 Increase
(1)	Health Care Price Increases in Excess of General Inflation	17.3%	19.8%	27.3%
(2)	Volume of Usage and Technology	82.7	80.2	72.7
(3)	Total	100.0%	100.0%	100.0%

The key point is that in order to restrain the growth in health care expenditures over the period since 1960, it would have been necessary to reduce the volume of services provided and the use of new technology, not health care prices alone.

Q. But wouldn't price constraints have discouraged usage and the diffusion of new technology?

A. Very likely. For example, if this had been done over the period since the 1960's, in order to have made a major impact on total health care costs, Federally set price constraints may have had to substantially reduce the usage of seven major new technologies which accounted for an estimated 30%-35% of the increase in real health care costs in excess of general inflation. These seven new technologies which have been introduced into medical practice in the late fifties and early sixties are listed in the table on the next page.

To effectively contain costs in the period 1965-1982, Federal regulators would have had to set prices to discourage the use of these seven new technologies and other forms of real usage.

The PPSS recommendations reflect the efficiency of free markets in accomplishing complex resource allocations.

In summary, PPSS recommended the following long-term improvements in Federal budgeting practices for health care spending:

Est. 1982 Hospital
Costs
($ Millions)

End stage renal disease treatment—dialysis and kidney transplants	$ 1,600
New diagnostic imaging—CAT scanning, nuclear medicine and ultrasound	3,430
Neonatal intensive care	2,100
Major cardiac surgery—bypass, valve and pacemaker installation	4,615
Hip and other joint replacements	1,680
Adult intensive care (ICU & CCU)	6,775
Inpatient parenteral nutrition	225
Total Seven Technologies	$20,425

- Restricting Federal Government spending on health care to a rate of increase in line with the overall growth rate of the U.S. economy.

- The goals of the major Federal entitlement programs would remain in force, for example, to ensure an acceptable and adequate level of health care coverage for the elderly, poor, and disabled. However, the Federal Government would be charged with the mission of accomplishing these basic goals within the budget restraint of increasing Federal expenditures no faster than the overall economic growth rate.

In addition to PPSS recommendations concerning long-term improvements in Federal health care financing through Medicare/Medicaid reimbursement, PPSS has analyzed other areas for improving Federal health care administration, as follows:

- *Excess hospital bed capacity* in both private and Veterans Administration (VA) facilities, which results in duplication of services and staff. VA hospitals operate at 75% of capacity, and some of the patients don't require intensive care hospitalization, but rather long-term care or outpatient treatment. The average hopital stay in a VA facility is 21 days compared to 7.2 days in a private hospital. There is a definite need for better planning and resource allocation in VA health care facilities. In addition, liberal reimbursement from Medicare and Medicaid for hospital construction encourages hospitals to build additional excess capacity. Hospitals can finance 50% or more of construction with debt capital from Medicare or Medicaid.

- *Duplicate payments in the Department of Defense (DOD), VA and Indian Health Service (IHS).* It is estimated that 15%-20% of all VA and IHS medical claims result in duplicate or erroneous payments—the same service is paid for twice, payment is made for unauthorized service, or service is billed to a third party such as Medicare. The DOD pays up to 80% of the health care costs of military dependents through the Civilian Health and Medical Program of the Uniformed Services (CHAMPUS). However, many persons eligible for CHAM-

PUS are also eligible for private health care cost coverage. The DOD does not actively pursue private insurers to regain the cost of medical care, even though it is, by law, the payor of last resort.

- *Duplicate facilities and services managed by each branch of the military and by the VA.* As currently structured, the Army, Navy, and Air Force each maintain separate hospital and medical service facilities under DOD's Military Health Care System (MHCS). The MHCS operates 161 hospitals and 310 outpatient clinics. In addition, the VA operates 172 hospitals, 276 outpatient clinics and 109 nursing and domiciliary care facilities. Both the VA and MHCS systems are underutilized and duplicative, and budgeted expenditures have increased over 400% over the past decade to $11.5 billion in FY 1983.

PPSS recommendations to improve efficiency of Federally administered health care can save $10.975 billion over three years. Major recommendations included the following:

- *Limit future excess hospital capacity* by restricting incentives to expand. Develop regulations that allow payments for closing or converting current excess capacity; limit reimbursement for interest and depreciation for underutilized hospitals; make construction financing less attractive. Cost savings are estimated to be $939 million over three years. In addition, the VA should convert its excess hospital capacity to long-term care facilities, substitute less costly outpatient care where appropriate and transfer patients who no longer require acute care to nursing homes.

- *Use fiscal intermediaries to process VA and IHS insurance claims.* Medicare and private sector claims are processed through a computerized system which automatically screens applicants to eliminate duplication. Fiscal intermediaries can process VA and IHS claims through a computer which will coordinate benefits across all medical claims programs, uncover duplication and significantly cut the cost of processing. Savings are estimated to be $1.131 billion over three years. In addition, to recover costs under the Civilian Health and Medical Program of the Uniformed Services (CHAMPUS), treatment and admission forms should be revised to include questions concerning health insurance coverage, and the DOD should actively pursue third party payors to recapture the cost of providing health care for military dependents with duplicate coverage. The Federal Government could recover $1.211 billion in costs over three years by adopting this recommendation.

- *Promote shared resources between the VA and the DOD* to minimize duplication and underuse of health facilities and personnel. These agencies could conceivably halve their costs by avoiding duplication.

Excess capacity results in duplication of services and staff, which drives up cost. In addition, excess capacity results in unnecessary utilization—admittance to the hospital though the illness doesn't really require hospitalization, or hospital stays that are longer than necessary.

A steady increase in capacity despite declining occupancy rates suggests an overbuilding of capacity during the last 15 years. In 1969, the occupancy rate was 78.8%, in 1980 that rate was 75.4%, a decline of (3.4)%. Even though utilization has been dropping, capacity has been increasing.

Excess hospital beds across the U.S. have been estimated to range from 68,887 to 264,000, and it is also estimated that each of these beds costs $33,281 annually—all of which must be covered in hospital charges to occupied beds. That means everyone is paying more for a hospital stay because of excess capacity.

Q. Why do hospitals build more capacity when the current capacity is underutilized?

A. Guaranteed reimbursement by Medicare and Medicaid of interest, depreciation, and amortized construction costs is the single most important incentive to build new, but unneeded, capacity. Hospitals can finance 50% or more of construction with debt capital from Medicare and Medicaid.

Q. That seems to be counterproductive. What did PPSS recommend to reduce this excess capacity and halt additional unnecessary construction?

A. PPSS recommendations were aimed primarily at limiting future excess capacity by restricting incentives to expand. First, develop regulations that allow payments to hospitals for closing or converting underutilized capacity—such hospitals are actually penalized under the current system. Second, limit reimbursement for interest and depreciation at hospitals where capacity falls below 85%.

PPSS also made recommendations aimed at halting new capacity by making financing less attractive, such as:

• Debt ratios for hospital construction of 80% or more are not uncommon. While it is unrealistic to penalize current indebtedness, standards for future debt levels should be incorporated into Medicare/Medicaid reimbursement formulas.

• Establish interest cost maximums in relation to the prime lending rate to finance new capital debt.

Q. How much would be saved by closing down excess capacity and limiting financing for new construction?

A. PPSS estimated cost savings of $939 million and revenue increases of $662 million over three years.

Q. Could the problems PPSS found in VA planning and resource allocation be elaborated?

A. The budget of the VA health care system has grown from $1.7 billion in 1970 to over $7 billion in 1983. Bed capacity—the number of beds available—has declined by 25% since 1966; but, even with declining capacity, the VA hospitals are operating at only 75% of capacity. And a large proportion of that capacity utilization may be unnecessary—patients' stays in VA hospitals average 21 days compared to 7.2 days in private hospitals. Some of these patients don't need hospitalization but long-term care facilities, and some could be treated at a lower cost as outpatients.

PPSS recommended that VA adopt case-mix/resource allocation and planning processes—i.e., minimize the length of stay for inpatient care, substitute less costly outpatient care for services which do not require hospitalization, and transfer patients who no longer need an acute level of medical and nursing care to less costly nursing homes. In addition, the VA should convert underutilized hospitals to long-term care facilities. Savings are estimated at $4.888 billion over three years.

It is estimated that 15–20% of all Veterans Administration (VA) and Indian Health Service (IHS) medical claims result in duplicate or erroneous payments—the same service paid for twice, payment made for unauthorized service, or service also billed to a third party, such as Medicare.

Duplicate payments persist because there are no procedures to identify patients with dual eligibility, and no efficient procedure for authorization of payments. To stop duplication, these two situations have to be rectified.

Q. How do you identify persons with dual eligibility?

A. The best way is to use a compatible computer system for all health care programs and identify patients by Social Security numbers. The key is shared information among the programs.

Q. Are medical programs—Medicare, private insurers, Medicaid, VA and IHS —computerized now?

A. Medicare and private sector claims are processed through a computerized system, and are automatically screened to eliminate duplication. The VA and IHS process claims manually, a very costly procedure. Currently, it costs VA up to $140 and IHS as much as $200 to process a claim. Private insurance companies and fiscal intermediaries expend about $6 per claim. A computer system compatible with Medicare is one solution to these high costs, but a more efficient solution is to use fiscal intermediaries (FIs).

Q. What are fiscal intermediaries?

A. Fiscal intermediaries (FIs) are private sector insurance processing firms with the computer capability to process claims and uncover duplication. Utilizing FIs would enable VA and IHS to impose safeguards, conduct pre- and post-audits, and coordinate benefits across all medical claims programs. PPSS estimated potential savings from reduced processing costs and elimination of duplication of $1.131 billion over three years—that's equivalent to the annual medical care costs of one million lower income retired couples in 1981, or 450,000 average hospital stays ($2,500 per stay).

DOD's Military Health Care System (MHCS) is comprised of the three separate hospital systems of the Army, Navy, and Air Force. The MHCS operates 161 hospitals and 310 outpatient clinics staffed with 151,000 personnel throughout the world. The total direct health care budget for FY 1983 was $4.5 billion. VA is a multifaceted health care system that provides a broad range of health services to an aging veteran population. The VA hospital system is characterized by inordinate length-of-stay averages that imply a large number of long-term patients occupying acute-care beds. PPSS recommended that VA and the Department of Defense (DOD) share their health resources. In addition both VA and DOD should improve their procedures for recovering medical costs from third party payors.

Q. What are the savings from sharing resources?

A. PPSS didn't quantify savings for this issue, but these agencies could conceivably halve their costs by avoiding duplication. The essential aspect of sharing health resources is the ability to more readily operate medical facilities at an effective occupancy rate, which would limit costly construction of new facilities and be a significant step toward a well-planned, consistent health policy.

Q. PPSS also recommended that VA and DOD improve procedures to collect medical costs from third party payors. Is this an example of dual eligibility problems?

A. Yes. There are many persons eligible for DOD and VA health care who also are eligible for other health cost coverage—military dependents, inactive military personnel and veterans. In fact, in 1981, only 33% of DOD hospital admissions were active duty personnel. The other 67% were dependents of active, retired and deceased military personnel.

Q. If the DOD doesn't provide hospital care for military dependents, who does?

A. Private medical care is available through the Civilian Health and Medical Program of the Uniformed Services (CHAMPUS). CHAMPUS assists eligible beneficiaries by reimbursing up to 80% of the cost of such care, depending on the type of beneficiary and applicable deductibles. However, unlike direct care provided to inactive beneficiaries, CHAMPUS is, by law, the last payor of this medical care. Thus, when a beneficiary is covered by private health insurance, the private insurance carrier is obligated to pay for such medical care. CHAMPUS, in turn, reimburses the beneficiary for any cost remaining after the applicable deductible has been satisfied.

Q. What PPSS concluded was that private health insurance and CHAMPUS cover military dependent hospital costs in private hospitals, but not in military hospitals. Is that correct?

A. Yes. But one of the main reasons is simply that DOD doesn't pursue third party payors when care is provided in military hospitals.

Q. What did PPSS recommend to collect funds from private insurers for care given in military hospitals?

A. PPSS recommended revising military health care system treatment and admission forms to include questions concerning health insurance coverage, revising DOD procedures to include recovery from privately insured inactive beneficiaries, proposing legislation to prohibit insurance company exclusionary clauses and developing a cost system that reflects the real cost of medical care.

Q. How much could be recovered in military medical expense by implementing PPSS recommendations?

A. PPSS estimated that the Federal Government can recover $1.211 billion in costs over three years.

The three-year total of all the recommendations in this section, after elimination of duplication and overlap among issues, is $115.361 billion—equal to the three-year taxes of 17.3 million median income families.

Government Lending Programs

PPSS reviewed the Federal Government's management of its lending programs and associated debt collection activities. Government lending programs are geared toward loan origination rather than loan management which is reflected in unacceptably high default rates in comparison to private sector standards. Despite these default levels, the magnitude of Federal credit supplied continues to increase—outstanding loans have increased by $307.7 billion or 45.5%, 1981-1984, from $676.3 billion to $984.0 billion.

PPSS recommended that loan program priorities be shifted from loan origination to loan management by providing increased incentives to Government loan officers to reduce defaults, by expanding the use of private sector collection agencies and reducing Federal direct lending by increasing the ratio of guaranteed-to-direct lending.

In FY 1983, the Government spent $31.1 billion in the specific areas covered by PPSS recommendations, with spending estimated to increase to $90.8 billion by the year 2000 if present policies are continued. Implementing PPSS recommendations would reduce spending to $29.4 billion in 2000, a saving of $61.4 billion, or 67.6%.

Direct and guaranteed loans outstanding under Federal lending programs are approaching *$1 trillion*, as follows:

Loans Outstanding Under
Federal Lending Programs
($ Billions)

		(1)	(2)	(3)	(4)
		Direct Loans			
	Fiscal Year	*Federal On & Off Budget*	*Government Sponsored Enterprises*	*Federally-Guaranteed Loans*	*Total Credit Outstanding Under Federal Programs*
(1)	1981	$185.0	$182.3	$309.0	$676.3
(2)	1982	207.8	225.6	331.2	764.6
(3)	1983E	227.4	281.1	387.0	895.5
(4)	1984B	210.9	337.3	435.8	984.0
	Average Annual Percent Increase				
(5)	1981–1984B	4.5%	22.8%	12.1%	13.3%

Direct lending by the Government starts out the same way as direct lending by a commercial bank—someone applies for a loan and is either accepted or denied—but that's where the similarity ends. Generally, interest rates on Federal loans are substantially below market rates, e.g., the average interest rate on the Farmers Home Administration's (FmHA) $20 billion housing loan portfolio is only 2.7%. New FmHA housing loan rates are 11 7/8%, which compares to current mortgage rates in the private sector of 13% to 14%. In addition, loan officer performance criteria in the Government are quite different from those applied to a private sector loan officer. In the Government, it's the number of loans in an employee's portfolio. In the private sector, it's how well the loans perform. To illustrate how these differing viewpoints affect loan quality, using FmHA as an example, 43% of its farm loans are delinquent, more than 10 times the average delinquency rate in the private sector.

The Government's loan programs perform poorly for several reasons. First, loan quality is not the foremost concern in the public sector. Indeed, many Federal lending programs establish as a prerequisite the denial of credit by a private sector lender. Second, once the Government's loan officers make a loan, its repayment is not nearly as important to them as it would be to a private sector lender. For example, when a loan made by the Department of Housing and Urban Development (HUD) is delinquent, HUD usually makes three attempts each year to collect the money, while in the private sector 24-36 attempts are made. In part, because the private sector is more aggressive in collecting its delinquent receivables, its success rate is 80%-85%, while the success rate of the Government is only 15%-20%.

Federal lending by on- and off-budget agencies is fairly straightforward. Not so clear are the lending activities of Government-sponsored enterprises. These agencies were created by the Government to fulfill specified credit functions—e.g., the Farm Credit Administration—and later to become "privately" owned. Privately owned means their activities are no longer controlled by the Government. However, these enterprises still carry out Federally-designed programs and receive special benefits from their close association with the Government, such as tax exemptions—the enterprises are exempt from Federal income taxes, and interest on their debt securities is exempt from state and local income taxes. Because of these special benefits and because these enterprises are perceived as being backed by the Government, they can generally borrow funds at rates only slightly higher than those of the Treasury. The Government estimates that these advantages save the enterprises one to three percentage points on their cost of borrowing.

While the Reagan Administration has attempted to control the growth of its direct lending programs, Government-sponsored enterprises have increased their loan portfolios by 22.8% per year, 1981-1984, to a budgeted $337 billion in FY 1984—1.6 times the level of total Federal direct loans outstanding. PPSS recommended that these enterprises go fully private, e.g., be taxed, to disassociate themselves from the Federal Government. To encourage this action, PPSS recommended institution of a fee which would increase each year that an enterprise continues to use the special privileges currently afforded. Ultimately, this change would put Government-sponsored lending on an equal footing with private sector lending in its ability to raise funds.

The third Federal credit program is Federally-guaranteed lending. This is an increasingly popular way for the Federal Government to provide credit to selected sectors of the economy, primarily for two reasons. First, it does not require the up-front use of Federal funds and, second, it reduces the overall risk to the Government. In loan guarantee programs, a private sector lender provides the money for the loan. The Federal Government then makes itself liable for the guaranteed portion of the loan if the borrower defaults. The private sector lender benefits because it has made a very low-risk loan and the Government benefits because it has not tied up its funds.

PPSS has made recommendations that would improve all three types of Federal credit programs. For example, PPSS recommended that interest rates on new direct Government loans be tied to the Treasury cost of borrowing.

Q. How would that reduce costs to the Government?

A. Currently, the Government may borrow in short-term markets—with more volatile interest rates—and use the money to fund loan programs such as Veterans Administration mortgages which may have 30-year maturities. As interest rates climbed in the 1970's, the spread between the Government's cost of borrowing and the interest rates on its loans widened, resulting in huge unanticipated costs and violating a basic banking principle—"never borrow short and lend long." PPSS recommended that the Government match the maturities and interest rates of its lending to those of its borrowing.

Q. How much difference would this change make?

A. PPSS estimates that it would generate $2.371 billion in additional interest revenue over three years. Revenues would increase in subsequent years as more and more loans are adjusted to higher interest rates.

Q. Did PPSS find loan programs which would be better administered by the private sector?

A. PPSS found that the Government was generally ill-suited to administer loans in comparison to private-sector lenders. Specifically, Farmers Home Administration direct loans and business loans made by the Small Business Administration should be phased out and replaced by guaranteed loan programs. Savings: $1.826 billion over three years.

At the same time these programs are being phased out, PPSS recommended that all other direct loan programs be reviewed for possible conversion to guaranteed loans.

Q. Should the Government be in the loan business at all?

A. As stated previously, the Government is the lender of last resort. When other sources of credit are unavailable, it makes loans to selected eligible borrowers. However, at the earliest time that loans prove to be viable, they should be transferred ("graduated") to the private sector. In this way, the Government ceases all its administrative responsibility for as well as any risk associated with the loan.

This action rarely takes place as planned for several reasons. Of most importance is the lower interest on most Government loans. Although interest rates rose during the 1970's, Federal loan rates generally did not adjust. As a result, Federal loans became more and more popular—the less the adjustment, the greater the popularity. This can be seen in the amount of Farmers Home Administration (FmHA) loans outstanding, which rose from $6.5 billion in 1970 to $58 billion in 1982—up 8.9 times in only twelve years. Another indicator of the popularity of Government loans is that 70% of borrowers from FmHA are not farmers. Remember FmHA is the Farmers Home Administration.

Q. What can be done?

A. One alternative, as mentioned previously, is for FmHA to guarantee loans only. In this way, loan administration as well as part of the risk would be transferred to the private sector. Another alternative that PPSS recommended is a firm policy that, for each loan made by the FmHA, one of its outstanding loans must be graduated, i.e., it must be sold to a private sector lender. Graduation would be on a loan for loan basis regardless of dollar amount. This would result in combined administrative and interest cost savings of $768 million over three years.

Q. PPSS recommended that Government-sponsored enterprises pay a fee for the special privileges that are now granted. Why is this recommendation being made if loans made by the agencies are not backed by the Government?

A. PPSS found these enterprises increased their lending 5.1 times faster than direct lending by the Government over the 1981-1984B period. Providing these agencies with easy access to lower cost credit distorts markets in favor of their activites, including home mortgages, student loans, and farm credit.

Q. What will happen to Government-sponsored enterprises if the PPSS recommendation that they go fully private is implemented?

A. They would become like any other financial institution with the same costs and the same opportunities to raise funds. In addition, until they go fully private, the Government would gain estimated revenues of $724 million over three years from the "special privileges" fee which was discussed previously.

Q. Guaranteeing lending programs appears to be a safe way for the Government to target credit. What did PPSS recommend in this area?

A. By guaranteeing a loan, the Government is agreeing to pay some portion of the principal, up to 100%, if the borrower defaults. Generally, the Federally-guaranteed portion is 90%. In addition, although it is common practice for private sector lenders to charge loan origination fees or points for loans made, there is no standard loan origination fee in the various Government lending programs.

PPSS believes that if Federal guarantees were lowered from 90% to a maximum of 75%, the benefits would be twofold. First, this would decrease Federal exposure on guaranteed loans. Second, it would provide the lender with greater incentive to collect on loans that are delinquent, by making the lender responsible for a greater portion of the loan principal.

Q. As of September 30, 1982, $6.5 billion, or 16.7%, of the $38.9 billion in Federal loans which were classified as current receivables on that date were delinquent. What can be done to improve debt collection efforts?

A. As part of an overall effort to improve the management of all Government receivables, the following actions are recommended:

   1. Develop uniform definitions for terms such as debt, delinquent debt, allowance for doubtful accounts, and write-offs. Establish allowances for potentially uncollectable accounts and write off accounts that are determined to be uncollectable.

   2. Coordinate debt collection efforts and establish uniform procedures among Government agencies. Establish a separate credit department in each agency.

   3. Identify loans due by degree of collectability, segregating accounts that are virtually uncollectable from those that could be collected through vigorous collection efforts. This will require computerizing current manual records and updating computer equipment; about half of the Federal Government's 17,000 computers are obsolete.

   4. Establish incentives for debt collection, tied to both individual and agency performance, e.g., allow agencies to retain a portion of the payments collected.

Q. How much would this save?

A. PPSS conservatively estimated that delinquent debt, other than that owed to the Internal Revenue Service, could be reduced by 25% over three years. This would accelerate collections by $8.1 billion and earn interest of $1.2 billion over three years.

   In addition, PPSS noted that delinquencies and defaults on Federal loans are not reported to credit bureaus. Thus, the borrowers' credit ratings remain unimpaired, allowing them to be eligible for additional Federal and private sector loans. As an incentive for borrowers to repay Federal loans, PPSS recommended that delinquent debtors be reported to credit bureaus. In addition, when all other means of collecting debt are exhausted, PPSS recommended that private sector collection agencies be used. These measures would increase collections by $1.489 billion, earning interest of $307 million over three years.

Q. Are there any other general measures that can be taken to encourage debtors to repay their loans on time?

A. Yes, there are. If all agencies charged a uniform interest penalty on delinquent debt, an estimated $1.085 billion could be earned over three years. In the past, most agencies did not charge interest penalties on delinquent debt despite a 1979 regulation that required them to do so. Indeed, the Veterans Administration did not even have the systems capability to compute such interest. However, the Debt Collection Act of 1982 puts into law the requirement that agencies compute and assess a penalty fee sufficient to cover the cost of processing and handling delinquent claims.

Another step that could be taken to improve the performance of loan officers is to establish uniform definitions of default throughout the Government and to maintain and report these statistics on a regular basis. When a loan officer's performance is appraised, the amount of loans made that have lapsed into default would be a key element in the appraisal. Because of the greater incentive to make better loans and to collect on loans that are currently delinquent, $626 million in receipts could be accelerated, earning interest of $137 million over three years.

In the Small Business Administration (SBA) alone, the use of collection agencies to recover Federal charged-off loans—which run at a rate three to four times as high as in the private sector—could save $118 million over three years. Reducing SBA's maximum loan guarantee to 75% from 90% would save another $72 million over three years.

Virtually all of the loan management problems discussed above were found by PPSS to exist in the Education Department's student loan programs. Student loans outstanding at the end of FY 1983 totaled approximately $30.5 billion, with $3.8 billion, or 12% of this amount, in default. The major programs through which student loans are made available are:

Student Loan Programs, FY 1983E

		(1) Amount Outstanding Including Defaults ($ Billions)	(2) Amount in Default	(3) Approximate Default Rate
(1)	Direct Loans (a)	$ 4.9	$1.6	33%
(2)	Guaranteed Loans (b)	25.6	2.2	9

(a) Primarily the *National Direct Student Loan* (NDSL) program, through which loans are made by the Federal Government through educational institutions.

(b) Primarily the *Guaranteed Student Loan* (GSL) program, through which loans are made by private sector lenders, insured by state agencies, and then reinsured for a fee by the Federal Government; and the *Federally Insured Student Loan* (FISL) program, through which loans are made by private sector lenders and insured for a fee by the Federal Government.

Under GSL and FISL, the Government is liable for all costs that are incurred because of borrower default, death, disability, and bankruptcy. The Government also pays an interest subsidy equal to the differential between the market rate and the stipulated guaranteed loan rate of 9%

during the life of the loan, in addition to all interest costs while borrowers are in school.

PPSS found that, of these three major student loan programs, the Guaranteed Student Loan program was the most cost effective. Since all the programs address the same goal—to provide financial assistance to students seeking post-secondary education—PPSS concluded that all the education loan programs should be consolidated into GSL.

Q. The default rate for direct loans is over three times greater than for guaranteed loans. What is wrong with the direct student loan program, NDSL?

A. PPSS found that the educational institutions which administer direct loans are poorly equipped to do so; particularly with regard to repayment. At the department level, administration is lacking as well. As an example, no one in the Department of Education could explain a $300 million discrepancy found by PPSS in its loans receivable records.

Q. How much would such a consolidation save?

A. Three-year savings are estimated at $870 million—enough to pay the average salaries of 15,934 elementary school teachers for three years. Savings would result from administrative cost savings, as well as from improved loan performance.

Q. What recommendations did PPSS make concerning the $3.8 billion in defaulted Education Department loans outstanding?

A. In this area, PPSS recommended that the Education Department:

1. Structure the collection operation as an independent unit with enough influence to deal effectively with other branches of Government. This would help collect $68 million in defaulted student loans from the 46,860 current and retired Federal employees who were identified in 1982 as holding such loans. Further, personnel should be trained periodically in the latest collection techniques.

2. Require parental or other cosigners for all student loans. Such a requirement made independently by a savings and loan bank in the Midwest has resulted in a default rate of less than 1%—i.e., 90% less than the national average for these loans.

Reducing the default rate on student loans would save the Government $495 million in the first three years.

While not specifically discussed in the preceding, there were twenty-two additional issues that PPSS reviewed in this area which can be categorized under the following recommendations:

• Improve the administration of Federal loan programs, emulating private sector lenders where appropriate. Three-year savings—$1.500 billion.

- Increase private sector participation in Federal loan programs. Three-year savings—$667 million.

- Improve debt collection efforts. Three-year savings—$414 million.

> The three-year total of all the recommendations in this section, after elimination of duplication and overlap among issues, is $12.931 billion—equal to the three-year taxes of 1.9 million median income families.

Research and Development

> Research and development (R&D) in the Federal Government is conducted primarily by five agencies which together accounted for 93.2% of the total FY 1983 R&D budget of $44.3 billion. Government laboratories account for 24% of Federally funded R&D, employing over 206,000 personnel in over 700 laboratories.
>
> PPSS noted that agency top management needs to become more actively involved in establishing specific goals for R&D in terms which are clear and, where possible, measurable. The lack of direction in substantive aspects of R&D and the budget process combine to create a system that does not have clear program priorities and that induces costly, abrupt changes.
>
> PPSS made the following recommendations to improve Federal R&D activities: develop clear and measurable R&D goals in Federal agencies; implement multiyear budgeting specifically for R&D activities and significantly reduce the current level of detail required for budgeting R&D programs; make greater use of "centers of excellence," a concept which concentrates research resources in specific areas; reduce the overhead costs of research grants to universities by establishing fixed overhead rates; and establish a centralized data base to provide access to all new, ongoing, and completed Federally-funded R&D.
>
> In FY 1983, the Government spent $22.9 billion in this area, with spending estimated to increase to $111.0 billion by the year 2000 if present policies are continued. Implementing PPSS recommendations would reduce spending to $81.4 billion in 2000, a saving of $29.6 billion or 26.7%.

Total spending for research and development (R&D) in the United States was $77.3 billion in 1982, with the Federal Government accounting for $36.1 billion, or 47%. Five Government agencies—the Department of Defense (DOD), National Aeronautics and Space Administration (NASA), Department of Energy (DOE), Department of Health and Human Services (HHS), and National Science Foundation (NSF)—accounted for more than 90% of the $36.1 billion total. The R&D funded by these agencies is conducted by industrial firms (52%), universities (11%), Federally-funded research and development centers (9%), and other non-Federal entities (4%), with the remaining 24% performed in-house by 206,000 personnel in more than 700 Government laboratories.

Despite the large scale of Federal research and development activities, clear and measurable goals and priorities have not been established, resulting in overlap and useless expenditures. PPSS has identified savings opportunities and formulated recommendations which could reduce Federal R&D costs by $45.074 billion over three years (before consolidating savings to remove overlap and duplication) primarily by improving managerial planning, evaluation, and control.

Federal R&D programs are intended to achieve three strategic objectives:

• to perform R&D for the Government's own use, i.e., to achieve the mission of the various Federal agencies;

• to provide a strong science and technology base for the nation's educational and development programs; and

• to expedite exploitation of technology beneficial to the economy.

In line with these objectives, Federal R&D strategies should:

• provide a climate for technological innovation that encourages private sector R&D investment, and

• focus R&D on areas with significant potential benefit to the nation, where the private sector is unlikely to invest.

Federal Government performance in R&D has been uneven, as summarized below:

• *Strategic Planning*—R&D management suffers from a lack of clearly defined goals. Existing planning activities do not adequately establish priorities for R&D programs, do not eliminate marginal programs, and do not serve as a base for operational management. Successful R&D programs substitute new research for old and discontinue spending on projects unlikely to achieve results.

• *R&D Management and the Budget Process*—The budget process is exceedingly cumbersome and time consuming, leading to program instability and associated cost excesses.

• *Management of Federal R&D Laboratories*—Some of the "labs" use outdated facilities and equipment, most have serious personnel problems, and there is no formal system for evaluating their performance or their contribution to agency programs. No R&D program can be successful in the short- and long-term without systematic evaluation and re-evaluation. Knowledge and technology change constantly and so should the programs.

• *Administration of Research Grants to Universities*—An increasing percentage of the money going to universities to conduct research for the Federal Government is used to meet administrative expenses. Efforts to control these costs have resulted in a financial reporting system that adds to the administrative expenses of the universities and has become a major area of contention between the Government and the universities.

• *Research Program Reporting*—Current efforts at reporting ongoing research efforts are incomplete, and the National Technical Information Service, which is responsible for processing data on research activities, does not have the necessary resources to expand reporting. Successful R&D is hard enough to accomplish when there is a sense of direction and when progress is continually monitored. Without specific goals and timely information, the Government's R&D program must overcome major and possibly insurmountable obstacles.

Since time constraints prevented review of all agencies with R&D budgets, PPSS concentrated on three Federal agencies—the Department of Defense (DOD), the National Aeronautics and Space Administration (NASA), and the Department of Energy (DOE). These three agencies together were budgeted to spend $36.2 billion on R&D in FY 1983, which represented 82% of the $44.3 billion total 1983 Federal R&D budget.

Q. The Office of Science and Technology Policy is responsible for developing an overall Federal R&D plan. Since centralized responsibility exists, why does the Federal Government lack specific R&D objectives?

A. The Office of Science and Technology Policy, established within the Executive Office of the President in 1976, is involved in overall Government R&D. However, that involvement is directed toward formulating policy and does not usually include developing specific R&D objectives for individual programs. The primary focus is on the supply of engineering and scientific manpower to support technological development; cooperation between the basic research efforts of the Government, universities, and industry; and the basic thrusts of overall science and technology efforts.

Q. As noted, PPSS reviewed three agencies which collectively account for 82% of 1983 budgeted R&D spending. How was the FY 1983 R&D budget apportioned among these three agencies?

A. DOD accounted for more than half (56.0%) of the Government funding for R&D, i.e., $24.8 billion. NASA and DOE accounted for 14.9%, or $6.6 billion, and 10.8%, or $4.8 billion, respectively (for a total of $11.4 billion). The remainder of the R&D budget 18.3%, or $8.1 billion, was for the Department of Health and Human Services

9.3%, or $4.1 billion, the National Science Foundation 2.2%, or $1.0 billion, and all other agencies 6.8%, or $3.0 billion.

Q. How is the DOD budget spent?

A. R&D funds for DOD are used to support the modernization of national defense forces through development of new strategic and tactical weapons and support systems. Nearly $25 billion of the total 1983 Federal R&D budget is accounted for by DOD, representing a 19% increase over the $20.8 billion spent in FY 1982. Approximately 46% ($11.4 billion) of defense-related R&D is conducted or sponsored by the Air Force, 26% by the Navy, 19% by the Army, and 9% by other DOD components.

Defense R&D program areas and FY 1983 budget obligations were as follows:

1983 DOD R&D Budget Obligations

		($ Billions)
(1)	Tactical Programs	$ 7.5
(2)	Strategic Programs	6.5
(3)	Technology Base	3.3
(4)	Program Management and Support	2.8
(5)	Intelligence and Communications	2.7
(6)	Advance Technology Development	0.9
(7)	Other Appropriations	0.7
(8)	R&D Facilities	0.4
(9)	Total Obligations	$24.8

The R&D expenditures of DOD, in addition to providing for the defense of the country, have a significant impact on the private sector, e.g., work on very high speed integrated circuits (VHSIC). Similarly, Government-funded R&D for the B-52 bomber was, in large part, responsible for the development of the commercial Boeing 707 airplane.

STRATEGIC PLANNING

Strategic planning techniques need to be applied more fully to Federal R&D to establish goals, formulate and evaluate programs for achieving those goals, select alternative projects within resource constraints, prepare and document implementation steps, and evaluate results.

Planning in the Federal Government is complicated by the absence of the private sector discipline of the profit motive. In the private sector, despite a strong "bottom-line" orientation, it is difficult to properly control R&D expenses. As a result, a good deal of R&D money is wasted by "giving the benefit of the doubt" to a scientific team. Without such bottom-line discipline in the Federal Government, the control problem is compounded. In conjunction with poorly defined goals and absent economic constraints, the Federal Government cannot adequately establish objectives, priorities and plans.

The Government's problems in the area of strategic planning can be summarized as follows:

- The lack of adequate and clear-cut goals, and inadequate strategies and tactics to achieve those goals, results in R&D programs that are too often funded on the basis of budget considerations rather than national priorities. In the private sector, successful R&D programs are directed toward achieving an objective which when reached or superseded results in the termination or reorientation of the program.

- Agencies establish spending requirements largely on the basis of local rather than overall planning. This results in unnecessary program duplication between laboratories and agencies and tends to continue programs of marginal value which originated in individual R&D facilities.

- Present techniques often do not include implementation plans and scheduled decision points, making it difficult to determine progress and make course corrections.

Most successful private sector R&D operations are disciplined with performance goals and yardsticks so that funds can be shifted from disappointing programs to ideas that offer greater probability for success. The key is to:

—closely monitor progress over time,
—determine the odds of success at each stage (the odds should be improving with time and money expended), and
—stop funding when the odds of success diminish.

- The budget process, external pressure from Congress, frequent changes in policy and leadership, and the lack of strategic focus equate to a short-term perspective in establishing Federal R&D priorities. Year-to-year planning is wasteful, particularly for R&D activities that tend to be long-term, as both time and money are consumed each year in rejustifying decisions from prior years.

PPSS has estimated that implementing a strategic planning process would reduce R&D costs by approximately 10% with three-year savings of $7.300 billion.

PPSS recommended that the Government:

- Develop improved strategic planning concepts and procedures. Each agency should adopt a strategic planning and control process specifically designed to meet its needs.

- Reexamine and, where necessary, redirect priorities to reflect national and agency goals.

- Ensure that new and updated strategic planning forms the basis for subsequent budgeting and operational management.

Q. What are the specific results of the deficiencies in Federal R&D discussed above?

A. There are a number of specific results:

- Many more R&D programs are initiated than can be funded to completion.

- R&D programs are not prioritized, which leads to inefficient use of development funds.

- Agency managers often are not able to terminate programs that do not meet cost and performance targets or that are no longer required to meet the mission and goals of the agency.

- In the absence of formal, top-down guidance on the nation's priorities, Federal R&D programs cannot effectively meet both near- and long-term technological requirements.

Q. What needs to be done to implement a goal-setting process in the Federal Government?

A. To implement a goal-setting process and have it become an integral part of the R&D management structure, PPSS recommended that each agency designate a senior official (at the Assistant Secretary level) to lead the internal effort and to coordinate with other agencies and the Executive Office of the President through the Office of Science and Technology Policy (OSTP). PPSS recommended that OSTP coordinate the goal-setting process and provide the necessary assistance to evaluate the consistency of those goals with National objectives. In the past, efforts to institutionalize strategic planning have focused on the budget process. This has not been very successful.

Q. How long will it take the Federal Government to implement a strategic planning process?

A. Industry experience indicates that implementing effective strategic planning for R&D will take three to five years. Agencies need to develop, refine, communicate, gain acceptance for, and achieve proficiency with respect to strategic planning. Top management must persistently emphasize and support the process if there is to be any hope of success; the process of strategic planning is a never-ending discipline that must be maintained and continuously improved upon to produce results.

Q. PPSS indicated that three-year cost savings of $7.300 billion could be achieved as a result of improved strategic planning. Isn't it difficult to quantify savings in this area?

A. It is very difficult to quantify the dollar impact of effective long-range strategic planning. The primary thrust of PPSS recommendations is improved management of the R&D process, focusing on goals and priorities within the context of available resources. This would necessitate R&D planning based on affordability which, in turn, would result in savings by eliminating marginal, duplicative and non-productive research.

Q. What impact does Congressional oversight have on the ability of the Executive Branch to reduce unnecessary R&D expenditures?

A. Congress has a significant impact. Executive Branch agencies can be forced to fund research projects even after demonstrating to Congress that a particular project would have more relevance to the mission of a different agency or that it will produce little value to the taxpayers or the Government. This occurs because of Congressional preoccupation with the interests of individual constituencies rather than broader national interests.

For example, officials of the Department of Health and Human Services (HHS) sought to terminate funding for a six-year economic research project. The project had first been funded in 1980, and, as of 1983, HHS had spent $667,000 supporting it. HHS officials decided not to request additional funding in 1983. However, Congress ordered HHS to "continue funding for this research effort at an amount necessary to keep the project on schedule, but no less than $400,000." HHS stated that "if every institution that wants a grant can go to the Congress directly to obtain it, a planned, rational program of research will be impossible to organize and maintain."

Strategic planning is the key to efficiency and achieving meaningful results. If, however, planning is subordinated to the needs of parochial interests, waste and inefficiency will result. Many R&D problems would not exist if there were good strategic planning.

The remaining four areas—R&D Management and the Budget Process, Improved Management of Resources in Federal Research Laboratories, Administration of Research Grants to Universities, and Research Program Reporting—are summarized below.

R&D MANAGEMENT AND THE BUDGET PROCESS

PPSS recommended the following actions to improve R&D management and the budget process, estimated to result in $3.670 billion in savings over three years:

- Initiate multiyear budgeting specifically for R&D activities.

- Reduce the current level of detail in budgeting for R&D programs.

- Shorten the budget preparation and review cycle.

- Reduce technical staff positions in R&D agencies.

Q. What impact does the lengthy budgeting process have on the effectiveness of R&D programs?

A. The lack of definition and the lead times involved result in changes in direction and scope and consequent cost increases.

In the fall of 1980, project managers began developing their detailed budget submissions for expenditures in FY 1983. Developing detailed funding plans for spending two to three years in the future presents many problems, particularly for new programs where specific project details are not fully defined. In many cases, the rush to get the project included in the budget prevents the kind of planning that should be done.

Q. Why is the budget process so lengthy?

A. One of the reasons is that the Congressional hearing process places significant burdens on Federal agencies. For example, there are 30 Congressional committees and subcommittees that have jurisdiction over some aspect of DOE. In the 97th Congress alone, DOE presented over 700 witnesses at more than 300 hearings. This problem is not unique to DOE. Defense agencies have appeared before the Interior and House Ways and Means Committees, in addition to numerous appearances before the Armed Services and Appropriations Committees, to discuss their R&D programs. Each of these hearings requires time for preparation of testimony. Further, considerable time is devoted to responding to written requests from Congressional committees.

MANAGEMENT OF FEDERAL R&D LABORATORIES

All Federal R&D literature cites the "over 700 Federal R&D labs" which are an integral part of the Government R&D program. PPSS found that 90% of the operating costs are incurred by the 146 labs with more than 100 employees. The remaining "labs" are small facilities, two-thirds of which have fewer than 25 employees.

Savings of $506 million could be realized over a three-year period in managing Federal R&D laboratories by:

- Establishing responsibility within the Executive Branch for evaluating laboratory performance and exploring for laboratory consolidations.

- Expanded use of "centers of excellence" (concentrating research efforts in a given area and centrally locating the resources to perform that research). This concept recognizes that some critical mass of resources is required to conduct first-rate research programs. Each center has a specific set of goals, concentrating its efforts on specific areas of expertise, thus avoiding non-productive R&D overlap among centers. Many organizations, including NASA, are using this concept. Additional centers of excellence would result in the following benefits:

—more intensive research on selected, priority technologies;
—greater purchasing power for sophisticated equipment;
—reduced duplication of work efforts within given technologies; and
—lower administrative and operating costs through better utilization of resources.

- Increased coordination among R&D laboratories to avoid excessive program overlap. DOD is emphasizing joint and cross-service programs to maximize the benefits of R&D investment. An Office of the Assistant for Directed Energy Weapons has been established to coordinate the efforts of the armed services and defense agencies to reduce duplication of effort and enhance productivity.

- Granting directors of Federal R&D laboratories more control over budget appropriations.

- Creating a scientific/technical personnel system at Government-operated laboratories independent of the current Civil Service personnel system through administrative and legislative actions.

- Establishing a set of guidelines which would define what constitutes an R&D laboratory, and reclassifying those facilities which do not meet the guidelines but which are now included in the list of 700 "laboratories."

- Expanding the use of private sector facilities for Government research. PPSS estimates that "contracting out" 5% of the current laboratory in-house budget would result in a 10% savings on such work.

Q. In the same area of discussion, why is it necessary to define what constitutes a Federal Research and Development Laboratory?

A. There are, as noted, over 700 facilities designated Federal R&D laboratories currently in operation. A number of these facilities are small and engaged in what would be more properly described as data gathering or monitoring functions, not basic or applied R&D. The U.S. Geological Survey, for instance, operates an extensive system of field offices to gather and apply data related to its mission. Another example is the VA, which operates 60 "R&D laboratories," each with ten or more personnel primarily engaged in studying problems involving the care of veterans.

These facilities differ sharply from more traditional R&D laboratories. The ten largest private sector laboratories, for instance, each employ a staff of more than 5,000 personnel. Overall, only 388 of the 700 Federal R&D laboratories have a staff of ten or more employees.

Q. What criteria should be used to define a Federal R&D laboratory?

A. Guidelines should be established which include requirements that the facility, as its primary activity, be engaged in basic research, applied research, development or management of R&D. Those organizations which should specifically be excluded from designation as Federal laboratories are those engaged primarily in routine quality control and testing, routine service activities, production, mapping and surveys, and information dissemination. This reclassification would take facilities now included in the category of R&D laboratories and identify them more appropriately as monitoring stations, sampling facilities, medical support facilities, etc. This reclassification would allow greater focus on R&D facilities.

ADMINISTRATION OF RESEARCH GRANTS TO UNIVERSITIES

An increasing percentage of the money going to universities to conduct research for the Federal Government is used to cover the indirect costs of that research, including departmental administration, general administration, and sponsored project administration. The time devoted to determining the allocation of administrative expenses by senior university administrators as well as senior Government officials is unwarranted.

PPSS recommended setting a negotiated fixed rate for administrative cost (indirect) elements. This would eliminate the burden associated with reporting actual rates. PPSS also recommended that the National Science Foundation, National Institutes of Health, Department of Defense, and other Federal agencies continue examining alternative funding mechanisms and research grant administration procedures to create greater institutional flexibility (in using grants), stability, responsibility, and accountability.

In conjunction with the agencies, OMB should develop a simplified method of institutional reporting. Savings in administrative time could be achieved for both universities and the Government without serious degradation of the information needed for program management.

In total, PPSS estimated that $388 million in savings over three years could be achieved by implementing these recommendations.

RESEARCH PROGRAM REPORTING

A significant number of research projects appear to duplicate each other, and there is a general lack of information sharing among agencies. Further, there is no central data base capable of providing ready access to all unclassified, new, ongoing and completed Federally funded R&D.

PPSS estimated savings of $225 million over three years by:

- Expanding the National Technical Information Service (NTIS) data base (consistent with limitations imposed by national security).

- Requiring contributions to and use of the expanded NTIS data base by Federal agencies and private sector recipients of grants and contracts.

- Including an explicit work statement on proposed and ongoing research projects which would confirm that a search has been made of the NTIS data base and that the study takes into account other work completed and reported.

Q. What is the NTIS, and what is currently included in its data base?

A. The National Technical Information Service (NTIS) is a self-sustaining organization under the auspices of the Department of Commerce.

The NTIS Bibliographic Data Base now serves as the central source for the collection and dissemination of non-classified Government-sponsored R&D and engineering reports submitted on a voluntary basis. The data base currently contains about 800,000 citations dating back to 1964 and is updated biweekly at a rate of about 65,000 new citations per year. However, the NTIS data base does not contain information on newly-established and in-progress Federal R&D projects.

Q. Did PPSS notice any examples of duplicated research effort?

A. Yes. For example, the different military services each undertake development of protective clothing and gear independently of one another. Each conducts separate studies of materials acceptability, reaction, etc. Also, several agencies are conducting parallel research on genetic engineering without cross-consultation. In a third example, a 1982 GAO report pointed out that eleven Federal agencies receive funding to conduct research regarding the National Marine Pollution Program, and that better coordination among the several agencies involved in that area of research is needed.

Other issues that PPSS identified for savings include defense procurement, funding levels for R&D activities, and the managerial structures for R&D programs.

Regarding defense procurement, a centralized, coordinated effort to distribute DOD research data among the services and the 75 DOD laboratories is necessary to provide an increased understanding of emerging weapons technologies. Also, the current administration and review system to reimburse DOD contractors for independent R&D costs is unnecessary. Savings of $1.925 billion over three years could be achieved by implementing PPSS recommendations in this area.

Improved management of R&D activities, such as by budgeting Department of Energy R&D in the National Laboratories on a three-year basis instead of the current annual review, centralizing policy and oversight responsibility for R&D conducted by the Department of Transportation, establishing a National Board to set goals and missions for Federally funded agricultural research, and reorganizing the Agricultural Research Service, could save $1.273 billion over three years.

Reduced, more efficient funding, or eliminating funding entirely, in such areas as National Institutes of Health research grants and contracts, National Laboratories research on nuclear fusion, social research in the Office of Human Development Services, and low-priority programs of State Agricultural Experiment Stations, could save $842 million over three years.

> The three-year total of all the recommendations in this section, after elimination of duplication and overlap among issues, is $15.413 billion—equal to the three-year taxes of 2.3 million median income families.

Wage-Setting Laws

> Laws that set wages on Federal construction projects have resulted in much higher costs to the Federal Government, as well as inhibiting competition at the local level and promoting the conditions that they were originally enacted to correct. PPSS recommended these laws be repealed.
>
> In FY 1983, the Government spent $37.5 billion in the specific areas covered by PPSS recommendations, with spending estimated to increase to $150.0 billion by the year 2000 if present policies are continued. Implementing PPSS recommendations would reduce spending to $110.2 billion in 2000, a saving of $39.8 billion, or 26.5%.

There are currently three major Federal laws that require Government contractors to pay their workers at least "prevailing" wages and benefits, as determined by the Department of Labor (DOL). While the term "prevailing" is not specifically defined in the laws, it has generally been interpreted to mean wages and benefits being paid for work of a similar nature in the area where the Federal work is to be performed. In many cases, to expedite the wage determination process, the Labor Department uses union-negotiated wage agreements. Union wages and benefits are frequently higher than non-union rates. In areas where union labor represents less than a majority of the local work force, use of union wage rates results in higher labor costs than would otherwise prevail. These laws, the Davis-Bacon Act (1931), the Walsh-Healey Act (1936), and the

Service Contract Act (1965), were ostensibly enacted to prevent cutthroat competition among contractors bidding for Federal work. Congress took the position that such competition should not be conducted at the expense of the workers' ability to earn a decent wage. Each law has operated to eliminate wages and benefits as factors in the Federal competitive bidding process.

The following excerpt from the legislative history of the Davis-Bacon Act, the first of the major Federal prevailing wage laws, sums up Congress' primary rationale for giving wage-setting power to the Federal Government, even though it conflicts with the long established Federal practice of awarding contracts on a competitive basis to the lowest bidder:

> Though the officials awarding contracts have faithfully endeavored to persuade contractors to pay local prevailing wage scales, some successful bidders have selfishly imported labor from distant localities and have exploited this labor at wages far below local rates.

> This practice . . . has resulted in a very unhealthy situation. Local artisans and mechanics, many of whom are men owning their own homes, and whose standards of living have long been adjusted to local wage scales, cannot hope to compete with this migratory labor. . . .

Similar rationales were applied to support the later passage of the Walsh-Healey and Service Contract Acts, described below.

Ironically, the basic conditions which prompted the passage of these laws—primarily imported labor undercutting local wage standards—have virtually disappeared in today's economy. To a large extent, the three wage laws now tend to create the very conditions they were originally enacted to eliminate. Yet they continue to be vigorously enforced, with a substantial detrimental effect on the nation's economic health.

Major features of these Acts are as follows:

Davis-Bacon. Applies to Federally-funded and assisted construction projects exceeding $2,000 in cost. If the $2,000 threshold, which was set in 1935, were adjusted to 1983 dollars, it would be approximately $16,500. Davis-Bacon has been extended by some 58 other Federal laws so that it now covers virtually every construction project even peripherally involved with the Federal Government, for example, those including Federal loan guarantees and insurance programs. Since these latter activities have increased rapidly in recent years, this means that the applicability of Davis-Bacon has similarly increased at a rapid pace. Workers on these projects must receive prevailing wages and benefits, as determined by the Secretary of Labor. The value of affected projects is more than $50 billion annually.

Walsh-Healey. Applies to Federal contracts in excess of $10,000 for the manufacture or furnishing of equipment, supplies, or other materials. The $10,000 threshold, enacted in 1936, equates to over $80,000 in 1983 dollars. A 1964 court decision forced the Labor Department to discontinue prevailing wage determinations, but the Act still sets eight hours as the daily maximum work that may be required before overtime pay is mandatory. Contracts affected by this law are valued at $90 billion annually.

Service Contract Act. Applies to Federal service contracts exceeding $2,500. This threshold, set in 1965, would equal $7,250 in 1983, adjusted for inflation. Employees must receive prevailing wages and benefits, as determined by the Department of Labor. A contractor must match the wages and fringe benefits paid by the previous contractor, even in cases where the service is to be performed in a different locality. The value of affected contracts is approximately $10 billion annually.

These three labor laws cover Federal projects and contracts totalling in excess of $150 billion annually, and the potential for savings is significant.

Some ways in which these Acts increase costs to the Federal Government include:

- Because it is virtually impossible for DOL to accurately determine what wages and benefits actually prevail in a given area, more often than not, the wage actually set is at or near the highest rate in an area, and frequently it exceeds the true local or market rate. (Davis-Bacon and Service Contract Acts)

- Because of inflexible provisions that overtime be paid after eight hours of work each day, companies that use four ten-hour days or other compressed work week options will not bid for Federal work, thereby minimizing competitive bidding. (Walsh-Healey)

- Provisions that successor contractors must pay wages established under previous wage agreements minimize the possibility that a given service will be performed more cheaply in a lower cost area. (Service Contract Act)

- The laws impose substantial administrative costs on both the Government and affected contractors, amounting to $185 million in 1982. (Davis-Bacon and Service Contract Acts)

PPSS recommended that, since the three Federal prevailing wage laws are no longer necessary or productive, they should be repealed. Federal and state labor standards protection laws passed or extended since the enactment of Davis-Bacon, Walsh-Healey, and the SCA provide adequate worker protection. Savings of $11.650 billion over three years would result if PPSS recommendations to repeal the laws are implemented.

A more detailed description of the Federal prevailing wage laws provides additional weight to the case for their repeal:

THE DAVIS-BACON ACT

This law was enacted in 1931, during a time when new construction spending in the United States had fallen from $10.8 billion in 1929 to $2.9

billion in 1933. The average annual earnings of construction workers during the same period fell from $1,674 to approximately half that level. By 1934, 59% of new construction was publicly financed. The Federal Government clearly dominated the construction markets, and Congress, reacting to claims of cutthroat competition, refused to make the Government a partner to "wage busting." By 1982, however, new construction spending had risen to $232.0 billion—with $51.1 billion, or 22%, publicly financed—and construction workers had become among the highest paid workers in the economy.

Q. Isn't it true that wages of construction workers rose less rapidly during the 1970's than did all private sector wages over the same period? Therefore, isn't Davis-Bacon necessary to protect the wages of construction workers?

A. Construction wages did not rise as rapidly as others during the 1970's, but that is a misleading defense of the Davis-Bacon Act. The following presents average wages for total private industry and construction workers 1970-1980:

Average Hourly Wages

		(1)	(2)	(3)
		Total Industry	Construction Workers	Construction as Multiple of All Industry Wages
(1)	1970	$3.23	$5.24	1.62X
(2)	1980	6.66	9.94	1.49
(3)	Average Annual Percent Increase	7.5%	6.6%	0.88X

As shown, the wages of all workers rose by an average 7.5% per year while construction wages rose 6.6% per year, but this difference in growth merely represents an evening out of wage levels among industries. Construction wages are still much higher than other wages. Despite the slower growth, construction wages were still 1.49 times as great as for all workers at the end of the 1970's, and 1.41 times as great as of August 1983. Furthermore, PPSS found that market rates are likely to prevail even in cases where Davis-Bacon wage determinations were lower. In other words, while there is strong evidence to show that Davis-Bacon artificially raises wage rates above local standards, there is no evidence to show that rates drop below the market where Davis-Bacon is not a factor.

Q. What about other justifications of the Davis-Bacon Act, for example, to ensure that local contractors are not excluded from Federal projects?

A. To the contrary, the evidence shows that Davis-Bacon accomplishes just the opposite. For example, a recent study of construction projects found that local contractors are used in only 28% of the projects in which Davis-Bacon applies, versus a 47% participation rate where Davis-Bacon is not involved.

Q. Why is there such a difference?

A. Local contractors tend to be smaller, non-union operations. These contractors do not want to risk good employee relations by paying some employees a higher wage just because they are working on a Federally-funded project. Therefore, these contractors will often not bid on a Federal project to avoid disrupting their regular employees. PPSS found that Davis-Bacon discriminates against smaller contractors and, thus, reduces competition.

Q. How much would the Government save if Congress repealed the Act?

A. PPSS estimated that savings would amount to $4.970 billion over three years. That amount would be enough to build 710 miles of rural highways in the United States.

THE WALSH-HEALEY ACT

Like the Davis-Bacon Act, Walsh-Healey was enacted during the Depression to prevent unscrupulous contractors from cutting wages on Government supply contracts. Because of a court decision and passage of other laws which have preempted its provisions, the only remaining practical effect of Walsh-Healey is to require that in any contract for Federal procurement exceeding $10,000 in value, employees must be paid overtime for hours worked in excess of eight hours per day.

Q. What is the practical impact of Walsh-Healey's 8-hour overtime restriction?

A. It prohibits or discourages employers who use increasingly popular compressed workweek schedules from bidding on Federal projects. This minimizes competition among Federal contractors and results in higher costs to the taxpayer.

Q. Isn't the Walsh-Healey 8-hour overtime requirement necessary to prevent employers from imposing "sweatshop" conditions?

A. In 1938, Congress passed the Fair Labor Standards Act. The FLSA sets wage and hour standards and requires employers to pay overtime for any work performed in excess of 40 hours a week. The FLSA applies to nearly all non-Federal contract workers and provides adequate protection to ensure against sweatshop conditions.

Q. What are some of the advantages of the compressed workweek?

A. Just some of the advantages of compressed workweeks include less traffic congestion, less pollution, less energy consumption, improved employee morale, more leisure time, safer workplaces, more accessibility for working mothers, decreased overtime costs, and reduced absenteeism.

Q. What is the projected three-year savings to the Federal Government if Walsh-Healey is repealed or changed to substitute the FLSA 40-hour a week overtime standard instead of the 8-hour a day restriction?

A. PPSS estimated a three-year savings to the Federal Government of $3.370 billion.

THE SERVICE CONTRACT ACT

The Service Contract Act, enacted in 1965, requires that contractors and subcontractors furnishing services to the Government under contracts exceeding $2,500 pay their employees prevailing wages and benefits as determined by the Department of Labor. The U.S. General Accounting Office, in a January 1983 Report to Congress, found that inherent problems exist in SCA's administration: SCA wage rates are generally inflationary; DOL cannot make accurate prevailing wage determinations; adequate labor protection to service employees can be provided through the FLSA. PPSS's study of the SCA resulted in similar findings.

Q. What does PPSS recommend?

A. The Service Contract Act should be repealed, which would result in savings to the Federal Government of $3.310 billion over three years.

REGULATORY REFORMS

Q. Don't recent regulatory changes to the three wage-setting laws take care of their cost raising impacts?

A. No. Although the Labor Department estimates its regulatory changes to the Davis-Bacon and Service Contract Acts could eventually result in a savings of over $700 million annually ($585 million for Davis-Bacon and $124 million for SCA), the revised regulations cannot remedy the inherent defects of these two laws. Further, because the Walsh-Healey eight-hour overtime restriction is statutory, it cannot be revised by regulatory changes. Finally, a different Administration could easily amend regulatory reforms and thus eliminate cost saving improvements.

CONCLUSION

Economic conditions have changed drastically since passage of the major Federal prevailing wage laws. Additional comprehensive labor protection legislation has been enacted. Federal contractors must now post performance bonds. The organized labor movement has developed into a major political and economic force. As a result of these developments, prevailing wage legislation is no longer necessary to protect the American worker, and, in fact, is having a negative impact on the economy. Moreover, the major wage laws now ironically actually cause the conditions they were enacted to eliminate. Thus, PPSS strongly recommended that the Davis-Bacon Act, the Walsh-Healey Act, and the Service Contract Act be repealed.

> The three-year total of all the recommendations in this section, after elimination of duplication and overlap among issues, is $11.650 billion—equal to the three-year taxes of 1.8 million median income families.

Insurance Programs

> The Federal Government has more than $2 trillion of insurance in force and PPSS determined that reserves are not actuarially funded and are thus inadequate to meet potential future claims. Further, premiums for insurance are not risk-related, and Federal programs duplicate insurance coverage readily available in the private sector.
>
> In FY 1983, the Government spent $6.1 billion in the specific areas covered by PPSS recommendations, with spending estimated to increase to $18.3 billion by the year 2000 if present policies are continued. Implementing PPSS recommendations would reduce spending to $9.0 billion in 2000, a saving of $9.3 billion, or 50.8%.

The Federal Government is by far the nation's largest insurer with $2.1 trillion of insurance in force at fiscal year end 1982, as summarized below:

Federal Insurance in Force
as of September 30, 1982

		(1)	(2)
		($ Trillions)	*As a %* *of Total(a)*
(1)	Deposit Insurance	$1.6	77.4%
(2)	Business-related Insurance	0.3	14.2
(3)	Other Insurance	0.2	8.4
(4)	Total	$2.1	100.0%

(a) Percents based on unrounded data.

Against this $2.1 trillion potential liability, PPSS found that the Government has accumulated reserves sufficient to cover only 1.0% of potential claims.

The PPSS review of Federal insurance programs addressed the following:

- Is Federal participation in these programs appropriate, or could the private sector provide coverage more efficiently?

- Are Federal risks and costs in the programs being adequately covered by revenues?

In its review of the deposit insurance programs, PPSS found that in the two major programs, Federal Deposit Insurance Corporation (FDIC) and the Federal Savings and Loan Insurance Corporation (FSLIC), which together account for $1.5 trillion, or 74.6% of all Federal insurance coverage, premiums did not adequately reflect the degree of risk associated with the institutions insured. The current practice of charging uniform premiums to all financial institutions does not provide incentive for the institutions to avoid high-risk or speculative lending.

If variable premiums were adopted, risk would be more carefully weighted, thus reducing potential Federal exposure in the event of bank failure. Further, PPSS recommended that the reserve levels of FDIC, FSLIC, and the National Credit Union Share Insurance Fund be increased to a level that would be comparable to that required of a private insurer.

The principal business-related insurance programs are the Aviation Insurance Revolving Fund, which insures commercial aircraft operating under contract to the Defense Department and the State Department, and Nuclear Risk Protection, which insures nuclear plants against losses resulting from plant accidents up to a maximum of $500 million per plant. Utilities pay $30 per kilowatt of generating capacity for the coverage. Recently, coverage by private sector insurers has been expanded in this area reducing the Government's involvement.

Other Federal insurance includes a wide variety of Government programs providing coverage against natural disaster, crime, etc.

Overall, PPSS recommended that Federal insurance programs be limited to those that are necessary, e.g., socially-desirable coverage unavailable from private sector insurers at acceptable rates. Moreover they should at a minimum operate at break-even levels after provision for the expenses of operating the plans. In addition, premiums should be risk related, i.e., higher risk policies should carry relatively higher premiums. This holds within programs as well as among programs.

Q. Insurance in the private sector is generally profitable to the seller even after prudent provision for future possible losses. In what ways are Federal insurance programs different?

A. Most private sector insurance programs actuarially structure premiums to earn a profit. There are two significant differences between public and private sector insurance programs, both relating to the relatively high risk skew of Government programs. First, the Government is often initiating a new type of insurance which has not been offered in the private sector and, second, it offers insurance for high risk occurrences, such as floods, for which the private sector cannot insure except at prohibitive rates. In order to meet the social objectives of its insurance programs, the Government establishes "affordable" premiums which generally do not cover the actuarial cost of the program.

For example, the National Flood Insurance Program, established in 1968, provides subsidized premium rates at less than full actuarial cost in order to encourage the purchase of flood insurance. The current premium rate is 40¢ per $100 of coverage, which is estimated to be about 80% of the actuarial rate. Moreover, a General Accounting Office review of the program revealed that even at these subsidized rates, an estimated $5 million per year is not collected because of improper procedures used by private sector underwriters contracted to administer the program. These underwriters are not liable for insurance losses which may result from their errors.

Further, the program *allows flooded communities to acquire flood insurance after the fact,* i.e., after flood damage has occurred. Even applying the most liberal interpretation, this is hardly insurance as the word is defined. While this provision can be used by a community only once, it discourages communities from undertaking appropriate flood plain management, i.e., no programs for loss prevention —a standard procedure in the private sector. As a result, the flood insurance program has consistently operated at a loss—$127 million in FY 1983, with a $118 million loss budgeted for FY 1984.

Q. How did PPSS recommend the program be improved?

A. Flood insurance should be limited to those areas that have instituted appropriate flood plain management procedures and the after-the-fact provision should be eliminated. Further, individuals should not receive disaster assistance for insurable items. The Federal Emergency Management Agency (FEMA), which administers the flood insurance program, should upgrade underwriting standards to arrive at proper risk ratings. In addition, FEMA should apply sanctions— through legal action where appropriate—against agents who abuse the program. Savings are estimated at $95 million over three years.

While not specifically identified as an "insurance program," PPSS did review the Pension Benefit Guaranty Corporation (PBGC) which insures the pensions of private sector employees. From its inception in 1974 to 1981, the PBGC ran a cumulative deficit of $200 million, and its liabilities, based on the value of future benefits of terminated private sector pension plans as well as from pending terminations, totaled $1.4 billion in FY 1983. This figure is exclusive of the massive liability of the Government for the benefits of all 29 million private sector employees currently covered by PBGC. PPSS review uncovered significant structural problems.

Q. What specific problems did PPSS find in its review of the Pension Benefit Guaranty Corporation?

A. In view of the continuing deficit that is being run by the PBGC, PPSS concluded that current premium levels are inadequate to fund the program properly and, thus, recommended the annual premium be increased from $2.60 per participant to $6.00.

PPSS also found that the PBGC premiums were not risk related and that existing legislation allows too much opportunity for abuse of the program—e.g., a large company could spin off a weak subsidiary with a substantial pension liability, which then could terminate the plan and transfer the liability to PBGC.

PPSS recommended a legislative initiative aimed at having the Congress close existing loopholes in the law and that PBGC premiums be adjusted to reflect the relative risk of insured pension plans, i.e., the premium on a 100% funded plan would be about half that of a 50% funded plan. Total savings from these recommendations over three years equal $3.548 billion—an amount equal to the present value of average lifetime pension benefits for 95,853 private sector employees.

Q. On what other Federal insurance programs did PPSS make recommendations?

A. The Agriculture Department's Federal Crop Insurance Corporation (FCIC) paid out $107 for every $100 of premium received in 1981—which was considered a good crop year—even though the Federal Crop Insurance Act of 1980 stipulates that premiums should be sufficient to cover losses *and* to establish a reasonable reserve against unforeseen losses. PPSS recommended that premiums be actuarially determined, and, assuming a 10% increase in premiums, estimated that additional revenues of $297 million over three years would be generated—enough to buy 122 million bushels of corn at 1982 prices.

Two other programs PPSS reviewed were Federal Crime Insurance and Federal Riot Insurance, which were found to be inappropriate for the Federal Government to administer. For example, 65% of all Federal crime insurance policies were written for coverage in New York. In FY 1981, New York policy holders paid $7.8 million in premiums but received $29.4 million in payments on claims—3.8

times the amount of premiums they paid. Again, no risk related premium setting procedures. Assuming a maximum 70% loss ratio to allow for expenses and reserves for future claims, the premiums should have been $42 million—$34.2 million higher than charged—equivalent to the annual taxes of 15,419 median income American families. The Federal Riot Insurance program should be discontinued because such insurance is readily available in the private sector. Discontinuing these two programs would save the taxpayers $37 million over three years.

Another area that is not specifically identified by the Government as an insurance program but which overlaps with insurance programs provided by the private sector is mortgage insurance. Currently, there are 15 private insurance companies which offer mortgage insurance. The main difference between these companies and the Government's Federal Housing Authority and Veterans Administration mortgage insurance has been that the Government insured 100% of the mortgage amount, while private mortgage insurance companies insured less than 100%.

An important advantage of mortgage insurance is that it allows a potential home buyer to acquire financing with a minimal downpayment (3%-5%) instead of the customary 20%.

PPSS recommended that Federal mortgage insurance be made available only to those who are ineligible for private mortgage insurance.

Other issues addressed in this area by PPSS, but not specifically discussed in the preceding, primarily relate to the funding levels of insurance programs that continuously run deficits. More business-like administration of these programs would raise revenues and produce savings of a combined $1.338 billion over three years.

> The three-year total of all the recommendations in this section, after elimination of duplication and overlap among issues, is $5.591 billion—equal to the three-year taxes of 840,246 median income families.

III. D. The Federal Employee: Managing the Work Force

Work force management determines the number of people and the skills necessary to accomplish an organization's objectives, and the actions necessary to obtain, develop, and motivate the work force. Work force requirements, however, have received little attention in Government because budget decisions are usually overriding, there is a lack of leadership from the Office of Personnel Management (OPM) and there is insufficient information to develop complete and integrated management systems. As a result, there is a need for human resource planning procedures that would allow for uniform decision making throughout the Federal Government regarding the size, composition, allocation, and development of work force needs.

This problem is pervasive throughout personnel procedures and controls. The Government lacks incentives to improve worker productivity, reduce overtime, eliminate thousands of unnecessary, temporary positions, establish adequate spans of control, reduce the number of managerial positions, and establish adequate training and development programs.

Regarding compensation, the Government is required by law to establish salaries for Federal employees that are comparable to those in the private sector. However, the surveys used to determine private sector wages are flawed, overstating private sector salaries. Further, the two major Federal retirement systems, the Civil Service and Military Retirement Systems, provide benefits that are approximately 3 and 6 times, respectively, as great as those in the private sector. Including retirement benefits, Federal fringe benefit costs (65.3% of payroll) are 28.2% points greater than costs in the private sector (37.1% of payroll).

PPSS recommended that OPM develop an adequate work force planning policy to be used by Federal agencies and that OMB develop and coordinate government-wide programs to improve productivity; that the surveys of private sector salaries be adjusted so they accurately reflect private sector wages; and that retirement, sick leave, and vacation costs be reduced so they are comparable to those in the private sector.

Compensation

In FY 1982, the Federal Government paid $102.8 billion in salaries to its 4.9 million civilian employees and military personnel. It is Federal policy that Government salaries be comparable to those in the private sector. However, as current surveys used to determine private sector wages are not accurate, this policy is not being followed. The structures of the Government's major pay systems "build in" pay increases above those in the private sector, in most cases. Federal executives, however, are underpaid in comparison to executives in the private sector. Military pay scales, while comparable to those in the private sector, are frequently perceived to be inferior because of the complicated pay system.

In FY 1983, the Government spent $22.0 billion in the specific areas covered by PPSS recommendations, with spending estimated to increase to $105.2 billion by the year 2000 if present policies are continued. Implementing PPSS recommendations would reduce spending to $83.1 billion in 2000, a saving of $22.1 billion or 21.0%.

At the end of FY 1982, the Executive Branch employed 4.9 million military personnel and civilian employees, 5.9 times the combined employment of Exxon and General Motors, and approximately the same number as in the top 40 companies of the Fortune 500. Federal direct compensation (salaries paid to employees) for 1982 was $102.8 billion, or more than double the $48.8 billion ten years ago, as follows:

Executive Branch
Employment and Compensation

		(1)	(2)	(3)
				1982 as a Multiple
	Fiscal Year-End	1972	1982	of 1972
	Employment (Millions)			
(1)	Civilian (Incl. USPS)	2.8	2.8	1.00X
(2)	Military	2.3	2.1	0.91
(3)	Total	5.1	4.9	0.96
	Direct Compensation (a) ($ Billions)			
(4)	Civilian (Incl. USPS)	$31.6	$ 65.8	2.08
(5)	Military	17.2	37.0	2.15
(6)	Total	$48.8	$102.8	2.11
	Average Compensation per Employee			
(7)	Civilian	$11,300	$23,500	2.08
(8)	Military	7,500	17,600	2.35
(9)	Total	$ 9,600	$21,000	2.19
	Memo:			
(10)	Consumer Price Index (1967 = 100)	125.3	289.1	2.31

(a) Accrual basis.

Average direct compensation costs have increased from $9,600 in 1972 to $21,000 in 1982, with civilian pay increasing somewhat less rapidly, (10.0%), and military pay somewhat more rapidly, 1.7%, than inflation.

PPSS reviewed the procedures by which the Federal Government determines civilian and military pay levels and found:

• Federal *white-collar* salaries (employees in professional, administrative, technical, and clerical positions) are compared annually to salaries in the private sector for similar positions. But the survey used to make these comparisons—the "comparability" survey—overstates average private sector wages by an estimated 4%, at a cost of $4.131 billion over three years to the Government.

- The proportion of Federal *white-collar* workers in middle- and upper-management positions is 2.8X as great in the Federal Government as it is in the private sector.

- Federal *blue-collar* employees (workers in craft, trade, and manual jobs) receive average salaries that are 8% higher than local private sector rates, costing taxpayers $1.787 billion over three years. About 85% of Federal *blue-collar* workers earn more than the salaries paid to private sector employees in comparable jobs. For every Federal employee receiving a wage comparable to those in the private sector, 5.7 Federal employees receive wages above those of their private sector counterparts.

- Almost half of the *Federal top-level executives* are underpaid (by about 50%) in comparison with their private sector counterparts. As a result, the attrition rate among these executives is very high.

- *Postal Service employees,* who negotiate for their wages, received hourly wages in 1982 that were, on average, $2.31, or 28%, more than the average salaries for their private sector counterparts in manufacturing, wholesale, trucking, and other blue-collar jobs. For the over 600,000 postal employees, this means additional wages of approximately $3.0 billion annually.

- *Military pay,* although equivalent to private sector wages on average, is *perceived* by both the public and military personnel to be lower than private sector salaries. Military pay is composed of six different elements: basic pay, allowances, incentives, special pay, separation pay, and the tax advantage resulting from the tax-exempt status of allowances. Typically, only basic pay is considered as salary when making comparisons to the private sector.

The overall conclusion that PPSS drew from its review is that compensation practices in the Government need to be extensively revised. Savings of $7.151 billion over three years could be achieved by implementing the following PPSS recommendations:

- Expand the type of positions covered in the comparability survey so that a direct comparison can be made with Federal *white-collar* positions. In addition, state and local government salaries and wages paid in nonprofit organizations should be included in the survey.

- Expand the survey of private sector *blue-collar* salaries to include state and local government employees and employees in nonprofit institutions. In addition, change the structure of the blue-collar pay system from a five-step system with parity to the private sector at step two (steps three, four and five receiving wages higher than those in the private sector), to a three-step system with parity at step two. This would eliminate the current 8% premium received by Federal blue-collar employees.

- Change the distribution of Federal *white-collar and blue-collar* workers so that the ratio of higher level to lower level positions more closely reflects that in the private sector.

- Increase the salary scales for *top-level executives* and reduce by approximately 50% the number of positions classified as "executive" in the Government.

- Use the 1984 wage negotiations between the *U.S. Postal Service* (USPS) and the postal unions to bring USPS salaries closer to comparable private sector salaries.

- Provide *military personnel* with earnings statements to show that total military compensation is comparable to salaries in the private sector.

PPSS reviewed the *General Schedule* (GS) pay system, which covers over 1.4 million civilian white-collar employees, approximately 50% of total Executive Branch civilian personnel. The GS consists of 18 levels or grades, each broadly defined in terms of tasks performed, responsibilities, and qualifications required. Salaries are adjusted annually. As of December 1982, GS salaries ranged from a minimum of $8,676 for GS-1 to a maximum of $63,800 for GS-18.

Q. Are Federal white-collar workers paid salaries comparable to those of their private sector counterparts?

A. The surprising answer is, nobody knows. The Government survey which compares Federal white-collar and private sector positions is not an accurate reflection of private sector wages. The Director of the Office of Personnel Management (OPM), one of the three people responsible for the comparability survey, stated before Congress in 1983 that the survey looks at the wrong jobs and the wrong occupations for the wrong companies in the private sector—"I can guarantee that the [comparability] survey is not an accurate survey." As the 1982 survey notes on the first page:

> "While the principle of pay comparability is reasonable, *its implementation in the existing law is seriously flawed.*"

In net, there is no definitive answer to the question of the comparability of private and public sector pay rates. However, there is near unanimity of opinion in the position that the inaccuracies and distortions inherent in the comparability survey render it useless for making this determination.

Q. What specifically is wrong with the white-collar comparability survey?

A. PPSS noted the following problems:

- The scope of the survey is extremely narrow. Out of approximately 1.4 million white-collar employees, 334,000, or 23.9%, were in positions directly comparable to the private sector jobs included in the 1982 survey. Only 4 Federal administrative positions were surveyed in 1982, although there are more than 150 different administrative positions in Government, which represent over 25% of the Federal work force.

• The survey currently includes only 24 occupations, less than 6% of the approximately 425 different occupations in the Federal Government. Additionally, highly skilled (and highly paid) Federal positions (e.g., lawyers, accountants, engineers, chemists, computer operators) represent over half the positions included in the survey —a serious imbalance.

• Many private and non-Federal government employees are excluded from the survey: state and local government employees (13.1 million as of 1982), although they account for 13.2% of the civilian workforce; workers in small and medium-size firms, eliminating over 96% of private sector companies; and employees in nonprofit institutions.

Q. Under the present system, proposed average salary increases from the comparability survey have been reduced ("capped") in five of the last six years. Hasn't this left Government employees with the impression that Federal white-collar salaries are not "comparable" with private sector wages?

A. That is precisely the point. If you accept the conclusions of the 1982 survey, Government white-collar workers were, on average, 18.5% behind their counterparts in the private sector. But the survey isn't valid, there's only an *impression* that average Federal pay lags private sector pay by 18.5%.

Further, 18.5% is the *overall* pay raise recommended by the survey. Employees in different occupations may be paid more or less than their private sector counterparts, according to the survey. For example, pay for entry-level engineers (GS-5 to GS-9) would have to increase 19.9%–40.7% to achieve comparability, as now defined, with pay in the private sector. On the other hand, pay for accountants in grades 9-12 would have to decrease by 5.8%–13.3% to achieve comparability, as now defined. Paying clerical and professional employees from the same schedule with only 18 grades has contributed to these discrepancies between Federal and private sectors.

Q. Since the increases proposed by the comparability survey have been implemented only once in the past six years, how will PPSS recommendations save the Government money?

A. At some point, the issue of comparability as presented by the survey will have to be addressed. Unless the survey is made credible, pay adjustments will continue to appear arbitrary and unrelated to private sector compensation, leading to worker dissatisfaction, decreased productivity, loss of personnel, etc. If white-collar salaries are actually behind those in the private sector, the Government will lose employees and applicants because of the higher wages offered elsewhere. Since, according to OPM, there are ten qualified applicants for each Federal job, PPSS does not believe that Federal salaries are generally inferior to those in the private sector. However, some entry-level positions and a limited number of executive positions at the highest level of Government pay salaries below those of their private sector counterparts. The savings estimate of $4.131 billion over three years assumes that at some point the comparability survey will once again become the basis for determining Federal pay increases (as in the early- to mid-1970's). When that occurs, PPSS recommended changes to the survey will result in savings.

Q. What have General Schedule increases been in recent years?

A. General Schedule (GS) increases are established by law. Since 1967, the basic salary scale (based on statutory increases in GS salaries) has increased 110.3%. However, *statutory* changes in Federal salaries alone are *not* an accurate reflection of *actual* salary increases. Average salaries increase as Federal employees advance into higher grade levels and as they advance in the 10 steps within 15 of the 18 GS grades. Average salaries have increased 136.8%, or by 24.0% more than the basic scale.

This 24.0% average salary premium primarily results from "grade creep"—the tendency of average GS grades to increase over time. The average grade of all employees in the GS classification system has increased more than 3 grades since the current system was established in 1949, as shown below:

Average GS Grade

(1)	1949	5.25	An increase of
(2)	1974	8.03	3.23 grades,
(3)	1981	8.48	or 61.5%

At FY 1983 average annual salaries of approximately $15,000 for a GS-5 level employee and $21,000 for a GS-8 level employee, the increase in average grades from 5.25 to 8.48—"grade creep"— would cost approximately $8.4 billion in 1983 for 1.4 million GS employees.

Also, the theoretical 18-year time period required to progress from step 1 to step 10 in the General Schedule is essentially unrealistic. Promotions (primarily to the next higher grade in an occupational sequence) speed up the process. Further, over 98% of those eligible to receive a within-grade step increase in a given year receive the increase.

Q. It was previously mentioned that there are too many Federal white-collar workers in high level positions. What are the comparable proportions of high level workers in Federal employment and in the private sector?

A. Only 26% of private sector middle and upper management personnel are employed at a level comparable to GS-11 and above, compared to 72% in the Federal Government—i.e., a Government concentration 2.8 times as great as that in the private sector.

PPSS conclusions are further supported by a review of the distribution of Federal professional positions in higher grade levels. Shown below is information for selected occupations, comparing the distribution in the Government with that in the private sector.

Percent Distribution of Employees

GS Grade Equivalents	(1) Federal Salary Range ($000) (FY 1983)	(2) Percent of Total Employees in High Level Grades — Private Sector	(3) *Ranked* — Federal	(4) Federal Distribution as Multiple of Private Sector
(1) Engineers GS 11–GS 15	$24.5–$63.1	61.4%	91.3%	1.5X
(2) Chemists GS 11–GS 14	24.5– 53.7	54.4	81.9	1.5
(3) Directors of Personnel GS 13–GS 14	34.9– 53.7	54.4	81.9	1.5
(4) Accountants GS 11–GS 13	24.5– 45.4	31.0	71.0	2.3
(5) Attorneys GS 13–GS 15	34.9– 63.1	41.2	68.8	1.7

As shown for these selected occupations, the proportion of Federal employees in high level (and high salaried) positions is 1.5X-2.3X the proportion in the private sector.

Q. Why has this concentration of Federal employees in high level positions occurred?

A. There are many contributing factors. For example, compensation is generally too low for entry level professional positions. The Government's ability to attract and retain professional employees, therefore, is adversely affected. To compensate for lower starting salaries, managers promote employees quickly, assigning them to higher grade levels (i.e., higher salary levels). With a GS system of only 18 grades and relatively rapid promotion, the opportunities for further advancement can be limited and career employees cluster at the upper grade levels.

Q. What changes did PPSS propose to bring General Schedule white-collar salaries in line with those in the private sector?

A. PPSS recommended the following:

1. Expand the scope of the survey to include more Federal positions.

2. Include state and local government and nonprofit institution workforce data, and smaller private sector firms, in the survey.

3. Change the distribution of employees in the General Schedule to bring the proportion of higher level (and higher salaried) employees to lower level (and lower salaried) employees more in line with the proportion in the private sector.

4. Increase the number of levels in the General Schedule from the eighteen now in use. Eighteen levels are too few to accommodate the approximately 425 different Federal occupations ranging from clerk to top management and which include professional, administrative, technical, and clerical occupations.

5. Set the pay rates of clerical and technical jobs according to local prevailing rates. Apply area wage scales to non-supervisory positions (mostly GS grades 1–12) that are recruited on a local basis.

Q. What savings would result from these recommendations?

A. Based on discussions with Federal compensation experts, PPSS concluded that expanding and modifying the pay comparability survey along the lines mentioned above would have resulted in a minimum 4% to 5% reduction in the 1982 comparability recommendation (18.5%), resulting in savings of $4.131 billion over three years—equivalent to the salaries of 69,000 employees earning $20,000 annually for three years.

Another area PPSS analyzed was the *Federal Wage System* (FWS). FWS employees work in blue-collar positions, including trade, craft, and labor occupations. Pay is established to match local prevailing rates; each of approximately 135 local wage areas adjusts pay once a year but at different times.

Typical positions are listed below for some grades in the FWS, together with average salaries for each grade.

FWS Pay Plan

	Grade	(1) Typical Positions	(2) Approx. Salary, Dec. 1981
(1)	1	Janitor; Porter	$12,800
(2)	5	Maintenance helper	16,500
(3)	6	Truckdriver, medium truck	17,800
(4)	7	Truckdriver, heavy truck	18,500
(5)	8	Truckdriver, tractor-trailer	19,300
(6)	9	Carpenter; Painter	20,600
(7)	10	Electrician	21,700

Unlike the GS pay plan, FWS does not provide for career progression by advancement to higher grades. A grade 8 employee would not progress to grade 9 or 10 unless he acquired the new skills necessary to enter a different profession. Career progression in the FWS occurs by advancing through the five levels or steps within each grade.   The FWS system includes a five step pay range within each grade, with the second step equal to the average private sector salary. The first, third, fourth, and fifth steps are, respectively, 96%, 104%, 108%, and 112% of the second step (the average private sector salary). The law also provides for advancement to the next higher step (with creditable service and satisfactory performance) as follows:

After 26 weeks at step 1 to step 2
After 78 weeks at step 2 to step 3
After 104 weeks at step 3 to step 4
After 104 weeks at step 4 to step 5.

Therefore, after 6 years at a given position, a Federal employee reaches the maximum level where he is paid 112% of the average private sector wage.

Q. The wage setting process for Federal blue-collar employees sounds straightforward. What problems has PPSS identified?

A. As of FY 1978, over 85% of the workers were in Steps 3, 4, and 5 and thus made more than average private sector workers in comparable positions. 55% of the blue-collar workforce were in the *Top Step*—Step 5—where they made *12%* more than average private sector workers.

The Federal Wage System is estimated by PPSS to result in an 8.0% wage premium based on the average FWS pay position at level 4, which is 108% of the comparable private sector average wage rate.

This 8.0% wage premium primarily results from the use of a five-step salary system, with step two at 100% of comparability and steps 3-5, where the majority of FWS employees are graded, at 104%-112% of comparability.

In addition, there are other problems with the FWS comparability process which distort private sector wages:

1. The use of out-of-area wage data when local data are unavailable (Monroney Amendment). This requirement can result in FWS wages in small cities and rural areas being based, in part, on private sector wages in more costly big-city areas. (For example, Macon, Georgia, wages are based in part on data from Atlanta.)

2. The exclusion from the survey of state and local government wage data and data from nonprofit institutions.

3. The use of Federal nationwide night-shift differentials which do not provide for differentials on the basis of local prevailing practices. Before enactment of the 1972 FWS legislation, night-shift differentials were determined in accordance with prevailing practices in the local wage area.

Q. How does the Monroney Amendment affect FWS salaries?

A. The use of out-of-area wage data (the Monroney Amendment) establishes pay rates when comparable and/or local area data are unavailable or unsuitable. Usually this means the use of wage data from large urban areas which tend to be higher than local rates. These imported data cannot be used to lower wages, but only to increase them. Further, they raise wages for all employees of a given grade in the wage area. Thus, including the pay of aircraft technicians (Grade 10) whose pay rate is determined in part by out-of-area data, results in a revised (and often higher) pay rate for all employees in Grade 10. Moreover, all grades can be affected by the increase because of the desire to maintain a uniform differential in pay rates among all grades. According to the CBO, in 1979 the Monroney Amendment raised wages in 20 of 135 wage areas, benefitting about 25% of the FWS work force. In the Macon, Georgia, area, the Monroney Amendment added approximately 15% to FWS wages.

Q. How do nationwide night-shift differentials affect FWS salaries?

A. Night-shift differentials add from 7.5% to 10.0% in pay depending on the time of night the employee works. Night-shift differentials based on *local* practices rather than a single national standard are generally used in the private sector. Further, Federal employees are paid overtime when they work in excess of 8 hours a day. This practice varies from that in the private sector which generally pays overtime based on 40 hour work weeks rather than 8 hour days.

Q. How much could be saved if these deficiencies in the FWS are eliminated?

A. PPSS estimated that redesigning the five-step pay scales to a three-step structure with comparability at step 2, eliminating the Monroney Amendment, eliminating national night-shift differentials, and including state and local Government and nonprofit institutions in the survey would reduce FWS salaries by 6% to 8%. Based on a conservative 6% reduction, savings are estimated at $1.787 billion over a three-year period—equivalent to the salaries of 30,000 employees at $20,000 annually for three years.

Q. The Monroney Amendment is an example of Congressional involvement in determining how much Federal workers get paid. Are there other examples?

A. Because of differences in the cost-of-living from city to city, wage scales for blue-collar workers can differ. In 1981, blue-collar workers at the McConnell Air Force Base in Wichita, Kansas claimed their pay was lower than that of counterpart workers in comparable cities such as Topeka and Oklahoma City. At the time, the blue-collar wage in Wichita was $7.69 an hour, compared to $8.53 at Topeka and $9.00 at Oklahoma City, 9.8% and 14.6% lower, respectively.

Congress, arguing that the survey used in setting wage scales was in error, exempted those workers from the 4.8% limit on pay raises that affected all other Federal employees. In January 1982, civilian blue-collar workers at the 184th Air National Guard Tactical Fighter Group, based at McConnell, received a 27.8% pay raise to $10.51 an hour. Based on a 40-hour work week, their new salaries were $420.40 a week, $49.28 ahead of comparable salaries in Topeka.

Another compensation area analyzed by PPSS was that for the Federal executive area. The term "executive" generally describes any of the approximately 11,000 positions paid at rates equal to or greater than the minimum $56,945 rate for a GS-16. There are three basic executive categories:

The Executive Schedule covers Cabinet Secretaries, Deputy or Under Secretaries, Assistant Secretaries, Congressmen, Senators, heads of independent agencies or major National programs, and Board or Commission members (approximately 3,000 members).

The Senior Executive Service (SES) results from the Civil Service Reform Act of 1978. Its creators envisioned it as the elite management corps of the Government. Currently, there are approximately 6,800 SES members.

The Super Grades (GS-16, 17, 18) primarily cover high-level staff aides, research scientists, administrative law judges, and heads of advisory bodies (approximately 1,000 members).

Salary ranges for the above "executive" categories are shown below:

Executive Pay, December 1982

General Schedule (GS. Super Grades)		Executive Schedule		Senior Executive Service	
		I.	$80,100		
		II.	69,800		
		III.	68,400		
		IV.	67,200	6.	$67,200
				5.	65,500
GS-18	$63,800	V.	63,800	4.	63,800
GS-17	63,800			3.	61,515
GS-16	56,945–63,800			2.	59,230
				1.	56,945

By law, Executive Schedule salaries for levels IV and V set the limit for salaries in the General Schedule and Senior Executive Service.

Q. What's wrong with executive pay in the $55,000–$80,000 a year range?

A. Top executives in the Government are underpaid in comparison to their private sector counterparts. Executive Schedule employees are responsible for agencies with as many as 150,000 employees and for budgets which may be over $100 billion. Yet, Federal executive salaries are approximately one-half to one-third of those in the private sector for senior management positions. A top private sector financial executive in a Fortune 500 company earns approximately $200,000 annually. Compare this amount to the *maximum* Executive Level salary of $80,100, which is 40.1% of $200,000.

In addition, increases in Federal executive salaries have lagged both the private sector and even increases granted Federal retirees. For example, the Comptroller General said in 1981:

> "In our opinion, the executive pay dilemma is one of the most critical but perhaps least understood and appreciated problems facing the Government today. Since March, 1977 (four years), the executive pay ceiling has been increased by only 5.5%. During that same period, *retired* Federal executives received annuity cost-of-living adjustments totaling 55%; Federal white-collar pay rates have been increased by 38% and private sector executive pay has gone up about 40%."

Further, between October 1969 and October 1979, executives in the Federal Government lost purchasing power, according to the GAO:

Executive Pay,
Loss in Purchasing Power

	Grade	(1) Salary Paid in Oct. 1969	(2) Salary Paid in Oct. 1979 — Current $	(3) Salary Paid in Oct. 1979 — Constant 1969 $	(4) % Salary Paid in 1979 Fav./(Unfav.) vs. 1969 — Current $	(5) % Salary Paid in 1979 Fav./(Unfav.) vs. 1969 — Constant 1969 $
(1)	ES Level I	$60,000	$69,630	$34,475	16.1%	(42.5)%
(2)	ES Level V	36,000	50,112	24,811	39.2	(31.1)
(3)	GS-16	25,044	47,889	23,711	91.2	(5.3)

As shown, although executive salaries have increased, 1969–1979, in 1969 dollars, executives have lost between (5.3)% and (42.5)% of their purchasing power. This has failed to motivate senior executives to achieve an improved level of operational efficiency and effectiveness—the incentive to excel is simply not there.

Q. In comparing salaries among Federal executive positions, there doesn't seem to be much of a gap between salary levels.

A. That's quite true. In the SES, going from level 3 to level 6 increases an employee's salary only $5,685, or 9.2%. With taxes taking half or more of that increase, there is no incentive for executives to strive for increased responsibilities, duties, and work. This is how salary or "pay compression" results in lost productivity and lack of incentive. If a promotion brings only a minimal pay increase, very few employees are going to try for that higher position or, if they do accept a promotion, they will lack the appropriate incentive to perform well.

Furthermore, it is possible to get a promotion and not get an increase in pay. In the General Schedule (for grades 18 and 17, for example) it is possible for a supervisor to make only as much as the person he supervises. Pay compression and pay limits, or "caps," are some of the major reasons executives are leaving Federal service, leading to the Government's "brain-drain."

Q. "Brain-drain" sounds ominous. What does it mean?

A. "Brain-drain" means that the best and brightest employees in the Government are leaving Federal service. The Government is losing its most valuable, experienced career executives. According to a study by the Comptroller General, experienced Federal executives at the peak of their managerial careers are retiring at an alarmingly high rate. For example, 3,137 career executives retired in 1980, compared with only 508 in 1977. The average Federal retirement age in 1981 was 59, compared to 63/64 in the private sector.

Q. What other problems result from pay compression?

A. SES was created in 1978 to improve the efficiency and effectiveness of the Federal Government. Those electing to join this elite cadre agreed to accept reassignments to areas where they were needed and give up some of the security offered other civil servants. In return, these executives became eligible for improved pay-setting procedures and a system of awards (including bonuses) which were based on their performance.

The high expectations with which the SES was established have not materialized. One problem is the difficulty of convincing executives to accept positions of greater responsibility that may involve moving to a different part of the country, and incurring expenses that are generally necessary in such a move, with no increase in salary. Furthermore, many Federal executives are reluctant to accept promotions because the increased responsibilities of the positions are not recognized with higher pay.

Personnel officials at Federal agencies consider low Federal executive salaries and infrequent adjustments as major sources of difficulty in recruiting well-qualified individuals from outside the Government. This is particularly evident in the medical, legal, and scientific fields. Conversely, the generally higher level of compensation in the private sector is an incentive for Government executives to leave public employment for positions in the private sector.

Q. Why have Federal executive salaries been compressed and capped?

A. The salaries of Congressmen and Senators are set at Level II of the Executive Schedule. Thus, any action taken by Congress to raise the rates in the Executive Schedule will result in the pay rates of Congress being increased. This is a political issue. Consequently, there have been long periods of drought between Executive Schedule pay adjustments. Since SES and GS super grade salaries are tied to the Executive Schedule, salary increases in these systems have also been stalled.

Q. What did PPSS recommend?

A. PPSS recommended:

1. Increasing Executive Schedule and SES salary rates by 20% to 30%, thus improving the prospects for recruiting, motivating, and retaining the best executives for top Federal positions;

2. Establishing a 10% to 15% differential between each of the five salary levels of the Executive Schedule;

3. Providing an annual or biannual review of Executive Schedule salaries; and

4. Separating the salary of the Congress from that of the Executive Schedule, and separating the link between SES and Executive Schedule pay.

In addition, as part of an effort to increase Federal productivity by providing incentives to an elite group of executive personnel, the Director of the Office of Personnel Management (OPM) should begin an in-depth study to determine which SES positions have the scope, accountability, and impact to warrant bonus eligibility and the higher salary schedule.

This would result in a relatively small group (1,000–3,500 managers) who would comprise the SES. The current positions deemed non-bonus eligible could be placed in the super grades (GS-16, GS-17, and GS-18).

Reducing the SES to 1,000–3,500 members would mean a small group of the best and the brightest employees compensated accordingly. The SES program would identify its participants as unique and distinctive and would represent a desirable goal towards which non-participating employees could aspire. The proposed SES contrasts to the current situation in which those nominated and recommended for membership often decline the opportunity.

The SES bonus program, which currently allows 20% of SES members in an agency to receive awards, should be structured so that bonuses are based on productivity and results. This program would be the counterpart of private sector bonus programs that base rewards upon performance—an incentive to accept promotions and responsibility with commensurate rewards.

Q. What savings would result from implementing these recommendations?

A. The savings associated with the foregoing recommendations cannot be measured in terms of dollars. As noted earlier, this issue centers on the Federal Government's ability to attract and retain key executive management personnel capable of effective and efficient management. Opportunities for savings are inherent in attracting the best executives into Federal service.

PPSS also analyzed *U.S. Postal Service (USPS)* compensation. In 1970, USPS, an independent agency in the Executive Branch of the Federal Government, replaced the Post Office Department. As a result, postal workers are part of the postal career service and are exempt from most laws relating to Federal employment. Postal salaries are determined by labor-management negotiations.

Q. Since the wages of Postal employees are determined through management-labor negotiations, it would seem that postal wages should closely reflect private sector rates. How do USPS salaries compare to specific blue-collar salaries in the private sector?

A.   USPS wage rates exceed the average salaries of workers in private sector industries by as much as $4 an hour, as shown below:

Comparison of Wage Rates and Salaries by Industry Classification
($ per hour and per year)

		(1)	(2)	(3)	(4)
				1982 Private Sector (Below) USPS Average:	
		Wage Rate 1982	Wage Rate		Salary
			Amount	Percent	
(1)	USPS Average Postal Salary	$10.61	—	—	—
	Private Sector				
(2)	Trucking & Warehousing	10.20	$(0.41)	(3.9)%	$ (853)
(3)	Communications	9.92	(0.69)	(6.5)	(1,435)
(4)	All Manufacturing	8.37	(2.24)	(21.1)	(4,659)
(5)	Wholesale Trade	7.93	(2.68)	(25.3)	(5,574)
(6)	Services	6.77	(3.84)	(36.2)	(7,987)
(7)	Finance, Insurance, Real Estate	6.59	(4.02)	(37.8)	(8,362)
(8)	Average, Private Sector Categories Shown Above	8.30	(2.31)	(21.8)	(4,805)

Average private sector wage rates are below those of USPS average postal salaries in every category. On a yearly basis, USPS workers average $4,805 more than workers in private industry.

Q.   What can be done to remedy this situation?

A.   The current collective bargaining agreements between USPS and its major unions will be renegotiated in 1984. These negotiations represent a major opportunity to reduce costs by emphasizing direct comparisons to the private sector. With over 600,000 employees, savings of even 10¢ an hour will result in lower payroll costs of approximately $125 million annually. Savings of $1.00 an hour can lead to annual cost reductions of over $1.2 billion.

In addition to civilian pay systems and salaries, PPSS also reviewed *military pay*. PPSS is committed to the proposition that total military compensation should be superior to that offered by the Nation's major employers. Superior salaries will stimulate recruitment and retention of quality personnel and recognize the need to compensate for potentially higher risk occupations.

As stated previously, military pay is currently composed of six different elements: basic pay, allowances, incentive pay, special pay, separation pay, and the tax advantage (allowances are tax-free). There are at least 32 different categories of pay and allowances, with several different levels of pay possible in most of these categories.

Q. The military is generally perceived as underpaid by the general public and by military personnel. Is this the case?

A. Definitely not. However, the complexity of the military pay system makes direct comparisons to the private sector difficult and creates the illusion that the military is underpaid.

Providing an annual statement to military personnel that includes all elements of their military pay would enhance the visibility of the total military compensation package and would facilitate private sector comparisons.

Q. On the subject of military pay, PPSS made recommendations regarding the bonus program for the Air Guard and Reserve and Civil Service pay to personnel on guard and reserve duty. Savings are estimated at $96 million over three years in these two areas. What problems did PPSS note?

A. PPSS found that the Government is not spending wisely almost $9 million annually on its Air National Guard and Air Force Reserve bonus programs for reenlistment. Bonus amounts are frequently too small to have much impact on reenlistment decisions. Further, the Government is similarly not spending wisely $20 million annually because it pays its civilian employees their full salaries while they are on military reserve active duty. This practice varies from the standard private sector practice of reducing salaries by the amount of reserve compensation.

The inadequacy of the Government's pay determination process for civilian employees, political restraints on executive salaries, and a lack of visibility in military compensation have adversely affected the Government's ability to attract, retain, and fairly compensate Federal employees. PPSS recommendations are intended to both save taxpayer money and improve the management of the Federal workforce.

In addition to the issues discussed above, there are several other issues dealing with compensation, with total three-year savings of $1.203 billion. Included in these issues are the following:

Incentive Pay. By limiting military aviation incentive pay and limiting Selective Reenlistment Bonus program payments to those skill areas where there are retention problems, savings of $887 million over three years are possible.

Foreign Service Personnel Management System. By correcting the skewed, top heavy personnel distribution and improving the personnel management system, three-year savings of $86 million are achievable.

Agricultural Stabilization and Conservation Service (ASCS) County Committee Elections. PPSS recommended that each of the 3,052 agricultural counties be split into 3 districts and that elections be held in each district only once every three years. Further, compensation for community committees should be eliminated. Three-year cost savings of $26 million are anticipated.

The three-year total of all the recommendations in this section, after elimination of duplication and overlap among issues, is $7.151 billion—equal to the three-year taxes of 1.1 million median income families.

Work Force Management

PPSS found serious deficiencies in the planning for and use of the Federal work force. These deficiencies are apparent in overstaffing, lack of employee motivation and low productivity. The problems are deep-rooted in the lack of a management structure to focus on human resource needs.

PPSS recommended that the Office of Personnel Management develop a systematic approach to formulating human resource policies and procedures for use by all Government agencies. These would have the purposes of assuring the application of high standards of personnel development.

In FY 1983, the Government spent $66.3 billion in the specific areas covered by PPSS recommendations, with spending estimated to increase to $357.0 billion by the year 2000 if present policies are continued. Implementing PPSS recommendations would reduce spending to $300.7 billion in 2000, a saving of $56.3 billion, or 15.8%.

In addition to analyzing the compensation of Federal employees, including retirement and fringe benefits, PPSS reviewed how Federal employees are managed, including the incentives provided to and the productivity of the Federal work force; staffing, grading (assigning salary levels to jobs), spans of control (number of workers per supervisor); and training and development.

INCENTIVES AND PRODUCTIVITY

A staff study prepared for Congress in 1979 stated: "If the overall Federal productivity could be increased by 10%, personnel costs could be reduced by more than $8 billion per year without a cutback in services."

Q. In what specific Government agencies are productivity improvements possible?

A. Social Security Administration (SSA) employees, for example, operate at about 50% of capacity because:

- Supervisors are not adequately controlling the flow of work through their units—employees have almost total control over the workflow.

- Supervisors have little or no responsibility for short-term planning.

- Supervisors have no incentive to increase productivity since improved productivity can decrease staff allocations and negatively affect the supervisor's compensation—a prime example of Federal procedures providing a disincentive to effective management.

- Upper management has not provided line supervisors with a standardized approach for organizing work, nor a specific approach to solving problems.

Q. What did PPSS recommend?

A. PPSS recommended a management system which would have supervisors develop and execute daily and weekly plans; a field office productivity system which would establish office productivity goals and would offer incentives for meeting or surpassing goals; and a reduction in the supervisory span of control from the current 15.4 employees for each supervisor to 9–12 employees per supervisor.

Projected savings of $1.266 billion over three years are based on raising productivity from 50% to 75%, thereby reducing staff levels by 16,000–18,000 employees. Productivity increases of this magnitude have been achieved in the private sector by instituting a supervisory planning and control system. In the private sector, this discipline, lacking throughout the Federal work force, is necessary to ensure the continued survival of the organization.

Q. In what other areas did PPSS find room for productivity improvements?

A. For one, in the area of real property maintenance, budgeted at $3.5 billion in FY 1983. In the past 30 years, there have been many efforts to use industrial engineering techniques to reduce maintenance costs in Government-owned facilities. Results have been less than successful—government-wide productivity in carrying out in-house maintenance still averages only 40%–45%. Productivity rates below 50% fall in the "low" range by private sector standards. PPSS found that:

- Maintenance productivity varies significantly from installation to installation; it ranged in a survey sample from 20% to 50%, indicative of the lack of Government productivity standards.

- Productivity in Government maintenance cannot be improved substantially unless present inadequacies in the areas of scheduling, estimating, and planning are corrected.

- There appears to be little, if any, incentive for managers to improve productivity, because neither rewards nor penalties are associated directly with this aspect of their jobs—promotions come customarily from being good mechanics rather than from displaying administrative skills.

Q.   What is the level of maintenance productivity in the private sector?

A.   Good productivity levels for maintenance in the private sector are in the range of 60% to 65%. Generally, high productivity in the private sector is associated with plants and facilities that use their own highly-skilled maintenance people and that use well-defined planning and scheduling programs.

PPSS recommended that:

- a government-wide program to raise the level of maintenance productivity be introduced;

- performance indices for property maintenance be established, both as a management tool and as performance incentives; and

- emphasis be placed on improving job estimates, plans, and detailed scheduling.

The Civil Service Reform Act of 1978 mandated a complete redesign of Federal systems for developing, motivating, and rewarding employees. The objective of the legislation was to materially improve Federal employee efficiency, responsiveness, and productivity through performance measurement systems (PMS) comparable to those used by private industry. The basic concept of all such plans is to measure employee performance against pre-established management goals and objectives.

Q.   Did PPSS review performance evaluations and their effect on productivity?

A.   Yes. Take the Veterans Administration (VA) as an example. Performance evaluations in VA claims processing can be greatly improved. The VA Department of Veterans Benefits (DVB) disbursed $15 billion in benefits to six million claimants in FY 1983 through 58 field stations.

The DVB work measurement system does not accurately measure individual and field station performance. A standard time for performing each major activity is used to measure productivity by comparing the standard to total time available. Since standards measure total elapsed time rather than the time taken to complete a task (i.e., standards include lost and unproductive time), the system overstates actual productivity and effectiveness.

Q. Can the DVB work measurement system be used effectively?

A. DVB productivity data has *not* been used to evaluate field station staffing levels or to project future personnel requirements. It is used to compare performance among stations and to ensure that they stay within an acceptable range. The current DVB productivity range of 65% to 92% is considered acceptable by DVB. The GAO, however, contends that the same productivity data indicate that field stations are overstaffed. The fact that since 1975 the claims work load has declined by 30%, while field station personnel have decreased only 22% and productivity, as measured by DVB's system, has *increased* 5%, supports GAO's conclusion.

Q. How does VA productivity compare with the private sector?

A. VA productivity figures can be put into perspective by comparing VA performance to the experience of private insurance companies. In the private sector, long-term disability claims are processed generally within 42 days compared to 98 days in 1981 for processing VA pension claims.

Q. How can VA's performance be improved?

A. To improve efficiency, the current VA productivity measurement system needs to be revised to conform to private sector standards. This measurement system should then be used as the basis for implementing a system of performance evaluations through annual reviews. Savings of $272 million over three years will accrue as a result of an estimated 30% reduction in direct labor necessary to process VA claims.

Q. Are there other agencies where the performance measurement system is not working as intended?

A. Yes. For example, in the Department of Labor's (DOL) work measurement system. Although 57% of supervisors indicated that most of their employees' work is measured, less than half feel that these measurements are a fair and equitable basis for evaluating individual performance. Further, only 30% believe that employees have control over the conditions affecting the quantity of work output. Fewer than one-half of supervisors believe that existing output measures, without improvement, can be used to appraise individual work performance.

Q.   What did PPSS recommend?

A.   The DOL management information systems do not produce the information needed to evaluate the performance of individual employees, nor do they identify the unit cost of major activities. Such data is vital to cost containment and productivity measurement.

Developing productivity measurement systems, holding managers accountable for meeting specific productivity improvement objectives, and providing managers with financial incentives for meeting these objectives would save $50 million over three years.

Q.   What is the primary obstacle to increasing productivity and improving work force planning?

A.   The Government has recognized that the major problem is disincentives to improve. For example, the GAO summarized the problem as follows:

> . . . disincentives, which were identified in previous GAO reports, include
>
> • across-the-board budget cuts, [in anticipation of] which . . . managers . . . keep staff above minimum levels in order to absorb the cuts and still perform the work;
>
> • tying grade levels to number of staff supervised; and
>
> • inability of managers to discipline employees who do not perform.

Q.   What solutions did PPSS propose to address these problems?

A.   OMB, within the broader framework of the strongly recommended Office of Federal Management, should be directed to establish programs to improve productivity throughout the Federal work force.

OMB, with assistance from OPM, should utilize existing incentive awards to recognize managers whose contributions to and participation in the program result in improved productivity.

Performance appraisals should include an evaluation of productivity improvement programs by managers and subordinates.

Staffing, Grading, and Spans of Control

PPSS noted that Government personnel policies fail to provide incentives to encourage efficient use of the Federal work force, resulting in:

• inordinate use of overtime;

• creation of thousands of unnecessary, temporary positions;

- assignment of inappropriate spans of control to managers;

- contracting of jobs to the private sector at a higher cost than could be accomplished internally (as opposed to Federal requirements that jobs be contracted out only when cost savings are possible); and

- excessive layering of management, including excessive use of deputies and assistants, duplicate organizational frameworks, and overgraded positions.

PPSS concentrated on staffing, grading, and spans of control.

Overstaffing can be viewed in terms of productivity. Eliminating excessive staff is a central aspect of productivity improvement and cost control. As an example, excessive staff exists in the Consumer Product Safety Commission (CPSC) and EPA.

Q. What problems are there in CPSC regarding excessive staff?

A. In comparison to other agencies, CPSC has proportionately more administrative staff relative to total employees as shown below:

		(1) Finance	(2) Admin. Services	(3) Personnel
(1)	CPSC	1:40	1:16	1:28
(2)	Average For Six Non-CPSC agencies	1:51	1:22	1:52
(3)	Average Non-CPSC As Multiple of CPSC	1.275X	1.375X	1.857X

The ratio of administrative to CPSC staff exceeds average non-CPSC staffing in these six agencies by 1.3X–1.9X for the administrative areas listed above. By eliminating 22 positions, CPSC would save $3 million over three years and achieve an administrative staff ratio that is the same as the average in the six non-CPSC agencies.

Q. What overstaffing problems exist in EPA?

A. EPA's ratio of personnel staff to employees, 2.8 per 100, is considerably higher than the median private sector ratio, which ranges from 0.7 to 1.0 per 100 employees. PPSS recommended that EPA achieve a ratio of 2 personnel staff per 100 employees by reducing the personnel staff by 101 employees. Savings of $13 million over three years are estimated.

In addition to overstaffing, there is excessive layering of positions such as deputies and assistants, whose functions are to free top management from the less important aspects of their jobs.

Q. What are some of the specific situations that PPSS found regarding overuse of deputy and assistant positions?

A. The Environmental Protection Agency (EPA), again, is an example where there is an unnecessarily large number of deputy and special assistant positions.

   PPSS found 41 special assistant and 41 deputy positions in EPA. The direct salaries of the special assistants amounted to $1.7 million, an average of over $42,000 each; direct salaries for the deputy positions were $2.3 million, an average of over $55,000 each.

   PPSS found that 30 of the 41 special assistant and half of the 41 deputy positions could be eliminated, with savings of $11 million over three years.

In addition, end-strength ceilings are numerical limitations placed on the civilian work force by the Office of Management and Budget (OMB) and Congress. The intent of these ceilings is to control the number of employees. However, civilian end-strength ceilings have been ineffective as management tools. Agencies have found ways to manipulate the ceilings, increasing staff over assigned limits and increasing personnel costs. Also, ceilings do not take into account personnel shortages that may exist in certain skills which impede efforts to accomplish agency functions.

Q. How do agencies manipulate end-strength personnel ceilings?

A. As of July 1982, the Air Force had approximately 260,400 civilian employees. Many of these were temporary employees who were taken off the books for one day, at year end, then "rehired." Others were "on call," career-conditional permanent employees who received full benefits but who could be taken off the rolls when necessary. The end-of-year ceiling process does not control the number of Air Force employees and does not take into account certain costs, such as the disruption of workflow as employees are "fired" and "rehired."

Q. Are there other specific problems resulting from the use of personnel ceilings?

A. PPSS found the following Air Force examples of major problems with personnel ceilings:

   More costly alternatives—Work which cannot be accomplished during regular hours is completed by paying overtime or by contracting out for the work at higher cost. The Air Force estimates that overtime in depot maintenance could be reduced by approximately 64% if the ceiling on civilian personnel were increased, saving $3.5 million annually.

   Cost of year-end terminations—To stay within year-end ceilings, agencies furlough employees and hire them back. There is a cost associated with furloughing an employee for the last day of a fiscal year and rehiring the employee one day later. The Air Force has estimated that this cost is about $150 per employee. Thus, despite an Air Force program to reduce its over-employment from 12,000 to 4,000 by the end of FY 1982, it still cost approximately $600,000 simply to terminate and rehire these 4,000 employees.

Work force imbalances—Ceilings create imbalances in the composition of the work force and shortages in certain skills. In the Air Force, one result of the ceiling has been a reversal in the planned conversion of 6,000 positions from military to civilian functions. This is contrary to established policy of conserving military personnel for military functions.

Reduced readiness—Work that has been funded but cannot be accomplished because of ceilings results in reduced readiness. In addition, the ability to "surge" to meet future crises is limited if overtime becomes the regular mode of operation.

Overall, PPSS identified $18–$40 million in possible annual cost savings to the Air Force alone if end-strength ceilings were eliminated, with savings over three years estimated at $96 million.

As discussed above, personnel ceilings are a flawed management tool and lead to inefficiencies. Other inefficient government-wide policies noted by PPSS are across the board personnel reductions and reduction-in-force (RIF) procedures.

Q. What damage do across-the-board staff reductions cause?

A. The Office of Revenue Sharing (ORS) of the Treasury Department is an example of an agency using across-the-board staff reductions inefficiently. The ORS has the same organizational structure today that it had in 1978, despite a 22% decrease in its work force.

Prior staff reductions have been across the board, reducing personnel in all divisions. This process may have severely weakened the organization by reducing some divisions to a point at which staffing is less than sufficient.

Reducing the ORS from seven to five divisions, with the attendant reduction of two division managers, will result in a more effective organization.

Future decreases in personnel, if required by additional reductions in manpower ceilings, can be achieved by abolishing whole units rather than eliminating staff across the board. This approach might be less devastating and more efficient than cutting staff on an equal division basis.

Q. How do reduction-in-force (RIF) procedures hinder efficient staffing?

A. When an agency determines a RIF is necessary, it must identify the positions to be abolished, determine which employees will lose or change jobs, determine whether employees who lose their jobs have rights to other positions, issue notices to the affected employees at least 30 days before the reduction is scheduled to take place, and assist employees in finding other jobs.

Some of the problems involved in current RIF procedures can be seen in RIFs undertaken by the Department of Health and Human Services (HHS) and by the Office of Personnel Management (OPM).

Q. What problems occurred during the RIF at HHS?

A. During FY 1982, 1,840 positions were abolished at HHS Headquarters and regional locations. In the process, 190 RIF separations took place, while 1,530 employees were affected by either reductions in grade or reassignments. *For each employee actually involuntarily separated, 8 employees were affected.* To abolish the 1,840 positions in Headquarters and the regions, HHS spent almost $5 million for staff time, administration, retraining, or relocation. In addition, there were large, incalculable costs associated with lost productivity, skills, and quality.

Q. What happened during the RIF at OPM?

A. During FY 1982, 278 positions with an average grade of GS-11 were abolished at OPM. Because employees in some of these positions were entitled to "bump" lower graded employees, the average grade of employees separated was GS-7, four grades below the positions that were abolished. The Agency experienced very heavy attrition during the two months prior to the RIF, and eventually only 113 persons were separated. The staff time to plan and execute OPM's 1982 RIF cost an estimated $222,000.

Q. What happens to employees who "bump" other employees or who are downgraded?

A. Downgraded employees assume the functions and responsibilities of the employees they replace. They are entitled to retain their previous salaries for two years, even though the jobs they now occupy are paid at lower rates. PPSS noted instances of highly paid professionals and managers performing jobs of low status and importance. The cost of this is evident. Of equal importance, however, is the effect on the morale of the downgraded employees, and those who work with them, doing the same work at a much lower rate of pay.

Q. Doesn't moving/downgrading employees from one position to another have a negative effect on agency efficiency?

A. Yes. Generally, unrestricted displacement of employees under the current system results in costly and counterproductive employee moves and substantially weakens agency organizations. Performance and efficiency under existing procedures carry little weight in determining retention rights. The quality and use of personnel retained in an agency after a RIF can become secondary under the current system of retention and reassignment.

Q. What does PPSS recommend to remedy present RIF procedures?

A. PPSS recommended:

- Assigning greater weight to performance and efficiency in determining employee ratings in RIF procedures. For example, veterans' preference has excessive weight in determining point assignments, while performance has too little weight.

- Limiting bumping and retreat rights (displacing employees with lower standing) to no more than one grade level lower than the position from which the RIF employee is released to prevent excessive and indiscriminate displacement and the loss of valuable employees.

- Designating separate retention lists by clerical and nonclerical classifications. Establishing lists on this basis will help lessen disruption by eliminating replacement of highly skilled clerical employees by marginally skilled or unskilled nonclerical employees.

PPSS estimated that the Government would have saved $43 million in 1982 if PPSS recommendations had been in place, or over one-third of 1982 RIF costs of $105 million.

Reorganizations help to determine what staff is necessary to an agency and how that staff should be organized. Studies are necessary to determine whether current structures meet agency needs and whether more efficient structures are possible. In many Government agencies, reorganizations would help define responsibilities, decrease personnel costs, and increase efficiencies. The private sector does this regularly.

Q. Did PPSS note any specific agencies where reorganizations would help reduce personnel costs?

A. EPA's policy on position management includes the following:

- A minimum number of managerial and supervisory positions are to be established.

- Fragmentation (unnecessarily splitting the organization into many small segments) is to be avoided.

- Narrow spans of control (providing more supervision than is necessary) are to be avoided.

However, EPA has not been following its own policy for position management. Some 161 small groups are scattered throughout EPA.

More than half consist of four or five employees, the remainder of three or less. This has led to an excessive number of managerial and supervisory positions, as well as to narrow spans of control.

Q. What did PPSS recommend?

A. EPA should concentrate on eliminating small organizational units by having senior officers submit reorganization plans as soon as possible. Reorganizing and reducing the number of small organizational units within the agency would result in long-term annual savings of $1.4 million. Organizational units should be large enough to prevent the tendency to inflate job grades artificially by proliferating the number of small units.

Q. Do fragmentation problems exist in some of the smaller agencies or bureaus?

A. Yes. In the Interstate Commerce Commission (ICC), the Office of Compliance and Consumer Assistance (OCCA) employs approximately 485 people. OCCA's personnel have not been reduced to reflect the greatly decreased regulatory mission of ICC as a result of 1980 legislation.

Staff positions help reduce personnel costs by increasing the efficiency of professionals and managers. However, in some agencies, there are not enough staff to support higher levels of management. Examples of the above were noted in the Department of Justice (DOJ) and the Department of Commerce (DOC).

Q. What is wrong with the ratio of professionals to staff in DOJ?

A. Paralegals are becoming an increasingly important resource for improving productivity and cost-efficiency in private legal practices. In the private sector, the ratio of attorneys to paralegals is about 5:1 compared to an average of 6:1 for all non-DOJ Executive Branch agencies. The ratio of attorneys to paralegals at DOJ legal divisions is 8:1, nearly 40% below the ratio in the private sector.

DOJ can save more than 50% in salary expenses for each attorney it replaces with a paralegal. Bringing the ratio of attorneys to paralegals in line with private sector practices within DOJ legal divisions would save the Government $13 million over three years.

Q. What about the Department of Commerce (DOC)?

A. The National Bureau of Standards (NBS) of DOC is a research laboratory whose primary mission is to provide measurement-related data and standards for use by industry, Government, academia, and the general public.

The 1983 budget for NBS calls for a staff that includes approximately five full-time professional employees for every one full-time technician (846 professional employees, 172 technicians). Typical industry research and development laboratories utilize one-to-one ratios of professionals to technicians.

To increase both the efficiency and effectiveness of NBS, a target of approximately three full-time professionals to one full-time technician is recommended.

Grade controls deal almost exclusively with grade escalation. Grade escalation is the tendency of average grades in the General Schedule to increase over time. Since 1949, the average grade in the General Schedule has increased as follows:

**Increase in General Schedule
Average Grade, 1949–1981**

	Year	
(1)	1949	5.25
(2)	1974	8.03
(3)	1981	8.48

Q. Are average grades in the Government comparable to those in private industry?

A. No. The current Federal classification system has resulted in large numbers of people in professional and administrative jobs being grouped in the higher GS grades. Approximately 70% of the exempt (from the Fair Labor Standards Act) positions are in grades 11 and above, and about 50% in grades 12 and above. As discussed under the "Compensation" section of this report, the resulting "inverted pyramid" distribution of exempt workers differs sharply from conditions in the private sector. In the private sector, only about 26% of the white collar work force is usually found in levels similar to GS-11—GS-15, as shown below:

Distribution of Management Personnel

	Grade	(1) Federal	(2) Private Sector	(3) Federal as Multiple of Private Sector
(1)	GS-11 and above	72%	26%	2.77X
(2)	GS-5 to 10	28	74	0.38

Q. Does this mean that Government grade controls, if any, are not effective?

A. Yes. A 1982 OPM study found that the net cost to the Government of positions that are incorrectly graded is *$682 million* annually. Furthermore, the study showed that 15.8% of all Federal positions are incorrectly graded, with another 8.9% having incorrect titles. The results of the survey are shown below:

Classification Errors, FY 1981

	Problem	(1) Number of Employees	(2) Percent of Total GS Employees
(1)	Overgrading	187,600	14.3%
(2)	Title Errors	116,800	8.9
(3)	Undergrading	19,700	1.5
(4)	Total	324,100	24.7%
(5)	Memo: Total Full- Time, Permanent General Schedule Employees	1,312,000	

As is clear from the above, the Federal Government has a large problem with grade controls and with personnel management—24.7% of all Government jobs have one of the three problems listed.

In the Washington, D.C. area, nearly one-third of all positions are overgraded and nearly half are misclassified with the wrong grade, occupation, or title.

Q. Are some agencies better than others at controlling grade misclassifications?

A. Yes. OPM noted that the Department of Defense (DOD) had fewer positions overgraded than other agencies, as shown below:

Misgrading, DOD and Non-DOD

		(1) Percentage DOD	(2) Percentage Non-DOD	(3) Non-DOD As Multiple of DOD
(1)	Overgraded	8.7%	16.7%	1.9X
(2)	Undergraded	0.4	2.3	5.8

Q. Why is DOD more effective than other agencies?

A. DOD has established procedures and controls to implement effective position management programs. DOD managers are required to issue internal program policies and procedures, conduct periodic compliance inspections or surveys, and commit sufficient resources to the program. Line managers and supervisors are evaluated at least annually for position management effectiveness.

As a result, the classification accuracy rate is much higher for DOD agencies than for other Federal agencies. Furthermore, DOD devotes more resources to classification work. The number of Position Classification Specialists in DOD is higher than in the other Federal agencies. In 1978, the ratio of DOD classifiers to employees was more than twice that of other agencies. In addition, the training program for Position Classifiers in DOD was considered by OPM to be more thorough than that of other Federal agencies.

Q. What changes did PPSS recommend to improve position classification accuracy?

A. Restructure the work force, reducing the average grade by one-half a grade. Average grade would then equal the value it had in 1974.

Intensify efforts to reduce overgrading, reducing overgrading to 5% of what now exists.

PPSS estimated that savings over three years could be $5.164 billion if the Federal position classification system were redesigned.

Q. How do promotion policies lead to grade escalation?

A. A 1976 study prepared for the Civil Service Commission shows that:

• The typical time between promotions for the Federal occupations surveyed is less than for the private sector. For example, in the three professional occupations which have career ladders (Accounting, Procurement, and Engineering), the typical time lapse between promotions in the private sector ranged from 41% to 93% longer than for promotions in the Federal Government.

• The percentage salary increase accompanying Federal promotions is larger than comparable increases in the private sector. For example, the percentage salary increases in each of the three professional occupations mentioned above were at least 40% higher in the Federal Government than in the private sector.

Furthermore, there is very little incentive to perform better since employees eligible for career ladder promotions whose performance is rated "outstanding," "highly effective," or "fully successful" are all promoted at about the same time.

Q. What did PPSS propose to change the present situation?

A. PPSS recommended relating promotional timing to individual performance, developing better promotion monitoring and auditing procedures, and ensuring a proper balance among mission needs, efficiency of operations, and effective employee utilization.

The question of *spans of control* (the number of employees per manager) is one of the many problems the Federal Government faces in position management. PPSS analyses in the Department of Energy (DOE) and the Public Health Service (PHS) of the Department of Health and Human Services provide examples of how various position management problems are connected.

Q. What problems exist in the Energy Department?

A. The 1982 average Department of Energy (DOE) salary of $31,200 per year is 30% higher than the Federal average. Furthermore, the average General Schedule (GS) grade level for all DOE employees in 1982 was 10.6—which is higher than all but 2 of the 17 agencies and departments surveyed by PPSS. Even a comparison of clerical employees showed that DOE's average annual salary and grade level at the end of 1981 was about $1,600 and a full GS level higher than that of the Government as a whole.

Q. Why are DOE salaries so high?

A. In percentage terms, DOE has more than twice as many employees in "supervisor" classifications as does the Federal Government overall. During 1982, the ratio of non-supervisory employees to first-level supervisors in the Department was 2.9:1, compared with the Federal average of 6.9:1. (A goal of 7:1 is standard in the private sector.)

Q. What problems do these small spans of control cause?

A. It is important from the standpoint of management efficiency to see that the proper amount of supervision is being provided at various levels. Too much management can be as bad as too little. Excessive "layering" of supervisory levels increases the number of employees, causes delays, and may actually lower the quality and consistency of the work. These problems are in addition to added personnel costs.

Q. Were similar problems evident in the Public Health Service (PHS)?

A. Yes. PPSS noted the following general problems which, in turn, result in specific problems in PHS:

• Civil Service "seniority" overvalues "experience" in a reduction-in-force mandate. The employee with the longest service record may not be the most productive.

• The widespread use of "Assistant" and "Deputy" positions is suspect. These positions, for the most part, are not the result of substantive or unique work requirements.

- The control over "grade creep" is weak for the administrative type operations, i.e., non-science disciplines. At present, there are GS-15s reporting to other GS-15s. There are too many GS-14s, GS-13s, etc. in the same group of administrative type employees.

- Responsibility for personnel actions has not always been coupled with corresponding authority at the agency level. The most common problem cited was the lengthy time involved in hiring high-quality scientists.

- The large number of sub-divisions, branches, and other organizational breakdowns adds to payroll costs and fragments responsibility.

- Current line/staff manning levels provide excess manpower at the current level of activity, and indicate that there are opportunities for productivity increases.

Q. What can be done to correct the situation?

A. PPSS recommended:

- upgrading RIF guidelines so that job performance is part of the criteria for job retention;

- allowing one year of retained pay and grade for those personnel who, after a RIF is completed, find themselves in a lower graded position than their former one. After one year, grade and pay should be adjusted to correspond to current job duties;

- eliminating some Deputy/Assistant positions and classifying employees based upon work performed to eliminate "grade creep"; and

- consolidating small organizational units, decentralizing authority and responsibility, and reducing staff.

PPSS recommendations would reduce PHS staff by 2,617 staff-years and result in three-year savings of $475 million.

Q. How do Congressional activities affect work force planning in the Executive Branch?

A. Congress can mandate minimum personnel levels or require that it be notified of pending reorganizations so as to prevent reductions in personnel.

Imagine the head of a $26 billion operation with over 200,000 employees who must get the approval of his board of directors for any reorganization plan that will affect as few as three employees—and have to wait eight months to implement it.

This is the situation in the Veterans Administration (VA). The VA Administrator must submit a detailed plan to Congress for any administrative reorganization plan that will affect 10% or more of the permanent full-time equivalent employees at a "covered office or facility." That last term includes any VA office or facility that has 25 or more permanent employees or is a free-standing outpatient clinic.

In addition, the Administrator must submit the plan to Congress the same day the President submits the next fiscal year's budget. Since that must be done in February, it means Congress gets until October 1, eight months later, when the new fiscal year starts, to analyze that plan.

While the VA was perhaps the only agency tied up in law in quite this way, many others find themselves with a myriad of personnel directives. The Environmental Protection Agency (EPA) is another example. As part of an effort to cut costs and refine operations, EPA proposed a budget of $540.4 million for employee salaries and expenses for FY 1984, a cut of $8.2 million, or 1.5%, from the 1983 appropriations of $548.6 million.

Congress increased the 1984 appropriation over the 1983 level by $26.3 million, or 4.7%, and increased spending above the Executive Branch proposal by $34.5 million, or 6.3%, to a total of $574.9 million.

In another instance, in 1983, Congress raised the funding level for the Consumer Product Safety Commission by $13 million, or 38%, over its current operations, and another $10 million over the ensuing four years, for a total increase of 68%.

But, even though the Commission said it did not need that much additional money, the real issue was a paragraph stating:

> The Commission shall employ on a permanent basis not fewer than the full-time equivalent of 650 officers and employees. Any decision of the Commission to employ more than the full-time equivalent of 650 officers and employees shall not be subject, directly or indirectly, to review or approval by any person within the Executive Office of the President.

In other words, the agency would not only be required to maintain a minimum number of employees on the payroll, whether or not they were needed, but would also be free to hire as many employees as it could justify to *Congress,* not the President.

TRAINING AND DEVELOPMENT

PPSS reviewed training and development programs and concluded that training and development have no central focus in the Government. This is a contributing factor to problems in human resource planning.

The law does not specifically authorize the Office of Personnel Management (OPM) to prescribe the types and methods of intra-agency training or to regulate the details of intra-agency training programs. As a result, agencies are duplicating efforts in the design, development, and delivery of generic supervisory and management level training programs. Many programs are very similar in course content and training approaches both among agencies, and between agencies and OPM.

PPSS found that no one in the Federal Government knows how much is being spent on training in total. Further, there are problems with the training systems in various agencies, aside from the area of duplication.

- In the Department of Education (ED), personnel development and training of employees was budgeted at $550,000 in 1983. Sixty percent of this amount was intended for professional development in the field of education, 10% for clerical work improvements, leaving only 30% of existing funds for badly needed training in management and technical skills. By changing the focus of training activities to support ED's mission, savings of $32 million over three years could be achieved.

- Improving EPA's programs for personnel training, development, and performance appraisal would redirect the $2.0 million training budget toward priority needs, strengthen management's ability to function in an increasingly complex environment, and reduce payroll costs. Recommended changes would result in significant management and program improvements, as well as reducing costs by $6 million over three years.

- No organized and sustained program exists to prepare Executive Level appointees for the complexities facing them in their jobs. A more comprehensive orientation program for these appointees is necessary.

- In the Army, permanent change of station (PCS) moves (with family relocations) are not necessary for attendance at advanced courses. By reducing the length of the courses, savings of $64.5 million over three years can be achieved.

- In 1981, unused training facilities in the Army cost $169.4 million. Additionally, it cost the Army $580.6 million to train personnel in occupational specialties it did not need.

Q. Why aren't agencies coordinating their training efforts?

A. Agencies are not subject to rigorous audits when it comes to spending discretionary funds for generic training, nor does it appear that they concern themselves too much with trying to avoid duplication of effort. This finding is supported by a review of contract actions and by PPSS interviews with agency training officers. There is no penalty for waste and no reward for avoiding it.

— 263 —

Q. What needs to be done to correct the present situation?

A. OPM needs to identify the training which is necessary to meet both the specific and general needs of the agencies. OPM should then develop courses to meet these needs. OPM and the Office of Management and Budget (OMB) should monitor agency training programs to prevent duplication.

Savings are estimated at $66 million over three years.

This cost savings is only a small part of the benefits that could result. A better trained work force will be more effective and efficient, saving many times the amount calculated above.

OTHER PROGRAMS

Among other personnel programs PPSS reviewed were:

• Feedback systems

• Grievance procedures in the U.S. Postal Service (USPS)

• USPS policies regarding official time off for Equal Employment Opportunity Commission (EEOC) grievances.

These areas offer opportunities not only for cost savings but, more significantly, for increasing productivity and job satisfaction and decreasing personnel-related costs by helping Government and Federal employees resolve work-related problems.

In addition to the issues discussed above, there are a number of other areas that present opportunities for cost savings.

Reorganizations/Reductions in Staff. In Health and Human Services (HHS), for example, weak delineation of responsibilities leads to duplicate staff, conflicting responsibilities, and lack of authority, inhibiting effective management. Reducing the size and role of central staff departments could lead to 1,461 fewer management staff personnel. Other examples of potential savings can be found in the Departments of Education, Labor, and Energy; Occupational Safety and Health Review Commission; Tennessee Valley Authority; Army Corps of Engineers; Federal Housing Authority; and Immigration and Naturalization Service. Estimated savings of $1.479 billion over three years are possible.

Better Management of Personnel Resources. Basic techniques, such as using a Management by Objectives system in the Public Health Service, revising the Housing and Urban Development system for tracking how employees use their time, developing cost/benefit analyses of IRS staff additions, and better management of permanent change of station moves (i.e., moving military personnel among installations), represent potential savings. Other examples can be found in the Department of Agriculture, the Foreign Service, Housing and Urban Development, and the U.S.

Synfuels Corp. Savings of $662 million over three years can be achieved by implementing PPSS recommendations.

Training. The Army could reduce costs by decreasing the number of permanent change of station moves involved in training programs and by cancelling Learning Resource Centers training programs since they do not further the Army's primary mission. Also, some of the civilian executive training centers should be relocated, and training staffs reduced from 4 or 5 to 3. Total estimated savings over three years are $168 million.

Productivity Improvement. One example of the need for productivity improvement is in correspondence handling within Health and Human Services (HHS). One piece of correspondence requiring the signature of the HHS secretary involves 55-60 people and requires approximately 47 days to complete. Productivity improvements are also possible in the Department of Education and in disseminating information about jobs with the Federal Government. Savings of $37 million over three years are estimated in these three areas.

> The three-year total of all the recommendations in this section, after elimination of duplication and overlap among issues, is $10.770 billion—equal to the three-year taxes of 1.6 million median income families.

Retirement Systems

> PPSS reviewed the two largest Federal retirement systems, the Civil Service Retirement System (CSRS) and the Military Retirement System (MRS), which together cover approximately 98% of all Government employees, and the Foreign Service Retirement System (FSRS), and concluded that the Government retirement plans provide benefits and incur costs three to six times as great as the best private sector plans.
>
> PPSS found that, in general, CSRS, MRS, and FSRS programs specify benefit formulas more liberal than can typically be found in the private sector; allow retirement, with unreduced benefits, at an earlier age than is typically found in the private sector; and provide full protection against inflation.
>
> PPSS recommendations would reduce Federal retirement costs to levels comparable to those in the private sector by increasing the normal retirement age from 55 for CSRS and about 40 for MRS to age 62, reducing benefits actuarially for retirement before age 62, reducing the credit granted for each year of service to levels comparable to those in the private sector, revising the benefit formula to define base earnings as the average of the highest five years salary

(versus three years currently), and revising cost-of-living adjustments to reflect prevailing private sector practices. PPSS also recommended that smaller pension plans (including FSRS) be revised to be consistent with those of CSRS.

In FY 1983, the Government spent $39.6 billion in the specific areas covered by PPSS recommendations, with spending estimated to increase to $227.7 billion by the year 2000 if present policies are continued. Implementing PPSS recommendations would reduce spending to $150.6 billion in 2000, a saving of $77.1 billion or 33.9%.

Retirement systems in both the public and private sectors are generally designed to fulfill three basic objectives—attracting, retaining and, ultimately, separating employees in a socially acceptable manner. While Federal retirement systems are similar in objectives to their private sector counterparts, both the benefits provided and the costs incurred are several times greater. PPSS is committed to the principle that Federal pensions should be both fair and equitable; as they are presently structured, they are neither.

To place the generosity of current Federal retirement programs in perspective, if American taxpayers had told Congress many years ago, "Federal Government employees are doing an excellent job, and we want a retirement plan for them which is comparable to the best the private sector has to offer—equal to typical plans in the top Fortune 500 companies," and Congress had provided just that, in the last 10 years the two biggest Federal retirement systems (the Civil Service and Military Retirement Systems) would have cost taxpayers *$103 billion less* than they actually did. Over the next ten years taxpayers would have *saved $314 billion*.

From 1973 to 1982 the Government paid out more than $200 billion in pension benefits to retired Civil Service and military personnel. Over the next ten years, 1983–1992, these costs are projected to increase to about $500 billion, 2.5 times as great as spending in the prior ten-year period.

These enormous expenditures are only part of the picture. The Government actually understates its retirement costs by failing to adequately provide for future benefits. The Government's shortfall, or the amount by which future costs exceed current assets and future contributions (unfunded liability), is more than a trillion dollars and has been increasing, on average, by $94 billion annually, 1979–1982. These costs must be paid for by current and future generations of taxpayers and, in many ways, are analogous to National Debt.

With the above perspective, PPSS estimates that Federal retirement costs for the CSRS and MRS would be $68 billion less over the three-year period 1984–1986 if prevailing private sector standards for pension costs and benefits had been previously adopted and fully implemented by the Government.

— 266 —

Savings which occur through changes in retirement benefits are usually long term, 10 to 20 years after implementation. As a result, there is little current political or financial incentive to apply restraints, and little has been done to change the benefits or to reduce the costs of Federal retirement systems. To provide an accurate assessment of cost reductions, savings from PPSS recommendations have been calculated based on payroll costs in the years 2001 to 2003 and have been discounted to their 1983 value. On this basis, PPSS savings for the CSRS ($30.000 billion) and MRS ($28.100 billion) come to $58.100 billion.

The three major factors contributing to the higher benefit levels and the higher costs of Federal plans are provisions which include liberal benefit formulas, early retirement ages, and cost-of-living adjustments (COLAs) which provide full inflation protection. These provisions:

- *specify liberal benefit formulas*—Civil Service Retirement System (CSRS) and Military Retirement System (MRS) benefits are computed based on the high three years average salary, versus high five years in the private sector, and the credit for service is about 40% to 60% greater in the public sector than in the private sector (1.7% to 1.9% per year in the public sector compared to 1.2% in the private);

- *allow retirement at an earlier age*—typically 55 and 40 in the Civil Service and military, respectively, versus 63/64 in the private sector; and

- *provide full protection against inflation*—as demonstrated from March 1977 to March 1982, when COLAs averaged 9.2%/year for Civil Service and military pensions, versus about 2%–3% for the private sector.

PPSS reviewed four retirement systems in the Federal Government out of the total of over 50 programs. These four programs are:

Civil Service Retirement System (CSRS)
Military Retirement System (MRS)
Foreign Service Retirement System (FSRS)
Railroad Retirement Board (RRB)

RRB provides pensions for private sector railroad retirees; it is the only private sector plan administered by the Government. The three other programs cover approximately 98% of all Federal military and civilian employees.

The costs of these programs are on the next page.

As shown, these retirement programs are very expensive. They amounted in 1982 to 8.7 times the total cost of running the Government in the year President Franklin D. Roosevelt took office (1933). In 1982, the four retirement systems reviewed by PPSS cost *$40.0 billion*. The two largest plans, CSRS and MRS, cost $34.4 billion in 1982. Not only are these costs enormous, but they have been increasing rapidly. Be-

Retirement Plan Outlays(a)
($ Billions)

		(1)	(2)	(3)	(4)
		1970	1982	1982 as Multiple of 1970	Average Annual % Increase
(1)	CSRS	$2.8	$19.5	7.0X	17.6%
(2)	MRS	2.8	14.9	5.3	14.9
(3)	FSRS	0.02	0.2	10.0	21.2
(4)	RRB	1.6	5.4	3.4	10.7
(5)	Total	$7.2	$40.0	5.6	15.4

(a) Includes administrative and other costs.

tween 1970 and 1982, the four retirement plans averaged annual increases of 15.4%, so that by 1982 outlays for these four retirement plans were 5.6 times 1970 spending. *At this rate of increase costs double in less than five years.* At the *17.6%* annual rate of increase for CSRS, 1970–1982, *costs double in only slightly more than four years.* This rate of increase results in the following actual and projected spending:

CSRS Outlays

		At an Average Annual Increase of 17.6% ($ Billions)
	Actual	
(1)	1970	$ 2.8
(2)	1982	19.5
	Projected	
(3)	1986	37.3
(4)	1990	71.3
(5)	1994	136.4
(6)	1998	260.9

In 1998, just 14 years from now, CSRS outlays could reach *$260.9 billion*—an economically unacceptable prospect.

PPSS analyzed and provided recommendations on several Government retirement programs, with attention primarily directed toward the two major systems, the Civil Service Retirement System and the Military Retirement System, which collectively cover about 98% of all Federal employees.

Most of the remaining retirement plans, such as the Foreign Service, U.S. Coast Guard, and the four-member U.S. Presidents Retirement System, are patterned after one of the two major plans. Proposed revisions to these two major programs are, therefore, equally applicable to the minor programs.

The table below compares private sector pension plans with the CSRS and MRS on the basis of benefit provisions:

Comparison of Pension Plan Provisions
Corporate Versus Civil Service and Military

		(1)	(2)	(3)	(4)	(5)
		Typical Private Sector Pension			Private Sector Fav./(Unfav.) to	
	Provisions		Civil Service	Military	Civil Service	Military
(1)	Most Common Retirement Age	63	55	40	(8 Years)	(23 Years)
(2)	Credit for Service	1.2%	1.7%	1.9%	(41.7%)	(58.3%)
(3)	Pay Base	Highest 5 Years	Highest 3 Years	Highest 3 Years	(2 Years)	(2 Years)
(4)	Early Retirement Reduction (% Per Year)	3%–6%	2%	(a)	(55.6%)	(a)
(5)	Indexing (% of CPI)	None	100%	100%	Infinite (b)	Infinite (b)
(6)	Vesting (Years of Service)	10	5	(a)	(5 Years)	(a)
(7)	Social Security (SS) Integration	Usually	No SS(c)	No	ND	ND

ND = Not Determinable.

(a) No early retirement provision; minimum 20 years service required.

(b) Depending on future inflation rates.

(c) Approximately 70% to 80% of all Civil Service retirees eventually qualify for Social Security, despite the non-participation of Civil Service employees in the Social Security system.

As shown in the table above, Federal employees in the CSRS and MRS can retire earlier than their private sector counterparts, receive more credit per year of service, are protected against inflation through cost-of-living adjustments (COLAs), and have their pensions reduced by less when they retire early (before the normal retirement age).

Retirement in the private sector usually means retirement from the work force and loss of salary. In contrast, the earlier Federal retirement age offers an opportunity for a second career in the private sector and qualification for a second and even a third pension (i.e., private sector pension and Social Security). For example, approximately 70%–80% of CSRS retirees will also receive Social Security retirement benefits, often as a result of jobs held outside Civil Service. In comparing the MRS and CSRS, and the other Federal pension plans, with private sector pension plans, this difference should be kept in mind.

Q. How did costs and benefits for CSRS and MRS get so far out of line compared to the private sector?

A. The rationale for establishing liberal public pensions was the perception in the 1920's that both civilian and military salaries were not competitive with the private sector. Rather than incurring the immediate cost of increased compensation, the "problem" of noncompetitive Federal salaries was solved by the more politically palatable solution of pushing the costs far into the future—establishing exceedingly generous pension systems. A dollar paid in future pension benefits has less immediate financial and political impact than a dollar paid in current salary. Therefore, more future benefit dollars have been promised in order to achieve personnel recruitment and retention objectives.

The Federal Salary Reform Act of 1962 dramatically changed the position of Federal salaries relative to those in the private sector by mandating pay comparability but made no compensating changes in Federal pensions. By the late 1960's public and private sector salaries were comparable; retirement benefits and costs, however, were not.

Q. How do typical Federal pension benefits compare to typical private sector pension benefits?

A. The following chart shows how lifetime pension benefits for typical retirees compare under the CSRS, MRS, and an average private sector pension plan:

Comparison of Lifetime
Pension Benefits
($000)

		(1)	(2)	(3)
	Pre-Retirement Salary	*Federal Benefits*	*Private Sector Pension Plus Social Security*	*Federal Benefits as Multiple of Private Sector*
		CSRS(a)		
(1)	$25,000	$ 542,000	$266,000	2.0X
(2)	50,000	1,085,000	398,000	2.7
		MRS(d)		
(3)	$25,000(b)	$1,072,000	$176,000	6.1
(4)	50,000(c)	1,679,000	252,000	6.7

(a) Retirement at age 55 with 30 years of service.
(b) Retirement at age 39 with 20 years of service.
(c) Retirement at age 43 with 20 years of service.
(d) Includes Social Security.

PPSS concluded that CSRS and MRS respective benefit levels are about 3 times and 6 times as great as the best private sector plans.

Q. How much do these higher CSRS and MRS pension payments cost the Federal Government compared to employer costs in the private sector?

A. The following summarizes cost comparisons as a percentage of payroll, including and excluding the funding of previously incurred pension plan liabilities (i.e., unfunded liabilities):

**Public and Private Sector
Comparisons of Employer
Retirement Costs
as a Percent of Payroll**

		(1)	(2)	(3)	(4)
				Amortization of Unfunded Liabilities	
					As Multiple of Private Sector
	Excluding Private Sector Thrift Plans	Excluded (Normal Cost)	Included (Total Cost)	Excluded	Included
(1)	Private Sector(a)	12%	14%	1.0X	1.0X
(2)	CSRS	30	85	2.5	6.1
(3)	MRS(a)	41	118	3.4	8.4
	Including Private Sector Thrift Plans				
(4)	Private Sector(a)	14%	16%	1.0X	1.0X
(5)	CSRS	30	85	2.1	5.3
(6)	MRS(a)	41	118	2.9	7.4

(a) Both MRS and private sector costs include Social Security.

Excluding the amortization of unfunded liabilities (i.e., normal cost), CSRS and MRS costs are, respectively, 2.5 and 3.4 times as great as in the private sector, excluding private sector thrift plan costs. The Government's retirement programs are, however, substantially underfunded—the CSRS and MRS have combined unfunded liabilities of more than a trillion dollars, increasing at the rate of $94 billion annually in the last three years.

Amortizing these liabilities in a manner consistent with private sector practices shows the Government's total costs as a percent of payroll to be 85% and 118% for CSRS and MRS, respectively, or 6 to 8 times the comparable private sector cost.

Q. Did PPSS analyses evaluate thrift/matching contribution plans which add to private sector annuities?

A. Thrift and profit-sharing plans would add about 2% points to the cost of private sector pension plans. Including thrift and profit-sharing plans, CSRS and MRS *normal costs* are, respectively, 2.1 times and 2.9 times as great as in the private sector, while *total costs* are, respectively, 5.3 times and 7.4 times as great.

Q. The amount of the unfunded liability of Federal pension plans has no effect on the current costs of these systems. Why is the unfunded liability of these plans important?

A. The unfunded liability represents money that will have to be paid out at some future date for retirement benefits. *These amounts are not potential costs, but actual costs that are accumulating and which future generations will have to pay.* In the private sector, companies provide for these costs by contributing more money than is necessary to cover current costs. The excess funds cover future costs.

Further, the unfunded liabilities of the MRS and CSRS understate costs, inhibiting the ability of Congress to make sound financial decisions regarding the plans. Understating retirement costs results in benefits which jeopardize the affordability of the retirement systems.

Over 50% of the current unfunded liability of the CSRS stems from the failure of the Federal Government to project the impact of salary increases and COLA increases on benefits.

Q. How much is the unfunded liability for all Federal pension systems?

A. The Government does not calculate the total cost of the unfunded liability for all its pension plans. However, the unfunded liabilities for the two largest Federal pension plans—CSRS and MRS—are available in published reports.

The unfunded liabilities of CSRS and MRS, as of September 30, 1982, were *$514.8 billion* and *$526.8 billion,* respectively. This $1,041.6 billion is the additional amount which would have to be contributed to CSRS and MRS to pay for the benefits promised to current employees and retirees, above employee and employer contributions—costs that will have to be paid by us, our children, and our grandchildren. At this writing, the unfunded liabilities of the CSRS and MRS total between $1.1 and $1.2 trillion.

Q. How much would it cost to amortize the unfunded liability?

A. In 1982, in addition to $23.6 billion in Government and employee contributions, *$30.0 billion in additional contributions would have been necessary to amortize the CSRS unfunded liability.* The $30 billion in amortization costs would have to be added to the normal retirement cost each year, for the next 40 years, in order to fully fund the CSRS. Total costs of *$53.6 billion* in 1982 are *91.9%* of covered payroll of $58.3 billion. Actual contributions of $23.6 billion include employee contributions of $4.2 billion, so that the total net cost to the Government of the CSRS was $49.4 billion, or 84.7% of payroll—*almost as much for pensions as for payroll.*

In 1982, the added cost of the MRS unfunded liability, amortized over 40 years, would have been $11.0 billion. In total, amortizing the CSRS and MRS unfunded liabilities in 1982 would have cost taxpayers an additional *$41.0 billion.*

Q. What accounts for the unfunded liability of pension plans in the Federal sector? How did this unfunded liability arise?

A. *The unfunded liabilities of Federal pension plans arise from inadequate funding resulting from the failure to adjust employer and employee contributions to reflect periodic improvements in Government pension plans.* The magnitude of the unfunded liability arises from the following factors:

- Federal plans provide unreduced retirement benefits earlier than the best private sector plans.

- Early retirement enables Federal employees to obtain benefits over a much longer period of time while allowing less time to accumulate the assets necessary to fund retirement benefits.

- Federal pensions are adjusted to reflect changes in the Consumer Price Index (CPI), allowing for annual increases in Federal pensions, a practice almost nonexistent in the private sector.

- Federal programs deliver higher annual pensions.

Q. Regarding the CSRS, doesn't the employee contribution of 7% of salary cover half the cost of employee pensions?

A. No. The CSRS is structured so that employees pay 7% of their salaries to the plan and employing agencies pay 7%, with the rest of the fund income coming from *interest and profit on investments and appropriations from the general fund of the U.S. Treasury*—the last, of course, coming ultimately from American taxpayers. The chart below presents the income for the CSRS for the period 1970-1982.

Total Government (taxpayer) contributions increased from $3.0 billion in 1970 to $27.3 billion in 1982, or at an average annual rate of 20.2%. At the same time, Federal employee contributions increased from $1.7 billion to $4.2 billion, an average annual rate of increase of 7.8%. Looked at another way, in 1970 employees accounted for 36.2% of the CSRS receipts; in 1982, employee contributions amounted to only 13.3% of CSRS receipts.

Q. How do COLAs affect CSRS and MRS pension costs?

A. Each 1% increase in the CPI in 1981 added approximately $190 million to CSRS outlays. Further, about one-half of military retirement system outlays result from cost-of-living adjustments. The MRS COLA cost alone was about $8 billion in 1983. If there is no

Civil Service Retirement Trust Fund(a)
($ Billions)

		(1)	(2)	(3)	(4)	(5)	(6)
		Employee Contribution	Employing Agency Contribution	U.S. Treasury Contribution	Interest & Profits(b)	Total Gov't	Total Receipts
(1)	1970	$1.7	$1.7	$ 0.2	$1.1	$ 3.0	$ 4.7
(2)	1982	4.2	5.0(c)	14.5	7.8	27.3	31.5

1982 Contributions only 2.47X the 1970 level, vs 9.1X for the Gov't.

1982 Contributions 9.1X the 1970 level, only 12 years earlier

	Avg. Ann. % Inc.						
(3)	1970– 1982	7.8%	9.4%	42.9%	17.7%	20.2%	17.2%

As a % of Total Receipts

(4)	1970	36.2%	36.2%	4.2%	23.4%	63.8%	100.0%
(5)	1982	13.3	15.9	46.0	24.8	86.7	100.0

Down 22.9% Pts.

Up 22.9% Pts.

(a) Cash basis.
(b) Includes interest and profits on employee and Government contributions.
(c) Includes $0.9 billion from U.S. Postal Service as payment for unfunded retirement expense.

change in the law and assuming a COLA of only 5% per year from 1989 on (less until then), the MRS *COLA costs* will be *$35 billion* by the year 2022.

Q. How do COLA benefits under CSRS and MRS, and typical private sector pension plans compare?

A. Federal benefits are adjusted for the full increase in the CPI, while only the Social Security portion of private sector pensions is adjusted for full CPI increases. COLA benefits available for Federal retirees under the current CSRS and benefits available to employees covered under private pension plans and Social Security are shown at the top of the next page.

On average, it is estimated that cost-of-living adjustments for the combination of Social Security with a private pension recover about 70% of increases in the Consumer Price Index.

Q. How have COLA increases affected Federal pensions?

COLA Increases

	Type of Retirement	Percentage Cost-of-Living Increases Recovered by Pension Adjustment
(1)	Civil Service/Military Service	100%
(2)	Combination of Private Pension and Social Security	70
(3)	Social Security	100
(4)	Private Pension	33

A. The table below compares increases in cost-of-living adjustments for Federal (General Schedule and Military) retirees, General Schedule salary increases, and increases in the Consumer Price Index for the period 1968 through 1982.

Increases in
Cost-of-Living Adjustments (COLAs)
For Federal Retirees, General Schedule Salaries,
and Consumer Prices

		(1) Index of COLA Increases to Annuitants	(2) Index of General Schedule Salary Increases	(3) Consumer Price Index
(1)	1968	100.0	100.0	100.0
(2)	1982	297.6	231.3	277.6
	Avg. Ann. % Inc.			
(3)	1968–1982	8.1%	6.2%	7.6%

Since 1968, increases in cost-of-living adjustments (COLAs) for Federal retirees have exceeded both increases in General Schedule salaries and the Consumer Price Index (CPI). A Federal employee retiring in 1968 would thus be receiving 3.0 times his 1968 average yearly annuity in 1982, while a General Schedule employee still working would be receiving 2.3 times his 1968 average yearly salary, assuming he were at the same grade. This means that an active employee, 1968-1982, received only 66.4% of the increases retired employees received (increases of 131.3% for active employees versus 197.6% for retirees). As a result, 1982 average annual annuities are 28.7% greater than if COLA increases had been similar to General Schedule increases over the same period. Further, 1982 pensions are 7.2% greater than they would be had COLA increases matched the increases in the CPI, 1968–1982.

Q. How would these increases affect the pension payments of retirees?

A. Here is a hypothetical example:

A CSRS employee retiring at the end of 1968 after 30 years of service and earning $18,700 in his last year would be entitled to a 1968 pension of approximately $10,000. In 1982, that pension would have risen to $29,800, 1.6 times his salary in 1968.

A CSRS employee earning $18,700 in 1968 who retired in 1982 after 30 years of service would be receiving a pension of $23,100, based on a salary of $43,300 in 1982—$6,700, or 22%, less than the 1968 retiree received in 1982.

The results compare as follows:

		(1)	(2)
		CSRS	
		1968 Retiree	1982 Retiree
		(Average Annual Amounts)	
(1)	1968 Salary	$18,700	$18,700
(2)	1982 Salary	NA	43,300
(3)	1968 Pension	10,000	NA
(4)	1982 Pension	29,800	23,100

The high cost of CSRS pensions is due in large part to COLAs, but also to granting full retirement benefits at earlier ages for Federal workers.

Q. How do retirement ages in the Government and the private sector compare?

A. A Congressional Budget Office study dated May 1981 included the following data:

Male Civil Service and Private Sector Retirees by Age at Retirement

		(1)	(2)	(3)	(4)	(5)
		As % of Total Retirements		CSRS as Multiple	Cumulative % of Total	
	Age at Retirement	CSRS	Private Sector	Of Private Sector	CSRS	Private Sector
(1)	Under 55	9.5%	1.1%	8.6X	9.5%	1.1%
(2)	55–59	39.6	6.3	6.3	49.1	7.4
(3)	60–61	14.5	12.6	1.2	63.6	20.0
(4)	62–64	18.1	42.1	0.4	81.7	62.1
(5)	65 and Over	18.3	37.9	0.5	100.0	100.0

As shown above, 63.6% of all male CSRS employees retire before age 62, compared to only 20.0% of private sector workers. The seven additional years over which CSRS provides unreduced benefits (and the COLA increases in each of those years) is a major contributing factor to the 1,891% increase in CSRS costs over the 1960–1981 period—more than nine times the rate of inflation. Further, the Office of Personnel Management reported that as of September 30, 1982, *"only 10% of employees who were eligible to retire before age 60 remained in active service at age 60."*

For perspective, the following shows the cost impact of provisions which allow retirement at a relatively early age in the public sector:

The Cost of Early Retirement

	Age	Cost Index	
(1)	65	1.0	
(2)	62	1.3	Costs 1.7X as great
(3)	60	1.5	with retirement at
(4)	55	2.2	55 instead of 62
(5)	45	3.4	
(6)	40	4.0	

Providing for early retirement at 40–45 years of age increases costs by 3.4X–4.0X.

To provide the same level of benefits at age 40, all else being equal, would cost four times as much as providing those benefits at age 65.

Q. Isn't there any incentive for Federal workers to keep working?

A. On the contrary, the Congressional Research Service has noted:

The combination of a) retirement opportunity with full benefits or with less than actuarial reductions; b) inflation protection; and c) second career possibilities with additional accrued benefits under both Social Security and a private pension strongly encourages Federal employees to aggressively pursue early retirement. This is unusually advantageous to the employee. It is clearly not in the best interest of the employer or the general taxpayer public and must be curtailed.

Q. How have disability provisions affected the CSRS?

A. To be eligible for disability retirement, an employee must have 5 years of service, be unable to satisfactorily and efficiently perform one function of the current position, and not be qualified for reassignment to a comparable position in the same agency.

The following chart is based on a 1978 Congressional Budget Office report and compares the rates at which CSRS and private sector annuitants retire under disability standards:

Disability Retirement Rates,
CSRS vs Private Sector Eligibility Standards

		(1)	(2)	(3)
		Rate of Disability per 100,000 Employees		CSRS Rate
	Attained Age	CSRS Standard	Private Standards	Greater Than Private Rate
(1)	30	1.4	0.9	55.6%
(2)	50	13.7	9.1	50.5
(3)	60	34.2	28.5	20.0
(4)	65	56.4	47.0	20.0

Between ages 30 and 50, the probability of a Federal employee retiring under CSRS provisions was over 50% greater than under private sector standards. Federal disability provisions have been tightened since the report was published. Nevertheless, retirees under "lenient" disability provisions in previous years contribute to the high costs of the CSRS. At the end of FY 1982, over 348,000 Civil Service retirees, nearly 27% of all retirees, retired under disability provisions.

Q. How do the liberal benefit formulas of the CSRS and MRS contribute to their high costs?

A. CSRS and MRS benefit provisions are much more liberal than those in the private sector, as shown below:

• *Credit for Service.* The percentage of pay per year of service in the benefit formula of the CSRS (1.9%—of which about 1.7% is the employer-paid portion) and the MRS (1.9% of BMC, Basic Military Compensation, a measure comparable to salary in the private sector) is high compared to a good private sector plan percentage of pay per year of service of 1.2%.

• *Average Salary.* The three-year average pay basis in the CSRS and MRS benefit formulas provides for a higher base salary, and hence higher benefits, than does the prevailing private sector practice of averaging salary over five years.

Q. What recommendations does PPSS propose to change the CSRS and MRS?

A. Some of the adjustments to the CSRS (which apply equally to the MRS) that would bring it more in line with private sector pensions are:

- Increase the age requirement for unreduced pension benefits to age 62;

- Reduce benefits actuarially for retirement before age 62, with no voluntary retirement before age 55;

- Revise the benefit formula to define base earnings as the average of the highest five years of salary;

- Reduce the credit granted for each year's service to levels comparable to those in the private sector (with the MRS benefit slightly higher than in the private sector);

- Increase the service requirement for vesting in the CSRS from 5 to 10 years. In the MRS, allow employees to vest after 10 years of service.

- Decrease COLAs in both the MRS and CSRS to reflect prevailing private sector practices; and

- Integrate CSRS and MRS with Social Security and eliminate provisions which allow "double dipping" (employees receiving two pensions, pay and a pension, or unreduced Federal pensions and full Social Security).

Q. What specific changes does PPSS propose to reduce Federal COLA provisions?

A. In general, COLA increases are recommended at 70% of inflation for Federal retirees without Social Security; for employees with Social Security, COLA increases are recommended at 33% of inflation. These adjustments conform to prevailing private sector practices. For purposes of determining how much of the *CSRS* pension should be fully indexed to inflation, a Social Security equivalent pension would be determined based on the employee's CSRS employment history. COLA increases equal to those under Social Security would be granted based on this amount—i.e., indexed at 100% of the CPI.

The difference between the actual CSRS pension benefit and the Social Security equivalent pension would be considered to be equivalent to a private sector pension. This pension would be adjusted for inflation in a manner consistent with private sector practices, currently 33% of the increase in the CPI.

Regarding the Military Retirement System, for annuitants under age 62 COLA increases would be limited to the lower of the CPI or the military "salary" increase. Since military personnel are covered under Social Security, for retirees age 62 and over the MRS pension benefit would be limited to COLA adjustments prevalent in the private sector, currently 33% of inflation on average.

Q. As a result of being included in the Social Security System, a new retirement plan is required for employees joining Civil Service after

January 1, 1984. How does the new plan affect PPSS recommendations?

A. The recently passed Social Security legislation includes a provision making it mandatory for new Federal Civil Service employees to be included in the Social Security retirement system starting January 1, 1984.

This legislation means that a new Civil Service Retirement System must be developed for new employees, with the present retirement system presumably closed to new entrants. This presents a unique opportunity to create a Civil Service retirement system for new employees which is fair not only to the employees but also to the taxpayers.

This new plan should be designed to be comparable in benefits and costs to good private sector plans. With appropriate protection of present participants (grandfathering and adjustments for differences in Social Security coverage), the CSRS should be modified to the same standard and permit transfer to the post-January 1984 plan.

There probably is no other retirement system which is as liberal and costly as the U.S. Military Retirement System. For this reason, among others, several major studies of the Military Retirement System have been made over the last few years. Many recommendations for reform have been proposed, some drastic, but *not one significant recommendation of these studies has yet been adopted by Congress.*

Military personnel can retire at any age with 20 years of service. The retiree receives an immediate annuity calculated as 2.5% of base pay for each year of creditable service, subject to a maximum of 75% of base pay. A member has no vested right in the retirement system, receiving no benefit if he retires before reaching the 20-year mark.

The Military Retirement System is relatively inefficient and not cost effective because:

- It provides no incentive to undertake hazardous duty—all personnel are eligible for 20-year retirement regardless of the nature of their service.

- It creates for many an arbitrary career length of 20 years, thus needlessly depriving the military of qualified personnel.

- Conversely, it causes less than optimal retention of personnel up to the 20-year point since there is no vesting until 20 years of service are completed.

- It provides limited incentive to join the military and lacks the flexibility to respond to short-term fluctuations in personnel needs, since benefits are paid after service is completed.

- It eventually provides benefits to only 13% of entering personnel.

Q. How does PPSS justify direct cost comparisons between private sector and military retirement systems, since they are radically different in their fundamental nature and purpose?

A. The primary difference between private sector retirement programs and the Military Retirement System is the use of the latter as a personnel management tool and not as a means of providing retirement income. To the extent both military and private sector retirement programs are intended to meet the financial needs of retired personnel, the cost and benefits provided are directly comparable. PPSS believes the MRS has limited value as a manpower management tool since, in essential aspects, it is counterproductive to the military's manpower requirements, e.g., the need to retain skilled personnel. The transition of military labor requirements from relatively unskilled to highly skilled is not reflected in the retirement system. Force management objectives could be better met by a combination of adjustments in other elements of the military compensation package, such as bonuses or salaries, and a revised retirement system.

Q. How does PPSS address arguments that high pensions are necessary to compensate for hazardous duty?

A. Retirement pay for hazardous duty is inequitable for two reasons. First, of those who enter the service only 13% ever collect retirement pay; the other 87% are not compensated in this way for hazardous and arduous duty. Second, the same retirement pay goes to all retirees of the same years of service and final pay, regardless of the degree to which each was subjected to hazardous and arduous duty during his military career.

Q. What changes does PPSS propose to the MRS?

A. In addition to changes already discussed, the system proposed by PPSS would replace 39% of Basic Military Compensation (BMC) after 30 years of service versus approximately 56% replaced under the current system. Also, COLA adjustments for those under 62 would be limited to the lower of the CPI or military salary increases. For those over 62, COLA adjustments would be equivalent to those received in the private sector, currently 33% of changes in the CPI.

In addition to the issues discussed above, PPSS reviewed the military's policy of allowing personnel to receive payment of base pay for accumulated unused annual leave, up to a maximum of 60 days, upon separation or retirement from military service. Simultaneous payment of accumulated unused leave and initial pension payments results in duplicate compensation to the retiring member for a period equal to the length of the unused leave. In general, private sector pension plans prohibit such duplicate payments. PPSS recommended that the effective date for the commencement of retirement pay be moved forward from the active duty termination date by the number of days of accumulated unused leave. Savings of $126 million over three years can be achieved if this recommendation is implemented.

As noted earlier in this section, PPSS reviewed four of the more than 50 retirement systems in the Federal Government. Provisions of one of these systems, the Foreign Service Retirement System (FSRS), were compared with the CSRS, and the FSRS was found to be much more liberal in the benefits it provides. Since the CSRS is much more liberal in its benefits than the best private sector plans, the FSRS is a *very* liberal program.

The cost of the Foreign Service Retirement System is increasing both in dollars and as a percent of pay. The Government's estimated budgeted cost of the system equaled 87% of pay in FY 1983. In contrast, the Government's cost for the U.S. Civil Service Retirement System, which covers most Federal civilian employees, is 30% of pay.

Q. How are FSRS benefits more liberal than those in CSRS?

A. Under the Foreign Service Retirement System, the normal retirement age (the age at which an employee may first retire on an unreduced pension) is 50 with 20 years of service, or 60 with 5 years of service, compared to CSRS provisions of age 55 with 30 years of service or age 60 with 20 years of service.

Foreign Service employees can retire at comparable or earlier ages than Civil Service employees. PPSS is not aware of any requirement of the Foreign Service that renders employees unable to perform their duties at age 50 or 60.

The Foreign Service Retirement System provides larger benefits than are provided under the Civil Service Retirement System for employees with equal records of service and salary for all except a small number of very long service employees. For an employee retiring after 20 years of service the Foreign Service System provides a benefit which is 10.3% greater than the Civil Service Retirement System would provide. The liberal provisions of the FSRS attempt to compensate for the hardships experienced by some Foreign Service officers during their careers. Foreign Service officers, and their families, typically live much or all of their working lives away from their own country. Some assignments are in desirable places like Paris, others in Moscow, where a normal life is nearly impossible. As is the case in the Military Retirement System, the same retirement pay goes to all Foreign Service officers of the same pay grade and years of service, regardless of the conditions under which the retiree spent his working years.

Q. What changes does PPSS propose?

A. The FSRS should be made equivalent to the CSRS. Proposed changes to the CSRS should, therefore, be incorporated into the

FSRS. Further, most other Federal retirement plans are patterned after either the CSRS or MRS. Revisions to these minor pension programs of the Government (including the FSRS) should be made so they conform with the PPSS-proposed revisions to the CSRS and MRS.

The Railroad Retirement Board administers the railroad industry's retirement system, Medicare, disability, unemployment, and medical insurance. The system currently affects about 450,000 active and one million retired railroad workers.

The RRB is essentially insolvent. At current benefit and tax levels the system was expected to run out of money in FY 1984. Declining employment has created a system where there are two retired employees for every active employee. The unfunded liability of RRB as of December 1980 was about $30 billion.

Q. How did this situation develop?

A. The history of railroad retirement is quite consistent. Benefits are periodically increased by Congress without adequate funding until a financial crisis occurs. Then Federal assistance is sought by the railroad community as part of a legislated package of benefits and funding.

Pension benefits to railroad retirees are among the most liberal in the nation. They include full retirement at age 60 for 30-year employees and payment of benefits to non-working spouses. Virtually all benefits are tax free. A 1981 Congressional Budget Office study on benefits and financing showed after-tax wages which are replaced in retirement as a percent of final salary (Replacement Rate) for railroad and other private sector pension plans as follows:

Retirement Benefit After-Tax Replacement Rates

		(1)	(2)
		Final Gross Salary(a)	
		$22,000	$30,000
	Married		
(1)	RRB	129%	105%
(2)	All Industries	97	76
(3)	RRB as Multiple of All Industries	1.3X	1.4X
	Single		
(4)	RRB	96%	79%
(5)	All Industries	83	66
(6)	RRB as Multiple of All Industries	1.2X	1.2X

(a) Gross salaries are shown for comparative purposes; replacement rates are for net, or after-tax, wages.

As shown above, RRB pensions are 1.2–1.4 times as generous as other private sector pensions. The present railroad retirement system has been exempted from Employee Retirement Income Security Act (ERISA) funding standards. Because RRB is a pay-as-you-go system, there are no financial reserves to cover future pension benefits already earned.

The 1981 tax increases and borrowing provisions, billed as a permanent solution to funding the RRB, have succeeded only in delaying insolvency into the mid-1980s. Again, labor and management are seeking ways of injecting more Federal money into the system.

Q. What changes does PPSS propose to the RRB?

A. PPSS proposes the following:

• All railroad workers and retirees should be brought into the Social Security system. The administration of the Social Security equivalent portion of railroad retirement should be turned over to SSA.

• The industry pension portion of railroad retirement should be turned into a private multi-employer pension plan.

• The Federal Government should provide financial security for the private pension fund without Federal subsidies by enacting a payroll tax on railroads.

• The tax-free status of RRB pension benefits should be changed. The benefits should be taxed on the same basis as all other private pension systems.

• This system should be turned into one which is run, managed, and financed by the industry and labor groups affected.

In summary, PPSS recommended major changes to Federal pension systems, involving almost *$61 billion* in savings over three years.

It is difficult to look at a pension system and say, "let's cut back on benefits." There are overtones of taking money away from employees at a time when regular paychecks stop and of breaking clear and longstanding agreements between employers and employees.

Federal retirement systems were originally intended to compensate for lower salaries and as mechanisms to help manage the work force. Although liberal pensions have never been a particularly effective tool for work force management, there was some logic to the system.

Since these pension plans were established, however, drastic changes have taken place:

• Salaries have increased to the extent that they are now comparable to those in the private sector (see previous section on Compensation).

• Costly benefits such as COLAs have been added to the plans.

• The number of retirees has increased, as have their lifespans.

PPSS is committed to the principle that Federal pensions should be "fair and equitable." These are the key words. PPSS recommendations will not leave Federal retirees deprived. *Federal pension plans are so generous and so costly that, after the changes proposed above are implemented, Federal pension plans will still be better than the plans covering the vast majority of American taxpayers.*

American taxpayers are the people paying for Federal pensions. Is it fair to ask them to pay for systems offering benefits 3 to 6 times as great as the best they can expect to receive?

> The three-year total of all the recommendations in this section, after elimination of duplication and overlap among issues, is $60.895 billion—equal to the three-year taxes of 9.2 million median income families.

Health and Other Fringe Benefits

> The Federal Government spent approximately $45.5 billion on fringe benefits for Executive Branch civilian personnel in 1982, 68.2% of total payroll costs. By 1987, fringe benefits are projected at 70.6% of total payroll. PPSS compared Federal fringe benefit costs and controls with standard private sector practices and concluded that mismanagement, inefficiencies, and abuse have led to excessive costs. In addition, the health benefit, vacation and sick pay policies of the Federal Government are more liberal than comparable private sector standards. Further, procedures and controls to detect fraud and abuse in disability benefits are inadequate. Regarding military health benefits and the military health care system, efficiencies need to be introduced to eliminate excess capacity, introduce cost containment measures, and coordinate health resources planning.
>
> PPSS recommendations are intended to reduce Federal fringe benefit costs by eliminating benefits which exceed prevailing private sector practices, introducing cost containment provisions in health plans, and de-liberalizing vacation and sick pay provisions. Military health benefit costs can be reduced by central coordination of health care systems and limiting access to non-military hospitals, increasing utilization of military health care facilities.
>
> In FY 1983, the Government spent $26.3 billion in the specific areas covered by PPSS recommendations, with spending estimated to increase to $149.1 billion by the year 2000 if present policies are continued. Implementing PPSS recommendations would reduce spending to $112.3 billion in 2000, a saving of $36.8 billion, or 24.7%.

Fringe benefit costs for the Executive Branch civilian work force are enormous—approximately $45.5 billion in 1982 (68.2% of total payroll) for 2.8 million employees, projected by PPSS to increase by $23.2 billion, or 51%, to $68.7 billion in 1987 (70.6% of total payroll).

Fringe benefits can be separated into two categories. First are those generally included as a payroll cost to the employer and paid to the employee—e.g., vacation and holiday pay, sick leave, administrative leave, work breaks, and cash awards. Second are those benefits which the employer generally does not pay to employees as salary—e.g., retirement pay, workmen's compensation, and health benefits.

Following is a breakdown of fringe benefits for FY 1979 and 1982, and as projected for 1987:

Fringe Benefit Costs
Executive Branch Civilian Employees(a)
($ Billions)

		(1)	(2)	(3)
	Fiscal Year	Payroll Related (b)	Non-Payroll Related (c)	Total Fringe Benefits
(1)	1979	$ 9.5	$ 20.9	$ 30.4
(2)	1982	12.1	33.4	45.5
(3)	1987E	17.6	51.1	68.7
(4)	1982 as % of 1979	127.4%	159.8% in 3 years	149.7%
	Avg. Ann. % Inc./(Dec.)			
(5)	1979–1982	8.4%	16.9%	14.4%
(6)	1982–1987E	7.8	8.9	8.6

(a) Cash basis.

(b) Fringe benefits generally *included* as a payroll cost to the employer and pay to the employee.

(c) Fringe benefits generally *excluded* as a payroll cost to the employer and pay to the employee.

Fringe benefit costs to the Government of $45.5 billion in 1982 were $15.1 billion, or about 50%, more than in 1979. From 1979–1982, fringe benefits increased at an average annual rate of 14.4%, the rapid growth resulting primarily from the 16.9% average annual increase in non-payroll related items. Over the five years, 1982–1987E, non-payroll related fringe benefits are expected to increase from $33.4 billion to $51.1 billion.

As shown on the next page, in 1982, fringe benefit costs accounted for 68.2% of total payroll costs (payroll and payroll related fringe benefits), an increase of 10.5% points from 1979.

From 1979 to 1982, fringe benefit costs increased 1.8 times as rapidly as total payroll costs, a 14.4% average annual increase as compared to 8.2%.

Total Personnel Costs
Executive Branch Civilian Employees(a)
($ Billions)

		(1)	(2)	(3)	(4)	(5)
					Fringe Benefits as % of Payroll,	
		Payroll			Including	
	Fiscal Year	Including Payroll Related Fringe Benefits(b)	Excluding Payroll Related Fringe Benefits(b)	Total Fringe Benefits	Payroll Related Fringe Benefits	Memo: Total Personnel Costs
(1)	1979	$ 52.7	$ 43.2	$ 30.4	57.7%	$ 73.6
(2)	1982	66.7	54.6	45.5	68.2	100.1
(3)	1987E	97.3	79.7	68.7	70.6	148.4
(4)	1982 as % of 1979	126.6%	126.4%	149.7%	118.2%	136.0%
	Avg. Ann. % Inc./(Dec.)					
(5)	1979–1982	8.2%	8.1%	14.4%	3.5% pts.	10.8%
(6)	1982–1987E	7.8	7.9	8.6	0.5	8.2

(a) Cash basis.
(b) Payroll related fringe benefits are those included as a payroll cost to the employer and pay to the employee. Non-payroll related fringe benefits are excluded as a payroll cost to the employer and not included as pay to the employee.

For perspective, the table on the following page shows the components of payroll-related and nonpayroll-related fringe benefits for 1979, 1982, and as projected for 1987.

Nonpayroll-related fringe benefits are projected to increase as a percent of payroll from 39.6% in 1979 to 52.5% in 1987, with increases in health benefit (up 125.0%) and retirement (up 27.5%) costs offset somewhat by decreases in workmen's compensation (down 21.1%) and cash allowances (down 10.0%).

As in the areas of compensation and retirement, PPSS compared Federal fringe benefit costs and controls with standard private sector practices and concluded that mismanagement, inefficiencies, overly liberal benefits, and abuse are costing taxpayers over $4 billion annually. A comparison for fringe benefits appears on page 289.

Employer Federal fringe benefit costs are *28.2% pts. greater* than average costs in the private sector. This results primarily from greater Federal costs for retirement, and vacation and sick leave used, offset somewhat by higher private sector costs for FICA, and thrift and profit sharing plans. Although *employer health insurance* costs in the private sector exceed Federal health insurance costs, *employer and employee* costs in the Federal Government exceed those in the private sector.

Regarding payroll related benefits, PPSS proposed changes in the Government's vacation and sick leave procedures which will be dis-

Fringe Benefits
(% of Total Payroll)

		(1)	(2)	(3)	(4)
					Percent Inc./(Dec.) 1979–
		1979	*1982*	*1987E*	*1987E*
	Payroll-Related:				
(1)	Vacation	7.3%	7.1%	7.1%	(2.7)%
(2)	Work Breaks	4.0	4.0	4.0	—
(3)	Sick Leave Used	3.1	3.4	3.4	9.7
(4)	Holidays	3.0	2.9	2.9	(3.3)
(5)	Administrative Leave	0.6	0.6	0.6	—
(6)	Cash Awards	0.1	0.1	0.1	—
(7)	Total Payroll-Related	18.1%	18.1%	18.1%	—
	Non-Payroll-Related:				
(8)	Retirement Benefits	32.4%	42.3%	41.3%	27.5%
(9)	Health Benefits	3.6	4.7	8.1	125.0
(10)	Workmen's Compensation (FECA)	1.9	1.5	1.5	(21.1)
(11)	Cash Allowances	1.0	0.9	0.9	(10.0)
(12)	All Other	0.7	0.7	0.7	—
(13)	Total Non-Payroll-Related	39.6%	50.1%	52.5%	32.6%
(14)	Total Fringe Benefits	57.7%	68.2%	70.6%	22.4%

cussed in more detail later in this section. Work breaks and holidays are already handled in a manner generally consistent with private sector practices.

Retirement benefits, the principal non-payroll related fringe benefit, are discussed as a separate section of this report. Health benefits and Workmen's Compensation are addressed later in this section.

Specific areas where PPSS noted possibilities for improving Federal controls and procedures are summarized below:

- The Federal Employee Health Benefits Program (FEHBP) costs 6.8% of total payroll including payroll related fringe benefits compared to health benefit costs of 5.8% in the private sector. This 1.0% pt. difference results from the design of the FEHBP which allows employees many plan choices and frequent opportunities to change plans ("adverse selection"—employees changing plans frequently in response to their needs for increased or decreased health insurance coverage). As a result, Government costs exceed comparable private sector costs by approximately $450 million annually.

- The amount of annual leave granted to Federal employees is from 1.2 to 1.9 times that granted in the private sector. The added yearly cost of annual leave is almost $1.3 billion.

Comparison of Private Sector
and Federal Fringe Benefits, 1981
(Employer Costs as a Percent of Total Payroll)

	Paid as a Part of Direct Payroll	(1) Federal	(2) Private Sector	(3) Federal Above/(Below) Private Sector
(1)	Vacation Used	6.99%	4.90%	2.09% pts.
(2)	Sick Leave Used and Short-Term Disability	3.95	1.70	2.25
(3)	Holidays (a)	2.80	3.40	(0.60)
(4)	Administrative Leave (a)	0.50	0.30	0.20
(5)	Work Breaks (a)	4.01	3.50	0.51
(6)	Cash Awards (a)	0.32	0.40	(0.08)
(7)	Total Payroll Benefits	18.57%	14.20%	4.37% pts.
	Paid in Addition to Direct Payroll			
(8)	Allowances	0.85%	0.70%	0.15% pts.
(9)	Retirement and Long-Term Disability (b)	39.65	5.80	33.85
(10)	Health Insurance (c)	4.25	5.80	(1.55)
(11)	Profit Sharing and Thrift	—	1.50	(1.50)
(12)	FICA (Social Security)	0.35	5.80	(5.45)
(13)	FECA (Workmen's Comp.)	1.31	1.60	(0.29)
(14)	Unemployment	—	1.40	(1.40)
(15)	Life Insurance	0.30	0.30	—
(16)	Total Non-Payroll Benefits	46.71%	22.90%	23.81% pts.
(17)	Total Fringe Benefit Costs	65.28%	37.10%	28.18% pts.

Note: Above does not include 6.29% of FY 1981 gross payroll for the present value of annual leave carried over or 23.2% for sick-leave carried over.

(a) When added together, holidays, administrative leave, work breaks, and cash awards in the Federal and private sectors are comparable in costs.

(b) Discussed under the Retirement section of this report.

(c) Employer cost only; employee and employer costs are 6.8% of total payroll.

- Federal employees take more than 1.6X the number of sick days as their private sector counterparts. As a result, annual Federal sick leave costs are approximately $1.2 billion higher than would be expected in the private sector.

- Procedures and controls to detect fraud and abuse in Federal Employment Compensation (FEC—disability benefits comparable to private sector workmen's compensation) are inadequate, costing taxpayers $95–$115 million annually.

PPSS also reviewed health care delivery systems in the Department of Defense and concluded that:

- Strong, centralized management is not in place to coordinate, plan, and oversee health care delivery and costs in the Department of Defense, wasting over $1 billion annually.

In general, PPSS recommended the following improvements:

- Regarding the FEHBP, control adverse selection (which results when employees who expect high medical costs concentrate in plans with extensive coverage) and improve program administration. (FEHBP administrative costs are less than 1/4 of 1% of premiums paid, compared to 1%-3% in the private sector.)

- Reduce annual leave and increase from 90 to 180 days the minimum service requirement for accruing initial vacation time so that Federal practices conform more closely to those in the private sector.

- Limit to 130 the number of sick days Federal employees can accumulate. (130 days is the number of days PPSS recommended as the qualifying period between occurrence of disability and eligibility for long-term disability payments. This qualifying period is comparable to that in the private sector.) Coupled with stricter supervision, this limit should reduce the amount of sick leave Federal employees use to a level comparable to that in the private sector.

- Reduce the number of employees receiving FEC benefits by implementing controls and reporting procedures typically found in private sector computerized disability payment systems. These controls and reports will help identify cases of fraud and abuse.

- Establish centralized authority and control over the DOD health care delivery system.

HEALTH BENEFITS

The FEHBP provides health insurance benefits to Federal employees and retirees, as well as to their dependents. Enrollment is voluntary. As of June 1981, FEHBP covered approximately 10 million people (2.4 million employees, 1.3 million annuitants and 6.3 million dependents). The program is contributory with employees and the Government sharing costs. Total FEHBP costs in 1981 were $4.2 billion, with the Government paying $2.6 billion, or 62%.

As of January 1982, there were 168 FEHBP options, including four programs available to all Federal employees, 19 plans available only to members of employee organizations and their families, and 145 comprehensive medical plans (health maintenance organizations (HMOs), most of which were available on a regional basis).

Each year, employees and annuitants are permitted to change plans or options in the FEHBP. Further, an employee may switch plans upon a change in marital status or loss of coverage, and may cancel a plan at any time.

Q. What accounts for the $450 million in higher FEHBP costs when compared to health benefit costs in the private sector?

A.   In addition to adverse selection, higher FEHBP costs result primarily from:

• A high ratio of high cost annuitants and their dependents in FEHBP resulting from the liberal early retirement provisions of the Civil Service Retirement System and generous survivor eligibility. 20% to 30% of Federal annuitants over 65 are not covered by Medicare. Aged annuitants without Medicare coverage use more FEHBP benefits and thus impose greater costs on the total FEHBP program than other participants. The Blue Cross/Blue Shield national FEHBP plan (covering approximately 51% of FEHBP participants) estimated that 1980 payments for aged annuitants without Medicare were 150% of that of the average participant, even though Medicare and non-Medicare covered participants pay the same FEHBP premiums.

• The difficulty of administering such a complex program and monitoring 168 separate plans, each with different benefits, claims handling standards, cost containment practices, and financial stability.

Q.   How does adverse selection cause health benefit costs to increase?

A.   "Adverse selection" allows employees to enroll in plans with high benefit provisions when they anticipate large medical expenses. Under FEHBP, an employee can change plans at least annually. For non-emergency medical treatments, employees can elect more comprehensive benefit plans when treatment is anticipated. They can subsequently switch to less comprehensive and less expensive coverage when treatment is completed. To put the number of employees changing plans in perspective, about 5% of total FEHBP participants change plans annually. However, one of the two Blue Cross/Blue Shield plans lost 234,000 participants in 1982, or 16% of total enrollment.

During annual open enrollment, Federal employees and annuitants may choose from many FEHBP plans. Federal employees in Washington, D.C., for example, have a choice among 22 plans. It is not uncommon for other Federal employees to have a choice among 12 or more plans. Their private sector counterparts, however, are offered a single plan (50% of the time) or a choice between two plans (30% of the time). The choice of many plans, the frequency of choice, and the widely varying plan benefits and premiums contribute to adverse selection.

Adverse selection by a minority of employees results in higher costs for the majority of employees and the Government. As an example, one of the government-wide plans has coverage valued at approximately 6% more than coverage under four other comparable FEHBP plans. Premiums, however, are 18% higher in the government-wide plan because of adverse selection. Since the plan is included in the formula for determining the Government's contribution, higher premiums increase Government costs. Also, the higher premium is unfair to employees who have not changed plans in anticipation of higher medical expenses and who are, therefore, overpaying for their coverage.

Q. How do FEHBP benefits compare to private sector benefits?

A. FEHBP does not specify standard or minimum coverage, and benefits, plan-to-plan, vary widely. On average, the six largest FEHBP plans cover 73% of medical expenses compared to 82% coverage in private sector plans.

Q. What is the total cost for FEHBP benefits?

A. The Federal Government and employees share the costs of the FEHBP. The table below shows employee and Government shares of total FEHBP costs, 1970-1981:

Total Premium Costs, FEHBP
($ Millions)

	Fiscal Year	(1) Employee Share	(2) Government Share	(3) Total	(4) Government as a % of Total
(1)	1970	$ 666	$ 250	$ 916	27.3%
(2)	1981	1,579	2,629	4,208	62.5
	Average Annual % Increase				
(3)	1970–1981	8.2%	23.8%	14.9%	3.2% Pts.

The cost to the Government for providing employee health insurance, 1970–1981, increased 23.8% per year, or about 40% faster than the comparable rate of increase in the private sector (16.9%). At the same time, the employee share increased only 8.2% annually, one-third as fast as the 23.8% increase in the Government share. The Government's share increased from 27.3% to 62.5% of total costs, an increase of 128.9% in 11 years.

Q. Does this mean that FEHBP costs per employee are greater than comparable costs in the private sector?

A. Yes. In 1981, the FEHBP average annual employee health care premium was $1,513. This compares to private sector costs as follows:

Annual Health Care Premiums Per Employee

		(1) Amount	(2) FEHBP as Multiple of Private Sector
(1)	FEHBP	$1,513	—
(2)	Chamber of Commerce	943	1.6X
(3)	236 Financial and Service Companies	1,116	1.4
(4)	Banks and Insurance Companies	1,295	1.2

FEHBP premiums are 1.2X-1.6X as expensive per employee as the private sector cost comparisons shown above.

Federal employees and the Government together pay more and get less coverage than the private sector for medical insurance.

Q. What improvements does PPSS recommend to reduce FEHBP costs and increase benefits?

A. PPSS recommended sixteen improvements to the FEHBP, including the following:

1. Conduct open enrollment only in alternate years; require enrollees to remain in a plan, once chosen, until the next open enrollment except in limited circumstances.

2. Require all plans to offer minimum benefits at least equal in value to those under Medicare. This would reduce the wide range of plan benefits, a factor contributing to the frequency with which employees change plans.

3. Obtain bids from insurance companies on the government-wide plans to ensure that cost containment ideas are explored.

4. Require that benefits for annuitants be included as part of the budget for the agency from which they retire, to focus attention on the high cost of those benefits. (Annuitants accounted for 37% of 1981 FEHBP participants.)

5. Bring annuitant and survivor eligibility requirements for FEHBP in line with stricter private sector practice.

6. Improve program administration by:

   1. Establishing or strengthening cost controls, e.g., setting minimum standards for the time in which claims are processed and auditing the rates at which different plans are used, replacing those that are not cost effective. These controls would help ensure that one plan does not have an advantage over another

in attracting Federal employees simply because it does not adequately control health care payments.

2. Improving the information distributed to FEHBP participants about the plans and the choices that are available. These improvements would help FEHBP participants make informed choices about the benefits and options available to them so that health benefits are used effectively.

By reducing FEHBP costs from 6.8% to 5.8% of payroll, savings will be $1.357 billion over three years, enough to pay for the health premiums of approximately 300,000 Federal employees for three years.

VACATION POLICY

The vacation policy for Federal employees is more liberal than in the private sector, specifically in regard to:

• Minimum length of service for first vacation;

• Length of vacation in relation to years of employment; and

• Maximum number of vacation days allowed to be carried over to the following year.

Employees of the Federal Government accrue vacation entitlement after three months of service. In comparison, employees at 53% of private sector firms do not accrue vacation pay until six months of service, and, at 22% of private sector firms, not until after twelve months—i.e., Federal vacation policy is more liberal than at least 75% of private sector firms.

Payroll and vacation costs 1979, 1982 and as projected for 1987 are shown below:

Payroll and Vacation Costs
($ Billions)

	Fiscal Year	(1) Vacation Cost	(2) Total Payroll Cost	(3) Vacation Cost as a % of Total Payroll Cost
(1)	1979	$3.8	$52.7	7.3%
(2)	1982	4.7	66.7	7.1
(3)	1987E	6.9	97.3	7.1
	Average Annual % Inc./(Dec.)			
(4)	1979–1982	7.3%	8.2%	(0.1)% pt.
(5)	1982–1987E	8.0	7.8	—

Annual vacation costs have increased 1.2 times from 1979 to 1982, from a level of $3.8 billion in 1979 to $4.7 billion in 1982 and are expected to increase 1.5 times, or to $6.9 billion, by 1987.

Q. How do Federal and private sector vacation allowances compare for specific lengths of service?

A. The following compares average Federal and private sector vacation days provided by length of service:

Vacation Benefit

		(1) Vacation Days Provided Private Sector	(2) Vacation Days Provided Federal	(3) Federal as % of Private Sector
	Length of Service			
(1)	6 months	4.8	6.5	135.4%
(2)	1–3 years	9.9	13.0	131.3
(3)	3–5 years	10.4	20.0	192.3
(4)	5–10 years	13.8	20.0	144.9
(5)	15–20 years	18.8	26.0	138.3
(6)	25–30 years	22.0	26.0	118.2
(7)	30 or more years	22.6	26.0	115.0

As shown, Federal employees receive between 115% and 192% of the vacation benefit received by private sector employees.

In addition, Federal employees can carry up to 30 days of vacation over to the following year. Private sector practices allow *no* carry-over in 54% of the companies surveyed, while 24% allow *less than* 16 days of carryover.

Q. What changes to Federal vacation policy did PPSS propose?

A. PPSS proposed three changes in Federal vacation policy:

• vacation time should be provided to employees only after 180 days of continuous employment—up from 90 days currently (savings of $298 million over three years);

• paid vacation time for Federal employees should be comparable to that granted in the private sector (savings of $3.486 billion over three years);

• unused annual leave should be forfeited (conservatively, no savings claimed since Federal employees would probably use their vacation allowance rather than lose it).

SICK LEAVE

Federal employees receive 13 days annually for sick leave. On the average, 9 of these days are taken each year and the remaining 4 days are accumulated. Nine days of sick leave used is excessive by private sector standards. The U.S. Chamber of Commerce reports that paid sick leave (sick leave plus short-term disability) totals 2.1% of gross pay (approximately 5.5 days per year) for nonmanufacturing industries—Federal employees take, on average, 63.6% more sick leave days than are taken in the private sector.

The following shows Federal payroll and sick leave costs for 1979, 1982, and projected for 1987:

Payroll and Sick Leave Costs
($ Billions)

	Fiscal Year	(1) Sick Leave Used	(2) Total Payroll Cost	(3) Sick Leave Used as a % of Total Payroll Cost
(1)	1979	$1.6	$52.7	3.1%
(2)	1982	2.2	66.7	3.4
(3)	1987E	3.3	97.3	3.4
	Average Annual % Inc./(Dec.)			
(4)	1979–1982	11.2%	8.2%	0.1% pt.
(5)	1982–1987E	8.4	7.8	—

Annual sick leave costs have increased 1.4 times, from $1.6 billion in 1979 to $2.2 billion in 1982, and are expected to increase 1.5 times to $3.3 billion by 1987.

Q. How can sick leave usage be controlled?

A. By providing that unused sick leave accumulates to a maximum of 130 days. That number of days will be needed to bridge the gap between the time when disablility occurs and when long-term disability benefits begin. This policy, coupled with stricter supervision, should reduce usage to a level comparable to that in the private sector.

Q. How much is the extra sick leave used by Federal employees costing U.S. taxpayers?

A. Savings from implementing PPSS recommendations are estimated at $3.690 billion over three years. Savings are based on the assumption that changes in sick leave benefits would bring Federal employee utilization rates and costs within the range of private sector costs. Private sector costs average 2.1% of gross pay while Federal Government costs are 61.9% higher at 3.4% (1983 estimate). Savings are based on the difference (1.3% pts.) as a percentage of gross payroll.

Q. How does sick leave usage in the Postal Service compare to usage in Federal agencies and in the private sector?

A. USPS average sick leave usage of 9 days per employee per year is the same as the government-wide average. Of 70 agencies for which OPM has accumulated data, *29 have sick day usage rates higher than USPS;* even though, on the whole, postal workers are more exposed to inclement weather and hazardous situations than other Federal workers. (More than 7,000 letter carriers, or 1 in 33, are bitten by dogs each year, for example.)

Nine sick days per Postal Service employee amount to a total of 21,734 work-years of lost productivity—$652 million annually.

Q. What can be done to reduce sick leave in the Postal Service?

A. A system of recordkeeping needs to be established to identify chronic absenteeism. The goal would be to correct the behavior of those who are habitually absent, as well as to ensure that other employees understand that management expects regular and consistent attendance.

WORKMEN'S COMPENSATION

In 1982, approximately $880 million in compensation benefits, excluding medical expenses, were paid to claimants under the Federal Employees Compensation (FEC) system (workmen's compensation). The system was found to be open to fraud and abuse because of an excessively permissive claims payment policy and because the current Automated Data Processing (ADP) systems are not effective.

Q. What are the main deficiencies in the FEC system which allow fraud and abuse to continue?

A. The main deficiencies that PPSS found were the following:

• The system does not correlate specific disabilities with recovery periods in order to identify those instances where absence exceeds established medical guidelines. The Government does not make use of comprehensive experience data to aid in identifying possible abuse.

• The current system does not require that the medical credentials of physicians certifying disability be verified as a prerequisite to claim payment.

• Claims submitted to more than one Region cannot be detected.

• There is no cross reference to other wage replacement systems (such as unemployment insurance, black lung compensation, etc.), and thus the possibilities for duplicate payment of benefits are great.

• The system does not verify wage earnings (available in 38 states) to identify individuals who may be employed while collecting benefits.

- Claims offices emphasize paying claims quickly with little emphasis on controlling potential abuse.

Q. What is the result of these deficiencies?

A. In 1980, 6.3% of Federal employees filed on-the-job injury claims, and 3.2% lost time from work. The corresponding figures for a large insurance company employing approximately 48,000 people in 1980 were 1.7% and 0.42%, respectively; so the experience in the Federal sector was 271% and 662% worse than in this representative private sector sample.

- For 1980, the Federal Government's experience of 3.2% of employees losing time does not compare favorably with the experience of other non-hazardous industries, e.g., banking (0.8%), communications (1.8%), and retailing (2.8%).

- The Assistant Postmaster General stated that an investigation of all postal workers receiving disability benefits found that 50% to 55% of these individuals were not totally disabled and could be performing some form of work.

- A 1982 investigation uncovered a number of extreme cases of fraud and abuse. In one instance, a letter carrier, who had been drawing benefits of more than $8,000 a year for total disability due to a knee injury, was running a pizza business. Another employee was receiving benefits of $14,000 a year while working in a flower shop. Another claimant was receiving benefits due to an elbow injury while operating a ceramics shop.

- Over the last 15 years, the Federal civilian work force has decreased slightly from 3.0 million to 2.8 million employees. During the same period, the number of long-term disability cases has grown from 20,000 to approximately 48,000 while the amount of annual disability compensation has increased from $75 million to $650 million. Since (a) the definition of a traumatic injury has not changed, (b) there is no evidence that job categories of a more dangerous nature have been added, and (c) there was no shift of employees to existing, presumably more dangerous jobs, the number of cases should have remained at about 20,000. Had this occurred, the total annual payout based on the current $13,600 per case average would be approximately $270 million, $380 million less than current costs of $650 million.

Q. What can be done to correct this situation?

A. Because FEC monitoring and control functions are inadequate to detect abuse, PPSS recommended that the Federal Government:

- Develop data and reporting systems to identify trends and supply the information necessary to assist in detecting abuse.

• Develop a system that correlates specific disabilities with specified time periods for recovery in order to identify instances where (a) disability status is not justified and (b) the length of disability has exceeded the established medical guideline.

PPSS estimated that the $380 million increase in FEC benefits can be reduced by 25%–30%, or $95–$115 million, in the third year after implementing PPSS recommendations. Savings of $189 million over the first three years are possible by implementing private sector procedures and controls.

DOD HEALTH DELIVERY SYSTEMS

DOD operates three direct health care systems, one for each of the three services. In addition, the Civilian Health and Military Program of the Uniformed Services (CHAMPUS) provides health care for civilian dependents of active duty personnel and for retired personnel and their dependents when health care is obtained from the private sector. The direct care system provides health care for active duty personnel, and for the dependents of active duty personnel, and for retirees and their dependents when space and resources are available.

Overall, the direct care hospitals are seriously underutilized, with average occupancy levels far below those considered marginal for civilian hospitals. While this should encourage diversion of CHAMPUS users to the direct care system, it has not. Because the direct care systems are budgeted within the Services and CHAMPUS is budgeted by the Office of the Secretary of Defense (OSD), financial incentives cause the direct care facilities to divert prospective patients to CHAMPUS.

To correct these problems, strong, centralized management must be put in place to coordinate, plan and allocate resources, and oversee health care delivery.

Q. What are some of the specific deficiencies in coordinating the CHAMPUS system with the direct health care systems of the Services?

A. Beneficiaries who live in catchment (surrounding) areas, i.e., within 40 miles of a military health care facility, are expected to get their inpatient care from that facility. Reimbursement via CHAMPUS for private sector inpatient care requires a nonavailability certificate (NAC) which must be obtained from the military direct care center. In FY 1979-1980, the military granted approximately 224,000 NACs.

The services do not have a specific coordinated policy on appropriate levels of approval or necessary documentation to support the NACs issued. An effective system for referrals to other direct care centers or other Federal health facilities has not been developed. If the present system is not changed, beneficiaries in catchment areas will continue to seek and obtain care from the private sector regardless of their proximity to military health care facilities. The lack of coordinated management between the direct care and CHAMPUS systems has led to inconsistent policy decisions and excessive costs.

Q. How much does CHAMPUS cost?

A. The estimated FY 1983 budget for CHAMPUS is $1.1 billion. DOD has estimated that approximately 55%, or $594 million, will represent expenditures for beneficiaries living within a catchment area. In fact, an additional appropriation of $110 million was requested for FY 1982 to fund the increasing use of the private sector for health care.

Q. Can the direct care system absorb the additional CHAMPUS patients? Are military hospitals operating at full capacity?

A. Only 77% of the operating bed capacity of military direct care hospitals in the continental United States is in use on an average day. Hospital administrators in the private sector use 85% as an optimal occupancy rate and 70% as a minimal rate, a criterion for closure. Using these criteria for the continental U.S. military direct care system, which includes 124 hospitals, only 6.5%, or eight hospitals, reach or exceed the optimal 85% utilization rate; 48 hospitals (38.7%) fall in the minimal category using 70% or less of operating bed capacity.

Q. What changes to CHAMPUS did PPSS recommend?

A. Nonavailability certificates (NACs) should not be issued for CHAMPUS beneficiaries who live within catchment areas except in emergency situations. The current 88% utilization rate of military health care facilities allows this change to be implemented with no strain on these facilities.

Q. What else can be done to increase the use of the military direct care system?

A. Under the existing DOD structure, four health care systems function independently of each other. A Defense Health Agency should be established. This agency should be responsible for managing all military treatment facilities worldwide. The potential benefits include: improved medical readiness and health care delivery; coordinated planning and budgeting for military health care resources; and development of uniform reporting and cost systems.

Q. Are there other ways in which DOD health care costs can be controlled?

A. Yes. Cost containment should become a priority in the management of military health care programs. Specifically, patients should be required to pay a greater share of health care costs. This would include charging for outpatient visits at direct care facilities, increasing the deductible for outpatient visits covered by CHAMPUS, and increasing patient payments for inpatient care at direct care facilities and under CHAMPUS.

Q. What savings did PPSS project from these recommendations regarding military health care costs?

A. Savings are estimated as follows over three years:

DOD Health Savings
($ Billions)

	Area	Amount
(1)	CHAMPUS NACs	$1.177
(2)	Defense Health Agency	0.943
(3)	Increasing Direct Care and CHAMPUS Patient Payments	0.934
(4)	Total	$3.054

Savings regarding CHAMPUS NACs are calculated based upon a 55% reduction in the $647 million spent in 1982 on non-psychotherapy and non-emergency claims, or 1982 savings of $356 million. Over three years, including inflation, savings would be $1.777 billion.

Establishing a Defense Health Agency would save 5% of direct health care costs ($5.7 billion in 1983), PPSS estimated. Over three years, savings would total $943 million.

Increasing patient payments for DOD supplied health care would yield three-year savings of $934 million. $773 million (or 83% of the $934 million) would result from charging a $10 fee for outpatient visits at direct care centers, with a $100 yearly maximum.

Savings in the Department of Defense from these three issues, estimated at $3.054 billion over three years, are enough to pay for over 300,000 hospital stays costing $10,000 each.

In addition to the issues described above, PPSS identified other fringe benefit areas where savings are possible. They represent estimated three-year savings of $24 million.

In FY 1982, 250 Air Force officers were projected to be involuntarily discharged for not achieving promotion grades within specific time periods. Severance pay costs were estimated at $30,000 each. PPSS recommended reducing severance pay to levels comparable to those in the private sector (which would result in severance pay of approximately $8,700 for each officer), saving $18 million over three years.

Army recruits discharged for "honorable" reasons during the first six months of service are entitled to accrued leave (vacation) pay. PPSS recommended delaying accrued leave benefits until a recruit demonstrates minimum suitability for the Army, a practice comparable to that in the private sector. Savings of $6 million over three years have been estimated.

Regarding Federal Workers' Disability Payments, PPSS recommended that a permanent capability to investigate cases on the rolls be established. Lack of adequate investigations in the past have resulted in abuse of benefits.

> The three-year total of all the recommendations in this section, after elimination of duplication and overlap among issues, is $12.092 billion—equal to the three-year taxes of 1.8 million median income families.

III. E. Other Opportunities with Significant Savings Potential Beyond PPSS

> There were many opportunities for cost savings or revenue enhancement that were only partially developed by PPSS Task Forces, and there were other areas which were not investigated at all. Nevertheless, these issues are valuable in that they demonstrate the continuing need to investigate the operations of the Federal Government. Savings opportunities identified by PPSS, although substantial, represent only a small part of the potential savings available across the Federal Government.
>
> In FY 1983, the Government spent $3.5 billion in the specific areas covered by PPSS recommendations, with spending estimated to increase to $16.3 billion by the year 2000 if present policies are continued. Implementing PPSS recommendations would reduce spending to $10.1 billion in 2000, a saving of $6.2 billion or 38.0%.

Inherent in a volunteer project such as PPSS are time constraints and personnel limitations which would preclude the comprehensive study of any organization, particularly one as large and as complex as the Federal Government. Accordingly, there were many opportunities for cost savings or revenue enhancement that were only partially developed by PPSS and other areas which were not investigated at all. In fact, many of the individual PPSS Task Force reports contain specific recommendations which, although reflecting careful thought, are not regarded as fully supported and defensible. Nonetheless, when viewed in total, these issues are valuable in that they demonstrate the continuing need to investigate the operations of the Federal Government.

Within the PPSS Task Force Reports, there are 54 recommendations with related three-year cost reduction and revenue enhancement opportunities of $8.557 billion, classified as "potentially justifiable and supportable." Due to time, personnel resources, and other limitations, recommendations in this category, while meritorious, are not regarded as fully supported by the Task Forces, but are deemed worthy of further analysis to determine the full extent of their merit.

In addition, the Task Forces identified about 190 potential opportunities which came to their attention during the review process. Unlike the "potentially justifiable and supportable" recommendations, these opportunities were not reviewed in depth by the Task Forces. However, taken as a whole, they represent important cost reduction opportunities for "further study."

Another source of opportunities for cost reduction is found in the Government's own GAO and OIG reports. Although the PPSS Task Forces used many of these reports in their reviews, these reports contain additional areas which were not specifically reviewed by the Task Forces.

Another avenue of additional savings and revenue enhancements is the extrapolation of savings identified by a specific Task Force government-wide. PPSS was divided into 36 Task Forces, each assigned to review either a specific agency, department, or a functional area, such as ADP. Task Forces worked independently of each other, but many recommendations developed by one Task Force have applicability within other governmental departments or agencies.

This government-wide applicability is a result of common structural, systemic, and procedural problems throughout the Government. For example, the Department of Labor (DOL) Task Force found that there were more telephones than employees within the DOL. As the usage of telephones is a common everyday practice, this issue was selected as having potential for extrapolation government-wide. Total savings from reducing the amount of telephone equipment across Government amount to $848 million.

A total of eleven issues were extrapolated across the Government, resulting in estimated three-year savings of $17.885 billion.

Q. In addition to reducing the amount of telephone equipment usage, what other recommendations were extrapolated government-wide?

A. The following chart presents major extrapolated savings opportunities uncovered by PPSS:

	Extrapolated Issues	Government-wide Three-Year Savings ($ Billions)
(1)	Enforce Implementation of Contracting Out	$ 7.390
(2)	Limit the Issuance of Tax-Exempt Bonds	5.174
(3)	Increase Competitive Bidding for 8(a) Contracts and Military Spare Parts	2.213
(4)	Increase Emphasis on Cost Containment	1.089
(5)	Other (7 Issues)	2.019
(6)	Total	$17.885

The recommendation to enforce the implementation of contracting out represents government-wide three-year savings of $7.390 billion. Due to the significance of the savings estimates and the impact on the operations of the Government, this issue is discussed in detail in the section, "Optimizing the Use of the Private Sector."

Q. How would reducing the amount of tax-exempt bonds generate $5.174 billion in savings?

A. Tax-exempt bonds, by definition, are a source of "lost revenues" to the Federal Government. In addition, the easy availability of tax-exempt bonds, primarily used to finance the construction of new hospitals or to modernize or expand existing hospitals, has contributed to the current excess supply of hospital beds. Limiting the amount of hospital revenue bonds issued will increase competition for these bonds and ensure that funds are allocated on a needs/merit basis which will reduce the amount of "lost revenues" to the Federal Government and prevent unnecessary construction. This can be accomplished by:

• changing tax-exempt revenue bonds to a general obligations basis,

• imposing a ceiling on the amount of tax-exempt revenue bonds, and/or

• providing financial justification for the issuance of tax-exempt bonds (e.g., on a rate of return basis).

Assuming that all tax-exempt revenue bonds could be limited by one of the above methods, it is estimated that in total tax-exempt revenue bonds will be decreased by 30% which will result in a three-year revenue enhancement of $5.174 billion.

Q. Better procurement procedures are a major PPSS recommendation, and it is discussed in detail in the section, "The Impact of Not Buying Prudently." Do savings estimates of $2.213 billion shown in the preceding table duplicate the section on not buying prudently?

A. No. The issues discussed here relate specifically to military spare parts and the 8(a) Program, which are not included in "The Impact of Not Buying Prudently." Currently, in the Defense department, spare parts are purchased directly from the original manufacturer of the equipment. This practice results in buying from the manufacturer without price competition from other producers. Major cost savings are projected if spare parts and their related technical specifications were to be incorporated into a formal reprocurement process which included competitive bidding. As this PPSS recommendation was made only in relation to one military agency, extrapolating these savings Defense-wide would result in potential three-year savings of $1.375 billion.

Additional procurement cost savings can be obtained by modifying the 8(a) Program. This program, which is administered by the Small Business Administration (SBA), currently sets aside procurement funds to be awarded to socially and economically disadvantaged companies. Cost savings opportunities arise because there is no competitive bidding among the 8(a) companies, and the procuring agency must always use SBA as a middleman. The effect of competitive bidding and the elimination of SBA's role as the middleman would result in cost savings of $838 million in procurement and administrative costs. In total, extrapolated procurement cost savings from the two recommendations regarding spare parts and the 8(a) Program total $2.213 billion.

Q. Procurement programs intended to achieve social objectives, like the 8(a) program, can increase costs to the Government because of reduced competition. Are there controls in place to ensure that costs do not escalate out of control?

A. Cost controls are only partially in place. The Army Task Force found that there is a backlog in the implementation of cost containment within the Army. If it is assumed that each military service has a backlog of cost containment programs, the opportunity to extrapolate savings Defense-wide is possible. Information supplied by the Department of Defense (DOD) revealed that the Air Force and the Navy have estimated backlogs on productivity enhancement programs valued at $100 million each. The potential savings resulting from these programs—60% of the one-time program cost annually over a ten-year average economic life—is extracted from the Army Task Force Report. Total three-year savings are estimated to be $1.089 billion.

Q. What are some of the other opportunities for cost savings that have been extrapolated across Government?

A. Reducing foreign exchange losses ($438 million), and eliminating Reserve forces dual pay ($331 million) are two defense-related issues which have potential three-year savings of $76.1 million when extrapolated Government-wide. The largest remaining extrapolated issue recommends more cost-effective shipment of goods, which would save $392 million over three years.

In total, the extrapolated savings opportunities represent $17.885 billion over three years, including the $7.390 billion in savings resulting from increased "contracting out."

The PPSS recommendations identified for further study offer additional opportunities to increase cost savings, revenue enhancements, and management efficiencies. The category "further study" is used to identify opportunities to eliminate waste and inefficiency within the Government, which, due to time and resource constraints, could not be thoroughly developed by PPSS.

Q.   How many opportunities for further study has PPSS identified?

A.   Hundreds. However, to cite every example would be too cumbersome and detailed. Instead, selected examples are shown to highlight additional areas for review. One area, for example, concerns consolidating programs and procedures with similar or overlapping functions or purposes. For example:

  • Equal Employment Opportunity (EEO) complaints filed by U.S. Postal Office (USPS) employees are handled by EEO specialists within USPS. If an employee's complaint is not successfully resolved at USPS, it can be refiled at the Equal Employment Opportunity Commission (EEOC). Thus, the EEO specialists function is duplicated within USPS and at the EEOC. Preliminary analysis reveals that by eliminating the EEO specialists in the USPS who perform the identical functions as the EEOC, the Government could save $252 million over three years.

In addition to eliminating duplicate programs, there is a recommendation by the Personnel Management Task Force to establish a central office to oversee productivity programs.

Q.   What benefits will a central office to oversee productivity programs produce?

A.   Substantial productivity gains could be realized by establishing a permanent office to develop, promote, and coordinate government-wide productivity programs. The success of these programs could be assured if performance appraisals of agency managers included an evaluation of their cooperation and participation in such programs. Based on Federal compensation costs of $63.6 billion in 1982, the Personnel Management Task Force estimates that a productivity increase of 5% would reduce personnel expenses by $10.521 billion over three years. Further study is needed to completely support a recommendation establishing a central office to increase productivity government-wide.

Q.   Are there other areas reviewed by PPSS where increased oversight could reduce costs?

A.   Yes. One area would be collective bargaining. Collective bargaining within the Government can cause wage differential problems for employees performing similar tasks. On average, Federal employees who bargain collectively for wages have higher rates of pay than employees under General Schedule (GS) and Federal Wage System (FWS) schedules. For instance, in FY 1981, the GAO determined that employees whose salaries were based on collective bargaining agreements averaged $4,857, or 26%, more per year than FWS employees in comparable jobs. Further study of this problem is recommended to ensure pay comparability for Federal employees who bargain collectively and FWS employees who perform similar tasks.

The existence of outdated and unwarranted programs is another result of the Government's lack of oversight. For example, the apparent objective of current farm legislation is to ensure adequate supplies of basic foodstuffs at affordable prices and to maintain minimum producer income at a modestly comfortable level, well above subsistence. A complicated system to maintain this "comfortable income level" is designed to shape market forces and stabilize farm supply and demand at price levels that will meet the objectives of producer income maintenance. The current programs have failed to meet these fundamental objectives.

Price Support program outlays in any given year are a function of several economic factors which make future program costs difficult to estimate. A wide range of estimates for FY 1983 and FY 1984 exists. The Congressional Budget Office (CBO) estimates $2.900 billion for the two-year period, while USDA estimates $5.100 billion.

Price Support programs have, in general:

- Induced record production and stocks at a time of stagnant domestic and world demand;

- Weakened the U.S. farmer's competitive position in world markets;

- Preferentially diminished the economic viability of the small, family-owned farm; and

- Committed the Federal Government to future crop support outlays well beyond those projected.

PPSS recommended that Government Price Support programs be restructured so as to provide producers with a "safety net" in cases of substantial, sharp, short-term price declines instead of providing income maintenance through supply/demand stabilization. Savings are estimated at $13.157 billion over three years.

Complex eligibility criteria and benefit determination formulas in transfer programs present a fruitful area for cost savings. Eliminating duplication, and changing the method of determining benefit levels, could ensure a more equitable distribution of benefits. For example:

- An estimated one million recipients of Aid to Families with Dependent Children (AFDC) reside in housing that is subsidized by HUD or by state agencies. These same recipients also receive a shelter allowance in their monthly AFDC benefit payment. Further study is warranted to determine the effect of discontinuing the duplication in shelter allowance payments by HUD and AFDC currently estimated to be $300 million annually.

- Short-term workers contribute a relatively small amount of Social Security tax because they have had little work in covered employment, but they receive a higher return on their contribution than the average wage earner. This is a result of the benefit formula. By spreading the short-term worker's covered earnings over a lifetime and applying the resulting artificially low average wage to the benefit formula, the low wage earner is favored. The GAO recommends revising the benefit formula to save $15 billion over the next decade.

Q. Are there other areas where further study could achieve substantial cost savings?

A. Yes. As one example, the costs of elective surgery and the number of operations performed under Medicare and Medicaid could be significantly reduced by requiring a second medical opinion. Getting a second medical opinion is generally recommended to ensure that surgery is necessary. Beneficiaries of Medicare and Medicaid, however, usually will not bother getting a second opinion to determine if surgery is necessary because the cost of the surgery is borne by the Government. The HHS Office of the Inspector General recommends that requiring second opinions could reduce the incidence of elective surgery by as much as 29% for Medicaid and 18% for Medicare. This would save the Government $157 million per year.

Inherent in the structure of an organization as large as the Federal Government, with its different and incompatible computer and accounting systems, is the difficulty of maintaining adequate financial and information controls. As a result, overpayments, misappropriations, and outright theft can go undetected. Examples follow:

• The Food Stamp program suffers from an inordinately high overpayment error rate of at least 9.8% when compared with other entitlement programs, due to theft, illegal trafficking, and fraudulent use of program benefits. In FY 1981, losses due to overpayment errors alone exceeded $1 billion. For example, food stamp dollars often find their way into the wrong pockets as a result of grocery stores giving their customers credit slips, rather than cash, for change of less than 50¢. The Inspector General for the U.S. Department of Agriculture (USDA) estimates that $30 million in food stamp money goes to grocery store owners each year because the credit slips were never redeemed by customers. Further study is necessary to recommend an alternative delivery system for the Food Stamp program which would help reduce fraud and administrative costs.

• The Unemployment Insurance Program (UIP) also lacks adequate procedures to prevent overpayments. For example, in FY 1983, nearly $30 billion was paid in UIP benefits. This represents more than a 100% increase since 1980. The Department of Labor (DOL) OIG found that state procedures for preventing, detecting, and recovering overpayments were inadequate and estimated that the overpayment error rate in the UIP is as high as 12%. Based on this rate, overpayments in FY 1983 are estimated at $3.7 billion.

• As another example, HUD has programs which provide rental units or rent subsidies to low and moderate income families. One program, the Public Housing Agencies (PHAs), uses inadequate cost data furnished by developers and owners to calculate rents. The HUD subsidy is determined in part by evaluating this information. The HUD OIG recommends that improving the cost data used by HUD to calculate subsidies could save $18 million annually.

Adequate supporting data is an everyday practice in the private sector. There are many effective business practices which the Government could institute to increase cost savings. The following three examples demonstrate common private sector practices which could be implemented in the Government.

• According to the HUD OIG, Public Housing Authorities (PHAs) have not adequately managed their cash balances. Available funds have been invested in low- or non-interest bearing accounts. The HUD OIG recommends that PHAs could realize substantial interest revenue by investing cash balances to realize the greatest return.

• Fixed-price, lump-sum contracts are those contracts which are bid and executed at a single price for a specified product. Components of the product are not broken out and are not priced individually on a unit basis. An issue arises for both the Government and the contractors when "change orders" become necessary in the course of work. Without unit pricing for specific components, any change order reopens the entire contract to negotiation. Further study is needed to determine the effect of establishing fixed profit margins in lump-sum contracts at the time of the contract award.

• Computer fraud in the Government is becoming an increasingly prevalent problem. According to the GAO, operators commonly tape access information to their terminals allowing anyone to illegally access that system. For example, a clerk used a Department of Transportation computer system to steal more than $800,000. The GAO recommends the implementation of a standard practice prohibiting display of access codes to minimize computer fraud.

Additional opportunities for cost savings would occur if the Government enforced existing laws.

• According to the GAO, the Government is losing millions of dollars in interest because the IRS is not enforcing laws that prohibit late deposits of weekly payroll taxes. By not following procedure, checks to pay these taxes may take up to two weeks beyond the due date to clear. During that time, companies earn interest on the float which should rightfully go to the Government. PPSS recommended that better enforcement of the law that prohibits these late deposits could save millions annually.

• A study by a Senate subcommittee found that fines assessed by judges have doubled since 1980 to nearly $100 million per year. Collection rates, however, are at an all time low of 35%. PPSS believes that increased efforts at the Department of Justice (DOJ) could help collect the estimated $180 million in delinquent fines.

Q. The majority of the previous examples represented cost savings. Are there any areas for further study which would increase revenues?

A. Yes. One significant area concerns the sale of off-shore leases. Currently, leasing of the Outer Continental Shelf (OCS), and the associated revenues from oil and gas exploration and development activities, provide the *largest source of non-tax revenues to the Federal Government*. Although only 5% of the total 1.0 billion OCS acreage has been offered for sale, in FY 1982 OCS revenues were $6.2 billion and represented 1.0% of total Government receipts. In FY 1983, OCS revenues are estimated to increase to $11.8 billion. In preparing the annual budget, OCS revenues from new lease sales cannot be estimated due to Congressional review of OCS's five year plan for lease sales. In FY 1982, Congress prohibited two lease sales which would have generated $5.7 billion in revenues. The Land/Facilities/Personal Property Task Force recommends making the Minerals Management Service (MMS), which centrally manages OCS, an independent, self-funding entity—i.e., requiring no appropriations. This would provide stability to both Government and private industry planning and budgeting processes, as Congress would only have to review the five year plan once. An additional benefit would be to minimize unplanned borrowing and the associated interest cost (conservatively estimated at *$460 million* for FY 1982) due to the unpredictable nature of these lease sales.

PPSS uncovered many instances where the Government could increase revenues by increasing user fees to recover operating costs. For example:

• In FY 1981, the Federal Government received $5.2 million, or about 2%, of the gross receipts collected by the approximate 530 concessioners operating in the national parks. This 2% franchise fee is insufficient to cover all repair and maintenance costs of the concessioners facilities. Consequently, taxpayers subsidize the costs to maintain these facilities instead of concessioners being charged user fees commensurate with operation and maintenance costs. PPSS recommended raising the franchise fee to a level that would cover costs. Increased revenues are estimated at $2 million over a three year period.

• The User Charges Task Force report recommends for further study that wastewater treatment facilities should at least charge user fees commensurate with costs. In FY 1978, approximately $1.8 billion, or

20% of the $9.1 billion required to operate and maintain 36 municipal wastewater treatment facilities, was not recovered by user fees. Unless these states raise their fees to cover costs, which are projected to exceed $200 billion by the year 2000, taxpayers will have to provide approximately $40 billion in subsidies.

- The Environmental Protection Agency (EPA) regulates, inspects, and analyzes conditions related to all forms of pollution. User charges, if any, to perform these tasks vary between programs and states. For example, air pollution control permit fees are levied by 21 states. However, these fees represent only 5% of the cost to operate Air Quality Programs. In contrast, user fees are not charged for ocean dumping, which costs $9 million per year. As user charges do not cover all costs, the States depend on the Federal Government for additional funds. Further study is required to determine the effect of the EPA requiring states to charge user fees commensurate with pollution control costs, which were at least $50 million in FY 1982.

Transferring responsibility for some Federal activities to the private sector could also prove expeditious and economical, for example:

- The EPA estimates that over $118 billion in Federal funding will be required for wastewater treatment facilities by the year 2000 to meet the goals of the Clean Water Act. As the Federal Government will not be able to provide these funds, one alternative is to use the private sector for the construction and ownership of these facilities. The Federal Construction Task Force states that the tax benefits of ownership and revenues from fees would provide an incentive/justification for private sector investment. PPSS findings indicate that privatization of the facilities would expedite construction and eliminate the need for the $118 billion Federal funding requirement.

- Costs per revenue dollar to operate a U.S. Postal Service (USPS) "contract station" range from 2.8¢ to 12.0¢, or less than half those of a regular post office window. Contract stations, which presently total 2,700, operate within an existing store or office, with the retailer providing USPS services. PPSS found that USPS could save $165 million over three years by using more contract stations.

And the list goes on and on. PPSS has only touched the tip of the iceberg; as all of this shows, there is more, much more, that needs to be done.

Given the opportunities identified in this section and elsewhere in the report, PPSS recommends the Office of Management and Budget (OMB) seek legislation to establish a series of public audit committees comprised of members from the private sector appointed by the President of the United States. The role of these public audit committees would be comparable to that of private sector audit committees, which serve in an advisory capacity to corporate boards of directors. The primary responsibility of the public audit committee would be to conduct thorough and independent reviews of Federal Government internal audit practices, procedures, and controls, and to evaluate the adequacy of the internal audit responsibilities, mission, and scope for the Federal Government. Many of the opportunities discussed in this report could have been realized earlier had, PPSS believes, the concept of a public audit committee been operational.

The private sector has increasingly come to recognize the positive value of a public audit committee as an instrument of control, as well as a means of enhancing the quality and acceptability of the internal audit process. A basic function of a corporate audit committee is to assist the board of directors in fulfilling its fiduciary responsibility relating to corporate accounting and reporting practices. Another major function of the committee is to maintain a direct and separate line of communication between the board of directors and the company's independent auditors. Through this role of communication, the audit committee develops information on an understanding of company activities which, through their advisory role with the board of directors, can be used to strengthen the board's control of company operations. PPSS believes that a properly structured Government-wide audit committee can assume a similar role and improve the overall control of Governmental operations. PPSS envisions a Public Audit Committee serving as the oversight committee for each of the individual public audit committees that would be established for each agency. This primary oversight Audit Committee would work with and through the Director of the PPSS-proposed Office of Federal Management (OFM) to the President. The agency-based audit committees would, in turn, work with and through the agency head to the oversight Public Audit Committee.

The oversight Audit Committee in concert with individual agency audit committees would provide the OFM with an independent assessment of overall management efficiency and control. The very complexity of the Federal Government's structure and operations increases the probability of breakdowns in internal control and policy compliance. Accordingly, these public audit committees would:

1. Focus on internal audit policies and procedures and on the mechanisms for internal control which ensure that operating policies are efficiently and effectively carried out.

2. Be concerned primarily with internal audit.

3. Work directly with the Director of the OFM in the case of the oversight Audit Committee, and heads of the various agencies and agency Inspectors General in the case of agency audit committees.

4. Allow staff members of internal review/audit groups (i.e., internal auditors) to have direct access to public audit committees without going through the agency head.

The oversight Public Audit Committee or individual agency public audit committees would review or offer guidance to top management in the following audit-related areas:

1. Policies for audit activity;

2. The development and execution of a comprehensive and coordinated long-term audit plan, including the prioritization of audit coverage in high dollar-risk environments such as social programs, procurement, inventory management, and financial management;

3. The effectiveness of and compliance with Government policies and procedures at all levels of management;

4. The effectiveness of management controls to increase operating economies and efficiencies;

5. The evaluation of internal controls and accomplishment of stated policy objectives;

6. Follow-up of management's implementation of audit recommendations;

7. Follow-up of various commission recommendations directed toward improvement of Government operations;

8. The need for updated computer and other state-of-the-art auditing techniques; and

9. The need for increased coordination between the various audit organizations in the selection of audit targets.

The benefits of a public audit committee can be far-reaching. For one, the committee's role reinforces the internal auditor's independence from management, thereby providing an additional degree of control over operating policies. An audit committee also forces both auditors and management to take a more aggressive approach toward problems that might otherwise go unresolved.

The committee's composition of private sector individuals assures the independent point of view that is so crucial to its effective functioning. While a knowledge of business and finance as they relate to Governmental activities is a distinct advantage to audit committee members, it is not essential for all members. Audit committee experience would be helpful criterion for committee membership. The committee composition should provide for diversity in outlooks among members.

PPSS recognizes that the use of public audit committees would be a unique approach, as no other Federal agency uses a private sector group in such a manner.

Legislation may be required to form an advisory group to the agency heads which is composed totally of members from outside the agencies.

Based on our knowledge of the operation of public audit committees in the private sector, we recommend that the legislation include the following provisions:

1. Appointment by the President of seven leaders from the private sector, with no more than four from any one political party for each public audit committee established. The committee members should serve for one term of six years and should not be reappointed unless the initial appointment was to fulfill an unexpired term of less than three years.

2. The President appoint three members for six years, two members for four years, and two members for two years (eligible for reappointment). Thereafter, all terms would be six years, except in situations where an unexpired term is filled. Anyone having served in the agency (for which the audit committee is being established) in the previous five years would not be eligible for membership on the audit committee. Members would serve without pay.

The primary duties and responsibilities of the public audit committees would be defined as follows:

1. The committees would be required to meet formally at least four times a year and submit a report of each meeting to the agency head and to the oversight Audit Committee. This oversight Audit Committee would, in turn, submit an annual report through the Director of OFM to the President. Meetings could be scheduled at any other times deemed appropriate by the committees.

2. The committees, on an individual or joint basis, would be accessible, through the agency or OFM, to receive reports, suggestions, questions, and recommendations from Government internal auditors and financial officers.

3. The committees would review the duties, responsibilities, and activities of the Inspectors General Offices, and other Government organizations with internal audit responsibilities.

4. The committees would review selected accounting policies and management plans and procedures and performance thereunder to assure compliance with agency and Government policy.

This is but one approach which, if implemented, could help restore sound fiscal and operations management to the Federal Government.

> The three-year total of all the recommendations in this section, after elimination of duplication and overlap among issues, is $8.557 billion—equal to the three-year taxes of 1.3 billion median income families.

IV

A SUMMARY OF PPSS RESULTS
AND A ROAD MAP FOR ACTION

Introduction

As clearly indicated in the preceding pages, PPSS has identified many and diverse opportunities for cost savings and management efficiencies in the Federal Government and cited specific examples of where these opportunities may be found and why they exist. PPSS believes it is now essential that a "road map for action" be developed to ensure the expeditious implementation of those recommended improvements.

Before proceeding further, it should be noted that, for purposes of *this* analysis, the focus is on total, three-year duplicated dollar savings and revenue enhancements—$544.985 billion—rather than net, unduplicated dollar opportunities—$424.351 billion. To comply with the intent of the Federal Advisory Committee Act and its provisions for ensuring public comment on the proposed findings, conclusions, and recommendations of Federal Advisory Committees, the 47 PPSS reports were released on an ongoing basis from April 1983 through January 1984. Accordingly, it was not possible to prevent the initial reporting of duplicated savings in reports concentrating on a specific department or agency and those reports focusing on functional issues which cut across the entire Federal Government. In addition, to have done so would have been to give an incomplete picture of the opportunities in specific departments or functional areas.

For some analytical purposes, however, the unduplicated savings are more useful, and they form the basis for a great deal of the overall impact analysis that appears throughout this Report.

As an example of duplicated opportunities, the recommendation to have the Department of Defense (DOD) "privatize" domestic commissary operations based on the private sector "warehouse" model was made by both the Office of the Secretary of Defense Task Force and the cross-cutting Privatization Task Force. Eliminating the duplication would have entailed removing the projected savings from one or the other of these reports, which would have resulted in an understatement of the potential for cost savings either through improvements in the management of DOD or through more extensive use of a Government-wide program of privatization.

Overview

There are a number of perspectives derived from a review of PPSS-identified opportunities and associated cost savings/revenue generation. For the development of a road map, PPSS has chosen to concentrate on the following:

• Authority for implementation

• Affected departments and agencies

• Management functions

with emphasis on the bottom-line impact, rather than the sheer number of opportunities identified.

Implementation—Although PPSS took care in identifying the responsible implementation authority, the complexities of the appropriations process could result in a change in these determinations.

The following table and graph show the breakdown of three-year savings/revenue by implementation authority:

Authority	Amount ($ Billions)	% of Total
Congress	$395.1	72.5%
Department/Agency	106.7	19.6
President	43.2	7.9
Total	$545.0	100.0%

The President can, of course, significantly influence department/agency actions (see chart IV-1).

In cases where more than one implementation authority is involved, savings/revenue have been categorized logically under the implementation authority with the power to render a "go" or "no-go" decision with respect to implementation. For example, when the President can initiate administrative action but legislative approval is required to implement it, the opportunity has been categorized under Congressional rather than Presidential authority.

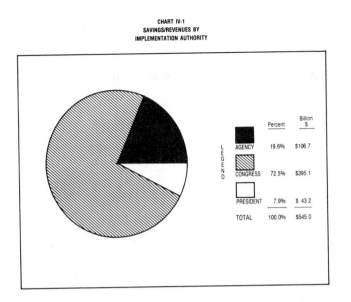

CHART IV-1
SAVINGS/REVENUES BY
IMPLEMENTATION AUTHORITY

Department and Agency Perspective—While the percentage of dollar opportunities actually under the control of the departments and agencies is significantly less than that under Congressional authority (27.5 percent versus 72.5 percent), PPSS believes that an identification of those departments and agencies where the greatest savings and revenue can be effected is important for purposes of developing a Government-wide plan of action.

PPSS has identified DOD and the three agencies with Government-wide oversight responsibility—the Office of Personnel Management (OPM), the Office of Management and Budget (OMB), and the General Services Administration (GSA)—as the agencies representing two-thirds of the three-year PPSS savings and revenue opportunities, or approximately $355.8 billion in total.

		($ billions)	% of Total
(1)	Department of Defense (DOD)	$165.7	30.4%
(2)	Office of Personnel Management (OPM)	66.2	12.2
(3)	Office of Management & Budget (OMB)	64.7	11.9
(4)	General Services Administration (GSA)	59.2	10.9
(5)	Subtotal	$355.8	65.4%
(6)	All Others	189.2	34.6
(7)	Total	$545.0	100.0%

Wherever functions are managed under guidelines set up and enforced by an oversight agency (such as OPM involvement with human resources management and GSA control of nonmilitary procurement), the savings opportunities have been categorized within the authority of that oversight agency.

The bar chart below presents a more complete breakdown of three-year projected cost savings and revenue enhancements on a department/agency basis.

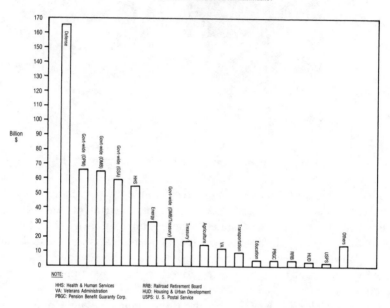

CHART IV-2
SAVINGS/REVENUES BY DEPARTMENT/AGENCY

NOTE:

HHS: Health & Human Services   RRB: Railroad Retirement Board
VA: Veterans Administration   HUD: Housing & Urban Development
PBGC: Pension Benefit Guaranty Corp. USPS: U. S. Postal Service

Major Management Functions—Although there are identifiable differences between the public and private sectors and the constituencies which they serve, there are, however, very real and numerous commonalities between the public and private sectors, such as:

a) human resources management
b) organization structures and procurement procedures and policies
c) financial controls
d) automated data processing
e) cash management
f) building services
g) transportation services
h) foreign exchange
i) overseas locations
j) hospital management
k) feeding (cafeterias)
l) retailing (consumers)
m) maintenance and repair

n) inventory and control of supplies
o) domestic and international shipment of goods
p) office automation
q) research and development
r) technology management
s) portfolio management
t) underwriting
u) insurance planning
v) lending
w) borrowing
x) budgeting
y) economic forecasting
z) expenditure control

Indeed, it was this commonality which provided the philosophical basis for the President's request that PPSS review and study Federal Government operations.

PPSS found that ten major management functions account for 90.5 percent of total PPSS three-year savings and revenue enhancements. Of these ten, five account for 68.6 percent, as shown in the following table, and may be compared to the private sector functions of human resources management, program/product management, fiscal management, and procurement.

		($ billions)	% of Total
(1)	Human Resources Management (HRM)	$125.9	23.1%
(2)	Subsidy Programs Management	99.0	18.2
(3)	Fiscal Management	53.8	9.9
(4)	Weapons Acquisition Management	49.9	9.2
(5)	Procurement Management (non-ADP)	44.7	8.2
(6)	Subtotal	$373.3	68.6%
(7)	Next Five Largest	119.7	21.9
(8)	Subtotal	$493.0	90.5%
(9)	All Others	52.0	9.5
(10)	Total	$545.0	100.0%

The following chart provides a graphic presentation of the savings and revenue impact of 14 major management functions.

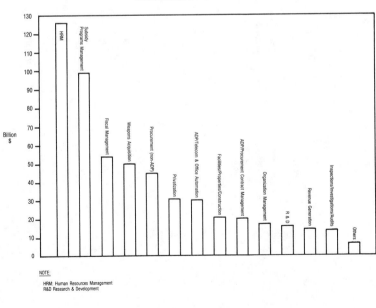

CHART IV-3
SAVINGS/REVENUES BY MAJOR MANAGEMENT FUNCTION

NOTE:
HRM: Human Resources Management
R&D Research & Development

TABLE IV-1
Management Function Categories
Recommendation Descriptions

1.

Human Resources Management
- productivity
- pensions
- compensation
- benefits
- staffing

2.

Subsidy Programs Management
- payment-in-kind value
- program consolidation
- administrative efficiency

3.

Fiscal Management and Control
- cash management
- debt management
- budget formulation
- portfolio investment

4.

Weapons Systems Acquisition
- multiyear contracting
- dual sourcing
- performance-based specifications

5.

Procurement/Contract Management (Non-ADP)
- contract labor rates
- A-76 procurement policy
- national contracting
- competitive bidding

6.

Privatization
- power marketing
- private sector contracting
- private sector participation

7.

ADP: Telecommunications and Office Automation Management
- ADP obsolescence
- ADP and OA planning
- computer matching
- claims/benefits automation

8.

Facilities, Property & Construction
- hospital bed needs analysis
- performance-based disposition
- fleet management
- maintenance productivity

9.

ADP: Procurement/Contract Management
- inventory management systems
- economic order quantity procurement

10.

Organization Management
- facilities consolidation
- structural consolidation
- structural streamlining

PPSS made specific recommendations about how the Federal Government can and should improve its management efficiency and effectiveness in each of the ten major categories which, as indicated earlier, account for 90.5 percent of total three-year PPSS savings/revenue. The areas covered in those recommendations are summarized in the table on page 320.

Setting Implementation Priorities—The preceding three analyses provide several different perspectives from which to view the PPSS recommendations. Using the major management functions described earlier as the "driver" to integrate the analysis by department/agency and by implementation authority, PPSS sought to create an action plan for implementing its recommendations. Specifically, it has attempted to identify:

• what the main opportunities are—by management function;

• where the opportunities exist—by department and agency; and

• who is responsible for pursuing them—by implementation authority.

The following ten charts (organized by management function with the greatest savings/revenue opportunities) provide such an integrated model, to be used as as a guide to implementing the 2,478 recommendations formulated by PPSS.

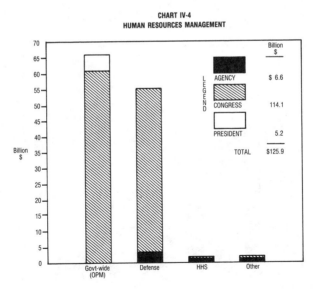

CHART IV-4
HUMAN RESOURCES MANAGEMENT

The opportunities in human resources management, the management function with the largest potential dollar savings ($125.9 billion), revolve around areas within the purview of OPM and the Department of Defense. Over 90 percent require Congressional authority for implementation.

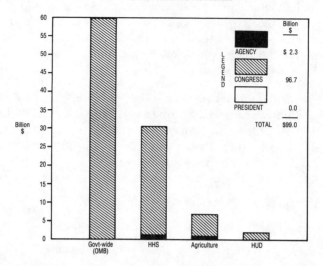

CHART IV-5
SUBSIDY PROGRAMS MANAGEMENT

It will take Congressional action to realize $96.7 billion in subsidy programs management improvement opportunities. Emphasis will be on programs within the jurisdiction of OMB and three other departments.

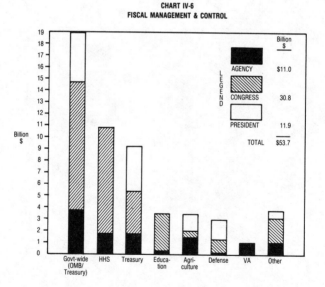

CHART IV-6
FISCAL MANAGEMENT & CONTROL

Savings and revenue opportunities in fiscal management and control appear throughout the Federal Government. The Treasury Department and OMB play a particularly significant role in this area as leaders and overseers of other departments.

CHART IV-7
WEAPONS SYSTEMS ACQUISITION

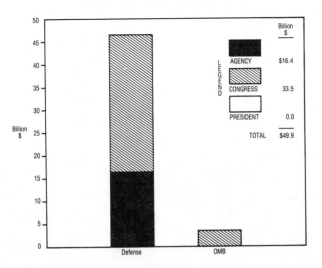

Improvements in weapons acquisition management are, understandably, concentrated in the Department of Defense, which can achieve approximately $16.4 billion in three-year savings on its own and an additional $33.5 billion over three years with the support of Congress.

CHART IV-8
PROCUREMENT/CONTRACT MANAGEMENT
(NON-ADP)

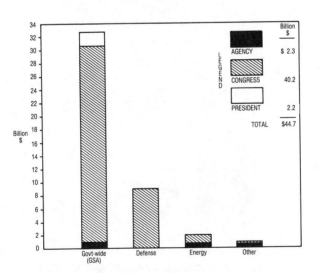

Congress can take action to implement improvements in procurement and contract management that could save $40.2 billion over three years. About three-quarters of the procurement opportunities ($33 billion) are within the purview of GSA, although $9.1 billion are specific to Defense.

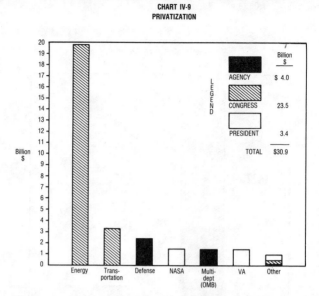

Savings and revenue opportunities through privatization of commercial functions and activities are often associated with specific departments. For each department there is generally only a single implementation authority involved—frequently Congress. Almost two-thirds of the three-year savings relate to the Department of Energy.

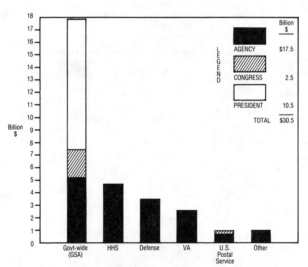

The Executive Branch is responsible for the implementation of most of the ADP recommendations in the telecommunications and office automation areas. Most departments can take action on their own, but Presidential initiatives are needed to achieve over $10 billion of the three-year savings through the key oversight agency in this category—GSA.

— 324 —

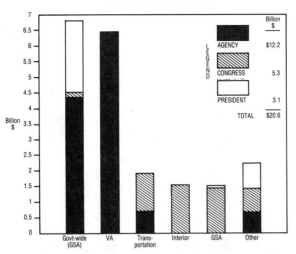

CHART IV-11
FACILITIES/PROPERTY/CONSTRUCTION

Through its own authority, the VA can save $6.5 billion over three years by improving the way it manages its facilities, properties, and construction projects. Government-wide, GSA can facilitate the saving of an additional $6.8 billion over three years.

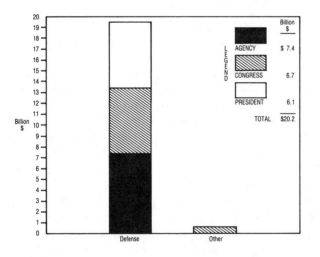

CHART IV-12
ADP: PROCUREMENT/CONTRACT MANAGEMENT

The Defense Department, with the cooperation of Congress and the leadership of the President, can save $19.5 billion over three years in procurement and contract expenses by implementing ADP procurement and contract management improvements.

CHART IV-13
ORGANIZATION MANAGEMENT

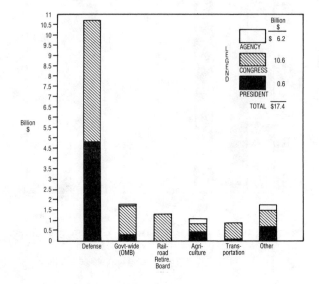

Over a three-year period, the Defense Department can save $10.7 billion by improving its organization planning and design. While departments such as Defense have some authority over their organization, Congress must give its approval before more than half of the savings can be realized.

The preceding charts focus on the ten most significant management functions, based on cost savings and revenue generation potential. Collectively, they account for 90.5 percent of the total three-year PPSS cost savings and revenue opportunities. Using this same approach, all functional improvements shown in Charts IV-4 through IV-13 can be tracked to specific departments and/or oversight agencies, as well as to the primary implementation authority involved.

Focus on Implementation Authority: Where the Big Payoffs Are—To develop a starting point for implementation, PPSS has prepared a table highlighting the key findings detailed in the ten charts, but reorganizing the data based on implementation authority. This reorganization creates a checklist of the five largest savings opportunities under each implementation authority, thus focusing attention on where the greatest and most immediate impact is possible. In addition to serving as a road map for implementing actions to realize the opportunities identified by PPSS, the following table presents additional information on the recommended solutions.

TABLE IV-2
Implementation Authority
Checklist

Implemen-tation Authority	Rank	Management Function	Department	Savings ($ billions)	Detail
A. *Congress*	1.	Human Resources Management	Govt-wide (OPM)	$ 60.970	Adjust Civil Service Retirement System. Change pay comparability and position classification procedures. Bring Federal employee annual leave and sick leave practices in line with private sector. Adjust employee health benefits program.
	2.	Entitlement Program Management	Govt-wide (OMB)	59.829	Include payments-in-kind as earnings for entitlement programs' analysis, definition of poverty, and IRS's determination of income. Improve entitlement program administration.
	3.	Human Resources Management	Defense	51.831	Adjust Military Retirement System. Revise pension formulas and payment schedules. Increase certain health care charges, deductibles, and co-payments. Eliminate dual pay for reserve duty.
	4.	Weapons Acquisition	Defense	30.088	Utilize common weapons system parts and standards. Increase use of dual sourcing and multiyear procurement. Improve development project management and budgeting and accounting procedures.
	5.	Procurement/ Contract Management (non-ADP)	Govt-wide (GSA)	29.716	Revise/repeal Davis-Bacon, Walsh-Healey, and Service Contract Acts.
		Subtotal		$232.434	

TABLE IV-2
Implementation Authority
Checklist (continued)

Implementation Authority	Rank	Management Function	Department	Savings ($ billions)	Detail
B. Agency	1.	Weapons Acquisition	Defense	$ 16.377	Navy should improve program stability; increase use of economic production rates, dual sourcing, and multiyear procurement; and facilitate modernization/productivity enhancements of contractors.
					Department-wide, procurement should be improved through better program planning, contracting, and management and through better weapons cost estimation and scheduling.
	2.	ADP: Procurement/ Contract	Defense	7.352	Increase use of economic order quantity system and improve inventory data systems.
	3.	Facilities/Property/ Construction	Govt-wide (GSA)	6.455	Improve efficiency of in-house maintenance and increase control of energy costs in Government buildings. Improve control of environmental mitigation outlays and use of value engineering in construction projects.
	4.	ADP/Telecommunications & Office Automation	Govt-wide (GSA)	5.164	Improve hardware and software resources management and improve payment processes in hospital systems.
	5.	Organization Management	Defense	4.757	Consolidate department's base support operations and centralize health care administration.
		Subtotal		$ 40.105	

C. *President*

1. ADP/Telecommunications & Office Automation	Govt-wide (GSA)	$ 10.480	Improve strategic planning, budgeting, and support for office automation systems. Coordinate Federal agencies' welfare recipient data and require standardized Federal and state recipient forms. Improve rail, freight traffic, and teleprocessing resources management.
2. ADP: Procurement/ Contract Management	Defense	6.074	Improve materials management systems.
3. Human Resources Management	Govt-wide (OPM)	5.164	Reduce overgrading and adopt position management plans. Review performance in these areas specifically.
4. Fiscal Management & Control	Govt-wide (OMB & Treasury)	4.216	Enforce Treasury's requirements for charging interest on all late loan payments. Decrease delinquent terms from 30 days to 15 days. Assess a non-refundable loan application fee to fully cover operating costs involved. Improve and coordinate agency debt collection procedures.
5. Fiscal Management & Control	Treasury	3.893	Improve collection of delinquent taxes through better classification of accounts, improved staffing, and more effective collection techniques.
Subtotal		$ 29.827	
Total in 15 Recommendations		$302.366	55.5% of duplicated savings of $545.0 billion.

A Strategy for Action

In the private sector, corporate strategy is viewed as a means of reducing general corporate objectives to manageable proportions, thus enabling employees across the company to work in unison toward the achievement of clearly identified goals and objectives. This unifying direction is critical for the successful coordination of management initiatives that cross departmental and functional boundaries, and for integrating disparate departmental projects.

The same principles apply to the public sector. If the President is to achieve the goal of sound fiscal management through improved efficiency in the Federal Government, then the Administration must develop and implement a strategy that will provide the required direction. With the understanding that sound fiscal management is indeed a goal of this Administration, PPSS has formulated hundreds of recommendations to improve specific Governmental operations. These recommendations have been summarized and grouped into a workable structure for analysis. It is now important that a Government-wide strategy for implementation be formulated.

PPSS believes that the Cabinet Council on Management and Administration (CCMA), working in concert with the Office of Cabinet Affairs, is the most effective group to lead the Administration's effort to restore principles of sound fiscal management to the Federal Government and, more specificallly, the implementation of PPSS's recommendations.

CCMA was established in September, 1982 and is the seventh of President Reagan's Cabinet Councils. The President has described the Cabinet Council system as a "means for deliberate consideration of major policy issues which affect the interest of more than one department or agency." CCMA's more specific directive is to control and supervise Reform 88, a long-term program to improve the management and administrative systems of the Federal Government. It also is charged with responsibility for monitoring and implementing the recommendations of PPSS. In addition, it formulates Government-wide policies pertaining to Executive Branch management, including administration and personnel issues.

In the view of PPSS, CCMA's membership makes it ideally suited to oversee the implementation of PPSS recommendations because it includes those with direct responsibility over most of the agencies and functions cited by PPSS as the major areas of opportunity. Collectively, this group has the authority to set priorities and articulate the Administration's strategy for realizing those opportunities.

PPSS, therefore, urges the President to call upon CCMA to make the implementation of PPSS recommendations its highest priority, and that he commit CCMA to the continued identification, formulation, and implementation of a Government-wide management strategy for the future, within its boundaries of authority.

V.

—◆—

A BASIS FOR HOPE

PPSS FINDINGS with respect to the state of Governmental machinery, the exorbitant costs of operation, and the overall financial picture provide no room for optimism that these problems will be solved without very difficult reversals in the trends of two decades.

When first requesting that this survey be undertaken, the President charged the members to scrutinize the Government with the same careful attention that they might give to a potential acquisition of another company. With the full results now in, what are the prospects?

As detailed in the preceding chapters, PPSS found that the Federal Government can be made a great deal more efficient. Costs can be contained and brought into line with revenues.

Most importantly, there are early indications, PPSS has found, of an eagerness on the part of the Executive Branch to move the PPSS recommendations into action.

Let us review the hopeful signs.

Executive Office of the President Response

The Executive Office of the President has developed a strategy, a structure, and a system to review and implement the PPSS recommendations. Specifically, the *strategy* is to hold each responsible agency accountable to review and act on each recommendation contained in the reports, stating either when implementation has or will take place or defending why it cannot.

The *structure* for reviewing the PPSS recommendations is as follows:

Following the PPSS Subcommittee hearings, the data are released in final form to the White House Office of Cabinet Affairs. The Office of

Cabinet Affairs distributes the reports to each affected department or agency, Office of Policy Development, and Office of Management and Budget (OMB) for review and comments.

1. The lead department/agency is asked to evaluate each issue and recommendation, indicating whether the item can be implemented as recommended or whether it, in the judgment of the department, requires modification.

2. The department/agency response is coordinated with OMB and the Office of Policy Development (OPD) prior to a meeting of a White House review group.

3. White House review groups have been established to consider department/agency responses. Cabinet members and agency heads as well as PPSS representatives are invited to participate in all review groups considering matters affecting their departments/agencies. It is the intent that most implementation decisions be made in these meetings.

4. Any issues which cannot be resolved by the review group may be appealed and later considered by the Cabinet Council on Management and Administration (CCMA) or in the budget review process.

5. It is the responsibility of the lead department/agency evaluating the individual issues and recommendations to present an implementation plan and schedule to the White House Office of Cabinet Affairs, so that progress can be monitored.

The *system* for keeping track of where the thousands of recommendations stand is a comprehensive automated data base developed by the PPSS Management Office. Initial classifications include the affected agency, program, function, savings potential, and implementation authority required. The White House then adds the agency implementation timetable and milestones.

Thirteen PPSS reports have been evaluated by the White House review process. There are approximately 250 issues in the 13 reports. The Executive Branch is in the process of implementing nearly 85 percent of these issues at some level. Implementation began in some cases during FY 1984. Others are incorporated in the proposed budget for FY 1985.

Thus, real progress has been made in the review of recommendations, and the pace of the review process should pick up now that the FY 1985 budget has been formulated and the PPSS Final Report has been submitted.

The strategy, structure, and system that have been set in place have established a viable mechanism for the review and implementation of PPSS recommendations. With its focus on the Cabinet Council on Management and Administration and the White House Office of Cabinet

Affairs, the implementation process is institutionalized in the key management structure of the Government.

In addition, OMB, in response to a PPSS recommendation that its functions of management and budget be integrated, conducted for the first time the FY 1985 budget review process with participation from the management review group. Significant OMB resources were applied to a management review of the PPSS recommendations as part of the FY 1985 budget review process. Decisions reached and actions taken are to be incorporated in the President's Budget Report to be released later this month or early next month. The OMB management group involvement in the budget process is viewed as a permanent and institutional change that will be carried out beyond the FY 1985 budget process and will provide an ongoing mechanism to assure follow-up and implementation of PPSS recommendations in the years ahead.

Agency Response

When PPSS Task Forces initially approached the agencies to begin their surveys, they encountered in nearly every instance a spirit of cooperation and support from agency officials. Agencies' attitudes throughout the survey have overwhelmingly reflected a basic and genuine interest in considering any proposals that might make their operations more efficient and effective.

PPSS, in turn, took on its task in the spirit of providing high quality professional analyses and recommendations of direct practical use. PPSS gave careful attention to agency declarations, but nonetheless exercised its own independent judgment of what was wrong or what was needed.

That professional relationship aided in formulating constructive solutions. Now it is furthering the implementation of the proposed solutions. Agencies already have accepted and are implementing many of the PPSS recommendations. Here are some examples:

- A series of PPSS cash management improvement recommendations are being carried out Government-wide, with estimated savings of $4.7 billion by FY 1985.

- A reduction of over 1,400 employees in the Department of Health and Human Services, as recommended by PPSS, is being made, with an estimated $172 million savings over three years.

- The Department of Education is implementing a PPSS recommendation for collecting delinquent student loans, with initial focus on 41,000 current or retired Federal employees owing more than $65 million in delinquent student loans.

- The Administration has initiated action to reduce the number of employees in grades GS/GM 11-15 by 40,000, as recommended by PPSS. Total estimated savings through FY 1988 is $1.4 billion.

- An aggressive Government-wide debt collection program which has been under way for nearly two years was reinforced by PPSS recommendations. Savings targets were established for FY 1983–FY 1988, with projected total collections of over $20 billion.

- GSA solicited bids from leading food service chains to set up a restaurant at its headquarters in Washington, D.C. If this test is successful, then competition for food service contracts is to be broadly extended, as recommended by PPSS.

- Recently, GSA announced that Federal employees would utilize Government-issued credit cards to pay for official travel, as recommended by PPSS. This is expected to save the Government $23 million annually through reduced processing of travel documents and elimination of the need to make cash advances.

- In conformity with PPSS recommendations, the Administration has announced the closing of 229 printing plants and duplicating centers, with estimated savings of $51 million.

In summary, the healthy attitude of agencies towards carrying out cost reduction actions is a favorable indication.

Congressional Response

Although PPSS is a commission established by Presidential Executive Order, 73 percent of its recommendations require the approval of Congress before they can be implemented. Congressional support for PPSS cost control efforts is, therefore, critical if the full savings impact is to be realized.

At the same time, projections of annual budget deficits of $200 billion a year and more over the foreseeable future have helped prompt the Congress as a body and members as individuals to take more than a passing interest in PPSS recommendations—which contain savings on the order of $120–140 billion a year and which over the 17 years to 2000 will prevent cumulative deficits and an increase in the national debt of $10.5 trillion.

Over the course of the past several months numerous hearings and briefings have been held at which PPSS representatives have discussed their findings and recommendations and responded to questions from members of Congress and their staffs. These sessions have in nearly all cases been marked by expressions of willingness to give a fair hearing to the recommendations and to consider how Congress might be involved in their implementation. Coming across clearly was a deep-seated concern with the burgeoning costs of Government and consequent openness to initiatives that give promise of moderating the problem.

The PPSS Chairman and his staff have provided testimony to both the

Senate and House Budget Committees and other committees as well. Other senior Survey officials have appeared before the House Budget Committee Task Force, the Subcommittee on Military Personnel and Compensation of the House Armed Services Committee, and staff members of the Senate Republican Policy Committee.

Representatives of many of the PPSS Task Forces have also briefed Committees and Subcommittees in both houses of Congress. The House Committee on Science and Technology, for example, invited representatives of the PPSS Task Forces on the Departments of Transportation, Commerce, and Energy, as well as those dealing with the Environmental Protection Agency and with the Government-wide functions of research and development, to present briefings. All of the military department Task Forces (Defense, Army, Navy, and Air Force) briefed the House Armed Services Committee's Subcommittee on Military Personnel and Compensation, while the Senate Budget Committee has been briefed by representatives of seven Task Forces and has plans to hear from nine more.

In addition to the receptivity to PPSS views indicated by the scheduling of these numerous hearings and briefings, many individual members of the Congress have taken a personal interest. A few examples follow.

- Representative Bob Livingston, a member of the House Appropriations Committee, wrote last autumn that "perhaps the largest potential budget savings for the government will derive from the President's Private Sector Survey on Cost Control." "What we've always thought, is true," he went on to say. "The government can be run more efficiently. The Reagan Administration, with its inspectors general and cash management programs, is beginning to achieve major savings. The Grace commission's cost control survey has given us a blueprint to achieve much more."

- Calling projected deficits "outrageous and unacceptable," Senator William Roth went on to point out in a recent article in *The New York Times* that the Grace Commission had "identified billions of dollars in possible savings over three years" and offered his opinion that "even if only a few of the commission's suggestions were implemented, the savings would be substantial."

- Senator William Armstrong has proposed that there be promulgated a Joint Congressional Resolution providing that each committee of the Senate consider and hold hearings on PPSS recommendations within its jurisdiction, then report on those hearings and any proposed implementing legislation.

While the major results cannot, of course, be expected until the Final Report has been transmitted to the President and the Administration accelerates its implementation activities, some Congressional actions have already taken place. A few examples follow.

- Senators Pete Domenici, Chairman, and Lawton Chiles, Ranking Minority Member, of the Senate Budget Committee jointly requested the Congressional Budget Office (CBO) to make a complete evaluation of all PPSS recommendations which require legislative action. Also they requested the General Accounting Office (GAO) to conduct a careful analysis of all major PPSS recommendations and related budgetary savings estimates. Both the CBO and GAO were to report their findings for Congress' use in the FY 1985 budget deliberations.

- Representative Delbert Latta, a member of the House Budget Committee, requested the Congressional Budget Office to publish and make available to every member of Congress a compendium of all PPSS recommendations. He indicated that the House Budget Committee would work with the Senate Budget Committee, CBO, and GAO to review these recommendations, declaring, "It is now our task in Congress to ensure that these recommendations are implemented to the maximum extent possible."

- Senator Robert Dole, while on "Meet the Press" a few months ago and in response to a question seeking his reaction to the need for establishing a Commission on budget deficits, responded that the Grace Commission recommendations provide sufficient basis for reducing costs without establishing a new commission.

- Representative Joseph Addabbo recently told the Service press that the House Appropriations Subcommittee on Defense, which he chairs, had adopted some of the cost-cutting recommendations of the PPSS.

- The Senate Appropriations Committee, acting to cut $100 million from the permanent change of station (PCS) account in the FY 1984 Defense Appropriations Bill, cited PPSS findings and further instructed the Department of Defense to consider these recommendations and report action taken to reduce PCS costs.

What final Congressional action will take place on the vast majority of PPSS recommended savings and revenue enhancements requiring action by that body remains to be seen, but it is clear from the activity that has already taken place that there is great interest in Congress—in both houses and on both sides of the aisle—in opportunities for economy in Government. This is consistent with the high level of interest in cost control elsewhere in society and provides the basis for a productive approach to solving this all-pervasive problem.

Public Response

As noted earlier, the implementation of any specific PPSS recommendation depends on whether the President and/or the Congress choose to exercise their authority to make the proposed changes in Federal Government operations. While they have the power to dismiss or accept the PPSS recommendations, in the end these two branches of Government are accountable for their actions—or their inaction—to the public that elects them, and they are necessarily responsive to the views of that public. In such a context, the extent to which PPSS recommendations are realized will depend greatly on the public's reaction to PPSS findings and conclusions.

There has been encouraging response from the media, the business community, and the general public as evidenced by the following:

a. Media

During the almost two years of the PPSS activity, there has been an apparent and growing media awareness of the unprecedented deterioration in the Nation's financial condition, for example:

U.S. News and World Report—July 25, 1983 issue cover story: "A City Without Guts—Why Washington is Losing the War on Waste."
Time—July 11, 1983 article on PPSS recommendations for "Rooting Out the Waste."
Barron's—Editorial Commentary in November 14, 1983 issue: "Structural U.S. Deficits? A Huge Amount Is Built-In Inefficiency and Waste."
Reader's Digest—January 1984 issue feature article: "How to Save Taxpayers $100 Billion a Year."
Newsweek—January 16, 1984 article on "Congressional Encroachment" titled "Congress in Dis-Grace."

The "$200 Billion Deficit" awareness has brought about greatly increased press coverage of spending, deficit, and tax issues, in the full spectrum of political and economic opinion. The ordinary citizen is being offered a wide range of commentary and advice, and often from the most expert journalists in the field. The ordinary citizen is becoming more knowledgeable in complicated economic areas.

Paul A. Volcker, Chairman of the Federal Reserve Board, has been quoted as saying, "I do not share the comfortable assumption of some that working forcefully and steadily toward better budgetary balance is a task that can wait a year or more."

In a more specific sense, concerning the efforts of PPSS itself, the various Task Force reports were made publicly available periodically starting in April 1983, and were presented at a series of well-attended press conferences. Many of the issues dealt with by PPSS are controversial and arouse opposition from special interest groups. PPSS expected opposition as well as approval; that PPSS has received some of each attests to the fact that our efforts did not flinch from some of the most contentious issues of the day.

b. Business Community

Private sector businesses are nearly unanimous in support of efforts to increase efficiency and reduce costs of the Federal Government. This is explained in part by the fact that businessmen know that business can thrive only in a climate of economic well-being, and that the current excessive costs of Government threaten the national economy. Their interest might also be explained by the fact that businessmen, as a group, are personally and occupationally attuned to efficiency and cost savings; they would like that same attention to be given to Government operations.

The business community has been enthusiastically behind the PPSS survey from the beginning. This is evidenced first by the strong commitment of the 161 appointed members of the executive committee, by their willingness to contribute key personnel in their organizations for long periods of time to conduct the necessary investigations, and by their companies' generous contributions exceeding $75 million. In addition there have also been cash contributions to support the Survey from numerous businesses not actively engaged in the Survey.

The major business organizations also are committed to supporting cost saving proposals. A letter to PPSS dated April 18, 1983 from Robert T. Thompson stated, "In my role as Chairman of the U.S. Chamber of Commerce I am going to push hard for early implementation of your recommendations."

Small businesses, as well as large, are supportive of this effort. Another letter received by PPSS states, "There are thousands of small businessmen such as myself who applaud you and . . . hope you . . . will pursue the initial objective since there is so much at stake in our economy and in our country."

It is important to note that businesses are willing to accept their fair share of the impact that far-reaching reforms would have. PPSS, composed mainly of business executives, looked at all Federal programs with the same objective eye and adopted numerous recommendations which might have a direct adverse financial impact on the private sector. A few such recommendations, showing the financial impact over a three-year period, include:

- Reduce progress payments to DOD contractors by $9.4 billion.

- Reduce operating subsidies to shipping companies by $75.4 million.

- Increase user fees paid by marine companies by $1.6 billion.

- Increase timber-cutting fees to logging companies by $99 million.

- Increase publication fees and document production fees; pharmaceutical firms, for example, would be charged an additional $13.5 million for documents obtained from the Government.

- Increase premiums charged corporations for Federal retirement benefit insurance by $324 million.

- Impose special assessments of $3.2 billion on corporations which underfund their own retirement benefit plans.

- Increase landing fees to airlines by $57 million.

It is a measure of the deep support in the business community for reducing Federal costs that it would endorse such actions as part of a major drive in the interest of good government and the overall economy.

c. Public

The cost-cutting proposals of PPSS have also attracted surprising public support. Thousands of letters have been received from the public. Some of them contained small donations, completely unsolicited, to advance the Survey goals. Most, however, simply expressed appreciation, urged continuing efforts to effect adoption of the recommendations, and in many cases offered personal assistance.

A representative statement from one of those letters declared: "We want you to know there are many, many of us out here in the silent majority who are applauding and urging you on in your great efforts on our behalf."

There have also been numerous public requests for speakers to address meetings and outline the major findings and recommendations of the Survey. The audience response at such meetings has been overwhelmingly supportive of eliminating waste, fraud, and abuses in Government.

Numerous specific PPSS recommendations would impact many Americans, including the salaries, annuities, or benefits that many receive and the rates, prices, and fees that many would pay. Because of this specificity, PPSS was braced to receive criticism. But, surprisingly, most of the public response has been favorable. There is a growing perception that our Government is in deep trouble and that some major reforms are essential.

The very fact that PPSS was mandated to survey the entire Governmental scene operated in its favor. Few citizens would willingly give up a benefit if they were in a small minority called upon to bear the cost. But a cut in benefits is easier to accept when one knows that all Americans are sharing in the same belt-tightening exercise, and that the result will be greater prosperity for all.

President Lincoln admonished us never to underestimate the basic intelligence of the American public. Implementation of many of PPSS's and other proposals for cost savings will ultimately depend upon the public's active participation in making the choices facing us as a nation. Perhaps the public receptivity to cost-cutting is founded upon a recognition that, if our Government can be made more efficient, smaller, and less expensive, then all of us will, in the long run, share in the far greater personal benefits that this will afford.

We are faced with a crisis, as PPSS findings have documented in detail. But, as the support for reform that exists in many quarters indicates, there is hope. Crises involve dangers, but also opportunities. Hopefully, the opportunities offered by PPSS will be fully explored and provide future generations of Americans with a basis for continued growth and well-being.

VOLUME II

VI.

THE WHO, WHAT, WHERE
AND WHEN OF PPSS

I place economy among the first and most important virtues, and public debt as the greatest of dangers to be feared. To preserve our independence, we must not let our rulers load us with perpetual debt . . . If we can prevent the government from wasting the labor of the people, under the pretense of caring for them, they will be happy.
—Thomas Jefferson

In establishing PPSS, the President drew not only upon his experience as Governor of California, but on a rich tradition of public-private partnership as well, as evidenced by such historical precedents as the Taft Commission on Economy and Efficiency (1910–1912), the Brownlow Committee (1936–1937), Hoover I (1947–1949) and Hoover II (1953–1955), the Ash Council (1969–1971), and the Carter Reorganization Project (1977–1979).

Q.   Why did President Reagan decide to establish the President's Private Sector Survey on Cost Control?

A.   The President has always had a long-standing philosophical commitment to the goal of conducting the affairs of Government according to principles of sound business and fiscal management, to reducing and ultimately eliminating the public debt, and to ensuring the worth and dignity of the people by guaranteeing that their labors will be both productive and fruitful.

Faced with an operating budget that exceeded revenues by $500,000 daily when he became Governor of California, Ronald Reagan asked leading representatives of the private sector to undertake a review of state operations for the purpose of identifying waste, inefficiency, overlap, and duplication. That effort was successful, with then Governor Reagan convinced that the methodologies of the private sector could be effectively applied to the many aspects of Government operations.

Fifteen years later as President and faced with a national debt of $1.25 trillion and no sign that rampant Government spending would abate in the near future, he announced, on February 17, 1982, the establishment of the President's Private Sector Survey on Cost Control. On June 30, 1982, he signed Executive Order 12369 formalizing its mandate and objectives.

Q.   What makes the private sector particularly qualified to undertake such a huge and challenging endeavor?

A.   Private sector management is driven by the need to ensure the enterprise's continued economic survival. This is a precondition for profit or any other measure of success and the satisfaction of this precondition requires constant attention to managerial efficiency and the effective use of resources in a competitive arena. The unforgiving tests of both the balance sheet and the marketplace must be met. Failure to meet the demands of either will, in time, bring the enterprise to an end, with the attendant consequences not only to management but to the investors, employees, suppliers, customers, and the community as well. In short, the private sector cannot operate with a continuing and growing deficit. Failure to operate efficiently and to ensure a satisfactory return to investors will cause the private sector enterprise to fail, with devastating effects on all its components—particularly its employees.

Government has no such incentive to survive, let alone succeed, nor any such test to meet. The Government, unlike private sector enterprise, is not normally managed as if it were subject to the consequences of prolonged managerial inefficiency or persistent failure to control costs. Such consequences have historically been avoided in the public sector—or, more accurately, postponed—by Government's propensity to increase tax revenues, engage in deficit spending, and spend yet more money on failed programs with the result of masking their ineffectiveness.

The members of the President's Private Sector Survey on Cost Control (PPSS) believe that the disciplines necessary for survival and success in the private arena *must* be introduced into Government to a far greater degree than previously has been the case. It is that belief which motivated the PPSS effort. A government which cannot efficiently manage the people's money and the people's business will ultimately fail its citizenry by failing the same inescapable test which disciplines the private sector: those of the competitive marketplace and of the balance sheet.

Q. But aren't there critical and fundamental differences between the goals and objectives of the public sector and those of the private sector?

A. Participants in PPSS recognized that the public sector performs roles which have no counterpart in the business community or, indeed, anywhere in the private sector. There are obviously *unique* Government functions involving such things as safeguarding the personal security and well-being of the people, the administration of justice, and the provision of numerous public services which cannot be strictly subjected to the same tests as in the private sector. The Survey, therefore, focused much of its attention on those critical factors which have a *comparable* impact upon both the management of Government and the management of the private sector, such as human resources management, fiscal management and control, procurement, automated data processing, etc. Indeed, in many ways, the Federal Government *is* the world's largest conglomerate—the largest power producer, insurer, lender, borrower, hospital system operator, landowner, tenant holder, holder of grazing land, timber seller, grain owner, warehouse operator, shipowner, and tank fleet operator.

In addition, the Executive Committee and other participants in PPSS represented both the for-profit and the not-for-profit sectors. As a consequence, the managerial views and perspectives of those whose primary objective is profit maximization were combined with those whose primary objective is the delivery of goods and services within identified constraints of survivability and efficiency, but where profit maximization is not the principal goal.

Q. When you talk about PPSS and the "private sector," exactly what do you mean?

A. PPSS was guided and directed in its survey by a 161-member Executive Committee, under the Chairmanship of J. Peter Grace. The 161 members of the Executive Committee, most of whom also served as Co-chairs of the Survey's individual Task Forces, constitute a major segment of the business leadership of the United States. About 80 percent are either chairmen, presidents, chief executive officers or chief operating officers of the Nation's leading corporations. The rest are principals of top law, accounting, investment and management consulting firms; former high-level Government officials; the heads of foundations and trade associations; and leaders from other private sector fields, including education, medicine, labor, and the media.

Among the Executive Committee members are representatives of:

• about a quarter of the *Fortune* top 100 companies;

— 345 —

- nearly a third of the top 50 commercial banks, including the five largest;
- the three largest insurance firms;
- three of the top ten diversified financial services firms;
- three of the top 30 retailers;
- the largest transportation company; and
- the largest advertising agency.

In addition to the Executive Committee, over 2,000 individuals participated in the Survey as Task Force members, Survey Management Office personnel, or PPSS advisors. A total of over 850 corporations, professional firms, and other private sector organizations contributed people, money, and/or services and equipment to the fulfillment of the President's mandate. A list of these participants is included at the end of this Report.

Because the numbers were so large, so varied in the skills represented, and stem from so many private sector sources, it seems safe to say that there is very little in the way of economic, social, financial, and managerial capabilities and experiences which did not exist somewhere in the Survey's reservoir of talent.

Q.   What criteria were used for selecting Executive Committee members? Was it really a nonpartisan effort?

A.   The President and the Chairman of the Executive Committee sought those individuals who had proven ability to effectively and efficiently manage their own enterprises—whether for-profit or not-for-profit. They sought and succeeded in recruiting the top business and managerial talent in America and asked those individuals to work like "tireless bloodhounds" in identifying waste and inefficiency in the Federal Government. Political affiliation was not a consideration for membership on the Executive Committee, nor was it a consideration in selecting PPSS Task Force members, Management Office personnel, etc. Instead, recruitment efforts were concentrated on finding "the best and the brightest" in the private sector, people who were willing to serve and provide needed resources and who could bring these resources and expertise to Washington in what was probably the most extensive, far-reaching demonstration of the public-private partnership to date.

Q.   What about conflicts of interest?

A.   Obviously, a private sector study on cost control and managerial efficiency in the Federal Government needed the help of private citizens who possessed the experience and the capacity to understand the processes of the Federal Government, analyze them intelligently, and recommend operational improvements in response to the President's mandate. Because of this understandable need to call upon people knowledgeable in the functions to be studied, the Survey was highly sensitive to possible conflicts of interest and took every reasonable step to avoid them, including the establishment of internal rules and standards that went beyond the requirements of the law. It is the Survey's view that it brought the best expertise of the private sector into the public analysis of Government, while avoiding compromise of the public trust.

Specifically, all members of the Executive Committee were cleared for appointment to that Committee by the White House Office of Legal Counsel. In addition, members of the Executive Committee who were asked to serve as Co-chairs of individual Task Forces were cleared for those assignments, not only by the White House Office of Legal Counsel, but also by the respective departments and agencies. In addition, Task Force members, who were not subject to the same conflict of interest statutes as were appointees to the Executive Committee, were subjected to an internal review for purposes of identifying and, if necessary, eliminating any potential or perceived conflicts of interest.

Q. What specifically did the President ask the private sector to do?

A. Specifically, the President directed PPSS "to conduct a Private Sector Survey on Cost Control in the Federal Government and . . . advise the President and the Secretary of Commerce, and other Executive Agency Heads, with respect to improving management and reducing costs."

PPSS's mandate, as stated by the President in those broad terms, was to review the operations of the entire Executive Branch of Government and to bring the experience and expertise of the private sector to bear on the management practices of the Federal Government. In a word, the President asked the PPSS Executive Committee to look at the component parts of the Executive Branch of Government with the same degree of detail and consideration with which a private company would consider a new acquisition.

Q. Given the size and complexity of the Federal Government, how did PPSS structure and organize such a massive undertaking by the private sector?

A. The first task was to divide the challenge into manageable pieces. Specifically, 36 Task Forces were established for purposes of reviewing some 98 percent of the Federal dollars and 100 percent of the Federal work force. Of the 36 Task Forces, 22 focused on specific departments and agencies and 14 were horizontal, cross-cutting Task Forces. In some instances, more than one Task Force was assigned a department or agency and in other instances a Task Force looked at a collection of departments and agencies (for example, those specifically focusing on business, banking, etc.). The horizontal, cross-cutting Task Forces focused on those issues which cut across all of Government, such as personnel, procurement, automated data processing, etc. In addition, the Survey Management Office issued a series of Selected Issues Reports on topics not covered by the Task Forces because of limited time and resources or, in some instances, on topics of sufficient import to warrant further study and a separate report.

Particular attention was devoted to coordinating the efforts of the Task Forces, so that overlap and duplication would be minimized and consistency ensured. Each Task Force was co-chaired by two or more members of the Executive Committee and had a full-time, Washington-based project manager who oversaw the day-to-day operations of the Task Forces.

Q. What did the Task Forces do?

A. Task Forces ranged in size from 20 to 90 members and divided their review of departments and agencies into four distinct phases: organization and start-up, diagnostic survey, in-depth survey, and report preparation.
The work of the Task Forces was monitored and coordinated by the Survey Management Office. Reporting to the Chairman, the Management Office consisted of a Director, Deputy Director (the sole Government employee designated as the Government liaison by the White House), Chief Operating Officer, and a staff of about 50 office personnel. Of particular importance were 12 "desk officers," most of whom were senior Washington-based executives with broad experience in working with the Federal Government. Each desk officer was responsible for the orientation of three to four Task Forces, guiding their efforts toward the most productive areas of review; coordinating planning and communications, monitoring progress, and assuring the quality of final Task Force reports. The work of this group supplemented and expanded upon that of a Government resources group, which included the Inspectors General offices, the Office of Management and Budget (OMB), the General Services Administration, and the Assistant Secretaries for Management. These two groups acted as a bridge between members of the Task Forces and the departments and agencies they reviewed.

Q. What was PPSS's focus—operations or policy?

A. It was not the principal purpose of PPSS to examine basic public policy, which reflects the major goals of the people as expressed through the democratic process. For example, PPSS did not focus on whether the Federal Government should concentrate its resources on defense, education, highways, health and welfare, or nutrition, nor did it address the question of what priority should be accorded each of these endeavors. PPSS concentrated, instead, on overall Government operations as distinguished from policy but included an examination of the execution of policy. Its primary concern was the degree of efficiency in the expenditure of tax resources and whether those expenditures achieved the desired public purpose at an acceptable cost through workable mechanisms and organizations equipped with the proper tools.

In carrying out its investigation, therefore, PPSS concentrated first and foremost on operations. At times, however, it was extremely difficult to draw a precise line clearly separating operations and policy. Indeed, there were numerous instances where a very significant overlap existed between operations and policy, with Task Forces unable to look at one without the other. It is interesting to note that many of the historical initiatives which preceded PPSS, particularly Hoover I and Hoover II, also found it difficult to make this differentiation. During the past decade, the separation of operations from policy has become even more difficult as policies have become more complex and as their administration has become more highly regulated.

Q. How were you received by the departments and agencies and by OMB? Wasn't PPSS, in effect, telling them they had not done their job properly and being critical of them simply by virtue of its presence?

A. The members of PPSS found a welcomed degree of receptivity in the departments and agencies. In addition, OMB was helpful in providing background data and continuing guidance to the members of the Task Forces.

The fact of the matter is that the press of business, at both the departments and agencies and OMB, simply precludes an in-depth, comprehensive survey, such as that conducted by PPSS. That certainly does not mean that the departments and agencies and OMB are not doing their job; it simply means that because of immediate needs departments and agencies and OMB find it difficult to address more than the issues "of the moment." Additionally, the value derived from a "fresh look" by outsiders with the capability to evaluate and recommend adoption of proven and cost effective private sector systems, techniques, and management tools could not be realized by an "in house" study.

The cooperative spirit which PPSS received from departments and agencies is demonstrated by the Central Intelligence Agency (CIA), which PPSS did not review. Following the completion of the Task Force reviews, the CIA contacted the Survey Management Office and asked for a listing of cross-cutting issues which might be applicable to the Agency, since it, too, wished to undertake an internal review based on PPSS findings.

In addition, a General Accounting Office report on PPSS noted:

> Most agency contacts viewed the task forces as positive attempts to identify cost savings. They generally viewed task force members as very talented experts who provided free advice and an objective view point. Given these perceptions, most agencies surveyed were willing to help the task forces and had an open mind on the findings.

Q. The Task Force reports contain some very precise calculations with respect to cost savings, revenue generation, and cash acceleration. How were these calculations derived and aren't the numbers duplicated in some instances?

A. A series of guidelines were provided to all of the Task Forces for purposes of standardizing calculations. Some of these guidelines were specifically suggested by OMB, such as the 10 percent inflation rate PPSS used at the beginning of the project (June 1982). Now, clearly, the current inflation rate is significantly lower, although it is unknown where it will go in the future. Accordingly, the Chairman's letter to the President contains certain economic forecasts which include an average annual inflation rate of 7 percent from now until the year 2000. In addition, some of the savings and revenue opportunities have been duplicated in individual Task Force reports. These duplications have been netted out for purposes of this Report to the President, but individual Task Force reports contain *all* savings and revenue opportunities identified by the Task Forces and including cash acceleration opportunities.

Of the total $544.985 billion in three-year cost savings and revenue generation identified in the 47 PPSS reports, approximately $120.634 billion represented duplications, resulting in net three-year savings and revenue of $424.351 billion.

Although PPSS has tried to be consistent and technically accurate in its calculations, its figures are, of necessity, of a *planning* rather than a *budget* quality. Emphasis, first and foremost, should be on the specific opportunity reported, with exact dollar savings and/or revenues to be a secondary effort and determined in concert with the departments and agencies and OMB.

Q. Given the calibre of the people who served on PPSS and the magnitude of their task, what percentage of waste, overlap, and duplication was PPSS able to identify?

A. Responding to this question requires that it be divided into two parts. In terms of how much PPSS found in total potential dollars that could be saved . . . it's probably about 35 percent. In terms of specifically identified opportunities for improvement . . . it's probably about 15 percent. That does not mean that those who were here did not work hard; it simply means that there are limits to what a volunteer effort can do. It also means that the problems which need to be addressed are numerous, complex, and overwhelming in nature. In short, all the Survey really did was provide a beginning and, it is hoped, leave behind a reservoir of sound management practices and ideas which can be applied to those areas which PPSS had neither the time nor the resources to address.

Unlike past attempts to improve the management of the Federal Government, and in contrast to the numerous Federal advisory committees and other private groups which at any given time are working to serve specific agency projects, this Private Sector Survey took a very broad look at the Executive Branch of the Federal establishment.

The broad scope of the Survey, and the relatively short time which could be devoted to Survey activities in view of the time and financial burdens imposed on its private sector participants, have understandably prevented the in-depth investigations demanded by complex situations. While over 2,000 private sector leaders and professionals donated many months of their time and significant resources to this intensive Survey, the subject is nevertheless too complex, and the public expenditures involved too huge, to permit complete investigation and full analysis of every cost saving and management improvement opportunity. However, patterns and examples were identified by the Task Forces and provided a basis for projecting cost saving opportunities to functions not specifically addressed by PPSS. Therefore, this effort is, in many respects, more truly a survey rather than an audit.

Q. What did this entire effort cost the Federal Government?

A. Except for the one full-time Government employee assigned it, PPSS cost the Federal Government *nothing*. A private, not-for-profit Foundation was established for purposes of raising gifts in kind as well as financial contributions to support the work of the Survey Management Office (including space, equipment, and support staff) and the overall administration of the Task Forces. Approximately $3.3 million was raised by the Foundation.

More specifically, members of the Executive Committee, the Survey Management Office and the Task Forces served without cost to the

Federal Government. All their salaries and expenses, including travel, hotel, and other out of pocket costs, were paid by their private sector employers who volunteered their services or by them personally. A rough calculation of private sector contributions in terms of time and personnel resources dedicated to the PPSS effort totals over $75 million. The extent to which PPSS was a private sector, volunteer, no-cost-to-the-Government effort makes it a particularly unique undertaking. Virtually all of its historical precedents were financed by Congressionally appropriated funds.

Q. Given some of its historical precedents, how unique is PPSS?

A. PPSS differs significantly from any previous study of the Federal Government in several ways. First, as noted, it has been funded and staffed entirely by the private sector and without cost to the taxpayers; second, it has concentrated upon applying the managerial experience and techniques of the private sector to the process of managing the national Government, rather than applying traditional public sector standards and techniques; and third, the sheer number and variety of Executive Committee members, senior advisors, and hundreds of Task Force participants, plus the broad scope of their combined experience and that of their firms, would indicate that PPSS's findings, conclusions and recommendations are representative of the views of the American business community, and, it is believed, the private sector as a whole.

With respect to the Reagan Administration, while PPSS is unique to the extent that it is a private sector effort, it is not unique in terms of the President's overall commitment to eliminating waste, duplication, and inefficiency in the Federal Government. Other initiatives the President has undertaken and which need to be viewed in concert with PPSS include the President's Council on Integrity and Efficiency, Reform 88, the Cabinet Council on Management and Administration and a greatly expanded and reinforced Inspector General program.

Q. What is the final end product of PPSS?

A. PPSS produced 36 Task Force Reports and 11 Management Office Selected Issues Reports, which contain a total of 2,478 recommendations which, as indicated earlier, represent $424.351 billion in three-year, unduplicated cost savings and revenue enhancements. An additional 54 recommendations and 188 issue areas for further study also were identified by PPSS. Three-year savings and revenue potential associated with the 54 specific recommendations for further study total $30.2 billion. The PPSS Task Forces also produced a series of appendices and a comprehensive set of working papers to supplement data contained in the Task Force reports. Executive

Summaries for each of the PPSS reports are contained in this Volume. Work papers and supplemental data are on file with the Department of Commerce.

Q. What is the time framework of the PPSS recommendations?

A. The work of PPSS focused on both short-term and long-term opportunities. In many instances, some of the PPSS recommendations can be easily and immediately implemented at the agency or department level. In other instances, implementation of PPSS recommendations will require Congressional legislation and, therefore, will take a much longer time period for implementation. For this reason, reference in the reports is made to "Year 1," "Year 2," and "Year 3," rather than to any specific fiscal year or time frame. PPSS considers its recommendations ageless.

Many of the major recommendations formulated by some of the historical precedents to PPSS took years to implement. For example, the idea of a unified national executive budget was first recommended by the Taft Commission on Economy and Efficiency in 1912 and implemented nine years later in the Budget and Accounting Act of 1921. The concept of a Senior Civil Service was recommended in the Second Hoover Commission Report of 1955, but was not implemented until 23 years later as part of the Civil Service Reform Act of 1978.

Q. What percentage of the PPSS recommendations can be implemented administratively and what percentage will require Congressional authority?

A. Approximately 73 percent of the duplicated dollar savings and revenue opportunities identified by PPSS will require Congressional approval before they can be realized. In addition, given the pervasive role which Congress plays in the affairs of the Executive Branch, particularly via the appropriations process, it is entirely possible that an even greater percentage will require Congressional concurrence.

Q. When do you think the PPSS recommendations will be implemented?

A. Many of the PPSS recommendations are already in the process of being implemented. Indeed, the White House has put together a comprehensive mechanism for the purpose of reviewing with the departments and agencies, OMB, and the Office of Policy Development each and every issue contained in the Task Force and Management Office reports. In addition, representatives from PPSS actively participate in those deliberations so as to ensure that the ultimate decision reflects the full input of the Survey.

Q. Many of the historical precedents to PPSS failed to have their recommendations implemented. Why does implementation seem to be moving so rapidly with respect to those recommendations contained in the PPSS reports?

A. In formulating its recommendations, PPSS sought to focus on specific and concrete examples and to be as detailed and precise as possible with respect to describing the problem, recommending the solution, projecting the potential cost savings/revenue enhancement, and indicating the appropriate implementation authority—Congressional, Agency, or President.

In addition, the timing is right. There is a growing awareness, both inside Government and out, that we no longer can afford the luxury of "business as usual."

Q. With the completion of the Task Force reports, the Management Office Special Issue Reports, and the Final Report to the President, what happens next?

A. Although the primary work of PPSS now obviously is completed, that does not mean that its work is over. Over 2,000 private sector volunteers spent a considerable period of time in Washington and PPSS is committed to advising them as to the implementation of their specific recommendations. Accordingly, key PPSS personnel will continue to work in close cooperation with the White House, OMB, and the departments and agencies so as to provide PPSS participants and the American people to whom this entire effort is dedicated with periodic status reports vis-a-vis their recommendations.

PPSS believes with the President that the hour is very late, and that a supreme effort to bring managerial and financial responsibility to the Federal Government is a matter of highest priority. It does not believe, however, that the situation is beyond recall, *provided* both the public and private sectors recognize the magnitude of the problem, understand its chief elements, and share a belief that prompt, effective, and well motivated action can create within the Federal establishment more responsible management and a greater respect for the people's money.

VII.

LONG-TERM ECONOMIC
IMPACT OF PPSS SAVINGS

THE FEDERAL GOVERNMENT comprises a major and growing share of the economy, with total Federal outlays—including transfer payments and interest—running at one-quarter of Gross National Product (GNP). Thus any significant shift in Federal finances cannot help but have a profound impact on the overall economy. Examples of such shifts in Federal finances in the post-World War II period are the Great Society program, started in the 1960s, and the Vietnam War, the impacts of which are shown in the table on page 356.

As the share of transfer payments tripled from the 4.0 percent average during 1947-1960 to 11.9 percent of GNP during 1981-1983 and net interest almost doubled from 1.5 percent to 2.6 percent over the same period, spending on national defense and other traditional functions of Government declined from 12.0 percent of GNP during 1947-1960 to 9.2 percent during 1981-1983. Initially, the increase in transfer payments appears to have helped to stimulate the economy, as real GNP growth accelerated to 3.9 percent per year during the 1960s from 3.1 percent in the earlier period. Similarly, industrial production edged up to 5.0 percent and inflation dropped from a 3.3 percent rate to 2.9 percent. However, at the same time that transfer payments were increasing, national defense spending remained relatively constant as a percent of GNP and other spending increased its share from 3.3 to 4.3 percent of GNP.

By the 1970s, much of the impetus provided by transfers had worn off, despite their continued growth, while defense and other expenditures were declining as a percent of GNP. Thus, real GNP growth slowed to 3.1 percent per year in the 1970s and 1.4 percent in 1981-1983, industrial production dropped even more sharply, and the rate of inflation more than doubled.

Also, the rate of unemployment has increased steadily in each period

Federal Spending and Economic Performance, 1947–1983

	(1)	(2)	(3)	(4)	(5)	(6)	(7)	(8)	(9)
		Federal Budget Outlays As a Percent of GNP							
Fiscal Year	National Defense	Trans-fer Pay-ments	Net Inter-est(a)	Other	Total	Real GNP	Indus. Prod.	Infla-tion	Unemploy-ment
		(Average for Period)				(Avg. Ann. % Increase)		(Avg. for Period)	
(1) 1947–1960	8.7%	4.0%	1.5%	3.3%	17.4%	3.1%	4.7%	3.3%	4.6%(b)
(2) 1961–1970	8.3	5.7	1.3	4.3	19.6	3.9	5.0	2.9	4.7
(3) 1971–1980	5.4	9.7	1.6	4.3	21.0	3.1	3.2	6.9	6.4
(4) 1981–1983	5.6	11.9	2.6	3.6	23.8	1.4	0.1	6.5	9.0

(a) Interest payments to non-Federal entities.
(b) 1948–1960

shown. This reinforces the fundamental condition that, as the Federal Government hands out money, the incentive to seek productive employment falls, lowering output. Since the money supply has been enlarged, however, prices are bid up.

In order to assess the economic ramifications of the changes in Federal finances proposed by PPSS, Federal revenues and outlays were forecast through the year 2000 by Data Resources Inc. (DRI) using their econometric model of the U.S. economy. As a first step, a basic forecast was produced, assuming the status quo of present policies. A further projection was made to take account of savings recommended by PPSS. The differences between these two cases are solely the result of the PPSS recommendations.

STATUS QUO OF PRESENT POLICIES

The following summarizes Federal finances from 1962 through 1983 and projected through 2000, assuming policies and programs in force continue in place and continue to evolve as they have in the past.

Federal Revenues and Outlays,
1962–2000: Status Quo of Current Policies
(\$ Billions)

		(1)	(2)	(3)	(4)
	Fiscal Year	Total Revenues	Total Outlays	Surplus/ (Deficit)	Outlays as a Multiple of Revenues
(1)	1962	\$ 99.7	\$ 106.8	\$ (7.1)	1.07X
(2)	1965	116.8	118.4	(1.6)	1.01
(3)	1970	192.8	195.7	(2.8)	1.01
(4)	1975	279.1	324.2	(45.2)	1.16
(5)	1980	517.1	576.7	(59.6)	1.12
(6)	1981	599.3	657.2	(57.9)	1.10
(7)	1982	617.8	728.4	(110.6)	1.18
(8)	1983	600.6	795.9	(195.4)	1.33
(9)	1985	754.8	939.9	(185.1)	1.25
(10)	1990	1,246.5	1,633.3	(386.7)	1.31
(11)	1995	2,089.2	2,864.6	(775.4)	1.37
(12)	2000	3,567.3	5,533.3	(1,966.0)	1.55
	Avg. Ann. % Inc./(Dec.)				
(13)	1962–1983	8.9%	10.0%	(17.1)%	NA
(14)	1965–1983	9.5	11.2	(30.6)	NA
(15)	1980–1983	5.1	11.3	(48.6)	NA
(16)	1983–2000	11.0	12.1	(14.5)	NA

Note: In this and subsequent tables, totals and percents have been calculated using unrounded numbers.

From the 1983 base of \$601 billion, revenues are projected to exceed \$1.2 trillion by 1990 and to climb further to \$3.6 trillion by 2000, averaging

Economic Environment
For DRI Projections:
Status Quo of Current Policies

	(1)	(2)	(3)	(4)	(5)	(6)	(7)	(8)	(9)	(10)	(11)	(12)	(13)
	Nominal GNP	Real GNP	Infla-tion	High Grade Corporate Bond Rate	3-Month T-Bill Rate	Unem-ployment Rate	Industrial Production	Real Business Fixed Invest-ment	Housing Starts	Federal Spending $ Billions	Federal Spending % of GNP	Surplus/(Deficit) $ Billions	Surplus/(Deficit) % of GNP
Fiscal Year	(Avg. Ann. % Inc/(Dec))			(Avg. For Period)			(Avg. Ann. % Inc/(Dec))		(Avg. For Period) (000)			(End of Period)	
(1) 1962–1983	8.8%	3.2%	5.5%	8.19%	6.54%	5.8%	3.4%	4.1%	1,558	$ 795.9	24.6%	$ (195.4)	(6.0)%
(2) 1962–1980	9.0	3.6	5.2	7.30	5.72	5.3	4.2	5.0	1,606	576.7	22.4	(59.6)	(2.3)
(3) 1962–1970	7.4	4.2	3.1	5.63	4.59	4.2	5.8	6.7	1,429	195.7	20.2	(2.8)	(0.3)
(4) 1970–1980	10.3	3.1	6.9	8.63	6.62	6.2	3.0	3.7	1,748	576.7	22.4	(59.6)	(2.3)
(5) 1980–1983	7.8	0.7	7.1	13.58	11.49	8.8	(1.5)	(1.3)	1,270	795.9	24.6	(195.4)	(6.0)
Projected													
(6) 1983–1985	9.2%	4.6%	4.4%	11.68%	9.37%	8.3%	7.8%	5.3%	1,704	$ 939.9	24.4%	$ (185.1)	(4.8)%
(7) 1985–1990	9.7	3.5	6.0	11.88	10.21	6.5	4.8	2.9	1,587	1,633.3	26.7	(386.7)	(6.3)
(8) 1990–1995	10.2	1.9	8.2	12.38	10.77	5.8	2.2	1.8	1,357	2,864.6	28.8	(775.4)	(7.8)
(9) 1995–2000	10.1	1.4	8.5	14.75	14.32	6.5	1.4	1.5	1,101	5,533.3	34.4	(1,966.0)	(12.2)
(10) 1983–2000	9.9	2.5	8.2	12.85	11.48	6.5	3.4	2.4	1,390	5,533.3	34.4	(1,966.0)	(12.2)

11.0 percent per year growth over 1983-2000. Over the same period, outlays are projected to grow 12.1 percent per year, i.e., 1.1 percentage points faster than revenues. This results in an increasing deficit which reaches $2.0 trillion by 2000. Even after adjusting for inflation of 7.1 percent per year, the deficit in 2000 is $605 billion in constant 1983 dollars.

As shown in column 4, as a multiple of revenues, outlays are projected in this case to reach a multiple of 1.55 in 2000 versus a multiple of 1.33 in 1983. Outlays as a multiple of revenues drop in 1985 to a multiple of 1.25 and then begin to rise over the projection period. This drop is a result of the continued economic recovery. During this period, some entitlement programs, such as unemployment insurance, are projected to drop, while certain tax revenues, such as corporate taxes, are projected to rise. These changes do not result from any changes to laws currently on the books but rather reflect economic conditions—e.g., corporate taxes rise because corporate profits are higher.

The table on page 358 summarizes the economic environment consistent with DRI's status quo projections.

As shown in the table, the projections for nominal GNP at 9.9 percent per year, 1983–2000, look about in line with recent past trends and are above the long-term 1962–1983 performance of 8.8 percent per year growth. However, as shown in columns 2 and 3, this is a misleading impression.

From a recovery-oriented growth, 1983–1985, the rate of growth of *real GNP* slows steadily over the forecast period to an average 1.4 percent per year in 1995–2000. Real growth averages 2.5 percent per year over the entire 1983–2000 period.

By contrast, real growth averaged 3.6 percent per year, 1962–1980, before slowing to 0.7 percent, 1980–1983. And that 1962–1980 period contained three recessions—two of which followed from the oil shocks of 1973–1974 and 1979–1980.

At the same time, inflation—stimulated by growing deficits—heats up to the 8.5 percent range in the 1990s from 4.4 percent per year, 1983–1985. On a year-by-year basis, inflation peaks at 8.7 percent in 1996/1997, and then edges down to 8.2 percent by 2000, as follows:

GNP Deflator
(% increase)

1983	4.4%
1985	4.6
1990	6.9
1995	8.6
1996	8.7
1997	8.7
1998	8.5
1999	8.3
2000	8.2

The lowering inflation during the late 1990s is not a healthy sign, but rather a symptom of a weak economy, reflecting the low level of real business fixed investment during the late 1980s and 1990s. The low level of fixed investment is responsible in large part for real GNP growing at only 1.4 percent per year, 1990–1995—i.e., less than two-thirds its potential—and it is this slack that takes the upward pressure off prices.

With inflation moving up again in the 1980s and early 1990s, it is not surprising that interest rates also rise. The high grade corporate bond rate, which is projected to hold reasonably steady for the rest of this decade at under 12 percent, rises to average 14.75 percent over 1996–2000. The three-month T-Bill rate is more reactive, averaging 10.77 percent, 1991–1995, and 14.32 percent, 1996–2000. However, even after adjusting for inflation, real interest rates remain very high as the continually growing deficits and rekindling of inflation lead to expectations of even higher rates of inflation. Following a modest drop during 1986–1995, real interest rates return to and surpass their current record levels as shown in the following table.

Nominal and Real
Interest Rates, 1963–2000:
Status Quo of Current Policies

		(1)	(2)	(3)	(4)	(5)
			High Grade Corp. Bond Rate		3-Month T-Bill Rate	
	Fiscal Year	Inflation	Nominal	Real	Nominal	Real
(1)	1963–1983	5.5%	8.21%	3.76%	6.57%	1.40%
(2)	1963–1980	5.2	7.32	3.35	5.75	0.83
(3)	1963–1970	3.1	5.62	3.44	4.55	1.85
(4)	1971–1980	6.9	8.68	3.27	6.71	0.01
(5)	1981–1983	7.1	13.58	6.21	11.49	4.86
	Projected					
(6)	1984–1985	4.4%	11.68%	5.84%	9.37%	5.16%
(7)	1986–1990	6.0	11.88	6.19	10.21	4.25
(8)	1991–1995	8.2	12.38	5.36	10.77	2.88
(9)	1996–2000	8.5	14.75	6.89	14.32	6.28
(10)	1984–2000	7.2	12.85	6.11	11.48	4.55
(11)	Memo: 2000	8.2	16.08	8.21	16.30	8.86

The 8.21 percent real rate projected for high-grade corporate bonds in 2000 compares to 4.45 percent in 1983 and 7.48 percent in 1982 while the 8.86 percent for T-Bills is 350 basis points above the 1981 record of 5.36 percent. This continuing high cost of credit puts a further damper on economic growth—in particular residential and non-residential investment, industrial production and, hence, employment. It is also significant that the spread between corporates and T-Bills narrows and then re-

verses, as Government is forced to go into the credit markets on an increasing basis to finance its growing debt. Thus, over the 1962–1983 period, the yield on corporates at 8.21 percent was 164 basis points above that on T-Bills. During the 1996–2000 period, the spread is projected to drop to 43 basis points on average, and in 2000 it is projected at (22) basis points—as T-Bills yield 16.30 percent to corporates' 16.08 percent.

The unemployment rate drops to a low of 5.8 percent in the 1990–1995 period and begins to rise after that.

Following the pattern of real GNP, industrial production, which averages 7.8 percent per year growth during the 1983–1985 recovery, drops to the 1.4–2.2 percent range over the 1990–2000 period, growth in real business fixed investment drops to 1.5 percent, 1995–2000, and housing starts average only 1.1 million units per year in the last five years of the projection period.

Both the slowdown in real activity and the run-up in inflation and interest rates result from the intrusion of the Federal Government on the private sector with spending in 2000 reaching 34.4 percent of GNP and the deficit reaching (12.2) percent of GNP.

The following table shows more detail on the revenue side of the projections.

Summary of Federal Revenues, 1962–2000: Status Quo of Current Policies
($ Billions)

	Fiscal Year	(1) Personal Income Taxes	(2) Revenues For Five Specially Funded Transfer Programs	(3) All Other	(4) Total
(1)	1962	$ 45.6	$ 17.0	$ 37.1	$ 99.7
(2)	1965	48.8	22.3	45.8	116.8
(3)	1970	90.4	44.4	58.0	192.8
(4)	1975	122.4	84.5	72.2	279.1
(5)	1980	244.1	157.8	115.2	517.1
(6)	1981	285.9	182.7	130.6	599.3
(7)	1982	297.7	201.5	118.5	617.8
(8)	1983	288.9	208.9	102.7	600.6
(9)	1985	332.1	272.5	150.3	754.8
(10)	1990	553.9	437.9	254.7	1,246.5
(11)	1995	965.5	762.4	361.2	2,089.2
(12)	2000	1,608.0	1,353.3	606.0	3,567.3
	Average Annual Percent Increase/(Decrease)				
(13)	1962–1983	9.2%	12.7%	5.0%	8.9%
(14)	1965–1983	10.4	13.2	4.6	9.5
(15)	1980–1983	5.8	9.8	(3.8)	5.1
(16)	1983–2000	10.6	11.6	11.0	11.0

Summary of Federal Revenues,
1962–2000: Status Quo of Current Policies *(continued)*
($ Billions)

	Fiscal Year	(1) Personal Income Taxes	(2) Revenues For Five Specially Funded Transfer Programs	(3) All Other	(4) Total
			As a Percent of Total		
(17)	1962	45.7%	17.1%	37.2%	100.0%
(18)	1965	41.8	19.1	39.2	100.0
(19)	1970	46.9	23.0	30.1	100.0
(20)	1975	43.9	30.3	25.9	100.0
(21)	1980	47.2	30.5	22.3	100.0
(22)	1981	47.7	30.5	21.8	100.0
(23)	1982	48.2	32.6	19.2	100.0
(24)	1983	48.1	34.8	17.1	100.0
(25)	1985	44.0	36.1	19.9	100.0
(26)	1990	44.4	35.1	20.4	100.0
(27)	1995	46.2	36.5	17.3	100.0
(28)	2000	45.1	37.9	17.0	100.0
			As a Percent of GNP		
(29)	1962	8.3%	3.1%	6.8%	18.2%
(30)	1965	7.4	3.4	6.9	17.7
(31)	1970	9.3	4.6	6.0	19.9
(32)	1975	8.3	5.7	4.9	18.9
(33)	1980	9.5	6.1	4.5	20.1
(34)	1981	9.9	6.3	4.5	20.8
(35)	1982	9.7	6.6	3.9	20.2
(36)	1983	8.9	6.5	3.2	18.6
(37)	1985	8.6	7.1	3.9	19.6
(38)	1990	9.1	7.2	4.2	20.4
(39)	1995	9.7	7.7	3.6	21.0
(40)	2000	10.0	8.4	3.8	22.2

The fastest growing segment of revenues through the year 2000 is expected to be revenues for the five specially funded transfer programs —old age and survivors and disability insurance (Social Security), hospital insurance (Medicare), railroad retirement, civil service retirement, and unemployment insurance (col. 2). These programs, which grew at 12.7 percent per year 1962–1983, are projected to rise 11.6 percent per year, 1983–2000. All personal income taxes are projected to grow 10.6 percent a year, 1983–2000, reaching $1.6 trillion in 2000, or 10.0 percent of GNP in 2000 versus 8.9 percent in 1983.

Because all three categories are projected to grow at roughly similar rates—i.e., 10.6 percent to 11.6 percent per year—their individual shares of total revenues do not change greatly. This is in sharp distinction to the period between 1962 and 1975 when social insurance taxes and contributions rose from a 17.1 percent share to 30.3 percent of total revenues and all other contributions except personal income taxes fell from 37.2 percent to 25.9 percent.

Of particular note, all three categories are projected to increase as a percent of GNP, i.e., the 9.9 percent growth of nominal GNP, 1983–2000, is slower than those for revenues.

The table on pages 364–365 summarizes outlays by major function.

The rates of increase of spending for education, training, health, and income security are all projected to slow from those of 1962-1983, while those for national defense, veterans' benefits, all other except interest, and net interest, are projected to accelerate.

National defense (col. 1), which was $210.5 billion in 1983, is projected to grow 11.2 percent per year to 2000—4.0 percentage points faster than during 1962–1983—reaching $1.3 trillion. As a percent of GNP, it is projected to rise from 6.5 percent in 1983 to 8 percent by 1990, and to remain at that level through 2000.

This forecast is in line with the Reagan Administration's budget plan through 1988, and is well below the peacetime experience between Korea and Vietnam, when defense averaged 9.8 percent of GNP. Furthermore, as a percent of total outlays, national defense expenditures are projected to fall from 26.4 percent in 1983 to 23.3 percent in 2000. They amounted to 45.9 percent in 1962—twice the forecast for 2000 and 1.74 times the 1983 level.

Veterans' benefits (col. 5) are projected to accelerate over the forecast horizon, from a 7.3 percent annual rate of increase, 1962–1983, to 8.2 percent per year, 1983–2000, when they are projected to reach $94.8 billion versus $24.8 billion in 1983. The acceleration primarily reflects rising medical costs and increasing claims from Vietnam veterans.

Net interest (col. 8) is, by far, the most rapidly rising expenditure category over the projection period, increasing 18.3 percent per year, compared to 12.9 percent per year, 1962–1983. Furthermore, by 2000 at $1.5 trillion, it is second in size—and a close second—only to income security.

It is interesting to examine the role that net interest plays in total spending and the deficit. While the overall growth of spending, 1983-2000, is 12.1 percent per year (col. 9), spending before interest (col. 7) grows at 10.7 percent per year, with net interest growing at 18.3 percent per year. This effect is shown clearly in the second tier, where interest, which was 11.0 percent of total spending in 1983 climbs to 27.5 percent of spending in 2000. Thus, spending before interest drops over the same period from 89.0 to 72.5 percent of total spending. As a percent of GNP, however, spending before interest rises from 21.9 percent in 1983 to 25.0 percent in 2000—again highlighting the slow growth of the economy. Total spending rises from 24.6 percent of GNP last year to 34.4 percent in 2000—i.e., over one-third of the whole economy accounted for by the Federal Government. The deficit as a percent of GNP, which was at (6.0)

Outlays by Function, 1962–2000:
Status Quo of Current Policies
($ Billions)

	(1) National Defense	(2) Education, Training, Employment & Social Services	(3) Health	(4) Income Security	(5) Veterans Benefits	(6) All Other Except Interest	(7) Subtotal Before Interest	(8) Net Interest	(9) Total	(10) Surplus/ (Deficit)
Fiscal Year										
(1) 1962	$ 49.0	$ 1.2	$ 1.2	$ 22.7	$ 5.6	$ 20.2	$ 99.9	$ 6.9	$ 106.8	$ (7.1)
(2) 1965	47.5	2.1	1.8	25.7	5.7	27.0	109.8	8.6	118.4	(1.6)
(3) 1970	78.6	8.6	12.1	43.1	8.7	30.2	181.3	14.4	195.7	(2.8)
(4) 1975	85.6	15.9	25.7	108.6	16.6	48.7	301.2	23.2	324.2	(45.2)
(5) 1980	135.6	30.8	55.2	193.1	21.2	88.4	524.2	52.5	576.7	(59.6)
(6) 1981	159.8	31.4	66.0	225.1	23.0	83.2	588.5	68.7	657.2	(57.9)
(7) 1982	187.4	26.3	74.0	248.3	24.0	83.6	643.7	84.7	728.4	(110.6)
(8) 1983	210.5	25.7	81.2	280.2	24.8	85.7	708.1	87.8	795.9	(195.4)
(9) 1985	268.6	28.0	98.1	306.5	27.5	90.2	819.0	120.9	939.9	(185.1)
(10) 1990	486.1	39.3	164.9	521.8	40.0	128.8	1,381.0	252.3	1,633.3	(386.7)
(11) 1995	796.9	54.1	288.2	920.4	62.0	202.0	2,323.7	540.9	2,864.6	(775.4)
(12) 2000	1,286.7	83.8	527.4	1,691.6	94.8	328.1	4,012.6	1,520.7	5,533.3	(1,966.0)
Avg. Ann. % Inc./(Dec.)										
(13) 1962–1983	7.2%	15.5%	22.2%	12.7%	7.3%	7.1%	9.8%	12.9%	10.0%	17.1%
(14) 1965–1983	8.6	14.8	23.6	14.2	8.5	6.6	10.9	13.8	11.2	30.6
(15) 1980–1983	15.8	(5.8)	13.7	13.2	5.5	(1.0)	10.5	18.7	11.3	48.6
(16) 1983–2000	11.2	7.2	11.6	11.2	8.2	8.2	10.7	18.3	12.1	14.5

As a Percent of Total

(17) 1962	45.9%	1.2%	1.1%	21.2%	5.3%	18.9%	93.6%	6.4%	100.0%	(6.7)%
(18) 1965	40.1	1.8	1.5	21.7	4.8	22.8	92.8	7.2	100.0	(1.3)
(19) 1970	40.1	4.4	6.2	22.0	4.4	15.5	92.7	7.3	100.0	(1.5)
(20) 1975	26.4	4.9	7.9	33.5	5.1	15.0	92.8	7.2	100.0	(13.9)
(21) 1980	23.5	5.3	9.6	33.5	3.7	15.3	90.9	9.1	100.0	(10.3)
(22) 1981	24.3	4.8	10.0	34.3	3.5	12.7	89.5	10.5	100.0	(8.8)
(23) 1982	25.7	3.6	10.2	34.1	3.3	11.5	88.4	11.6	100.0	(15.2)
(24) 1983	26.4	3.2	10.2	35.2	3.1	10.8	89.0	11.0	100.0	(24.5)
(25) 1985	28.6	3.0	10.4	32.6	2.9	9.6	87.1	12.9	100.0	(19.7)
(26) 1990	29.8	2.4	10.1	32.0	2.5	7.9	84.6	15.4	100.0	(23.7)
(27) 1995	27.8	1.9	10.1	32.1	2.2	7.1	81.1	18.9	100.0	(27.1)
(28) 2000	23.3	1.5	9.5	30.6	1.7	5.9	72.5	27.5	100.0	(35.5)

As a Percent of GNP

(29) 1962	8.9%	0.2%	0.2%	4.1%	1.0%	3.7%	18.2%	1.3%	19.5%	(1.3)%
(30) 1965	7.2	0.3	0.3	3.9	0.9	4.1	16.7	1.3	18.0	(0.2)
(31) 1970	8.1	0.9	1.3	4.4	0.9	3.1	18.7	1.5	20.2	(0.3)
(32) 1975	5.8	1.1	1.7	7.3	1.1	3.3	20.4	1.6	21.9	(3.1)
(33) 1980	5.3	1.2	2.1	7.5	0.8	3.4	20.4	2.0	22.4	(2.3)
(34) 1981	5.5	1.1	2.3	7.8	0.8	2.9	20.4	2.4	22.8	(2.0)
(35) 1982	6.1	0.9	2.4	8.1	0.8	2.7	21.1	2.8	23.8	(3.6)
(36) 1983	6.5	0.8	2.5	8.7	0.8	2.7	21.9	2.7	24.6	(6.0)
(37) 1985	7.0	0.7	2.5	8.0	0.7	2.3	21.3	3.1	24.4	(4.8)
(38) 1990	8.0	0.6	2.7	8.5	0.7	2.1	22.6	4.1	26.7	(6.3)
(39) 1995	8.0	0.5	2.9	9.3	0.6	2.0	23.4	5.4	28.8	(7.8)
(40) 2000	8.0	0.5	3.3	10.5	0.6	2.0	25.0	9.5	34.4	(12.2)

Net Interest and the Deficit,
1962–2000: Status Quo of Current Policies
($ Billions)

	(1)	(2)	(3)	(4)	(5)	(6)	(7)
		Outlays			Surplus/(Deficit)		Net
Fiscal Year	Total Revenues	Ex-cluding Interest	Net Interest	Total Outlays	Before Net Interest	In-cluding Interest	Interest as a % of the Deficit
(1) 1962	$ 99.7	$ 99.9	$ 6.9	$ 106.8	$ (0.3)	$ (7.1)	96.4%
(2) 1965	116.8	109.8	8.6	118.4	7.0	(1.6)	537.5
(3) 1970	192.8	181.3	14.4	195.7	11.5	(2.8)	505.2
(4) 1975	279.1	301.2	23.2	324.2	(22.1)	(45.2)	51.3
(5) 1980	517.1	524.2	52.5	576.7	(7.1)	(59.6)	88.1
(6) 1981	599.3	588.5	68.7	657.2	10.8	(57.9)	118.6
(7) 1982	617.8	643.7	84.7	728.4	(25.9)	(110.6)	76.6
(8) 1983	600.6	708.1	87.8	795.9	(107.5)	(195.4)	45.0
(9) 1985	754.8	819.0	120.9	939.9	(64.2)	(185.1)	65.3
(10) 1990	1,246.5	1,381.0	252.3	1,633.3	(134.4)	(386.7)	65.2
(11) 1995	2,089.2	2,323.7	540.9	2,864.6	(234.5)	(775.4)	69.8
(12) 2000	3,567.3	4,012.6	1,520.7	5,533.3	(445.2)	(1,966.0)	77.4
Avg. Ann. % Inc./(Dec.)							
(13) 1962–1983	8.9%	9.8%	12.9%	10.0%	33.3%	17.1%	NA
(14) 1965–1983	9.5	10.9	13.8	11.2	ND	30.6	NA
(15) 1980–1983	5.1	10.5	18.7	11.3	147.4	48.6	NA
(16) 1983–2000	11.0	10.7	18.3	12.1	8.7	14.5	NA

percent in 1983, more than doubles to (12.2) percent of GNP—exceeded only by the years during World War II.

Obviously, the deficit is the result of the whole mix of spending and tax policies currently in place. However, it is interesting to note that of the $1.8 trillion *increase* in the deficit 1983–2000, $1.4 trillion or 80.9 percent of the increase is accounted for by the *increase* in net interest, i.e., only 19.1 percent of the increase in the deficit is being used to fund programs, with the remaining 80.9 percent simply servicing debt. This highlights the cost of continuing large deficits as shown in the table on page 366.

Net interest is projected to account for about two-thirds of the total deficit during 1985–1995 and then rise to 77.4 percent—over three-fourths—by 2000.

An alternative way of looking at Federal outlays is to group them as payments for individuals (or transfer payments) and other outlays—including net interest, the purchase of goods and services, and other expenditures related to the traditional functions of Government. The following table shows transfer payments and other outlays.

Transfer Payments and Other Outlays,
1962–2000: Status Quo of Current Policies
($ Billions)

	Fiscal Year	(1) Total Transfer Payments (a)	(2) Net Interest	(3) National Defense (a)	(4) All Other Outlays	(5) Total Outlays
				Other Outlays		
(1)	1962	$ 29.5	$ 6.9	$ 48.1	$ 22.2	$ 106.8
(2)	1965	33.7	8.6	46.1	30.1	118.4
(3)	1970	66.0	14.4	75.7	39.6	195.7
(4)	1975	156.6	23.2	79.3	65.1	324.2
(5)	1980	283.0	52.5	123.7	117.5	576.7
(6)	1981	330.3	68.7	146.0	112.1	657.2
(7)	1982	363.5	84.7	172.5	107.7	728.4
(8)	1983	402.8	87.8	194.3	111.0	795.9
(9)	1985	452.6	120.9	250.4	116.0	939.9
(10)	1990	764.0	252.3	454.1	162.9	1,633.3
(11)	1995	1,338.9	540.9	741.3	243.5	2,864.6
(12)	2000	2,440.0	1,520.7	1,194.8	377.8	5,533.3

		Average Annual Percent Increase/(Decrease)				
(13)	1962–1983	13.2%	12.9%	6.9%	8.0%	10.0%
(14)	1965–1983	14.8	13.8	8.3	7.5	11.2
(15)	1980–1983	12.5	18.7	16.2	(1.9)	11.3
(16)	1983–2000	11.2	18.3	11.3	7.5	12.1

(a) Military pensions are a transfer payment and, hence, are excluded from national defense outlays in this table.

Transfer Payments and Other Outlays,
1962–2000: Status Quo of Current Policies (*continued*)
($ Billions)

	Fiscal Year	(1) Total Transfer Payments (a)	(2) Net Interest	(3) National Defense (a)	(4) All Other Outlays	(5) Total Outlays
				Other Outlays		
				As a Percent of Total		
(17)	1962	27.7%	6.4%	45.1%	20.8%	100.0%
(18)	1965	28.4	7.2	38.9	25.4	100.0
(19)	1970	33.7	7.3	38.7	20.2	100.0
(20)	1975	48.3	7.2	24.4	20.1	100.0
(21)	1980	49.1	9.1	21.4	20.4	100.0
(22)	1981	50.3	10.5	22.2	17.1	100.0
(23)	1982	49.9	11.6	23.7	14.8	100.0
(24)	1983	50.6	11.0	24.4	13.9	100.0
(25)	1985	48.2	12.9	26.6	12.3	100.0
(26)	1990	46.8	15.4	27.8	10.0	100.0
(27)	1995	46.7	18.9	25.9	8.5	100.0
(28)	2000	44.1	27.5	21.6	6.8	100.0
				As a Percent of GNP		
(29)	1962	5.4%	1.3%	8.8%	4.1%	19.5%
(30)	1965	5.1	1.3	7.0	4.6	18.0
(31)	1970	6.8	1.5	7.8	4.1	20.2
(32)	1975	10.6	1.6	5.4	4.4	21.9
(33)	1980	11.0	2.0	4.8	4.6	22.4
(34)	1981	11.5	2.4	5.1	3.9	22.8
(35)	1982	11.9	2.8	5.6	3.5	23.8
(36)	1983	12.5	2.7	6.0	3.4	24.6
(37)	1985	11.7	3.1	6.5	3.0	24.4
(38)	1990	12.5	4.1	7.4	2.7	26.7
(39)	1995	13.5	5.4	7.5	2.4	28.8
(40)	2000	15.2	9.5	7.4	2.4	34.4

As discussed above, net interest is projected to be the most rapidly increasing expenditure category, rising 18.3 percent per year, 1983–2000. National defense and transfer payments are projected to grow almost in lock step at 11.3 percent and 11.2 percent, respectively, while all other outlays slow to just 7.5 percent per year, barely keeping pace with inflation. Together, transfer payments and interest are projected to total $4.0 trillion in 2000—equal to 71.6 percent of total outlays, i.e., almost $3 out of every $4 spent by the Government is simply a redistribution of income and makes no net contribution to GNP. And despite total Federal outlays growing at 12.1 percent per year, 1983–2000—2.2 percentage points more rapidly than GNP—productive expenditures by the Government are projected to grow at only 10.1 percent—just 0.2 percentage point faster than GNP. This is shown in the bottom tier where the sum of national defense and all other outlays remains almost constant as a percent of GNP, going from 9.4 percent in 1983 to 9.8 percent in 2000.

The following table shows details on payments for individuals.

Transfer Payments, 1962–2000:
Status Quo of Current Policies
($ Billions)

		(1)	(2)	(3)	(4)	(5)	(6)	(7)	(8)	(9)	(10)
	Fiscal Year	Social Security	Railroad Retirement	Civil Service Ret.	Unemployment Assist.	Hospital Insurance	Subtotal	Memo: Revenues	Memo: Surplus/(Deficit)	All Other Transfers	Total Transfers
					Five Specially Funded Social Programs						
(1)	1962	$ 13.9	$ 1.0	$ 1.1	$ 3.8	—	$ 19.8	$ 17.0	$ (2.8)	$ 9.7	$ 29.5
(2)	1965	16.9	1.1	1.4	2.8	—	22.3	22.3	—	11.4	33.7
(3)	1970	29.6	1.6	2.8	3.4	$ 5.0	42.3	44.4	2.1	23.7	66.0
(4)	1975	65.2	3.1	7.1	13.5	10.6	99.4	84.5	(14.9)	57.2	156.6
(5)	1980	117.1	4.7	14.7	18.0	24.3	178.8	157.8	(21.0)	104.2	283.0
(6)	1981	137.9	6.0	17.6	19.7	29.2	210.4	182.7	(27.7)	119.9	330.3
(7)	1982	153.9	5.7	19.4	23.8	34.9	237.7	201.5	(36.2)	125.8	363.5
(8)	1983	170.1	6.2	20.7	29.8	38.7	265.5	208.9	(56.6)	137.3	402.8
(9)	1985	200.6	7.6	23.9	17.4	47.7	297.2	272.5	(24.7)	155.4	452.6
(10)	1990	357.4	10.5	43.1	26.0	81.8	518.7	437.9	(80.8)	245.3	764.0
(11)	1995	641.1	16.6	75.7	41.7	156.6	931.7	762.4	(169.3)	407.2	1,338.9
(12)	2000	1,177.1	26.1	137.4	76.7	306.2	1,723.6	1,353.3	(370.3)	716.4	2,440.0
	Avg. Ann. % Inc./(Dec.)										
(13)	1962–1983	12.7%	8.9%	15.2%	10.3%	ND	13.1%	12.7%	15.4%	13.5%	13.2%
(14)	1965–1983	13.7	9.9	16.0	14.1	ND	14.8	13.2	51.0	14.8	14.8
(15)	1980–1983	13.3	9.4	12.1	18.2	16.8%	14.1	9.8	39.2	9.6	12.5
(16)	1983–2000	12.1	8.8	11.8	5.7	12.9	11.6	11.6	11.7	10.2	11.2

Transfer Payments, 1962–2000:
Status Quo of Current Policies (continued)
($ Billions)

		(1)	(2)	(3)	(4)	(5)	(6)	(7)	(8)	(9)	(10)
			Five Specially Funded Social Programs								
	Fiscal Year	Social Security	Railroad Retirement	Civil Service Ret.	Unemployment Assist.	Hospital Insurance	Subtotal	Memo: Revenues	Memo: Surplus/ (Deficit)	All Other Transfers	Total Transfers
						As a Percent of Total					
(17)	1962	13.0%	1.0%	1.0%	3.6%	—	18.6%	16.0%	(2.6)%	9.1%	27.7%
(18)	1965	14.3	1.0	1.2	2.4	—	18.8	18.8	—	9.6	28.4
(19)	1970	15.1	0.8	1.4	1.7	2.5%	21.6	22.7	1.1	12.1	33.7
(20)	1975	20.1	0.9	2.2	4.1	3.3	30.6	26.1	(4.6)	17.6	48.3
(21)	1980	20.3	0.8	2.5	3.1	4.2	31.0	27.4	(3.6)	18.1	49.1
(22)	1981	21.0	0.9	2.7	3.0	4.5	32.0	27.8	(4.2)	18.2	50.3
(23)	1982	21.1	0.8	2.7	3.3	4.8	32.6	27.7	(5.0)	17.3	49.9
(24)	1983	21.4	0.8	2.6	3.7	4.9	33.4	26.2	(7.1)	17.3	50.6
(25)	1985	21.3	0.8	2.5	1.9	5.1	31.6	29.0	(2.6)	16.5	48.2
(26)	1990	21.9	0.6	2.6	1.6	5.0	31.8	26.8	(4.9)	15.0	46.8
(27)	1995	22.4	0.6	2.6	1.5	5.5	32.5	26.6	(5.9)	14.2	46.7
(28)	2000	21.3	0.5	2.5	1.4	5.5	31.1	24.5	(6.7)	12.9	44.1
						As a Percent of GNP					
(29)	1962	2.5%	0.2%	0.2%	0.7%	—	3.6%	3.1%	(0.5)%	1.8%	5.4%
(30)	1965	2.6	0.2	0.2	0.4	—	3.4	3.4	—	1.7	5.1
(31)	1970	3.1	0.2	0.3	0.3	0.5%	4.4	4.6	0.2	2.5	6.8
(32)	1975	4.4	0.2	0.5	0.9	0.7	6.7	5.7	(1.0)	3.9	10.6
(33)	1980	4.5	0.2	0.6	0.7	0.9	6.9	6.1	(0.8)	4.0	11.0
(34)	1981	4.8	0.2	0.6	0.7	1.0	7.3	6.3	(1.0)	4.2	11.5
(35)	1982	5.0	0.2	0.6	0.8	1.1	7.8	6.6	(1.2)	4.1	11.9
(36)	1983	5.3	0.2	0.6	0.9	1.2	8.2	6.5	(1.8)	4.3	12.5
(37)	1985	5.2	0.2	0.6	0.5	1.2	7.7	7.1	(0.6)	4.0	11.7
(38)	1990	5.8	0.2	0.7	0.4	1.3	8.5	7.2	(1.3)	4.0	12.5
(39)	1995	6.4	0.2	0.8	0.4	1.6	9.4	7.7	(1.7)	4.1	13.5
(40)	2000	7.3	0.2	0.9	0.5	1.9	10.7	8.4	(2.3)	4.5	15.2

The first seven columns relate to the five specially funded transfer programs. Within that group, unemployment assistance particularly stands out, growing only 5.7 percent per year 1983–2000. This results from the reduced unemployment rate expected in the future versus the postwar record 1983 level of 10.2 percent.

Hospital insurance, or Medicare, is projected to continue to be the fastest growing of the funded transfer programs, with outlays rising at 12.9 percent per year, 1983–2000, when they are expected to reach $306 billion, or 5.5 percent of total outlays. The two major retirement programs—Social Security and Civil Service Retirement—are each projected to grow at 12 percent per year, 1983–2000, when together they will total $1.3 trillion, or 23.8 percent of all outlays. Railroad Retirement, the smallest of the funded programs, is projected to increase at 8.8 percent per year, in line with its historical growth.

Of note, the total spending for these five programs (col. 6) is expected to reach $931.7 billion by 1995—about equal to the *total projected spending* only ten years earlier in 1985. As a percent of GNP, these five programs are projected to be at 10.7 percent in 2000 versus 3.6 percent of GNP in 1962, a multiple of 3.0. The deficit of these five programs is projected at $(169.3) billion in 1995. This deficit, which is the net of the spending in these five programs and the revenues taken in for these five programs, is only $16 billion less than the record 1983 deficit for the *entire Government*. By 2000 this deficit is projected to be $(370.3) billion, or 2.3 percent of GNP.

The total of payments for individuals (col. 10) was $403 billion in 1983, and is projected to exceed $2.4 trillion in 2000—more than the whole country's GNP in 1979. These programs will account for 15.2 percent of GNP in 2000 versus 12.5 percent in 1983 and 5.4 percent in 1962.

The table on page 372 breaks out the major unfunded transfer programs shown in column 9.

The fastest growing transfer payments programs since 1962 have been Medicaid, Food Stamps, Supplemental Medical Insurance, Housing Assistance, and Guaranteed Student Loans, all of which grew in excess of 20 percent per year. Together these programs now total over $60 billion, and they are projected to rise at 11.5 percent per year to $384.5 billion in 2000—virtually equal to personal income taxes plus all other receipts by the Federal Government in 1983 excluding those earmarked for the specially funded transfer programs.

The table at the top of page 373 summarizes the outlook for transfer payments, interest, and personal income taxes.

Of particular note is the last column, showing Federal contributions to transfer programs (i.e., excluding the revenues from the five specially funded programs) plus net interest as a percent of personal income taxes. This measure stood at 42.5 percent in 1962. The 1983 level was at 97.5 percent—almost all the income taxes are expended in these programs. By 2000 this percentage is expected to rise to 162.1 percent.

**Unfunded Payments for
Individuals, 1962–2000:
Status Quo of Current Policies**
($ Billions)

		(1)	(2)	(3)	(4)	(5)
				Ranked	Average Annual % Increase/(Decrease)	
		1962	1983	2000	1962–1983	1983–2000
(1)	Federal Employee Retirement & Insurance Excl. Civil Service	$3.0	$ 26.7	$133.4	11.0%	9.9%
(2)	Medicaid	0.1	19.1	123.0	28.3	11.6
(3)	Public Assistance, etc.	4.0	24.3	110.5	9.0	9.3
(4)	Food Stamps	0.01	12.2	93.3	38.0	12.7
(5)	Supplemental Medical Insurance	—	17.7	90.9	21.4(a)	10.1
(6)	Housing Assistance	0.2	9.6	49.5	21.3	10.1
(7)	VA Medical Care	1.0	7.5	35.7	10.2	9.6
(8)	Guaranteed Student Loans	—	2.2	27.9	71.5(b)	16.1
(9)	Child Nutrition	0.2	3.4	26.9	15.3	13.0
(10)	Other	1.3	14.6	25.3	12.3	3.3
(11)	Total	$9.8	$137.3	$716.4	13.5%	10.2%

(a) 1967–1983 Growth Rate
(b) 1970–1983 Growth Rate

PPSS SAVINGS

PPSS identified savings possibilities both within individual agencies and across Government. This approach inevitably resulted in some overlapping or duplication of savings recommended in different reports. Also, although this scheme of reporting makes it easy to determine where, and by whom, action should be taken, it does not correspond precisely with the Federal budget system of identifying outlays by function and subfunction. Conversely, the DRI model corresponds exactly to the Federal system of accounts.

In order to put the savings recommendations in a form in which they could be analyzed using the DRI model, several steps were taken.

• Each recommendation was determined to be either a one-time saving or an ongoing saving. One-time savings are primarily cash accelerations, while ongoing savings are generally cost reductions or revenue generations. In some cases the recommendation resulted in savings over several years, but fewer than the 17-year time horizon of PPSS. Here the present value of the saving stream was calculated and treated as a one-time saving.

• All recommendations touching on the same or related activities were carefully screened for overlaps and duplications, which were then eliminated—i.e., the savings were only counted once.

	Fiscal Year	(1) Personal Income Taxes	(2) Total Transfers	(3) Net Interest	(4) Total Interest and Transfer Payments	(5) Federal Contributions to Transfer Programs plus Interest Amount	(6) As a % of Personal Income Taxes
(1)	1962	$ 45.6	$ 29.5	$ 6.9	$ 36.4	$ 19.4	42.5%
(2)	1965	48.8	33.7	8.6	42.3	20.0	41.0
(3)	1970	90.4	66.0	14.4	80.4	36.0	39.9
(4)	1975	122.4	156.6	23.2	179.9	95.3	77.9
(5)	1980	244.1	283.0	52.5	335.5	177.7	72.8
(6)	1981	285.9	330.3	68.7	399.0	216.3	75.7
(7)	1982	297.7	363.5	84.7	448.2	246.7	82.9
(8)	1983	288.9	402.8	87.8	490.7	281.8	97.5
(9)	1985	332.1	452.6	120.9	573.5	301.0	90.6
(10)	1990	553.9	764.0	252.3	1,016.3	578.4	104.4
(11)	1995	965.5	1,338.9	540.9	1,879.8	1,117.4	115.7
(12)	2000	1,608.0	2,440.0	1,520.7	3,960.7	2,607.4	162.1
	Avg. Ann. % Inc./(Dec.)						
(13)	1962–1983	9.2%	13.2%	12.9%	13.2%	13.6%	NA
(14)	1965–1983	10.4	14.8	13.8	14.6	15.8	NA
(15)	1980–1983	5.8	12.5	18.7	13.5	16.6	NA
(16)	1983–2000	10.6	11.2	18.3	13.1	14.0	NA

• After being divided into the one-time and ongoing categories and after eliminating duplications, all savings were phased in over a five-year period beginning in 1984, as follows:

Savings Implementation

Fiscal Year	One-Time	Ongoing
1984	10%	10%
1985	20%	30%
1986	30%	60%
1987	20%	80%
1988	20%	100%

• Finally, the savings were assigned to specific subfunctions in the Federal budget system.

Each recommendation clearly falling under a specific subfunction in the Federal accounts was assigned to that subfunction. In cases where a recommendation covered more than one subfunction, the savings were allocated. In cases such as Personnel, savings were allocated to subfunctions based on the payroll associated with each subfunction; or for general Research and Development (R&D), savings were allocated based on obligations earmarked for R&D by agency—e.g., NASA.

The following summarizes actual Federal finances from 1962 through 1983 and projected through 2000, assuming all the PPSS recommendations are implemented, but nothing else in the economy changes from the Status Quo of Present Policies Case, e.g., no increases or decreases in tax rates.

Federal Revenues and Outlays,
1962–2000: PPSS Savings
($ Billions)

	Fiscal Year	(1) Total Revenues	(2) Total Outlays	(3) Surplus/ (Deficit)	(4) Outlays as A Multiple of Revenues
(1)	1962	$ 99.7	$ 106.8	$ (7.1)	1.07X
(2)	1965	116.8	118.4	(1.6)	1.01
(3)	1970	192.8	195.7	(2.8)	1.01
(4)	1975	279.1	324.2	(45.2)	1.16
(5)	1980	517.1	576.7	(59.6)	1.12
(6)	1981	599.3	657.2	(57.9)	1.10
(7)	1982	617.8	728.4	(110.6)	1.18
(8)	1983	600.6	795.9	(195.4)	1.33
(9)	1985	758.5	894.2	(135.7)	1.18
(10)	1990	1,173.2	1,199.8	(26.6)	1.02
(11)	1995	1,807.8	1,870.3	(62.6)	1.03
(12)	2000	3,052.7	3,089.9	(37.1)	1.01
	Avg. Ann. % Inc./(Dec.)				
(13)	1962–1983	8.9%	10.1%	17.1%	NA
(14)	1965–1983	9.5	11.2	30.6	NA
(15)	1980–1983	5.1	11.3	48.6	NA
(16)	1983–2000	10.0	8.3	(9.3)	NA

From $600.6 billion in 1983, revenues are projected to increase to $3.1 trillion in 2000, a 10.0 percent per year annual increase. Outlays are projected to increase at 8.3 percent per year over the period—1.7 percentage points slower than revenues—and to reach $3.1 trillion in 2000. This more rapid growth of revenues compared to outlays is projected to decrease—but not eliminate—the deficit to $37 billion by 2000.

As brought out in column 4, Outlays as a multiple of revenues are projected to drop from the peak of 1.33 in 1983 to 1.18 in 1985, and then remain in the 1.01–1.03 range during 1990–2000. The surge in 1983 to 1.33 occurred as tax revenues fell and unemployment and other transfer payments increased because of the recession.

The following table summarizes the economic environment consistent with DRI's PPSS savings projections.

Economic Environment
For DRI Projections: PPSS Savings

	(1)	(2)	(3)	(4)	(5)	(6)	(7)	(8)	(9)	(10)	(11)	(12)	(13)
										Federal Spending		Surplus/(Deficit)	
Fiscal Year	Nominal GNP	Real GNP	Inflation	High Grade Corporate Bond Rate	3-Month T-Bill Rate	Unem-ployment Rate	Industrial Production	Real Business Fixed Investment	Housing Starts	$ Billions	% of GNP	$ Billions	% of GNP
	(Avg. Ann. % Inc/(Dec))			(Avg. For Period)			(Avg. Ann. % Inc/(Dec))		(Avg. For Period) (000)	(End of Period)			
(1) 1962–1983	8.8%	3.2%	5.5%	8.19%	6.54%	5.8%	3.4%	4.1%	1,558	$ 795.9	24.6%	$(195.4)	(6.0)%
(2) 1962–1980	9.0	3.6	5.2	7.30	5.72	5.3	4.2	5.0	1,606	576.7	22.4	(59.6)	(2.3)
(3) 1962–1970	7.4	4.2	3.1	5.63	4.59	4.2	5.8	6.7	1,429	195.7	20.2	(2.8)	(0.3)
(4) 1970–1980	10.3	3.1	6.9	8.63	6.62	6.2	3.0	3.7	1,748	576.7	22.4	(59.6)	(2.3)
(5) 1980–1983	7.8	0.7	7.1	13.58	11.49	8.8	(1.5)	(1.3)	1,270	795.9	24.6	195.4	(6.0)
Projected													
(6) 1983–1985	8.4%	3.8%	4.4%	11.19%	8.09%	8.7%	6.4%	4.9%	1,728	$ 894.2	23.6%	$(135.7)	(3.6)%
(7) 1985–1990	8.5	3.5	4.8	9.95	6.22	7.4	4.9	5.1	1,690	1,199.8	21.1	(26.6)	(0.5)
(8) 1990–1995	8.8	2.4	6.2	10.05	6.78	6.7	2.9	3.1	1,606	1,870.3	21.6	(62.6)	(0.7)
(9) 1995–2000	9.3	1.9	7.3	11.33	8.99	7.1	2.3	2.4	1,521	3,089.9	22.8	(37.1)	(0.3)
(10) 1983–2000	8.8	2.7	5.9	10.53	7.42	7.2	3.7	3.7	1,620	3,089.9	22.8	(37.1)	(0.3)

As shown, the long-term projections to 2000 for nominal and real GNP and, hence, inflation are all in line with the 1962–1983 experience:

- Nominal GNP projected up 8.8 percent per year vs. 8.8 percent, 1962–1983.

- Real GNP projected up 2.7 percent per year vs. 3.2 percent, 1962–1983.

- Inflation projected at 5.9 percent vs. 5.5 percent, 1962–1983.

All of these long-term projections are quite favorable to the recent past, with nominal GNP growing at 7.8 percent per year, real GNP up 0.7 percent per year, and an inflation rate of 7.1 percent, all 1980-1983 (line 5, cols. 1–3).

Yields on Treasury Bills are also expected to return to close to historical levels, dropping from an 11.49 percent average during 1980–1983, to 8.09 percent, 1983–1985, and 7.42 percent, 1983–2000. Corporate bond rates are projected to continue to remain high, however—although lower than current levels—as follows:

Nominal and Real Interest Rates, 1963–2000: PPSS Savings

	Fiscal Year	(1) Inflation	(2) High Grade Corp. Bond Rate Nominal	(3) Real	(4) 3-Month T-Bill Rate Nominal	(5) Real
(1)	1963–1983	5.5%	8.21%	3.76%	6.57%	1.40%
(2)	1963–1980	5.2	7.32	3.35	5.75	0.83
(3)	1963–1970	3.1	5.62	3.44	4.55	1.85
(4)	1971–1980	6.9	8.68	3.27	6.71	0.01
(5)	1981–1983	7.1	13.58	6.21	11.49	4.86
	Projected					
(6)	1984–1985	4.4%	11.19%	5.36%	8.09%	3.95%
(7)	1986–1990	4.8	9.95	4.75	6.22	1.26
(8)	1991–1995	6.2	10.05	4.35	6.78	0.53
(9)	1996–2000	7.3	11.33	4.66	8.99	1.85
(10)	1984–2000	5.9	10.53	4.68	7.42	1.54
(11)	Memo: 2000	7.3	12.15	5.24	10.33	3.19

Real rates for high-grade corporates are projected to average 4.68 percent over the 1984–2000 period—92 basis points above the 1963-1983 average—as they first decline, then rise to 5.24 percent by 2000. Real rates for T-Bills are projected to average 1.54 percent—14 basis points above the 1963–1983 average—as they fall to an average 0.53 percent during 1991–1995, before rising to 3.19 percent.

The healthy economy and lower real interest rates combine to stimu-

Federal Government Receipts
by Type, 1962–2000: PPSS Savings
($ Billions)

	Fiscal Year	(1) Personal Income Taxes	(2) Five Specially Funded Social Programs	(3) All Other	(4) Total
(1)	1962	$ 45.6	$ 17.0	$ 37.1	$ 99.7
(2)	1965	48.8	22.3	45.8	116.8
(3)	1970	90.4	44.4	58.0	192.8
(4)	1975	122.4	84.5	72.2	279.1
(5)	1980	244.1	157.8	115.2	517.1
(6)	1981	285.9	182.7	130.6	599.3
(7)	1982	297.7	201.5	118.5	617.8
(8)	1983	288.9	208.9	102.7	600.6
(9)	1985	348.7	270.3	139.5	758.5
(10)	1990	551.6	416.5	205.1	1,173.2
(11)	1995	907.9	665.4	234.5	1,807.8
(12)	2000	1,546.8	1,118.4	387.5	3,052.7
		Average Annual Percent Increase/(Decrease)			
(13)	1962–1983	9.2%	12.7%	5.0%	8.9%
(14)	1965–1983	10.4	13.2	4.6	9.5
(15)	1980–1983	5.8	9.8	(3.8)	5.1
(16)	1983–2000	10.4	10.4	8.1	10.0
		As a Percent of Total			
(17)	1962	45.7%	17.1%	37.2%	100.0%
(18)	1965	41.8	19.1	39.2	100.0
(19)	1970	46.9	23.0	30.1	100.0
(20)	1975	43.9	30.3	25.9	100.0
(21)	1980	47.2	30.5	22.3	100.0
(22)	1981	47.7	30.5	21.8	100.0
(23)	1982	48.2	32.6	19.2	100.0
(24)	1983	48.1	34.8	17.1	100.0
(25)	1985	46.0	35.6	18.4	100.0
(26)	1990	47.0	35.5	17.5	100.0
(27)	1995	50.2	36.8	13.0	100.0
(28)	2000	50.7	36.6	12.7	100.0
		As a Percent of GNP			
(29)	1962	8.3%	3.1%	6.8%	18.2%
(30)	1965	7.4	3.4	6.9	17.7
(31)	1970	9.3	4.6	6.0	19.9
(32)	1975	8.3	5.7	4.9	18.9
(33)	1980	9.5	6.1	4.5	20.1
(34)	1981	9.9	6.3	4.5	20.8
(35)	1982	9.7	6.6	3.9	20.2
(36)	1983	8.9	6.5	3.2	18.6
(37)	1985	9.2	7.1	3.7	20.0
(38)	1990	9.7	7.3	3.6	20.6
(39)	1995	10.5	7.7	2.7	20.8
(40)	2000	11.4	8.3	2.9	22.5

late investment. At 3.7 percent per year, business fixed investment is the fastest growing sector of the U.S. economy over the 1983–2000 period. Industrial production also grows at 3.7 percent per year, 1983–2000, 8.8 percent faster than the 1962–1983 rate of 3.4 percent, and a sharp reversal from the (1.5) percent per year decline, 1980–1983.

Employment benefits, as the unemployment rate trends down from an average of 8.8 percent during 1980–1983 to 6.7 percent during 1990–1995. During 1995–2000, the unemployment rate moves back up to 7.1 percent.

As a percent of GNP, Federal spending drops from the 1983 level of 24.6 to 21.1 percent in 1990, before rising to 22.8 percent in 2000. The deficit as a percent of GNP virtually disappears, falling from 6.1 percent in 1983 to 0.3 percent in 2000, its lowest level since 1969—when there was a surplus.

The table on page 377 provides more detail on the revenue side of the projections.

Personal income taxes (col. 1) and revenues for the five specially funded transfer programs (col. 2)—Social Security, Medicare, Railroad Retirement, Civil Service Retirement, and Unemployment Insurance—are each projected to increase an average 10.4 percent per year, 1983–2000. All other revenues (col. 3)—chiefly corporation income taxes, but also including excise taxes, estate and gift taxes, customs duties, deposits of earnings by the Federal Reserve System, and other miscellaneous receipts—are projected to increase at just 8.1 percent per year.

All three categories are projected to retain their current approximate shares of total revenues because of their roughly similar growth rates—i.e., 8.1 to 10.4 percent per year. In contrast, from 1962 to 1983, revenues earmarked for the five specially funded transfer programs more than doubled as a percent of total, increasing from a 17.1 percent share to 34.8 percent. The share of personal income taxes also rose over this period—largely because of bracket creep—from 45.7 percent in 1962 to 48.1 percent in 1983. Thus, the share of other revenues in the total fell by 54 percent—from 37.2 percent in 1962 to 17.1 percent in 1983.

Both personal income taxes and revenues earmarked for the five specially funded transfer programs are projected to increase as a percent of GNP, but other revenues edge down from 3.2 percent in 1983 to 2.9 percent in 2000, i.e., the 8.8 percent growth of nominal GNP projected for 1983–2000 is slower than those for income taxes and social insurance and only slightly faster than that for other revenues.

The table on pages 380–381 summarizes outlays by function.

Except for national defense, the rate of increase of spending is projected to slow from the 1962–1983 period. National defense, which was $210.5 billion in 1983, is projected to grow at 9.2 percent per year to 2000 when it will reach $937 billion. The projected rate is 2.0 percentage points faster than during 1962–1983 but (6.6) percentage points less rapid than the 15.8 percent rate of 1980–1983.

Despite the acceleration from its long-term growth trend, defense spending is projected to remain fairly constant as a percent of GNP, rising from 6.5 percent in 1983 to about 6.9 percent in 2000. In contrast, during the 1962–1971 period, defense outlays ranged from 7.2 percent of GNP to 9.4 percent. As a percent of total outlays, defense expenditures are projected to rise from 26.4 percent in 1983 to 30.3 percent in 2000.

While the other categories of expenditures are projected to decelerate, the major social programs are still expected to increase rapidly. Thus, expenditures for health programs (col. 3) which grew at 22.2 percent per year, 1962–1983, and 13.7 percent per year, 1980–1983, are projected to increase 9.6 percent per year, 1983–2000, reaching $385 billion or 12.5 percent of total outlays. Income security programs—the largest component of total outlays—are projected to slow from 12.7 percent per year growth during 1962–1983 and the 13.2 percent rate of 1980–1983 to 10.3 percent, 1983–2000, and reach $1.5 trillion, or 47.7 percent of the total.

Alone among the expenditure categories shown, net interest (col. 8) is projected to decrease over the projection period, falling (0.9) percent per year compared to a 12.9 percent per year average increase during 1962–1983 and 18.7 percent per year, 1980–1983. At $75.1 billion in 2000, it accounts for only 2.4 percent of total outlays, compared to 11.0 percent in 1983. By contrast, outlays before interest grow at 8.9 percent, 1983–2000—9.8 percentage points faster than net interest—and rise from 89.0 percent of total spending in 1983 to 97.6 percent in 2000.

As a percent of GNP, net interest decreases by 2.1 percentage points from 2.7 percent in 1983 to 0.6 percent by 2000, compared to a 1.8 percentage point decrease in total outlays from 24.6 percent of GNP in 1983 to 22.8 percent in 2000, while spending before interest increases slightly, from 21.9 percent in 1983 to 22.3 percent in 2000. The deficit as a percent of GNP drops quickly from 6.0 percent in 1983 to 3.6 percent in 1985 and 0.5 percent in 1990—and then remains between 0.3 and 0.7 percent of GNP through 2000. The table on page 382 provides further perspective on the relation of interest, total spending, and the deficit.

Except for interest on the debt, the Federal Government would have surpluses of $62.6 billion in 1990 and $37.9 billion in 2000, instead of deficits of $(26.6) billion and $(37.1) billion, respectively. Looked at another way, net interest as a percent of the deficit is projected to jump from 45.0 percent in 1983 to 335.1 percent in 1990, drop to 99.7 percent by 1995, and then jump to 202.1 percent in 2000.

An alternative way of looking at Federal expenditures is to group them into payments for individuals, or transfer payments, and other outlays—i.e., net interest, the purchase of goods and services, etc., as shown in the table on page 383.

Outlays by Function, 1962–2000: PPSS Savings
($ Billions)

	(1) National Defense	(2) Education, Training, Employment & Social Services	(3) Health	(4) Income Security	(5) Veterans Benefits	(6) All Other Except Interest	(7) Subtotal Before Interest	(8) Net Interest	(9) Total	(10) Surplus/(Deficit)
Fiscal Year										
(1) 1962	$ 49.0	$ 1.2	$ 1.2	$ 22.7	$ 5.6	$ 20.2	$ 99.9	$ 6.9	$ 106.8	$ (7.1)
(2) 1965	47.5	2.1	1.8	25.7	5.7	27.0	109.8	8.6	118.4	(1.6)
(3) 1970	78.6	8.6	12.1	43.1	8.7	30.2	181.3	14.4	195.7	(2.8)
(4) 1975	85.6	15.9	25.7	108.6	16.6	48.7	301.2	23.2	324.2	(45.2)
(5) 1980	135.6	30.8	55.2	193.1	21.2	88.4	524.2	52.5	576.7	(59.6)
(6) 1981	159.8	31.4	66.0	225.1	23.0	83.2	588.5	68.7	657.2	(57.9)
(7) 1982	187.4	26.3	74.0	248.3	24.0	83.6	643.7	84.7	728.4	(110.6)
(8) 1983	210.5	25.7	81.2	280.2	24.8	85.7	708.1	87.8	795.9	(195.4)
(9) 1985	250.9	26.5	94.7	306.5	25.6	76.8	781.0	113.3	894.2	(135.7)
(10) 1990	365.8	30.0	137.8	483.8	27.4	65.8	1,110.6	89.2	1,199.8	(26.6)
(11) 1995	588.8	34.6	218.7	842.4	37.6	85.9	1,808.0	62.3	1,870.3	(62.6)
(12) 2000	937.4	45.1	385.4	1,474.9	53.8	118.1	3,014.8	75.1	3,089.9	(37.1)
Avg. Ann. % Inc./(Dec.)										
(13) 1962–1983	7.2%	15.5%	22.2%	12.7%	7.3%	7.1%	9.8%	12.9%	10.0%	17.1%
(14) 1965–1983	8.6	14.8	23.6	14.2	8.5	6.6	10.9	13.8	11.2	30.6
(15) 1980–1983	15.8	(5.8)	13.7	13.2	5.5	(1.0)	10.5	18.7	11.3	48.6
(16) 1983–2000	9.2	3.4	9.6	10.3	4.7	1.9	8.9	(0.9)	8.3	(9.3)

As a Percent of Total

	Year											
(17)	1962	45.9%	1.2%	1.1%	21.2%	5.3%	18.9%	93.6%	6.4%	100.0%	(6.7%)
(18)	1965	40.1	1.8	1.5	21.7	4.8	22.8	92.8	7.2	100.0	(1.3)
(19)	1970	40.1	4.4	6.2	22.0	4.4	15.5	92.7	7.3	100.0	(1.5)
(20)	1975	26.4	4.9	7.9	33.5	5.1	15.0	92.8	7.2	100.0	(13.9)
(21)	1980	23.5	5.3	9.6	33.5	3.7	15.3	90.9	9.1	100.0	(10.3)
(22)	1981	24.3	4.8	10.0	34.3	3.5	12.7	89.5	10.5	100.0	(8.8)
(23)	1982	25.7	3.6	10.2	34.1	3.3	11.5	88.4	11.6	100.0	(15.2)
(24)	1983	26.4	3.2	10.2	35.2	3.1	10.8	89.0	11.0	100.0	(24.5)
(25)	1985	28.1	3.0	10.6	34.3	2.9	8.6	87.3	12.7	100.0	(15.2)
(26)	1990	30.5	2.5	11.5	40.3	2.3	5.5	92.6	7.4	100.0	(2.2)
(27)	1995	31.5	1.8	11.7	45.0	2.0	4.6	96.7	3.3	100.0	(3.3)
(28)	2000	30.3	1.5	12.5	47.7	1.7	3.8	97.6	2.4	100.0	(1.2)

As a Percent of GNP

	Year											
(29)	1962	8.9%	0.2%	0.2%	4.1%	1.0%	3.7%	18.2%	1.3%	19.5%	(1.3%)
(30)	1965	7.2	0.3	0.3	3.9	0.9	4.1	16.7	1.3	18.0	(0.2)
(31)	1970	8.1	0.9	1.3	4.4	0.9	3.1	18.7	1.5	20.2	(0.3)
(32)	1975	5.8	1.1	1.7	7.3	1.1	3.3	20.4	1.6	21.9	(3.1)
(33)	1980	5.3	1.2	2.1	7.5	0.8	3.4	20.4	2.0	22.4	(2.3)
(34)	1981	5.5	1.1	2.3	7.8	0.8	2.9	20.4	2.4	22.8	(2.0)
(35)	1982	6.1	0.9	2.4	8.1	0.8	2.7	21.1	2.8	23.8	(3.6)
(36)	1983	6.5	0.8	2.5	8.7	0.8	2.7	21.9	2.7	24.6	(6.0)
(37)	1985	6.6	0.7	2.5	8.1	0.7	2.0	20.6	3.0	23.6	(3.6)
(38)	1990	6.4	0.5	2.4	8.5	0.5	1.2	19.5	1.6	21.1	(0.5)
(39)	1995	6.8	0.4	2.5	9.7	0.4	1.0	20.8	0.7	21.6	(0.7)
(40)	2000	6.9	0.3	2.8	10.9	0.4	0.9	22.3	0.6	22.8	(0.3)

Net Interest and the Deficit,
1962–2000: PPSS Savings
($ Billions)

	(1)	(2)	(3)	(4)	(5)	(6)	(7)
		Outlays			Surplus/(Deficit)		Net
Fiscal Year	Total Revenues	Ex-cluding Interest	Net Interest	Total Outlays	Before Net Interest	In-cluding Interest	Interest as a % of the Deficit
(1) 1962	$ 99.7	$ 99.9	$ 6.9	$ 106.8	$ (0.3)	$ (7.1)	96.4%
(2) 1965	116.8	109.8	8.6	118.4	7.0	(1.6)	537.5
(3) 1970	192.8	181.3	14.4	195.7	11.5	(2.8)	505.2
(4) 1975	279.1	301.2	23.2	324.2	(22.1)	(45.2)	51.3
(5) 1980	517.1	524.2	52.5	576.7	(7.1)	(59.6)	88.1
(6) 1981	599.3	588.5	68.7	657.2	10.8	(57.9)	118.6
(7) 1982	617.8	643.7	84.7	728.4	(25.9)	(110.6)	76.6
(8) 1983	600.6	708.1	87.8	795.9	(107.5)	(195.4)	45.0
(9) 1985	758.5	781.0	113.3	894.2	(22.5)	(135.7)	83.5
(10) 1990	1,173.2	1,110.6	89.2	1,199.8	62.6	(26.6)	335.1
(11) 1995	1,807.8	1,808.0	62.3	1,870.3	(0.2)	(62.6)	99.7
(12) 2000	3,052.7	3,014.8	75.1	3,089.9	37.9	(37.1)	202.1
Avg. Ann. % Inc./(Dec.)							
(13) 1962–1983	8.9%	9.8%	12.9%	10.0%	33.3%	17.1%	NA
(14) 1965–1983	9.5	10.9	13.8	11.2	ND	30.6	NA
(15) 1980–1983	5.1	10.5	18.7	11.3	147.4	48.6	NA
(16) 1983–2000	10.0	8.9	(0.9)	8.3	ND	(9.3)	NA

Transfer Payments and
Other Outlays, 1962–2000: PPSS Savings
($ Billions)

		(1)	(2)	(3)	(4)	(5)
		Total		Other Outlays		
	Fiscal Year	Transfer Payments	Net Interest	National Defense(a)	All Other Outlays	Total Outlays
(1)	1962	$ 29.5	$ 6.9	$ 48.1	$ 22.2	$ 106.8
(2)	1965	33.7	8.6	46.1	30.1	118.4
(3)	1970	66.0	14.4	75.7	39.6	195.7
(4)	1975	156.6	23.2	79.3	65.1	324.2
(5)	1980	283.0	52.5	123.7	117.5	576.7
(6)	1981	330.3	68.7	146.0	112.1	657.2
(7)	1982	363.5	84.7	172.5	107.7	728.4
(8)	1983	402.8	87.8	194.3	111.0	795.9
(9)	1985	446.0	113.3	233.6	101.4	894.2
(10)	1990	678.4	89.2	340.8	91.3	1,199.8
(11)	1995	1,148.6	62.3	549.1	110.3	1,870.3
(12)	2000	1,998.4	75.1	874.5	142.0	3,089.9
		Average Annual Percent Increase/(Decrease)				
(13)	1962–1983	13.2%	12.9%	6.9%	8.0%	10.0%
(14)	1965–1983	14.8	13.8	8.3	7.5	11.2
(15)	1980–1983	12.5	18.7	16.2	(1.9)	11.3
(16)	1983–2000	9.9	(0.9)	9.3	1.5	8.3
		As a Percent of Total				
(17)	1962	27.7%	6.4%	45.1%	20.8%	100.0%
(18)	1965	28.4	7.2	38.9	25.4	100.0
(19)	1970	33.7	7.3	38.7	20.2	100.0
(20)	1975	48.3	7.2	24.5	20.1	100.0
(21)	1980	49.1	9.1	21.4	20.4	100.0
(22)	1981	50.3	10.5	22.2	17.1	100.0
(23)	1982	49.9	11.6	23.7	14.8	100.0
(24)	1983	50.6	11.0	24.4	13.9	100.0
(25)	1985	49.9	12.7	26.1	11.3	100.0
(26)	1990	56.5	7.4	28.4	7.6	100.0
(27)	1995	61.4	3.3	29.4	5.9	100.0
(28)	2000	64.7	2.4	28.3	4.6	100.0
		As a Percent of GNP				
(29)	1962	5.4%	1.3%	8.8%	4.1%	19.5%
(30)	1965	5.1	1.3	7.0	4.6	18.0
(31)	1970	6.8	1.5	7.8	4.1	20.2
(32)	1975	10.6	1.6	5.4	4.4	21.9
(33)	1980	11.0	2.0	4.8	4.6	22.4
(34)	1981	11.5	2.4	5.1	3.9	22.8
(35)	1982	11.9	2.8	5.6	3.5	23.8
(36)	1983	12.5	2.7	6.0	3.4	24.6
(37)	1985	11.8	3.0	6.2	2.7	23.6
(38)	1990	11.9	1.6	6.0	1.6	21.1
(39)	1995	13.2	0.7	6.3	1.3	21.6
(40)	2000	14.8	0.6	6.5	1.0	22.8

(a) Military pensions are a transfer payment and, hence, are excluded from national defense outlays in this table.

As shown in the table, transfer payments and outlays for National Defense—excluding military pensions—are both projected to grow between 9 and 10 percent per year, 1983–2000. All other outlays except interest—those which along with National Defense comprise the traditional functions of Government—are projected to increase at only 1.5 percent per year, i.e., 4.4 percentage points slower than inflation. This slow growth is a direct result of the Task Force recommendations, which enable economies to be realized in these programs. Thus, after increasing at 8.0 percent per year, 1962–1983, All Other Outlays are projected to fall (17.7) percent between 1983 and 1990—(2.7) percent per year. Modest growth then resumes in these programs and spending increases 3.8 percent per year, 1990–1995, and 5.2 percent per year, 1995–2000. As a percent of total, these outlays fall by (66.9) percent, from 13.9 percent in 1983 to 4.6 percent in 2000, and as a percent of GNP they drop from the 3.4–4.6 percent range they occupied during 1962–1983 to just 1.0 percent in 2000.

As noted above, net interest is projected to drop 0.9 percent per year, 1983–2000, as a result of the PPSS recommendations and to account for only 2.4 percent of total outlays in 2000. By comparison, transfer payments at $2.0 trillion in 2000 are projected to account for 64.7 percent of all outlays, and 14.8 percent of GNP—both all-time highs. The table on pages 385–386 shows details on payments for individuals.

The first seven columns refer to the five specially funded transfer programs—Social Security, Medicare, Unemployment Insurance, Civil Service Retirement, and Railroad Retirement. Within that group, Social Security and Medicare—by far the two largest—are projected to grow at 11.7 and 10.9 percent per year, 1983–2000. At the other end of the scale, unemployment assistance—which was exceptionally high during 1983 because of the record postwar unemployment rate of 10.2 percent—is projected to increase at only 4.7 percent per year to 2000. After Social Security and Medicare, Civil Service Retirement—the other major retirement program—is projected to grow at 9.1 percent per year. Railroad Retirement, the smallest of the funded programs, is projected to grow at 5.4 percent per year, 1983–2000.

In total, these programs are projected to grow at 10.7 percent per year, compared to 13.1 percent during 1962–1983 and 14.1 percent per year, 1980–1983, and to reach $1.5 trillion in 2000—48.6 percent of total expenditures and 11.1 percent of GNP. Since revenues for these specially funded programs are projected to increase at 10.4 percent per year—(0.3) percentage point slower than outlays—the deficit incurred by these trust funds widens from $(56.6) billion in 1983 to $(383.7) billion in 2000—10.3 times the total deficit of $(37.1) billion.

All other transfer programs are projected to grow at 7.8 percent per year, 1983–2000, compared to 13.5 percent per year, 1962–1983. In 2000,

Transfer Payments, 1962–2000: PPSS Savings
($ Billions)

	(1)	(2)	(3)	(4)	(5)	(6)	(7)	(8)	(9)	(10)
Fiscal Year	Social Security	Railroad Retirement	Civil Service Ret.	Unemployment Assist.	Hospital Insurance	Subtotal	Memo: Revenues	Memo: Surplus/(Deficit)	All Other Transfers	Total Transfers
				Five Specially Funded Social Programs						
(1) 1962	$ 13.9	$ 1.0	$ 1.1	$ 3.8	—	$ 19.8	$ 17.0	$ (2.8)	$ 9.7	$ 29.5
(2) 1965	16.9	1.1	1.4	2.8	—	22.3	22.3	—	11.4	33.7
(3) 1970	29.6	1.6	2.8	3.4	$ 5.0	42.3	44.4	2.1	23.7	66.0
(4) 1975	65.2	3.1	7.1	13.5	10.6	99.4	84.5	(14.9)	57.2	156.6
(5) 1980	117.1	4.7	14.7	18.0	24.3	178.8	157.8	(21.0)	104.2	283.0
(6) 1981	137.9	6.0	17.6	19.7	29.2	210.4	182.7	(27.7)	119.9	330.3
(7) 1982	153.9	5.7	19.4	23.8	34.9	237.7	201.5	(36.2)	125.8	363.5
(8) 1983	170.1	6.2	20.7	29.8	38.7	265.5	208.9	(56.6)	137.3	402.8
(9) 1985	201.5	7.1	22.6	20.1	46.0	297.4	270.3	(27.1)	148.6	446.0
(10) 1990	345.1	7.3	33.0	29.0	68.4	482.9	416.5	(66.3)	195.5	678.4
(11) 1995	621.7	10.2	52.4	45.6	118.9	848.7	665.4	(183.3)	299.9	1,148.6
(12) 2000	1,107.6	15.2	90.5	65.0	223.8	1,502.1	1,118.4	(383.7)	496.3	1,998.4
Avg. Ann. % Inc./(Dec.)										
(13) 1962–1983	12.7%	8.9%	15.2%	10.3%	ND	13.1%	12.7%	15.4%	13.5%	13.2%
(14) 1965–1983	13.7	9.9	16.0	14.1	ND	14.8	13.2	51.0	14.8	14.8
(15) 1980–1983	13.3	9.4	12.1	18.2	16.8%	14.1	9.8	39.2	9.6	12.5
(16) 1983–2000	11.7	5.4	9.1	4.7	10.9	10.7	10.4	11.9	7.8	9.9

Transfer Payments, 1962–2000: PPSS Savings (continued)
($ Billions)

		(1)	(2)	(3)	(4)	(5)	(6)	(7)	(8)	(9)	(10)
	Fiscal Year	Social Security	Railroad Retirement	Civil Service Ret.	Unemployment Assist.	Hospital Insurance	Subtotal	Memo: Revenues	Memo: Surplus/ (Deficit)	All Other Transfers	Total Transfers
		Five Specially Funded Social Programs									
As a Percent of Total											
(17)	1962	13.0%	1.0%	1.0%	3.6%	—	18.6%	16.0%	(2.6)%	9.1%	27.7%
(18)	1965	14.3	1.0	1.2	2.4	—	18.8	18.8	—	9.6	28.4
(19)	1970	15.1	0.8	1.4	1.7	2.5%	21.6	22.7	1.1	12.1	33.7
(20)	1975	20.1	0.9	2.2	4.1	3.3	30.6	26.1	(4.6)	17.6	48.3
(21)	1980	20.3	0.8	2.5	3.1	4.2	31.0	27.4	(3.6)	18.1	49.1
(22)	1981	21.0	0.9	2.7	3.0	4.5	32.0	27.8	(4.2)	18.2	50.3
(23)	1982	21.1	0.8	2.7	3.3	4.8	32.6	27.7	(5.0)	17.3	49.9
(24)	1983	21.4	0.8	2.6	3.7	4.9	33.4	26.2	(7.1)	17.3	50.6
(25)	1985	22.5	0.8	2.5	2.3	5.1	33.3	30.2	(3.0)	16.6	49.9
(26)	1990	28.8	0.6	2.8	2.4	5.7	40.2	34.7	(5.5)	16.3	56.5
(27)	1995	33.2	0.5	2.8	2.4	6.4	45.4	35.6	(9.8)	16.0	61.4
(28)	2000	35.8	0.5	2.9	2.1	7.2	48.6	36.2	(12.4)	16.1	64.7
As a Percent of GNP											
(29)	1962	2.5%	0.2%	0.2%	0.7%	—	3.6%	3.1%	(0.5)%	1.8%	5.4%
(30)	1965	2.6	0.2	0.2	0.4	—	3.4	3.4	—	1.7	5.1
(31)	1970	3.1	0.2	0.3	0.3	0.5%	4.4	4.6	0.2	2.5	6.8
(32)	1975	4.4	0.2	0.5	0.9	0.7	6.7	5.7	(1.0)	3.9	10.6
(33)	1980	4.5	0.2	0.6	0.7	0.9	6.9	6.1	(0.8)	4.0	11.0
(34)	1981	4.8	0.2	0.6	0.7	1.0	7.3	6.3	(1.0)	4.2	11.5
(35)	1982	5.0	0.2	0.6	0.8	1.1	7.8	6.6	(1.2)	4.1	11.9
(36)	1983	5.3	0.2	0.6	0.9	1.2	8.2	6.5	(1.8)	4.3	12.5
(37)	1985	5.3	0.2	0.6	0.5	1.2	7.8	7.1	(0.7)	3.9	11.8
(38)	1990	6.1	0.1	0.6	0.5	1.2	8.5	7.3	(1.2)	3.4	11.9
(39)	1995	7.2	0.1	0.6	0.5	1.4	9.8	7.7	(2.1)	3.5	13.2
(40)	2000	8.2	0.1	0.7	0.5	1.7	11.1	8.3	(2.8)	3.7	14.8

they are projected to reach $496 billion, or 16.1 percent of total outlays. The following table breaks out the major unfunded transfer programs.

Unfunded Payments for
Individuals, 1962–2000: PPSS Savings
($ Billions)

		(1)	(2)	(3)	(4)	(5)
				Ranked	Average Annual % Increase/(Decrease)	
		1962	1983	2000	1962–1983	1983–2000
(1)	Federal Employee Retirement & Insurance Excl. Civil Service	$3.0	$ 26.7	$ 96.1	11.0%	7.8%
(2)	Public Assistance, etc.	4.0	24.3	92.0	9.0	8.1
(3)	Medicaid	0.1	19.1	89.9	28.3	9.6
(4)	Supplemental Medical Insurance	—	17.7	66.4	21.4(a)	8.1
(5)	Food Stamps	0.01	12.2	62.0	38.0	10.1
(6)	Housing Assistance	0.2	9.6	34.0	21.3	7.7
(7)	Other	1.3	14.6	18.8	12.3	1.5
(8)	Child Nutrition	0.2	3.4	17.9	15.3	10.3
(9)	VA Medical Care	1.0	7.5	11.1	10.2	2.3
(10)	Guaranteed Student Loans	—	2.2	8.1	71.5(b)	7.9
(11)	Total	$9.8	$137.3	$496.3	13.5%	7.8%

(a) 1967–1983 Growth Rate
(b) 1970–1983 Growth Rate

The fastest growing of these programs are expected to be Child Nutrition, Food Stamps, and Medicaid, which are projected to increase at between 9.6 and 10.3 percent per year, 1983–2000. Together these three programs are projected to total $170 billion in 2000—equal to 96.4 percent of total Federal receipts except for personal and corporation income taxes and the revenues earmarked for the specially funded transfer programs.

The table on page 388 shows the outlook for transfer payments, interest, and personal income taxes.

As shown in the last column, Federal contributions to transfer programs—i.e., outlays for the unfunded programs plus an amount equal to the deficit of the funded programs—increased from 42.5 percent of personal income taxes in 1962 to 97.5 percent in 1983, i.e., there was virtually no money left for any other Government activity. If the PPSS recommendations are implemented, however, this percentage is projected to drop to about 60 percent of personal income taxes, the lowest since 1970.

**Transfer Payments, Interest, and
Personal Income Taxes, 1962–2000: PPSS Savings**
($ Billions)

	Fiscal Year	(1) Personal Income Taxes	(2) Total Trans- fers	(3) Net Inter- est	(4) Total Interest and Transfer Payments	(5) Federal Contributions to Transfer Programs plus Interest Amount	(6) As a % of Personal Income Taxes
(1)	1962	$ 45.6	$ 29.5	$ 6.9	$ 36.4	$ 19.4	42.5%
(2)	1965	48.8	33.7	8.6	42.3	20.0	41.0
(3)	1970	90.4	66.0	14.4	80.4	36.0	39.9
(4)	1975	122.4	156.6	23.2	179.9	95.3	77.9
(5)	1980	244.1	283.0	52.5	335.5	177.7	72.8
(6)	1981	285.9	330.3	68.7	399.0	216.3	75.7
(7)	1982	297.7	363.5	84.7	448.2	246.7	82.9
(8)	1983	288.9	402.8	87.8	490.7	281.8	97.5
(9)	1985	348.7	446.0	113.3	559.2	288.9	82.9
(10)	1990	551.6	678.4	89.2	767.6	351.1	63.7
(11)	1995	907.9	1,148.6	62.3	1,210.9	545.5	60.1
(12)	2000	1,546.8	1,998.4	75.1	2,073.4	955.0	61.7
	Avg. Ann. % Inc./(Dec.)						
(13)	1962–1983	9.2%	13.2%	12.9%	13.2%	13.6%	NA
(14)	1965–1983	10.4	14.8	13.8	14.6	15.8	NA
(15)	1980–1983	5.8	12.5	18.7	13.5	16.6	NA
(16)	1983–2000	10.4	9.9	(0.9)	8.8	7.4	NA

EFFECTS OF PPSS SAVINGS

Since the Status Quo of Current Policies Case and the PPSS Savings Case use identical assumptions relating to the economy and Federal policies—except for the PPSS recommendations themselves—the impact of implementing the recommendations can be readily determined by comparing the two cases. The following table summarizes projected Federal finances during 1983–2000 for the two cases.

As shown in the table, the net effect of the PPSS recommendations would be to save the Federal Government $1.9 trillion per year by 2000 (col. 3, line 15) and $10.5 trillion over the entire 1984–2000 period (col. 3, line 18). Initial savings would, of course, be more modest. Outlays in the PPSS Savings Case are lower than those in the Status Quo Case by $46 billion in 1985 (line 7)—while recommendations are still being implemented. The savings due to the recommendatons then increase to $433

		(1) Status Quo of Current Policies	(2) PPSS Savings	(3) PPSS Fav./(Unfav.) to Status Quo Amount	(4) %
	Revenues				
(1)	1983A	$ 600.6	$ 600.6	—	—
(2)	1985	754.8	758.5	$ 3.6	0.5%
(3)	1990	1,246.5	1,173.2	(73.4)	(5.9)
(4)	1995	2,089.2	1,807.8	(281.4)	(13.5)
(5)	2000	3,567.3	3,052.7	(514.6)	(14.4)
	Outlays				
(6)	1983A	$ 795.9	$ 795.9	—	—
(7)	1985	939.9	894.2	$ 45.7	4.9%
(8)	1990	1,633.3	1,199.8	433.5	26.5
(9)	1995	2,864.6	1,870.3	994.3	34.7
(10)	2000	5,533.3	3,089.9	2,443.4	44.2
	Deficit				
(11)	1983A	$ (195.4)	$ (195.4)	—	—
(12)	1985	(185.1)	(135.7)	$ 49.3	26.7%
(13)	1990	(386.7)	(26.6)	360.1	93.1
(14)	1995	(775.4)	(62.6)	712.8	91.9
(15)	2000	(1,966.0)	(37.1)	1,928.8	98.1
	Cumulative, 17 years 1984–2000				
(16)	Revenues	$ 29,731.5	$26,479.1	$(3,252.4)	(10.9)%
(17)	Outlays	41,370.5	27,585.9	13,784.6	33.3
(18)	Deficit	(11,639.0)	(1,106.9)	10,532.2	90.5

billion in 1990, $994 billion in 1995, and $2.4 trillion in 2000, and total $13.8 trillion, 1984–2000 (lines 8–10 and 17). These outlay reductions are partially offset by lower revenue projections (lines 3–5 and 16) to arrive at the net savings figure—which is the reduction in the deficit.

The seeming paradox of lower revenues resulting from the PPSS recommendations—which include revenue enhancements—can be explained by two factors: the loss of stimulus near term resulting from lower Government spending and the lower rate of inflation in the PPSS Case—5.9 percent per year, 1983–2000, vs. 7.2 percent in the Status Quo Case. The following table shows the same annual data in constant 1983 dollars.

Summary Federal Finances,
1983–2000: Status Quo of
Current Policies vs. PPSS Savings
(Constant 1983 $ Billions)

		(1)	(2)	(3)	(4)
				PPSS Fav./(Unfav.) to Status Quo	
		Status Quo of Current Policies	PPSS Savings	Amount	%
	Revenues				
(1)	1983A	$ 600.6	$ 600.6	—	—
(2)	1985	692.1	696.1	$ 4.0	0.6%
(3)	1990	854.7	850.8	(3.9)	(0.5)
(4)	1995	966.9	971.2	4.3	0.4
(5)	2000	1,098.2	1,154.3	56.0	5.1
	Outlays				
(6)	1983A	$ 795.9	$ 795.9	—	—
(7)	1985	861.8	820.7	$ 41.1	4.8%
(8)	1990	1,119.8	870.1	249.7	22.3
(9)	1995	1,325.8	1,004.8	321.0	24.2
(10)	2000	1,703.5	1,168.3	535.2	31.4
	Deficit				
(11)	1983A	$ (195.4)	$ (195.4)	—	—
(12)	1985	(169.7)	(124.6)	$ 45.1	26.6%
(13)	1990	(265.1)	(19.3)	245.8	92.7
(14)	1995	(358.9)	(33.6)	325.3	90.6
(15)	2000	(605.2)	(14.0)	591.2	97.7

By eliminating the effect of differing rates of inflation, it is made clear that in real terms the recommendations do result in higher revenues—up by $56 billion in 2000 (constant 1983 dollars) as shown in column 3, line 5. The $4.0 billion increase in 1985 (col. 3, line 2) largely reflects the phased-in impact of cash accelerations. The lower revenues in 1990 (line 3) result from the loss of fiscal stimulus caused by lower Government spending in the late 1980s. By 2000, however, the stimulus provided to the private sector by lower interest rates more than compensates for the decreased Federal spending.

The table on pages 391–392 shows the impact of the recommendations on inflation, interest rates, and other key economic indicators.

As shown in lines 1–5 of the table, nominal GNP growth in the PPSS Savings Case consistently runs below that in the Status Quo of Current Policies Case. This is, however, due solely to the more favorable—i.e., lower—rate of inflation that occurs if the PPSS recommendations are implemented.

Thus, as shown in lines 6–10, although *real* GNP in the PPSS Savings

Comparison of Key Economic Variables,
Status Quo and PPSS Savings Cases

		(1)	(2)	(3)	(4)
		Status Quo of Current Policies	PPSS Savings	PPSS Fav./(Unfav.) to Status Quo	
				Amount	%
	Nominal GNP	\multicolumn{4}{l}{Average Annual % Incr./(Decr.)}			
(1)	1983–1985	9.2%	8.4%	(0.8)% pts.	(8.7)%
(2)	1985–1990	9.7	8.5	(1.2)	(12.4)
(3)	1990–1995	10.2	8.8	(1.4)	(13.7)
(4)	1995–2000	10.1	9.3	(0.8)	(7.9)
(5)	1983–2000	9.9	8.8	(1.1)	(11.1)
	Real GNP				
(6)	1983–1985	4.6%	3.8%	(0.8)% pts.	(17.4)%
(7)	1985–1990	3.5	3.5	—	—
(8)	1990–1995	1.9	2.4	0.5	26.3
(9)	1995–2000	1.4	1.9	0.5	35.7
(10)	1983–2000	2.5	2.7	0.2	8.0
	Inflation				
(11)	1983–1985	4.4	4.4	—	—
(12)	1985–1990	6.0	4.8	1.2% pts.	20.0%
(13)	1990–1995	8.2	6.2	2.0	24.4
(14)	1995–2000	8.5	7.3	1.2	14.1
(15)	1983–2000	7.2	5.9	1.3	18.1
	High-Grade Corporate Bond Rate	\multicolumn{4}{l}{Average for Period}			
(16)	1984–1985	11.68%	11.19%	0.49% pts.	4.2%
(17)	1986–1990	11.88	9.95	1.93	16.2
(18)	1991–1995	12.38	10.05	2.33	18.8
(19)	1996–2000	14.75	11.33	3.42	23.2
(20)	1984–2000	12.85	10.53	2.32	18.1
	3-Month T-Bill Rate	\multicolumn{4}{l}{Average for Period}			
(21)	1984–1985	9.37%	8.09%	1.28% pts.	13.7%
(22)	1986–1990	10.21	6.22	3.99	39.1
(23)	1991–1995	10.77	6.78	3.99	37.1
(24)	1996–2000	14.32	8.99	5.33	37.2
(25)	1984–2000	11.48	7.42	4.07	35.4
	Unemployment Rate				
(26)	1984–1985	8.30%	8.65%	(0.35)% pts.	(4.2)%
(27)	1986–1990	6.46	7.40	(0.94)	(14.6)
(28)	1991–1995	5.82	6.68	(0.86)	(14.8)
(29)	1996–2000	6.50	7.10	(0.60)	(9.2)
(30)	1984–2000	6.50	7.25	(0.75)	(11.5)

Comparison of Key Economic Variables,
Status Quo and PPSS Savings Cases *(continued)*

		(1)	(2)	(3)	(4)
				PPSS Fav./(Unfav.) to Status Quo	
		Status Quo of Current Policies	PPSS Savings	Amount	%
	Industrial Production	Average Annual % Incr./(Decr.)			
(31)	1983–1985	7.8%	6.4%	(1.4)% pts.	(18.0)%
(32)	1985–1990	4.8	4.9	0.1	2.1
(33)	1990–1995	2.2	2.9	0.7	31.8
(34)	1995–2000	1.4	2.3	0.9	64.3
(35)	1983–2000	3.4	3.7	0.3	8.8
	Real Business Fixed Investment				
(36)	1983–1985	5.3%	4.9%	(0.4)% pts.	(7.6)%
(37)	1985–1990	2.9	5.1	2.2	75.9
(38)	1990–1995	1.8	3.1	1.3	72.2
(39)	1995–2000	1.5	2.4	0.9	60.0
(40)	1983–2000	2.4	3.7	1.3	54.2
	Housing Starts	Average for Period (000 Units)			
(41)	1984–1985	1,704	1,728	24	1.4%
(42)	1986–1990	1,587	1,690	103	6.5
(43)	1991–1995	1,357	1,606	249	18.4
(44)	1996–2000	1,101	1,521	420	38.2
(45)	1984–2000	1,390	1,620	230	16.6

Case grows more slowly than in the Status Quo Case through 1985, by the 1990–1995 period, it is growing 0.5 percentage point, or 26.3 percent, more rapidly. For the entire 1983–2000 period, the average growth rate of 2.7 percent projected under the PPSS scenario is 0.2 percentage point, or 8.0 percent, more rapid than the 2.5 percent of the Status Quo Case. The initially faster growth in the Status Quo Case is, as noted earlier, a result of the stimulus provided by Government spending.

In both cases, inflation rekindles in the 1990s. In the Status Quo of Current Policies scenario, the renewed inflation results from continuing deficits—which by the late 1990s are in the $1–$2 trillion range. This leads to inflation rising to 8.6 percent per year in 1995 and averaging 8.5 percent per year, 1995–2000. The lower deficits of the PPSS scenario lead to correspondingly lower inflation—rising to only 7.3 percent, per year, 1995–2000. Over the entire forecast period, inflation in the PPSS Case averages 5.9 percent per year, 1.3 percentage points, or 18.1 percent, favorable to the Status Quo.

As would be expected, with lower inflation, interest rates are lower as well. In the PPSS Case, the rate for high-grade corporates drops steadily from 11.17 percent in 1983 to 9.30 percent in 1990 before inflation pushes it back to 12.15 percent by 2000. The rate on T-Bills is more reactive, dropping fom 8.40 percent in 1983 to 5.82 percent in 1990, then rising to 10.33 percent by 2000. By comparison, in the Status Quo Case, yields increase steadily to average 14.75 percent on corporates and 14.32 percent on T-Bills during 1995–2000. Real rates are also lower in the PPSS Case as shown in the following table.

Real Interest Rates,
1983–2000: Status Quo of
Current Policies vs. PPSS Savings
(Avg. for Period)

		(1)	(2)	(3)	(4)
				PPSS Savings Fav/(Unfav) to Status Quo	
		Status Quo	PPSS Savings	Amount	%
	High-Grade Corporate Bonds				
(1)	1983 Act.	4.45%	4.45%	—	—
(2)	1984–1985	5.84	5.36	0.48% pts.	8.2%
(3)	1986–1990	6.19	4.75	1.44	23.3
(4)	1991–1995	5.36	4.35	1.01	18.8
(5)	1996–2000	6.89	4.66	2.23	32.4
(6)	1984–2000	6.11	4.68	1.43	23.4
(7)	Memo: 2000	8.21	5.24	2.97	36.2
	Treasury Bills				
(8)	1983 Act.	4.06%	4.06%	—	—
(9)	1984–1985	5.16	3.95	1.21% pts.	23.4%
(10)	1986–1990	4.25	1.26	2.99	70.4
(11)	1991–1995	2.87	0.53	2.34	81.5
(12)	1996–2000	6.28	1.85	4.43	70.5
(13)	1984–2000	4.55	1.54	3.01	66.2
(14)	Memo: 2000	8.86	3.19	5.67	64.0

As shown, real interest rates on both shortand long-term debt are projected to be in a generally rising trend—except for the early 1990s—under the Status Quo, rising to over 8 percent by 2000. The decline during the early 1990s reflects the slowing down of the economy as the burden of large deficits begins to overwhelm the fiscal stimulus they provide.

In contrast, in the PPSS Savings Case, the real rate on high-grade corporates remains in a fairly narrow range, with no discernable trend until the late 1990s when it rises to 5.24 percent in 2000. For the entire 1984–2000 period, the real rate in the Savings Case averages 4.68 percent, 143 basis points, or 23.4 percent, lower than the Status Quo.

T-Bills, on the other hand, show a sharp decline in real yields, again followed by an increase in the late 1990s. From 4.06 percent in 1983, the real yield on Treasury Bills drops to an average 0.53 percent during 1991–1995 before rising to 3.19 percent in 2000. Over the 1984–2000 period, the average real yield on T-Bills is 1.54 percent in the PPSS Savings Case, 301 basis points, or 66.2 percent, favorable to the Status Quo.

The lower real interest rates resulting from the PPSS recommendations lead to more rapid growth of both industrial production (lines 31-35 of the Comparison of Key Economic Variables table) and real business fixed investment (lines 36-40) than occurs given the Status Quo of Current Policies. Industrial production, mirroring real GNP, grows more slowly at first in the PPSS Case, although growth of 6.4 percent per year, 1983–1985, is still healthy. By the late 1990s, however, when the economy stalls under the Status Quo, industrial production growth in the PPSS Case is 2.1 percent per year—0.7 percentage point or 50 percent higher. Over the entire 1983–2000 period, industrial production in the PPSS Case grows at 3.7 percent per year, 0.3 percentage point or 8.8 percent faster than under the Status Quo.

The pickup in industrial production has a multiplier effect on real business fixed investment. From 1983 to 1985, fixed investment grows 4.9 percent per year, (0.4) percentage point slower than under the Status Quo. This accelerates to 5.1 percent per year, 1985–1990, 1.76 times the Status Quo rate. During the 1990–1995 period, investment growth slows to 3.1 percent per year, but this is still 1.3 percentage points or 72.2 percent faster than under the Status Quo.

Housing starts (lines 41–45) also benefit from the lower interest rates and are consistently higher if the PPSS recommendations are implemented. The difference is slight at first—just 24,000 starts per year—or 1.4 percent—during 1984–1985. By 1996–2000, however, there are an average 420,000 more starts per year—38.2 percent higher—in the PPSS Savings Case than under the Status Quo.

Unlike the other key economic variables, the unemployment rate (lines 26–30) is higher as a result of the recommendations than it would have been under the Status Quo. This is true for all periods shown, with unemployment averaging 7.2 percent, 1984–2000, in the PPSS Savings Case—0.7 percentage point, or 11.5 percent, higher than the Status Quo. It is important to realize, however, that this higher unemployment rate does not reflect fewer people working, but rather more people in the labor force, as shown in the following table.

The (0.2) percentage point unfavorable variance in the unemployment rate resulting from the PPSS recommendations reflects an additional 0.5 million people looking for work. There are, however, 2.2 million more people already at work as a result of the recommendations. This situation arises because the more rapidly growing real GNP and business fixed

Labor Supply and Employment, 2000:
Status Quo of Current Policies vs. PPSS Savings
(Millions, Except Percent)

		(1)	(2)	(3)	(4)
				PPSS Fav/(Unfav) to Status Quo	
		Status Quo	*PPSS Savings*	*Amount*	*%*
(1)	Population	267.6	267.6	—	—
(2)	Civilian Labor Force	136.1	138.8	2.7	2.0%
(3)	Labor Participation Rate	65.5%	66.8%	1.3% pts.	2.0
(4)	Employed	126.7	128.9	2.2	1.7
(5)	Unemployed	9.4	9.9	(0.5)	(5.3)
(6)	Unemployment Rate	6.9%	7.1%	(0.2)% pt.	(2.9)

investment induce more people to join the labor force, as shown in the following:

Labor Force Composition, 2000:
Status Quo of Current Policies vs. PPSS Savings
(Millions)

		(1)	(2)	(3)	(4)
				Ranked PPSS Above/(Below) Status Quo	
		Status Quo	*PPSS Savings*	*Amount*	*%*
(1)	Females, 25–54	44.3	46.6	2.3	5.2%
(2)	Males, 55 and over	9.0	9.3	0.3	3.3
(3)	Males, 25–54	52.6	52.6	—	—
(4)	Males, 16–24	12.2	12.2	—	—
(5)	Females, 16–24	11.2	11.2	—	—
(6)	Females, 55 and over	6.8	6.8	—	—

The entry of 25- to 54-year-old women and older men into the labor force reflects the large pool available. At 44.3 million in 2000, the labor force participation rate is only 75.4 percent for 25- to 54-year-old women against 90.3 percent for comparably aged men. Similarly, among men who are 55 and over, the participation rate is only 37.6 percent in the Status Quo Case.

As noted above, one of the effects of the PPSS recommendations is a lower rate of inflation. This has the effect of greatly distorting the apparent savings when the PPSS outlays are subtracted from the Status Quo outlays. To assess the impact of the recommendations on Federal revenues and outlays accurately, this differential inflation effect has to be eliminated. The rest of the analysis in this section, therefore, is presented in constant 1983 dollars, unless stated otherwise.

The following table shows detail on Federal revenues under the Status Quo and PPSS Savings Cases.

Federal Receipts, 1983 and 2000:
Status Quo of Current Policies vs. PPSS Savings
(Constant 1983 $ Billions)

		(1)	(2)	(3)	(4)	(5)
				2000		
					PPSS Fav/(Unfav) To Status Quo	
		1983	Status Quo	PPSS Savings	Amount	%
(1)	Personal Income Taxes	$288.9	$ 495.1	$ 584.8	$ 89.8	18.1%
(2)	Revenues for Five Specially Funded Transfer Programs	208.9	416.6	422.9	6.3	1.5
(3)	All Other	102.7	186.6	146.5	(40.0)	(21.5)
(4)	Total	600.6	1,098.2	1,154.3	56.0	5.1
	Avg. Ann. % Inc./(Dec.) 1983–2000					
(5)	Personal Income Taxes		3.2%	4.2%	1.0% pt.	31.3%
(6)	Revenues for Five Specially Funded Transfer Programs		4.1	4.2	0.1	2.4
(7)	All Other		3.6	2.1	(1.5)	(41.7)
(8)	Total		3.6	3.9	0.3	8.3

Thus in 2000, the PPSS recommendations produce $56 billion (in 1983 dollars), or 5.1 percent more revenues for the Federal Government than it would receive under the Status Quo. Increased personal income tax receipts of $89.8 billion more than account for the total, and increased receipts for the specially funded transfer programs account for a further $6.3 billion.

All other receipts are lower by $40.0 billion in real terms because of decreased corporation income tax collections. The drop in corporate taxes reflects sharply lower corporate profits in the PPSS Case—in large measure the result of increased depreciation resulting from the increased business investment stimulated by lower interest rates. This is true both before and after adjusting for the different rates of inflation, as shown in the following table.

Corporate Profits and Taxes, 1983 and 2000:
Status Quo of Current Policies vs. PPSS Savings
($ Billions)

		(1)	(2)	(3)	(4)	(5)
					2000	
					PPSS Fav./(Unfav.) to Status Quo	
			Status	PPSS		
		1983	Quo	Savings	Amount	%
				Current Dollars		
(1)	Pre-Tax Profits	$187.1	$1,468.1	$ 923.2	$(544.9)	(37.1)%
(2)	Taxes	65.1	524.0	286.7	(237.3)	(45.3)
(3)	Profits After Tax	122.0	944.1	636.5	(307.6)	(32.6)
(4)	Memo: Cash Flow	289.3	1,464.5	1,264.1	(200.4)	(13.7)
				Constant 1983 Dollars		
(5)	Pre-Tax Profits	$187.1	$ 452.1	$ 350.9	$(101.2)	(22.4)%
(6)	Taxes	65.1	161.4	109.0	(52.4)	(32.5)
(7)	Profits After Tax	122.0	290.8	241.9	(48.9)	(16.8)
(8)	Memo: Cash Flow	289.3	451.0	480.4	29.4	6.5

As shown, in 2000, pre-tax corporate profits are $(545) billion, or (37.1) percent, lower in the PPSS Savings Case than under the Status Quo before adjusting for inflation and $(101) billion, or (22.4) percent, lower in constant 1983 dollars. Similarly, taxes paid—to state and local as well as to the Federal Government—are lower by (45.3) percent in nominal terms, and by (32.5) percent in real terms. Cash flow is also lower in the PPSS Savings Case, but only in nominal terms. After adjusting for inflation, net cash flow in 2000 is projected higher in the PPSS Savings Case than under the Status Quo by $29.4 billion (1983 dollars), or 6.5 percent.

In terms of growth rates, personal income taxes are projected to increase 4.2 percent per year in real terms in the PPSS Case, 1.0 percentage point or 31.3 percent more rapidly than under the Status Quo. Little variation between the two cases appears in the revenues collected for the five specially funded transfer programs, however, which increase only 0.1 percentage point, or 2.4 percent, more rapidly as a result of the PPSS recommendations.

The higher level of real personal income tax receipts reflects both specific revenue generating recommendations made by PPSS and greater personal income because of the stronger economy in the PPSS Savings Case, as shown in the table on the following page.

As shown, aggregate personal income in 2000 is projected at $2.1 trillion in 1972 dollars—$108.5 billion, or 5.3 percent, higher as a result of the PPSS recommendations (line 1, cols. 3–5). The effective personal

Personal Income and Taxes, 1983 and 2000:
Status Quo of Current Policies vs. PPSS Savings
(Constant 1972 $ Billions except Per Capita)

		(1)	(2)	(3)	(4)	(5)
				2000		
					PPSS Above/(Below) Status Quo	
			Status Quo	PPSS Savings		
		1983			Amount	%
(1)	Personal Income	$1,273.0	$2,034.1	$2,142.6	$108.5	5.3%
(2)	Disposable Personal Income:					
	Total	1,081.8	1,704.3	1,775.3	71.0	4.2
(3)	Per Capita	4,630.0	6,369.0	6,634.3	265.3	4.2
(4)	Personal Tax and Non-Tax Payments	191.2	329.8	367.3	37.5	11.4
(5)	Effective Personal Tax Rate	17.9%	20.6%	21.2%	0.6% pt.	2.9

tax rate (line 5) is also higher—by 0.6 percentage point, or 2.9 percent. These result in higher tax payments of $37.5 billion, or 11.4 percent, in the PPSS Case compared to the Status Quo. Despite this higher level of taxation, individuals are still better off, as shown in line 3, where real per capita disposable income is projected at $6,634 in the PPSS Savings Case —$265 or 4.2 percent higher than under the Status Quo.

The following table shows the impact of the PPSS recommendations on outlays by function.

By far, the largest savings occur in the net interest function. By 2000, net interest in the PPSS Savings Case is projected at $28.4 billion in 1983 dollars—$(439.8) billion, or (93.9) percent less than under the Status Quo (col. 8, lines 9, 13, 17). The $440 billion in interest savings accounts for 82.2 percent of the reduction in total outlays of $535.2 billion, and 74.4 percent of the $591.2 billion reduction in the deficit, as shown in the table on page 400.

Excluding interest, outlays are projected to rise to $1.14 trillion (1983 dollars) in the PPSS Savings Case by 2000, $95.4 billion or 7.7 percent favorable to the Status Quo (col. 2, lines 9, 13, 17). This results in a real surplus before interest of $(14.3) billion (col. 5, line 9) which is $151.4 billion favorable to the Status Quo.

After interest, the largest savings in percentage terms occur in Education, Veterans' Benefits, and Other (cols. 2, 5, 6 of the Outlays by Function table) with reductions of 33.9 percent, 30.3 percent, and 55.8 percent, respectively, in 2000. Health programs are reduced by 10.3 percent in 2000, and National Defense by 10.5 percent.

Status Quo of Current Policies vs. PPSS Savings
(Constant 1983 $ Billions)

	(1) National Defense	(2) Education, Training, Employment & Social Services	(3) Health	(4) Income Security	(5) Veterans Benefits	(6) All Other Except Interest	(7) Subtotal Before Interest	(8) Net Interest	(9) Total	(10) Surplus/(Deficit)
Fiscal Year										
(1) 1983	$210.5	$25.7	$ 81.2	$280.2	$24.8	$ 85.7	$ 708.1	$ 87.8	$ 795.9	$(195.4)
Status Quo of Current Policies										
(2) 1985	$246.3	$25.7	$ 90.0	$281.0	$25.3	$ 82.7	$ 751.0	$110.8	$ 861.8	$(169.7)
(3) 1990	333.3	26.9	113.1	357.8	27.5	88.3	946.8	173.0	1,119.8	(265.1)
(4) 1995	368.8	25.0	133.4	426.0	28.7	93.5	1,075.5	250.3	1,325.8	(358.9)
(5) 2000	396.1	25.8	162.4	520.8	29.2	101.0	1,235.3	468.2	1,703.5	(605.2)
PPSS Savings										
(6) 1985	$230.2	$24.4	$ 86.9	$281.2	$23.5	$ 70.5	$ 716.7	$104.0	$ 820.7	$(124.6)
(7) 1990	265.3	21.8	99.9	350.8	19.9	47.7	805.4	64.7	870.1	(19.3)
(8) 1995	316.3	18.6	117.5	452.6	20.2	46.1	971.3	33.5	1,004.8	(33.6)
(9) 2000	354.5	17.1	145.7	557.7	20.4	44.6	1,139.9	28.4	1,168.3	(14.0)
Amount PPSS Favorable/(Unfavorable) to Status Quo										
(10) 1985	$ 16.2	$ 1.4	$ 3.1	$ (0.2)	$ 1.7	$ 12.2	$ 34.3	$ 6.9	$ 41.1	$ 45.1
(11) 1990	68.0	5.2	13.2	6.9	7.6	40.6	141.4	108.3	249.7	245.8
(12) 1995	52.5	6.4	15.9	(26.6)	8.5	47.4	104.2	216.8	321.0	325.3
(13) 2000	41.7	8.7	16.7	(36.9)	8.8	56.4	95.4	439.8	535.2	591.2
Percent PPSS Favorable/(Unfavorable) to Status Quo										
(14) 1985	6.5%	5.3%	3.4%	(0.1)%	6.9%	14.8%	4.6%	6.2%	4.8%	26.6%
(15) 1990	20.4	19.1	11.7	1.9	27.7	45.9	14.9	62.6	22.3	92.7
(16) 1995	14.2	25.8	11.9	(6.2)	29.6	50.7	9.7	86.6	24.2	90.6
(17) 2000	10.5	33.9	10.3	(7.1)	30.3	55.8	7.7	93.9	31.4	97.7

Interest and the Deficit, 1983–2000:
Status Quo of Current Policies vs. PPSS Savings
(Constant 1983 $ Billions)

		(1)	(2)	(3)	(4)	(5)	(6)	(7)
				Outlays		Surplus/(Deficit)		Net Intere
						Before		Intere as a
	Fiscal Year	Total Revenues	Excluding Interest	Net Interest	Total Outlays	Net Interest	Including Interest	of th Defi
(1)	1983	$ 600.6	$ 708.1	$ 87.8	$ 795.9	$(107.6)	$(195.4)	45.
Status Quo of Current Policies								
(2)	1985	$ 692.1	$ 751.0	$110.8	$ 861.8	$ (58.8)	$(169.7)	65.
(3)	1990	854.7	946.8	173.0	1,119.8	(92.2)	(265.1)	65
(4)	1995	966.9	1,075.5	250.3	1,325.8	(108.5)	(358.9)	69
(5)	2000	1,098.2	1,235.3	468.2	1,703.5	(137.1)	(605.2)	77
PPSS Savings								
(6)	1985	$ 696.1	$ 716.7	$104.0	$ 820.7	$ (20.6)	$(124.6)	83
(7)	1990	850.8	805.4	64.7	870.1	45.4	(19.3)	335
(8)	1995	971.2	971.3	33.5	1,004.8	(0.1)	(33.6)	99
(9)	2000	1,154.3	1,139.9	28.4	1,168.3	14.3	(14.0)	202
Amount PPSS Favorable/(Unfavorable) to Status Quo								
(10)	1985	$ 4.0	$ 34.3	$ 6.9	$ 41.1	$ 38.2	$ 45.1	15
(11)	1990	(3.9)	141.4	108.3	249.7	137.6	245.8	44
(12)	1995	4.3	104.2	216.8	321.0	108.4	325.3	66
(13)	2000	56.0	95.4	439.8	535.2	151.4	591.2	74
Percent PPSS Favorable/(Unfavorable) to Status Quo								
(14)	1985	0.6%	4.6%	6.2%	4.8%	65.0%	26.6%	23
(15)	1990	(0.5)	14.9	62.6	22.3	ND	92.7	67
(16)	1995	0.4	9.7	86.6	24.2	99.9	90.6	95
(17)	2000	5.1	7.7	93.9	31.4	ND	97.7	96

Interestingly, income security programs (col. 4) are larger on a constant dollar basis as a result of the PPSS recommendations, amounting to $557.7 billion (1983 dollars) in 2000—$36.9 billion or 7.1 percent more than under the Status Quo. The difference between the two cases for individual income security programs is detailed in the following table.

The increased outlays for Social Security (line 1) and Other Income Security (line 3) reflect the traditional policy of the Federal Government of expanding these programs as the ability to pay increases.

The lower interest rates, greatly reduced deficit, and generally stronger economy in the PPSS Savings Case all lead to this increased ability. This is also part of the reason for the increase in unemployment

Income Security Programs, 1983 and 2000:
Status Quo of Current Policies vs. PPSS Savings
(Constant 1983 $ Billions)

		(1)	(2)	(3)	(4)	(5)
					2000	
					PPSS Above/ (Below) Status Quo	
			Status Quo	PPSS Savings		
		1983			Amount	%
(1)	Social Security	$170.8	$362.5	$417.3	$54.8	15.1%
(2)	Unemployment Compensation	29.9	23.6	24.6	0.9	4.0
(3)	Other Income Security	21.3	30.6	31.4	0.8	2.6
(4)	Housing Assistance	9.7	15.4	13.0	(2.4)	(15.7)
(5)	Food and Nutrition Assistance	18.3	38.0	31.3	(6.7)	(17.6)
(6)	Federal Employee Retirement Disability	20.6	41.7	33.7	(8.0)	(19.1)
(7)	Other General Retirement and Disability	7.9	8.9	6.4	(2.5)	(28.5)

compensation, but here the higher unemployment rate—7.1 vs. 6.9 percent under the Status Quo in 2000—also contributes to larger outlays. The other programs all show decreased outlays as a result of the PPSS recommendations.

An alternative way of looking at Federal expenditures is to group them into payments for individuals, or transfer payments and other outlays—i.e., net interest, the purchase of goods and services, etc., as in the table at the top of page 402.

As shown, the real value of transfer payments is projected to increase as a result of the PPSS recommendations. In 2000, transfer payments at $755.6 billion (1983 dollars) are $4.4 billion, or 0.6 percent, above what they would have been under the Status Quo (col. 1, lines 9, 13, 17). This increase is primarily due to larger Social Security outlays in real terms, as discussed above. As an example of how the different inflation rates in the Status Quo and PPSS Cases can distort comparisons, in nominal terms transfer payments are lower in the PPSS Case, as shown in the table at the bottom of page 402.

As shown, measured in nominal dollars, there is an apparent savings of $442 billion, or 18.1 percent, in transfer payments by 2000 as a result of the PPSS recommendations. However, because the recommendations also lead to an 18.6 percent reduction in total inflation over the 1983–

Transfer Payments and Other Outlays, 1983–2000:
Status Quo of Current Policies vs. PPSS Savings
(Constant 1983 $ Billions)

		(1)	(2)	(3)	(4)	(5)
		Total		Other Outlays		
	Fiscal Year	Transfer Payments	Net Interest	National Defense(a)	All Other Outlays	Total Outlays
(1)	1983	$402.8	$ 87.8	$194.3	$111.0	$ 795.9
Status Quo of Current Policies						
(2)	1985	$415.0	$110.8	$229.6	$106.4	$ 861.8
(3)	1990	523.8	173.0	311.3	111.7	1,119.8
(4)	1995	619.7	250.3	343.1	112.7	1,325.8
(5)	2000	751.2	468.2	367.8	116.3	1,703.5
PPSS Savings						
(6)	1985	$409.3	$104.0	$214.4	$ 93.0	$ 820.7
(7)	1990	492.0	64.7	247.2	66.2	870.1
(8)	1995	617.1	33.5	295.0	59.3	1,004.8
(9)	2000	755.6	28.4	330.6	53.7	1,168.3
Amount PPSS Favorable/(Unfavorable) to Status Quo						
(10)	1985	$ 5.7	$ 6.9	$ 15.2	$ 13.3	$ 41.1
(11)	1990	31.8	108.3	64.1	45.4	249.7
(12)	1995	2.6	216.8	48.1	53.4	321.0
(13)	2000	(4.4)	439.8	37.2	62.6	535.2
Percent PPSS Favorable/(Unfavorable) to Status Quo						
(14)	1985	1.4%	6.2%	6.6%	12.5%	4.8%
(15)	1990	6.1	62.6	20.6	40.7	22.3
(16)	1995	0.4	86.6	14.0	47.4	24.2
(17)	2000	(0.6)	93.9	10.1	53.9	31.4

(a) Military pensions are a transfer payment and, hence, are excluded from national defense outlays in this table.

Transfer Payments, 2000:
Status Quo of Current Policies vs. PPSS Savings
($ Billions)

		(1)	(2)	(3)	(4)
				PPSS (Above)/Below Status Quo	
		Status Quo	PPSS Savings	Amount	%
(1)	Current Dollars	$2,440.0	$1,998.2	$441.8	18.1%
(2)	GNP Deflator (1983 = 100)	324.8	264.5	60.3	18.6
(3)	Constant 1983 Dollars	$ 751.2	$ 755.6	$ (4.4)	(0.6)%

Transfer Payments, 1983–2000:
Status Quo of Current Policies vs. PPSS Savings
(Constant 1983 $ Billions)

	Fiscal Year	(1) Social Security	(2) Railroad Retirement	(3) Civil Service Ret.	(4) Unemployment Assist.	(5) Hospital Insurance	(6) Subtotal	(7) Memo: Revenues	(8) Memo: Surplus/(Deficit)	(9) All Other Transfers	(10) Total Transfers
				Five Specially Funded Social Programs							
(1)	1983	$170.1	$6.2	$20.7	$29.8	$38.7	$265.5	$208.9	$(56.6)	$137.3	$402.8
Status Quo of Current Policies											
(2)	1985	$183.9	$7.0	$21.9	$16.0	$43.7	$272.5	$249.9	$(22.7)	$142.5	$415.0
(3)	1990	245.1	7.2	29.5	17.8	56.1	355.7	300.2	(55.4)	168.2	523.8
(4)	1995	296.7	7.7	35.0	19.3	72.5	431.2	352.9	(78.3)	188.5	619.7
(5)	2000	362.4	8.0	42.3	23.6	94.3	530.6	416.6	(114.0)	220.5	751.2
PPSS Savings											
(6)	1985	$184.9	$6.5	$20.8	$18.5	$42.3	$272.9	$248.1	$(24.9)	$136.3	$409.3
(7)	1990	250.3	5.3	24.0	21.1	49.6	350.2	302.1	(48.1)	141.8	492.0
(8)	1995	334.0	5.5	28.1	24.5	63.9	456.0	357.5	(98.5)	161.1	617.1
(9)	2000	418.8	5.7	34.2	24.6	84.6	568.0	422.9	(145.1)	187.6	755.6
Amount PPSS Favorable/(Unfavorable) to Status Quo											
(10)	1985	$ (1.0)	$0.5	$ 1.2	$(2.5)	$ 1.4	$ (0.4)	$ (1.8)	$ (2.2)	$ 6.1	$ 5.7
(11)	1990	(5.2)	1.9	5.6	(3.3)	6.5	5.5	1.8	7.3	26.4	31.8
(12)	1995	(37.3)	2.2	6.9	(5.2)	8.6	(24.7)	4.6	(20.1)	27.4	2.6
(13)	2000	(56.4)	2.3	8.1	(0.9)	9.6	(37.3)	6.3	(31.1)	32.9	(4.4)
Percent PPSS Favorable/(Unfavorable) to Status Quo											
(14)	1985	(0.5)%	6.9%	5.0%	(15.7)%	3.3%	(0.1)%	(0.7)%	(9.8)%	4.3%	1.4%
(15)	1990	(2.1)	26.2	18.6	(18.3)	11.6	1.5	0.6	13.2	15.7	6.1
(16)	1995	(12.6)	28.6	19.7	(26.7)	11.9	(5.7)	1.3	(25.7)	14.5	0.4
(17)	2000	(15.6)	28.8	19.1	(4.0)	10.2	(7.0)	1.5	(27.2)	14.9	(0.6)

2000 period—equivalent to a 1.2 percentage points per year reduction—the real value of the payments is greater by $4.4 billion, or 0.6 percent.

Other outlays all decline in real terms. As discussed above, net interest is lower by $439.8 billion, or 93.9 percent, and accounts for 82.2 percent of the reduction in total outlays. The savings to National Defense, excluding outlays for military retirement which are included with transfers, are $37.2 billion, or 10.1 percent, while All Other Outlays are lower by $62.6 billion, or 53.9 percent.

The table on page 403 shows details on payments for individuals.

As discussed earlier, Social Security and Unemployment Assistance outlays are higher as a result of the PPSS recommendations because the Government is presumed to follow its traditional policy of increasing payments as its ability to pay increases. Thus, as trust fund revenues increase, so do outlays—although after 1990 they increase more rapidly than revenues, so that the deficit for the five specially funded transfer programs expands from $(114.0) billion (1983 dollars) under the Status Quo (col. 8, line 5) to $(145.1) billion (col. 8, line 9).

Unfunded Payments to Individuals, 1983 and 2000:
Status Quo of Current Policies vs. PPSS Savings
(Constant 1983 $ Billions)

		(1)	(2)	(3)	(4)	(5)
						Ranked
					2000	
					PPSS (Above)/ Below Status Quo	
		1983	Status Quo	PPSS Savings	Amount	%
(1)	Guaranteed Student Loans	$ 2.2	$ 8.6	$ 3.1	$ 5.5	64.3%
(2)	VA Medical Care	7.5	11.0	4.2	6.8	61.8
(3)	Food Stamps	12.2	28.7	23.4	5.3	18.3
(4)	Child Nutrition	3.4	8.3	6.8	1.5	18.3
(5)	Housing Assistance	9.6	15.3	12.9	2.4	15.7
(6)	Federal Employee Retirement & Insurance, Excl. Civil Service	26.7	41.1	36.3	4.7	11.5
(7)	Medicaid	19.1	37.9	34.0	3.9	10.2
(8)	Supplemental Medical Insurance	17.7	28.0	25.1	2.9	10.2
(9)	Other	15.1	7.8	7.1	0.7	9.1
(10)	Public Assistance, etc.	24.3	34.0	34.8	(0.8)	(2.2)
(11)	Total	$137.8	$220.7	$187.7	$32.9	14.9%

The reductions in the other specially funded programs as a result of the PPSS recommendations are projected to range from 19.1 percent in the case of Civil Service Retirement to 29.5 percent for Railroad Retirement Benefits—the smallest of the funded programs. All Other Transfer Programs—i.e., the unfunded ones—are projected to be cut by $32.9 billion, or 14.9 percent. The table on page 404 compares the major unfunded programs.

Guaranteed Student Loans and VA Medical Care are by far the unfunded transfer programs where the greatest percentage savings occur—with outlays lower by 64.3 and 61.8 percent, respectively, as a result of the PPSS recommendations. These two programs also have the largest

Transfer Payments, Interest,
and Personal Income Taxes, 1983–2000:
Status Quo of Current Policies vs. PPSS Savings
(Constant 1983 $ Billions)

	(1)	(2)	(3)	(4)	(5)	(6)
						Federal Contributions to Transfer Programs plus Interest
				Total Interest and Transfer Payments		*As a % of Personal Income Taxes*
Fiscal Year	*Income Taxes*	*Total Transfers*	*Net Interest*		*Amount*	
1983	$288.9	$402.8	$ 87.8	$ 490.6	$281.7	97.5%
·us Quo of Current Policies						
1985	$304.5	$415.0	$110.8	$ 525.9	$276.0	90.6%
1990	379.8	523.8	173.0	696.8	396.5	104.4
1995	446.9	619.7	250.3	870.0	517.2	115.7
2000	495.1	751.2	468.2	1,219.4	802.7	162.1
·S Savings						
1985	$319.9	$409.3	$104.0	$ 513.2	$265.2	82.9%
1990	400.7	492.0	64.7	556.7	254.6	63.5
1995	484.6	617.1	33.5	650.6	293.1	60.5
2000	584.8	755.6	28.4	784.0	361.1	61.7
·ount PPSS Favorable/(Unfavorable) to Status Quo						
1985	$ 15.5	$ 5.7	$ 6.9	$ 12.6	$ 10.8	7.8% pts.
1990	20.9	31.8	108.3	140.1	141.9	40.9
1995	37.7	2.6	216.8	219.5	224.1	55.3
2000	89.8	(4.4)	439.8	435.4	441.6	100.4
·cent PPSS Favorable/(Unfavorable) to Status Quo						
1985	5.1%	1.4%	6.2%	2.4%	3.9%	8.6%
1990	5.5	6.1	62.6	20.1	35.8	39.1
1995	8.4	0.4	86.6	25.2	43.3	47.7
2000	18.1	(0.6)	93.9	35.7	55.0	61.9

dollar savings. Most other programs have savings between 10 and 20 percent, but Public Assistance and Related Payments—including AFDC and SSI—actually increases slightly as a result of the PPSS recommendations. As with Unemployment Compensation, this reflects a higher unemployment rate than under the Status Quo.

The table on page 405 shows the outlook for transfer payments, interest, and personal income taxes.

As shown in the last column, as a result of the PPSS recommendations, Federal contributions to transfer programs plus interest as a percent of Personal Income Taxes are projected at 61.7 percent in 2000—(100.4) percentage points, or (61.9) percent below the Status Quo. By comparison, in 1983 these unproductive Federal expenditures ate up 97.5¢ of every dollar of personal income tax.

VIII.

EXECUTIVE SUMMARIES OF PPSS REPORTS

On June 30, 1982, President Reagan signed Executive Order 12369 formally establishing the President's Private Sector Survey on Cost Control (PPSS). Briefly stated, the President directed PPSS to:

- Identify opportunities for increased efficiency and reduced costs achievable by Executive action or legislation.

- Determine areas where managerial accountability can be enhanced and administrative controls improved.

- Suggest short- and long-term managerial operating improvements.

- Specify areas where further study can be justified by potential savings.

- Provide information and data relating to Governmental expenditures, indebtedness, and personnel management.

To carry out this assignment, the Foundation for the President's Private Sector Survey on Cost Control was established. It formed a Survey Management Office, which organized 36 Task Forces, each of which was co-chaired by two or more members of the Executive Committee. In addition, the Management Office prepared and released 11 Management Office Selected Issues Reports.

Twenty-two of the 36 Task Forces were assigned to study specific departments and agencies, and the remaining 14 studied functions cutting across Government, such as personnel, data processing, and procurement. Management Office Selected Issues Reports focused on those issues which the Task Forces did not have time to address because of limited resources, as well as those issues which, after a review of all Task Force reports, deserved special consideration because of their considerable scope and impact.

A listing of the 36 Task Forces follows:

Agriculture
Air Force
Army
Automated Data Processing/Office Automation
Boards/Commissions—Banking
Boards/Commissions—Business Related
Commerce
Defense—Office of Secretary
Education
Energy (including Federal Energy Regulatory Commission and Nuclear Regulatory Commission)
Environmental Protection Agency/ Small Business Administration/ Federal Emergency Management Agency
Federal Construction Management
Federal Feeding
Federal Hospital Management
Federal Management Systems
Financial Asset Management
Health & Human Services— Department Management/Human Development Services/ACTION

Health & Human Services—Public Health Service/Health Care Financing Administration
Health & Human Services— Social Security Administration
Housing & Urban Development
Interior
Justice
Labor
Land, Facilities, and Personal Property
Low Income Standards and Benefits
Navy
Personnel Management
Privatization
Procurement/Contracts/Inventory Management
Real Property Management
Research and Development
State/AID/USIA
Transportation
Treasury
User Charges
Veterans Administration

Management Office Selected Issues Reports were as follows:

Vol. I: Publishing, Printing, Reproduction, and Audiovisual Activities
Vol. II: Travel and Traffic Management
Vol. III: Financial Management in the Federal Government
Vol. IV: Wage Setting Laws: Impact on the Federal Government
Vol. V: Anomalies in the Federal Work Environment
Vol. VI: Federal Retirement Systems
Vol. VII: Information Gap in the Federal Government
Vol. VIII: The Cost of Congressional Encroachment
Vol. IX: Federal Health Care Costs
Vol. X: Opportunities Beyond PPSS
Vol. XI: Federally Subsidized Programs

Each of the Task Forces prepared a draft report and, with few exceptions, an appendix supporting the recommendations contained in the Task Force report. Those appendices are on file with the Department of Commerce's Central Reference and Records Inspection Facility. It should be noted that recommendations relating to any one Federal agency may be included not only in the appropriate agency Task Force report, but also in the reports of the functional cross-cutting Task Forces, as well as the Management Office Selected Issues Reports.

The Executive Summaries which follow represent the major findings and conclusions contained in each of the Task Force and Management Office Selected Issues Reports. In reviewing the cost saving opportunities identified in the Executive Summaries, it is important to note that cost savings, revenue, and cash acceleration opportunities may duplicate similar opportunities reported in other reports. Thus, there may be instances of double counting of dollar opportunities between reports. These duplications have been netted out in Section III, Volume I of this Report.

PPSS believes that the majority of the recommendations contained in individual reports are fully substantiated. However, it would be misleading to allege that each and every recommendation is rooted in a uniformly high level of research, analysis, and substantiation. Various time limitations, business resources, and other constraints did not permit achievement of the desired uniformity objective.

PPSS has evaluated, therefore, the "supportability" of the recommendations on their management merits and has grouped them into the following three categories.

- Category I   *Fully substantiated and defensible.* Recommendations in this category are, in the opinion of the Task Force, convincing and deserving of prompt implementation.

- Category II   *Substantially documented and supportable.* Recommendations in this category may not be fully rationalized or documented in the report, but all indications point to the desirability and defensibility of proceeding with their implementation.

- Category III *Potentially justifiable and supportable.* Recommendations in this category, while meritorious, are not regarded as fully supported in the report, due to time, personnel resources, and other constraints, but are deemed worthy of further analysis to determine the full extent of their merit.

These category descriptions do not take into account political, social, or economic conditions which may alter the supportability of these recommendations for implementation. *Cost savings and revenue enhancements indicated in the Executive Summaries reflect only those associated with Category I and Category II recommendations.*

Dollar estimates in the reports are based on reasonable and defensible assumptions, including standard three-year projections based on when first, second, and third year partial or full implementation will occur, and not specific fiscal years. Accordingly, estimated savings or revenue opportunities are understandably of a "planning" nature and not of a "budget'' quality. Therefore, the reader should guard against drawing conclusions or making dollar projections based on the disclosures contained only in a given report.

The standard three-year projections of cost savings and revenues include 10 percent inflation in years two and three. On revenue accelerations and cash accelerations, savings are claimed on the interest avoided, which is estimated at 10 percent. These rates reflect generally prevailing rates at the time the Task Force and Management Office Selected Issues Reports were prepared, and the impact of alternative inflation rates has been indicated in the Chairman's letter to the President.

In addition to identifying specific opportunities for cost control and improved efficiency, PPSS sought to identify the appropriate implementation authority for each recommendation. Because of the complexities of the appropriations process, as well as historical precedents, however, further data could result in a change on PPSS-identified authority.

All of the PPSS reports were considered and acted upon in meetings open to the public by a Subcommittee of the Executive Committee of PPSS, along with other statements and recommendations. Written comments submitted by the public, if any, were forwarded to the White House along with the final PPSS reports.

Note: Titles and corporate affiliations of Co-chairs are current as of date of report submission and approval.

Task Force on
The Department of Agriculture*

CO-CHAIRS:	William B. Graham Chairman Baxter Travenol Laboratories, Inc.	*NUMBER OF ISSUES:* 58 *NUMBER OF* *RECOMMENDATIONS:* 154
	William Wood Prince President F. H. Prince & Co., Inc.	*3-YEAR* *COST SAVINGS:* $12.237 ($ billions)
PROJECT *MANAGER:*	Clifton B. Cox Chairman of the Board Cox, Lloyd Associates, Ltd.	*3-YEAR* *REVENUE GENERATION:* $.606 ($ billions)
NUMBER OF *TASK FORCE* *MEMBERS:* 27		*3-YEAR* *CASH ACCELERATION:* $5.846 ($ billions)

* The U.S. District Court found that certain of the Task Force's recommendations exceeded the authority of the Executive Committee.

Overview

The U.S. Department of Agriculture (USDA) assists farmers by providing research, credit, insurance, price supports, production and market information, and marketing assistance. USDA also assists consumers with nutritional information, regulations on safety and health, and food for low-income persons. In FY 1983, USDA outlays were approximately $45.0 billion and Department employees totaled approximately 112,000.

The principal focus of the Task Force's effort was on management and administrative operations at USDA. The scope and magnitude of many USDA programs, however, necessarily led the Task Force to consider the extent to which inefficiency and duplication in the underlying policies and programs affect operations.

Issues and Recommendations

The Task Force studied 58 issues and formulated recommendations which could result in cost savings of $12.237 billion, revenue generation of $606 million, and cash acceleration of $5.846 billion over a three-year period, resulting in a 10 percent reduction in annual outlays. In addition, over $8 billion of Government lending would be transferred to the private sector, reducing the Government risk of losses and its need to enter credit markets.

Farmers Home Administration—The Farmers Home Administration (FmHA) administers loan and grant programs to rural Americans. FmHA has grown exponentially in the number of borrowers and outstanding loans. More than 55 percent of the agency's outstanding loans are to nonfarm borrowers.

Due to program growth and diversification, FmHA has not adequately met the needs of farmers, and an overall delinquency rate of 43 percent has developed in the farm loan programs. Task Force recommendations would result in cost savings of $1.342 billion, revenue generation of $141.4 million, and cash acceleration of $821.0 million over a three-year period and included improving management information systems, upgrading the quality and management of the loan portfolio, and transferring the FmHA housing function to the Department of Housing and Urban Development.

Food and Nutrition Service—USDA's Food and Nutrition Service (FNS) administers food assistance to families and children in cooperation with state and local governments, and includes the Food Stamp Program and the National School Lunch, School Breakfast, and Summer Food Programs. FNS expenditures account for over 50 percent of USDA's budget. The Task Force found that Congress has specified operating practices that prevent programs from evolving with economic changes and recommended updating the Thrifty Food Plan, adjusting economies-of-scale used in determination of food stamp allotments, and reducing overlaps between child nutrition benefits and food stamp benefits.

Task Force recommendations, when implemented, will result in cost savings of $6.739 billion over a three-year period.

Foreign and Domestic Commodity Programs—Farm price support programs have resulted in record production and stocks at a time of stagnant domestic and world demand. They have weakened the U.S. farmer's competitive position, diminished the viability of the family-owned farm, and committed funds well beyond projections.

Task Force recommendations are estimated to result in cost savings of $1.897 billion over a three-year period. These included eliminating USDA commodity donations to other Government agencies and the requirement that 50 percent of P.L. 480 commodity shipments be carried on U.S. flag vessels. The Task Force also recommended further study of the general area of price supports.

Forest Service—The Forest Service, with over 190 million acres and 42,000 employees, posted losses of $1.0 billion in FY 1983. To offset this deficit, the Task Force recommended initiatives with projected cost savings of $1.038 billion, revenue generation of $404.4 million, and cash acceleration of $4.725 billion over a three-year period.

Task Force recommendations included changes in timber sales; increased recreation and grazing fees; reductions in staff, construction, and research activities; and implementation of a flat payment schedule for selected USDA goods and services where market conditions permit a realistic test.

Rural Electrification Administration—Electricity and telephones are now available to 99 percent of rural America. Yet, the Rural Electrification Administration is still making low-interest loans.

Task Force recommendations included reductions in generation and transmission loans, Government financing of cooperatives, and USDA regulations.

Projected cost savings of these recommendations are $102.6 million, with revenue generation of $33.1 million and cash acceleration of $300.0 million over a three-year period.

Other—The Task Force also examined other relatively small but important opportunities for cost savings and revenue generation (duplication in meat, dairy, and poultry inspection requirements; changes in county office structure; and reductions in USDA research activities) which are estimated to yield $1.146 billion in cost savings and $27.4 million in revenue in the first three years of implementation.

Implementation

Of the 154 Task Force recommendations, 94 (61 percent) are within the purview of USDA, 17 (11 percent) involve Presidential action, and 43 (28 percent) will need Congressional approval.

Task Force on
The Department of the Air Force

CO-CHAIRS:	James H. Evans Chairman and CEO Union Pacific Corp.	*NUMBER OF ISSUES:*	22
	Robert W. Galvin Chairman and CEO Motorola, Inc.	*NUMBER OF* *RECOMMENDATIONS:*	50
	Paul F. Oreffice President and CEO Dow Chemical Co.	*3-YEAR* *COST SAVINGS:* ($ billions) Air Force Budget	$12.523
PROJECT *MANAGER:*	Charles L. Eaton Senior Vice President Union Pacific Corp.	Other Agency Budgets Total Savings	$15.080 $27.603
NUMBER OF *TASK FORCE* *MEMBERS:*	36		

Overview

The mission of the Air Force as part of the Department of Defense (DOD) is to deter war and, if deterrence fails, to employ air power effectively to assist in concluding any conflict on terms favorable to the United States. In 1983, the Air Force employed 812,056 people and maintained and operated a fleet of 9,180 aircraft. Its FY 1983 budget was approximately $78.4 billion.

The Task Force focused on inefficiencies associated with the implementation of policy, not the shaping of policy. Improvements in management and operating procedures were seen as opportunities to help reduce budget deficits, fund additions to America's defense system, and finance other high priority nondefense programs.

Issues and Recommendations

The Task Force examined 22 specific issues and made 50 recommendations broadly grouped into four categories. Three-year projected cost savings totaled $27.603 billion, of which $12.523 billion pertains directly to the Department of the Air Force.

Pay, Personnel, and Retirement—The Task Force concluded the Air Force retirement system is too liberal in its benefit provisions. For example, officers who retired in 1972 receive more retirement pay today than officers of the same rank on active duty. The Task Force identified opportunities to reduce DOD retirement costs paid to Air Force retirees by an estimated $4.550 billion annually. Cost savings would be reflected in the DOD budget.

The Task Force also found that current Air Force severance pay far exceeds that of the private sector and that, unlike the private sector, Federal employees receive full salary as well as military pay while on annual Air Guard/Reserve active duty. The Task Force recommended that Air Force severance pay be adjusted to more closely reflect private sector practices and that Federal employees receive either full Federal pay or Air Guard/Reserve active duty pay, whichever is higher.

Total three-year cost savings from all recommendations pertaining to pay, personnel, and retirement issues amount to $15.271 billion.

Financial Management—The Air Force has no periodic, formal, high-level review of spending performance against budget commitments despite its sophisticated Planning, Programming, and Budget System (PPBS) and Program Objective Memorandum (POM). To correct the accounting problems and eliminate duplicate efforts, the Task Force recommended that funds be appropriated on an accrual basis and that the program and budget reviews be consolidated. The Task Force also recommended that the Comptroller's Office be reduced in size and that per diem travel expenses be revised.

Implementation of these recommendations would result in cost savings of $1.213 billion over a three-year period.

Procurement, Contracting, and Weapons Systems Acquisition—In general, the Task Force found that additional costs were imposed on the Air Force by the Davis-Bacon, Walsh-Healey, and Service Contract Acts, which contain provisions outdated by social and economic trends. Repeal or amendment could reduce costs significantly, increase competition, and improve productivity. The Task Force also recommended improvements in the Small Business Act dealing with awarding of Section 8(a) contracts to economically and socially disadvantaged small firms.

Based on its analysis of specific procurement practices, the Task Force recommended a formal weapons systems acquisition process which allows for selection of spare parts contractors and increasing the use of multiyear procurement. The Task Force also emphasized the cost advantages of dual sourcing between contractors and awarding production quantities on the basis of product quality and cost.

Although the Air Force leads other agencies in contracting out and implementation of OMB Circular A-76, the Task Force found it nonetheless did not fully implement the FY 1983 objectives for contracting out and that it lacked effective controls and uniform management of OMB Circular A-120, which regulates the procurement of consulting, research, management, and advisory services. Concerted compliance with these two directives and the implementation of internal controls would result in improved cost savings.

Implementation of all Task Force recommendations in the procurement area would result in three-year cost savings of $10.307 billion.

Organizational Management—The Task Force identified improvements related to travel, automated data processing (ADP) systems at the

Air Force Logistics Command (AFLC), and consolidation of the Air Reserve and Air National Guard. Three-year cost savings of $69.5 million could result by simplifying travel reimbursement procedures, levying fines for no-shows, and requiring non-DOD agencies to use Military Air Command (MAC) overseas services and to negotiate additional route discounts with U.S. flag carriers. With respect to AFLC and its inventory of 900,000 items, the Task Force projected that three-year net savings of $580.6 million would occur by implementing a comprehensive ADP modernization program. Finally, preliminary review of Air National Guard and Air Reserve facilities and overall operations indicated potential three-year cost savings of $163.8 million.

Implementation

Of the 50 recommendations formulated by the Task Force, 12 are within the authority of the Agency, 2 require Presidential involvement, and 36 will need Congressional approval.

**Task Force on
The Department of the Army**

CO-CHAIRS:	Roger E. Birk Chairman, President, and CEO Merrill Lynch & Co., Inc.	*NUMBER OF ISSUES:* 21 *NUMBER OF* *RECOMMENDATIONS:* 78
	John L. Horan Chairman Merck & Co., Inc.	*3-YEAR* *COST SAVINGS:* $13.400* ($ billions)
	William A. Marguard Chairman, President, and CEO American Standard Inc.	* Includes $.692 billion in cost savings which will accrue to the Department of Defense, rather than to the Department of the Army.
	Lewis T. Preston Chairman Morgan Guaranty Trust Co. of New York	
PROJECT MANAGER:	Richard H. Francis Vice President and Chief Financial Officer American Standard Inc.	
NUMBER OF TASK FORCE MEMBERS:	51	

The Department of the Army was created to contribute to the deterrence of warfare and, if deterrence fails, to contribute to concluding any conflict on terms favorable to the United States. In FY 1983, the Army had a budget of approximately $60 billion and over 1,785,000 full-time Government employees.

The Task Force identified several key factors that affect the Army's ability to carry out its mission, including: Army tradition; the issue of combat readiness; transition to high technology; management structure; visibility to outside experts; accountability to Congress, including the annual budget process; and Administration control vs. policy management.

Issues and Recommendations

The Task Force studied 21 issues from which 78 specific recommendations were formulated. These recommendations are projected to result in cost savings of $13.4 billion over three years, including savings of $692 million that will accrue to the Department of Defense (DOD) rather than to the Department of the Army. Recommendations were broadly grouped into three areas: personnel, materiel, and administrative management.

Personnel—In FY 1983, personnel compensation by the Army totaled $17.5 billion or 29 percent of its FY 1983 budget. In its review of Army personnel policies, the Task Force found that Army training programs and their requirements are not adequately coordinated, resulting in underutilization and shortages of trained personnel in designated skill areas. Certain personnel policies, including family moves in European tours, 20-year retirement, and "up-or-out" promotion systems; regimental rotation; staffing of mandated programs; and use of learning resource centers were found to foster inefficient use of resources.

To redress identified deficiencies in the Army's personnel systems, the Task Force recommended improved procedures in the recruitment, training, and assignment of new enlistees; an increase in the length of overseas tours for new enlistees, as well as for accompanied and unaccompanied officers; and a reduction in family moves related to overseas tours. The Task Force also recommended that the Army study options for modifying the current "up-or-out" retirement policy, as well as the retirement system as a whole, and recommended changes in the current accrued annual leave policy.

Implementation of these recommendations would result in better management and improved efficiency of personnel resources, with projected cost savings of $1.293 billion over a three-year period.

Materiel—During the next four years, it is expected that the Army will spend more than $100 billion to acquire modern weapons and meet its readiness goals. In its review of the Army's weapons procurement and management programs, the Task Force found that failure to incorporate realistic cost estimates in the budget of major weapons systems results in the postponement of difficult affordability decisions and creates instability in the Army's procurement programs. The Task Force also found that the storage of idle equipment is excessive, with 30–40 percent of stored weaponry inoperable or obsolete, and that war reserve inventories are poorly designed and managed.

Accordingly, the Task Force recommended that the Army incorporate cost growth data and sound technical management in new weapons system decision-making and that the cost of equipment storage and the size of war reserve stockpiles be reduced by eliminating unnecessary items and contracting with private vendors. The Task Force also identified cost control opportunities which would result from identifying and selling excess real estate, improving the maintenance of combat vehicles, and modernizing and streamlining the Corps of Engineers.

Implementation of these recommendations is projected to result in cost savings of $10.262 billion over a three-year period, of which $692 million will accrue to DOD rather than to the Department of the Army.

Administrative Management—In its analysis of Army support services, the Task Force found them to be neglected relative to combat-related activities, resulting in the use of obsolete and inefficient systems when new, cost-effective administrative support systems are available. To provide more cost-effective management support, the Task Force recommended that the Army modernize management equipment and coordinate its application, particularly in the areas of data processing, cost containment programs, and cash management.

Implementation of these recommendations would result in cost savings of $1.845 billion over a three-year period.

Implementation

Of the 78 Task Force recommendations, 52 (67 percent) fall within the implementation authority of the Department of the Army and 26 (33 percent) require Congressional action. Congressional influence is felt acutely in the review of Army budgeting processes where policy-making occurs through control of national budget allocations. For the most part, recommendations aimed at reorganizing personnel and management systems can be implemented directly by the Army. Those recommendations which fall under Congressional purview involve increasing funding, revision of public law, or approval of extensive reorganization across agency boundaries.

Task Force on
Automated Data Processing/Office Automation

CO-CHAIRS:	William Agee Former Chairman Bendix Corp.	*NUMBER OF ISSUES:* 18
	Joseph Alibrandi President and CEO Whittaker Corp.	*NUMBER OF* *RECOMMENDATIONS:* 58 *3-YEAR* *COST SAVINGS:** $19.063
	Donald E. Procknow President Western Electric Co., Inc.	($ billions) * *Note:* In addition to specific cost savings opportunities, the Task Force also identified
PROJECT *MANAGER:*	John K. Kerr President Medicus Systems Corp.	ADP/OA recommendations in other PPSS reports that would result in additional three- year cost savings/revenue generation/cash acceleration of $11.316 billion.
NUMBER OF *TASK FORCE* *MEMBERS:* 42		

Overview

With over 17,000 computers and a work force of more than 250,000, Federal automated data processing operations dwarf those of even the largest private sector users. Key legislation involving Federal automated data processing/office automation (ADP/OA) operations include the Brooks Act (P.L. 89–306) and the Paperwork Reduction Act (P.L. 96–511), both of which require the Office of Management and Budget (OMB) to develop a policy for the Government's management of information.

Issues and Recommendations

As a result of its review, the Task Force formulated 58 recommendations which, when fully implemented, will result in three-year cost savings of $19.063 billion. The Task Force also prepared a compendium issue of ADP-related recommendations contained in other PPSS reports which result in additional three-year cost savings/revenue generation/cash acceleration totaling $11.316 billion.

Administrative Management—The Federal Government has failed to develop a coherent system for ADP planning and management and, as a result, has not capitalized on substantial opportunities for cost savings and improved effectiveness. The Task Force recommended that the position of Federal Information Resource Manager (FIRM) be established within the PPSS-recommended Office of Federal Management to oversee ADP/OA throughout the Government. Serving as a Presidential appointee, the FIRM would be responsible for establishing and chairing a Government-wide Information Technology Steering Committee, which would be the primary body for establishing Federal goals and directives in ADP, developing short- and long-term plans for upgrading information technology, and addressing the challenges and opportunities posed by emerging new technologies. The Task Force also recommended that a qualified Senior Executive Service career professional oversee ADP/OA management in each department or agency.

Precise quantification of savings from management recommendations is difficult, if not impossible. However, the magnitude of savings will outweigh any requisite resource allocation.

Resource Management—The average age of Government computers is six to seven years, almost twice the private sector experience, which requires many of them to be maintained by specially trained Federal personnel rather than the manufacturer. Upgrading Government ADP systems or replacing them with current technology would reduce operating expenses, enhance revenue collection, and facilitate sharing technical resources. To address this problem, each department and agency should examine the obsolescence of its ADP operations, how well these operations serve the agency mission, and available means of consolidating and enhancing the ADP systems within the agency. Implementation of Task Force recommendations in the area of resource management would result in three-year savings of $4.030 billion.

In reviewing teleprocessing (TP) activities, the Task Force found that TP costs generally are not clearly identified apart from overall telecommunications costs and are not allocated to end users. The Task Force recommended that OMB Circular A-121 on TP policies and procedures be amended to require more precise delineation of TP expenditures. Implementation of Task Force recommendations would result in three-year cost savings of $517.0 million.

In assessing the Government's management of OA resources, the Task Force recommended improved management of OA and stressed its use by managerial/professional personnel. It found that individual agencies suffer from one or more of the following OA problems: procurement of duplicate and/or incompatible systems; underused OA equipment; fragmented planning and procurement; focus on clerical rather than professional staff; and no inventory of existing OA equipment to allow coordination with new procurements.

Task Force recommendations to address these problems included requiring departments to prepare annual OA plans and status reports and asking GAO to perform independent reviews, and would result in three-year savings of $6.537 billion.

Personnel Recruitment and Management—Central to the Task Force's recommendations was the need to improve salaries and hiring procedures for ADP personnel. Government ADP salaries, work environment, and technical sophistication are currently insufficient to attract the quantity and quality of ADP personnel needed. For example, applicants with college degrees in computer fields typically are hired by the Government at a starting salary of $12,854. Entry-level ADP positions in the private sector frequently pay in excess of $20,000. Government salaries at the upper levels are now 25 percent below those of the private sector.

Although the Task Force did not attempt to quantify specific savings, it was convinced that problems in ADP resource allocation and management cannot be resolved without attracting and retaining high quality personnel.

Agency-Specific Recommendations—In addition to its Government-wide recommendations, the Task Force studied in-depth ten agency-specific issues and prepared a compendium consisting of an additional 49 issues contained in other PPSS reports. Three-year cost savings from the ten in-depth agency-specific issues total $7.979 billion, with the compendium accounting for an additional $11.316 billion in three-year cost savings/revenue generation/cash acceleration. Recommendations at the agency-specific level included increased use of ADP systems at the Customs Service, Internal Revenue Service, and Department of Defense; consolidation of ADP activities at the Department of Transportation, Environmental Protection Agency, and Health Care Financing Administration; and improved systems management procedures at the Department of the Army, Department of Transportation, and Health Care Financing Administration.

Implementation

Of the 57 major Task Force-specific recommendations (excluding the compendium), 43 (75 percent) can be implemented directly by Agency officials, 10 (18 percent) will require Presidential action, and 4 (7 percent) will require Congressional authorization.

Task Force on
Boards/Commissions—Banking

CO-CHAIRS:	Fletcher L. Byrom Retired Chairman Koppers Co., Inc.	*NUMBER OF ISSUES:* 41
	John H. Tyler McConnell Chairman and CEO Delaware Trust Co.	*NUMBER OF RECOMMENDATIONS:* 84
	Robert T. Powers Chairman Nalco Chemical Co.	*3-YEAR COST SAVINGS:* $1.617 ($ billions)
PROJECT MANAGER:	Donald R. Caldwell Executive Vice President and COO Atlantic Financial Federal	*3-YEAR REVENUE GENERATION:* $7.782 ($ billions) *3-YEAR CASH ACCELERATION:* $ .554 ($ billions)
NUMBER OF TASK FORCE MEMBERS: 34		

Overview

The Task Force reviewed 13 agencies associated with banking and investment: the five financial industry regulatory bodies—the Federal Reserve System (Bank Regulation Section only), the Office of Comptroller of the Currency, the Federal Deposit Insurance Corporation, the Federal Home Loan Bank Board, and the National Credit Union Administration; the three secondary mortgage-related agencies—Federal National Mortgage Association (FNMA), Government National Mortgage Association, and the Federal Home Loan Mortgage Corporation; as well as the Farm Credit Administration; the Pension Benefit Guaranty Corporation; the Railroad Retirement Board; the U.S. Synthetic Fuels Corporation; and the Export-Import Bank.

The overall objective was to identify opportunities for cost control and improved management effectiveness. The Task Force also sought to (1) generate revenue where it appeared a group was receiving favored status, and (2) decrease the overall burden of Government that the regulatory approaches represent.

Issues and Recommendations

The Task Force reviewed 41 issue areas and made 84 recommendations. These recommendations would result in three-year cost savings of $1.617

billion, revenue generation of $7.782 billion, and cash acceleration of $554.3 million.

The single most significant suggestion was the privatization of the quasi-governmental agencies which retain special privileges such as favored tax status (except FNMA) and the ability to borrow either from the Federal Financial Bank (FFB), the Treasury, or in the public markets with agency status. The Task Force recommended that such quasi-private bodies be subject to some form of income tax; a user charge on borrowing with agency status or from the FFB or the Treasury; and a restriction on investment alternatives to Treasury obligations to eliminate any opportunity for arbitrage.

Other principal findings and recommendations, grouped by principal agency, follow.

Pension Benefit Guaranty Corporation (PBGC)—The Task Force identified an inadequacy in premium levels, loopholes in Title IV of the Employees Retirement Insurance Security Act (ERISA), and the need for accelerated collection of insurance premiums and effective administration of pension plans. Task Force recommendations included increasing single-employer premiums to $6, amending ERISA to prevent abusive claims and adverse selection, accelerating and improving premium collection, and developing a risk-related premium structure.

Implementation of these recommendations would result in three-year cost savings of $84.2 million, revenue generation of $3.651 billion, and cash acceleration of $262.0 million.

Export-Import Bank (Eximbank)—Opportunities exist for reducing Eximbank's exposure and costs by promoting private sector involvement in export credit insurance, reviewing interior rate structures and avoiding exposure to interest rate fluctuations, reducing space usage, and establishing formal management planning. Although savings were quantified only for space utilization ($1.6 million over three years), significant management efficiencies could result from all recommendations.

Railroad Retirement Board (RRB)—The RRB has two principal components: a private pension/unemployment program, which has a $30 billion unfunded liability, and a separately administered social security system. The former should be privatized and the latter be turned over to the Social Security Administration. The Task Force also recommended an increase in tax rates, a reduction in benefits, the placing of Medicare beneficiaries under the Health Care Financing Administration, and the restructuring of disability programs. Implementation would result in three-year cost savings of $1.375 billion, revenue generation of $2.319 billion, and cash acceleration of $259.0 million.

Federal Reserve System (FRS), Office of Comptroller of the Currency (OCC), the Federal Deposit Insurance Corporation (FDIC), the Federal Home Loan Bank Board (FHLBB), and the National Credit Union Administration (NCUA)—The Task Force identified the need for more uniform and systematic policies and procedures, as well as structural changes in the regulatory system itself. Specifically, it called for consolidating the regulatory arm of FRS, OCC, and FDIC on the grounds that, with minor exceptions, their mission is the same, differing only in the corporate structure of the banks they regulate.

Task Force recommendations called for the FHLBB system to be charged a user fee for its agency status, a limit on district bank investments to Treasury obligations, and a reduction in the number of district banks. Recommendations stressed the need also to re-evaluate the tax-exempt status of credit unions.

Implementation of recommendations pertaining to the regulatory bodies would result in three-year cost savings of $136.8 million, revenue generation of $379.0 million, and cash acceleration of $33.3 million.

Federal National Mortgage Association (FNMA), Federal Home Loan Mortgage Corporation (FHLMC), and Government National Mortgage Association (GNMA)—The Task Force recommended the elimination of FHLMC's Federal tax exemption, the establishment of a fee for use of agency status by FNMA and FHLMC, a phasing-out by GNMA of the FNMA servicing of the Mortgage Backed Securities Program, and an increase in GNMA fees. Implementation of these recommendations would result in three-year cost savings of $0.4 million and revenue generation of $61.0 million.

Farm Credit Administration (FCA)—The Task Force called for elimination of the Federal tax exemption for certain entities of the Farm Credit System and, based on its review of FCA, establishing a Government-wide fee for use of agency status. Implementation would result in revenue generation of $1.372 billion over a three-year period.

U.S. Synthetic Fuels Corporation (SFC)—As a result of its survey of SFC, the Task Force concluded that administrative expenses could be reduced via a more efficient use of personnel resources and by changing to an "outreach type" procurement process. Three-year cost savings from such an approach would be $18.2 million.

Implementation

Of the 84 recommendations formulated by the Task Force, 34 (41 percent) are within the purview of the agencies, 2 (2 percent) involve Presidential action, and 48 (57 percent) require Congressional approval.

**Task Force on
Boards/Commissions—Business**

CO-CHAIRS:	George H. Dixon President First Bank System, Inc.	*NUMBER OF TASK FORCE MEMBERS:* 84
	Edward Donley Chairman and CEO Air Products and Chemicals, Inc.	*NUMBER OF ISSUES:* 96 *NUMBER OF RECOMMENDATIONS:* 289
	Robert A. Pritzker President The Marmon Group, Inc.	*3-YEAR COST SAVINGS:* $2.367 ($ billions)
	John M. Regan, Jr. Chairman and CEO Marsh & McLennan Companies, Inc.	*3-YEAR REVENUE GENERATION:* $ .929 ($ billions)
	Thomas I. Storrs Chairman NCNB Corp.	*3-YEAR CASH ACCELERATION:* $ .034 ($ billions)
	Rawleigh Warner, Jr. Chairman and CEO Mobil Corp.	
PROJECT MANAGER:	William Duggan, Jr. Vice President Marsh & McLennan Companies, Inc.	

Overview

The Boards and Commissions Business Task Force studied the U.S. Postal Service, the Tennessee Valley Authority, eight business-oriented regulatory commissions—the Civil Aeronautics Board, Commodity Futures Trading Commission, Consumer Product Safety Commission, Federal Communications Commission, Federal Maritime Commission, Federal Trade Commission, Interstate Commerce Commission, and Occupational Safety and Health Review Commission—and selected Federal insurance programs. Task Force recommendations to improve the operations of the business-related boards and commissions are agency or program specific and focus on human resource management, fiscal management and control, organizational management, and automated data processing (ADP).

The Task Force studied 96 issue areas and formulated 289 recommendations which, when fully implemented, will result in cost savings of $2.367 billion, revenue generation of $929.0 million, and cash acceleration of $33.5 million over a three-year period.

U.S. Postal Service (USPS)—Changes in planning, organizational structure, and systems could produce significant cost savings and management efficiencies at USPS. Specifically, USPS needs improved use of hurdle rates in working capital investment decisions; the development of a comprehensive human resources plan; and the establishment of centralized organizations for marketing, procurement, and transportation.

Although the Task Force found most aspects of USPS financial operations to be sound, borrowing restrictions, cash management practices, and erosion of equity have weakened USPS's financial position. Given that 84 percent of USPS operating expenses are personnel related, recommendations were offered in the use of overtime and sick leave, comprehensive personnel planning to ensure the proper skills mix, and greater involvement of postal workers in Postal Service decisions. The Task Force called for USPS to devote more attention to product management, account management, new product research, and increased internal and external marketing to improve acceptance of the ZIP+4 program, presort programs, central delivery, and other special services.

Implementation of Task Force recommendations pertaining to USPS would result in three-year cost savings of $2.031 billion, revenue generation of $369.8 million, and cash acceleration of $23.5 million.

Tennessee Valley Authority (TVA)—As a result of its review of the TVA, the Task Force recommended elimination of duplications within the Office of Engineering Design and Construction, reductions in personnel support staff, improved efficiencies in generating plants and related support systems, and changes in compensation and benefit plans. The Task Force also recommended a three-year phase-in of user charges for services currently provided under the National Fertilizer Development Center program.

Implementation of the above recommendations would result in three-year cost savings of $214.0 million and revenue generation of $83.8 million.

Regulatory Commissions—The Task Force formulated over 100 recommendations calling for changes in the organization, systems, and staffing levels of the regulatory commissions, particularly in light of recent Government regulatory reforms. Recommendations included changes in personnel management, improved cost accounting systems, consolidation of offices, streamlined adjudicatory and rule-making processes, and the institution of user fees.

Implementation of Task Force recommendations pertaining to regulatory commissions would result in three-year cost savings of $27.6 million and revenue generation of $178.0 million.

Federal Insurance Programs—The Task Force recommended relating insurance premiums to risk, thereby building reserves against catastrophic loss; using guaranteed loans rather than direct lending; and abandoning certain Federal reinsurance practices. Program-related recommendations included the phasing out of certain insurance programs which, in the view of the Task Force, should be left to the private sector; increasing premiums; and improving financial management and personnel systems.

Insurance program changes would produce cost savings of $93.9 million, revenue generation of $297.4 million, and cash acceleration of $10 million over three years.

Implementation

Of the 289 recommendations made by the Task Force, 232 (80 percent) can be implemented by the respective boards and commissions, 6 (2 percent) require Presidential action, and 51 (18 percent) need Congressional approval.

**Task Force on
The Department of Commerce**

CO-CHAIRS:	Amory Houghton, Jr. Chairman and CEO Corning Glass Works	*NUMBER OF ISSUES:* 12
	Robert V. Van Fossan Chairman and CEO Mutual Benefit Life Insurance Co.	*NUMBER OF RECOMMENDATIONS:* 29
		3-YEAR COST SAVINGS: $.259 ($ billions)
PROJECT MANAGER:	George B. Bennett Chairman Braxton Associates	*3-YEAR REVENUE GENERATION:* $.471 ($ billions)
NUMBER OF TASK FORCE MEMBERS: 27		*3-YEAR CASH ACCELERATION:* $.015 ($ billions)

The Department of Commerce (DOC) encourages, serves, and promotes the nation's international trade, economic growth, and technological advancement, and fosters the national interest through a competitive free enterprise system. In FY 1983, it had a staff of 34,000 and a budget of approximately $1.4 billion. Included within the Department are the International Trade Administration (ITA), the Bureau of the Census, the Economic Development Administration (EDA), the Patent and Trademark Office (PTO), the National Bureau of Standards (NBS), and the National Oceanic and Atmospheric Administration (NOAA).

Although the Secretary of Commerce and his staff are making important efforts to reduce waste and inefficiency, opportunities exist for improvement. The Task Force also concluded that the Department's role in the formulation and implementation of domestic and international economic policy is an issue of critical importance.

Issues and Recommendations

The Task Force studied 12 issues and formulated 29 recommendations which, when fully implemented, will result in cost savings of $259.0 million, revenue generation of $471.0 million, and cash acceleration of $15 million over a three-year period.

The Task Force identified five areas of opportunity: organizational and human resources management, research and development, procurement of equipment and automated data processing (ADP) systems, financial management, and revenue generation and privatization.

Organization and Human Resources Management—The Task Force focused particular attention on the need to reorganize as well as restructure staff and staff operations in ITA so as to achieve a substantial gain in overall effectiveness while significantly reducing the budget allocated to its activities. Specific recommendations included integrating the Office of Trade Development and the U.S. Commercial Service into a single organization structured around industry sectors; integrating the functions of the International Economic Policy Group and the Foreign Commercial Service into a single organization responsible for developing country-specific and multilateral trade policies and negotiating positions from a Washington, D.C. base; and appointing a Presidential Task Force to develop a restructuring plan and implementation schedule for the recommended reorganization. Implementation of the Task Force's recommendations would result in three-year cost savings of $68.3 million.

Other organizational and human resources management recommendations focused on the NBS and Patent Office. With respect to the NBS, the Task Force recommended increasing the ratio of technicians to professionals in NBS laboratories, using more university students as NBS technicians, and developing a system for private sector evaluation of NBS. Task Force recommendations pertaining to the PTO called for a reduction in the proposed PTO hiring goals and increasing instead the use of industrial engineering techniques to reduce patent pendency time. Implementation of the Task Force recommendations would result in three-year cost savings of $9.4 million.

Research and Development Activities—NBS managers must contend with several sources of policy direction from within the Government, with resulting confusion over the expansion of NBS program activity beyond traditional areas of measurement science. Reasonably so, the NBS technically trained staff is not capable of independent assessment of the appropriateness of NBS research activity based solely upon technical explanations. To remedy this problem, the Task Force proposed that a three-year review process and a private sector Project Evaluation Committee be established. Implementation of the Task Force recommendations would result in cost savings of $45.0 million.

Procurement of Equipment and Automated Data Processing Systems —The Census Bureau's present plan for information technology improvements is estimated to cost $95.3 million through FY 1988. It is recognized that the agency needs to take advantage of new computer technology and provide greater automation and integration of various operations. After reviewing the Census Bureau's plan, however, the Task Force concluded that the proposed procurement is too large in scope and includes unnecessary costs. The Task Force also found planned equipment procurements for the PTO excessive.

Based on its review, the Task Force recommended adopting an alternative procurement plan for the Census Bureau, reassessing work station needs for the PTO, and ranking technology projects according to cost/benefit analysis results.

Implementation of the Task Force recommendations would result in cost savings of $14.8 million over a three-year period.

Financial Management—EDA is responsible for ten different grant, loan, and loan guarantee programs. The Task Force studied the Public Works Program, a collection of four grant programs, and found that of $3.5 billion in grants, over $600 million in grant projects have not been completed. The Task Force also found a delinquent loan rate of 41 percent in 1981. To redress this situation, the Task Force recommendations included separating EDA credit granting and collection functions, formalizing debt collection procedures, improving pre- and post-approval financial analysis, and returning loan approval authority to regions.

Implementation of Task Force recommendations pertaining to EDA would result in three-year cost savings of $63.3 million and cash acceleration of $15.0 million.

Revenue Generation and Privatization—The Task Force also examined the possibility of NOAA's recovering a substantial portion of the Government's investment in civilian land remote sensing satellite systems (LANDSAT) and the phasing out of the NOAA Weather Radio Program. The Task Force recommended that the Government sell LANDSAT data and pricing rights and eliminate Federal funding for the NOAA Weather Radio Program.

Implementation of these recommendations would result in cost savings of $58.0 million and revenue generation of $471.0 million over a three-year period.

Implementation

Of the 29 recommendations made by the Task Force, 24 (83 percent) can be implemented by the Agency, 3 (10 percent) require Presidential action, and 2 (7 percent) need Congressional approval.

Task Force on
The Office of the Secretary of Defense

CO-CHAIRS:	Robert A. Beck Chairman and CEO The Prudential Insurance Company of America	*NUMBER OF* *TASK FORCE* *MEMBERS:* 40

	Carter L. Burgess
	Chairman, Executive
	  Committee
	Foreign Policy
	  Association
		NUMBER OF ISSUES: 40
		
		NUMBER OF
		RECOMMENDATIONS: 73

	James E. Burke Chairman and CEO Johnson & Johnson	*3-YEAR* *COST SAVINGS:* $44.508 ($ billions)
	Carl D. Covitz President Landmark Communities, Inc.	*3-YEAR* *REVENUE GENERATION:* $.248 ($ billions)
PROJECT *MANAGER:*	William H. Tremayne Vice President The Prudential Insurance Company of America	

Overview

The mission of the Department of Defense (DOD) is to deter war and, if deterrence fails, to conclude any conflict on terms favorable to the United States. All functions in DOD and its component agencies are performed under the direction of the Office of the Secretary of Defense (OSD). DOD's estimated obligational authority for FY 1983 was $239.4 billion. DOD employs two million military personnel and has approximately one million civilian employees—more than any other free world organization.

Management of DOD is an awesome task, which is compounded by the fact that the military Services never really believed that central management by the Secretary of Defense was needed. In addition, Congress often restricts DOD's management prerogatives, subjecting weapon choices, base deployment, and other major management decisions to political pressures.

Issues and Recommendations

The Task Force focused on 40 key issues and formulated 73 recommendations which would result in cost savings of $44.508 billion and revenue generation of $248.2 million over a three-year period.

Logistics—Logistics issues involve the acquisition of goods for the field, the transportation of goods and people, and base operations and support. The Task Force found Service predilection for full control of logistics pertaining to that Service, resulting in duplication of central staff support, failure to take advantage of the economic benefits of large volume orders, and costly functional and geographic overlap.

Significant cost saving opportunities in inventory management, base support, base realignment, and contracting out were identified by the Task Force, which recommended improved traffic procedures and depot operations, demilitarization of ammunition, and the reduction of military bases and support services for bases. Implementation would result in three-year cost savings of $11.996 billion.

Weapons Procurement—In the area of weapons procurement, the Task Force found a need for DOD to modernize and streamline the acquisition process. Specific recommendations included consolidation of the acquisition process under a newly created position of Under Secretary of Defense for Acquisition; simplification of regulatory processes; consolidation of all contract administration and functions; and related improvements in the area of research and development, data exchanges, use of common parts, and the number of new weapons systems started each year.

Task Force recommendations will result in three-year savings of $18.256 billion when implemented.

— 430 —

Retirement—The Military Retirement System allows military personnel to retire after 20 years of service with an immediate and unreduced benefit. The most common age at retirement is 43 for officers and 39 for enlistees. The Task Force developed two alternative approaches for reducing the cost of military retirement. One alternative proposes delaying payment of benefits until 30 years from Service entry date. The other proposes reduced benefits via an earned income offset during the transition to civilian employment for retirees under age 62, with full benefits paid at age 62. Based on the first alternative and related recommendations calling for benefits to be based on the average of the highest 36 months of base pay, integration with Social Security, and payment for unused leave, the Task Force projects cost savings of $6.893 billion over three years.

Personnel—In its review of other Service-related benefits, the Task Force concluded that commissaries were no longer meeting their original objective of providing food to officers at frontier posts and recommended terminating commissary operations with a three-year cost savings of $972.7 million. The Task Force also recommended restricting Selective Reenlistment Bonus payments to critical need organization categories and restricting Aviation Career Incentive Program payments to those actually performing flying duty required by orders. Implementation of these recommendations, in addition to reductions in the number of Permanent Change of Station moves, would result in three-year cost savings of $1.218 billion.

Health—DOD's health care costs have risen significantly over the past few years. The situation is exacerbated by the interplay and lack of coordination between the direct care system and the Civilian Health and Medical Program of the Uniformed Services (CHAMPUS) for civilian dependents and retired personnel and dependents.

Direct care military hospitals are seriously underutilized. Because direct care systems are budgeted within the Services and CHAMPUS is budgeted by OSD, financial incentives cause the direct care facilities to push prospective patients to CHAMPUS. Task Force recommendations included consolidating the military health care system, transferring CHAMPUS users to direct care facilities, and requiring patients to pay a greater portion of health care costs. Implementation of these recommendations would result in three-year savings of $3.169 billion.

Finance—OSD has virtually no usable financial management information system. Without ready access to management information, frequent resort is made to special studies, creating delays in obtaining relevant data. Furthermore, because of the operational deficiencies of the basic accounting system, great reliance must be placed upon financial controls and internal auditing. The Task Force recommended the establishment of a Procurement Audit Service to perform internal reviews of DOD procurement practices, appointment by the President of an audit committee for DOD, and improvements in post-payment freight bill audit practices.

Implementation of these recommendations would result in three-year cost savings of $1.872 billion.

The Task Force called for changes in Government-furnished material (GFM) and the pricing policy of foreign military sales (FMS). Task Force recommendations included extending the use of inventory control managers to GFM, and assigning the DOD Comptroller responsibility for formulating, implementing, administering, and monitoring FMS pricing and financial management. Implementation of these recommendations would result in three-year cost savings of $132.4 million and revenue generation of $248.2 million.

Organization—The Task Force also identified the need for the establishment of a Defense Executive Office and the elimination of separate staffs reporting to the Service Secretaries. It also recommended the creation of a new position, Under Secretary of Defense for Acquisition, which would be separated from the Under Secretary of Defense for Research and Engineering.

Implementation

Of the 73 recommendations made by the Task Force, 30 (41 percent) can be implemented by the Department. The remaining 43 (59 percent) will require Congressional approval.

**Task Force on
The Department of Education**

CO-CHAIRS:	Spencer F. Eccles Chairman, President, and CEO First Security Corp.	*PROJECT MANAGER:*	Donald B. Summers Vice President, Human Resources Delmed, Inc.
	Alfred H. Kingon Former Editor-in-Chief Financial World Magazine	*NUMBER OF TASK FORCE MEMBERS:* 32	
	Nathan R. Owen Chairman and CEO General Signal Corp.	*NUMBER OF ISSUES:* 9 *NUMBER OF RECOMMENDATIONS:* 60	
	Robert H. Willis Chairman and President Connecticut Natural Gas Corp.	*3-YEAR COST SAVINGS:* $2.828 ($ billions)	
		3-YEAR CASH ACCELERATION: $5.841 ($ billions)	

Overview

In 1980, education-related activities of other agencies were consolidated with the Department of Health, Education and Welfare's Office of Education to form a Cabinet-level Department of Education. The Department's purpose is to strengthen the Federal commitment to equal educational opportunity for all individuals, including the disadvantaged and underprivileged. Emphasis over the past 20 years has been on vocational training and financial aid to students in post-secondary education. The Department had a staff of over 5,000 employees and funding of $14.8 billion in FY 1983.

The Task Force found that problems related to the consolidation in 1980 have been compounded by increasing financial aid to education at all levels. Although it is now, through its loan programs, a financial institution of substantial proportions, the Department lacks the experienced financial management, staff, and information systems characteristic of successful commercial banks.

Issues and Recommendations

The Task Force studied nine issue areas and formulated 60 recommendations which would result in cost savings of $2.828 billion and cash acceleration of $5.841 billion over a three-year period.

With a view toward improving the cost-effectiveness of existing services and their administration, the Task Force focused on those management functions common to Government and business: organizational and human resources management, fiscal management, and automated data processing (ADP).

Organization and Management—Organizational structure has been unnecessarily complicated by the elaborate network of projects created by legislatively mandated programs. Moreover, the absence of a clear mission and concerns about the Department's future have resulted in inadequate guidance for structural reorganization.

Task Force recommendations to alleviate these problems included expediting the standardization, consolidation, and termination of targeted programs; strengthening the staff, skills, and resources of the Information Resources Management Service; and establishing measurable goals, creating more realistic job descriptions, and returning support functions to program offices in order to redefine the Department's mission to conform with existing programs. Cost savings associated with these recommendations would total $805.0 million over three years.

Human Resources Management—During the period 1978–1980, Department employment increased more than 50 percent. The preponderance of educators and administrators with little or no experience in personnel oversight and contract management has led to ineffective utilization of human resources, low morale, and low productivity. To address the problem of inadequately trained personnel, the Task Force recommended revitalizing the Horace Mann Learning Center, which has responsibility for Departmental training needs, and contracting out for specialized skills, particularly in the area of ADP. Viewing the Department's two-year "manpower freeze" as counterproductive, the Task Force recommended manpower ceilings, tighter budgets, and revised job classifications.

Implementation of the Task Force's recommendations would result in cost savings of $14.5 million over a three-year period.

Fiscal Management—Emphasis on prompt delivery of appropriated funds in an overly complex organization has encouraged poor management of financial resources, with the Department's loan programs suffering a 10 percent default rate. Task Force recommendations focused on simplifying the disbursement and collection of loans; increasing the degree of monitoring of those programs; and requiring lenders to apportion loans as students need money, rather than disbursing annual lump sums, as is now the practice. The Task Force also recommended that states share responsibility for ensuring the availability of loans to all qualified students by making changes in state regulations. To redress the problem of $2.2 billion in uncollected loans in default, the Task Force recommended shifting control of loan delinquencies in the program from educational institutions to the Department.

Task Force recommendations would result in cost savings of $1.994 billion and cash acceleration of $5.841 billion over a three-year period.

ADP and Office Automation Management—The ADP function is badly fragmented, out-of-date, and without reliable data bases. These shortcomings have resulted in waste, fraud, abuse, and error. In addition to conducting an in-depth study of existing management information systems and internal controls, the Task Force recommended revision of the general ledger account structure in order to present information compatible with Treasury accounts for ease in reconciliation and management decisions.

Projected three-year cost savings associated with these Task Force recommendations are $14.0 million.

Implementation

Of the 60 recommendations proposed by the Task Force, eleven require Congressional action. Although moves toward loan program consolidation will involve both Congress and the Department, 48 of the recommendations fall within the purview of the Department. One recommendation involves Presidential action.

**Task Force on
The Department of Energy,
the Federal Energy Regulatory Commission,
and the Nuclear Regulatory Commission**

CO-CHAIRS:	John W. Hanley Chairman and CEO Monsanto Company Roger Milliken President and CEO Milliken & Company	*NUMBER OF ISSUES:* 21 *NUMBER OF* *RECOMMENDATIONS:* 82 *3-YEAR* *COST SAVINGS:* $2.790 ($ billions)
PROJECT *MANAGER:*	Walter R. Pettiss Vice President and Assistant Treasurer Milliken & Company	*3-YEAR* *REVENUE GENERATION:* $1.291 ($ billions)
NUMBER OF *TASK FORCE* *MEMBERS:* 67		*3-YEAR* *CASH ACCELERATION:* $ .089 ($ billions)

Overview

The Department of Energy (DOE) was established in 1977. It includes nuclear research and defense production, the five Power Marketing Administrations, programs in energy conservation and renewable energy, the regulation of petroleum pricing and allocations, and the Strategic Petroleum Reserve. The FY 1983 budget obligation for DOE was $15.7 billion. The staff includes approximately 16,000 full-time Government employees and over 100,000 contract employees.

The Federal Energy Regulatory Commission, a semi-autonomous part of DOE, succeeded the Federal Power Commission. Its FY 1983 budget was $93 million; it has 1,800 employees. The Nuclear Regulatory Commission is an independent, Presidentially appointed Commission, with an FY 1983 budget of $480 million and 3,300 employees.

Although staffed with dedicated and competent people, DOE faces an overriding need for a much sharper focus on its mission. The lack of mission focus exacerbates micromanagement, the most prevalent problem at DOE.

Issues and Recommendations

The Task Force studied 21 issue areas and formulated 82 recommendations which, when fully implemented, will result in three-year cost savings and revenue generation of $4.081 billion and cash acceleration of $89 million.

Organization and Staffing—DOE suffers from micromanagement in supervising its employees and contractors. The supervisory span of control frequently is too low, and selected DOE offices are characterized by unnecessary staffing "layers." Low salaries also exacerbate organization and staffing problems. Specific Task Force recommendations would result in three-year cost savings of $18.6 million and included broadening the span of control; reducing management layers; strengthening reporting systems and long-range planning; institutionalizing "value analysis"; and developing incentives for attracting and retaining qualified personnel.

Procurement and Contracting—More than 85 percent of DOE operating personnel are involved in procurement and contracting. The Task Force identified duplicative and counterproductive layers of management and regulation and the need to expand and streamline DOE's use of contracted goods and services. The Task Force recommended eliminating unnecessary co-management of Government-Owned Contractor-Operated (GOCO) facilities, and increasing emphasis on "contracting out" and the use of competitive bidding. Three-year cost savings of $731.1 million would result from implementation of these recommendations.

Strategic Petroleum Reserve (SPR)—The Task Force recommended making facilities construction and operation of the Reserve a GOCO activity and continuing to fill the Reserve at its present rate until new underground caverns are ready, instead of requiring interim storage. It also proposed exempting the massive SPR purchases from the Cargo Preference Act. Implementation of these recommendations would result in three-year cost savings of $1.281 billion.

Internal Accounting Controls—DOE's internal accounting controls require consistency and modernization. Specific recommendations were made to improve and coordinate accounting systems, share ADP resources, and increase the number of auditors and funding for audit activities, with three-year cost savings opportunities estimated at $131.9 million, plus cash acceleration of $89.4 million.

Research and Development (R&D)—R&D is hampered by duplication of effort; unseemly competition for funds; and, most significantly, no authoritative and specific outline of an overall R&D mission. To rectify these major problems, the Task Force recommended clarification of DOE's R&D mission by the Secretary, with clear bipartisan Congressional backing. Potential associated cost savings amount to $413.7 million over three years.

Defense-related Programs—Indicating its clear support for defense-related DOE programs, the Task Force called for prompt and decisive action to ensure FY 1984 initial funding for a new production reactor (NPR) and the Defense Waste Processing Facility, thereby avoiding potential cost escalations. It also recommended that R&D programs on magnetic fusion aimed at the ultimate production of peaceful energy be narrowed to two competitive programs in FY 1984, that security procedures be revised, and that policies and procedures be standardized. Implementation of overall recommendations would result in three-year cost savings of $183.5 million.

Power Marketing Administrations (PMAs)—In addition to supporting continued exploration of privatizing PMAs, the Task Force recommended a revised and more businesslike approach to amortization of that portion of the Federal Government's capital investment allocated to power production and increased fees to recover the full cost of the Government's investment in PMAs. Implementation of these and related recommendations would result in revenue generation of $1.290 billion over three years.

The Federal Energy Regulatory Commission (FERC) and the Nuclear Regulatory Commission (NRC)—FERC's regulatory mission—to ensure energy supplies at just and reasonable prices—can be expedited by de-emphasizing case-by-case decisions by the Commissioners, and by delegating increased authority to staff directors, administrative law judges, and FERC's Office of Opinions and Reviewers. Potential three-year cost savings total $29.7 million.

NRC's role is to license civilian use of nuclear energy to ensure public health and safety. The Task Force specifically focused on the need to interrelate cost-effectiveness and prudence with respect to health and safety in the nuclear field. Although no specific cost savings were claimed, opportunities for improved management efficiencies are significant.

Implementation

Of the 82 major recommendations formulated by the Task Force, 58 (71 percent) are within the purview of DOE/FERC/NRC, 2 (2 percent) involve Presidential action, and 22 (27 percent) need Congressional approval.

**Task Force on
Environmental Protection Agency,
Small Business Administration, and
Federal Emergency Management Agency**

CO-CHAIRS:	William H. Bricker Chairman, President, and CEO Diamond Shamrock Corporation	*NUMBER OF ISSUES:* 28 *NUMBER OF RECOMMENDATIONS:* 78
	Ben F. Love CEO Texas Commerce Bancshares, Inc.	*3-YEAR COST SAVINGS:* $1.660 ($ billions) *3-YEAR*
PROJECT MANAGERS:	Roger P. Batchelor, Jr. Independent Consultant	*REVENUE GENERATION:* $ .199 ($ billions)*
	Lee E. Straus Vice President and Chief Administrative Officer Texas Commerce Bancshares, Inc.	*3-YEAR CASH ACCELERATION:* $ .315 ($ billions)*
NUMBER OF TASK FORCE MEMBERS:	74	

This summary consists of an agency-by-agency analysis.

ENVIRONMENTAL PROTECTION AGENCY

Overview

Since its formation in 1970, the Environmental Protection Agency (EPA) has grown rapidly. The Agency's initial budget of $303 million reached $3.7 billion in FY 1983 (including $2.4 billion for construction grants); it employs 10,925 full-time equivalent employees. The Agency is organized around four program offices: Air, Noise, and Radiation; Pesticides and Toxic Substances; Solid Waste and Emergency Response; and Water. Ten regional offices serve as EPA's link to the states and territories.

EPA currently is the product of segmented growth and crisis-oriented responses to the laws it administers. The Task Force recognized that many needed management reforms have been instituted, but found additional opportunities to enhance efficiency.

Issues and Recommendations

The Task Force studied 12 issues and formulated 36 recommendations which, when fully implemented, will result in three-year cost savings of $480.3 million.

Delegation—The concept underlying most environmental legislation is that the states will ultimately assume administrative responsibility for the programs. While EPA management is striving to reach this objective, progress is slow. Washington remains heavily involved, particularly in the construction grant program, causing duplicate efforts and time-consuming delays. Task Force recommendations included clarifying roles and responsibilities of headquarters and regional personnel, and developing uniform oversight programs, which would result in three-year savings of $64.1 million.

Consolidation—EPA's history of segmented growth has created numerous opportunities for consolidating its facilities or activities. The Task Force found that EPA administers separately 17 categorical state financial grants and operates more laboratories than it needs. The automated data processing (ADP) system was developed on an "as needed" basis and is riddled with redundancies and incompatible systems. The consolidation of categorical grants, closing of selected laboratories, and integration of ADP systems would result in savings of $311.1 million over three years.

General Management—The Task Force found a need for an improved cost accounting system, better supervision and coordination of contract management, and more effective use of training funds and performance evaluation systems. Task Force recommendations included the development of an Agency-wide cost accounting system, improved financial systems and procedures, simplified procurement processes, and upgraded training and evaluation programs. Implementation of Task Force recommendations in this area would result in three-year cost savings of $105.1 million.

Implementation

Of the 36 Task Force recommendations, 28 (78 percent) are within the purview of the Agency, and 8 (22 percent) require Congressional action.

Overview

The Small Business Administration (SBA) was created by the Small Business Act of 1953. Its purpose is to aid, counsel, assist, and protect the interests of small businesses in order to preserve free competitive enterprise. Activities include making direct and guaranteed loans, providing management assistance, and helping small businesses secure Government contracts. In FY 1983, the Agency had 4,000 employees and a $245.0 million budget.

A principal SBA activity is making direct and guaranteed loans to small businesses that are unable to obtain credit elsewhere. This activity is carried out primarily through the 7(a) program, which had a FY 1983 budget of $85 million for direct loans and $2.01 billion in guaranty loans (banks typically make the loans, and the SBA guarantees up to 90 percent). Out of a $17.1 billion loan portfolio, $9.2 billion is in guaranty loans, $1.7 billion is in direct and immediate participation loans, and $6.2 billion is in disaster loans.

Issues and Recommendations

The Task Force studied 12 issues and formulated 31 recommendations which, when fully implemented, will result in three-year cost savings of $231.7 million, revenue generation of $199.3 million, and cash acceleration of $315.0 million. The Task Force placed principal focus on improving the quality of the SBA loan portfolio and reducing Agency costs.

A majority of the identified savings would result from the SBA's transferring more responsibility for its programs to the private sector. By requiring and encouraging banks in the private sector to make more of the loan decisions, make better loan decisions, and participate more in collecting and liquidating problem loans, the Task Force believes the SBA can reduce its overhead and net credit losses. In addition, by utilizing private collection services to work charged-off loans, the SBA can dramatically increase its loan recoveries. Since Congress has not permitted the SBA to contract out for private collection services and since the SBA does not have the resources to work charged-off loans properly, the Task Force found that problem loans are basically ignored once the SBA charges them off.

Other Task Force recommendations included reducing the maximum loan guaranty percentage from 90 to 75 percent and the maximum guaranty in the Surety Bond Guaranty Program from 90 to 85 percent, thereby reducing SBA's exposure on each loss and encouraging banks to make sounder lending decisions. The Task Force also called for discontinuing

SBA disaster loans for flood-related losses that are insurable by businesses and individuals.

In addition to the above cost-saving opportunities, significant revenue enhancements would result from increasing the SBA's front-end loan guaranty fee from 1 to 2 percent. This fee is passed along by the lending bank to the borrower and would have a minimal impact on the net cost of the borrower. Imposing a 1 percent user's fee on Small Business Investment Company (SBIC) borrowings would produce additional revenues. Finally, the Task Force concluded that the SBA should increase its charge to contractors in the Surety Bond Guaranty Program from 0.5 to 1 percent.

Implementation

Of the 31 recommendations, 12 (39 percent) are under the purview of the Agency, 3 (10 percent) require Presidential action, and 16 (51 percent) require Congressional approval.

FEDERAL EMERGENCY MANAGEMENT AGENCY

Overview

The Federal Emergency Management Agency (FEMA), formed in 1979, consolidated the emergency preparedness and recovery functions of four agencies. FEMA had an FY 1983 budget of $892.0 million and 2,549 employees.

After an initial review of Agency activities, the Task Force chose to concentrate its attention on disaster assistance programs.

Issues and Recommendations

The Task Force studied four major issues and formulated 11 recommendations which, when fully implemented, will result in three-year cost savings of $948.3 million.

National Flood Insurance Program (NFIP)—NFIP was established to provide adequate indemnification for the loss of property in flood-prone areas, where private insurance protection is unavailable or unaffordable. The Task Force found that the empowering legislation is inadequate to ensure that the program is run efficiently and on a sound financial basis. In addition, responsibility for flood insurance, flood hazard mitigation, and flood-related disaster assistance rests with three separate offices at FEMA. To make the NFIP actuarially sound and self-supporting, the Task Force recommended increasing deductibles, reducing the ratio of subsidized to actuarial rates, and overall rate increases. Other recommendations included.establishing an advisory committee with oversight control and requiring the Office of Management and Budget and FEMA to make an annual, consolidated analysis of the effect of flood insurance, flood hazard mitigation, and flood disaster assistance. Implementation of these recommendations would result in three-year savings of $662.2 million.

Other disaster assistance programs were found to be duplicative, inefficient, and inequitable. Recommendations included launching a national campaign to sell flood insurance, making it mandatory in high-hazard flood zones, and eliminating direct assistance grants for insurable items. Implementation of these recommendations would result in cost savings of $276.0 million over three years.

United States Fire Administration (USFA)—USFA's mission is to establish fire prevention and control plans, programs, and systems to ensure effective joint action by the public, industry, governments, and the fire services to reduce losses caused by fire. Approximately 75 percent of USFA's total funding is spent in the form of grants to state and local fire services. The Task Force found that USFA has never received the funding levels necessary to fulfill its mission, and that its original scope and goals are too broad and not achievable. Consequently, the Task Force recommended phasing out USFA with a cost savings of $10.3 million over three years.

Strategic and Critical Materials Stockpile Management—Although the General Services Administration (GSA) is responsible for stockpile management, responsibility for stockpile policy rests with FEMA. Budgeting and purchasing responsibilities reside with GSA, including control of the Stockpile Transaction Fund. The Task Force recommended that FEMA be given control of the Fund for purposes of acquisition and disposal, with GSA remaining responsible for managing the Stockpile. No specific savings were claimed.

Implementation

Of the 11 recommendations formulated by the Task Force, 3 (27 percent) are within the purview of FEMA, 2 (18 percent) require Presidential action, and 6 (55 percent) will need Congressional approval.

Task Force on
Federal Construction Management

CO-CHAIRS:	Robert J. Buckley Chairman and President Allegheny International, Inc.	*PROJECT* *MANAGER:*	Edwin K. Isely Former Manager A. T. Kearney, Inc.
	Raymond C. Foster Chairman, President, and CEO Stone & Webster, Inc.	*NUMBER OF* *TASK FORCE* *MEMBERS:* 93 *NUMBER OF ISSUES:* 23	
	Melvyn N. Klein President and CEO Altamil Corp.	*NUMBER OF* *RECOMMENDATIONS:* 23	
	John W. Kluge Chairman, President, and CEO Metromedia, Inc.	*3-YEAR* *COST SAVINGS:* $5.446 ($ billions)	
	Frederick P. Rose Chairman Rose Associates, Inc.		
	Paul J. Schierl President and CEO Fort Howard Paper Co.		

Overview

Under Federal authority granted to 26 agencies, the Federal Government undertakes or sponsors virtually every type of construction ranging from residential and industrial facilities to wastewater treatment plants, hospitals, and office buildings. The Task Force focused on direct construction which the Government performs for its own accounts, as well as construction grants and cost-sharing arrangements with state or local entities. Construction programs generated by Federal agencies involved outlays in excess of $30 billion annually during FY 1981 to 1983.

Federal construction projects are characterized by mismanagement and confusion at all stages of the construction process. Key problems include diffusion of authority and responsibility to initiate construction, Federal requirements that hamper effective program management and increase costs, legislation with mixed goals unrelated to construction, and lack of clear guidelines for handling construction design and value engineering.

The Task Force examined 23 specific issues broadly grouped into four major categories and formulated recommendations which, when fully implemented, will result in cost savings of $5.446 billion over a three-year period.

Construction and Management Quality Control—Diffusion of authority and responsibility is a significant and recurring problem. Federal construction projects suffer from inadequate project planning, scoping, and design. Emphasis is on short-term results rather than long-term benefits, and unnecessary project delays occur because of breaks in management continuity and lengthy approval time for even minimal design changes.

The Task Force recommendations, with cost savings of $286.5 million over a three-year period, include establishing pilot project manager/program management systems and procedures for selected major construction projects and requiring grantees for construction programs at state and local levels to define clearly the roles, authorities, responsibilities, and liabilities of all parties involved in a given project.

Design and Procurement—Few incentives exist for Federal officials to hold down the cost of construction. Compensation of professional employees is not related to efficiency. Similarly, while state or local governments have responsibility for minimizing costs in Federal grant programs, there is little incentive to do so because design and construction costs are ultimately borne by the Federal Government.

Rectifying problems in contract design and procurement would result in cost savings of $1.986 billion over a three-year period. PPSS recommendations included increasing the use of performance specifications to elicit innovative responses from industry, institutionalizing the concept of "value engineering" for evaluating all stages of the construction life cycle, and modifying the Environmental Protection Agency construction grants program to rely more on private financing.

Environment—With respect to construction projects, there are 45 different environmental laws containing requirements that are difficult to administer effectively and that greatly increase the cost of construction. Even after requirements of the National Environmental Policy Act (NEPA), an umbrella statute, are fulfilled, a Federally funded construction program must still search out the applicable requirements from the 44 other environmental laws, sometimes causing delays as long as five or ten years. It is estimated that environmental issues increased construction costs by almost 400 percent during the 1970s and are expected to continue to cause additional increases throughout the 1980s.

Implementation of the Task Force's recommendations relating to the impact of environmental legislation on Federal construction would result in cost savings of $3.030 billion over a three-year period. Among the recommendations are the consolidation of a majority of special purpose environmental reviews and assessments under NEPA, the creation of a single review process, and greater "scoping" during the Environmental

Impact Statement process to allow interested agencies or parties the opportunity to identify and discuss at one point in time all environmental concerns.

Privatization and Contracting Out—PPSS found that many Federal agencies underestimate the value of contracting out for construction activities. Current cost comparisons are typically biased toward the Government and often fail to take into account the loss of tax revenue in estimating the cost of keeping construction activities in-house.

The Task Force estimated that the acceleration of privatization/contracting out of construction activities would result in three-year cost savings of $143.0 million.

Implementation

Of the 23 major recommendations formulated by the Task Force, 13 (56 percent) are within the purview of Federal agencies, 5 (22 percent) involve Presidential action, and another 5 (22 percent) require Congressional approval.

**Task Force on
Federal Feeding**

CO-CHAIRS:	H. J. Cofer, Jr. President Rich-SeaPak Corp.	*NUMBER OF ISSUES:* 6
	Henry H. Henley, Jr. Chairman and CEO Cluett, Peabody & Co., Inc.	*NUMBER OF* *RECOMMENDATIONS:* 15 *3-YEAR* *COST SAVINGS:** $.260 ($ billions)
	Edward L. Hutton President and CEO Chemed Corp.	*3-YEAR* *REVENUE GENERATION:* $.039 ($ billions)
	Carl Karcher Chairman and CEO Carl Karcher Enterprises, Inc.	* *Note:* This Report contains a compendium issue covering Federal feeding issues from other reports. The compendium includes 15 recommendations with additional three-year fully/partially supportable cost savings/ revenue generation of $11.368 billion.
	Edward W. Whittemore Chairman and CEO American Brands, Inc.	
PROJECT *MANAGER:*	George J. Schramm Former Vice Chairman American Brands, Inc.	
NUMBER OF *TASK FORCE* *MEMBERS:*	30	

Nearly every Federal agency is involved in some type of feeding activity, including administration and management of cafeterias; hospital and prison feeding programs; national school lunch programs; women, infants, and children feeding programs; summer feeding programs; food storage and distribution programs; open mess; and troop feeding programs. Aggregate net costs for Federal feeding (FY 1981) were $21.1 billion.

Most Federal feeding programs have developed independently of each other. With a few exceptions, the programs are relatively small. Collectively, however, they amount to a major expenditure item.

The Task Force found that: (1) no one agency maintains comprehensive data, nor has oversight, for Federal feeding activities; (2) efforts to improve management will succeed if specific agencies and opportunities for improvement are targeted; and (3) greater private sector competition must be encouraged for food service and supply contracts.

Issues and Recommendations

Five issue areas were studied, and 15 recommendations developed pertaining to policy and management information, use of commercially available products, soy protein extender in ground beef, food service contracts, and troop feeding. In addition, the Task Force prepared a compendium issue identifying Federal feeding issues contained in other PPSS reports with recommendations for $11.368 billion in three-year cost savings/revenue generation.

Implementation of the recommendations would result in cost savings of $260 million and revenue generation of $39 million over three years.

Management Information—Federal feeding programs are both complex and diverse, yet no Federal agency maintains comprehensive information on their total scope and cost. The Task Force was severely hampered in its review by what it termed the "information gap." The size of Federal feeding activities, combined with the lack of unified policy or even a Government-wide data base, makes a strong case for strengthened central control and oversight. Specific savings were not quantified by the Task Force, but it strongly recommended the establishment of a uniform Federal feeding policy, including systems for reporting and accountability.

Substitution of Commercially Available Products for Federal Specification Products—Traditionally, the Federal Government has used lengthy, detailed specifications to purchase food products, even though similar commercial products are less expensive. Despite existing policy aimed at increasing the use of commercially available products, only 73 of approximately 600 Federal food items have been converted from Government specifications to commercial item descriptions (CID). The Task Force recommended that all covered products not already converted be converted to CIDs and that the Office of Federal Procurement Policy be given regulatory authority to ensure agency compliance with CIDs.

Implementation of these recommendations would result in cost savings of $8.4 million over a three-year period.

Soy Protein Extender in Ground Beef—Purchases of ground beef by the Department of Agriculture (USDA) serve two objectives. Not only are they donations to the National School Lunch Program, but they also remove surplus beef from the marketplace (price supports). To reduce costs, the Task Force recommended that the Secretary of Agriculture issue an order for USDA-procured ground beef products to contain 20 percent soy protein extender. The soy extender detracts from neither the nutritional value nor palatability. Use of soy extender would yield cost savings of $83.9 million over a three-year period.

Food Service Contracts—The General Services Administration (GSA) administered contract food operations in Government-owned buildings with gross sales of $65 million in FY 1983.

The Task Force found that GSA fails to charge market prices for space rental (1.5 percent of sales versus the 7.5 percent more frequently found in other institutions) and does not solicit competitive bids on commission rates for food service contracts. The Task Force recommended that GSA adopt a nationwide policy of allowing qualified bidders to bid competitively on commission rates, adopt a more flexible attitude toward requests for cafeteria price increases, and reevaluate cafeteria rental rates. Implementation of Task Force recommendations would result in revenue generation of $38.8 million over three years.

Troop Feeding—In FY 1983, the Department of Defense purchased $1.392 billion worth of food, primarily for troop feeding. The Task Force found that budget preparation, menu planning, and actual food served are often unrelated, and that excessive food allowances and inefficient delivery encourage waste and discourage accountability.

The Task Force recommendations, when implemented, will result in cost savings of $167.3 million over a three-year period.

Implementation

Of the 14 major recommendations formulated by the Task Force (excluding the compendium), 12 (86 percent) are within the purview of the departments and agencies, 1 (7 percent) will require Presidential involvement, and 1 (7 percent) will necessitate Congressional action.

Task Force on
Federal Hospital Management

CO-CHAIRS:	Raymond A. Hay President LTV Corp.	*NUMBER OF* *TASK FORCE* *MEMBERS:* 19
	William B. Johnson Chairman IC Industries, Inc.	*NUMBER OF ISSUES:* 13
	James L. Ketelsen Chairman and CEO Tenneco, Inc.	*NUMBER OF* *RECOMMENDATIONS:* 60

	Henry E. Simmons, M.D.
	National Director,
	  Health Care Consulting
	  Programs
	Peat, Marwick, Mitchell
	  & Co.
		3-YEAR
		COST SAVINGS: $9.191
		($ billions)
		
		3-YEAR
		REVENUE GENERATION: $2.721
		($ billions)

PROJECT *MANAGER:*	Jack Whitelaw Officer Manager Vought Corporation	

Overview

The Federal hospital system consists of the Military Health Care System (MHCS) of the Department of Defense (DOD) and the Veterans Administration (VA) Hospital System. MHCS is composed of three distinct hospital systems: Army, Navy, and Air Force. MHCS operates 161 hospitals and 310 outpatient clinics, employs 151,000 persons, and has an annual budget (FY 1983) of $4.5 billion. The VA Hospital System consists of 172 hospitals providing medical, surgical, geriatric, and psychiatric services. The FY 1983 budget for this 89,000-bed system was $7 billion.

Without underestimating the Federal system's complexity, the Task Force found that Federal hospitals have not kept pace with the private health care system's delivery of services. Specifically, the Federal health care system is especially deficient in the areas of automated management information systems necessary for health care resource allocations, accurate determination of patient care costs, and management incentives for cost-efficient decisions.

Issues and Recommendations

The Task Force assessed 13 issues grouped into three major categories: planning and resource allocation, procurement and supply activities, and third-party reimbursements and duplicate payments.

Sixty recommendations projected three-year cost savings of $9.191 billion and revenue generation of $2.721 billion.

Planning and Resource Allocation in DOD—Lacking any central control or authority, MHCS is characterized by inefficiency and large-scale duplication of services. A disproportionate number of hospitals are underutilized and there are shortages of technical and professional personnel. Construction and renovation projects are planned without regard for staffing needs, demand, and proximity of other armed services' hospitals. Services and equipment are not shared among the branches, resulting in waste and duplication. Major Task Force recommendations included freezing construction funds for 27 small, underutilized hospitals and 20 larger, underutilized hospitals, and appointing a full-time Director of Shared Health Resources to ensure that procurement, automated data processing, and shared hospital bed opportunities are more effectively pursued to eliminate underuse and waste.

These recommendations are projected to yield $1.497 billion in cost savings over a three-year period.

Planning and Resource Allocation in the VA Hospital System—Excessive length of stay averages indicate many long-term patients occupy costly acute care beds. Systems fail to properly account for VA's unique mix of patient cases, resulting in a process which rewards inefficiency. Resource allocation and construction and renovation plans are based on occupancy averages that are grossly inflated by long lengths of stay. Construction costs within the VA system greatly exceed comparable private sector projects.

To rectify these discrepancies, the Task Force recommended that the VA allocate resources and plan budgets for its hospitals based on hospital case-mix using a Diagnosis Related Group (patient categories based on efficient use of hospital resources) bed-need projection and resource consumption model. The Task Force also recommended that the VA cease constructing nursing homes and convert underutilized hospital beds to nursing home beds.

These actions would yield cost savings of $5.864 billion over a three-year period.

Procurement and Supply Activities—MHCS and VA operate a costly, anachronistic depot system for distributing medical supplies. High maintenance costs of the depot system outweigh bulk ordering advantages. Despite the depot system, some 40 percent of supplies are purchased from expensive local dealers.

VA should phase out its depot system and DOD should reduce its depot-held supplies to $100 million in medically unique items. In addition, both should reduce the supplies purchased on the open market from over 40 percent to 15 to 25 percent.

Implementation of these recommendations will yield cost savings of $699.1 million over a three-year period.

Third-Party Reimbursements and Duplicate Payments—VA and

MHCS frequently provide health care service to militarily eligible beneficiaries who also have private insurance. Health care benefits are also provided to beneficiaries insured by third parties. Minimal effort is expended to recover health care costs from private insurers.

These problems led to the following recommendations: that DOD establish a central claims authority to aggressively pursue recovery from third-party payers of the cost to treat individuals who are injured or diseased due to the negligence or irresponsibility of a third party; that DOD collect the cost of providing care to militarily inactive beneficiaries who are also covered by private health insurance; that the VA contract with fiscal intermediaries, such as private insurance carriers, to process claims more efficiently; and that the VA actively pursue recovery health care costs from insured, non-service connected veterans and establish a means test for free health care.

Total recommended actions would yield cost savings of $1.311 billion and revenue generation of $2.721 billion over a three-year period.

Implementation

Of the 60 recommendations formulated by the Task Force, 45 (75 percent) are entirely within the purview of DOD and the VA, 2 (3 percent) involve Presidential action, and 13 (22 percent) will require Congressional approval.

**Task Force on
Federal Management Systems**

CO-CHAIRS:	Joseph E. Connor, Jr. Senior Partner Price Waterhouse	*NUMBER OF TASK FORCE MEMBERS:* 29
	Harry E. Figgie, Jr. Chairman and CEO Figgie International, Inc.	*NUMBER OF ISSUES:* 10
	John E. Fisher Chairman Nationwide Mutual Insurance Co.	*NUMBER OF RECOMMENDATIONS:* 35
	Daniel W. Lufkin Chairman of the Finance Committee Columbia Pictures Industries, Inc.	*Note:* Because of the far-reaching nature of its recommendations, the Federal Management Systems Task Force did not attempt to quantify cost savings, revenue generation, or cash acceleration.
	J. Paul Sticht Chairman R. J. Reynolds Industries, Inc.	
PROJECT MANAGER:	Lewis J. Krulwich Partner Price Waterhouse	

Overview

The report on Federal Management Systems recommends significant changes in Federal management, designed to provide the central guidance and direction necessary to develop well-coordinated and effective processes and structure. The Task Force identified serious structural and procedural problems in Executive Branch organization; information flow; budgeting, planning, and evaluation methods; continuity characteristics; and communication practices. In a fundamental sense, the recommendations of all the PPSS Task Forces address symptoms of these problems.

The Government's size amplifies its need for effective management. The Federal Government had FY 1982 outlays of $728 billion—more than double the combined sales of Exxon, Mobil, General Motors, Texaco, and Standard Oil of California (the top five U.S. companies in sales). In addition, the Government owns one-third of all the U.S. land mass and 2.6 billion square feet of building space. Operational complexity being proportional to size, such complexity critically calls for managerial effectiveness.

Although there are differences in operating styles and requirements between the public and private sectors of the economy, it is imperative that the management of the Executive Branch take a businesslike approach.

Issues and Recommendations

Ten issues were analyzed and 35 recommendations formulated. They can be broadly grouped into the areas of organization management, financial management, and management information systems. No attempt was made to calculate specific dollar savings and revenue opportunities due to the far-reaching nature of the recommendations.

Organizational Management—Responsibility for developing and implementing administrative policies is not clearly assigned. Duplications, conflicts, and blurred lines of authority abound. Direction and coordination are lacking in key areas, resulting in span-of-control problems with multiple administrative departments and agencies reporting to the President and Executive Office of the President. In addition, the Executive Branch suffers because objectives, plans, and accomplishments are not communicated effectively. Problems of continuity exacerbate these shortcomings: key appointees change, on average, every 18 to 24 months, a condition endemic to the political process.

In response to these problems, the Task Force recommended the establishment of an Office of Federal Management (OFM) within the Executive Office of the President. OFM will be responsible for policy development and direction in the area of financial management, budgeting and planning, human resources, administration (including information resources management, procurement, and property management), and management improvement. OFM would include the budget functions of the Office of Management and Budget and otherwise serve as the President's management staff. The General Services Administration and Office of Personnel Management would report directly to OFM for policy direction. Key OFM officials would be appointed on a long-term basis to increase the potential for management continuity and achievement of objectives. One of OFM's high priority projects would be the development of a comprehensive communications program designed to convey goals and objectives to Federal employees.

Financial Management—Meaningful budgeting, planning, and evaluation are generally lacking at both the agency and central Government levels. Specifically, the budget is not fully used as a management tool. Budget preparation is stressed instead of budget execution and control; accounting for actual expenditures is separated from budget preparation; and budget appropriation classifications are not related to the needs of agency management. Further, time constraints on the budget process help misdirect budget focus, and the annual budget and appropriations process focuses concern on only the subsequent fiscal year.

The Task Force recommended that OFM assume overall responsibility for financial management. Specifically, OFM should direct the implementation of a planning system by which long-term goals and activities would be identified, communicated, and implemented. Plans and budgets should be strengthened to enhance the capabilities of capital asset and budget analysis as managerial tools. Potential means of strengthening include revising classifications to match management needs, integrating the financial management and budget process, and adopting a biennial budget approach to add time for consideration of long-term management needs. The Task Force also recommended the establishment of an audit support division within OFM to strengthen the reliability of underlying financial data.

Management Information Systems—Automated data processing (ADP) efficiency suffers from a lack of coordinated development, incompatible data, and functionally obsolescent hardware. Departments and agencies have developed independent systems and procedures, taking little advantage of the experience or work of other departments and agencies.

The Task Force recommended that OFM develop common Government-wide ADP software systems and related procedures for use in such administrative areas as payroll, accounts receivable, and fixed asset accounting.

Implementation

Of the 35 major recommendations formulated by the Task Force, 30 (86 percent) involve Presidential action and the remaining 5 (14 percent) require Congressional approval. To reiterate, no specific amount of savings were identified due to the far-reaching nature of the recommendations.

**Task Force on
Financial Asset Management**

CO-CHAIRS:	Edward W. Duffy Chairman and CEO Marine Midland Banks, Inc.	*NUMBER OF ISSUES:* 35
	Wilson S. Johnson Chairman National Federation of Independent Businesses	*NUMBER OF* *RECOMMENDATIONS:* 90 *3-YEAR* *COST SAVINGS:* $13.777 *($ billions)*
	Edward B. Rust President State Farm Fire & Casualty Co.	*3-YEAR* *REVENUE GENERATION:* $ 9.726 *($ billions)*
PROJECT *MANAGER:*	Bruce G. Fielding President Fielding, Locksley & Storek Accountancy Corp.	*3-YEAR* *CASH ACCELERATION:* $48.647 *($ billions)*
NUMBER OF *TASK FORCE* *MEMBERS:* 51		

Overview

The stated debt of the U.S. Government is $1.25 trillion. Annual collections and disbursements total over $1.7 trillion. At an annual interest rate of 10 percent, 20 cents of every dollar of Government revenue is required for debt service. Despite these huge amounts, the Federal Government is many years behind the private sector in computer techniques, financial management information systems, and accounting records.

The Task Force found Government-wide deficiencies in the area of financial asset management, policies, and procedures. Agency personnel often lack financial management skills, inadequate accounting systems lead to mismanagement of cash flow, and lack of uniform definitions causes confusion and duplication. The Task Force concluded that: significant amounts of cash can be more effectively managed by accelerating collections and decelerating disbursements, major deficiencies in debt collection and default prevention warrant immediate attention, Government loans can become more like those that private lenders would make by increasing fees and interest rates, and the increasing scope of Federal credit activities needs to be addressed.

Financial Asset Management issues examined by the Task Force were grouped into five major categories: cash management, direct Government lending, guaranteed Government loans, debt collection, and Government securities. Implementation of the 90 Task Force recommendations would yield cost savings of $13.777 billion, revenue generation of $9.726 billion, and cash acceleration of $48.647 billion over a three-year period.

Cash Management—While Federal cash management is beginning to receive increased attention, the Task Force recommended additional improvements which would result in better utilization of funds and reduce interest expense to the Federal Government.

Recommendations proposed by the Task Force would result in total cash accelerations and decelerations of $30.589 billion and net interest savings of $9.642 billion over three years. However, the amounts reported as cash acceleration have a one-time-only impact. Absent an increased level of acceleration in the second year, the Federal deficit would return to the first year's balance. Specific recommendations included accelerated collection and deposit of receipts; increased use of electronic funds transfers (EFT); adoption of a Government-wide accounts payable system; revised progress payments to defense contractors; and use of payment on due date and checks-paid letters-of-credit to slow cash disbursement. The Task Force also emphasized the need for Agency-specific incentives for improved cash management.

Direct Government Lending—Direct loans are cash payments secured by a mortgage, bond, debenture, or promissory note. Federal direct loan obligations have increased dramatically in the last 30 years, from $3.5 billion in FY 1950 to $61.4 billion in FY 1980, causing serious concerns as to the impact on interest rates, inflation, economic growth, and productivity.

Recommendations in the area of Governmental direct lending were projected to yield cost savings of $1.356 billion, revenue generation of $5.258 billion, and cash acceleration of $6.218 billion over a three-year period. Recommendations included increasing fees and interest rates on direct loans; upgrading credit training programs and exploring private sector loan models for credit decision-making; encouraging increased private sector participation in direct loan programs; and establishing new default levels on Government loans.

Guaranteed Government Loans—Guaranteed Government lending is a popular form of credit assistance because, in the absence of default, budgetary costs are minimal. In FY 1978, new net primary guaranteed loans totaled $39.5 billion, while in FY 1983 they will total an estimated $87.7 billion, a 122 percent increase.

Task Force recommendations included moving from direct to guaranteed loans at the Farmers Home Administration and the Small Business

Administration; increasing the Guaranteed Student Loan origination fees from 5 to 10 percent; and restructuring the guaranteed loan program to encourage the private sector to assume a larger share of the risk. Implementation of Task Force recommendations pertaining to guaranteed loans would result in three-year cost savings of $332.3 million, revenue generation of $3.384 billion, and cash acceleration of $142.1 million.

Debt Collection—Debt owed to the Federal Government arises from hundreds of Government activities which generate receivables. Of the $219 billion in receivables due the Government as of June 30, 1982, the majority (85 percent) were loan receivables.

Recommendations offered by the Task Force were projected to yield cost savings of $1.933 billion, revenue generation of $1.085 billion, and cash acceleration of $11.698 billion over a three-year period. These recommendations included contracting for debt collection services, offsetting debt owed to the Government against Internal Revenue Service refunds due borrowers, and strictly enforcing interest and penalty charges on delinquent debt.

Government Securities—The Secretary of the Treasury borrows funds from the public to finance Federal deficits and refinance maturing public debt. Management improvements recommended by the Task Force and projected to yield cost savings of $513 million during a three-year period included discontinuing coupon-type and registered securities and using electronic funds transfers for payment of interest and principal on Government securities.

Implementation

Of the 90 major recommendations formulated by the Task Force, 40 (44 percent) are within the purview of associated agencies, 25 (28 percent) involve Presidential action, and 25 (28 percent) require Congressional approval.

**Task Force on
The Department of Health and Human Services:
Department Management, Office of Human
Development Services, ACTION**

CO-CHAIRS:	Michael D. Dingman
Chairman of the Board
and CEO
Wheelabrator-Frye, Inc. | *NUMBER OF ISSUES:* 8

*NUMBER OF
RECOMMENDATIONS:* 117 |
| | Forrest N. Shumway
Chairman of the Board
and CEO
The Signal Companies,
Inc. | *3-YEAR
COST SAVINGS:* $.602
($ billions) |
| *PROJECT
MANAGER:* | Andrew J. Chitiea
Board of Directors and
Senior Vice President
The Signal Companies,
Inc. | *3-YEAR
CASH ACCELERATION:* $.477
($ billions) |
| *NUMBER OF
TASK FORCE
MEMBERS:* | 23 | |

Overview

In FY 1983, expenditures by the Department of Health and Human Services (HHS) totaled $268 billion, or about one-third of all Federal outlays. HHS employees numbered over 135,000 in 1983, compared to 35,000 in 1953. Because of the size, complexity, and scope of HHS-administered programs, three PPSS Task Forces reviewed HHS. This Task Force focused on HHS Department Management, the Office of Human Development Services (HDS), and the independent ACTION agency.

HDS provides social services for the elderly, children, and youth; Native Americans; and persons with developmental disabilities through grants to state, local, and private agencies. The FY 1983 budget for HHS Department Management was $267 million; for HDS, $4.931 billion; and for ACTION, $117 million. ACTION's mission is to advocate and support the voluntary efforts of citizens and public and private organizations to help solve the problems of the poor, disabled, elderly, and youth with special needs.

The Task Force found that different, and sometimes conflicting, management philosophies have been imposed in the endless effort to manage the increasingly cumbersome and unwieldy scope of program operations. The Department exhibits characteristics of both centralized and decentralized management systems. Together in one organization they guarantee inefficiency and conflict.

The Task Force examined eight issues and made 117 recommendations which would result in cost savings of $601.7 million and $477.0 million in cash acceleration over a three-year period.

Department Management—The Task Force found problems of layering, duplication, conflicting responsibilities and authorities, and lack of accountability in HHS's Department Management which result in expenditures of substantial time and resources with disappointing results. To clarify responsibilities and authority, the following actions were proposed: restructuring and reducing the size of Department Management, adopting a decentralized organization concept and operating philosophy, and reducing the size and scope of various staff functions.

Implementation of the Task Force recommendations would yield three-year cost savings of $247.6 million.

Responsibility and accountability for correspondence within HHS are inadequately defined. This lack is manifested in lower productivity and poor quality. To remedy these deficiencies, the Task Force recommended actions which would result in a $7.1 million cost savings over a three-year period.

ACTION—ACTION is overstaffed, with an organizational structure that predates the Peace Corps 1982 split-out. The Agency has neither revamped its organization nor pared down overhead expenditures to match its narrowed mission. Task Force recommendations, which would result in three-year cost savings of $26.7 million, include reducing staff from 603 to 360 and placing increased emphasis on managerial skills in future employees.

Human Development Services (HDS)—The Task Force concluded that HDS's structure and the distribution of functional responsibilities and accountability should be revised and clarified to avoid duplication, fragmentation, overlap of functions, and excessive organizational layers for effective management. Task Force recommendations would result in cost savings of $56.3 million over a three-year period.

The Task Force also found that since research results cannot be directly associated with program, policy, or legislative changes, the cost of HDS's investment in social research may exceed the benefits. Moreover, studies continue to be funded in heavily researched areas, even though most HDS programs are mature and should not require significant research funding to sustain established levels of service. The Task Force recommended that a moratorium be declared on new research projects for FY 1984 and that the social research management process also be improved. In addition, it recommended the elimination of policy research being undertaken by HHS's Department Management because sufficient research is already being performed within HHS's operating divisions. Three-year cost savings were projected at $112.2 million.

Fiscal Management—In fiscal management, the Task Force found significant opportunities for improvement, particularly with respect to "delay of drawdown." When funds for the Federal Government's share of Medicaid are transferred to any state, a balance of excess Federal funds, or float, builds up before funds are disbursed. This float costs the Federal Government interest to finance, and the state can invest the funds from this float in the short-term market and gain windfall interest income.

Under the delay-of-drawdown program, the Government estimates the number of days between the issuance of check and presentation of that check for payment. Thirty states have volunteered to go onto the program and agreed to delay drawing down Federal funds. Twenty states have procrastinated or refused.

Failure to meet the delay-of-drawdown implementation schedule for all states has resulted in substantial costs to the Federal Government. The Task Force strongly recommended that all 20 remaining states be brought under the delay-of-drawdown program immediately, and that ultimately a checks-paid letter-of-credit approval be implemented for the Federal Government's advance to Aid to Families with Dependent Children and Medicaid funds.

Implementation of Task Force recommendations would result in cost savings of $158.9 million and cash acceleration of $477.0 million over a three-year period.

Implementation

Of the 117 recommendations formulated by the Task Force, 111 (95 percent) can be implemented by Agency authority—including all of the recommendations involving cost savings of $.602 billion—1 (1 percent) can be implemented through Presidential action, and 5 (4 percent) require Congressional approval.

Task Force on
The Department of Health and Human Services:
the Public Health Service and
the Health Care Financing Administration

CO-CHAIRS:	Samuel H. Armacost President and CEO Bank of America	*NUMBER OF ISSUES:* 18
	Edward L. Hennessy, Jr. Chairman, President, and CEO Allied Corp.	*NUMBER OF* *RECOMMENDATIONS:* 71 *3-YEAR* *COST SAVINGS:* $12.677 ($ billions)
	Charles J. Pilliod, Jr. Chairman and CEO Goodyear Tire & Rubber Company	*3-YEAR* *REVENUE GENERATION:* $.662 ($ billions)
PROJECT *MANAGER:*	Albert F. Ritardi Director, Medical and Environmental Services Allied Corp.	*3-YEAR* *CASH ACCELERATION:* $.052 ($ billions)
NUMBER OF *TASK FORCE* *MEMBERS:* 31		

Overview

The Department of Health and Human Services (HHS) is the Federal agency most directly concerned with personal welfare and human concerns. HHS is the largest department of the Executive Branch in budget expenditures, with an FY 1983 budget of $268 billion and a full-time equivalent staff of 141,000. The Task Force Report on the Health Care Financing Administration (HCFA) and the Public Health Service (PHS) is one of three PPSS reports focusing on HHS.

HCFA, created in 1977, primarily administers oversight of Medicare and Medicaid programs which together accounted for $75.3 billion of HCFA's FY 1983 budget of $87.8 billion. HCFA has about 4,200 employees.

The major functions of PHS are to assist states and communities with the development of local health resources and education programs for health professions; to improve the delivery of health services to all Americans; to conduct and support research in the medical and related sciences and to disseminate scientific information; to protect the health of the nation against impure and unsafe foods, drugs and cosmetics, and other potential hazards; and to provide national leadership for the prevention and control of communicable disease. PHS employees number about 49,000 and its total FY 1983 budget was $7.782 billion.

A major reorganization of the existing financial structure of the health care system is needed to contain spiraling health care costs. Between 1960 and 1980, total public and private spending for health grew from $27 billion to $244 billion and, as a share of Gross National Product, from 5.3 percent to 9.5 percent. The Federal Government share grew over 2,000 percent from $3 billion to $71 billion.

Administration of Medicare and Medicaid requires a stable, continuous, and highly competent top management team. The Task Force found that HCFA suffers from an exceptionally high turnover of key management staff, and that top officials spend two or three days a week in Washington, D.C., instead of directing operational management functions at HCFA's Baltimore, Maryland, headquarters. At PHS, the Task Force found administrative redundancy and wasteful practices.

Issues and Recommendations

The Task Force identified 18 issues and 71 specific recommendations which, when implemented, will result in three-year cost savings of $12.677 billion, revenue generation of $662.0 million, and cash acceleration of $51.7 million.

HCFA—Medicare costs represent a growing burden to the Federal budget and a major contribution to health care cost inflation. In 1983, the Medicare program grew about 16 percent, compared to a budget growth of 4.5 percent. The urgency of controlling costs is exacerbated by the difficulties facing the Social Security system. The Medicare Hospital Insurance Trust Fund faces bankruptcy in 1987 unless the funding/benefit basis is changed.

The Task Force criticized cost control disincentives built into the HCFA system, such as paying hospitals regardless of the validity of costs from an efficiency standpoint; paying physicians on a usual, customary, and reasonable (UCR) basis; and allowing reimbursement of costs associated with excess hospital capacity.

Recommendations were made to counter these disincentives without reducing benefits or raising taxes. These included changing to a national prospective system for Medicare hospital reimbursement; adopting a fixed fee prospective system for Medicare physician reimbursement; and developing regulations for incentives to close or convert excess hospital capacity, such as the elimination of tax-free bonds to finance hospital construction.

Successful implementation of suggested recommendations depends largely on HCFA's developing an effective, experienced, and highly competent top management team. To strengthen HCFA's leadership, the Task Force recommended improvements in internal communications, operational planning, retention of competent Civil Service employees, efforts to minimize duplication among departments, manpower planning, and overall proactive execution.

Implementation of Task Force recommendations regarding HCFA would result in three-year cost savings of $10.833 billion and revenue generation of $622 million.

PHS—PPSS found instances of redundant positions and overstaffing causing operational inefficiencies. Specific recommendations included eliminating some 4,600 redundant positions, revising reduction-in-force procedures, dissolving the Office of Assistant Secretary for Health and integrating it with the Office of the Secretary, and decentralizing overall authority and responsibility in PHS.

With respect to fiscal management and control, the Task Force identified a need for improving collections from PHS scholarship and loan programs, revising reimbursement procedures to contract care providers of the Indian Health Service, instituting a cost control management-by-objectives program, and changing the eligibility criteria for Indian Health Service coverage and benefits.

The Task Force also found inefficient administration of research and development at PHS, including substantial cost variations in similar grants and contracts, lack of adequate controls on equipment purchases by NIH grant recipients, and duplicative or unnecessary programs and facilities. Task Force recommendations included establishing ceilings on administrative costs for grants and contracts; reducing overhead costs, eliminating equipment funding, and systematically reviewing research grants at recipient institutions; and eliminating planned construction.

Implementation of Task Force recommendations relevant to PHS operations would result in three-year cost savings totaling $1.843 billion.

Implementation

Of the 71 recommendations formulated by the Task Force, 45 (63 percent) are within Agency authority and 26 (37 percent) will need Congressional approval.

Task Force on
The Department of Health and Human Services
Social Security Administration

CO-CHAIRS:	John J. Byrne Chairman, President, and CEO GEICO Corp.	*NUMBER OF* *TASK FORCE* *MEMBERS:* 30
	Joseph P. Downer Vice Chairman Atlantic Richfield Co.	*NUMBER OF ISSUES:* 10 *NUMBER OF* *RECOMMENDATIONS:* 56
	Harold A. Eckmann Chairman and CEO Atlantic Mutual Insurance Co.	*3-YEAR* *COST SAVINGS:* $8.407 ($ billions)
	George P. Jenkins Former Chairman and CEO Metropolitan Life Insurance Co.	*3-YEAR* *REVENUE GENERATION:* $.980 ($ billions)
PROJECT *MANAGER:*	John J. Byrne Assistant Vice President The Atlantic Companies	*3-YEAR* *CASH ACCELERATION:* $4.661 ($ billions)

Overview

The Social Security Administration (SSA), one of the four operating divisions of the Health and Human Services Department (HHS), has grown significantly since its inception in the late 1930s. SSA programs include Old Age and Survivors Insurance, Disability Insurance, Supplemental Security Income, and Aid to Families with Dependent Children (AFDC). SSA is also responsible for processing Medicare beneficiary entitlement and premium information for the Health Care Financing Administration. SSA had an FY 1983 budget of $189 billion and employed 81,690 people representing 70 percent of the HHS budget authority and 59 percent of HHS personnel. The HHS-Social Security Administration Task Force was one of three PPSS Task Forces to review HHS.

Issues and Recommendations

The Task Force reviewed ten issues and formulated 56 recommendations which would result in three-year cost savings of $8.407 billion, revenue generation of $980 million, and cash acceleration of $4.661 billion. The issues and recommendations fall into three principal categories: automated data processing (ADP), major operational issues, and administrative law judges.

Automated Data Processing—The most critical situation within SSA is the computer operation, which is trying to fulfill its key role using obsolete systems and hardware. The Task Force focused on the current Systems Modernization Plan (SMP), developed in an effort to modernize SSA computer operations. Although the Task Force supported the aggressive initiatives undertaken to implement SMP, it concluded that implementation will take longer than the proposed five years and will cost significantly more than the half billion dollars currently estimated.

Despite specific problems, the Task Force was encouraged to find that SSA has initiated a process of change and growth and has institutionalized a structure for managing that process. Although the Task Force did not identify specific cost savings in the area of ADP, cost-saving recommendations presented elsewhere in the Report depend on the availability of an effective, modern computer system in SSA.

Operational Issues—The greatest number of recommendations developed fell into the category of operational issues. Line supervisors are not actively involved in the daily control of work flow, have no standardized means of organizing work within the office, and are rarely provided with quantitative/objective goals by management. The Task Force recommended the implementation of a supervisory productivity management system which ultimately would lead to a system for managing office activity throughout SSA. Concluding that the current network of SSA field offices was too large and too complex, it recommended that the 1,343 district/branch offices be reduced to approximately 500 and that resident/contact stations (3,476) and teleservice centers (33) be eliminated.

In order to reduce erroneous payments at AFDC, which in FY 1983 totaled $370 million, the Task Force recommended enforcement of the Michael Amendment which requires the Government to impose fiscal sanctions on states which fail to achieve legislated error rate targets. The Task Force also called on HHS to consider withholding an estimated sanction amount from state AFDC grants based upon a projection of the state's benefit payment base and payment error rate.

With respect to SSA's Annual Earnings Test, which is designed to ensure that recipients of Old Age and Survivors Insurance (OASI) and Disability Insurance (DI) do not earn outside income in excess of the maximum amount allowable, the Task Force found SSA's error rate reports to be complicated, untimely, and lacking in any useful data for trend analysis. As a result, the Task Force recommended the preparation of computer tapes of all OASI beneficiaries aged 62 to 69 and DI beneficiaries in order to facilitate the mailing of annual reporting forms, the adjustment of benefits at the beginning of the calendar year, accelerated enforcement of rules and procedures pertaining to overpayments, and the collection of interest from beneficiaries receiving overpayments. The Task Force also proposed simplifying and auditing SSA's Program Operating Manual and eliminating all future Federal Fiscal Liability Payments.

Implementation of recommendations pertaining to operations management would result in three-year cost savings of $4.760 billion, revenue generation of $980 million, and cash acceleration of $4.661 billion.

Administrative Law Judges—In its review of the appellate system for Social Security disability claims, the Task Force found that although the SSA process of review is called appellate, it is not, since new evidence may be introduced at all levels of the review process. The process is characterized by high reversal rates, with the Disability Determination Service (DDS) denying 70 percent of the claims and the SSA Administrative Law Judges reversing 60 percent of the denied claims that reach them. Further, when engaged in continuing disability investigations, DDS terminates benefits already awarded in almost 50 percent of the cases. By contrast, the Administrative Law Judges reverse almost 80 percent of the cases taken on appeal. In the view of the Task Force, the high reversal rate is due to inconsistent criteria used throughout the appellate process, a problem exacerbated by increasing work loads, lengthy time frames for processing claims, and increasing administrative costs. The Task Force recommended that SSA establish one set of operative standards for all levels of adjudication; strengthen the role and procedures of DDS; eliminate the opportunity to provide new data at each level of appeal; and limit the number of permissible refilings.

The Task Force estimated that implementation of its savings would result in three-year cost savings totaling $3.647 billion.

Implementation

SSA can implement 54 of the 56 recommendations (96 percent). The remaining two recommendations (4 percent) will require action by the Congress.

Task Force on
Housing and Urban Development

CO-CHAIRS:	Frank T. Cary	*NUMBER OF ISSUES:*	10
	Chairman of the		
	Executive Committee	*NUMBER OF*	
	IBM Corporation	*RECOMMENDATIONS:*	50
	Richard Cooley	*3-YEAR*	
	Chairman, President, and	*COST SAVINGS:*	$2.460
	CEO	($ billions)	
	Seattle First National		
	Bank	*3-YEAR*	
	Barry F. Sullivan	*REVENUE GENERATION:*	$ .358
	Chairman and CEO	($ billions)	
	First National Bank of		
	Chicago	*3-YEAR*	
		CASH ACCELERATION:	$ .667
PROJECT	Richard J. Borda	($ billions)	
MANAGER:	Executive Vice President		
	Wells Fargo Bank		
NUMBER OF			
TASK FORCE			
MEMBERS:	41		

Overview

Established in 1965, the Department of Housing and Urban Development (HUD) administers more than 60 programs, including mortgage insurance, rental subsidies for low-income families, anti-discrimination regulations, and rehabilitation and preservation activities. HUD is essentially a financial institution with a social mission.

HUD estimated outlays in FY 1983 were $13.0 billion. Of the total 15,122 employees, 4,081 are located in Washington and 11,041 serve in regional and field offices.

The Task Force found that HUD's concentration on its social mission —program delivery—has turned attention away from cost-effective administration. This emphasis has led to the extension of programs to ineligible recipients and a corresponding neglect of accounting systems. A lack of automated systems has inflated staff numbers and resulted in management layering and inefficient debt collection.

Issues and Recommendations

The Task Force selected ten issue areas for study and proposed 50 recommendations which, when implemented, will result in a cost savings of $2.460 billion, revenue generation of $358 million, and cash acceleration of $666.7 million over three years. The ten issue areas studied can be aggregated into three main categories: financial management; internal organization and administrative procedures, including the management of the 2,700 Public Housing Authorities (PHAs); and the acquisition, management, and disposition of real estate holdings.

Financial Management—Accounting practices and internal financial controls at HUD are materially deficient. Accounting systems are primarily manual and, even where automated, are mostly outdated. No one area of HUD has been given total responsibility and authority for coordinating and developing Department-wide financial management practices and procedures. Problems over lump-sum disbursement have not been resolved with suitable accounting methods. Generally accepted accounting practices and procedures are not followed in administering Federal Housing Administration (FHA) insurance loans. Departmental review and verification of financial information is limited or non-existent.

To correct unsound financial management, the Task Force recommended the establishment of an Office of the Assistant Secretary for Financial Management with responsibility for coordinating and developing Department-wide financial management practices and procedures. Other recommendations included the automation of current manual financial systems; the development and implementation of an aggressive cash management program; contracting out, where necessary, for cash management systems and debt collection; and improved management of HUD's loan portfolio.

Implementation of these recommendations would result in cost savings of $2.302 billion, revenue generation of $318.9 million, and cash acceleration of $666.7 million over a three-year period.

Organization and Administration—Frequent management turnover and changes in program direction have resulted in overlap and duplication of functions and management layering. The Time Reporting System, which is overly complex, provides questionable benefits. Disparity in the nature and size of PHAs makes performance evaluation difficult and the current formula for calculating PHA operating subsidies provides no incentive for reducing operating costs. In particular, HUD and PHA management personnel generally lack the skills necessary to employ more sophisticated management techniques.

In addition to specific actions, the Task Force recommended that an evaluation team be created to review all major programs, support areas, and field offices of management and/or administration, with specific targeting of overlap and duplication.

Three-year cost savings of $69.6 million are projected.

Acquisition/Management/Disposition of Real Estate—Problems exist despite progress in the reduction of inventory. Lack of qualified personnel, decentralized responsibility and authority, poor internal communications, complex regulations, and the absence of incentives to meet property disposition goals have discouraged cost-effective management.

No formal tracking system exists to monitor progress in the foreclosure process. Existing evaluation procedures are inconsistent and the disposition process is further hampered by lack of reliable data systems and unnecessary legal delays.

Task Force recommendations included establishing a centralized monitoring system to track foreclosures and expedite the acquisition of properties for foreclosure; establishing a disposition and sales program which is more evenly distributed throughout the year; enacting amendments to the Internal Revenue Service Code relative to cash accounting and depreciation; and changing the current "sell as is" policy in the sale of single family properties.

Implementation of these recommendations would result in a three-year cost savings of $89.1 million and revenue generation of $38.6 million.

Implementation

Of the 50 Task Force recommendations, 47 (94 percent) can be implemented directly by agency officials and 3 (6 percent) will require Congressional authorization.

**Task Force on
The Department of the Interior**

CO-CHAIRS:	George D. Anderson President Anderson ZurMuehlen & Co.	*NUMBER OF TASK FORCE MEMBERS:* 24
	William T. Coleman, Jr. Partner O'Melveny & Myers	*NUMBER OF ISSUES:* 9
	Morley P. Thompson President Baldwin-United Corp.	*NUMBER OF RECOMMENDATIONS:* 27 *3-YEAR COST SAVINGS:* $ .271 ($ billions)
	Hays T. Watkins Chairman and CEO CSX Corporation	*3-YEAR REVENUE GENERATION:* $1.022 ($ billions)
PROJECT MANAGER:	Robert C. Hacking Manager, State and Local Government Ernst & Whinney	*3-YEAR CASH ACCELERATION:* $ .231 ($ billions)

Overview

The Department of Interior, established in 1849, is one of the Government's oldest departments. Its FY 1983 budget (obligational authority) was $6.7 billion and employees totaled close to 73,000. As the nation's principal conservation agency, Interior has responsibility for most of the nationally owned public lands and natural resources.

In performing its mission, the Department frequently is placed in conflicting roles—conservator and developer, trustee and program manager. Opportunities identified for cost control focused on improved management practices, stricter adherence to current policies, and changes which would put some of Interior's operations on a more businesslike basis. Opportunities for revenue generation primarily involve the sale of unneeded public lands.

Issues and Recommendations

The Task Force studied nine issues and formulated 27 recommendations which, when fully implemented, will allow the Department to achieve three-year savings of $271.2 million and revenue generation of $1.022 billion. Identified issues and recommendations can be grouped into three major categories: land management, National Park Service (NPS) operations, and fiscal management and control.

Land Management—With adequate advance planning, some $900 million in net revenue and $146 million in interest savings could be generated from the sale of excess public lands during the first three years. The sale of excess land would represent less than 1 percent of lands under the control of the Bureau of Land Management (BLM). Federal law and regulations provide reasonable and adequate safeguards over disposal of excess lands. Parks and wilderness areas, environmentally sensitive areas, and similar lands would not be sold.

With respect to rangeland management, the Task Force concluded that transfer of the rangeland to private ownership could save an estimated $93.1 million over three years. Given the total acreage of public rangeland and the potential controversy involved with its direct transfer to the private sector, the Task Force proposed as an alternative long-term grazing permits of 99 years duration which can accomplish the same objective. Under this approach, the maintenance, management, and improvement of the rangelands would be shifted to the permit holder. Under either alternative, the Task Force believes that safeguards on use and access can and should be established.

The Task Force also found that grazing fees were $2.30 per animal unit in 1981, while comparable charges were $5 to $15 on commercial rangeland and on lands owned by the Bureau of Indian Affairs and the Department of Defense. An increase in BLM fees to market rates could result in $19.5 million of added revenues over a three-year period. In addition, the Task Force identified but did not claim savings for other cost control opportunities in the area of Environmental Impact Statement preparation, payments in lieu of taxes to state and local governments, and consolidation of selected land management activities now performed by both BLM and the Forest Service.

In addition to Interior, the Environmental Protection Agency, the Coast Guard, and the Army Corps of Engineers are involved in monitoring resource development on the Outer Continental Shelf (OCS), resulting in duplication and delays in the permit issuing process. The Task Force estimated that by consolidating 30 percent of the currently required inspections and eliminating certain required OCS reporting to Congress, three-year cost savings of $5.5 million could result.

National Park Service Operations—During 1981, the NPS operated 333 parks and charged entrance fees at only 64 of them. Operating costs in the national park system rose 296 percent between 1971 and 1981. Revenue increased 11 percent and entry fee revenues as a percentage of operating costs declined from 7 to 2 percent. Adjusted for inflation, entry fees declined over 50 percent.

The Task Force recommended repealing the current Congressional freeze on NPS entrance fees and increasing revenues generated by camping, tour, and entrance fees.

The Task Force also identified cost control opportunities in concession management practices at parks. Currently, the average franchise fee is 2 percent of gross receipts, significantly below the private sector standard. In addition, a need exists for better contract administration, negotiation, and renegotiation. The Task Force recommended strengthening the Office of Concessioner Management, increasing concessioner competition, and adopting the Visitor Facility Fund Bill which earmarks a portion of concessioner fees for repair and maintenance facilities.

The Task Force calculated that three-year revenue generation of $102.6 million would occur as a result of implementation of its recommendations.

Fiscal Management and Control—Substantial improvements are required in the debt collection activities of the Bureau of Indian Affairs, where 77 percent of the delinquent loans have been delinquent longer than 180 days, even though policy sets 90 days as the maximum. The Task Force also recommended instituting block grants in the Fish and Wildlife Service and improving cash management practices, including use of lock boxes. Implementation of the Task Force recommendations would result in three-year cost savings of $26.6 million and cash acceleration of $230.5 million.

Implementation

The Task Force's survey of nine issues resulted in the formulation of 27 recommendations of which 15 (56 percent) can be implemented by the Agency, 10 (37 percent) by Congress, and 2 (7 percent) by the President.

**Task Force on
The Department of Justice**

CO-CHAIRS:	Weston R. Christopherson Chairman and CEO Jewel Companies, Inc.	*NUMBER OF TASK FORCE MEMBERS:* 12	
	Frederick Deane Chairman and CEO Bank of Virginia	*NUMBER OF ISSUES:* 10 *NUMBER OF RECOMMENDATIONS:* 37	
	Jewel S. Lafontant Senior Partner Lafontant, Wilkins, Jones & Ware, P.C.	*3-YEAR COST SAVINGS:* $.183 ($ billions)	
	Arthur Levitt, Jr. Chairman and CEO American Stock Exchange, Inc.	*3-YEAR REVENUE GENERATION:* $.667 ($ billions)	
PROJECT MANAGER:	Clarence S. Wilson, Jr. Member of Firm Lafontant, Wilkins, Jones & Ware, P.C.	*3-YEAR CASH ACCELERATION:* $.288 ($ billions)	

Overview

The overall mission of the Department of Justice (DOJ) is to enforce the law in the public interest, to represent the United States in all Supreme Court cases, to represent the Federal Government in legal matters generally, and to render legal advice and opinions to the President and to the heads of Executive departments. DOJ is headed by the Attorney General. In FY 1983, DOJ employed 56,000 people. Its proposed FY 1984 budget is $3.4 billion. The Immigration and Naturalization Service (INS) is part of the Department.

The Task Force compared DOJ to other Federal agencies and private law practices, using general principles of good management. The Task Force identified opportunities for improvements in planning, reporting, systems efficiency, and maximizing the use of personnel.

Issues and Recommendations

The Task Force identified nine issues for review and formulated 32 recommendations specifically focusing on DOJ. The tenth issue and accompanying five recommendations addressed the Offices of Inspectors General (IG), who are independent auditors in departments and agencies. When fully implemented, the recommendations will result in cost savings of $183.2 million and revenue generation of $666.9 million over a three-year period, in addition to a cash acceleration of $288.4 million.

Organizational and Human Resources Management—The Task Force identified Agency-wide opportunities for improvements in the use of paralegals. Currently, DOJ has an 8:1 ratio of attorneys to paralegals; the ratio found in the private sector is 5:1. The Task Force recommended increasing personnel ceilings for paralegals and establishing a paralegal coordination office to act as a liaison among paralegals, attorneys, and managers of the different divisions.

To improve resource management by the INS and the port-of-entry inspection services, the Task Force recommended that INS reduce central and regional office staffing by 298 positions and that the Office of Management and Budget (OMB) assume responsibility for coordinating and ultimately consolidating the activities of the various port-of-entry inspection services for entering passengers and cargo. It also recommended promoting technological advances to speed port-of-entry processing for passengers.

When implemented, recommendations in the areas of organizational and human resources management will result in a three-year cost savings of $87.5 million.

Fiscal Management and Control—Cost savings opportunities exist in the Department's revenue collection efforts, asset seizure and forfeiture practices, travel procurement procedures, and investment of excess profits by Federal Prison Industries, Inc. (UNICOR).

DOJ acts as a collection attorney for other Federal agencies and as an attorney on behalf of the United States in the collection of civilian fines and claims. To improve cost efficiency in these activities, the Task Force recommended the use of private collection agencies and the adoption of a uniform reporting system for claims forwarded to DOJ for legal action. It also recommended improved management of seized assets.

Improvements in the area of travel procurement, including the use of personal credit cards as a pilot program, and the remittance to the U.S. Treasury of excess UNICOR profits earned in the next three years also were recommended by the Task Force.

Implementation of the Task Force's recommendations would result in three-year cost savings of $58.4 million, with three-year revenue generation of $666.9 million and cash acceleration of $288.4 million.

Automated Data Processing Systems—DOJ is in need of improved automated legal support systems to facilitate the availability of information necessary to plan and manage litigation. Recommendations included the implementation of a coordinated systems development effort, with specific emphasis on the identification of user needs and requirements.

Implementation of the recommendations would result in cost savings of $37.3 million over a three-year period.

Improvements in Inspector General Operations—The Task Force's review of the IGs indicated a lack of a common perception of their roles, insufficient coordination among IGs in different departments and agencies, and inadequate technical support for the IGs at a central level in the Executive Branch. To correct these problems, the Task Force recommended organizational and procedural changes, including coordination of systems development among constituent agencies, improved acquisition procedures, strong ADP leadership, and a central office to be responsible for coordinating the activities of the IGs.

Specific savings were not quantified for this issue, although the Task Force recognized that savings will accrue from improved IG operations, including further reductions in waste, fraud, and abuse.

Implementation

Of the 32 recommendations pertaining specifically to DOJ, 19 (59 percent) fall within DOJ's purview; 8 (25 percent) require Presidential involvement; and 5 (16 percent) require Congressional action.

**Task Force on
The Department of Labor**

CO-CHAIRS:	James S. Kemper, Jr. Chairman Kemper Corporation	*NUMBER OF TASK FORCE MEMBERS:* 32
	Francis C. Rooney, Jr. CEO Melville Corporation	*NUMBER OF ISSUES:* 14
	Richard R. Shinn Chairman and CEO Metropolitan Life Insurance Co.	*NUMBER OF RECOMMENDATIONS:* 49
	Luke G. Williams CEO American Sign & Indicator Corp.	*3-YEAR COST SAVINGS:* $3.718 ($ billions)*
PROJECT MANAGER:	Max Hirschhorn Independent Consultant	

Overview

The purpose of the Department of Labor (DOL) is to promote and develop the welfare of American wage earners, improve their working conditions, and advance their opportunities for profitable employment. DOL administers over 130 Federal labor laws. During FY 1982, DOL employed approximately 18,000 persons full time. For FY 1982, it obligated approximately $37 billion.

The Task Force found that the Department already had under way aggressive programs for reducing costs and had achieved substantial cost savings. In initiating such constructive change, the Secretary and the DOL management team have established a climate for improvement. The Task Force approach was to select areas where private sector expertise could add to management initiatives.

Issues and Recommendations

The Task Force selected 14 issues to study and formulated 49 recommendations, which are projected to result in three-year cost savings of $3.718 billion. Areas studied include: the Federal Disability Program, automated data processing (ADP) and telecommunications, wage setting laws and area wage scales, and human resources and organizational management.

Federal Employment Disability Program—Under the Federal Employment Compensation Act approximately $650 million was paid in 1981 in compensation to claimants experiencing long-term (45 days or longer) traumatic injuries, and about $170 million was paid to cover medical expenses. The Task Force identified opportunities to improve claims investigation and monitor the payment of legitimate claims, and recommended changes in the payment of workers' compensation medical bills.

Task Force recommendations would result in three-year cost savings of $190.3 million.

Automated Data Processing and Telecommunications—To utilize DOL's current and about-to-be-acquired ADP systems more effectively, the Task Force recommended designating the Assistant Secretary of Administration and Management to exercise central control over the acquisition and management of all ADP equipment, services, and personnel. It was further recommended that DOL replace the planned and current procurements for ADP equipment with a single procurement plan.

Implementation of recommendations in this area would result in three-year cost savings of $16.2 million.

Wage Setting Laws—The Secretary of Labor establishes regulations and procedures to administer and enforce certain wage laws, namely, the Davis-Bacon, Walsh-Healey, and Service Contract Acts.

The Davis-Bacon Act originally was aimed at protecting local contractors from outside contractors. Today, local contractors perform only 28 percent of the Davis-Bacon projects, but 47 percent of the non-Davis-Bacon projects. The Walsh-Healey Act requires overtime pay for time worked in excess of eight hours per day, thus failing to take into consideration new alternative work schedules. The Service Contract Act (SCA), which sets minimum wage standards for service employees, has subsequently been extended by regulation to cover such service workers as highly paid, high-technology employees.

To address the adverse consequences of these wage setting laws, the Task Force recommended: raising the threshold for application of Davis-Bacon Act requirements from $2,000 to $25,000; amending the Walsh-Healey Act to remove eight hours as the threshold for overtime pay for a single work day, but retaining the 40-hour-a-week threshold; and excluding ADP and high-technology contracts from SCA coverage. The Task Force estimated three-year cost savings of $3.227 billion as the result of its recommendations.

Area Wage Scales—The Federal Pay Comparability Act of 1970 requires that Federal pay rates be comparable with private sector pay rates for the same level of work. The basic pay system for Federal white-collar employees, the General Schedule, is a national pay system that has no provision for pay variations based upon local salary conditions. About 90 percent of the larger multi-establishment private sector companies use pay scales for non-supervisory white-collar employees based upon local salary conditions.

The Task Force recommended that the Secretary of Labor, functioning as the President's Pay Agent, propose legislation calling for the introduction of area wage scales on a city-by-city basis.

Implementation of the recommendations formulated by the Task Force would result in cost savings of $203.1 million over a three-year period.

Human Resources and Organizational Management—The Task Force studied opportunities to make DOL more efficient and effective in the accomplishment of its mission through better utilization of human resources and improved organizational management. Specific recommendations included reducing the number of regional offices, increasing the supervisory span of control, developing standardized measures of work performance, and providing managers with work incentives. Additional recommendations called for improved oversight of procurement activities and improved training and development programs.

Implementation of these and other recommendations would result in cost savings of $81.4 million over a three-year period.

Implementation

Of the 49 major recommendations formulated by the Task Force, 39 (80 percent) are within the purview of DOL, none involves Presidential action, and 10 (20 percent) will need Congressional approval. The authority of Congress is required to amend the three wage-setting Acts, and to introduce area wage scales for Federal civilian non-supervisory white-collar workers.

Task Force on
Land/Facilities/Personal Property

CO-CHAIRS:	John F. McGillicuddy Chairman and CEO Manufacturers Hanover Trust Co.	*NUMBER OF* *TASK FORCE* *MEMBERS:* 41
	Donald G. McNeely Chairman Space Center, Inc.	*NUMBER OF ISSUES:* 3
	Donald W. Nyrop Former CEO Northwest Airlines, Inc.	*NUMBER OF* *RECOMMENDATIONS:* 9 *3-YEAR* *COST SAVINGS:* $ .201
	Joseph J. Pinola Chairman and CEO First Interstate Bancorp	*($ billions)* *3-YEAR* *REVENUE GENERATION:* $ .426
	Darwin E. Smith Chairman and CEO Kimberly-Clark Corp.	*($ billions)*
PROJECT *MANAGER:*	Paul A. Jones Executive Vice President and Secretary Kimberly-Clark Corp.	

Overview

The Task Force identified specific opportunities for cost control and improved efficiency in its cross-cutting review of the Federal Government's management of its land, facilities, and personal property resources. In undertaking its review, the Task Force worked in close cooperation with the General Services Administration (GSA) and other PPSS Task Forces and concluded that the Department of the Interior's management of mineral resources is hampered unnecessarily by Congressional interference, that the Federal vehicle fleet suffers from decentralized management, and inactive Government files are stored longer than necessary.

Issues and Recommendations

Nine recommendations were made by the Task Force, with projected cost savings of $200.7 million and revenue generation of $426.2 million over a three-year period.

Offshore Minerals Management—The Federal Government owns the entire Outer Continental Shelf (OCS), an area with one billion acres and the greatest oil and gas potential of all Federal lands. Responsibility for administering the OCS rests with Interior's Mineral Management Service (MMS).

Since 1954, less than 23 million acres have been leased out by the Federal Government. Despite the considerable alarm raised in response to Interior's five-year plan to accelerate development of this national asset, the Task Force found that adequate safeguards in the law and in the plan make the program effective in the long run. The Task Force endorsed Interior's OCS plan. It did, however, recommend two lease changes which could increase Federal revenues without a loss of private sector incentives; namely, utilization of optimum royalty rate systems to maximize Federal revenues and use of seven-year primary terms for leases in harsh environments.

In the area of OCS management, the Task Force found that the OCS plan is vulnerable to unpredictable interruptions. Because long-range planning cannot be effective without predictability and finality, the Task Force recommended management changes designed to segregate Congressional policymaking from Interior's implementation of that policy. Specifically, it recommended making the MMS an independently funded entity using proceeds from OCS and repealing the requirement of annual Congressional reviews of finalized five-year plans.

Implementation of Task Force recommendations pertaining to management of OCS would result in three-year revenue generation of $410.4 million.

Motor Vehicle Management—The 318,000 Federal vehicles (excluding the U.S. Postal Service fleet) are divided among more than 100 Federal divisions, each operating its own motor pool independently. Virtually no cooperation or coordination exists among the fleet managers, resulting in inefficient, duplicative, and costly vehicle operations. Further, there is a serious lack of adequate data to make cost comparisons among agencies or with private fleets. As a result, the fundamental question of whether the Federal Government should be in the vehicle fleet business at all is unanswered.

The Task Force recommended that opportunities for standardization of procedures and management improvements be identified and implemented by all fleet agencies, that a Government-wide management information system be established to address the Government's continued ownership and operation of a motor vehicle fleet, that the current vehicle procurement process be revised to contract out for all new vehicles a year at a time, and that a reconditioning program be implemented for all decommissioned vehicles.

Implementation of Task Force recommendations would result in three-year savings of $146.1 million and revenue generation of $15.8 million.

Federal Records Management—Functioning under GSA, the National Archives and Records Service (NARS) is responsible for operating 14 record storage centers for inactive files, managing archival programs of significant historical value, providing technical training on records to other agencies, operating seven Presidential libraries, and publishing certain official documents. The Task Force found no major problems with the archival, publishing, and library functions, and focused on record management and technical training programs.

The cost of storing Government records is increasing faster than necessary. Contributing to this unnecessary proliferation are records without retention schedules, records with long retention schedules, and NARS's inability to require agencies to seek technical assistance and training. Poor record management is largely due to the lack of commitment from top agency officials. The Task Force recommended that departments and agencies be required to establish retention periods that do not exceed the useful life of records and, with GSA guidance, that record management practices be assessed and improvements implemented.

Implementation of recommendations in the area of record management would result in cost savings of $54.6 million over three years.

Implementation

Of the nine recommendations developed, four are within the purview of affected agencies, four involve Presidential action, and one requires Congressional approval.

**Task Force on
Low Income Standards and Benefits**

CO-CHAIRS:	Bennett Archambault CEO Stewart-Warner Corporation	*NUMBER OF TASK FORCE MEMBERS:* 24
	Richard J. Flamson, III Chairman and CEO Security Pacific National Bank	*NUMBER OF ISSUES:* 9 *NUMBER OF RECOMMENDATIONS:* 24
	Robert A. Schoellhorn Chairman and CEO Abbott Laboratories	*3-YEAR COST SAVINGS:* $5.887 ($ billions)
	Robert K. Wilmouth President and CEO National Futures Association	
PROJECT MANAGER:	Richard W. Strauss Manager, Washington Operations Stewart-Warner Corporation	

Overview

The Federal Government administers 64 entitlement programs with qualification criteria based on income and/or assets. In FY 1982 expenditures for these programs totaled $86.2 billion. The Low Income Standards and Benefits Task Force studied the following programs, which comprise 71 percent ($61.3 billion) of total entitlement expenditures: Medicaid; Aid to Families with Dependent Children (AFDC); Supplemental Security Income (SSI); Veterans Administration (VA) Pensions; Emergency Assistance and Low Income Home Energy Assistance (LIHEA); Food Stamps; Low-Rent Public Housing and other Housing Subsidies; Low Income Housing Assistance; Special Food Supplement to Women, Infants, and Children; and Child Nutrition.

The Task Force aimed at reducing administrative costs, minimizing overlap and duplication of benefit payments, and reducing fraud and abuse. These aims are the important objectives in targeting benefit payments more efficiently and improving the quality of service to those actually in need.

Issues and Recommendations

The Task Force made 24 recommendations which can be broadly grouped into three areas, with implementation of recommendations in cost savings of $5.887 billion over three years.

Program Coordination and Consolidation—The multiplicity of needs-based programs has created a complex situation in which many agencies in different departments perform distinct but overlapping functions, giving rise to a cumbersome welfare bureaucracy at state, local and Federal levels. The problem is exacerbated by the fact that state administrative costs for many programs (Food Stamps, AFDC, and Medicaid) are reimbursed on a 50 percent Federal open matching basis, thus reducing incentives to keep administrative costs down. State costs varied from $20 to $126 per average monthly case load in FY 1981.

The Task Force endorsed the 1982 Combined Welfare Administration (CWA) proposal to place Federal funding for administrative costs under a single block grant. Instead of setting the Federal share of state administrative costs at 95 percent of the FY 1982 amount, however, it suggested procedures be developed to adjust the amount of the grant based on anticipated case loads for the three programs and by cost level increases. Adoption of a modified CWA proposal by the Congress would limit the rapid growth of administrative costs, reduce and simplify the current reporting requirements, and result in three-year cost savings of $929.0 million.

Although not specifically addressing the veterans' pension program, the Task Force concluded that the very size of the program (exactly

1,901,101 veterans and veterans' survivors received benefits at a program cost of $3.786 billion) required close control over program operations. Task Force concurred with the PPSS Task Force on the VA, which recommended an independent analysis of eligibility and payment errors and the use of corrective action, including computer matching.

With respect to the Energy and Emergency Assistance programs and weatherization programs, the Task Force recommended program consolidation. At present, fewer than half the states participate in the Emergency Assistance program. Energy Assistance block grants are being transferred to other assistance programs, suggesting that original appropriations were overstated and that states have other priorities for these funds. Eliminating the Emergency Assistance program and terminating transfers from Energy Assistance to other programs would yield projected cost savings of $290.3 million over three years. In addition, it recommended merging most existing weatherization programs into the Community Block Grant Program administered by HUD.

Eligibility Verification/Automation—The Census Bureau reported that in 1981 over 14.5 million households (17 percent of total households) received one or more selected, means-tested, public noncash benefits. In spite of similarities in goals, procedures, and requirements, each program operates in a highly independent manner. Current estimates indicate $4.1 billion in overpayments were made in 1983 in five programs: AFDC, Food Stamps, SSI, Medicaid, and Section 8 Housing.

Although automation of data on public assistance recipients has been shown to be beneficial, legislative restrictions inhibit the development of fully integrated automated data processing (ADP) systems. Access to certain types of income information, for example, is restricted by law. To remove these restrictions, the Tax Reform Act of 1976 should be amended to allow needs-based programs to use Internal Revenue Service and Social Security Administration data, including income from self-employment and from military and Federal employment, as well as unearned income. In the Task Force's view, access to this information is fundamental to any effective integrated ADP systems.

The Task Force conservatively estimated three-year cost savings of $3.637 billion.

Improved Payment and Administrative Control—Substantial savings could ensue from the institution of payment systems, distribution methods, and/or simplified eligibility criteria that provide for increased control and accountability. SSI eligibility criteria are overly complex, the benefits formula is too inflexible, and the Medicaid open-ended reimbursement method provides no incentives for hospitals to be efficient since all costs are reimbursed as incurred. The Task Force recommended reducing the sensitivity of the SSI benefit formula to changes in recipients' circumstances, adopting a prospective payment system, and improving prescreening and case management.

The Task Force's recommendations would result in cost savings of $1.031 billion over a three-year period.

Implementation

Of the 24 recommendations formulated by the Task Force, 13 (54 percent) are within the jurisdiction of departments and agencies, 3 (13 percent) require action by the President, and 8 (33 percent) will need Congressional approval.

**Task Force on
The Department of the Navy**

CO-CHAIRS:	Nicholas T. Camicia Chairman and CEO The Pittston Company	*NUMBER OF TASK FORCE MEMBERS:* 33
	Maurice R. Greenberg President and CEO American International Group, Inc.	*NUMBER OF ISSUES:* 16 *NUMBER OF RECOMMENDATIONS:* 69
	Stanley Hiller, Jr. Chairman Hiller Investment	*3-YEAR COST SAVINGS:* $7.185 ($ billions)
	Thomas M. Macioce President and CEO Allied Stores Corp.	
PROJECT MANAGER:	Robert M. Cockrill Partner Coopers & Lybrand	

Overview

The Department of the Navy had an FY 1983 budget in excess of $86.0 billion, a military force of 755,000, and a civilian staff of 328,000. It maintains deployable fleet and air elements and conducts other activities which contribute to national security and the defense of the United States and its interests worldwide.

The Task Force found a lack of managerial skills compared to those in a well-run private corporation. It found a lower level of individual productivity and efficiency and a much higher cost of corporate (headquarters) overhead than in the private sector. Procedural requirements are burdensome, reviews are lengthy and excessive, and decision-making is fragmented.

The Task Force reviewed 16 issues and made 69 recommendations, which would result in three-year cost savings of $7.185 billion. Issues chosen for study were limited to those of importance to the Navy which could be compared to private sector business enterprises. These involved six major categories: weapons systems acquisition, supply and inventory management, implementation of systems for automated data processing (ADP), aircraft maintenance and overhaul, cash management, and career development.

Weapons Acquisition—The Task Force concluded that problems relating to program stability and economic production schedules, multiyear procurement, dual sourcing, and contractor incentives have resulted in significant cost increases and management inefficiencies. Specific problems included the disruptive factors of inconsistent and constantly changing fiscal and program guidance from the Office of the Secretary of Defense, the proclivity of the Navy to allow production of more weapons than it can fund at economic rates, and the extent and costly impact of program stretch-outs. In addition, failure to engage in multiyear procurement and dual sourcing has resulted in significant cost overruns and a less-than-optimal production base, while the absence of performance-based incentives for contractors, inadequate assessment, and late introduction of training requirements exacerbate costs.

The Task Force recommended limiting the number of programs put into production, establishing a two-year budget cycle, placing greater emphasis on multiyear contracting and dual sourcing, integrating production requirements and training needs, and improving incentives for contract performance.

Three-year cost savings associated with the Task Force's recommendations were estimated at $6.265 billion.

Supply and Inventory Management—Numerous problems and insufficiencies confront the Navy with respect to its vast supply network and inventory control points. Specifically, supply facilities on ships are monitored by unreliable computer-tracking systems, with inaccurate issues and receipts the result. The six Naval Supply Centers are plagued by inaccurate inventory records, excessive adjustments, unreliable management information, and inventory losses that amounted to $133.0 million in FY 1980 and $330.0 million in FY 1981. Specific recommendations included more effective training and work standards development; standardization of components at supply and weapons centers; and extension of officer tours at weapons stations, supply centers, and inventory control points for greater continuity and experience in the management of those operations. Cost savings of approximately $200.0 million over three years would result from implementation of these recommendations.

Automated Data Processing—Most Navy computers were installed in the mid-1960s and early 1970s and represent technology and operating systems that are obsolete. Equipment is difficult and expensive to maintain, and diminishing reliability causes frequent malfunctions and reduces productivity. The Navy is installing some new computer systems, but the estimated time required for completion of these projects is excessive. It was recommended that the Navy improve management of ADP assets and functions by consolidating reviews for the ADP-approval cycle, encouraging purchase of general purpose computers, making full use of delegated procurement authority and umbrella contracts, and establishing an office with overall responsibility. Recommendations, upon implementation, would produce cost savings of approximately $180.0 million over three years.

Aircraft Maintenance and Overhaul—Aircraft maintenance management is divided in the Navy. Fleet commanders who operate the aircraft have no control over the work content, duration, or funds spent at the depot level. At Naval Air Rework Facilities, the Task Force questioned what appeared to be excessive frequency of heavy aircraft overhauls. Comparison of private airline service programs with the Navy's program revealed order of magnitude differences in maintenance expenditures. The number of man-hours funded for maintenance engineering by the Navy was also found to be higher than anticipated, while analysis of Navy engineering staffs indicated that the Navy staffing levels are higher than those of all the civilian airlines combined, on a comparable basis. The Task Force recommended giving aircraft fleet commanders responsibility for in-service, life-cycle aircraft maintenance management; extending time intervals between aircraft overhauls; and reducing technical staff at rework facilities. Cost savings of $510.0 million over three years would result from these recommendations.

Cash and Career Management—Reducing Federal borrowing requirements by reducing cash held by $50 million and prompt deposit of cash receipts would yield savings, as would career management innovations, including longer lengths of tour duty and special talent pools. Total estimated savings are $30.0 million over three years.

Implementation

Of the 69 major recommendations made by the Task Force, 66 (96 percent) are within the authority of the Department of the Navy to implement. One (1 percent of the total) requires Presidential action and two (3 percent) need Congressional approval.

**Task Force on
Personnel Management**

CO-CHAIRS:	Robert Hatfield President New York Hospital	*NUMBER OF TASK FORCE MEMBERS:* 21
	Donald R. Keough President The Coca-Cola Company	*NUMBER OF ISSUES:* 18 *NUMBER OF*
	John A. Puelicher Chairman and CEO Marshall & Ilsley Corp.	*RECOMMENDATIONS:* 95 *3-YEAR COST SAVINGS:* $39.270
PROJECT MANAGER:	Sy B. Pranger Independent Consultant	($ billions)

Overview

The Office of Personnel Management (OPM) is a small, independent agency responsible for overseeing the execution and administration of laws, rules, and regulations covering over 2.1 million Federal civilian employees (excluding the Postal Service). In FY 1982, it had a staff of 5,000 and an operating budget of $157.0 million. OPM administers the Civil Service Retirement Fund, the Federal Employees Health Benefits Fund, and the Federal Employees Life Insurance Fund, which in the aggregate are responsible for $41.7 billion of benefit obligations.

The Task Force studied the cost-effectiveness and efficiency of Government-wide personnel programs, focusing on employee benefits, compensation levels, and service contracting guidelines. It concluded that significant and far-reaching opportunities exist for cost control and improved management efficiencies. The Task Force did not address personnel issues related to the military forces or the U.S. Postal Service.

Issues and Recommendations

Eighteen issues were studied and 95 recommendations formulated, which would result in three-year cost savings of $39.270 billion.

Civil Service Retirement System (CSRS)—The Task Force found that the CSRS is more costly than comparable private sector programs. The average cost of pensions (as a percent of payroll) to an employer in the private sector is 14 percent; in the Federal Government it is 29 percent.

This unfavorable differential does *not* reflect the unfunded CSRS pension liability of $500 billion. In contrast, private sector retirement plans are fully funded. Amortization of this unfunded liability over a 40-year period would raise Government pension costs to 85 percent of payroll.

To control costs, the Task Force recommended raising the normal retirement age to 62, discontinuing the practice of crediting unused sick leave as extra service, reducing benefits for early retirees, replacing the CSRS disability provision with a separate long-term disability plan, and eliminating overindexing in cost-of-living adjustment practices.

Three-year cost savings from the implementation of these and other recommendations would be $15.890 billion.

Federal Employees Health Benefits Program (FEHBP)—The Federal Government spends an inordinately large percent of payroll on health care when compared to the private sector. An extremely complex health insurance package offers 168 separate plans, with different costs and benefits. The 3.7 million employees and annuitants may change plans annually. FEHBP health benefit plans cost more per beneficiary due to adverse selection, caused by the numerous plan choices, the high ratio of more costly annuitant beneficiaries, and the difficulty in administering such a complex program.

Proposed actions include limiting open enrollment to alternate years, strengthening cost containment programs, and streamlining benefit packages. In total, recommendations would result in three-year cost savings of $1.357 billion.

Pay Comparability—Pay comparability is overstated for Federal employees under both the General Schedule (GS) system and Federal Wage System (FWS).

The GS pay comparability system, which covers 1.4 million Federal employees, should expand its pay survey to include the salaries of workers in state and local governments, nonprofit organizations, and small and medium-sized firms, and be conducted every other year instead of annually. Local pay rates should be used for certain locally recruited jobs.

To improve wage comparability for 450,000 blue-collar workers under FWS, the Task Force recommended the redesign of the current five-step pay range to a three-step structure; the repeal of the Monroney Amendment, which provides for out-of-area data in wage surveys; and elimination of nationwide night-shift differentials.

The Task Force estimated that three-year cost savings of $5.918 billion would result from implementation of these recommendations.

Organization Management—The Federal Position Classification System is not applied or administered adequately. Costly overgrading is common due primarily to the system's inflexibility, as well as its complex and out-of-date classification standards.

The Task Force recommended that OPM intensify efforts to reduce overgrading by using flexible special rates, incentive awards, and quality step pay increases; by providing agencies with technical guidance and evaluation; by clearly defining responsibility for classification within OPM; and by working with the Office of Management and Budget to enforce agency cooperation.

When implemented, these and other organizational management recommendations will result in three-year cost savings of $5.321 billion.

Pay for Time Not Worked—The cost of employee annual and sick leaves is significantly higher in the Federal Government than the private sector.

The Task Force recommended legislative changes to require a minimum of 180 days' service prior to a first vacation, less liberal vacation schedules, limits on accrued vacation, and limitation of accrued sick leave to not more than 130 days, resulting in three-year cost savings of $7.474 billion.

Contract Management—The Task Force concluded that Government agencies are not adequately pursuing opportunities for private sector contracting of Federal functions. It recommended agencies perform cost comparisons and contract for goods and services when so justified. Three-year savings of $3.310 billion would result from implementation of these and other recommendations.

Implementation

Of the 95 recommendations formulated by the Task Force, 59 (62 percent) fall within the purview of the OPM Director, 34 (36 percent) require Congressional action, and 2 (2 percent) need Presidential approval.

**Task Force on
Privatization**

CO-CHAIRS: Bruce J. Heim
              Vice President
              F. Eberstadt & Co.,
                 Inc.

              Paul F. Hellmuth
              Retired Managing
                 Partner
              Hale & Dorr

              Edward L. Hutton
              President and CEO
              Chemed Corporation

              Paul E. Manheim
              Advisory Director
              Lehman Brothers, Kuhn,
                 Loeb, Incorporated

              Eben W. Pyne
              Retired Senior Vice
                 President
              Citibank, N.A.

              David L. Yunich
              Retired Vice Chairman
              R. H. Macy & Co., Inc.

PROJECT   Leo Kramer
MANAGERS: President
              Kramer Associates, Inc.

              Paul Taff
              Senior Associate
              Kramer Associates, Inc.

*NUMBER OF
TASK FORCE
MEMBERS:* 28

NUMBER OF ISSUES: 9

*NUMBER OF
RECOMMENDATIONS:* 22

*3-YEAR
COST SAVINGS*:* $11.191
($ billions)

*3-YEAR
REVENUE GENERATION:* $17.226
($ billions)

*Note: In addition to these cost savings/
revenue generation opportunities, the Task
Force identified numerous privatization
opportunities contained in other PPSS Task
Force reports.

Overview

Privatization means to turn over a Federal activity, or part of a Federal
activity, to a non-Federal entity. By allowing Government to *provide*
services without necessarily *producing* them, privatization increases
Federal efficiency. In the view of the Privatization Task Force, scarce
resources are better utilized, Government responsibilities are fulfilled at
a cost savings, and management reaps the benefits of success and carries
the responsibility of failure when services are privatized.

Issues and Recommendations

The Task Force urged establishment of a uniform policy for formalizing
privatization at each agency, including the establishment of an administrative structure for assessing privatization opportunities.

   Nine issues were studied and 22 recommendations formulated yielding cost savings of $11.191 billion and revenue generation of $17.22 billion over a three-year period.

Power Marketing Administrations (PMAs)—The PMAs of the Department of Energy operate 123 hydroelectric dams and 622 substation and employ 4,900 persons. In FY 1982, they sold 45 percent of the nation's hydroelectric power. PMA revenues do not repay Federal investment, pricing mechanisms are unsound, and independent auditors report that PMAs do not conform to generally accepted accounting principles. The Task Force recommended that the Government begin an orderly process of disengaging from participation in commercial electric power marketing.

Task Force recommendations would yield cost savings of $3.535 billion and revenue generation of $16.302 billion over a three-year period.

National Space Transportation System (NSTS)—Privatizing space launching services could help the U.S. increase its economic base, compete more effectively with foreign manufacturers, and strengthen its space leadership.

Cost savings of $1.523 billion are projected over a three-year period.

Veterans Administration (VA) Hospital Management—The VA Hospital System provides medical, surgical, geriatric, and psychiatric services at over 172 locations. Obsolete facilities, excessive construction costs, and inefficient and costly management practices result in unnecessarily high health care costs.

The Task Force recommended phasing out the construction of VA hospitals, stopping plans for the construction of new nursing homes, and contracting out hospital management services to the private sector on a trial basis.

Task Force recommendations would yield cost savings of $1.437 billion over a three-year period.

Commissary Operations in the Department of Defense—Resembling warehouse-style retail grocery stores, military commissaries date back to the early 19th century. FY 1983 subsidization approached $590 million. The Task Force found fragmented management, a failure to charge indirect costs to commissary operations, and frequent noncompetitive prices vis-a-vis private sector warehouse stores rather than retail supermarkets. The Task Force recommended comparing commissary costs, retail prices, and product mix with local warehouse stores, and privatizing commissary operations where appropriate.

Cost savings of $2.064 billion and revenue generation of $383.2 million would be realized over a three-year period.

Metropolitan Washington Airports (MWA)—National and Dulles Airports are the only two commercial airports in the U.S. owned by the U.S. Government. The Task Force concluded that operating MWA is incompatible with the Federal Aviation Administration's primary role of ensuring air safety, and recommended that MWA be sold to a local airport authority with three-year cost savings of $113.0 million and revenue generation of $341.5 million.

Federal Vehicle Fleet Management—The Federal fleet is composed of approximately 436,000 autos, trucks, buses, and specialty vehicles. Lacking both central control and a coherent Management Information System (MIS), the Federal fleet is plagued by an information gap in determining aggregate costs. The Task Force also concluded that the fleet was underutilized.

The Task Force recommended that the Office of Management and Budget develop an MIS for all departments and agencies; that the fleet be pared by 100,000 vehicles, and that private sector options be applied to improve the operation of the remaining vehicles where possible. These recommendations would yield cost savings of $1.260 billion and revenue generation of $200.0 million over a three-year period.

Coast Guard Services—The Coast Guard's primary missions are law enforcement and search and rescue (SAR). The Task Force recommended that the Coast Guard continue to use the private sector for vessel inspection and measurement services and that private firms conduct non-life-threatening SAR operations as well as repairs and maintenance work required for marine and inland buoys. These recommendations would result in cost savings of $1.259 billion over a three-year period.

Implementation

Of the 22 major recommendations, 6 are within the purview of associated agencies, 9 involve Presidential action, and 7 require Congressional approval.

Task Force on
Procurement/Contracts/Inventory Management

CO-CHAIRS:	Willard C. Butcher Chairman The Chase Manhattan Bank, N.A.	*NUMBER OF* *TASK FORCE* *MEMBERS:* 39
	Edward S. Finkelstein Chairman and CEO R. H. Macy & Co., Inc.	*NUMBER OF ISSUES:* 22 *NUMBER OF* *RECOMMENDATIONS:* 57
	Clifton C. Garvin, Jr. CEO Exxon Corporation	*3-YEAR* *COST SAVINGS:* $20.271 ($ billions)
PROJECT *MANAGER:*	Edgar A. Robinson Senior Vice President Exxon Company, U.S.A.	

Overview

The Federal Government engages in some 18 million procurement actions per year totaling more than $159 billion (FY 1982). Items purchased by or for the Department of Defense (DOD) accounted for about $125 billion or 78.6 percent. Government agencies hold more than $88 billion worth of items in inventories stored in hundreds of locations. The procurement process is extremely complex, involving a wide variety of goods and services, a maze of statutory and regulatory rules, and more than 130,000 Federal procurement personnel.

In Government, procurement funds are subject to rigid budgetary restrictions, and procurement officials are closely proscribed by a complex set of laws and regulations that severely limit their flexibility. Two basic laws govern all Federal procurement: (1) the Armed Services Procurement Act (1947), and (2) the Federal Property and Administrative Services Act (1949), which applies to civilian procurement. In addition, the Government procurement process is utilized as a powerful vehicle for social change. Some 80 socioeconomic programs affect the procurement process.

Issues and Recommendations

The Task Force studied 22 issues and formulated 57 recommendations, which will result in three-year cost savings of $20.271 billion when implemented.

Overall Procurement Issues—The most comprehensive Task Force recommendation pertaining to overall procurement activities called for fuller integration of the Office of Federal Procurement Policy (OFPP) into the budget and program review processes of the Office of Management and Budget (OMB) so as to strengthen its policy development role and impact.

The Task Force also endorsed support of OFPP's 1982 proposal for the Uniform Federal Procurement System, designed to unify procurement policies, increase competition, etc. The Task Force also recommended that a major study of the most pervasive socioeconomic programs be undertaken to seek means of reducing their burdens on the procurement process without altering their basic objectives. Three-year cost savings of $847 million would be achieved as a result of implementing these recommendations.

Weapons Acquisition—Although the "Carlucci Initiatives" in DOD seek major improvements in the weapons acquisition process, the Task Force found that they have not been expeditiously implemented and that one of the most important—multiyear contracting—has made little progress. The Task Force recommended actions to further the implementation of multiyear contracting for weapons systems and expand the concept to other high payout areas. In addition, the Task Force emphasized the need for program prioritization within the acquisition process.

The Task Force specifically addressed how DOD/Services might conduct the acquisition process in a more efficient and effective manner. It found that Program Management Plans are not fully effective as management tools and sometimes are nonexistent; roles, responsibilities, and authorities are not always well defined; and program management and acquisition strategies are often developed from the top down and are frequently limited in scope. With respect to contracting, insufficient emphasis is placed on the potential "total" cost of a major weapons program and inadequacies exist in the source selection process, performance evaluation, and scheduling estimates.

To redress the shortcomings, the Task Force recommended more comprehensive and timely program planning; strengthening cost/schedule development to produce a "most likely result" and improving "early warning" indicators; enhancing the selection of prime contractors and upgrading subcontracting activities; and increasing the effectiveness of program managers and the program management organizations.

Proposed recommendations in the area of weapons acquisition would result in three-year cost savings of $11.255 billion.

Inventory Management—Almost all of approximately $40 billion worth of materiel is under DOD's inventory control. The Task Force focused on methods to optimize the quantities to be purchased and the frequency of purchases—the "Economic Order Quantity" (EOQ) system; management of inventory data once the materiel is in the Government's supply system; inventory-taking techniques; and consolidation of base support services. The Task Force found the EOQ system frequently is overriden by inventory managers, inventory carrying costs are not fully assessed, the level of accuracy in demand forecasting is unsatisfactory, and 40 to 50 percent of inventory is over a year old, raising questions of quality deterioration and readiness. In addition, inter-Service and intra-Service sharing opportunities are not exploited. Accordingly, the Task Force recommended DOD compliance with the EOQ system; interim measures to augment inventory management computer systems, pending completion of longer term modernization programs; implementation of a program to institute "wall-to-wall" inventory-taking techniques at major facilities; and consolidation of base support activities.

Three-year cost savings would total $6.089 billion, with a one-time reduction in inventory of approximately $4.540 billion.

Procurement Efficiency Issues—The Task Force identified several issues that could have significant procurement cost savings, including expanding reliance on the private sector for goods and services, consolidating certain DOD contract administration and procurement activities, and implementing advances in ADP.

Implementation of recommendations would result in three-year savings of $2.006 billion.

Civilian Procurement—The General Services Administration (GSA) influences all civilian procurement through its policymaking authority to establish regulations for procurement practices and mandate when GSA is the required source of supply. Total civilian procurement was $29.7 billion in FY 1981.

The Task Force concluded that GSA's acquisition and distribution responsibilities should be broadened by requiring most civilian agencies to utilize GSA's services, resulting in the greatest possible economies of scale in the procurement process. GSA should be relieved of the responsibility for policy development so it can concentrate on its operational mission, with policy matters being handled by OFPP in OMB. Over three years, $74.0 million would be saved as a result of the Task Force's recommendations.

Implementation

Of the 57 recommendations, 45 (79 percent) can be implemented by the individual agencies. Six recommendations require Congressional action and six require action by the President.

Task Force on
Real Property Management

CO-CHAIRS:	Robert A. Georgine President Building and 　Construction 　Trades Department AFL-CIO	*PROJECT* *MANAGER:*	John N. Sherman Manager Business Planning, 　Plastic Products 　Business Center Hercules Incorporated
	Alexander F. Giacco Chairman, President, and 　CEO Hercules Incorporated	*NUMBER OF* *TASK FORCE* *MEMBERS:* 23	
	Donald P. Kelly Chairman, President, and 　CEO Esmark, Inc.	*NUMBER OF ISSUES:* 10 *NUMBER OF*	
	Donald B. Marron Chairman and CEO Paine Webber 　Incorporated	*RECOMMENDATIONS:* 52 *3-YEAR* *COST SAVINGS:* $2.362 ($ billions)	
	Nathan Shapell Chairman Shapell Industries, Inc.		

Overview

The U.S. Government owns buildings valued at $42 billion, based on acquisition costs. Although there is no central office specifically designated as the manager of real property, the General Services Administration (GSA) is known as "the Government's landlord." The Department of Defense (DOD) also manages extensive real property holdings.

Federal budget allocations are not consolidated for real property management. Real property management expenditures for GSA and DOD are quite substantial, however. For example, GSA spent $224 million for utilities, $190 million for janitorial services, $100 million for maintenance, and $779 million for rent during FY 1983. For its part, DOD spent approximately $2.5 billion for utilities, $1.5 billion for janitorial services, and $3.2 billion for maintenance, also in FY 1983.

Issues and Recommendations

The Task Force identified ten major areas for study and formulated 52 recommendations which, when fully implemented, will result in three-year cost savings of $2.362 billion. To target management functions common to Government and business, the study focused on: organization and staffing, facilities/property/construction management, procurement and contracting, and leasing procedures and practices.

Organization and Staffing—Management of real property suffers from the excessive duplication of effort and substandard productivity levels in both the management and maintenance functions. Effective management is stifled by a lack of basic goals, planning, role identification, and regular performance measurements. Task Force recommendations would result in an approximate three-year cost savings of $1.187 billion and included: establishing clear, concise goals for Federal real property management; eliminating unnecessary duplication between GSA and tenant agencies in facility management functions; and introducing a comprehensive maintenance incentive and productivity program.

Facilities/Property/Construction Management—The Task Force identified inadequacies in meeting office space use goals and in locating and disposing of surplus real property owned by Federal agencies.

At DOD, the Task Force found that the policy of minimizing new housing construction is not being fully practiced. It also found little incentive for Federal agencies to identify and report surplus property. Implementation of Task Force recommendations would result in three-year cost savings of $443.8 million. Specific recommendations included: reevaluating surplus property sales goals, providing incentives for agencies to cooperate in the disposal program, declaring a moratorium on DOD housing construction while strengthening the Variable Housing Allowance, and upgrading the quality of information provided by the Federal Government's real property data base.

Additional cost control opportunities exist in the area of Federal energy management programs. By building Energy Management Control Systems (ECMS) to commercial specifications and basing decisions about new ECMS investments on potential dollar savings, the Task Force estimates three-year cost savings at $385.1 million.

Procurement/Contract Management—Opportunities for cost savings can be generated by revising wage determinations under the Service Contract Act (SCA) and by stressing management discretion in contracting out for maintenance requiring highly skilled personnel. Task Force recommendations would result in three-year cost savings of $135.0 million. Major recommendations included: revising wage determination procedures to make Government contract wages comparable to those in the private sector and revising Office of Management and Budget Circular A-76 guidelines to permit more management discretion in contracting out high-skill maintenance.

Leasing and Acquisition/"Prospectus" Procedures—The Task Force concluded that GSA needs to modernize its system of leasing and to streamline its lease prospectus procedures. Specifically, changing the threshold on lease prospectuses from a dollar basis to a size basis would enable GSA to take advantage of favorable leasing conditions. Implementation of the Task Force recommendations would result in three-year cost savings of $210.7 million.

Implementation

Of the 52 major recommendations, 28 (54 percent) can be implemented under existing agency authority, 7 (13 percent) can be implemented under Presidential authority, and the remaining 17 (33 percent) will require Congressional action.

Task Force on
Research and Development

CO-CHAIRS:	William F. Ballhaus President Beckman Instruments, Inc.	*NUMBER OF* *TASK FORCE* *MEMBERS:* 29
	Karl D. Bays Chairman and CEO American Hospital Supply Corp.	*NUMBER OF ISSUES:* 8 *NUMBER OF* *RECOMMENDATIONS:* 25
	James L. Ferguson Chairman and CEO General Foods Corp.	*3-YEAR* *COST SAVINGS:** $12.090 ($ billions)
	David Packard Chairman of the Board Hewlett-Packard Co. Edson W. Spencer Chairman and CEO Honeywell, Inc.	* *Note:* This Report contains a compendium issue covering R&D issues from other PPSS reports. It includes 97 recommendations with additional three-year cost savings and revenue generation of $32.984 billion.
PROJECT *MANAGER:*	Dr. Eugene E. Yore Corporate Director, Design Automation Honeywell, Inc.	

Overview

Research and development (R&D) in the Federal Government is conducted primarily by five agencies which account for 93.2 percent of the total FY 1983 R&D budget of $44.3 billion—Department of Defense (DOD), National Aeronautics and Space Administration (NASA), Department of Energy (DOE), Department of Health and Human Services (HHS), and National Science Foundation (NSF). The R&D funded by these agencies is conducted by industrial firms (52 percent), Government laboratories (24 percent), universities (11 percent), Federally funded research and development centers (9 percent), and others (4 percent). Over 700 laboratories employing 206,000 conduct the 24 percent of the R&D performed in-house.

The Task Force found a need for top R&D management to become much more actively involved in establishing the specific goals for R&D. The current system, which is inhibited by the budget process, cannot establish program priorities and, thus, results in program instability.

Issues and Recommendations

In the seven issue areas surveyed, the Task Force formulated 25 recommendations which, when implemented, could result in three-year savings opportunities of $12.09 billion. In addition, a compendium of R&D issues from 14 other PPSS task forces listed 97 recommendations with potential cost savings and revenue generation of $32.984 billion.

Strategic Planning—R&D management suffers from a lack of clearly defined goals. Existing planning efforts do not establish priorities for R&D programs, cannot eliminate marginal programs, and do not serve as a base for operational management. Specific Task Force recommendations to alleviate the above findings would result in three-year cost savings of $7.3 billion. These recommendations included: focusing efforts by top agency management on the development of clear, measurable statements of R&D goals; developing systems necessary to translate goal statements into complete plans; and committing to the use of effective strategic planning to guide the operations of each agency.

R&D Management and the Budget Process—The budget process used to obtain funding for R&D programs is too cumbersome and time consuming and is a factor in the significant cost growth experienced in R&D programs. To remedy these deficiencies, the Task Force made recommendations, which would result in $3.67 billion in savings opportunities over three years. These recommendations included implementing multiyear budgeting specifically for R&D activities.

Privatization—The Task Force highlighted opportunities to privatize Federal R&D efforts described in other PPSS task force reports, including private funding for the fifth space shuttle. Although no specific additional cost savings were claimed, the Task Force believed a concentrated analysis of privatization opportunities could result in billions of dollars of potential savings.

Management of Federal R&D Laboratories—In reviewing some of the major labs, the Task Force found some with outdated facilities and equipment, all with personnel problems, and no formal system for evaluating the laboratories' contribution to the agency's program(s). Of the 700 labs, more than 300 have fewer than ten employees and budgets under $300,000. The Task Force made seven recommendations to improve lab performance, including greater use of "centers of excellence," a concept which concentrates research resources to achieve a critical mass in selected areas. Savings opportunities of $506.4 million over three years were identified.

Administration of Research Grants to Universities—An increasing percentage of money going to universities to conduct research for the Federal Government is used to cover the indirect costs of the research, particularly the administrative components. The Task Force recommended that a fixed rate be used to reimburse these costs and estimated savings opportunities of $387.9 million over a three-year period.

Research Program Reporting—The Task Force found that current efforts at reporting ongoing research efforts are incomplete and that the National Technical Information Service, which processes the data, does not have the tools to expand the reporting. Three-year savings opportunities of $225 million would occur if use of the data base were made mandatory and requirements were implemented to ensure research performers supplied the necessary information, thus eliminating costly duplication of research activities.

NASA Cost Reporting—Project cost data reported by NASA were found to be significantly understated, since NASA does not include Civil Service and other essential cost elements in its reporting. The Task Force recommended that all project costs be managed and reported in the same system. No specific savings were claimed by the Task Force.

Implementation

Of the 25 major recommendations formulated by the Task Force (excluding the compendium), 17 (68 percent) are within agency purview and 8 (32 percent) will require Congressional action.

Task Force on
The Department of State/AID/USIA

CO-CHAIRS:	J. Rawles Fulgham Retired Vice Chairman InterFirst Corporation George L. Shinn Retired Chairman and CEO First Boston Corp.	*NUMBER OF ISSUES:* 10 *NUMBER OF* *RECOMMENDATIONS:* 31 *3-YEAR* *COST SAVINGS:* $.383 ($ billions)
PROJECT *MANAGER:*	Arthur M. Scutro, Jr. Vice President First Boston Corp.	*3-YEAR* *REVENUE GENERATION:* $.360 ($ billions)
NUMBER OF *TASK FORCE* *MEMBERS:* 25		*3-YEAR* *CASH ACCELERATION:* $.056 ($ billions)

Overview

The Department of State (State), the United States Information Agency (USIA), and the Agency for International Development (AID) have a common international focus and coordinated international roles. The President's FY 1983 budget "to protect and advance the interests of the United States and its people in international affairs" approximated $18.1 billion. State, USIA, and AID comprise 46 percent of the budget. Employment at those agencies for FY 1983 was estimated at nearly 38,000 people in the United States and abroad.

Issues and Recommendations

The Task Force formulated 31 recommendations in ten issue areas which, when implemented, will result in three-year cost savings of $382.8 million, revenue generation of $360 million, and cash acceleration of $55.9 million.

Department of State—The Task Force's review of the personnel system disclosed that the distribution of Foreign Service Officers (FSOs) is skewed toward senior FSOs; that supervising management and members of the American Foreign Service Association (the elected bargaining agent for the State Department) can be the same people; and, with rare exception, that the Foreign Service System provides larger retirement benefits than are provided by the Civil Service Retirement System (CSRS) for Federal employees with equal records of service and salary. Specifically, while the Government's cost for CSRS in FY 1981 was 32.7 percent of payroll, the cost of the Foreign Service Retirement System was 86.7 percent of payroll.

The Task Force recommended that State review the current ranking of positions and realign personnel, redesign and improve the performance evaluation system, eliminate the current conflict of interest situation in labor-management practices, increase the retirement age, and change the retirement benefit formula to be consistent with the CSRS standard.

Implementation of these recommendations would result in three-year cost savings of $200.4 million.

U.S. Government property holdings under State's Office of Foreign Buildings (FBO) total more than 2,700 buildings and long-term lease holdings at 287 foreign locations. In addition, FBO maintains $5 billion in real property holdings. Yet, it does not have a comprehensive real property management information system to monitor progress, measure performance, and identify developing problems. The Task Force recommended the establishment of a comprehensive management information system at FBO and the development of guidelines for identifying surplus properties. Savings, while not quantified, would be substantial.

Cost control opportunities in improved fiscal management practices and controls at FBO also exist. The present financial management system does not identify all costs associated with the maintenance and operation of an individual building. No system exists for forecasting and reporting foreign currency expenditures; purchases of foreign currencies are always on a "spot basis" with no hedging by the Department; and foreign currency transactions by State always involve purchases, never sales. To prevent losses due to foreign currency fluctuations, an accounting system should be developed to identify foreign currency needs and a currency futures/forward desk established.

Additional opportunities for improved fiscal management were targeted in the Bureau for Refugee Programs, where the Task Force found deficiencies in the management and control of loan programs.

Implementation of Task Force recommendations would result in three-year cost savings of $25.8 million, with an additional $55.9 million in cash acceleration.

Agency for International Development (AID)—The management process for development projects is less efficient than at other national donor agencies, as indicated by its high operating expenses as a percent of total disbursements (13.5 percent) and the average time elapsed to develop and approve a project (16.7 months). In addition, interest on AID loans has not reflected the true cost of borrowing by the U.S. Government and thus represents hidden foreign aid.

Recommendations included improving the project planning process by utilizing block grants, returning deobligation/reobligation authority to AID, and moving to a two-year budget submission cycle; establishing a minimum base lending rate for all AID loans which would be adjusted according to quantitative criteria; eliminating the cargo preference requirement; and enforcing AID policies that mandate four-year tours of duty. These recommendations will result in three-year cost savings totaling $156.6 million, with an additional $360 million in revenue generation.

United States Information Agency (USIA)—As a complement to the diplomacy conducted by State, USIA serves the national interest through the performance of public diplomacy, especially in broadcasting U.S. information to foreign countries.

The Task Force concluded that program evaluation of educational and cultural activities is decentralized, subjective, and often incomplete; planning and goal-setting at overseas missions are too broad and available monitoring mechanisms are not used; and international broadcasting programs suffer from a lack of performance standards and evaluation. Task Force recommendations included establishing an analytical resource capability within USIA, developing an agency-wide program review system, and deferring program expansions planned for FY 1984. No specific savings were quantified by the Task Force.

Implementation

Of the 31 recommendations, 21 (68 percent) can be implemented by Agency authority, 9 (29 percent) require Congressional action and 1 (3 percent) needs Presidential approval.

Task Force on
The Department of Transportation

CO-CHAIRS:	Coy G. Eklund
	Chairman and CEO
	The Equitable Life
	  Assurance Society of
	  the United States
		NUMBER OF
		TASK FORCE
		MEMBERS: 11
		
		NUMBER OF ISSUES: 22

	Thomas G. Pownall Chairman and CEO Martin Marietta Corp.	*NUMBER OF* *RECOMMENDATIONS:* 69
	William H. Spoor Chairman and CEO Pillsbury Co.	*3-YEAR* *COST SAVINGS:* $2.712 ($ billions)
	Terry Townsend Immediate Past Chairman American Society of Association Executives	*3-YEAR* *REVENUE GENERATION:* $1.705 ($ billions)
	L. Stanton Williams Chairman and CEO PPG Industries, Inc.	*3-YEAR* *CASH ACCELERATION:* $ .436 ($ millions)

PROJECT
MANAGER:
	William T. McCaffrey
	Vice President and Area
	  Executive Officer
	The Equitable Life
	  Assurance Society of
	  the United States	

Overview

The Department of Transportation (DOT), with a FY 1983 budget of nearly $19 billion, has approximately 99,000 employees. Both numbers represent a three-year downward trend. More than two-thirds of the present DOT budget is devoted to grants. Principal activities are in four areas: staff, land, sea, and air. The principal entities within DOT include the Office of the Secretary (OST), Federal Highway Administration

(FHWA), Federal Railroad Administration (FRA), Urban Mass Transportation Administration (UMTA), National Highway Traffic Safety Administration (NHTSA), Research & Special Programs Administration (RSPA), United States Coast Guard (USCG), Maritime Administration (MarAd), and Federal Aviation Administration (FAA). DOT's stated purpose is to develop policies and programs conducive to efficient, convenient, and low-cost transportation.

Issues and Recommendations

Twenty-two issues were analyzed and 69 recommendations were formulated which, when fully implemented, will result in three-year cost savings of $2.712 billion, revenue generation of $1.705 billion, and cash acceleration of $436 million.

Staff—The Task Force identified potential improvements in R&D strategic planning, administrative support, data processing operations, grant administration, and cash management.

The Task Force recommended establishing an entity responsible for R&D policy, goal-setting, and monitoring to focus the R&D effort and reduce noncritical projects. To improve administrative support, the Task Force suggested that DOT consolidate its currently existing ten regions into six and cut headquarters personnel by at least 276 people. Consolidation of the ADP functions of OST were also recommended, along with greater use of DOT's own time-sharing facilities. To improve grant administration and cash management, the Task Force recommended enforcing DOT regulation against early payment of bills and unwarranted drawdowns by grantees, and requiring a check-paid method for making DOT grant distributions.

Implementation of the Task Force's recommendations for staff improvements would yield $683.5 million in cost savings and $436 million in cash acceleration over a three-year period.

Land—The Task Force recommended changes in the resource allocation methods to improve the cost effectiveness of the Federal highway programs including a significant reduction in the number of program categories from 40 to 12. Additional savings in the Federal highway program could be realized by adopting the Task Force's recommendations for streamlining the regulatory requirements.

The Task Force also found that FHWA, FRA, RSPA, UMTA, and NHTSA have similar land-based missions and recommended they be functionally reorganized to reduce the cost of common services. The Task Force also recommended that DOT combine the safety functions of FHWA, UMTA, NHSTA, and RSPA into one Land Transportation Safety Administration. FHWA would then be consolidated with UMTA to form the Surface Transporation Administration. Additional recommendations included integrating overlapping legislation and implementing a policy of user fees.

Implementation of the above recommendations would result in savings of $1.269 billion and revenue generation of $66.4 million over three years.

Air—In analyzing opportunities within FAA to improve cost efficiency without compromising air travel safety, the Task Force recommended that FAA consolidate the nine current regional offices into seven and the 20 Air Route Traffic Central Centers into 15. It called for FAA to increase fees at MWA, to reduce hours of operation at low volume airports, and to consolidate Flight Service Stations.

The Task Force found redundant managerial overhead and excess service capacity created by technological improvements in automated controlling systems. In addition, FAA bears the cost of legislated control over agency operating policy, particularly with regard to the MWA (Metropolitan Washington Airports), which suffer from poor operating margins, and at low-volume local airports that use FAA services disproportionate to their activity and safety requirements.

Implementation of these recommendations would result in $635.9 million in cost savings and $57.6 million in revenue generation over three years.

Sea—The Coast Guard uses general tax revenues to fund certain benefits for specific user groups, rather than charging an appropriate user fee. The Task Force recommended instituting user fees to recoup the operating and support costs of providing services to identifiable groups of marine users. In addition, it suggested that the USCG consider using commercial towing services in non-life-threatening situations, use private maintenance of short-range navigational aids, and turn over Vessel Traffic Safety systems to local authorities. Reducing U.S. Merchant Marine Academy appointments and instituting cost-sharing tuition for students also were recommended.

The implementation of these recommendations is projected to provide total three-year cost savings of $123.8 million and revenue generation of $1.582 billion.

Implementation

Of the 69 recommendations formulated by the Task Force, 39 (57 percent) are under Agency purview and 30 (43 percent) involve Congressional action.

**Task Force on
The Department of the Treasury**

CO-CHAIRS:	Alfred Brittain, III Chairman of the Board Bankers Trust Company, Inc.	*NUMBER OF ISSUES:* 23 *NUMBER OF RECOMMENDATIONS:* 63
	William H. Donaldson Chairman Donaldson Enterprises, Inc.	*3-YEAR COST SAVINGS:* $2.367 ($ billions)
	John H. Filer Chairman and CEO Aetna Life and Casualty Company	*3-YEAR REVENUE GENERATION:* $2.994 ($ billions)

*PROJECT
MANAGER:*
	Robert G. Maxon
	Vice President/Corporate
	  Comptroller
	Aetna Life and
	  Casualty Company
		*3-YEAR
		REVENUE ACCELERATION:* $6.145
		($ billions)

NUMBER OF TASK FORCE MEMBERS: 47		

Overview

The Department of the Treasury may be characterized as a collection of disparate functions: large, people-intensive operations, such as the Internal Revenue Service (IRS) and the U.S. Customs Service (Customs), deal directly with individuals in their revenue-collecting activities, while small organizations, such as the Offices of Fiscal Management and Revenue Sharing, handle large dollar responsibilities. Spending by the Department in FY 1983 totaled $146.1 billion and included some $133.2 billion of interest paid on the public debt. Treasury employs 122,900 people.

Treasury is the closest thing the Federal Government has to a private sector financial management function—the Federal money manager. In undertaking its review, the Task Force concluded that the greatest benefits will accrue from revenue-oriented measures rather than expense cuts. The measure of successful implementation of its recommendations will be Treasury's contribution to narrowing the Federal deficit, rather than merely reducing its budget.

Issues and Recommendations

The Task Force studied 23 issue areas and made 63 recommendations which, when fully implemented, will result in three-year cost savings of $2.367 billion, revenue generation of $2.994 billion, and revenue acceleration of $6.145 billion. Issues studied by the Task Force can be grouped into funds flow management, operational performance, and systems management and development.

Funds Flow Management—The Task Force found that the Federal process for collecting delinquent payments and other accounts receivable is neither aggressive nor sophisticated when compared to the private sector. In addition, useful management information enabling the Treasury Department to forecast its cash needs is lacking. Generalizing from specific issues studied, both problems involve information as well as management priorities. Federal agencies lack useful information on the amounts and nature of their accounts receivable to support aggressive collection efforts. Furthermore, system interfaces and other communication tools are inadequate to manage funds flow on the basis of current and reliable information on day-to-day Federal cash revenues and outlays.

With respect to delinquent taxes, as of June 30, 1982, the IRS estimated that its accounts receivable backlog reached a record level of $23.2 billion. In addition, the backlog of appeals in Tax Court—78,000 cases as of July 31, 1982—further delays tax revenue collection. Task Force recommendations to expedite the collection of delinquent taxes included an improved mix of clerical to professional staff so as to maximize professional skills; more aggressive collection techniques, including use of credit bureaus, payroll deductions, and automatic bank transfers in collecting installment agreements; and classification of delinquent accounts. Establishment of a decentralized appellate tax board of approximately 75 administrative law judges, resident in appropriate cities, also would alleviate the problem of backlogged tax cases.

The Task Force also identified opportunities for improved funds management in Customs procedures and collection of the Retail Alcohol Occupational Tax, including improved ADP systems, Customs collection by account rather than by shipment, and prohibition of sales of alcoholic beverages to retailers who have no occupational tax stamp.

Implementation of Task Force recommendations in the area of funds management would result in three-year cost savings of $1.702 billion, revenue generation of $81.9 million, and revenue acceleration of $6.145 billion.

Operational Performance—A wide range of Treasury operations reveal numerous opportunities for cost control and improved management efficiencies.

— 503 —

The Task Force recommended Department-wide, cost-benefit analysis for all new personnel additions and, with respect to the IRS, elimination of functional overlap, the establishment of a volunteer taxpayer service, and an increased enforcement presence. Opportunities for consolidations in the border management activities of Customs and Immigration and Naturalization Services were identified, along with the proposed consolidation of Customs' enforcement operations. Management reorganizations were proposed for the Bureau of Alcohol, Tobacco, and Firearms and the Office of Revenue Sharing, along with revised compliance procedures. Other operations-based recommendations included the use of offset printing for the back of $1 notes, adoption of a common Federal Reserve seal, space consolidation in the Bureau of Government Financial Operations, and changes in and relocation of selected functions of the Bureau of the Mint.

The Task Force estimated that implementation of its recommendations regarding operational performance would result, over three years, in savings totaling $608.3 million and revenue generation of $2.897 billion.

Systems Management and Development—The Federal Government's lack of integrated systems management and development is strikingly apparent at Treasury, where the lack of systems standards to ensure an automated and timely flow of fiscal information handicaps the Department in fulfilling its functions. All of these problems are exacerbated by a lack of ADP expertise within Treasury, as well as obsolete systems. The Treasury operations most in need of improved ADP systems management and development include the IRS; the Bureau of Alcohol, Tobacco, and Firearms; the Office of Revenue Sharing; and the Bureau of Public Debt. Recommendations included development of systems planning, reductions in the number of service centers, upgrading of equipment, and increased automated functions.

Three-year cost savings from the Task Force's recommendations total $56.1 million, with revenue generation totaling $15.5 million.

Implementation

Of the 63 recommendations made by the Task Force, 41 (65 percent) can be implemented by the Department, 6 (10 percent) require Presidential involvement, and 16 (25 percent) need Congressional approval.

**Task Force on
User Charges**

CO-CHAIRS:	James Stewart Chairman (Retired) Frank B. Hall & Co., Inc.	*NUMBER OF ISSUES:* 22
	Eugene J. Sullivan Chairman and CEO Borden, Inc.	*NUMBER OF RECOMMENDATIONS:* 57 *3-YEAR REVENUE GENERATION:** $10.211 ($ billions)*
PROJECT MANAGER:	James B. Clawson Independent Consultant	
NUMBER OF TASK FORCE MEMBERS: 28		* *Note:* This Report also contains a compendium issue containing user charges issues from other PPSS reports which, when implemented, would result in additional three- year revenue generation of $10.764 billion, for a total of $20.975 billion.

Overview

User charges are fees collected from beneficiaries of Government programs that provide services, products, or other benefits not shared by the general public. When user charges fail to recover the full costs or are not assessed at all, taxpayers must absorb the costs of these programs. There are approximately 1,500 user charge programs in the Federal Government, which in FY 1981 raised approximately $40 billion in revenue.

Issues and Recommendations

PPSS Task Forces identified total user charge opportunities with a potential three-year revenue generation of $20.975 billion. Approximately $10.211 billion are associated with the 56 recommendations in the User Charges Task Force Report, excluding the compendium issue which identified additional user charge opportunities which would result in three year revenue totaling $10.764 billion.

 Recreation—The Federal Government owns and administers a large number of recreation areas. The agencies with the largest number of visitor hours for nonfee units are the Army Corps of Engineers (Corps) and the Forest Service (FS). The Corps is prohibited from charging entrance fees at its water resource recreation areas by the Land and Water Conservation Fund Act (LWCFA), which also limits fee charges for FS. Furthermore, in 1979 Congress enacted legislation freezing entrance fees for the National Park Service and prohibiting the collection of fees at all nonfee sites. The Task Force recommended lifting the Congressional freeze and amending LWCFA to allow greater flexibility in the collection of entrance fees at recreation sites. When implemented, Task Force recommendations will result in three-year revenue generation of $527.5 million.

Sales—Federal Government products include electricity, grazing lands, publications, firewood, and military equipment. In the sale of products, pricing is the greatest difficulty. Most often prices are too low or nonexistent. Key PPSS recommendations included requiring the Department of Energy to impose a user fee on the hydroelectric power generated by the Power Marketing Administrations so as to ensure full cost recovery, establishing either an auction-bid system or a new fee formula that would more closely recover fair market value for the forage on grazing lands, charging a minimum of $10 for a firewood permit and an additional fee of $5 per cord taken from Government land, and ensuring full cost recovery with respect to Foreign Military Sales. When implemented, the recommendations will result in three-year revenue generation of $5.09 billion.

Inspection and Grading—The Government conducts numerous inspection and grading activities. Many are mandatory and for the benefit of the general public; others are voluntary and are performed at the request of the user. Voluntary activities are conducted primarily through the Agricultural Marketing Service, Federal Grain Inspection Service (FGIS), and Manufactured Home Inspection. Recommendations included instituting full cost recovery user fees for cotton grading and cotton warehouse licensing, adjusting FGIS fees annually to recover 100 percent of costs, and authorizing the use of user charge receipts to offset the administrative costs of inspection and enforcement of the Manufactured Housing Program. When implemented, these recommendations will result in revenue generation totaling $36.8 million over a three-year period.

Regulatory and Licensing—The Federal Communications Commission (FCC) regulates interstate and foreign communications by radio, television, wire, and cable but does not collect user fees for these services. In addition, the Federal Energy Regulatory Commission (FERC), an agency within the Department of Energy, regulates certain interstate aspects of the natural gas, hydroelectric, oil pipeline, and electric industries, and provides special services to identifiable beneficiaries. Its user fees fail to fully cover the cost of services. The Task Force recommended that FCC and FERC support proposals for expanded authority from Congress to collect user fees. Implementation of Task Force recommendations pertaining to FCC and FERC will result in three-year revenue enhancement of $209.2 million.

Special Services—Special services to identifiable beneficiaries include those related to the Freedom of Information Act, the Coast Guard, and the Customs Service. Task Force recommendations would result in three-year revenue generation of $1.013 billion, and included instituting hourly rates for processing Freedom of Information Act requests commensurate with expertise used to perform the service, implementing user fees for Coast Guard services to identifiable beneficiaries (non-life-threatening search/rescue efforts, ice breaking, recreational boating safety, etc.), and instituting user fees for Customs Services for aircraft entry, clearance, etc.

Transportation—While the cost of providing transportation-related services or products can be determined in most cases, the means of collecting the fee from the user presents special problems.

Key recommendations to help solve these problems included recovering 100 percent of the cost of operation, maintenance, and construction of deep draft harbors; gradually instituting full cost recovery for Corps and Tennessee Valley Authority expenditures related to the nation's inland waterways system; and instituting a management information system by the Federal Highway Administration to provide sufficient data to maintain a current pricing mechanism for user charges. Implementation of these recommendations would result in three-year revenue generation of $3.334 billion.

Implementation

Of the 56 Task Force-specific recommendations (excluding the compendium), 24 (43 percent) are within the purview of the agencies, 6 (11 percent) involve Presidential action, and 26 (46 percent) will need Congressional approval.

Task Force on
The Veterans Administration

CO-CHAIRS:	William C. Douce President and CEO Phillips Petroleum Company	*NUMBER OF ISSUES:* 8
	Hans W. Wanders Chairman and Chief Operating Officer Wachovia Corp.	*NUMBER OF RECOMMENDATIONS:* 24
		3-YEAR COST SAVINGS: $2.120 ($ billions)
	William L. Wearly Chairman of the Executive Committee Ingersoll-Rand Co.	*3-YEAR REVENUE GENERATION:* $0.953 ($ billions)
PROJECT MANAGER:	John R. Babson Consultant Ingersoll-Rand Co.	*3-YEAR CASH ACCELERATION:* $0.208 ($ billions)
NUMBER OF TASK FORCE MEMBERS:	32	

Overview

The Veterans Administration (VA) administers a system of benefits to veterans and their dependents, including compensation payments, pensions, education and rehabilitation programs, home loan guarantees, burial insurance, and a comprehensive medical program. (VA hospital operations are covered separately by the PPSS Task Force Report on Federal Hospital Management.) The VA employs approximately 218,493 people and operated with an FY 1983 budget of $28.9 billion, including VA hospitals.

Although VA employees demonstrated genuine concern for the welfare of veterans, the Task Force found program operation efficiency less than adequate. Analysis concentrated on internal problems such as automated data processing (ADP), compensation and insurance programs, central office management, debt collection activities, claims processing, and the operation of mortgage guarantee programs.

Issues and Recommendations

The Task Force studied 8 issue areas and formulated recommendations which, when fully implemented, will result in three-year cost savings of $2.120 billion, revenue generation of $953.3 million, and cash acceleration of $208 million.

Organization and Human Resources Management—The Task Force found a lack of role definition with respect to administrative staff, poor prioritization of staff activities, and ineffective manpower control. Claims processing suffers from overabundant staff and poor productivity levels.

The Task Force recommended that the Administrator clearly define the roles and responsibilities of line and staff organizations; realign and consolidate staff into functional areas (management support, administrative support, and legal); and implement an agency-wide work load management system to replace the current hiring freeze. To improve claims processing, the Department of Veterans Benefits (DVB) should revise the current work measurement system to one that utilizes pace-rating and a smaller allowance for slack time and that could be used to forecast work load and staffing needs, measure results, and evaluate productivity.

The Task Force estimated that its recommendations to improve claims processing would result in three-year savings of $271.7 million.

Fiscal Management and Control—The VA does not optimally manage and control its loan portfolio or debt collection practices. Specifically, uncollectible "old debt" masks the collection process and diverts resources from current, more readily collectible debt. All VA debt collection is hampered by an ineffective, untimely debtor communication process and by lax collection enforcement.

The Task Force recommended that the VA assign all debt over one year old to outside collection agencies and that current debt cases be assigned to field offices to facilitate timely communication and collection. In addition, the VA should raise the monetary limit for transferring debt collection jurisdiction to the Department of Justice. To improve loan portfolio management, the Task Force called on the VA to schedule frequent sales, thus minimizing exposure to interest rate fluctuations, and to simplify loan pooling by performing issuer's duties and pursuing the establishment of a "dealer syndicate."

When implemented, these recommendations would result in savings and revenue generation of $1.007 billion and cash acceleration of $208 million over three years.

ADP/Telecommunications and Office Automation—The Task Force found incompatible computing resources, obsolete computer hardware without adequate vendor support, and lack of technologically advanced telecommunication networks linking the VA locations to computer locations. The Task Force also identified a need to improve ADP management in the benefit plan and hospital care areas. The Task Force recommended the creation of a steering committee at the Administrator's level to establish ADP policies and strategies, direct future development, and guide systems integration. It also recommended the use of computer matching techniques and improved quality and control in benefit payments.

The Task Force estimated three-year cost savings of $1.485 billion, although it did not quantify savings with respect to benefits and hospital care.

Insurance Programs—VA's National Service Life Insurance Program (NSLI) and Veterans Special Life Insurance Program (VSLI) pay excessive dividends because administrative costs are absorbed in the general VA budget. The Task Force recommended that NSLI and VSLI be required to cover these costs, as do other VA insurance programs. This recommendation would not affect policyholder benefits and would result in three-year savings to the VA of $84.8 million.

Facilities/Property/Construction Management—The VA inadvisably purchases properties under the Guaranteed Loan Program, submitting bids that frequently do not take into account factors such as local market conditions and repair costs. The Task Force recommended that the VA bid only when other bids entered are clearly not representative of current market value. This could result in savings of $225.1 million over a three-year period.

Implementation

Of the 24 recommendations formulated by the Task Force, 22 (92 percent) can be implemented by the Agency and 2 (8 percent) will require Congressional approval.

Management Office Selected Issues Report

Volume I: Publishing, Printing, Reproduction, and Audiovisual Activities

PROJECT DIRECTOR:	F. David Gorman Independent Attorney	*NUMBER OF ISSUES:* 7
NUMBER OF COMMITTEE MEMBERS:	4	*NUMBER OF RECOMMENDATIONS:* 29 *3-YEAR COST SAVINGS:* $1.463 ($ billions) *3-YEAR REVENUE GENERATION:* $ .265 ($ billions)

Overview

The Federal Government spent nearly $2.5 billion in FY 1982 on printing ($880 million), publishing ($836 million), reproduction ($676 million), and audiovisual production ($91 million). These numbers were based on data collected by PPSS, as no single Government source maintains such information, a problem exacerbated by the fact that virtually every major agency or sub-agency is involved in publishing, printing, reproduction, and/or audiovisual production.

Issues and Recommendations

PPSS studied seven issues and formulated 29 recommendations which, when implemented, will result in three-year cost savings and revenue generation of $1.728 billion.

Publications Management—In 1981, the Government saved $46.8 million as a result of the Office of Management and Budget's (OMB) Bulletin 81-16, which required departments and agencies to eliminate unnecessary publications. The Bulletin expired in 1982, however, and has no continuing authority. PPSS recommended that OMB reissue and expand the authority of Bulletin 81-16, which could yield savings exceeding $300 million over three years. PPSS also recommended that OMB issue guidelines on publications management, exercise oversight of agency publication programs, revise job classifications for publishing professionals, and develop accounting procedures to identify hidden publishing costs.

In a related area, PPSS estimated that over $1 billion in costs went unrecovered in 1982 due to restrictions on user fees, and concluded that even a modest program of user fees could generate revenue of at least $264.8 million over three years. It also determined that better mailing list management could result in three-year cost savings of $95.9 million, and that an additional three-year savings of $549.5 million would result if agencies followed the General Services Administration guidelines for mailing publications.

Printing Production—PPSS identified a lack of central coordination in the management of the Federal Government's 235 individual printing plants and recommended consolidating underutilized agency printing plants, creating central printing facilities, establishing auditing procedures to capture full costs, and increasing commercial procurement of printing services. Implementation of PPSS recommendations would result in three-year cost savings of $158.9 million, in addition to significant but difficult-to-quantify management efficiencies.

Reproduction—Despite the existence of some 60,000 copiers and 4,000 duplicators in the Federal Government, PPSS found inefficiencies in the acquisition and utilization of reproduction equipment, including decentralized management; lack of information regarding equipment inventory, production volume, and related costs; and an absence of budgetary accountability for reproduction services. PPSS recommendations included directing OMB to provide centralized direction and budgetary control; centralizing copying and duplicating management within agencies; and coordinating the management of word processing, printing, and automated data processing. Implementation of PPSS recommendations would result in three-year cost savings of $327.7 million.

Audiovisual Activities—PPSS's investigation of audiovisual activities led it to conclude that expenditures in this area are lower than has been conjectured, and that these activities are now being managed effectively. Recommendations were made for additional management improvements, however, in an effort to help maintain the high product quality and cost-efficient operations achieved thus far.

Implementation

Of the 29 recommendations, 4 (14%) can be implemented by the affected agency, 21 (72%) can be implemented through Presidential action, and 4 (14%) will require Congressional approval.

Management Office Selected Issues Report

Volume II: Travel and Traffic Management

PROJECT DIRECTOR:	F. David Gorman Independent Attorney	*NUMBER OF ISSUES:* 4
NUMBER OF MEMBERS: 6		*NUMBER OF RECOMMENDATIONS:* 11
		3-YEAR COST SAVINGS: $1.850 ($ billions)
		3-YEAR CASH ACCELERATION: $ .032 ($ billions)

Overview

In FY 1982, the Federal Government spent over $9.4 billion on travel and freight transportation functions. PPSS found that the Federal Government's lack of centralized control and monitoring of travel and freight procurement produces management inefficiencies, unnecessary costs, and missed savings opportunities. PPSS focused its review on those agencies that have the greatest responsibility for incurring or managing travel and transportation services and expenditures: the Department of Defense, the General Services Administration, and the Office of Management and Budget.

Issues and Recommendations

PPSS studied four issues and formulated 11 recommendations which, when fully implemented, will result in three-year cost savings of $1.850 billion and cash acceleration of $32.1 million.

   Federal Travel Procurement—As a result of its analysis, PPSS concluded that Federal studies and test programs instituted to improve travel arrangements and achieve travel discounts have failed to create a Federal travel procurement system capable of capitalizing on new opportunities offered by airline deregulation. It recommended that the Government develop a centralized travel contracting and negotiating staff and that it consolidate existing travel service personnel and related hardware and software into "in-house" travel centers. Estimated cost savings from improved travel procurement and administration would amount to $984 million over three years.

Travel Expense Accounting and Reimbursement—PPSS found the Federal Government's travel expense accounting and reimbursement process to be inefficient and recommended the establishment of an integrated expense reporting system which would ensure that travelers and agencies process expense accounts expeditiously. In addition, it concluded that revised travel reimbursement policies, such as the use of flat-rate, locality-based per diem subsistence allowances, would speed up the accounting and reimbursement process, as would the use of personal charge cards. When implemented, PPSS recommendations in this area would result in three-year cost savings of $171.2 million.

Federal Traffic Management—In the view of PPSS, the Federal Government is not transporting its shipments efficiently and is not obtaining the lowest rates possible. PPSS recommended greater cooperation between agencies and increased use of automated systems to achieve Government-wide traffic management efficiencies, including selection of optimum routing and rates, consolidation of shipments, and the negotiation of volume-based rates. PPSS estimated that $529.6 million over three years would be saved as a result of these recommendations.

Transportation Audit—PPSS estimated that the Federal Government is losing approximately $65 million a year in unrecovered rate overcharges. Unlike the private sector, the Federal Government is legally precluded from making prepayment rate audits. PPSS found that on a post-payment audit basis, the Government recovers about 0.37% of its freight charges (compared to a recovery rate of 1.75% in the private sector) and that there is an 18-month backlog of unaudited freight bills. PPSS recommended that the Government make use of private sector freight auditing services and that statutory prohibition against full rate auditing prior to payment be repealed. An estimated three-year cost savings of $165.2 million would occur as a result of improved collection of freight overcharges.

Implementation

Of the 11 recommendations, 4 (36 percent) can be implemented by the affected agency; 2 (18 percent) can be implemented through Presidential action; and 5 (46 percent) will require Congressional approval.

Volume III: Financial Management in the Federal Government

PROJECT DIRECTORS:	Gregory C. Carey Assistant to the Chairman W. R. Grace & Co. Richard A. Goodman Assistant to the Chairman W. R. Grace & Co.	*NUMBER OF ISSUES:* 4 *NUMBER OF RECOMMENDATIONS:* 13 *3-YEAR COST SAVINGS:* Potential savings are identified in other PPSS reports and no new savings are claimed in this report.
NUMBER OF PROJECT MEMBERS: 3		

Overview

The report on Financial Management in the Federal Government analyzes shortcomings and opportunities in four key financial areas: the true size of the Federal budget, accounting systems, cash management, and debt collection. PPSS's approach in undertaking its review was to compare Federal Government practices with those of large American corporations.

Issues and Recommendations

PPSS studied four major issues and formulated 13 recommendations in the area of Government-wide financial management. Identified savings are *not* incremental to those contained in previously released PPSS reports.

The True Size of the Federal Budget—Federal Government expenditures significantly understate the true level of Federal activity because they exclude or only partially include major spending commitments. If the budget reflected all Government spending commitments (including off-budget entities, guaranteed loans, Government-sponsored enterprises, and the proper funding of retirement plans), FY 1984 budgeted expenditures would be $1,812 billion, more than twice the official budget of $849 billion, and the Federal debt would stand at $4.025 trillion, rather than the currently reflected $1.444 trillion. PPSS recommended including offsetting collections in both revenue and outlay totals, placing off-budget Federal entities back onto the budget, including guaranteed loans and Government-sponsored enterprises in budget outlays, and including the full cost to fund the liabilities of Federal retirement plans.

Accounting Systems—PPSS found that almost one-third of the accounting systems in the Federal Government lack approval of the General Accounting Office (GAO). There is no central controlling entity with responsibility and authority to ensure that agency accounting systems contain adequate internal controls over receipts, disbursements, and assets and that agency managers have timely, accurate, and useful financial information. In addition, obsolete, incompatible, and independent Federal Government ADP systems contribute to inadequate accounting systems. PPSS recommended establishing a central controllership function within the Office of Federal Management, as proposed by the PPSS Federal Management Systems Task Force. It also recommended that strong controllership functions be established in each agency; that the central controller, working with agency controllers, develop comprehensive accounting policy, financial reporting, and internal control standards; that legislation be introduced to require agencies to comply with GAO's accounting systems approval process; and that a timely and comprehensive form of annual external reporting for the Government be developed.

Cash Management—PPSS found that cash management practices in the Federal Government lag significantly behind those in the private sector due to a lack of adequate incentives and controls. PPSS recommended using the budget process to establish incentives for cash management improvements and creating a Financial Management Department to improve direction, coordination, and administration of the financial management function throughout Government. PPSS estimated that the Federal Government can reduce by three days the "float" on its $7 billion in cash flow per working day, resulting in an incremental improved cash flow of $21 billion, with interest savings of $7 billion over a three-year period.

Debt Collection—As of September 30, 1982, the Federal Government was owed $301 billion, of which 30% was due immediately or within a year (current receivables). Of the $92.7 billion in current receivables, about $37.8 billion were delinquent. Despite renewed emphasis on debt collection, PPSS found many agency accounting systems are not adequate to support credit management and debt collection activities. PPSS recommended that the Government accelerate data collection to provide immediate information on delinquencies, establish more effective performance standards, create a permanent debt collection staff, and encourage private institutions extending credit under guaranteed loan programs to upgrade their own collection efforts.

Implementation

Authority for implementing these recommendations rests with the Congress.

Management Office Selected Issues Report

Volume IV: Wage Setting Laws:
Impact on the Federal Government

PROJECT	G. John Tysse	*NUMBER OF ISSUES:* 3	
DIRECTOR:	Director, Labor Law		
	U.S. Chamber of	*NUMBER OF*	
	Commerce	*RECOMMENDATIONS:* 13	
NUMBER OF		*3-YEAR*	
PROJECT		*COST SAVINGS:* $11.65	
MEMBERS:	8	($ billions)	

Overview

PPSS conducted an analysis of the major Federal prevailing wage laws: the Davis-Bacon Act, the Walsh-Healey Act, and the Service Contract Act. Principal focus was on their costs and effects on Government and private contractors, with PPSS concluding that they cannot be effectively administered, significantly increase the cost of Government, and impose administrative burdens on contractors.

Issues and Recommendations

PPSS recommended that all three prevailing wage laws be repealed, with three-year cost savings to the Government estimated at $11.65 billion.

   The Davis-Bacon Act—In addition to the Federal Davis-Bacon Act (1931), there are some 37 state prevailing wage laws called "little Davis-Bacon" acts. Davis-Bacon requires the Secretary of Labor to determine the "prevailing wage" on Federally funded and assisted construction projects. The law was originally intended to prevent unscrupulous outside contractors from successfully bidding Federal projects by importing cheap labor, and covered only direct Federal construction. It has been extended by Congress over the last 50 years to cover virtually any construction project where there is some Federal connection. In application, Davis-Bacon removes wages and benefits as a factor in the competitive bidding process.

   The task force found that the Davis-Bacon Act is not and cannot be fairly and effectively administered, operates largely in direct contravention to its original purpose, discriminates against smaller contractors, and has anticompetitive effects. Absent repeal, PPSS recommended the dollar threshold be increased to $1 million, the prevailing wage be defined to mean the range of wages within a local area, and the law be amended to

— 516 —

permit the unlimited use of semiskilled helpers and to proscribe the use of urban rates for rural areas and *vice versa.*

PPSS estimated that the repeal of Davis-Bacon would result in three-year cost savings of $4.97 billion, with minimal disruption of the construction industry.

The Walsh-Healey Act—The Walsh-Healey Act applies to all Federal contracts exceeding $10,000 for the manufacture or furnishing of materials, supplies, articles, or equipment and was enacted for reasons similar to those which led to the passage of the Davis-Bacon Act. Its principal effect is in its provisions requiring overtime pay for work in excess of eight hours a day, which effectively prevents the use of flexible work schedules.

PPSS concluded that the Act is obsolete, reduces competition, and drives up labor costs. Its repeal would result in three-year cost savings of $3.37 billion. If total repeal cannot be effected, PPSS recommended that the daily eight-hour threshold for overtime pay be repealed, the dollar threshold be increased from $10,000 to $1 million, and contracts between the Federal Government and businesses with 100 or fewer employees be exempt from coverage.

The Service Contract Act—The Service Contract Act (SCA) was enacted in 1965. It requires that employees working under Federal Government service contracts over $2,500 be paid prevailing wages and benefits as determined by the Secretary of Labor. SCA's rationale was similar to that for the Davis-Bacon and Walsh-Healey Acts.

PPSS found that SCA prevailing wage rate determinations result in the importation of foreign wage rates into the locality where the work actually is performed, that data sources available to the Department of Labor are inadequate for making accurate prevailing wage determinations, and that the Department of Labor fails to adjust prior wage determinations downward to reflect lower prevailing wage rates.

PPSS projected that repeal of SCA would result in three-year cost savings of $3.31 billion. If repeal cannot be achieved, the Act should be amended to raise the threshold to $100,000, white collar application should be eliminated, and successorship provisions should be stricken.

Implementation

Implementation of PPSS recommendations to repeal the major prevailing wage laws will require Congressional approval.

Management Office Selected Issues Report

Volume V: Anomalies in the Federal Work Environment

PROJECT DIRECTOR:	George S. Goldberger Assistant to the Chairman W. R. Grace & Co.	*NUMBER OF ISSUES:* 22 *NUMBER OF RECOMMENDATIONS:* 56
NUMBER OF TASK FORCE MEMBERS:	11	*3-YEAR COST SAVINGS:* Specific anomalies, including recommendations and cost savings, are discussed in detail in individual PPSS reports and no new savings are claimed in this report.

Overview

In examining Government operations, PPSS identified examples of mismanagement, inefficiency, and lack of coordination among departments and agencies, all of which are exacerbated by the massive size of the Federal Government. The term "anomalies" is based on a comparison between sound, commonly accepted management practices and procedures and those found in the Federal Government.

Issues and Recommendations

In this report, PPSS focused on the Federal Government's need for a comprehensive and integrated strategy; an efficient and well-managed organizational structure; effective and responsive management systems; and competent, qualified, and properly motivated employees.

Management Operations—PPSS found management operations characterized by functionally obsolescent and incompatible automated data processing (ADP) systems; an absence of cost-consciousness in building and property management; inadequate information and support systems for financial management, budgeting, planning, and evaluation; employee benefits which exceed the best of those found in the private sector; and overly complex and rigid procurement policies and procedures. For example:

- Government ADP systems are so old that manufacturer maintenance is no longer possible and instead requires the use of specially trained Federal employees at an annual cost to the taxpayer of approximately $600 million.

- In 1982, the Federal Government had loans and guarantees outstanding of about $791 billion, but it cannot determine how long $35 billion in delinquent debt has been on the books; the totals in idle Federal cash held by grantees; cash balances; and total Federal funds granted to individual states and localities.

• Under the General Service (GS) classification system in Washington, nearly one-third of all positions are misclassified with the wrong grade, occupation, or title, costing the taxpayer $682 million annually.

Program Operations—The Federal Government has not been able to develop accounting and data processing systems adequate to keep up with and manage the phenomenal growth of the nation's subsidized programs. Other cost savings could occur if the Government collected fees from beneficiaries of Government services, products, or benefits *not* shared by the general public and if certain activities were turned over to non-Federal entities, i.e., privatized. For example:

• HUD disbursed more than $5 million of Community Development Block Grant Program funds to the city of Boston, which in turn spent the funds for payroll and administrative expenses unrelated to HUD programs.

• The military commissary system—established in the 1800s to serve soldiers in frontier posts—currently consists of 238 commissaries in the continental US, including six in such "outposts" as Washington, D.C. Privatizing commissary operations could result in $2.4 billion in three-year savings and revenue.

• Of the 238,000 Department of Education loans submitted before September 15, 1979, at least 55,000 lacked information on original loan amounts and dates, repayments, and Social Security numbers of the borrowers.

Implementation

For many of the PPSS recommendations, implementation is within the purview of the departments and agencies; others will require action by the President and/or the Congress.

Management Office Selected Issues Report

Volume VI: Federal Retirement Systems

PROJECT DIRECTORS:	John J. Gish Director, Special Projects Business Economics Group W. R. Grace & Co.	*NUMBER OF PROJECT MEMBERS:* 4 *NUMBER OF ISSUES:* 9
	Henry James Lawler Director, Corporate Plans Monsanto Corporation	*NUMBER OF RECOMMENDATIONS:* 27 *3-YEAR*
DEPUTY PROJECT DIRECTOR:	Raphael Kaminer Senior Business Analyst Business Economics Group W. R. Grace & Co.	*COST SAVINGS:* $58.1 ($ billions)

Overview

During 1973–1982, the Federal Government paid out more than $200 billion in pension benefits to retired civil service and military personnel. The Office of Personnel Management (OPM) and the Department of Defense (DOD) estimate that during 1983–1992, these costs will increase to $500 billion.

Despite these massive expenditures, the Government understates its retirement costs by failing to adequately provide for future benefits. The Government's shortfall, i.e., unfunded liability, is more than a trillion dollars and has been increasing, on average, by $94 billion annually. Ultimately, these costs will have to be borne by the taxpayer.

Issues and Recommendations

PPSS studied nine issues and formulated 27 recommendations which, when implemented, will result in three-year cost savings totaling $58.1 billion.

PPSS reviewed the two largest Federal retirement systems, the Civil Service Retirement System (CSRS) and Military Retirement System (MRS), which jointly cover approximately 98% of all Government employees. It concluded that Government retirement plans provide benefits and incur costs three to six times as great as the best private sector plans. This large differential does not fully recognize the $1.1 trillion cost of unfunded future Government pension liabilities. Based on full funding, CSRS and MRS are 6.1 and 8.4 times the cost of private sector plans, respectively. In its analysis, PPSS relied heavily upon two authoritative industry studies: the Bankers Trust, *Corporate Pension Plan Study—A Guide for the 1980s*, and the Hay-Huggins, *Noncash Compensation Comparison*. Attention was focused on retirement age, long-term disability provisions, benefit formulas, inflation protection, integration of Federal pension programs, and pension accounting and investment practices.

PPSS found that, in general, CSRS and MRS programs specify benefit formulas more liberal than typically found in the private sector; allow retirement, with unreduced benefits, at an earlier age than typically found in the private sector; and provide full protection against inflation.

The impact of liberal CSRS and MRS provisions can be summarized by comparing lifetime pension benefits in the public and private sectors: Assuming retirement at age 55, which is typical of the CSRS retiree, and at a preretirement salary of $50,000, lifetime benefits paid would be $1,085,000, or 2.7 times the pension and Social Security benefits paid to the private sector retiree. Assuming retirement at age 43 with 20 years of service, which is typical of an officer retiring under MRS, and a preretirement salary of $50,000, lifetime benefits paid would be $1,679,000, or 6.7 times the benefits paid to the private sector retiree (both including Social Security).

To make the Government's retirement costs comparable to those of the private sector, PPSS recommended: increasing the normal retirement age from 55 for CSRS and about 40 for MRS to age 62, reducing benefits actuarially for retirement before age 62, reducing credit granted for each year's service to levels comparable to those in the private sector, revising the benefit formula to define base earnings as the average of the highest five years of salary, and revising cost-of-living adjustments to reflect prevailing private sector practices.

Implementation

All PPSS recommendations concerning retirement will require Congressional approval. PPSS recommended that the Administration, through OPM, DOD, and the Office of Management and Budget, prepare the necessary legislation for Congressional approval as soon as possible so as to minimize the lead time before significant savings can be realized.

Management Office Selected Issues Report

Volume VII: Information Gap in the Federal Government

PROJECT
DIRECTORS:
	Richard V. Horan
	President
	Citizens Public
	   Expenditure
	   Survey, Inc.
	
	Keith S. Kendrick
	Assistant to the President
	Chemed Corporation
		NUMBER OF ISSUES: 5
		
		NUMBER OF
		RECOMMENDATIONS: 14
		
		3-YEAR COST SAVINGS/
		REVENUE GENERATION: *

NUMBER OF *TASK FORCE* *MEMBERS:* 8		* *Note:* Three-year cost savings and revenue generation total $78.598 billion. Because they have been drawn entirely from other PPSS reports, they are not again claimed here.

Overall Perspective

When President Reagan established PPSS, he asked the private sector executives to look at the various departments and agencies as if they were candidates for a merger or takeover. In responding to this request, the private sector found that key information regarding Government services, personnel, facilities, equipment, performance, and cost often was not available and, when available, frequently was out of date, inaccurate, or incomplete. These information "gaps" made the concept of looking at the Federal Government as a merger or acquisition candidate impossible, since information necessary to make a buy or no-buy decision was not available.

"Information gap" is defined as a collapse in the communication or reception of knowledge. The "gap" extends to all types of information and permeates virtually every department and agency of the Federal Government and every functional area of operation and program management.

PPSS found that in the area of financial reporting systems, the Federal Government has over 300 separate accounting systems and does not prepare balance sheets, statements of operations, statements of changes in financial position and cash flow, and interim financial statements. Project management data, where it exists, are incomplete, inaccurate, and improperly defined for purposes of effective management.

Issues and Recommendations

From the private sector's acquisition analysis, it became clear that the information gap deficiency in Government is the result of a broad and systematic management failure, which may be summarized in terms of a structural leadership void and four roadblocks that halt orderly processes. The roadblocks include: (1) no focused identification of the information needed for effective management; (2) poor accuracy, timeliness, and consistency of data; (3) inadequate manual and automated systems; and (4) failure to utilize available information to support decision-making. From a structural perspective, no single person or office is coordinating the selection and flow of management information.

Closing the gaps identified in the 126 issues from other PPSS task force reports would lead to three-year cost savings and revenue generation of $78.598 billion. This dollar amount duplicates savings and revenues previously reported by PPSS and is presented here to provide a perspective on the scope and significance of the problem.

Individual task forces recommended specific solutions to the information gaps they identified. In this report, the focus was on the development of a corrective program that would include an agency-by-agency needs assessment; collection standards in the areas of relevance, completeness, accuracy, timeliness, and consistency; a systems approach to information processing; improved utilization of data, including an assessment of agency performance and sharing of relevant data between agencies; and a structure to facilitate the information management process. Such a program is designed to provide a systematic, incremental approach that establishes an ongoing structure and process to upgrade the information that Government decision-makers have available to them.

Implementation

The 14 recommendations concerning information gap are within the authority of the Executive Branch and should be implemented in conjunction with the recommendations of the PPSS Federal Management Systems Task Force which call for the establishment of an Office of Federal Management and the centralization of key management functions.

Management Office Selected Issues Report

Volume VIII: The Cost of Congressional Encroachment

PROJECT DIRECTOR:	Paul Clark Vice President National Center for Legislative Research	*NUMBER OF ISSUES:* 5
		NUMBER OF RECOMMENDATIONS: 32
NUMBER OF TASK FORCE MEMBERS:	6	*3-YEAR COST SAVINGS:* $7.775 ($ billions)
		3-YEAR REVENUE GENERATION: $1.070 ($ billions)

PPSS acknowledged that Congress has every constitutional right to exercise its lawmaking powers, not only with respect to setting funding levels and policy guidelines for programs, but even with respect to mandating administrative procedures. It also recognized that it had no competence or desire to argue constitutional issues, and that the complexities of the Federal checks and balances system makes analogies between the public and private sector imperfect. Nonetheless, the PPSS findings demonstrate that Congress has expanded the scope of its concern for Executive Branch activities to include the most minute details of operations—from dictating the size and style of agency wall calendars, to overruling a Treasury Department decision on a mailbox address for payments of tobacco taxes, to requiring an attorney in a Government office in Stillwater, Oklahoma.

Based on its professional private sector experience, PPSS concluded that such top level involvement with day-to-day decisions reduces operating management's effectiveness and productivity. In effect, the cost of this decrease in efficiency should be taken into account when Congress decides how far down the administrative ladder to exercise its legislative powers.

Many PPSS reports contained instances in which Congressional involvement with day-to-day program operations have delayed or prevented program management from achieving proposed efficiencies. In this regard, it is relevant to note that over 70 percent of the cost saving/revenue enhancement opportunities identified in the PPSS reports will require Congressional approval. This special report further analyzed the issue by focusing on the basic management functions that must be successfully executed by the Executive Branch if efficiency and cost-effectiveness of operations are to be attained.

Issues and Recommendations

PPSS studied four major management categories—strategy, structure, systems, and people—and identified 32 opportunities for corrective action which, when fully implemented, could result in three-year cost savings of $7.775 billion and revenue generation of $1.070 billion.

Among the examples of excessive Congressional involvement in Executive Branch operations identified in the report were the following:

- Over the last 20 years, numerous programs to close some of DOD's most unnecessary, inefficient, and uneconomical military bases have been blocked by the efforts of Congressmen from affected areas.

- The 231 military commissaries across the U.S. rely on taxpayer subsidies of more than $750 million a year, unlike the self-supporting

Post Exchanges. These commissaries are not necessary at military installations in large metropolitan areas, and phasing out the subsidy would still enable patrons to purchase food at savings of 15 percent or more.

- Under a 1981 law, the Veterans Administration must submit a detailed plan to Congress for any organizational change that will affect as few as three employees.

- Programs to increase the use of contracting out for services rather than having them performed by Federal employees have been continually thwarted, even though using outside contractors could result in annual savings in the billions of dollars, and in many cases improve service.

To redress this situation, PPSS strongly recommended that the President be given item veto power, such as is available to the governors of 43 states. This would enable a President to separate approval of major legislation from disapproval of unrelated—and unnecessarily costly—elements included in a bill. Of course, Congress would still be able to exercise its Constitutional right to override that veto.

Implementation

Implementation of the corrective actions indicated above and the PPSS recommendation that the President be given the item veto will require Congressional approval.

Management Office Selected Issues Report

Volume IX: Federal Health Care Costs

PROJECT DIRECTORS:	Joseph C. Hoffman Special Consultant on the Health Care Industry W. R. Grace & Co.	*NUMBER OF ISSUES:* 1 *NUMBER OF RECOMMENDATIONS:* 5
	Anthony J. Mangiaracina Executive Vice President, General Development Group W. R. Grace & Co.	*3-YEAR COST SAVINGS:* $28.9 ($ billions)
NUMBER OF TASK FORCE MEMBERS: 1		

Overview

Total U.S. health care expenditures grew from $41.7 billion in 1965 to $322.4 billion in 1982, or by 12.8 percent per year, about 40 percent faster than the overall economic growth rate of 9.2 percent in total Gross National Product (GNP). Health care costs have absorbed a larger and larger portion of total GNP, increasing from 4.4 percent in 1950 to 6.0 percent in 1965 and 10.5 percent in 1982.

Present Government financing arrangements tie Government expenditures to a dynamic growth industry, since Federal, state, and local governments pay for a substantial share of total health care costs. In 1982, tax levy funds financed 42.4 percent of the country's total health care bill (Federal Government, 28.9 percent; and state and local governments, 13.5 percent). From a base of $5.5 billion in 1965, Federal expenditures on health care increased to $93.1 billion by 1982, up by 18.1 percent per year.

PPSS concluded that linking Federal spending and health care expenditures under the present reimbursement financing arrangements is undesirable. Specifically the current system raises several key long-term issues, including what can be done to address the fiscal problems caused by rapid growth in health care spending and how Federal budget problems can be addressed without destroying the fundamental economic and technological advances which underlie the growth in health care expenditures.

Issues and Recommendations

PPSS formulated five recommendations which, when implemented, would result in three-year cost savings of $28.9 billion. An additional $16.2 billion in three-year cost savings were identified in other PPSS reports dealing with health care expenditures. Based on its findings and conclusions, PPSS sought to develop recommendations that would generate savings from long-term reforms of Federal health care financing and reimbursement systems, so as to reduce Federal expenditures on health care and improve the overall efficiency and quality of the health care delivery system.

Specifically, PPSS recommended establishing a fiscally acceptable limitation on total Federal health care expenditures. This fiscal "cap" would be such that Federal expenditures on all health care programs would be restricted to increases no greater than the overall rate of growth in the U.S. economy, i.e., by approximately 8 percent to 10 percent per year. In addition, expenditures would be based on per capita spending rates for the population served by each program and would be structured to prevent year-to-year reductions in real per capita expenditure levels for program population groups.

PPSS further proposed geographic allocation of expenditures based on the number of persons served by Medicare and Medicaid in each region. Designation of the geographic areas would be based on the current health care catchment areas, i.e., the local markets including the health care facilities and providers used by a majority of the residents, with some allowance for major regional differences in per capita health care costs resulting from climate or other environment variations, as well as basic economic factors, such as regional differences in the cost of living and the scale of health care facilities serving each broad geographic area. However, it is PPSS's intention to reduce as much as possible the extent to which Government agencies must make regulatory decisions affecting differences in regional health care spending.

PPSS further recommended that the Federal Government invite competitive bids from the private sector and state and local health care systems to provide services to its beneficiaries. Privatization of these services would mean the interposition of an intermediary which would assume the financial and managerial responsibilities for ensuring that the Medicare and Medicaid services are covered at a cost to the Federal Government (and the beneficiaries) no greater than the contractually agreed expenditure levels. In most cases, this would not represent a change in the actual health care provider.

Finally, PPSS recommended the institutionalization of consumer choice. Bidders would be free to submit plans with premium costs which are more than the maximum per capita amount which the Federal Government will finance. Consumers, in turn, would be free to choose these more costly plans, provided they pay the excess of premium costs over the Government allowance. In addition, there would be periodic enrollment periods when enrollees would be given the opportunity to change their form of coverage.

Implementation

Implementation of the above PPSS recommendations will require Congressional approval.

Management Office Selected Issues Report

Volume X: Opportunities Beyond PPSS

PROJECT DIRECTOR:	George S. Goldberger Assistant to the Chairman W. R. Grace & Co.	*NUMBER OF ISSUES:* 11
		NUMBER OF RECOMMENDATIONS: 12
NUMBER OF TASK FORCE MEMBERS: 18		*3-YEAR COST SAVINGS:* $15.947 ($ billions)

Overview

Inherent in a volunteer project such as PPSS are time constraints and personnel limitations which would preclude a comprehensive study of any organization, particularly one as large and as complex as the Federal Government. Accordingly, there were many opportunities for cost savings or revenue enhancements that were only partially developed by PPSS and other areas which were not investigated at all. The purpose of this report is to illustrate that the savings opportunities identified by PPSS, although substantial, represent only a small part of the potential savings available across the Federal Government.

Extrapolated Savings Opportunities

Many of the savings opportunities uncovered by a particular Task Force may have been identified by another Task Force. The converse, however, is that there may also be opportunities identified by one Task Force that could be applied across other areas of the Federal Government. Eleven issues were selected for their applicability to other areas of the Government and illustrate how a single cost saving measure can be extrapolated to yield greater benefits. These 11 issues initially showed three-year savings of $6.083 billion. Extrapolation of these issues across Government shows incremental savings of $11.802 billion over three years.

On a Government-wide basis, total savings for these issues amounts to $17.885 billion over three years. Of the 11 issues, eight, with three-year savings of $15.947 billion, are categorized as fully substantiated or substantially documented and are included in total PPSS savings. The remaining three issues, whose three-year savings of $1.938 billion are not included in PPSS savings overall, are classified as potentially justifiable and supportable.

For example, extrapolation of the Tax Exempt Bonds issue amounts to total three-year savings of $5.174 billion. This issue extrapolates an HHS–Public Health/HCFA Task Force report recommendation which proposes that "tax-exempt hospital bonds be general obligation issues of the Governmental unit issuing them rather than revenue bonds." As presented in the Task Force report, the intent of this recommendation was to limit the amount of tax-exempt hospital bonds issued by converting them to general obligations at the State level. Because State and local governments place a ceiling on funds in this category, competition would increase as hospitals vie for a limited pool of tax-exempt financing. The extrapolation of this recommendation Government-wide involves reducing the amount of tax-exempt bonds issued in all financing categories by changing them to general obligation bonds, imposing a ceiling on the amount of tax-exempt revenue bonds, and requiring financial justification.

This section of the report presents selected issues worthy of further analysis to determine additional savings opportunities. These issues have been extracted from work done by PPSS as well as reports of the General Accounting Office (GAO) and the Office of the Inspector General (OIG).

Within the PPSS reports are two specific areas which designate additional opportunities for savings. The first area represents the issues entitled, "Category III—Potentially Justifiable and Supportable." These recommendations total 54 in number with related three-year savings of $30.158 billion. The second area represents issue subjects defined as "Cost Control Opportunities for Further Study." These subject areas represent potential opportunities for savings which the Task Force could not investigate in detail. Approximately 188 opportunities of this nature are contained in the reports. While these issues do not represent a comprehensive list of areas identified for further study by PPSS, the GAO, or the OIG, they underscore opportunities for additional cost savings in the Federal Government.

PPSS also studied military reserve forces and identified several areas that are worth further study. Three issues with estimated savings of $1.485 billion over three years include civilianization of training, revisions in the retirement systems, and termination of dual pay practices.

Implementation

Of the 12 specific recommendations, 5 (42 percent) are within the purview of the departments and agencies, and 7 (58 percent) will require Congressional action.

Management Office Selected Issues Report

Volume XI: Federally Subsidized Programs

PROJECT DIRECTOR:	Jesse L. Koontz Vice President, Economic Analysis, Natural Resources Group W. R. Grace & Co.	*NUMBER OF ISSUES:* 1
		NUMBER OF RECOMMENDATIONS: 4
NUMBER OF PROJECT MEMBERS: 10		*3-YEAR COST SAVINGS:* $58.900 ($ billions)

Overview

Federal expenditures may be distinguished between non-targeted outlays for traditional Government functions (national defense, the administration of justice, etc.) and non-traditional outlays targeted to specific groups of individuals, businesses, or institutions. From 1962 to 1982, targeted outlays grew at an average annual rate of 5.9 percent in constant dollars, compared with the 2.4 percent growth rate for traditional expenditures, and were a driving force in the uncontrolled growth of Federal spending.

Issues and Recommendations

As a result of its study of subsidy programs, PPSS formulated four recommendations which would result in three-year cost savings of $58.9 billion. The overriding conclusion reached by PPSS is that, despite the magnitude of the dollars expended on these non-traditional areas, adequate information does not exist to determine the degree to which intended recipients are receiving sufficient benefits, or, conversely, the degree to which benefits are going to undeserving recipients to the detriment of all taxpayers.

PPSS also found shortcomings in subsidy management, including multiple and overlapping programs; decentralization of responsibilities; lack of coordination among administrative and legislative functions; and complex, inconsistent, and sometimes conflicting program eligibility criteria.

Based on data obtained by PPSS, this lack of program control has resulted in significant mistargeting of benefits, as exemplified by the following:

Means-Tested Programs—In 1982, the pre-transfer payment poverty gap was $50.1 billion. However, even after expenditures of $124.0 billion in 1982 on means-tested programs for the poor, a poverty gap of $12.7 billion still existed. In theory, the $124 billion not only should have brought all households out of poverty, but should have brought all households to 125 percent of the poverty level, with $47.5 billion to spare. Further, an Office of Management and Budget analysis showed that in 1981, 42.4 percent of those receiving benefits from major means-tested programs had total incomes in excess of 150 percent of the poverty line.

Subsidies for the Elderly—Despite massive unfunded liabilities, $76.1 billion in social insurance payments (primarily Social Security) were made to elderly persons who were above the poverty line. Since this $76.1 billion in social insurance payments is in excess of what these retirees and their employers paid in, including interest, they are properly considered a Federal subsidy.

Farm Subsidies—There appears to be no ongoing data collection on total subsidy benefits ($14.3 billion in FY 1982) received by each family or corporate farmer. It has been estimated that as much as 50 percent of the Farmers Home Administration loan portfolio could be assumed by private sector lenders.

User Charges—Due in part to unclear administrative policies and insufficient data regarding the full cost to the Government, many users of Government goods and services pay only a fraction of the actual cost, with the taxpayer absorbing the majority of the expense. PPSS identified $21.0 billion in potential revenue over three years due to new or increased user charges.

PPSS recommended that a form, similar to the W-2 form issued to wage-earners, be issued to each recipient of a Government subsidy, with a copy provided to the Internal Revenue Service. All Federal payments shown on this form would be added to the beneficiary's earnings to arrive at total income, thus enabling determination of the extent to which targeted outlays are meeting stated objectives. PPSS further suggested that consideration be given to the consolidation of benefit programs; that agency accounting systems be significantly upgraded to accurately provide data on administrative costs, currently estimated at $13.2 billion for the 15 largest subsidy programs; and that Federal poverty statistics be redefined to include the value of in-kind transfer payments, such as Food Stamps. Including the value of such non-cash benefits would have reduced the poverty rate from 15 percent to 9.6 percent in 1982.

Implementation

Implementation of PPSS recommendations pertaining to subsidy programs will require Congressional action.

IX

Summary Spreadsheets of PPSS Reports

Task Force Reports	Number of Issues	Number of Recommendations	3-Year* Cost Savings	3-Year* Revenue Generation	Total 3-Year* Cost Savings/ Revenue	3-Year* Cash Acceleration
The Department of Agriculture	58	154	$ 12.237	$ .606	$ 12.843	$ 5.846
The Department of the Air Force	22	50	27.603	—	27.603	—
The Department of the Army	21	78	13.400	—	13.400	—
Automated Data Processing/ Office Automation	18	58	19.063	—	19.063	—
Boards/Commissions—Banking	41	84	1.617	7.782	9.399	.554
Boards/Commissions—Business	96	289	2.367	.929	3.296	.034
The Department of Commerce	12	29	.259	.471	.730	.015
The Office of the Secretary of Defense	40	73	44.508	.248	44.756	—
The Department of Education	9	60	2.828	—	2.828	5.841
The Department of Energy, The Federal Energy Regulatory Commission and the Nuclear Regulatory Commission	21	82	2.790	1.291	4.081	.089
The Environmental Protection Agency/The Small Business Administration/The Federal Emergency Management Agency	28	78	1.660	.199	1.859	.315
Federal Construction Management	23	23	5.446	—	5.446	—
Federal Feeding	6	15	.260	.039	.299	—
Federal Hospital Management	13	60	9.191	2.721	11.912	—
Federal Management Systems	10	35	a	a	a	a
Financial Asset Management	35	90	13.777	9.726	23.503	48.647

Task Force Reports	Number of Issues	Number of Recom- menda- tions	3-Year* Cost Savings	3-Year* Revenue Generation	Total 3-Year* Cost Savings/ Revenue	3-Year* Cash Accel- eration
The Department of Health and Human Services—Department Management, Office of Human Development Services, ACTION	8	117	.602	—	.602	.477
The Department of Health and Human Services— Public Health Service/ Health Care Financing Administration	18	71	12.677	.662	13.339	.052
The Department of Health and Human Services— Social Security Administration	10	56	8.407	.980	9.387	4.661
The Department of Housing and Urban Development	10	50	2.460	.358	2.818	.667
The Department of the Interior	9	27	.271	1.022	1.293	.231
The Department of Justice	10	37	.183	.667	.850	.288
The Department of Labor	14	49	3.718	—	3.718	—
Land/Facilities/Personal Property Management	3	9	.201	.426	.627	—
Low Income Standards and Benefits	9	24	5.887	—	5.887	—
The Department of the Navy	16	69	7.185	—	7.185	—
Personnel Management	18	95	39.270	—	39.270	—
Privatization	9	22	11.191	17.226	28.417	—
Procurement/Contracts/Inventory Management	22	57	20.271	—	20.271	—
Real Property Management	10	52	2.362	—	2.362	—
Research and Development	8	25	12.090	—	12.090	—
The Department of State/AID/ USIA	10	31	.383	.360	.743	.056
The Department of Transportation	22	69	2.712	1.705	4.417	.436
The Department of the Treasury	23	63	2.367	9.139	11.506	—
User Charges	22	57	—	10.211	10.211	—
The Veterans Administration	8	24	2.120	.953	3.073	.208
Management Office Selected Issues Reports						
Volume I—Publishing/Printing Reproduction and Audio- Visual Activities	7	29	1.463	.265	1.728	—
Volume II—Travel and Traffic Management	4	11	1.850	—	1.850	.032
Volume III—Financial Management in the Federal Government	4	13	b	b	b	b

Summary Spreadsheets of PPSS Reports
(continued)

Task Force Reports	Number of Issues	Number of Recommendations	3-Year* Cost Savings	3-Year* Revenue Generation	Total 3-Year* Cost Savings/ Revenue	3-Year* Cash Acceleration
Volume IV—Wage Setting Laws: Impact on the Federal Government	3	13	11.650	—	11.650	—
Volume V—Anomalies in the Federal Work Environment	22	56	a	a	a	a
Volume VI—Federal Retirement Systems	9	27	58.100	—	58.100	—
Volume VII—Information Gap in the Federal Government	5	14	b	b	b	b
Volume VIII—The Cost of Congressional Encroachment	5	32	7.755	1.070	8.825	—
Volume IX—Federal Health Care Costs	1	5	28.900	—	28.900	—
Volume X—Opportunities Beyond PPSS	11	12	10.773	5.174	15.947	—
Volume XI—Federally Subsidized Programs	1	4	58.900	—	58.900	—
PPSS Totals	784	2,478	$470.754	$74.230	$544.984	$68.449

* Duplicated Numbers; Dollar amounts represent Category I and Category II (fully and partially support-able) only.

a No savings/revenue/cash acceleration claimed.

b Identified savings specifically claimed in other PPSS reports and not claimed herein.

X

PPSS Participants and Contributors

**PRIVATE SECTOR SURVEY ON COST CONTROL
IN THE FEDERAL GOVERNMENT
EXECUTIVE COMMITTEE**

—CHAIRMAN—

Mr. J. Peter Grace
Chairman and Chief Executive Officer
W. R. Grace & Co.

—MEMBERS—

* Mr. William Agee
Former Chairman
Bendix Corporation

* Mr. Joseph Alibrandi
President and Chief Executive
Officer
Whittaker Corp.

* Mr. George D. Anderson
President
Anderson, ZurMuehlen & Co.

* Mr. Bennett Archambault
Chief Executive Officer
Stewart-Warner Corporation

* Mr. Samuel H. Armacost
President and Chief Executive
Officer
Bank of America

* Dr. William F. Ballhaus
President
Beckman Instruments, Inc.

---

* = Co-chair; title and company affiliation at time reports were completed and approved.
** = Communications Committee Member.
° = Simon Field Coordinating Group Member.
• = Chairman's Staff Member.

— 540 —

— 541 —

— 542 —

STAFF

I. *Management Office*

Director

James W. Nance
(February 1982–March 1983)

Chief Operating Officer

J. P. Bolduc
Booz·Allen & Hamilton Inc.
W. R. Grace & Co.

Deputy Director

Janet Colson
Special Assistant to the President

*Key Group Members**

Jean C. Batcheller
Paul F. Bennett
Melody M. Brooks
Francesco A. Calabrese
Frederick C. Cue
Steven Dely
Francis A. DiBello
Tracy L. P. Finn
John K. Giannuzzi
Robert H. Harrison
William J. Hemphill
Jeffrey A. Jones
Gerald D. Kasper
Charles Katsainos
Regina I. Kidd
Lewis J. Krulwich
Jerome M. Lewis
William M. Lucianovic
Andrew J. Lynch
Edward A. Lynch
J. T. Michelson
Robert L. Moon
George T. Pappas
Robert E. Pedigo
Robert P. Pikul
Judith E. Selvidge
Lewis Sorley
Andrea L. Tyndall

II. *Economic Analysis and Senior Review Group*

Group Director

Leonard Kamsky
W. R. Grace & Co.

Deputy Group Director

Duncan Bailey
W. R. Grace & Co.

*Key Group Members**

Michael Berman
Joseph Boshart
Gregory C. Carey
David B. Elkin
John J. Gish
George S. Goldberger
Patrick P. Grace
Raphael Kaminer
Annette B. Lanouette
Dorothy M. Ott
Edwin S. Rubenstein
John R. Sico
Carmel A. Urgo
Timothy S. vanBlommesteyn

---

* Additional participants included in "Management Office and Other Professional and Support Staff" listing.

III. *Public Relations Group*

Group Director

Antonio Navarro
W. R. Grace & Co.

Deputy Group Director

Frederick E. Bona
W. R. Grace & Co.

*Management Office
Communications Officers*

James M. DiClerico
Burson-Marsteller

Murray Sanders
Martin Marietta Corp.

Key Group Members *

Luis Castillo
Stephen B. Elliott
Corinne A. Forti
Richard L. Moore
John J. O'Connell, Jr.
Bonnie C. Sullivan
Chris G. Tofalli

IV. *Legal Affairs Group*

Group Director

Albert A. Eustis
W. R. Grace & Co.

*Management Office
Legal Counsel*

R. Stanley Harsh
Independent Attorney

Key Group Members *

Paul H. Frankel
Harmon G. Lewis

Special Counsel

Jeffrey P. Altman
Herbert L. Fenster
McKenna, Conner, & Cuneo

V. *Foundation for PPSS*

Board of Trustees

Albert A. Eustis, Chairman
Patrick J. Christmas

Allen D. Cors
Robert J. McIntosh

Officers of the Foundation

President
  Francis D. Flanagan
Vice President and Treasurer
  Kenneth Y. Millian
Vice President and Controller
  William B. Hansen
Vice President
  Klaus G. Scheye

Secretary
  Harmon G. Lewis
Assistant Secretary
  John N. Thurman
Assistant Treasurer
  Priscilla N. Myerson

Key Group Members *

Barbara L. Rollinson
Danielle M. Werchowsky
Suzette L. M. Wu

* Additional participants included in "Management Office and Other Professional and Support Staff" listing.

— 546 —

Jeanne R. Abate
John Acher
Charlotte H. Adams
John P. Addis
Mary Jo Allen
Mary K. Anglin
David C. Arpee
Joan Atkins
Patti Jo Baber
Howard E. Barash
John Joseph Barbati
Irene N. Bariga
Catherine S. Barron
Janet T. Basedow
Patrice Beckett
David R. Belle-Isle
Audrey M. Benford
John J. Bennett
Frank P. Bergen
Lisa D. Berger
Bedford Berrey
Edward F. Beyer
James R. Bianchi
Sheila B. Bindman
Michael E. Birkett
Donna Black
Anita Bloom
Edward E. Boehme
Debora Andrea Bond
William Bonesso
Joseph Boshart
Michelle A. Botts
Liesbeth Boxman
Dennis Bradshaw
Betty E. Bremby
Kenneth V. Brooks
John C. Brooman
Barbara Etta Brown
Ellen E. Brown
Veronica Andre Brown
Warren M. Brown
Sandra Brown-Tucker
Henry Bullock
Jerry J. Burcham
John M. Burgess
Winifred M. Burns
Claudian W. Burton
Angel M. Caban
Kathleen Callahan
Maureen Cannell
Gregory C. Carey
Blanche L. Hite Carr
Thomas Carrier
Ellen Carton

Intisar Chaudhry
L. Sanders Clagg
Bernard W. Clark
Paul Clark
Phyllis Ann Clark
James Clawson
Beverly J. Coates
William F. Cody
Eileen A. Colon
Lee A. Conrad
Debra A. Contrastano
Clyde F. Coombs
Robert J. Cornish
Stella M. Correia
Mary E. Costello
Susan Cunningham
Jyretha Darden
Annette Davis
Walter G. Davis
Norma Dawson
Edgar S. Day
Mark A. de Bernardo
Jean de Luxembourg
Brenda Dent
Thomas M. Dersch
Olga D. DiDomenico
Paul Dietrich
Catherine Ditoto
Carroll Doherty
Stephen R. Drapeau
Geoffrey H. Dreyer
Teresa R. Driver
Den Drumwright
Dorothy A. Duffy
Vernice Duncan
Henry L. D. Ebert
Nicholas Eftimiades
Lawrence M. Eichorn
Betsy Eisendrath
Wenda Ellington
Christine W. Engbrecht
Linda P. Erdberg
Stephen M. Erhart
Marie R. Errick
Theresa A. Ezzo
Paul Feser
Mark Fiddes
Elaine Finger
Randall Truman Fitzgerald
Donna J. Flannery
William D. Flannigan
Nancy L. Fox
Benjamin Frank
Mary T. Gale

Sharon Lea Gardine
Rose A. Gargiulo
Richard Garner
Marlin G. Geiger
Jeffrey L. Geller
George Gerung
Gregory E. Gieber
Louise Gimple
John J. Gish
Sarah G. Glover
Stephen D. Goddard
Alba Goebel
Edward J. Gogol
George S. Goldberger
Robert D. Gonda
Mary Gonzales
Richard A. Goodman
Ralph J. Gorden
F. David Gorman
Mary E. Gose
Geneese Gottschalk
Christopher G. Grace
Patrick P. Grace
Byron A. Grant
Frank M. Graves
Nina Graybill
Richard Greenberg
Henry L. Greenfeld
William C. Greenough
Brian D. Gregory
Mary K. Groseclose
George B. Gudz
Katherine L. Guest
Beverly J. Guilford
Charlotte Haberaeker
Ellen M. Haight
Vincent T. Hall
Mary Frances Hamill
Alan G. Hammersmith
James R. Handy
Charles E. Hansen
Elizabeth Hanson
Linda A. Harley
Eleanor Harms
Beverly Harris
Joan Harris
Mary R. Harris
Nicole Harris
Sean F. Harris
John A. Harrison
R. Stanley Harsh
Patricia A. Hartnett
Anna D. Hartsfield
Timothy C. Hassett

Cara L. Haynie
Michael L. Hays
Raymond E. Herzog
Edward F. Heymann
Irving Heymont
Joanne Hill
Timothy Hill
Toni Yvette Hill
Andrew W. Hodge
Paul S. Hoff
Joseph C. Hoffman
Jeanette E. Holbrook
Reid L. Holloway
Richard V. Horan
Lynn Ann Hornig
Mary V. Hornig
Cindy E. Horowitz
Holly B. Howell
Gina Hyman
Marion Ivey
Deborah Jackson
Keith R. Jacobson
June Jakubowski
Richard C. Jelinek
Christine A. Jennings
Jerry Jernigan
Brenda M. Johnson
Carmen J. Jones
Lavone Jones
Lon Jones
Patricia A. Jones
Prenell P. Jones
Arlene A. Kainz
Raphael Kaminer
Estelle M. Kane
Mary M. Kase
John B. Keeley
Elsie T. Kelly
Keith S. Kendrick
Signora A. Kennie
Andrew S. Kenward
Charlene V. King
Hubert M. King, Jr.
Sarah T. King
James R. Knickman
John A. Knubel
John R. Knudsen
Steve L. Komar
Jesse L. Koontz
John Korbel
Patricia A. Koshinski
Charles D. Kuehner
Steven S. Lakin
Annette B. Lanouette
Elizabeth Larson

Eileen M. Lavin
Henry J. Lawler
Thomas M. Lawlor
Marjorie Lawrence
Judy Lynn Lawson
Jean E. LeGrand
Ronald Lense
Gregory C. Lentz
Beth R. Lerner
Mary Alice Lessler
Helen M. Lewis-Wistner
Paul Liebow
Gerald Lipson
Lula Little
Mildred Kay Little
Martha J. Lockhart
Marybeth M. Long
Kenneth J. Luchs
J. M. Luke
Lisa H. Lyle
Patricia A. McAndrews
William J. McCaffrey, Jr.
Patrick G. McCann
Linda McCready
William A. McCulloch
Cathy A. McDonald
Gail L. McDonald
Donna Lee McGee
Jeffrey C. McGuiness
Jane E. McGuinness
Annette McKee
Peter McLaughlin
Andrew A. R. McWilliams
Rosemary B. Machalek
Cheryl C. Mackey
Dorothy K. Mady
Veronica Makell-Spriggs
Anthony J. Mangiaracina
Maria Mannarino
Madeline T. Manzo
Roy Markon
Eugene Marshall
Joanne Martin
Richard M. Martin
Joan L. Mashburn
E. Ines Matos
Susan B. Maurizi
L. Ralph Mecham
Jolie Melanson
Paul J. Merck, Jr.
Paul David Messina
Jeffrey J. Michael
Anne M. Middaugh
Marylin Mikuta
Carol Miller

Pamela S. Miller
Barbara B. Minich
Debora A. Mood
Robert L. Moon
Allison I. Moore
Janet Moore
Richard L. Moore, Jr.
Mary E. Moranzoni
Martha D. Morris
Spencer J. Morris
Deborah Odell Moss
Karen M. Mudd
Stephan C. Mulvihill
Catherine M. Murphy
Linda Myers
Andrew Nance
L. David Narrow
Antoinette Neal
Barbara B. Neesham
Cynthia Neeves
Daniel L. Nettuno
David M. Nicholas
Lillian Nicolich
Emma G. Nogales
Dargie Norman
Lynne E. Nuber
Keith C. Nusbaum
John J. O'Connell, Jr.
Colum P. O'Donnell
Judith A. O'Gorman
S. Lynn O'Gorman
William M. O'Reilly
Dorothy Ott
Rebecca Paquette
David Clement Parker
Thomas A. Peacock
Edgar Allen Peden
May C. Pena
Linda W. Petrie
Brenda Peyton
Kamau S. Philbert
Howard J. Philipp
Wendy B. Pierce
Sharon D. Piper
Sandra F. Pittman
Rhall Pope
Darby L. Prentiss
Ted Princiotto
Renee Pugliesi
Robert L. Putman
Stuart A. Rado
Edward Ramsey
Sharon J. Rawls
Kerri A. Raymond
Thomas K. Reilly

Rosemarie Rennick
Sharon R. Reynolds
Beverly Ann Rhodes
Deborah L. Ridgeway
Joseph W. Rio
Suzanne P. Ripley
Patricia N. Rogers
Alice O. Rollinson
Amy C. Rollinson
Mary Ross
Bernard D. Rostker
Daniel S. Rothblum
John C. Runyan
Mark V. Rutecki
Francis B. Ryan
Beatriz Sainz
Raymond L. Sanders
Edwald W. Sanjek
Eliza Ruffin Saunders
Klaus G. Scheye
James P. Schlicht
Allen D. Schmidt
Eric M. Schneck
Alfred M. Schneider
John Schroeder
Leslie G. Schultz
Gordon Scott
Charles Sharp
Amy E. Shaunessy
Christopher L. Shea
Diane E. Sherwood
John Sico
Charles F. Silvernail
Karen A. Simms
Anne A. Simpkinson
Mary Linda Sippel
Georgiana E. Slaughter
Norma E. Slaveter
Mitchell L. Smith
Janice M. Sokil
William Scott Soost

Martin Sorkin
John F. Spellman
Patricia A. Spinosa
Mark M. Spradley
Elisabeth M. Squire
Colleen L. Stanford
Gene D. Steiker
Helen L. Stewart
Patrick J. Stewart
Shannon Stibi
E. Clinton Stokes
Mindy D. Strominger
Joseph B. Sullivan, Jr.
Michael M. Sullivan
Ann C. Tasseff
Cynthia J. Templeton
Mary Germaine Thier
Orpha B. Thomas
Regina G. Thomas
Ruby T. Thomas
David L. Thompson
Stephen A. Thompson
Kimberly Thorne
Carrol H. Thornton
Frank Tibolla
Cynthia Y. Tillar
Louis C. Tinelli
Lisa Y. Tong
Julietta Torres
Timothy Tremel
Darrell W. Trimble
Tony A. Trujillo, Jr.
Robert D. Tye
Andrea L. Tyndall
G. John Tysse
Roger Ueltzen
James M. Ulcickas
Harlan K. Ullman
Timothy S. vanBlommesteyn
Scott Douglas Vining

Ram Viswanathan
Joyce Vogel
Norman Waks
Joel M. Wallinga
Karen L. Walsh
Jerry B. Ward
David L. Warner
James P. Wayne
Andrea Weaver
Sandra L. Webb
Richard Wegman
Stephen A. Weitzman
Mary Beth Welch
W. Harrison Wellford
Judith Whalen
Karen E. Wieckert
David J. Wilbur
Michael Wilkins
Cheryll B. Williams
Doris A. Williams
Kim T. Williams
Rodney L. Williams
Rosita Williams
Sharon M. Williams
Edward M. Willis
Jacqueline M. Willis
Vanessa Witherall
Alem Woldehawariat
Farrell J. Wolfson
Laura Wong
Marjorie T. J. Wong
Suzanne H. Woolsey
J. B. Worthington
Charles R. Wright
Willie Wright
Barbara A. Yastine
Richard B. Young
Thane Young
John F. Zaehringer
Michael S. Zarin

PPSS TASK FORCES

The Department of Agriculture

Co-Chairs

William B. Graham
Chairman
Baxter Travenol
  Laboratories, Inc.

William Wood Prince
President
F. H. Prince & Co., Inc.

Project Manager

Clifton B. Cox
Chairman of the Board
Cox, Lloyd Associates, Ltd.

Task Force Members

Kathleen S. Bittermann	Gerald F. Heisinger
Bartley P. Cardon	Daniel T. Kaschak
Thomas G. Cody	Gregory A. Knott
Mary B. W. Coe	Robert W. Kohlmeyer
Aberlardo S. Curdumi	A. J. Marcussen
Douglas J. DeMartin	Paul E. Marsh
Richard D. Donoghue	William E. Marshall
Paul C. Fiduccia	John E. Matthews
Michael E. Fitch	Horst J. Metz
Ross W. Gorte	Karl H. Ottolini
John S. Grimshaw	Allan Jeff Reinking
Donald H. Haider	Ian A. Schapiro
Bill L. Harriott	John A. Stewart
Augustin S. Hart, Jr.	

The Department of the Air Force

Co-Chairs

James H. Evans
Chairman and Chief
  Executive Officer
Union Pacific Corp.

Robert W. Galvin
Chairman and Chief
  Executive Officer
Motorola, Inc.

Paul F. Oreffice
President and Chief
  Executive Officer
Dow Chemical Co.

Project Manager

Charles L. Eaton
Senior Vice President
Union Pacific Corp.

Task Force Members

Joseph J. Adams	Richard de C. Hinds
Paul J. Andrews	John D. Kettelle
Thomas I. Betts	Christopher M. Klein
Jerald Blizin	Richard J. Kuehl
Burton M. Cohn	Richard K. Long
Edgar S. Day, Jr.	Herbert H. Lyon
John P. Deasey	John F. Lyons
Michael J. Deutch	Robert O. McAlister
John E. Diegelman	John J. McGonagle, Jr.
James F. Dobson	Ira George Morrison
William C. Drake	L. Richard Myers
Christina Eubank	Terrence M. Quirin
William M. Foulks	J. John Rhodes
Victor L. Friedrich	David W. Selzer
Peter M. Frolick	Mark M. Shaklee
J. S. Gentle	George P. Smith, II
Jerry C. Gose	William M. Watterworth
Vera S. Hannigan	Robert W. Wright

The Department of the Army

Co-Chairs

Roger E. Birk
Chairman, President and Chief
   Executive Officer
Merrill Lynch & Co., Inc.

William A. Marquard
Chairman, President and Chief
   Executive Officer
American Standard Inc.

John J. Horan
Chairman
Merck & Co., Inc.

Lewis T. Preston
Chairman
Morgan Guaranty Trust Co. of New
   York

Project Manager

Richard H. Francis
Vice President and Chief Financial
   Officer
American Standard Inc.

Task Force Members

John B. Artopoeus	David Holty	Donald P. Maroney
Elizabeth Boucher	Robert E. Imowitz	Emmett F. Meyer
Clinton D. Burdick	George N. Johnson, Jr.	Ed J. Morehouse
Julia Busalacchi	Hayes Q. Johnson	William E. Mullin
Nancy Felshaw Carden	Paul Kayser	Kenneth L. Rider
Clayton Christensen	Joseph F. Kelly	Donald B. Robinson
Richard M. Cohen	Stephen B. King	Rudolph Ruda
Jeffrey C. Constantz	David E. Kinney	Linda D. Scheuplein
Steven Darien	Robert C. Koche	Gregory L. A. Thomas
Daniel J. Donahue	Bernard N. Levin	Paula J. Hans Todd
Henry C. Ellison, III	Gail Milgram Levy	Michael C. VanderZwan
Robert Erickson	John W. Liska	Steven A. Wein
Irene Ann Etzkorn	Douglas A. Love	Dorothy Wilfong
John Farrell, Jr.	James V. McGee, Jr.	Roger C. Wilson
Leo F. Fenzel	Daniel J. McLaughlin	Lewis E. Wise
William L. Hauser	Gerald F. McQuade	Elizabeth Woole
Delores I. Holmes	Daniel J. Malachuck, Jr.	Blondell E. Wylie

Automated Data Processing/Office Automation

Boards/Commissions—Banking

Boards/Commissions—Business

Co-Chairs

George H. Dixon
President
First Bank System, Inc.

John M. Regan, Jr.
Chairman and Chief Executive Officer
Marsh & McLennan Companies, Inc.

Edward Donley
Chairman and Chief Executive Officer
Air Products and Chemicals, Inc.

Thomas I. Storrs
Chairman
NCNB Corp.

Robert A. Pritzker
President
The Marmon Group, Inc.

Rawleigh Warner, Jr.
Chairman and Chief Executive Officer
Mobil Corporation

Project Manager

William Duggan, Jr.
Vice President
Marsh & McLennan Companies, Inc.

Task Force Members

Kerry E. Adams	Walter J. Hatcher	Barbara B. O'Leary
Charles T. Albright	M. Thomas Hatley, Jr.	William C. Oliva
Paul H. Barton	William C. Heilbrun	Steven G. Penansky
Roger G. Bast	F. Bruce Hijikata	James R. Posner
Donald J. Beaulieu	Peter A. Horowitz	Michael A. Putetti
Dr. Jesse D. Bennett	Roger L. Huss	Susan M. Putnam
Richard A. Bill	William Ilnyckyj	Thomas E. Reinert, Jr.
Thomas E. Blythe	Donald M. Jenkins	O. C. Rittenhouse
Michael P. Cantoli	David C. Keehn	Stacy N. Rowley
E. Marty Carhart	Cheryl F. Keller	James L. Ruane
James W. Colby	William J. Kendrick	Otto C. Schenk
Thomas B. Collins	Sally Ann Kirkpatrick	Thomas A. Scott
Donald R. Crowell	Arthur W. Kleinrath	Sylvia S. Small
Lewis I. Dale	John M. Lavin	Thomas M. Smitley
Stephen I. Danzansky, Esq.	Willa Lisa Lebedoff	Louis A. Sonzogni, Jr.
Charles H. Ebersole	Arthur Lemay	John F. Spevacek
David P. Edstrom	Charles Liotta	Adrian L. Steel, Jr.
Jodie M. Einbinder, Esq.	Judith G. Lowe	Margaret L. Stueben
Raleigh D. Ellis, Jr.	Robert W. Lundgren	Richard B. Sullivan
Thomas G. Evancie	Martin E. Luther	M. Anne Swanson
John H. Evers	Patricia Maher, Esq.	Cynthia Taylor
Susan D. Falkson, Esq.	Peter W. C. Mather	Alfred B. Thacher
Richard J. Favretto	Charles A. McCrann	E. Carl Uehlein, Jr.
Wayne A. Fletcher	Adrian Miller	William E. Walton
Charles W. Freeman	Francis Milone	David H. Ward
Richard J. Funck	Barry L. Molnar	Miner H. Warner
Marc Gary	Brent C. Moore	John R. Weddle, Jr.
Louis W. Hart	Terrence T. O'Horo	George Weisendanger

The Department of Commerce

Co-Chairs

Amory Houghton, Jr.
Chairman and Chief Executive Officer
Corning Glass Works

Robert V. Van Fossan
Chairman and Chief Executive Officer
Mutual Benefit Life
 Insurance Co.

Project Manager

George B. Bennett
Chairman
Braxton Associates

Task Force Members

Julian H. Allen
James A. Carroll
Frank Cassidy
Paul T. Clark
Paul V. Daverio
Helen Doo
David M. Earls
John A. Elie
Robert W. Foster
William Givens
Charles E. Grenier, Jr.
F. Philip Hunt
Mary Alice Johnson
Joan G. Kirkendall

John T. Klug
Owen Knox
Daniel J. Lammon
Jerome M. Lewis
Gregory D. Luther
Frank J. Wesley Miles, Sr.
Eileen A. Moran
Clarence R. Patty, Jr.
Rosemary Polk
Jean M. Suda
Dennis Vignola
Thomas Waaland
Audrey H. Whitcomb

Consultants

Richard E. Buten
Dr. Jack Byrd, Jr.
Hoyt H. Chaloud
Richard E. Cocks
Hassan Hammami
James Rulmyr
Allan Stoecker

The Office of the Secretary of Defense

Co-Chairs

Robert A. Beck
Chairman and Chief Executive Officer
The Prudential Insurance Company of
America

Carter L. Burgess
Chairman, Executive Committee
Foreign Policy Association

James E. Burke
Chairman and Chief Executive Officer
Johnson & Johnson

Carl D. Covitz
President
Landmark Communities, Inc.

Project Manager

William H. Tremayne
Vice President
The Prudential Insurance Company of
America

Task Force Members

Duncan K. Alexander
Jeffrey P. Altman
Frank J. Bane
Eugene K. Brown
Robert N. Brown
Graham M. Brush, Jr.
Patricia C. Conroy
Alisa D. Cullum
Edward T. Dougherty
Stephen R. Drapeau
Joseph F. Egan
Nancy L. Fox
Dale W. Gasch
Martin A. Glick
Donald S. Grenough

Thomas F. X. Grover
Susan M. Hodges
Oscar A. Hoffman
Dale L. Johnson
Jeffrey A. Kuchar
Robert G. Lynch
Keith Y. Miyahira
Robert K. Moore
Jacob B. Pankowski
Louis N. Parent
Alan L. Parker
Bruce H. Pauly
Charles J. Payne
Peter S. Pinkham
Norris M. Plumley

Patrick D. Raudenbush
Ernest Sackman
Eliza R. Saunders
Edward A. Singletary
Richard C. Smith
Charles H. Snyder
Walter B. Stevenson
Penny R. Thompson
Colby Ward
Dianna E. Waters
Signe Weber
Jean Welcker
John Wos

The Department of Education

Co-Chairs

Spencer F. Eccles
Chairman, President, and Chief
   Executive Officer
First Security Corp.

Alfred H. Kingon
Former Editor-in-Chief
Financial World Magazine

Nathan R. Owen
Chairman and Chief Executive Officer
General Signal Corp.

Robert H. Willis
Chairman and President
Connecticut Natural Gas Corp.

Project Manager

Donald B. Summers
Vice President, Human Resources
Delmed, Inc.

Task Force Members

Dana Sue Alder
John J. Bennett
Robert L. Bourne
Scott M. Cleary
David J. Cohen
Justine Denise Couchoud
Philip R. Fortune
Reginald G. Fuller
James W. Garrett
Geoffrey C. Gould
Erika Graf-Webster
Courtney Hall

Robert M. Hallman, Esq.
Byron A. Hartley
R. Bruce Hillier
Michael R. Jacqmin
Scott H. Jaggar
Mark H. Johnston
Russell F. Leavitt, Jr.
R. Gillem Lucas
Donald H. Ludington
James N. Martin
Michael D. Mendelson
Sammy W. Pearson

Frank X. Pesuth
Robert L. Richardson
Frank H. Roby
Patrick J. Russo
Daniel A. Sill
Harold A. Strickland
Perley A. Swasey, Jr.
Michael R. Zucchini

Consultant

Clark S. Judge

The Department of Energy, the Federal Energy Regulatory Commission,
and the Nuclear Regulatory Commission

Co-Chairs

John W. Hanley
Chairman and Chief Executive Officer
Monsanto Company

Roger Milliken
President and Chief Executive Officer
Milliken & Company

Project Manager

Walter R. Pettiss
Vice President and Assistant
 Treasurer
Milliken & Company

Task Force Members

John D. Anderson	Leonard Geller	Hugh R. O'Farrell
Fred H. Balluff	Joseph P. Glas	Diarmuid F. O'Scannlain
Craig D. Bedle	Theodore Hamburger	Alfred H. Ostrand
Bernie Bohlmann	R. M. Harbour	Fred W. Pardee
Donald B. Bolger	Sy Herman	John C. Phillips
George E. Bollibon	Edward C. Holland	Robert H. Porter
Pamela A. Bollig	Milton E. Key	Joseph Clark Powers
O. Jack Burkland	Kenneth Kilderry	John F. Proctor
Elbert W. Burr	Otto A. Klingler	Francis E. Reese
Vaughan Chambers	S. Paul Kovich	Eric Reichl
John D. Chiquoine	Frank E. Kruesi	Marcus A. Rowden
Ernest A. Conrads	Robert Kupp	Bernard Rusche
Joseph Cunning	Ralph E. Leonberger	John M. Ryder
Donald B. Dixon	Alexander Luft	Monroe Sadler
Daniel Donoghue	J. P. McFadden	Edward H. Schneider
D. Jane Drennan	Charles King Mallory	Paul V. Tebo
Dr. John J. Drysdale	Cecil J. Marty	John Utley
Joseph M. Dukert	Charles N. Masten	James Van Reenen
Robert H. Dunlap	Gerald E. Meetze	Dr. James Wei
Mark R. Dusbabek	W. Leroy Miller	Clive G. Whittenbury
Donald L. Eby	William J. Mottel	William Zimmermann
Edwin L. Field	Joseph E. Myers	
Robert J. Gallick	Raymond J. O'Connor	

The Environmental Protection Agency,
the Small Business Administration, and the
Federal Emergency Management Agency

Co-Chairs

William H. Bricker
Chairman, President and Chief
  Executive Officer
Diamond Shamrock Corporation

Ben F. Love
Chief Executive Officer
Texas Commerce Bancshares, Inc.

Project Managers

Roger P. Batchelor, Jr.
Independent Consultant

Lee E. Straus
Vice President and Chief
  Administrative Officer
Texas Commerce Bancshares, Inc.

Task Force Members

Glenn Affleck
Nicholas Alicino
William R. Austin
Robert J. Becker
F. Douglas Bess
Dr. B. Peter Block
Kenneth Braud
William J. Burgess
Paul L. Carll
R. L. Mark Chambers
Warren W. Cole
Roger P. Cottrell
Ronald J. Cracas
Gerard W. Daigre
Mary V. Davis
Harold J. Dean
Henry A. Dudley
Lucinda A. Edmonds
Bennett E. Elrod
Oliver M. Fike
Robert J. Gallo
John A. Garman
Joseph F. Gentile
Owen L. Gentry
Steven A. Ginsburgh

Kenneth S. Harlan
Dr. Donald J. Harvey
Kenneth A. Haseley
LaVern Heble
Dr. Charles W. Hinman
Dr. Thomas Houtman, Jr.
James K. Hull
Donna M. Hunt
William C. Hutton
Robert L. Jacks
Graham H. Jackson
Gene L. Jessee
Virgil A. Johnson
Robert M. Johnston
Sam P. Kamas
Elisa S. Kaplan
Paul J. Klebba
Henry S. Kramer
Albert E. Lewis
William V. Lightsey
Dr. E. Victor Luoma
Michael J. McAfee
Michael P. Mauzy
David L. Mendez
Frances M. Miller

James T. Norman
Richard E. Parsels
Dr. Jerry B. Pausch
George M. Pettee
Tibor Polgar
Anne B. Pouns
John D. Rice
Richard E. Rings
John Roorda
Ann-Marie Schuknecht
Peter M. Schwab
Dr. James G. Smith
E. C. Sommer
Dan Spence
Donald R. Talbott
Antonio Torres
H. Neal Troy
Anthony G. Tummarello
Robert M. Walter
Fred B. Warburton
Lawrence J. Washington
David C. Williams
Robert B. Yates
Douglas M. Yeager

Federal Construction Management

Co-Chairs

Robert J. Buckley
Chairman and President
Allegheny International, Inc.

Raymond C. Foster
Chairman, President and Chief
  Executive Officer
Stone & Webster, Inc.

Melvyn N. Klein
President and Chief Executive Officer
Altamil Corp.

John W. Kluge
Chairman, President and Chief
  Executive Officer
Metromedia, Inc.

Frederick P. Rose
Chairman
Rose Associates, Inc.

Paul J. Schierl
President and Chief Executive Officer
Fort Howard Paper Co.

Project Manager

Edwin K. Isely
Former Manager
A. T. Kearney, Inc.

Task Force Members

Joel I. Abrams
E. F. Andrews
Edward R. Bajer
Warren H. Barkley
Peter L. Beal
Donald Berman
Francois G. Bernardeau
William I. Bracken
Anthony J. Branca
Ralph W. Browning
Keith J. Brunette
Edward K. Bryant
John J. Burke
Jack N. Carter
Barbara A. Cebuhar
Rama Rao V. Cherukuri
Louis F. Cohn
Bruce V. Cole
William P. Cotellese
Mary E. Creevy
James A. D'Agostino
Danielle C. Daniels
Thomas E. Debruycker
Brian P. Deery
James F. Diulus
Don S. Domgaard
Barbara J. Douglas
Alan M. Dunn
Roy H. Eno
Steven G. Farkas
Harvey J. Goldman

James R. Graham
W. William Graham, Jr.
Samuel L. Hack, Esq.
Donald R. Hague
Robert D. Halverstadt
Edward D. Hamm
Thomas W. Harrison
Sharon B. Holcombe
Stuart S. Holder
Alfred H. Hunter
Michael J. Hurley
Robert W. James
Max R. Janairo, Jr.
William M. Johnstone
Susan T. Keller
Thomas M. Kurek
Victor F. Leabu
T. Cynthia Lebrun-Yaffe
Peter M. Lehrer
David R. Levin
Robert A. Lincoln
Edward J. Markus
Jean M. Martin
Ernest R. McCamman
Kenneth E. McIntyre
Anna R. McManamon
J. William Melsop
Adam A. Miller
Sandra Mokuvos
John W. Morris
David W. Mueller

Neil J. Munro
Leonard J. Murgi
Edward G. Murphy
John M. Mylin
William M. Newman
Patricia M. Overton
David C. Peters
Neal R. Peterson
Theresa A. Peterson
Edgar F. Pohlmann
Keith M. Poore
Clyde J. Poppell
Robert G. Rhodes
Jerome L. Rosenberger
Ralph Rossini
William J. Shalkham
Kiprian M. Skavinski
John K. Smith
Philip L. Smith
James M. Sprouse
Philip J. Stassi
Warner S. Strang
Bernard Strassner
James S. Sykes
William B. Taylor
Romolo Testarmata
Mary Lee Vigilante
Norma J. Walde
Charles E. Wallace
Cheryll B. Williams
Ralph O. Wilson, Jr.

Federal Feeding

Co-Chairs

H. J. Cofer, Jr.
President
Rich-SeaPak Corporation

Henry H. Henley, Jr.
Chairman and Chief Executive Officer
Cluett, Peabody & Co., Inc.

Edward L. Hutton
President and Chief Executive Officer
Chemed Corporation

Carl Karcher
Chairman and Chief Executive Officer
Carl Karcher Enterprises, Inc.

Edward W. Whittemore
Chairman and Chief Executive Officer
American Brands, Inc.

Project Manager

George J. Schramm
Former Vice Chairman
American Brands, Inc.

Task Force Members

Joseph S. Adomakoh, Jr.
William P. Benes
Lillan Brueggemeyer
Arthur G. Busher
Robert T. Chancler
Richard M. Cochrane
Daniel A. Conforti
Thomas M. Dersch
Michael J. Giuffrida
Thomas C. Hassett

Mary V. Hornig
Fred E. Karhohs
Edward R. Kienle
Keith Swor Kendrick
William H. Kohler
Edward T. Kohlmeir
Charles J. Krause
Mary M. Leonard
Allen R. Maxwell
Rose Mary Mims

Patricia L. Phillips
Joseph W. Rio
Karen Ross
Mary Ann Royal
Salomon Schildhaus
Paul Shang
Susan K. Shea
Alice F. Skelsey
David Lee Slusher
Marjorie T. J. Wong

Federal Hospital Management

Co-Chairs

Raymond A. Hay
President
LTV Corp.

William B. Johnson
Chairman
IC Industries, Inc.

James L. Ketelsen
Chairman and Chief Executive Officer
Tenneco, Inc.

Henry E. Simmons, M.D.
National Director, Health Care
Consulting Programs
Peat, Marwick, Mitchell & Co.

Project Manager

Jack Whitelaw
Office Manager
Vought Corporation

Task Force Members

Michael M. Barch
Thomas E. Batey
Shirley S. Boone
Gretchen K. Flack
Kristofer Garmager
Timothy R. Garmager
Thomas V. Gillen
Beverly Guilford

Lorraine D. Johnson
William H. Johnson
Mark E. Lindsey
Maxine D. Llewellyn
Edward J. Mausser, Jr.
Fallon J. Mikula
Kristine St. Andrae
Promod K. Seth

Thomas F. Streff
Linda Strevig
Herbert E. Wellborn

Consultant

David Tilson

Federal Management Systems

Co-Chairs

Joseph E. Connor, Jr.
Senior Partner
Price Waterhouse

Harry E. Figgie, Jr.
Chairman and Chief Executive Officer
Figgie International, Inc.

John E. Fisher
Chairman
Nationwide Mutual Insurance Co.

Daniel W. Lufkin
Chairman of the Finance Committee
Columbia Pictures Industries, Inc.

J. Paul Sticht
Chairman
R. J. Reynolds Industries, Inc.

Project Manager

Lewis J. Krulwich
Partner
Price Waterhouse

Task Force Members

Edward P. Arter
William R. Beshire
R. Thomas Blanchard
Katherine H. Cardulla
Thomas J. Carrier
Edward P. Chait
Dennis Durden
Gregory L. Freehauf
Robert A. Freeman
Jeffrey W. Galginaitis

Mark K. Galloway
Nancy A. Gravatt
Charlotte A. Haberaecker
Edward J. Haller
Ralph W. Jordan
Mary E. Keegan
Sandra L. LaFevre
Daniel J. Lammon
Ronald J. Lynch
Bruce W. McCuaig

J. T. Michaelson
Douglas M. Piper
I. Theresa Poletto
Michael J. Schaub
F. James Seaman
David S. Shapland
John S. Sobczyk
Alyse W. Unterburger
W. James Wintzer

Consultants

Ross Conner
Emmet E. Delay
William M. Hall
John W. Heilshorn

Henry Jaenicke
Nancy Kingsbury
Jack McGill
Robert H. Ourant

Robert A. Rennie
Leonard Rutman
Gilbert Simonetti, Jr.
William E. Thompson

Financial Asset Management

Co-Chairs

Edward W. Duffy
Chairman and Chief Executive Officer
Marine Midland Banks, Inc.

Wilson S. Johnson
Chairman
National Federation of Independent
  Businesses

Edward B. Rust
President
State Farm Fire & Casualty Co.

Project Manager

Bruce G. Fielding
President,
Fielding, Locksley & Storek
Accountancy Corp.

Task Force Members

Vincent Beggs	Charles C. Hubbard	William G. Onsted
Charles J. Cardwell	Margaret R. Johnson-Orrick	Laura Onsted
Elaine R. Carlis	Mark Johnston	Martha S. Peyton
Leona Del Prete	Virgil Jones	Carol E. Pokodner
Louis R. Del Prete	Hiromi Kayama	Carl Pompei
Art Denzau	Theodore Kuchenriter	Joe Potosky
John E. Doner	Ralph Leal	Gordon Schroeder
Gerritt L. Ewing	Kevin Lew-Hansen	David G. Schultes
John J. Fawley	David Linnowes	Eileen Shake
Evelyn L. Fielding	Susan C. London	Charles T. Smith
Deborah Figart	Meredith McKay	Kent Stone
Clarence Frame	Fred A. Marcussen	Bruce Thompson
Lesley Ann Frowick	Brant L. Massman	Lucie Todd Torrance
Ellen S. Goldberg	Hartwell Morse	Dick Vanderbosch
Scott Gray	Frank L. Nemiroff	Deborah Williams
Jim Herr	George M. Niesyty	Jennifer Wirick
Miriam H. Herr	Mary Ann O'Connor	Marlene Wray

The Department of Health and Human Services:
Department Management,
Office of Human Development Services, ACTION

Co-Chairs

Michael D. Dingman
Chairman of the Board and Chief
   Executive Officer
Wheelabrator-Frye, Inc.

Forrest N. Shumway
Chairman of the Board and Chief
   Executive Officer
The Signal Companies, Inc.

Project Manager

Andrew J. Chitiea
Board of Directors
Senior Vice President
The Signal Companies, Inc.

Task Force Members

Ra Nae Allen	Charles R. Englert	Anna R. Pusateri
Tina Marie Bateman-Cassetta	Thomas M. Foley	Catherine L. Barker-Roth
Carol S. Bowman	Steven P. Foote	Robert R. Ruprecht
Patrick M. Brand	John G. Gantz, Jr.	Don Sabanos
Deidre C. Bruton	Edward F. Greenberg	Gary M. Sullivan
Edward S. Cowden	Carol E. Hamilton	Philip H. Turnock
Robert D. Cully	James P. Honohan	Dale L. Ziegler
Steven F. Cunningham	Jeffrey U. Price	

The Department of Health and Human Services:
Public Health Service, Health Care Financing Administration

Co-Chairs

Samuel H. Armacost
President and Chief Executive Officer
Bank of America

Edward L. Hennessy, Jr.
Chairman, President and Chief
   Executive Officer
Allied Corp.

Charles J. Pilliod, Jr.
Chairman and Chief Executive Officer
Goodyear Tire & Rubber Company

Project Manager

Albert F. Ritardi
Director, Medical and Environmental
   Services
Allied Corp.

Task Force Members

James H. Abrams	Joseph H. Gilchrist	Richard R. Robert
Donald G. Anderson	James A. Hathaway	Madeline C. Sprague
Frank W. Armstrong	Gordon J. Hewitt	Terry N. Stewart
Charles B. Breuer	Joseph F. Hutchinson	Robert J. Tivey
Ruth N. Bruns	John C. Longstreth	Terry Lee Turner
Brewster P. Campbell, Jr.	Gregory E. Madsen	Patrick J. Vath
Vito A. Caravito	Richard M. Martin	G. Howard Vocke
Russell L. Creighton	Jeanne I. Owers	Willard W. Wecker
Michael L. T. Didier	Hollis Paschen-Andersen	Michael C. Wolff
Rosemary C. Dimler	Barbara J. Pettis	
Ralph M. Esposito	William E. Rinehart, Sc.D.	

The Department of Health and Human Services:
Social Security Administration

Co-Chairs

John J. Byrne
Chairman, President and Chief
  Executive Officer
GEICO Corp.

Joseph P. Downer
Vice Chairman
Atlantic Richfield Co.

Harold A. Eckmann
Chairman and Chief Executive Officer
Atlantic Mutual Insurance Co.

George P. Jenkins
Former Chairman and Chief
  Executive Officer
Metropolitan Life Insurance Co.

Project Manager

John J. Byrne
Assistant Vice President
The Atlantic Companies

Task Force Members

James Abell	David Graham	Ann Mercurio
William Birmingham	Charles Grenier	Beth Nelson
B. Bowersox	Peter Hanley	R. Robinson
Ronald Buckley	Burke Hansen	Len Schiller
Connie Cottingham-Goggins	John Jarrett	James Streff
Charles R. Davies	Madison Jones III	Jean Suda
Dennis Dolan	Tim Kilcullen	Paul Talbott
David Earls	K. Lindner	D. Van Norman
Winston Foster	Mike Madden	Robert Warden
A. Franck	James Maloney	Robert Yarnall

The Department of Housing and Urban Development

The Department of the Interior

Co-Chairs

George D. Anderson
President
Anderson ZurMuehlen & Co.

Morley P. Thompson
President
Baldwin-United Corp.

William T. Coleman, Jr.
Partner
O'Melveny & Myers

Hays T. Watkins
Chairman and Chief Executive Officer
CSX Corporation

Project Manager

Robert C. Hacking
Manager, State and Local
  Government
Ernst & Whinney

Task Force Members

Mark G. Aron	Walter G. Johnson	Allen J. Sinisgalli
Theodore C. Barreaux	Brenda H. Kelley	Paul G. Sittenfeld
Maria T. Beck	Salvatore La Spada	John W. Snow
Donald T. Bliss, Jr.	Joseph F. Moraglio	Stephen Sobotka
Michael F. Brimmer	Denise M. Palmer	Robert N. Steinwurtzel
Jon T. Brown	William C. Pitt, III	J. Thomas Tidd
Jeffrey R. Finci	James C. Schultz	W. Edward Whitfield
Susan E. Janicki	Nelle Seckinger	Carol A. Zuckerman

The Department of Justice

Co-Chairs

Weston R. Christopherson
Chairman and Chief Executive Officer
Jewel Companies, Inc.

Frederick Deane
Chairman and Chief Executive Officer
Bank of Virginia

Jewel S. Lafontant
Senior Partner
Lafontant, Wilkins, Jones & Ware,
  P.C.

Arthur Levitt, Jr.
Chairman and Chief Executive Officer
American Stock Exchange, Inc.

Project Manager

Clarence S. Wilson, Jr.
Member of Firm
Lafontant, Wilkins, Jones & Ware,
  P.C.

Task Force Members

Laura V. Banks	Jeffrey Gordon	Charles M. Moritz
James Wilson Bush	T. Gaylon Layfield, III	Christopher M. Randall
Philip D. Fowler	Charles Lewis	Gordon Stewart
Wenda S. Freeman	Rev. Harold Thomas Lewis	David J. Vidal

The Department of Labor

Co-Chairs

James S. Kemper, Jr.
Chairman
Kemper Corporation

Francis C. Rooney, Jr.
Chief Executive Officer
Melville Corporation

Richard R. Shinn
Chairman and Chief Executive Officer
Metropolitan Life Insurance Co.

Luke G. Williams
Chief Executive Officer
American Sign & Indicator Corp.

Project Manager

Max Hirschhorn
Independent Consultant

Task Force Members

Wallace R. Baker
Joseph A. Bourdon
Thomas E. Callahan
Charles P. Carroll
Daniel J. Cavanagh
Eugene M. Frein
Paul Garfinckel
Dorri J. Gitlin
Geoffrey M. Hanford
Gerard F. Harrison
Arthur Korman

Alexandra P. Lappas
Richard L. McClellan
Elizabeth H. Maurer
Barbara I. Nitzberg
William Norton
Donald A. Odell
Arthur R. Owens
Pearl Percak
Joseph Pfenning
Darby L. Prentiss
Franklin H. Rogers

Richard R. Sachs
Stephen A. Schlazer
Charles J. Sokolski
Harvey Sontag
John F. Ward
Howard B. Warren
Robert R. Wehner
Ralph C. Weisgerber
Myra D. West-Allen
Richard F. Wiseman

Land/Facilities/Personal Property

Co-Chairs

John F. McGillicuddy
Chairman and Chief Executive Officer
Manufacturers Hanover Trust Co.

Donald G. McNeely
Chairman
Space Center, Inc.

Donald W. Nyrop
Former Chief Executive Officer
Northwest Airlines, Inc.

Joseph J. Pinola
Chairman and Chief Executive Officer
First Interstate Bancorp

Darwin E. Smith
Chairman and Chief Executive Officer
Kimberly-Clark Corp.

Project Manager

Paul A. Jones
Executive Vice President and
  Secretary
Kimberly-Clark Corp.

Task Force Members

Richard J. Archer
Joan Atkins
Brad L. Bates, Esq.
George H. Bigelow
Laura M. Boldosser
Hal Bowman
Judith G. Caratenuto
Marcia K. Cowan
Daniel R. DeBord
Donald H. Denison
Judith A. Forsythe
Robert E. Freer, Jr.
Richard Greenberg
Melissa Ann Guye

Michael H. Haller
Ruth Hertzfeld
Denise A. Jones
Malcolm W. McDonald
Elaine MacNichol
Mike D. Mark
Paul Messina
Roger A. Murch
Michael Nemeroff
Joanne P. S. Ongman, Esq.
Sumner Parker
Barbara Peters
William R. Ransom
John C. Ritter

A. X. Robbins
Don Rodich
Renee Rollins
Mark Rutecki
Patricia Gail Scott
Leslie Sloan
Teresa L. Spalding
Ram Viswanathan
Bonnie B. Wan
Mike Wilkins
Sue Woolsey
Thane Young
Sharon L. Zeigler
Wayne R. Zwickey

Low Income Standards and Benefits

Co-Chairs

Bennett Archambault
Chief Executive Officer
Stewart-Warner Corporation

Robert A. Schoellhorn
Chairman and Chief Executive Officer
Abbott Laboratories

Richard J. Flamson III
Chairman and Chief Executive Officer
Security Pacific National Bank

Robert K. Wilmouth
President and Chief Executive Officer
National Futures Association

Project Director

Richard W. Strauss
Manager, Washington Operations
Stewart-Warner Corporation

Task Force Members

Jeffrey A. Alspaugh	Jay W. Howard	Ivison W. Rhodes
Michael B. Barr	John W. Jerome	Claudia S. Ringel
Mellen Candage	Richard W. Kasperson	Roger D. Rutz
James M. Cloney	William H. McCloskey	Victoria S. Shain
Sarah E. Collins	Nancy J. Olson	Richard E. Steen
David Crosland	Walter J. Olson	William F. Turner
John J. Duffy	David J. Reene	Ray G. Vanheusden
Edward M. Hallinan	Rebecca J. Reid	Garry W. Vosahlik

The Department of the Navy

Co-Chairs

Nicholas T. Camicia
Chairman and Chief Executive Officer
The Pittston Company

Stanley Hiller, Jr.
Chairman
Hiller Investment

Maurice R. Greenberg
President and Chief Executive Officer
American International Group, Inc.

Thomas M. Macioce
President and Chief Executive Officer
Allied Stores Corp.

Project Manager

Robert M. Cockrill
Partner
Coopers & Lybrand

Task Force Members

Dale R. Babione
Richard Beaumont
William Benson
Murray Bovarnick
John W. Boyd
Gerald J. Brown
Herbert C. Clayman
Norman Clement
Roy Clester
Norman Dargie
Joseph Dore, III

Paul C. Keenan, Jr.
Robert E. Lay
Charles Lee
Donald H. Lichty
James S. Lyles
Thomas D. Matteson
John Maurer
James McCoy
John McCreight
J. Wade Miller
Klein E. Mitchell

Charles B. Molster
Michael Murphy
Eric T. Oster
James Phillips
Robert A. Rosen
James Ryan
Leon Schneider
Susan J. Shindell
Phillip Silverman
Roger D. Wiegley
Emmanuel Zimmer

Personnel Management

Co-Chairs

Robert Hatfield
President
New York Hospital

Donald R. Keough
President
The Coca-Cola Company

John A. Puelicher
Chairman and Chief Executive Officer
Marshall and Ilsley Corp.

Project Manager

Sy B. Pranger
Independent Consultant

Task Force Members

Joyce A. Akers
Edward A. Brinkley
Robert J. Brookhiser
Irvine H. Dearnley
Katherine E. Douglass
Kathleen C. Dudek
Belinda O. Fairhall
William B. French
Walter C. Gansser
Jerry Greenberg

C. William Isaacson
Wilburt A. Koontz
John A. Lersch
William L. Lucianovic
Jon L. Manetta
James T. Ray
Whatley S. Scott
David P. Siebold
William T. Smith
John E. Stehr

John E. Toole
Victor Zink

Consultants

Frank J. Alosa
H. Geoffrey Andrews
Robert P. Buczkowski
Carl Smith

Privatization

Co-Chairs

Bruce J. Heim
Vice President
F. Eberstadt & Co., Inc.

Paul F. Hellmuth
Retired Managing Partner
Hale & Dorr

Edward L. Hutton
President and Chief Executive Officer
Chemed Corporation

Paul E. Manheim
Advisory Director
Lehman Brothers, Kuhn, Loeb,
    Incorporated

Eben W. Pyne
Retired Senior Vice President
Citibank, N.A.

David L. Yunich
Retired Vice Chairman
R. H. Macy & Co. Inc.

Project Managers

Leo Kramer
President
Kramer Associates, Inc.

Paul Taff
Senior Associate
Kramer Associates, Inc.

Task Force Members

Adm. Herbert Anderson
Catherine S. Barron
William Benes
A. Mark Berlin
Bruce R. Collins
Thomas M. Dersch
Bernard DiFiore
Elisabeth Harding
Anthony J. Hope

Brad Hummell
Thomas S. Karwacki
Keith S. Kendrick
Douglas E. Mackay
Jeffrey J. Michael
Mark D. Mishler
George T. Pappas
Joseph W. Rio
Eliza R. Saunders

William Scofield
David L. Slusher
Dr. Leo Tansky
Paula Todd
Eileen Torbeck
James Van Reenan
Robert E. Weiner
Judith M. Whalen
Marjorie T. J. Wong

Procurement/Contracts/Inventory Management

Co-Chairs

Willard C. Butcher
Chairman
The Chase Manhattan Bank, N.A.

Edward S. Finkelstein
Chairman and Chief Executive Officer
R. H. Macy & Co., Inc.

Clifton C. Garvin, Jr.
Chief Executive Officer
Exxon Corporation

Project Manager

Edgar A. Robinson
Senior Vice President
Exxon Company, U.S.A.

Task Force Members

Nellie Bannister	Donald F. Hagan	Robert A. Pinzuti
Steven Braunstein	Clyde D. Hart, Jr.	Herbert Rackoff
D. Bruce Brunson	Dwight F. Holloway	Lee R. Raymond
George W. Cadwallader	Thomas G. Horst	John A. Redmond
Marshall N. Carter	Joel Katzman	Frank R. Reilly
Charles A. Cooper	Stephen I. Kelly	Gregory J. Robers
Peter T. Crichton	John A. Knubel	Richard A. Rosenberg
Alfred R. Crosby	Carol J. Lewis	Barry J. Sharp
Katherine L. Davis	Michael Luciuk	Henry Sinason
Deborah C. Diamond	Thomas A. McWalters	Richard M. Voripaieff
Donald Eugene	Joseph M. Miscione	Harold T. Wright
Jack A. Feitelberg	Warren T. Olde	Percy Wu
Alice B. Haemmerli	Manuel Peralta	Eileen Wynne

Real Property Management

Co-Chairs

Robert A. Georgine
President
Building and Construction Trades
    Department
AFL-CIO

Alexander F. Giacco
Chairman, President and Chief
    Executive Officer
Hercules Incorporated

Donald P. Kelly
President, Chairman and Chief
    Executive Officer
Esmark, Inc.

Donald B. Marron
Chairman and Chief Executive Officer
Paine Webber Incorporated

Nathan Shapell
Chairman
Shapell Industries, Inc.

Project Manager

John N. Sherman
Manager
Business Planning
Plastic Products Business Center
Hercules Incorporated

Task Force Members

Michael Anderson
Gary J. Bausom
George H. Bigelow
Terry A. Buller
Elizabeth A. Dawson
Alan M. DiSciullo
Joseph M. Dukert
Parker T. Fernald

Karl Haas
Ray W. Hodges, Jr.
Gretchen Hoekenga
Thomas W. Hunsberger
Kenneth K. Jones
Anne Marie Kane
Walter B. Kulikowski
Samuel A. Mabry

Robert Mallock, Sr.
George L. Moore, Jr.
Frank J. O'Brien
Grant R. Patrick
Mark Perechocky
Stephen W. Price
James B. Weaver
Barbara Wyman

Research and Development

Co-Chairs

William F. Ballhaus
President
Beckman Instruments, Inc.

David Packard
Chairman of the Board
Hewlett-Packard Co.

Karl D. Bays
Chairman and Chief Executive Officer
American Hospital Supply Corp.

Edson W. Spencer
Chairman and Chief Executive Officer
Honeywell, Inc.

James L. Ferguson
Chairman and Chief Executive Officer
General Foods Corp.

Project Manager

Dr. Eugene E. Yore
Corporate Director, Design
  Automation
Honeywell, Inc.

Deputy Project Manager

Steven Malevich
Manager, Emerging Issues Program
Beckman Instruments, Inc.

Task Force Members

Ronald H. Abrahams
R. Glenn Affleck
Dr. Walter R. Beam
John C. Beckett
John L. Bilangi
Sarah Messengale Billock
Clyde F. Coombs, Jr.
James L. Copenhaver
Stuart N. Davidson
Walter Donner

Maurice E. Esch
Stephen F. Hirshfeld
Grace M. Holden
Linda K. Holt
George A. Issac, III
John W. James
Virginia L. Jamison
Donald A. Klein
Ralph E. Lee
Edward J. Marteka

Thomas H. Morton
Oksana Orel
William T. Ryan
August Schellhammer
William G. Schmick
Roger N. Schmidt
Stephen S. Thaxton
Sam D. Walker
Florence M. Zeller

The Department of State/AID/USIA

Co-Chairs

J. Rawles Fulgham
Retired Vice Chairman
InterFirst Corporation

George L. Shinn
Retired Chairman of the Board and
    Chief Executive Officer
First Boston Corp.

Project Manager

Arthur M. Scutro, Jr.
Vice President
First Boston Corp.

Task Force Members

A. John Allen
Louise S. Armstrong
Dr. C. Cary Barton
Robert B. Calhoun, Jr.
James E. Connor
K. Craig Gallehugh
David Glazer
Donald S. Grubbs, Jr.
Peter F. Heuzey

Nancy J. Holland
James A. Hynes
Dr. Charles Katsainos
Stacie McGinn Kivimae
Alice W. Lorillard
Michael L. McAllister
Cheryl M. Neimuth
Robert A. Pikul
Dr. Fred O. Pinkham

Robert J. Reynolds
William Rita
Mack F. Rossoff
Lawrence A. Silverstein
Chris D. Simpson
Robert J. Starry
G. William Vining

The Department of Transportation

Co-Chairs

Coy G. Eklund
Chairman and Chief Executive Officer
The Equitable Life Assurance Society
    of the United States

Thomas G. Pownall
Chairman and Chief Executive Officer
Martin Marietta Corp.

William H. Spoor
Chairman and Chief Executive Officer
Pillsbury Co.

Terry Townsend
Immediate Past Chairman
American Society of Association
    Executives

L. Stanton Williams
Chairman and Chief Executive Officer
PPG Industries, Inc.

Project Manager

William T. McCaffrey
Vice President and Area Executive
    Officer
The Equitable Life Assurance Society
    of the United States

Task Force Members

Dale S. Alexander
David R. Belle-Isle
Robert E. Bowles
Joseph Cafaro
Joseph P. Guasconi
Paul E. Hall

N. Thomas Harris
Franklin C. Jesse, Jr.
Winston W. Marsh
Eugene F. Ritzenthaler
Paul Stepner

Consultants

Anthony J. D'Anna
George T. Pappas

The Department of Treasury

Co-Chairs

Alfred Brittain, III
Chairman of the Board
Bankers Trust Company, Inc.

William H. Donaldson
Chairman
Donaldson Enterprises, Inc.

John H. Filer
Chairman and Chief Executive Officer
Aetna Life and Casualty Company

Project Manager

Robert G. Maxon
Vice President/Corporate Comptroller
Aetna Life and Casualty Company

Task Force Members

Christopher L. Bergstrom
Lyman J. Bishop
Paul A. Brodict
Francesco A. Calabrese
Theresa A. Carpentieri
James D. Converse
Ralph E. Cyr
Stephen M. DuBose
Deborah G. Faber
Donald E. Flannery
Marc A. Gardiner
R. Frank Gooden
M. Jacqueline Gordon
Esteban Hnyilicza
Herschel B. Hoffenberg
R. James Huber, Jr.
Karl E. Ideman

Tracye D. Johnson
John M. Jureller
Kathleen A. Krueger
Sondra D. Levin
J. Robert McAfee
James J. McEntee
David W. McFadden
J. Howard McKee
Andrew M. Miller
John F. Moore
John M. Mueller
John W. Nostrand
Jeffrey J. Park
Harold C. Passer
Deborah L. Penharlow
Lewis W. Pogue
Michael J. Prendergast

Nancy M. Saltojanes
Paul J. Sarosy, Jr.
Raymond J. Sibiga
David W. Small
Ann E. Thomas
Joyce G. Thompson
James T. Todd
Deane B. Turner
Thomas J. Vogel
William D. Walston, Jr.
Rebecca L. Wilson
Desmond C. Wong
Lawrence J. Young

Consultants

Nicholas F. Schauer
Frank Wolpe

User Charges

Co-Chairs

James Stewart
Chairman (Retired)
Frank B. Hall & Co., Inc.

Eugene J. Sullivan
Chairman and Chief Executive Officer
Borden, Inc.

Project Manager

James B. Clawson
Independent Consultant

Task Force Members

Catherine S. Barron
W. Bailey Barton
Richard A. Berman
Ronald J. Duych
Carmel Fauci
William P. Frankenhoff
Charles H. Granger
J. William Harsch
William B. Harwood, Jr.
George W. Koch

William L. Lew
George R. Lyon
Thomas J. Malloy
Anthony P. Manforte
K. H. Mao
Edward Margolin
James T. McCory
Allan L. Miller
Bernard Nemtzow
Robert L. Purvin

Ludwig Rudel
Randall C. Runk
James R. Selwood
Thomas C. Seoh
Celia Q. Sherred
J. Berry Wallace
Joseph E. Warden
Cynthia F. Wilchcombe

The Veterans Administration

Co-Chairs

William C. Douce
President and Chief Executive Officer
Phillips Petroleum Company

Hans W. Wanders
Chairman and Chief Executive Officer
Wachovia Corp.

William L. Wearly
Chairman of the Executive Committee
Ingersoll-Rand Co.

Project Manager

John R. Babson
Consultant
Ingersoll-Rand Co.

Task Force Members

Alan Atwater
Robert V. Bakalian
Andrea M. Cadematori
Gregory D. Dalton
Richard H. Elcock
Sharon Fonville
Al L. Hall
John K. Hollan
Henry A. Johnson
Richard D. Johnson
Charles King

David R. Kirchman
Bruce Lesher
Roy E. Levi
Cynthia A. Linderer
Edward A. Lynch, Jr.
Stephen Madden
Thomas M. Martinsen
Michael J. Ostronic
Elizabeth A. Patton
Lawrence Petree
Lori L. Rones

Gordon B. Santee
Leslie D. Sari
Joyce E. Scheuermann
Patricia A. Smith
Richard H. Snelsire
William T. Stewart
Paul E. Taylor
Paula A. Verkuilen
Leslie R. Watson
Roy W. Wegen
H. A. Wiegand

VOLUME I
Publishing, Printing, Reproduction,
and Audiovisual Activities

Project Director	*Project Members*
F. David Gorman Independent Attorney	Rosemary Machalek Andrew McWilliams George Pappas Stephen Weitzman

VOLUME II
Travel and Traffic Management

Project Director	*Project Members*
F. David Gorman Independent Attorney	Joan Atkins Richard Greenberg George Pappas Mark Rutecki Ram Viswanathan Michael Wilkins

VOLUME III
Financial Management in the Federal Government

Project Director	*Project Members*
Gregory C. Carey Assistant to the Chairman W. R. Grace & Co. Richard A. Goodman Assistant to the Chairman W. R. Grace & Co.	Lee A. Conrad Jeffrey L. Geller Byron A. Grant

VOLUME IV
Wage Setting Laws:
Impact on the Federal Government

Project Director	*Project Members*
G. John Tysse Director, Labor Law U.S. Chamber of Commerce	Mark de Bernardo Dennis Bradshaw Donna Lee McGee Jeffrey McGuiness John Runyan James Schlicht Patrick Stewart David Thompson

VOLUME V
Anomalies in the Federal Work Environment

Project Director

George S. Goldberger
Assistant to the Chairman
W. R. Grace & Co.

Project Members

Howard E. Barash
Warren M. Brown
Stephen M. Erhart
Robert D. Gonda
Patrick P. Grace
Reid L. Holloway
Robert L. Moon
John J. O'Connell, Jr.
Colum P. O'Donnell
Christopher L. Shea
Barbara A. Yastine

VOLUME VI
Federal Retirement Systems

Project Directors

John J. Gish
Director, Special Projects
Business Economics Group
W. R. Grace & Co.

Henry James Lawler
Director, Corporate Plans
Monsanto Corporation

Deputy Project Director

Raphael Kaminer
Senior Business Analyst
Business Economics Group
W. R. Grace & Co.

Project Members

Joseph Boshart
Dorothy Ott
Klaus G. Scheye
John Sico

VOLUME VII
Information Gap in the Federal Government

Project Directors

Richard V. Horan
President
Citizens Public Expenditure Survey,
  Inc.

Keith S. Kendrick
Assistant to the President
Chemed Corporation

Project Members

Thomas M. Dersch
Mary V. Hornig
Rosemary B. Machalek
Jeffrey J. Michael
Joseph W. Rio
Tony A. Trujillo, Jr.
Andrea L. Tyndall
Marjorie T. J. Wong

VOLUME VIII
The Cost of Congressional Encroachment

Project Director

Paul Clark
Vice President
National Center for Legislative
  Research

Deputy Project Directors

Gerald Lipson
Chairman
The Washington Information Group

Randall Truman Fitzgerald
Independent Consultant

Project Members

Lisa Diane Berger
R. Stanley Harsh
Steven Scott Lakin
Janice Marie Sokil

VOLUME IX
Federal Health Care Costs

Project Directors

Joseph C. Hoffman
Special Consultant on the Health Care
  Industry
W. R. Grace & Co.

Anthony J. Mangiaracina
Executive Vice President, General
  Development Group
W. R. Grace & Co.

Project Member

James R. Knickman

VOLUME X
Opportunities Beyond PPSS

Project Director

George S. Goldberger
Assistant to the Chairman
W. R. Grace & Co.

Project Members

William F. Cody
Jean de Luxembourg
Christopher G. Grace
Patrick P. Grace
R. Stanley Harsh
Irving Heymont
John B. Keeley
John Knubel
Annette B. Lanouette
S. Lynn O'Gorman
Thomas K. Reilly
Bernard D. Rostker
Christopher L. Shea
Lewis Sorley
Joseph B. Sullivan, Jr.
James M. Ulcickas
Harlan K. Ullman
Timothy S. vanBlommesteyn

VOLUME XI
Federally Subsidized Programs

Project Director

Jesse L. Koontz
Vice President, Economic Analysis
Natural Resources Group
W. R. Grace & Co.

Deputy Project Director

Joan L. Mashburn
Independent CPA

Project Members

Catherine Barron
Gregory C. Carey
Blanche L. Hite Carr
Richard A. Goodman
Elizabeth Hanson
Edgar Allen Peden
E. Clinton Stokes
Stephen A. Thompson
David Wilbur

CONTRIBUTORS TO THE PPSS EFFORT *

AFIA Worldwide Insurance
AFL-CIO Building & Construction Trades
  Dept.
A. M. Trucking Associates
AMF Foundation
ARA Services, Inc.
AVCO Corp.
Abbott Laboratories
Acushnet Foundation, Inc.
Adams, Charlotte H.
Aetna Life and Casualty Company
Aetna Life Insurance Co.
Air Products and Chemicals, Inc.
Allegheny International, Inc.
Allegretti & Co.
Allen and Associates, Inc.
Louis A. Allen Associates, Inc.
Alliance of American Insurers
Allied Corp.
Allied Stores Corp.
Allis-Chalmers Corporation
Allstate Insurance Co.
Altamil Corp.
Alumax, Inc.
Aluminum Co. of America
Amax Foundation, Inc.
American Apparel Association
American Brands, Inc.
American Can Company
American Council on Life Insurance
American Consulting Engineers
American Controlled Industries, Inc.
American Cyanamid Co.
American Enterprise Institute
American Equipment Co., Inc.
American Express Co.
American Financial Corp.
American General Contractors of America
American Hospital Supply Corporation
American Institute of Certified Public
  Accountants
American International Group, Inc.
American Paper Institute
American Petrofina Foundation
American Sign & Indicator Corp.
American Society of Association
  Executives
American Standard, Inc.
American Stock Exchange, Inc.
American Telephone & Telegraph Co.
American Trucking Associations, Inc.
American University

Americar Rental Systems
Ampco Printing
AmSouth Bancorporation
Anderson ZurMuehlen & Company
Anheuser-Busch, Inc.
M. L. Annenberg Foundation
Archer-Daniels-Midland Co.
Archicorps
Arthur Andersen & Co.
Ashland Oil, Inc.
Associated Builders and Contractors
Associated General Contractors
Association of American Railroads
Atlantic Bancorporation
Atlantic Companies
Atlantic Financial Federal
Atlantic Mutual Insurance Co.
Atlantic National Bank of Florida
Atlantic Richfield Co.
Austin Co.
Automatic Data Processing, Inc.
BASF Wyandotte Corp.
BDC Corporation
BDM Corporation
Bache, Halsey, Stuart, Shields
Baker & Hostetler
Baker International
Michael Baker, Jr., Inc.
Baldwin-United Corp.
Baltimore Gas & Electric Co.
Bank of America
Bank of California
Bank of New York
Bank of Virginia
BankAmerica Foundation
BankAmerica International New York
Bankers Trust Co.
Barnett Banks of Florida, Inc.
Robert Basil International
C. Cary Barton Associates, Inc.
Baxter Travenol Laboratories, Inc.
Bear Stearns & Company
Bendix Corporation
Beneficial Corporation
Beneficial Management Corp.
Bentley College Graduate School
Berk-Boh Incorporated
Bernardeau and Associates, Inc.
Bernhard, Arnold
Bethlehem Steel Corp.
Betz Laboratories, Inc.
Bindon Farm

*As of January 31, 1984.

Black & Decker Manufacturing Co.
Blue Cross & Blue Shield of Texas
Boeing Co.
Boise Cascade Corp.
Bolduc, J. P.
Booz·Allen & Hamilton Inc.
Borden, Inc.
Borden Foundation
Boston Consulting Group
Boston University
Braxton Associates, Inc.
Bristol-Myers Co.
Brokaw Capital Management Company
O. Frederick Brown Foundation
Brown, Roady, Bonvillan & Gold
George B. Buck Actuarial Consultants
Buck Consultants, Inc.
Burgess, Carter L.
Burlington Industries Foundation
Burlington Industries, Inc.
Burroughs Corporation
Burson-Marsteller
CACI, Inc.
CBS, Inc.
CPC International
CPM Partnership
CSX Corporation
C. U. Companies
CVS/Melville Corporation
CWI Temporaries
Cahill, Gordon and Reindel
Howard H. Callaway Foundation
Cameron Iron Works, Inc.
Campbell Soup Company
Capital Cities Communications, Inc.
Capital Cities Foundation, Inc.
Capital Gazette Communications
Career Temporaries
Cargill Incorporated
Carleton University, School of Social Work
Carolina Power & Light Co.
Carpenter Technology Corporation
Catholic University of America
Caterpillar Foundation
Celanese Fibers Operation
Celanese Corp.
Champion International Corp.
Champion Spark Plug Co.
Champlin Petroleum Co.
Charles River Associates
Charter Foundation, Inc.
Chase Manhattan Bank, N.A.
Chemed Corp.
Chemical Bank
Chesapeake & Potomac Telephone Co.
Chesebrough-Pond's, Inc.

Chevron U.S.A., Inc.
Chicago Board of Trade
Chrysler Corporation Fund
CIGNA Corporation
Cincinnati Milacron, Inc.
Citibank, N.A.
Citicorp
City Investing Co.
City Investing Co. Foundation
Cleary, Gottlieb, Steen & Hamilton
Clorox Co.
Cluett, Peabody & Co., Inc.
Coca-Cola Company
Thomas Cody & Associates
Coleman, William T.
Collier, Shannon, Rill & Scott
Colt Industries, Inc.
Columbia Pictures Industries, Inc.
Combustion Engineering, Inc.
Commercial Union Insurance Co.
Committee on the Handicapped
Common Sense Management Inc.
Commonwealth Edison Co.
Connecticut Bank & Trust Co., N.A.
Connecticut General Corp.
Connecticut Natural Gas Corp.
Conoco, Inc.
Consolidated Edison Company
Contemporaries, Inc.
Continental Grain Company
Continental Group, Inc.
Continental Group Foundation, Inc.
Continental Illinois National Bank & Trust
    Co. of Chicago
Continental Telecom, Inc.
Continental Telephone Co.
Controller Services Company
Coopers & Lybrand
Copperweld Corporation
Corning Glass Works
Corning Glass Works Foundation
Country Companies
Cox Lloyd Associates
Crocker National Bank
Crocker National Corporation
Cross & Trecker Foundation
D. W. Associates
DAKA Corporation
City of Dallas, Texas
Daniel Construction Company
Dart & Kraft, Inc.
Dartmouth College
Data Resources, Inc.
Day & Currie Construction Company, Inc.
Deere & Company
Delaware Trust Co.

Delmarva Power & Light Co.
Delmed, Inc.
Deloitte, Haskins & Sells
Dersch Oil Company, Inc.
Detroit Edison Co.
Dick DeVoe Buick Cadillac, Inc.
Dexter Corp.
Diamond Shamrock Corp.
Digital Equipment Corp.
Domgaard Associates
Donaldson Enterprises, Inc.
R. R. Donnelley & Sons Co.
Dow Chemical Co.
Dow Corning U.S.A.
Dravo Corp.
Dreadnaught Programs, Inc.
Dresser Industries, Inc.
Drexel University
Drug, Chemical & Allied Trades
    Association, Inc.
DuBois Chemicals
DuBois International
Duke Power Co.
Dun & Bradstreet Corp.
Dun & Bradstreet Corp. Foundation
E. I. Du Pont de Nemours
ES Products
East Ohio Gas Company
Eastman Kodak Co.
Eaton Corporation
F. Eberstadt & Co., Inc.
Eckerd Corp.
Eckmann, Harold A.
Daniel J. Edelman, Inc.
Editorial Consultants, Inc.
El Paso Products Co.
Elgin National Industries, Inc.
Emerson Electric Co.
Engbrecht, Christine W.
Ensco, Inc.
Equitable Life Assurance Society of the
    United States
Erickson Group of Companies
Ernst & Whinney
Esmark, Inc.
Ethicon, Inc.
Evaluation Research Society
Ex-Cell-O Corp.
Exchange National Bank
Executive Counselors, Inc.
Exxon Company, U.S.A.
Exxon Corporation
Exxon Research & Engineering Co.
FMC Corporation
Falk Corp.
Farmers Alliance Mutual Insurance Co.

Federal City Council
Federated Department Stores, Inc.
Field Enterprises, Inc.
Fielding, Locksley & Storek
Polly Fields Associates, Inc.
Figgie International, Inc.
Financial World Magazine
Firestone Tire & Rubber Co.
First Bank System, Inc.
First Boston Corp.
First Interstate Bancorp
First Interstate Bank of California
First National Bank of Atlanta
First National Bank of Birmingham
First National Bank of Boston
First National Bank of Chicago
First Oklahoma Bancorporation, Inc.
First Security Bank of Utah, N.A.
First Security Corp.
Fisher, John E.
Fisher Scientific Co.
Fluor Corp.
Fluor Foundation
Folds, Charles W.
Ford Aerospace & Communications Corp.
Ford Agency
Ford Enterprises, Ltd.
Ford Motor Co.
Ford Motor Co. Fund
Foremost-McKesson, Inc.
Fort Howard Paper Co.
W. P. Frankenhoff, Inc.
Freeport-McMoRan, Inc.
Fried, Frank, Harris, Schriver &
    Kampelman
Fuqua Industries, Inc.
GAF Corp.
GEICO Corp.
GK Technologies, Inc.
GTE Corp.
Garrett Automotive Products Co.
General Dynamics Corp.
General Electric Co.
General Foods Corp.
General Mills Foundation
General Mills, Inc.
General Motors Corporation
General Motors Foundation
General Reinsurance Corp.
General Signal Corp.
General Telephone & Electronics Corp.
General Tire & Rubber Co.
George Washington University
George Washington University Hospital
Georgetown University
Georgia-Pacific Corporation

Georgia-Pacific Foundation
Georgia Power Co.
Gestetner Corporation
Gibson, Dunn & Crutcher
Giddings & Lewis Foundation, Inc.
Giddings & Lewis, Inc.
Giffels Associates, Inc.
Gilbane Building Co.
Gilbert & Bennett Mfg. Co.
Glendale Corporation
B. F. Goodrich Company
B. F. Goodrich Research Center
Goodyear Tire & Rubber Company
Goss & Marcussen
Gould Foundation
Grace, J. Peter
W. R. Grace & Co.
W. William Graham, Jr., Inc.
Grain Processing Corp.
W. W. Grainger, Inc.
Grammarians, Inc.
Charles Granger Consulting Services
Granite Construction Co.
Alexander Grant & Company
Gravatt Public Affairs
Frank M. Graves Associates
Great Lakes Chemical Corp.
Great Northern Nekoosa Corporation
Green International, Inc.
Greif Bros. Corp.
Greiner Engineering Sciences
Grey, Lyon & King
Grocery Manufacturers of America
Grumman Corp.
M. J. Giuffrida & Associates, Inc.
Gulf Oil Corp.
Gulf & Western Industries, Inc.
HPI Hospital Pharmacies, Inc.
Jeanne Hale Temporaries
Frank B. Hall & Co., Inc.
Frank B. Hall of New York, Inc.
Handy and Harmen Foundation
Hartford Insurance Group
Hartford National Bank & Trust Co.
Harvard Business School
Harvard University Law School
Hearst Business Communications, Inc.
Helicon Group, Ltd.
Hellmuth, Paul F.
Help Unlimited
Hercules Incorporated
Heritage Foundation
Herr's Potato Chips
Hershey Foods Corp.
Heublein, Inc.
Hewlett-Packard Co.

Hill & Knowlton, Inc.
Hiller Investment
Hines Industrial
Max Hirschhorn Consulting
Holiday Inns, Inc.
Holland & Knight
Honeywell, Inc.
Honeywell, Avionics Division
Hospital Corp. of America
Houston Natural Gas Corp.
Howard University Hospital
Howrey & Simon
Harvey Hubbell Foundation
Hughes Tool Company
Hunton & Williams
Hydril Company
IC Industries, Inc.
ICI Americas, Inc.
I.D.S.
Idanta Partners
Illinois Water Treatment Co.
Indiana National Bank
Indianapolis Water Co.
Industrial Valley Bank & Trust Co.
Ingersoll-Rand Co.
Insilco Corp.
Institute of Medicine
Insurance Company of North America
Intel Corp.
InterFirst Corp.
International Business Machines Corp.
International Coal Refining
International Executive Service Corp.
International Minerals & Chemical Corp.
International Telephone & Telegraph Corp.
InterNorth, Inc.
InterNorth Foundation
Interpublic Group of Companies, Inc.
J. M. Foundation
JMS Associates
Jacobs Engineering Group, Inc.
James River Corporation
Jenkins, George P.
George W. Jenkins Foundation
Jewel Companies, Inc.
Jewish Communal Fund of New York
John Hancock Mutual Life Insurance Co.
Johnson, Howard B.
Johnson & Johnson
KBA International
Kaler, Worsley, Daniel, & Hollman
Kansas City Power & Light Co.
Carl Karcher Enterprises, Inc.
A. T. Kearney, Inc.
Kelco Company
Kellogg Co.

M. W. Kellogg Constructors, Inc.
Kelly Services, Inc.
Kemper Corporation
Kemper Group
Kerr-McGee Foundation
Ketron, Inc.
Keywell Industries
Kidde, Inc.
Kimberly-Clark Corp.
Kirkland & Ellis
Kirkpatrick, Lockhart, Hill, Christopher & Phillips
Koppers Co., Inc.
Korn/Ferry International
Kramer Associates
LTV Corp.
Labor Policy Association
Lafontant, Wilkins, Jones & Ware, P.C.
Lance, Inc.
Landmark Communities, Inc.
Landmark Industries
Landrum & Brown
Larkin, Felix E.
Lavin & Leonard
Lazard Freres & Co.
Lear Siegler Foundation
Lear Siegler, Inc.
Lehman Brothers, Kuhn, Loeb, Incorporated
Lehrer-McGovern
Lehrman Corporation
Lehrman Foundation
Leslind Marketing Services
Kenneth Leventhal & Company
Levi Strauss & Co.
Lewco Securities Co.
Liberty Corporation
Liberty Corporation Foundation, The
Liberty National Life Insurance Co.
Lifemark Corporation
Linbeck Construction Corp.
Lincoln Electric Co.
Lincoln National Corp.
Lincoln National Life Insurance Co.
Arthur D. Little, Inc.
Litton Industries
Lockheed Corp.
Loctite Corp.
Lodi Iron Works, Inc.
Logan Temps
Long Island Lighting Co.
Lord, Day & Lord
Nancy Low & Associates
Lubrizol Corp.
Lufkin, Dan W.
Lummus Company, The

V. Lummus Corporation
Macaione Company
John and Catherine MacArthur Foundation
McDonnell Douglas Foundation
McGraw-Edison Co.
McGraw-Hill, Inc.
McGraw-Hill Foundation, Inc.
Mack Trucks, Inc.
McKenna, Conner & Cuneo
McKinsey & Company
Macro Communications, Inc.
R. H. Macy & Co., Inc.
Main Hurdman CPA's
Management Analysis Center
Management Analysis Company
Management Counsel, Ltd.
Manheim, Paul
Manufacturers Hanover Trust Co.
Mapco, Inc.
Marcy Gymnasium Equipment Company
Marine Midland Banks, Inc.
Marmon Group, Inc.
Marriott Corporation
Marsh & McLennan Companies, Inc.
Marshall & Ilsley Bank Foundation, Inc.
Marshall & Ilsley Corp.
Marshall's, Inc.
Martin Marietta Corp.
Maryland Casualty Co.
Massachusetts Institute of Technology
Matsco Division
Mayer, Brown & Platt
Mead Corporation Foundation
Medicus Systems Corporation
Mellon Bank, N.A.
Mellon-Stuart Co.
Melville Corporation
Mercantile Bank at Dallas
Mercantile Stores Co.
Merck & Co., Inc.
Merrill Lynch & Co., Inc.
Merrill Lynch Private Capital, Inc.
Metcalf & Eddy, Inc.
Metromedia, Inc.
Metropolitan Life Foundation
Metropolitan Life Insurance Co.
Middle South Utilities, Inc.
Miller, August J.
Milliken & Company
Minnesota Mining & Manufacturing Co.
Mitre Corp.
Mobil Corporation
Monsanto Company
Montgomery Ward & Co., Inc.
Monyco, Inc.
J. P. Morgan & Company, Inc.

Morgan Guaranty Trust Co. of New York
Morgan, Lewis & Bockius
Morgan Stanley, Inc.
Morrison-Knudsen Co., Inc.
Motorola, Inc.
Mutual Benefit Life Insurance Co.
Mutual Life Insurance Co. of New York
NBK Corporation
NCNB Corp.
NCR Corp.
NL Industries Foundation
Nalco Chemical Co.
Nalco Foundation
National Academy of Sciences
National Association of Realtors
National Can Corp.
National Car Rental System, Inc.
National Distillers & Chemical Corp.
National Economics Research Association
National Federation of Independent
  Businesses
National Steel Corp.
National Fisheries Institute
National Futures Association
National Loss Control Service Corp.
National Network of Youth Advisory
  Boards
National Savings & Trust Bank
National Steel Corp.
Nationwide Mutual Insurance Co.
New York City Board of Education
New York Life Insurance Co.
New York State Housing Authority
New York Times Company
New York University
Newmont Mining Corp.
Norfolk Southern Corp.
North American Philips Corp.
North Carolina National Bank
North Star Universal, Inc.
Northern Telecom, Inc.
Northern Trust Company
Northrop Corp.
Northwest Airlines, Inc.
Northwest Bancorporation Foundation
Northwestern National Life Insurance Co.
Northwestern University
Norton Simon, Inc.
ORC, Inc.
ORG, Resource Counselors
ORI, Inc.
Oak Partners, Inc.
Oakland Press
O'Connor & Hannan
Oklahoma Bancorporation
John M. Olin Foundation

O'Melveny & Myers
Omnicare, Inc.
W. G. Onsted & Associates
Oppenheimer Capital Corporation
Organization Resources Counselors
Ortho Pharmaceutical Corporation
Owens-Corning Fiberglas Corp.
Owens-Illinois, Inc.
Owens-Illinois, Inc., Fund
PHH, Inc.
PPG Industries Foundation
PPG Industries, Inc.
PSA Airlines
Paccar Foundation
Pacific Western Realty and Development
  Corp.
Paine Webber Incorporated
Paine, Webber, Jackson & Curtis, Inc.
Pan American World Airways, Inc.
Pandick, Inc.
Office of Daniel Parker
H. G. Parks, Inc.
Peat, Marwick, Mitchell & Co.
Penn Central Corp.
Penn, Ralph S.
J. C. Penney, Inc.
Pennwalt Corp.
Peoples Gas Light & Coke Co.
Pepper, Hamilton & Scheetz
Pepsico Foundation
Pepsico, Inc.
Peterson, Howell & Heather, Inc.
Petrolane, Inc.
Pfizer, Inc.
Pfizer Foundation, Inc.
Philadelphia National Bank
Phillips Petroleum Company
John H. Phipps Broadcasting Stations, Inc.
Pillsbury Co.
Pillsbury, Madison & Sutro
Pitney Bowes, Inc.
Pittsburgh National Corp.
Pittston Company
Planning Research Corp.
Pogo Producing Co.
Pope, Charles R.
Population Crisis Committee
Port Authority of New York & New Jersey
Potomac Electric Power Co.
Pratt & Whitney
Preston State Bank
Price Waterhouse
F. H. Prince & Co., Inc.
Prince Foundation
Princeton University
Printing Industries of America
Procter & Gamble Co.

Procter & Gamble Fund
Project HOPE
Protemp
Provident Charitable Trust
Prudential Foundation
Prudential Insurance Co. of America
Public Service Electric & Gas Co.
Puelicher, John A.
Robert L. Purvin & Associates
Pyne, Eben W.
Quaker Oats Co.
R&S Research & Statistics
Ragen, Roberts, O'Scannlain
Rama Rao & Alfred, Inc.
Rand McNally & Company
Raytheon Co.
Reich, Joseph H.
Republic Bank
Research-Cottrell, Inc.
Rexnord Foundation
R. J. Reynolds Industries, Inc.
John Rhodes & Company
H. Smith Richardson Charitable Trust
Richardson-Vicks, Inc.
Rich-SeaPak Corporation
Riggs National Bank of Washington, D.C.
Roberts, Charles C.
Rockwell International Corporation
Rockwell International Corporation Trust
Rocky Mountain Energy of Union Pacific
Rogers and Wells
Roper Corporation
Rose Associates, Inc.
Rosen Associates
Royal Crown Companies, Inc.
Royal Insurance
Rust International Corporation
Ryan Enterprises
SEI Information Technology
Safeway Stores, Inc.
St. Joe Minerals Corporation
St. Monica's Church (Washington, D.C.)
St. Paul Companies
Salomon Brothers, Inc.
Salomon, Richard
Santa Fe Industries, Inc.
Santarelli & Gimer
Satellite Business Systems
Ingrid Saunders Selectemps
Schering-Plough Corp.
Science Applications, Inc.
Scott Paper Co.
Sears, Roebuck and Co.
Seattle First National Bank
Securities Industry Automation Corp.
Security Pacific Finance Corp.

Security Pacific Finance System, Inc.
Security Pacific National Bank
Sentry Insurance
Shannon & Luchs
Shapell Industries, Inc.
Shearman & Sterling
Shell Companies Foundation
Shell Oil Company
Sidley & Austin
Siegel and Gale
Signal Companies, Inc.
SmithKline Beckman Corp.
Sobotka Associates
Sobotka & Company Inc.
Southern Bell
Southern California Edison Co.
Southern Pacific Co.
Space Center, Inc.
Spaceplex, Inc.
Sperry Corp.
Sperry Electronic Systems
Spiegel, Inc.
A. E. Staley Manufacturing Co.
Standard Brands, Inc.
Standard Oil Co.
Stanford University Graduate School of
    Business
Stanley Works
State Farm Insurance Companies
State Farm Fire & Casualty Co.
State Farm Mutual Automobile Insurance
    Co.
J. P. Stevens & Co., Inc.
Stewart, James
Stewart-Warner Corporation
Stewart-Warner Foundation
S. M. Stoller Corp.
Stone & Webster, Inc.
Storage Technology Corp.
Sullivan & Cromwell
Sun Company, Inc.
Sunshine Biscuits, Inc.
Sunstrand Corporation
Sunstrand Corporation Foundation
K. S. Sweet Associates
Sybron Corporation
Syncronet, Inc.
Syscon Corp.
TAC/Temps
TRW, Inc.
Taft Broadcasting Co.
Tampax, Inc.
Tandy Corp.
Temporary Secretaries, Inc.
Tendler, Black & Biggins
Tenneco, Inc.

Tennessee Eastman Co.
Texaco U.S.A.
Texas American Bancshares, Inc.
Texas Commerce Bank
Texas Commerce Bancshares, Inc.
Texas Instruments, Inc.
Texas Motor Transportation Association
Texas Oil & Gas Corp.
Texas Utilities Company
Textron, Inc.
J. Walter Thompson
Law Firm of Thompson, Mann & Hutson
Time, Inc.
Today's Office
Todd Shipyards Corp.
Touche Ross & Company
Towers, Perrin, Forster & Crosby, Inc.
Transco Companies, Inc.
Transcontinental Gas Pipe Line Corp.
Travelers Corp.
Travelers Insurance Co.
Trust Co. Bank
Twain Braxton International
UMC, Inc.
UOP, Inc.
Underground Construction Co., Inc.
U.S. Chamber of Commerce
U.S. Fidelity & Guaranty Corp.
U.S. Gypsum Foundation
USLife
U.S. Steel Corp.
Union Camp Corporation
Union Carbide Corp.
Union Oil Co. of California Foundation
Union Pacific Corp.
Union Texas Petroleum Corporation
United Air Lines, Inc.
United Parcel Service, Inc.
United States Fidelity & Guaranty Co.
United States League of Savings
  Institutions
United Technologies Corp.
United Telecommunications, Inc.
Universal Leaf Tobacco Co., Inc.
University of Albuquerque
University of Arizona
University of Arizona, College of
  Agriculture
University of California (Irvine)
University of Cincinnati
University of Maryland
University of Pittsburgh
Upland Industries Corporation
Vanderbilt University
Velo-Bind, Inc.

Velsicol Chemical Corp.
Veratex Corp./Omnicare, Inc.
Villa Park, Illinois, School District
Vought Corp.
Vulcan Materials Co.
WCTV Channel 6
Wachovia Bank and Trust Co., N.A.
Wachovia Corp.
Warner, Rawleigh
Warner-Lambert Company
William K. Warren Foundation
Washington Gas Light Co.
Washington National Insurance Co.
Washington Post Co.
Washington University of St. Louis, Center
  for Study of American Business
Wayne State University
Weitzman & Rogal
Wellford, Wegman, Hoff, Krulwick & Gold
Wells Fargo Bank
Wells Fargo Foundation
Werchowsky, Danielle Marie
Wesray Corp.
K. S. S. West Associates
West Virginia University
Western Electric Co., Inc.
Westinghouse Electric Corp.
Roy F. Weston, Inc.
Westvaco Corporation
Wheelabrator Foundation, Inc.
Wheelabrator-Frye, Inc.
Whirpool Corporation
Whitco Chemical Corporation
Whittaker Corp.
Wiegand Consulting, Inc.
Willco Foundation
Clyde E. Williams & Associates
Williams, Luke G.
Williams Companies
Williams Companies Foundation, Inc.
Willkie, Farr & Gallagher
Winn-Dixie Stores Foundation
Winn-Dixie Stores, Inc.
Winston & Strawn
Wisconsin Public Service Corp.
Witco Chemical Foundation
F. W. Woolworth Co.
Xerox Corp.
Arthur Young & Company
Young & Rubicam, Inc.
Young, Thomas F.
Yunich, David L.
H. B. Zachry Co.
Zimmer, Fishbach & Hertan
Zork Hardware Co.